W9-DCJ-217

CONTINUITY AND CHANGE IN CONTEMPORARY CAPITALISM

In the early 1980s, many observers, including authors and editors of this book, argued that powerful organized economic interests and social democratic parties created successful mixed economies promoting economic growth, full employment, and a modicum of social equality. The present book reexamines this argument from the vantage point of the second half of the 1990s, finding that the conventional wisdom no longer adequately reflects political and economic realities. Advanced democracies have responded in path-dependent fashion to such novel challenges as technological change, intensifying international competition, new social conflict, and the erosion of established patterns of political mobilization. Nevertheless, the book rejects the currently widespread expectation that "internationalization" makes all democracies converge on similar political and economic institutions and power relations. Diversity among capitalist democracies persists, though in a different fashion than in the "golden age" of rapid economic growth after World War II.

Herbert Kitschelt is Professor of Political Science at Duke University and specializes in European party system and post-Communist politics. His recent books include *The Transformation of European Social Democracy* (Cambridge University Press, 1994), *The Radical Rights in Western Europe* (University of Michigan Press, 1995), and *Post-Communist Party Systems* (forthcoming, Cambridge University Press).

Peter Lange is Professor of Political Science at Duke University. His previous publications include *Unions, Change and Crisis: French and Italian Union Strategy and the Political Economy, 1945–1980* (with George Ross and Maurizio Vannicelli) and "Political Responses to Interdependence: What's Left for the Left?" (with Geoffrey Garrett), in *International Organization* (Fall 1991).

Gary Marks is Professor of Political Science at the University of North Carolina at Chapel Hill and Director of the UNC Center for European Studies. His previous publications include *Unions in Politics: Britain, Germany, and the United States in the Nineteenth and Early Twentieth Century* (Princeton University Press, 1989), *The Crisis of Socialism in Europe* (Duke University Press, 1992) coedited with Christiane Lemke, and *Reexamining Democracy* (Sage, 1992).

John D. Stephens is Professor of Political Science and Sociology at the University of North Carolina at Chapel Hill. He is the author of *The Transition of Capitalism to Socialism* (1979) and coauthor of *Democratic Socialism in Jamaica* (with Evelyne Huber Stephens, 1986) and of *Capitalist Development and Democracy* (with Dietrich Rueschemeyer and Evelyne Huber Stephens, 1992).

CAMBRIDGE STUDIES IN COMPARATIVE POLITICS

General Editor
PETER LANGE   Duke University

Associate Editors
ROBERT H. BATES   Harvard University
ELLEN COMISSO   University of California, San Diego
PETER HALL   Harvard University
JOEL MIGDAL   University of Washington
HELEN MILNER   Columbia University
RONALD ROGOWSKI   University of California, Los Angeles
SIDNEY TARROW   Cornell University

OTHER BOOKS IN THE SERIES

CONTINUITY AND CHANGE IN CONTEMPORARY CAPITALISM

Edited by

HERBERT KITSCHELT

PETER LANGE

GARY MARKS

JOHN D. STEPHENS

CAMBRIDGE
UNIVERSITY PRESS

PUBLISHED BY THE PRESS SYNDICATE OF THE UNIVERSITY OF CAMBRIDGE
The Pitt Building, Trumpington Street, Cambridge CB2 1RP, United Kingdom

CAMBRIDGE UNIVERSITY PRESS
The Edinburgh Building, Cambridge CB2 2RU, UK   http: //www.cup.cam.ac.uk
40 West 20th Street, New York, NY 10011-4211, USA   http: //www.cup.org
10 Stamford Road, Oakleigh, Melbourne 3166, Australia

First published 1999

Printed in the United States of America

Typeface Garamond no. 3 11/13 pt.   *System* DeskTopPro$_{/UX}$® [RF]

*A catalog record for this book is available from
the British Library*

Library of Congress Cataloging-in-Publication Data
Continuity and change in contemporary capitalism / edited by Herbert
Kitschelt . . . [et al.].
p.   cm. – (Cambridge studies in comparative politics)
"This volume grows out of conferences at the University of North
Carolina, Chapel Hill, in September 1994 and Humboldt University,
Berlin, in May 1995" – Pref.
Includes bibliographical references and index.
ISBN 0-521-62446-0. – ISBN 0-521-63496-2 (pbk.)
1. Economic history – 1990– – Congresses.   2. Capitalism –
History – 20th century – Congresses.   3. Technology transfer –
Economic aspects – Congresses.   4. Comparative economics –
Congresses.   5. Comparative government – Congresses.   6. Comparative
industrial relations – Congresses.   7. Foreign trade and employment –
Congresses.   8. Democratic – Congresses.   I. Kitschelt, Herbert.
II. Series.
HC59.15.C66   1999
330.12'2'0904 – dc21   98-21651
                                                                  CIP

ISBN 0 521 62446 0 hardback
ISBN 0 521 63496 2 paperback

CONTENTS

LIST OF CONTRIBUTORS

Gøsta Esping-Andersen is Professor of Comparative Social Systems at the University of Trento (Italy). He has formerly taught at European University and at Harvard University. He is the author of *Politics against Markets (1985)*, *The Three Worlds of Welfare Capitalism* (1990), and the forthcoming *The New Political Economy of the Welfare State*.

Miriam Golden is Professor of Political Science at the University of California at Los Angeles. Her publications include *Heroic Defeats: The Politics of Job Loss* (1997) and an edited volume with Jonas Pontusson entitled *Bargaining for Change: Union Politics in North America and Europe* (1992). With Peter Lange and Michael Wallerstein, she is completing a book manuscript reporting and analyzing data on unions, employers, collective bargaining, and industrial relations in sixteen OECD countries from 1950 to 1992.

Peter A. Hall is Professor of Government and Senior Associate at the Center for European Studies, Harvard University. He is the author of *Governing the Economy* (1986) and numerous articles on political economy and policy making in Europe and editor of *European Labor in the 1980s* (1987), *The Political Power of Economic Ideas* (1989), and, with Jack Hayward and Howard Machin, *Developments in French Politics* (1992).

Liesbet Hooghe is Assistant Professor in Political Science at the University of Toronto and Jean Monnet Fellow, European University Institute, Florence (1996–1997). Her publications include *Separatisme* (1989), *A Leap in the Dark: Nationalist Conflict and Federal Reform in Belgium* (1991), and *Cohesion Policy and European Integration: Building Multi-Level Governance* (1996). She has published articles on comparative federalism and nationalism, European integration, EU regional policy and subnational mobilization, and the role of the European Commission. She is currently working on a book on role perceptions of senior officials of the European Commission.

Evelyne Huber is Morehead Alumni Professor of Political Science and director of the Institute for Latin American Studies at the University of North Carolina at Chapel Hill. She is the author of *The Politics of Workers' Participation: The Peruvian Approach in Comparative Perspective* (1980) and coauthor of *Democratic Socialism in Jamaica* (with John D. Stephens, 1986) and of *Capitalist Development and Democracy* (with Dietrich Rueschemeyer and John D. Stephens, 1992). She is currently working on social policy in Latin America and, with John D. Stephens, on a book on the social democratic welfare state.

Desmond King is Professor of Politics and a Fellow of St. John's College, Oxford University. His publications include *The New Right: Politics, Markets, and Citizenship* (1987), (as coeditor) *Preferences, Institutions and Rational Choice* (1995), *Actively Seeking Work? The Politics of Unemployment and Welfare Policy in the United States and Britain* (1995), and *Separate and Unequal: Black Americans and the US Federal Government* (1995).

Herbert Kitschelt is Professor of Political Science at Duke University. He is the author of *The Logics of Party Formation* (1989), *The Transformation of European Social Democracy* (1994), and *The Radical Right in Western Europe* (1995). He is presently completing a book manuscript on the formation of party systems in east central Europe.

Jytte Klausen is Associate Professor of Comparative Politics at Brandeis University and Fellow at the Minda de Gunzberg Center for European Studies, Harvard University. She is coeditor (with Louise A. Tilly) of *European Integration in Social and Historical Perspective, 1850 to the Present* (1997) and author of *War and Welfare: Europe and the United States, 1945 to the Present* (1998). She is currently working on a study of the representation of women by conservative, liberal, and socialist parties in late nineteenth- and twentieth-century European democracies.

Hanspeter Kriesi is Professor of Political Science at the University of Geneva, Switzerland. He has published several books on the mobilization of social movements in western Europe. Most recently he coauthored (with Ruud Koopmans, Jan Willem Duyvendak, and Marco Giugni) a comparative volume on new social movements in western Europe (1995), and edited (with Urs Altermatt) a volume on the extreme right in Switzerland (1995). He is currently working on the formation of public opinion on ecological issues.

Peter Lange, Professor and Chair, Department of Political Science at Duke University, recently published "Internationalization, Institutions and Domestic Change" (with Geoffrey Garrett), in R. Keohane and H. Milner, eds., *Internationalization and Domestic Politics* (1996). His earlier publications include *Unions, Change and Crisis: French and Italian Union Strategy and the Political Economy, 1945–1980* (with George Ross and Maurizio Vannicelli) and "Political Responses to Interdependence: What's Left for the Left?" (with Geoffrey Garrett) in *International Organization* (Fall 1991). Lange is currently working on a long-term large data-collecting and analysis project (financed by the National Science Foundation) on the relationship between globalization and changes in the strength and structure of national trade-union movements across the advanced industrial democracies and the consequences of these changes for national economic performance and the distribution of income. The project will result in a coauthored book with his collaborators, Miriam Golden (UCLA) and Michael Wallerstein (Northwestern University), to be published in 1999.

Gary Marks is Professor of Political Science at the University of North Carolina at Chapel Hill, and director of the UNC Center for European Studies. His publications include *Unions in Politics: Britain, Germany, and the United States in the Nineteenth and Early Twentieth Centuries* (1989), *The Crisis of Socialism in Europe* (1992) coedited with Christiane Lemke, and *Reexamining Democracy* (1992) with Larry Diamond. His most recent book is *Governance in the European Union* with Fritz Scharpf, Philippe Schmitter, and Wolfgang Streeck (1996).

Timothy J. McKeown is Associate Professor of Political Science at the University of North Carolina at Chapel Hill. He has written extensively on international political economy, foreign policy decision making, and business-state relations. His next book is *The High Politics of Aid* (forthcoming).

Karl Ove Moene is Professor of Economics at the University of Oslo. He has worked extensively with Michael Wallerstein on the politics of egalitarian policies. In addition Moene has done work on comparative economic institutions. He is editor of the *Scandinavian Journal of Economics.*

Leonard Ray finished his doctorate at the University of North Carolina at Chapel Hill in 1998 and is now Assistant Professor of Political Science at Binghamton University. His research ranges from the role of subnational governments in the European Union to theories of altruism. He is a coauthor of "Competencies, Cracks and Conflicts: Regional Mobilization in the European Union" (*Comparative Political Studies*, 1996) and the author of

"Why We Give" (forthcoming in *Polity*). He is currently investigating the link between political parties and public support for European integration.

Beth A. Simmons is a Professor of Political Science at the University of California at Berkeley, specializing in international political economy and international law and institutions. Formerly on the faculty of Duke University, she spent 1995–1996 working in the Capital Markets and Financial Studies Division of the International Monetary Fund as an International Affairs Fellow, sponsored by the Council on Foreign Relations. Her work has been published in *International Organization* and *World Politics,* and in 1995 her book, *Who Adjusts? Domestic Sources of Foreign Economic Policy during the Interwar Years, 1923–1938* (1994) was awarded the American Political Science Association's Woodrow Wilson Award for the best book published in the United States on government, politics, or international affairs and APSA's Section on Political Economy Award for the best book or article published in the past three years. Professor Simmons received her Ph.D. from Harvard University.

David Soskice is Director of the Research Division "Employment and Economic Change" of the Social Science Research Centre, Berlin (the WZB), and Emeritus Fellow of Economics, University College, Oxford University. He is coauthor of *Unionism, Economic Stabilisation and Incomes Policies: European Experience* (1983) with Robert Flanagan and Lloyd Ulman, and coauthor with Wendy Carlin of *Macroeconomics and the Wage Bargain: A Modern Approach to Employment, Inflation and Exchange Rates* (1990). He is currently working on innovation strategies of companies and their human resource and technology transfer requirements within and across different systems of advanced capitalism; and the relation between microeconomic company performance and macroeconomic fiscal and monetary management and employment outcomes.

John D. Stephens is Professor of Political Science and Sociology at the University of North Carolina at Chapel Hill. He is the author of *The Transition from Capitalism to Socialism* (1979) and coauthor of *Democratic Socialism in Jamaica* (with Evelyne Huber Stephens, 1986) and of *Capitalist Development and Democracy* (with Dietrich Rueschemeyer and Evelyne Huber Stephens, 1992). With Evelyne Huber, he is currently working on a book on the historical development and current impasse of the social democratic welfare state.

Kees van Kersbergen is Professor of National Political Systems and Dutch Politics at the University of Nijmegen. He is the author of *Social Capitalism: A Study of Christian Democracy and the Welfare State* (1995). He is currently working on a study of the politics of adjustment in contemporary welfare states.

Michael Wallerstein is Professor of Political Science at Northwestern University. He has written and coauthored many articles on comparative industrial relations and social democratic labor market institutions. He is currently working with Karl O. Moene on the politics of egalitarian policies and with Miriam Golden and Peter Lange on changes in wage-setting institutions in sixteen advanced industrial economies in the postwar period.

Stewart Wood took a First in philosophy, politics, and economics at Oxford University in 1989. After completing his doctorate at Harvard University, he was elected a Research Fellow of St. John's College, Oxford University, and, in 1996, became an Official Fellow and Tutor in Politics at Magdalen College, Oxford. His publications include (as coauthor) *Options for Britain* (1995) and articles in professional journals such as *Political Studies*. His thesis, currently being revised for publication, is on "Capitalist Constitutions: Supply-Side Reform in West Germany and the United Kingdom, 1960–1990."

PREFACE

This volume grows out of conferences at the University of North Carolina, Chapel Hill, in September 1994 and Humboldt University, Berlin, in May 1995. It is the tangible result of long-standing and close relations of cooperation between members of the political science departments at UNC Chapel Hill and Duke University. Our desire to understand the dynamic patterns of political governance in advanced capitalist democracies brought us together. We embarked on this joint book project because we shared the belief that the mid-1990s offers a vantage point from which to assess the momentous political-economic changes of the preceding decade and a half.

In the early 1980s, all of us accepted the view that the presence of powerful organized economic interests and social democratic parties successfully created mixed economies promoting economic growth, cushioning economic investment risks, and protecting wage earners through comprehensive welfare states. By furnishing a distribution of life chances acceptable to the vast majority of citizens, such arrangements offered the best prospect for advancing social peace and stable democracy. From the perspective of the second half of the 1990s, we began to reexamine this view and set out to explore the extent to which conditions for economic growth, social peace, and political governance have changed. In discussions over a period of several months, we jointly identified key social conditions, international and domestic economic processes, political institutions, and mechanisms of policy making that amounted to what some may nostalgically call the "golden age" of post–World War II capitalism. We then invited scholars whose work has focused on these issues to join us in our enterprise to assess continuity and change of contemporary capitalist democracies. Three years and two conferences later, this book is the result of our collaborative effort.

Our project would not have been possible without the seed money provided by the Department of Political Science and the Center for International Studies of the University of North Carolina at Chapel Hill. The Council for European Studies promoted our efforts by a CES Research Planning Group grant. At Duke, the Trent Foundation supported our first conference in Chapel Hill. We wish to thank Barbara Hicks, William Keech, and Thomas Oatley for providing detailed comments at that meeting and Ruth Pitts for administering it. Our second conference took place in Berlin because one of the Duke-based editors, Herbert Kitschelt, at the time held a joint appointment with Humboldt University and we intended to tap into the analytical capabilities of our Berlin colleagues to improve our analysis. In particular, we would like to thank Thomas Cusak, Klaus Eder, Michael Kreile, Claus Offe, and Jeffrey Sellers for helpful contributions to our debates in Berlin and Regina Klingenberg for her administration. For the Berlin conference, the CES grant and support from the Thyssen Foundation were essential. Subsidies from Humboldt University in Berlin and from the Science Center in Berlin covered the remaining expenses. We would like to thank all funding agencies for their contributions. John Stephens would also like to thank the Swedish Collegium for Advanced Study in the Social Sciences for providing the time to work on his chapter and the conclusion. As always, they bear no responsibility for the final product.

INTRODUCTION

Herbert Kitschelt, Peter Lange, Gary Marks, and John D. Stephens

The point of intellectual departure for this volume is the end of the postwar period of rapid growth and the breakdown of postwar social contracts and institutional arrangements that were the central topics of comparative political economy from the 1960s to the 1980s. In the two decades following World War II, advanced capitalist democracies were characterized by rapid economic growth, expanding welfare state entitlements, apparently frozen party systems, class- and religion-based voter alignments, highly institutionalized systems of industrial relations, and a stable, if tense, system of international relations. Many, perhaps most, social scientists regarded these as permanent features of modern society. Not one of these features survived the decades of the 1970s and 1980s. The initial expression of the transformation that took place was "stagflation," a phenomenon that stimulated several academic conferences and a host of papers that concluded that countries with social democratic governments and highly centralized systems of national collective bargaining – in short, "neocorporatist" societies – were the most successful in producing low levels of unemployment, modest inflation, and economic growth, and could best defend welfare state entitlements (Goldthorpe 1984; Lindberg and Maier 1985). However, it later became clear that the early 1980s represented merely a temporary holding pattern. In the intervening years we have witnessed a transformation not only of the economies of advanced capitalist democracies, but also of their systems of labor relations, party systems, and voter alignments. In one region, western Europe, these have been accompanied by a partial redesign of authoritative decision making in the process of political integration.

Contrary to the view of a decade ago, social democracy, far from being uniquely able to manage these changes, now appears to be incapable of pursuing its traditional policy goals as one government after another has decided to prioritize price stability over employment. But the current situation is hardly rosy for conservative parties and employers either, as they also have yet to find policies that promote economic growth as effectively as the policies of state interventionism did in the postwar decades.

For these reasons, a reassessment of the conclusions of the studies of the mid-1980s is overdue. This volume represents an effort by social scientists working in diverse, but interrelated, fields to reanalyze the trajectories of the political economies of advanced capitalist societies.

THE SOCIAL AND POLITICAL ORDER IN THE MID-1960s

The most salient policy outcomes of the political economies of advanced capitalist societies during the mid-1960s were rapid growth, low unemployment, modest inflation, and expansion of the welfare state. Governments manipulated fiscal and monetary policy in pursuit of these goals and, under the Bretton Woods system of fixed but flexible exchange rates, they could resort to devaluation should domestic inflation begin to threaten competitiveness and thus employment. The main energy source for advanced capitalist economies was oil, and its real price declined in these years. Each country fashioned its own version of a compromise between capital and labor. Economic growth, based on impressive gains in labor productivity, facilitated the incorporation of organized labor into national policy making. Though the terms of compromise varied across countries according to the strength of labor and the left, in every country labor received increasing real wages and welfare state entitlements – pensions, unemployment insurance, and, in most cases, health care and sick pay.

Domestically, class compromise rested on the ability of workers to establish unions that could bargain effectively with employers in the labor market and social democratic parties that could exert leverage in politics. The chief cleavage in most Western societies was between workers and employers, and this was reflected in the arrangement of major parties along a left-right spectrum. In the view of Stein Rokkan and Seymour Martin Lipset, which was almost universally accepted by political scientists, this common organization of political space came about because, with the exception of the United States, the industrial revolution produced parties of organized labor. Historic religious and, to a lesser extent, ethnic and regional divisions explained differences between countries, and the resulting patterns of party systems and voter alignments, again in Rokkan and Lipset's widely accepted view, were "frozen" since the 1920s. Internationally, national control of economic policy was based on the Bretton Woods system, which in turn rested on American economic hegemony and on a degree of economic insulation sufficient to allow fiscal and monetary policy to be effective within national borders.

POLITICAL ECONOMY AFTER THE GOLDEN AGE: THE VIEW FROM THE MID-1980s

The collapse of Bretton Woods in 1971 and the first oil shock of 1973 marked the end of the so-called golden age of vigorous growth and political stability, and the onset of "stagflation" and political uncertainty. The economic problems of the period were the focus of many studies of comparative political economy; indeed, this was the period of the flowering of comparative political economy as a field. John Goldthorpe's 1984 edited volume, *Order and Conflict in Contemporary Capitalism*, was an intellectual milepost in this field, bringing together leading scholars of comparative political economy to take stock of, and analyze, the transformation of advanced capitalist democracies in the post–golden age era. The book summarized and refined the thinking of this period, and it serves as a point of departure for this volume.

The basic finding of *Order and Conflict* was that countries led by social democratic governments with highly centralized systems of industrial relations (i.e., neocorporatist societies) were most effective in dealing with post-OPEC disturbances in their political economies. Cross-national research found that such countries had lower levels of unemployment, lower strike levels, more egalitarian social policies, and similar levels of inflation and economic growth. The reasons for this are twofold. Social democratic participation in government opened a political channel for trade unions to exchange wage moderation for favorable public policy, including legal protection of unions, economic policies engendering full employment, and egalitarian social welfare. Second, union centralization allowed unions to overcome the collective-action problems of restraining their wage demands to keep their side of the bargain. Neocorporatist bargaining benefited workers (despite some earlier claims to the contrary, especially from neo-Marxist writers) by expanding the welfare state, producing a fairer distribution of economic reward, and sustaining long-run economic growth.

The social democratic model demanded that national governments be able to stimulate the economy fiscally or monetarily to sustain high levels of employment while restraining wages and thus controlling domestic inflationary pressures (Cameron and Scharpf in Goldthorpe 1984). At the same time, however, most neocorporatist societies had small, open economies that were heavily trade dependent and thus, far from being threatened by openness to the international economy, saw international competitiveness as their lifeblood.

The point of departure of the Goldthorpe volume (in common with much of the comparative political economy of this period, but going back at least to Shonfield) is that modern capitalism is heterogeneous. Distinctive institutional matrices produce diverse responses to similar economic problems. In his conclusion, Goldthorpe examined – and rejected – the sociological theory of the "logic of industrialism," which posits convergence of industrial societies. He argued that there were two basic responses to the "crisis" of the 1970s: social democratic neocorporatism and dual labor market policy exemplified in the U.S. and liberal political economies.

In saying that the Goldthorpe volume was an intellectual marker for the period, we note the following themes: (1) social democratic success in promoting a universalistic, solidaristic, and redistributive welfare state (Esping-Andersen and Korpi in Goldthorpe 1984; Cameron 1978; Stephens 1979; Korpi 1983; Esping-Andersen 1985); and (2) the virtues of "neocorporatism," centralized bargaining, union centralization, and/or the combination of centralized bargaining, union strength, and leftist government in promoting growth, low levels of unemployment, and modest inflation (articles by Cameron, Lange, Lehmbruch, and Schwerin in Goldthorpe 1984; Olson 1982; Garrett and Lange 1991; Katzenstein 1984; 1985; Lange and Garrett 1985; Marks 1986; Schmitter 1981; Scharpf 1987).

POLITICAL ECONOMY, AND POLITICS, AFTER THE GOLDEN AGE: THE VIEW FROM THE MID-1990s

The limitations of the Goldthorpe volume and the school of thought it exemplified reflect the time in which it was written. Parties, unions, and businesses initially reacted to the economic shocks of the 1970s as if they were cyclical economic downturns. They applied the policy instruments that they had used in the previous era – demand stimulation, interest rate manipulation, wage restraint – but with greater intensity. From the 1980s, however, it became clear that the economic problems facing advanced capitalist economies were rooted in a set of fundamental and interconnected changes, in particular, the internationalization of markets for goods and finance (particularly currencies); the relative decline of industrial production and rise of the service sector; the shift away from "Fordist," semi-skilled assembly line production toward "flexible specialization" and skill differentiated production. The drastic effects of these changes for capitalist political economies were reinforced by the end of the Bretton Woods system and the two oil price shocks of 1973–1974 and 1979–1980.

By the early 1980s, it was clear that the bases of economic policy had shifted. Aggregate monetary and fiscal instruments were devalued as a means for enhanced economic performance. National instruments of macroeconomic policy, in particular interest rates and fiscal policy, were strait-jacketed by the response of international capital. Reducing interest rates or increasing government spending to put idle productive resources to work could stimulate capital outflows having the opposite effect. Governments could fix currency exchange rates, but it was prohibitively expensive to do so in the face of countervailing international pressures, as François Mitterrand's socialist government found in the early 1980s when its fiscal and monetary expansionary policies led to capital flight, increased imports that crowded out domestically produced goods, and three currency depreciations in two years (Cameron 1987; Moravcsik 1991; Hall 1986).

Neocorporatist approaches to economic policy making began to unravel from the late 1970s even in countries where the working class had sufficient political and industrial power to bargain effectively. The reasons for this are diverse and are examined in several chapters of this volume. Employers came to place great stress on flexibility in response to changes in the technology of production and growing diversity of consumption, and they were increasingly unwilling to subscribe to labor market coordination at the national level (Hall, this volume; see also Streeck 1992; Sandholtz and Zysman 1989; Piore and Sabel 1984). The labor force became increasingly heterogeneous as the proportion of women, white-collar, and professional employees grew and blue-collar manufacturing employment declined (Klausen, this volume). Trade unions representing increasingly diverse groups of employees found it difficult, and sometimes impossible, to unify behind bargained wage restraint. Class ties and identities, which bound employees together while pitting them against employers, declined sharply in most European countries in these years (Esping-Andersen, this volume). One consequence of this was that labor was less and less able to act as a cohesive political entity in interclass bargaining. The problems facing advanced capitalist societies were two sided: international economic pressures increased; the capacity of governments to coordinate functional interests in response to them declined.

Relative economic decline and the perceived failure of national Keynesianism set the stage for innovation. The directions it took were shaped by the stock of ideas available, prior institutions, and power relations among relevant groups (Hall 1993). Two broad streams of innovation were preeminent: first, a shift toward neoliberalism, involving some measure of privatization, deregulation (especially of financial markets), and cutting budget deficits, most marked in the U.K. and Anglo-American democracies (King and Wood, this volume), but influencing even societies where neocorporatism was entrenched; second, in western Europe, the reinvigoration of European integration in an attempt to intensify international competition within Europe by restricting nontariff barriers and create a capacity for problem solving at the European level (Hooghe and Marks, this volume).

In retrospect, it is clear that the Goldthorpe volume gave us a snapshot of a situation that was changing rapidly. Some of the most important conclusions of the volume did not hold five years later. From the point of view of policy prescription, social democratic market interventionism, far from being the cutting edge, was on the defensive from the mid-1980s.

As we convened a group of scholars to reanalyze the transformation of the advanced capitalist democracies since the end of the golden age, it was apparent to us that we would have to cast our net considerably wider than had the Goldthorpe group. The earlier work focused exclusively on political economy, neglecting other aspects of the political system, even ones that arguably had considerable political economic effect. Within political economy, furthermore, the focus was narrowly on unions and wage bargaining. This is readily understood. Analyses of the period focused on distributive conflicts in the context of short-term cyclical forces and price and wage cost shocks. In this context, a focus on restraining wage pressures through labor market and governmental policies designed to promote restored growth with lower unemployment and inflation made sense. But with longer hindsight, neither the analysis nor the prescriptions were sustainable.

Recent work by two of the editors and their coauthors (Garrett and Lange 1991, 1995; Huber and Stephens 1997) convinced us that there had been a fundamental misunderstanding of even the narrow area of social democratic unemployment and growth policy. Previous analysis implied that social democratic economic policy in the golden age consisted primarily of demand-side stimulation. Our work had shown that it was, instead, primarily supply side, including public investment directly in human and physical capital and facilitating private investment in physical capital through low interest rates and subsidized interest rates, made possible by the relatively closed financial markets that characterized the period and by labor market institutions that incorporated the organized labor movement. Contrary to the popular wisdom, fiscal policy of social democratic governments was actually relatively austere. Thus, while labor market institutions would still figure prominently in the contributions to our volume (Golden, Wallerstein, and Lange; Moene and Wallerstein; Klausen), we wanted to solicit contributions that would cover a wider range of institutions of the political economy that influence economic growth and stagnation, extending to the entire "production regime" (Hall; King and Wood; Soskice; all this volume). Moreover, we recognized that the production regime cannot be fully understood without examining its interlinks with the "welfare state regime," and several of the contributions address this interface (King and Wood; Soskice; Stephens, Huber, and Ray).

It also appeared to us that, given the increasing importance of economic internationalization for the development of capitalist societies, the international setting itself merited greater attention than it had received in the Goldthorpe book, which included only one contribution on the topic. Given the very different magnitudes of change in trading and financial regimes, we considered it essential that these be dealt with in separate contributions (McKeown; Simmons). Furthermore, given the shake-up of European political economy with the deepening of the European Community, it was clear that we would not be able to treat capitalist political economy exclusively from the standpoint of decision making within individual countries. The changes we were concerned with affected not only political-economic outcomes, such as economic growth, unemployment, or public policy, but the structuration of political authority (Hooghe and Marks).

The recent work of another of the editors (Kitschelt 1994a) alerted us to another weakness of the Goldthorpe volume, the absence of any discussion of politics and its interface with political economy. Parties, party alignments, political behavior, social movements hardly appear in the volume despite their obvious importance for many of the concerns of the contributions to the book. The organizational structure and electoral appearance of leftist parties, for example, is critical to any understanding of the feasibility of neocorporatist arrangements in advanced capitalist democracies. Or, to take another example, occupational structure changes and the growth of public employment clearly have profound implications for the wage bargaining process that was so central to much of the work in comparative political economy of the early 1980s. Three of the contributions to Part III of this volume (King and Wood; Kitschelt; van Kersbergen) are centrally concerned with the interaction of politics and political economy. The remaining two (Esping-Andersen; Kriesi) address the broad theme of the interconnection between the massive changes in social structure, especially occupational and class structure, and political behavior and party systems.

PART I

THE INTERNATIONAL SETTING FOR POLITICAL-ECONOMIC STRATEGIES

THE GLOBAL ECONOMY, POST-FORDISM, AND TRADE POLICY IN ADVANCED CAPITALIST STATES

Timothy J. McKeown

B y now it is generally agreed that the markets for goods and services of most nations of the world, particularly the advanced capitalist nations, are more closely connected to and affected by the global economy than they ever have been. If openness is measured in the simplest way, by the ratio of imports to gross domestic product, then in general the openness of the advanced capitalist states surpassed that of 1914 during the early 1970s; since then world trade has grown twice as fast as world income, and trade in manufactures three times the rate (McKeown 1991; GATT 1993).[1] For the developed countries, this change is particularly important, because they historically have specialized in the export of manufactured goods. Measured in terms of the value of goods shipped, in 1992 manufactures comprised 73 percent of world trade (GATT 1993: 2). While the collapse of oil prices in the early 1980s partly accounts for this statistic, the succession of post–

---

[1] Measuring openness by the ratio of imports to GDP is admittedly problematic, because the measure is sensitive to factor endowments and the pattern of demand for importables, apart from the way that conscious policy choices alter it (Leamer 1988). However, a discussion that focuses on changes in this ratio is less vulnerable to this criticism, simply because the underlying economic characteristics are unlikely to change nearly as quickly as the policy can.

World War II multilateral tariff reductions that concentrated on lowering tariffs on manufactures also led to greatly increased intraindustry trade among the Organization for Economic Cooperation and Development (OECD) countries (see Table 1.1).[2]

In this chapter I first outline the consequences of changes in the international trading system for the economies of advanced capitalist states, with particular reference to the "post-Fordist" thesis that the industrial structure of these countries is evolving away from the mid-twentieth-century pattern dominated by the employment of large numbers of workers in assembly line production systems driven largely by economies of scale. I address in turn changes at the subnational and the national levels, though the difference between them is more a matter of emphasis and convenience than logic. I then present and discuss some recent empirical research by economists on the links between the trade regime and wage growth and distribution. This provides the backdrop for an examination of commonalities in the evolution of trade policy across western Europe, North America, and Japan. The extent of the commonalities among this institutionally diverse set of states suggests the merit of considering how similar factor endowments and exposure to global economic events shape the policy responses of these countries. The conclusion section emphasizes the multifaceted effects of an open trading system, suggests some reasons for caution in assessing its effects, and speculates on some novel political responses to continued openness.

THE ECONOMIC CONSEQUENCES OF INCREASING OPENNESS

SUBNATIONAL EFFECTS

Greater openness in goods markets is thought to have several effects that are generally consonant with those posited for "post-Fordist" advanced economies. Indeed, it is plausible to trace many "post-Fordist" developments directly to changes in the trading system.

Within the neoclassical theory of international trade, the mainline Hecksher-Ohlin-Samuelson theory posits that trade will equalize returns to factors of production across national boundaries. This conclusion rests

---

[2] The increase in trade cannot be attributed to decreases in freight and insurance costs. These costs can be roughly estimated by comparing the value of exports going to Country X f.o.b. (free on board) and imports arriving in Country X c.i.f. (cost including insurance and freight). Doing so for 1954 and 1992 yields the following ratios of insurance and freight costs to value of shipments: 2.4 and 3.2 percent. (International Monetary Fund 1979, 1993).

Table 1.1. *Trade openness of the advanced capitalist states, 1960–1989*

	1960–1973	1974–1979	1980–1989
Social democratic welfare states			
Sweden	45	58	63
Norway	82	89	82
Denmark	60	61	69
Finland	45	55	60
Austria	53	66	75
Mean	57.0	65.8	69.8
Christian democratic welfare states			
Belgium	75	101	132
Netherlands	92	96	110
Germany	39	51	61
France	26	39	45
Italy	31	41	42
Switzerland	61	66	73
Mean	54.0	65.7	77.2
Liberal welfare states			
Canada	39	48	52
Ireland	77	101	112
United Kingdom	41	55	53
United States	10	17	18
Mean	41.8	55.3	58.8
Japan	20	26	28
Australia	30	31	33
New Zealand	46	55	63

Source: IMF, *International Financial Statistics Yearbook* (various years).

on assumptions of uniform technologies, decreasing returns to scale, and initial factor endowments that are not excessively dissimilar (Helpman and Krugman 1985: 13–16). When these assumptions are violated, current theory suggests that returns to factors do not always equalize, but as a rule of thumb it is still wise to presume that the effect of greater openness is to reduce the importance of nation-specific factor returns. In labor markets, this implies that, controlling for skill levels, wages will tend to equalize across national boundaries; a similar verdict holds for profits.[3] In developed

[3] This argument abstracts from the existence of an international capital market, or the effects of creating or liberalizing such a market. The effect of capital market liberalization on returns to capital was initially thought to be fairly straightforward: the new rate of return would be intermediate between the high return in the formerly capital-scarce

countries, this in turn implies that openness depresses the wages of the unskilled and elevates the wages of the highly skilled and the profits of capital, since the former are more abundant in the global economy as a whole than they are in their national economies, while the opposite is true for skills and capital. This creates a situation where international wage *convergence* (again, controlling for skill level) occurs simultaneously with national wage *divergence* (between skill levels); the effect of this on political unity between skilled and unskilled labor in a single nation, and on their attitudes toward trade policy, are easily surmised.

The effects of trade openness on national labor markets are generally accentuated by international factor movements. Wilfred Ethier (1986)

economy and the low rate of return in the formerly capital-abundant economy (Gale 1974; Karekan and Wallace 1977). At a high level of abstraction, one can construct a general equilibrium model of the international economy consistent with either neoclassical or Marxian assumptions that utilizes migration and international capital flows to equilibrate marginal returns on a global basis (Roemer 1983). However, the introduction of issues from the theory of finance (principally, the theory of portfolios) significantly changes the verdict: when agents inhabit an economy subject to stochastic disturbances, and when they must decide how much to save and where to invest, "Capital market integration changes the proximate determinants of relative factor returns from savings rates to the elements that underlie portfolio allocation decisions and other factors; that is, from rates of time preference and levels of risk aversion to relative asset riskiness, overall productivity levels, and even relative populations" (Osler 1991: 89). Savings rates in turn are affected by different patterns of time preference for consumption, different levels of business cycle fluctuation across countries, which give rise to different levels of variance in earnings; or different levels of risk aversion. Whereas under capital market autarky any difference in capital stocks between economies of equal size is simply a function of different savings rates, with trade in capital the portfolio allocation decisions of agents facing uncertainty will affect capital stocks, real output, and factor prices. "As a result, factor prices can move in many different ways upon [an international opening of capital markets]. They could move towards each other, but they could also move in parallel, both rising or both falling; they could diverge, even if they were initially equal; finally, it is even possible that the ranks of relative factor prices be reversed, so that the lowest becomes the highest and vice versa. The paths actually followed by factor returns depend on whether and how countries differ initially and on the direction of consumers' savings response to changes in uncertainty" (Osler 1991: 89).

It is clear both from her empirical results and from Osler's model that increasing openness need not bring about convergence of capital-market results so long as important national differences of the kind noted by Osler continue to exist. And if "anything can happen" in terms of factor returns, then similarly "anything can happen" as far as actors' political responses to these changing factor returns. The empirical situation is of course further complicated by the fact that many securities constitute claims on a spatially diversified asset portfolio: buying shares of a multinational corporation that produces in many different countries, and whose performance is not closely linked to any one national market, means that even Osler's account – in which capital is always "pure" national capital – is still a simplification. Finally, it should be noted that in Osler's model the welfare consequences of opening could easily be Pareto-inferior as Pareto-superior to autarky in capital markets: Everyone could lose, or everyone could win.

presents extensions of Ricardian and Heckscher-Ohlin-Samuelson trade frameworks to accommodate the free international movement of one factor. As might be expected, national returns to factors are more readily equalized when international factor movements occur in addition to international goods movements, and many of the qualifying factors mentioned by Helpman and Krugman no longer prevent the equalization of returns across different national markets. Of course, returns in national labor markets would equalize without any trade liberalizations at all, if there were no barriers to migration. Because barriers to the migration of skilled labor are considerably less than for the unskilled, they tend to accentuate the disparity in the effects of increasing trade openness on these two groups.

Along with changes in the relative fortunes of the skilled and unskilled, the greater openness of the goods market changes the mix of economic activities taking place in each nation. Import-competing sectors contract; exporting sectors expand, and the proportion of the economy that is involved in the international economy increases (i.e., the traded-goods sector increases in importance compared to the nontraded-goods sector). Because sectors are often tied to specific geographic regions (Cassing, McKeown, and Ochs 1986), or to specific political parties (Kurth 1979), and because labor-union strength may be concentrated in either rising or declining sectors, an increase in openness can have quite far-reaching effects, but also ones that are difficult to predict from within the confines of extant general theories and without any country-specific knowledge.

A third connection between international trade and "post-Fordist" production lies in the effects of the changes in the trading system on the very nature of production. A more open trading system means that an exporter faces an industry demand curve that has shifted outward – the smaller the national market, and the greater the amount of international opening, the more pronounced the shift. This development in turn means that the potential for mass production is actually *increased*, since longer production runs are possible before demand is saturated. It has long been recognized that if an industry has significant fixed costs, its profitability is critically dependent on the length of its production runs (or, what often amounts to the same thing, its level of capacity utilization). Because of this, Moran (1973) argued that firms with high fixed costs that are operating in an environment characterized by significant technological change would be the natural supporters of policies designed to create an open world trading system.

At the same time, import-competing firms must contend with more domestic demand being satisfied by imports, so they are less able to sustain long production runs, or high levels of capacity utilization in factories that were formerly sized to serve the national market without competition from imports – unless the domestic market is growing so rapidly that both increased imports and high levels of domestic sales can grow simultaneously. (This, of course, is a contingency that is a good deal more unrealistic in recent times than it was in the 1960s.) If import-competing firms do not exit the market, and they cannot match foreign producers on production costs, these firms may radically change their production techniques or attempt to differentiate their products. The former implies in general that they will substitute capital goods for labor; the latter implies that they will become "niche" producers, seeking to survive in markets for specialized goods, while ceding domination of mass market items to imports. Knowledge of the local market (particularly, rapid acquisition of information about changes in tastes) and an established and efficient distribution system may be much more valuable comparative advantages for a "niche" producer than for a foreign mass-market producer (Gereffi and Wyman 1991). So-called flex-spec (flexible-specialized) production is thus one way to respond to import competition.

A second effect of greater openness on mass production runs contrary to the effect of increased demand. Because the market is now larger, it becomes possible to write off research and development costs over more units sold; this in turn stimulates investments in research and development, which reduces the time between innovations. The product cycle (in the sense of Vernon 1966) thus becomes shorter. (This intuition is developed and formalized in Grossman and Helpman 1990.) Such a development would of course imply that investments in machines and people that were multipurpose rather than being optimized for a relatively narrow range of production possibilities would become relatively more attractive, since the amount of time available in which to capture scale economies from a given product or process is shrinking. For nationally concentrated industries, the opening of the goods market to imports may well increase competition; this in turn may render infeasible any collusive "foot dragging" on changes in product or process technology for oligopolized industries such as autos (casual observation of Detroit's behavior over the past thirty years suggests there is something to this). This also has favorable implications for "flex-spec."

Finally, declining employment in assembly lines does not necessarily mean the disappearance of the lines themselves so much as the disappearance of labor from them. Changes that are not closely connected to short-term increases in trade openness (the cheapening of producers' goods, particularly those with some computing capacity; the increase in the supply of skilled labor) could lead to this result in any case. Technological change may also have very uneven effects on labor, particularly for those whose skill portfolio is narrow and undiversified. In the United States, for example, the computer industry boasts one of the fastest growing occupations, computer engineer, but also one of the most quickly declining ones, computer operators (Bureau of the Census 1996: 409). Such developments undercut the capacity of labor to act as a unified coalition, even within a single industry.

ECONOMY-WIDE EFFECTS

Aside from its effects on particular sectors or social groups, changes in trade openness or in trade patterns can have economy-wide effects. It has been recognized since at least the time of Keynes that increases in exports or decreases in imports in the presence of idle workers and equipment are a painless way to increase output and incomes – so long as foreign governments do not take offsetting actions. (Even if an offsetting reaction is anticipated, the political benefits from protection in a period of idle workers and equipment can still be larger than when resources are more fully employed [Cassing, McKeown, and Ochs 1986; Wallerstein 1987].) An even older insight, found in any conventional international economics textbook, is that protection in the presence of scarcity creates misallocations of resources that reduce welfare. Taken together, these insights suggest that commercial policy can play a countercyclic role; the historical association of protection with depression suggests that indeed governments have exploited this possibility. Finally, changing the level of protection entails adjustment costs, and, because agents hold undiversified or imperfectly diversified portfolios of assets (particularly irreversible investments in skills), they often experience very sizable windfall gains or losses.

Beyond these elementary observations, there are a set of additional macroeconomic considerations. To do full justice to this topic would require an excursion into open-economy macroeconomic theory, but a few useful things can still be said nonetheless.

One issue is raised by the presence of trade imbalances. As long as there are international capital flows, the short-term balance-of-payments pressures maintaining a balance of imports and exports are weak: in the presence of a surplus on the capital account (due to new borrowing from foreigners or remittances from previous foreign investments), a nation can run a deficit on the current account for an extended period of time. Likewise, a surplus of exports over imports can be sustained for a lengthy period if the income is invested abroad to produce a capital outflow that matches the current account inflow. (If the flows are in equilibrium, the price of foreign exchange will be stable.) While a chronic trade deficit can be associated with slow growth and unemployment (as in interwar Britain [Cairncross and Eichengreen 1983]), it can also be viewed as part of "normal" capitalist development for an economy that is either relatively capital poor (and hence attracting new capital from abroad) or else the recipient of substantial foreign investment income. Conversely, chronic trade surplus can be associated with above-normal rates of income growth, as in Japan from 1950 to 1990, but it can also be associated with chronic repayment of debt and unspectacular growth performance, as in the case of Latin America in recent years.

Because restricting or liberalizing trade can affect external balance (through its immediate effect on the current account and induced effects on capital flows or the exchange rate) or internal balance (through its employing or disemploying effects in national labor markets), one can extend the traditional discussion of the trade-offs between monetary and fiscal policy to include commercial policy as an additional instrument. This insight has been developed the furthest by Magee, Brock, and Young (1989), who investigated the evolution of the level of protection of the American economy and who presented both a theory and empirical results suggesting that the level of protection is partly determined by choices made on fiscal and monetary policy. Decreasing protection can be a way of counteracting inflation, while increasing or not decreasing it will tend to accommodate it. (Correspondingly, as noted earlier, increasing protection can be used to counteract unemployment, while leaving protection unchanged is a way of accommodating it.) If consumers spend most of their money on tradable goods, and trade is sufficiently open so that the price of these goods is near the world market price, then the domestic price level can only increase if the home currency is devalued.

Apart from its one-time effect on allocative efficiency, some recent work on incorporating international trade effects into growth models has argued that trade liberalization leads to an extended period of higher growth. The example given earlier in which trade liberalization shortens the product cycle in technology-intensive industries can be seen as a particular instance of a more general phenomenon − trade policy can alter the quantity of investment as well as the return on investment. If it initially improves returns to capital (as it would in capital-rich countries), then increases in savings would cause the capital stock to grow more quickly for a time than it otherwise would. To show this formally requires a model in which the capital stock is endogenously determined, rather than being treated as exogenous as in the original Stolper-Samuelson (1941) formulation. In such a model one possible result is that trade liberalization has no long-run effect on returns to factors – all of the effects of liberalization are realized by changes in the quantities of factors and of output rather than their prices (Baldwin 1992).

Unfortunately, the relatively rosy implications of such models for the capital-rich countries are undercut by consideration of the *location* of these new investments. In a very simple model of the location of investments in a global-market economy (one in which there are no financial instruments and hence no separation of financial and "real" variables), Lucas (1990) notes that simple rate-of-return considerations would cause capital to flow from capital-rich to capital-scarce countries, and that the observed size of the capital flows, even in recent times, is much too small to be consistent with the likely disadvantages in productivity in the capital-poor countries. His solution to this puzzle – barriers to the entry of foreign capital by native capitalists in the capital-poor countries – is becoming less and less historically relevant as the prevalence of neoliberal policies in the less developed world increases. If significant differences in rates of return persist, while barriers to entry are removed from investments in the less developed world, and the trading system is opened so that all markets for manufactured goods are accessible from capital-poor countries, then the only forces pulling investment in manufacturing into capital-rich countries would be lower risks (i.e., lower variability of returns) in the developed world, the presence in the developed world of increasing-returns industries that enjoyed "first mover" advantages, or the presence of place-specific assets in these countries. Aside from natural resources and infrastructure, the most obvious such asset is human capital endowments. Hobson's (1965 [1938]: 364–365) vision of a "rentier" society, in which industry and agriculture in the metropole are largely extinguished in favor of service activities, no longer seems entirely implausible (although he does seem to neglect the fact that downward pressure on wages in the advanced states and upward pressures in the exporting NICs can mitigate, halt, or even reverse this process). Hobson's spotlighting the importance of China in the consummation of such a process seems quite prescient: Taiwan and the People's Republic of China account for about 9.1 percent of world exports, and Chinese exports are growing at about 20 percent per annum. This is not only a much higher growth rate than that of any other leading exporter (GATT 1993:3, 4),[4] but the much larger low-wage population of China

---

[4] The computation is for 1992 and excludes intra-EC trade from world trade. It also assumes that all Hong Kong reexports come from China, which is not strictly true. Including intra-EC trade would lower the Chinese share to 6.9 percent, and leave it the

implies that the length of time required for Chinese exports to level off will be much longer than in the case of Japan or the "four tigers" (Korea, Taiwan, Hong Kong, and Singapore). The latter countries are now experiencing rates of export growth close to the global average; indeed, some countries on the European periphery are experiencing significantly higher rates of export growth (see Table 1.2). However, barring protection in the developed states or political upheaval in China itself, double digit Chinese export growth will probably persist for an extended period.[5]

In this context it is easy to make sense of the neoliberals' stress on infrastructure (e.g., the "information highway"), education, and retraining as recipes for the advanced capitalist states; if one presumes that open trade and investment patterns are going to persist, these are obvious strategies to prevent further declines in wages and salaries. While developed countries may still enjoy an advantage in terms of lower political risks, the removal of protection, by opening domestic economies more fully to disturbances in the global economy, ought to increase the variability of returns to nation-specific assets in the liberalizing country, particularly those involved in producing traded goods. Of course, at the same time expropriations and other forced takings in the less developed world are quite out of fashion, so their perceived riskiness as investment sites is likely declining.

THE EXPERIENCE OF THE ADVANCED STATES UNDER INCREASING GLOBAL OPENNESS

Economists have already begun to argue about the consequences of declining trade barriers for growth and the distribution of income, particularly in the advanced countries. In the United States, this debate was spurred by public consideration of the North American Free Trade Agreement; a

---

fourth largest exporter, after the United States, Germany, and Japan.

[5] Consideration of trade in services modifies the picture somewhat. Trade in services is growing almost twice as fast as merchandise trade (12 percent versus 6.3 percent in 1992), and the United States, western Europe, and Japan continue to dominate (the majority of world service exports is generated by just seven developed countries: the United States, France, Italy, Germany, the United Kingdom, Japan, and Spain). Interestingly, Italy and Spain are experiencing the most rapid growth in service exports. The American edge in share of service exports is considerably more pronounced than in merchandise exports: service exports in the United States exceed those in France by more than 60 percent (GATT 1993: 5). American aggressiveness in seeking removal of trade barriers in services is thus easy to comprehend.

Table 1.2. *Value in billions of U.S. dollars, global share, and growth rate of merchandise exports for selected countries during 1992*

Country	Exports	Share (%)	Growth rate (%)
United States	448.2	12	6.3
Germany	430.0	11	6.8
Japan	339.9	9.1	8.0
Italy	178.2	4.8	5.1
Hong Kong			
Exports	119.5	3.2	1.8
Reexports	89.4	2.4	29.6
China	85.0	2.3	18.2
Taiwan	81.5	2.2	7.0
South Korea	76.6	2.1	6.6
Singapore	40.8	1.1	5.9
Sweden	56.1	1.5	1.6
Mexico	46.2	1.2	7.7
Austria	44.4	1.2	8.0
Malaysia	40.6	1.1	18.3
Denmark	39.6	1.1	10.1
Russian Federation	37.0	1.0	Not computed
Brazil	36.1	1.0	14.2
Norway	35.2	0.9	3.1
Thailand	32.5	0.9	14.2
Ireland	28.3	0.8	16.9
Portugal	18.3	0.5	12.4
Turkey	14.7	0.4	7.9
World average			6.3

Source: General Agreement on Tariffs and Trade (1993).

number of economists have sought to address the relation of the historically poor performance of American real wage growth over the past twenty-odd years to the changes in the international trading system (Leamer 1992; Murphy and Welch 1991, 1992; Bound and Johnson 1992; Lawrence and Slaughter 1993). There is no consensus about this relationship. While some, such as Leamer and Murphy and Welch, argue for a relationship between the changing trade pattern and wages, others, most notably Lawrence and Slaughter, contend that there is no evidence to link changes in trade to changes in growth and distribution of earned income within the United States.

A second area of investigation has focused on the degree and rate of international convergence. While some have studied this directly, an equally promising alternative is to study convergence in regions of a single trading system that is highly integrated. The implicit argument is that, by establishing the rate at which convergence occurs under the most propitious conditions, we can at least develop an upper limit to the estimate of the rate of economic convergence among areas that are less tightly linked by economic and political bonds. Barro and Sala-i-Martin's (1991) study of convergence among the fifty states of the United States from 1880 to 1988 and seventy-three "regions" (provinces) in West Germany, the United Kingdom, Italy, France, Netherlands, Belgium, and Denmark from 1950 to 1985 found that in both instances interregional differences gradually shrank at a rate of about 2 percent of the difference per year. Williamson's (1992) data on real wages for unskilled labor in a set of fifteen countries that approximates the OECD[6] reveals considerable converging in 1850–1890 and 1956–1984, but insubstantial converging or even diverging in other periods (including 1984–1988). His evidence on the effect of trade liberalization on wage convergence in the European Community (EC) countries finds convergence rates comparable with that of the different regions of the United States, even with the presence for much of his sample period of substantial barriers to migration within the EC. Since in both the American and the western European cases the effects of migration and capital flows on the equalization of returns to factors are probably accentuating the convergence due simply to the integration of the goods markets, it seems safe to say that convergence among countries where barriers to capital and labor flows persist will be even slower.

Recent developments in growth theory also suggest that where differences between countries are substantial, openness need not bring about convergence. This could occur in a situation in which different types of countries travel along different growth paths, and the interconnections between the different types provided by flows of goods or factors are not sufficient to move countries from one path to another. Durlauf and Johnson (1992) analyze subgroups of countries with similar initial income or literacy rates (based on 1988 data) and generate statistical results that are consistent with the hypothesis that there are several equilibrium growth rates in their sample of countries. Thus, similar countries may converge as the system opens, but a global convergence need not occur. This is another reason why one ought to hesitate in generalizing from studies of

---

[6] No doubt because of data availability problems, the only less developed country included is Argentina. It is the strongest outlier in a regression of wages in 1870 against real wage growth in the subsequent 118 years (see Williamson 1992: figure 2), and it is also an outlier in the relation of real wages to population growth.

convergence within the developed world to convergence between developed and less developed countries. Indeed, since the dispersion of national per capita incomes on a global basis has been increasing since the 1950s at the same time that the trading system has generally become more open (Ben-David 1991), it is apparent that any model that seeks simply to apply the factor price equalization theorem to historical situations without regard to other within-nation or between-nation processes is too inaccurate to be useful.

An even more skeptical position is offered by Lawrence and Slaughter (1993), who argue that there is no evidence linking increased trade openness to declining real wages for unskilled workers in the United States. Their empirical analysis is multifaceted and complicated, but it rests fundamentally on the lack of changes in goods prices (and of terms of trade), which the neoclassical theory takes to be the mechanism whereby changes in the trade regime affect returns to factors. They argue that the source of low wage growth lies in slow rates of growth in marginal physical productivity, and they point in particular to slow productivity growth in American service industries (which tend more often to be nontraded goods producers) as the culprit.

Their argument is ultimately deficient because of their excessive reliance on the analytical apparatus of neoclassical theory (particularly the Stolper-Samuelson theorem). This body of theory was designed for a world of "national capital," in which goods production takes place within single countries (rather than with a production process utilizing several countries) and international capital flows are not treated. American firms in the post-1945 era have been the most active in foreign direct investment, which is consistent with the United States being the high-wage economy for most of this period. Unbundling the production process for manufactured goods so that much of the physical production takes place abroad in low-wage economies, while nonproduction activities are left in the United States, would have the following results:

1. The ratio of nonproduction to production workers in American industry increases.
2. Since "production" tends to map onto "unskilled and "semiskilled," while nonproduction tends to map onto "skilled," the demand in manufacturing for skilled labor relative to less skilled labor increases substantially.
3. Because much of the physical production process is now overseas, the capital investments in increasing the marginal physical productivity of workers in that process also occur overseas. As a result, the marginal

physical productivity of American manufacturing (i.e., manufacturing within the geographical confines of the United States but *not* manufacturing by "American" firms) does not grow as quickly as it did previously.

4. Slow productivity growth portends slow wage growth. However, if one measures wages in terms of how large a bundle of manufactured goods the wages can purchase (the way Lawrence and Slaughter measure them), then wages are seemingly increasing more rapidly, because manufacturing workers can now purchase more of their output with their wage than they could previously. The cost decline in these goods, however, is due to globalization, which so reduces production costs that firms practicing it can hold down price increases in their goods, increase expenditures on nonproduction workers, and still make more profits. The U.S. terms of trade do not change because the increased imports of semifinished manufactures are still low-cost, low-value-added goods, and the increased exports of finished goods are still high-cost, high-value-added goods.

5. The unskilled labor released from domestic manufacturing drives down wages for unskilled labor in the rest of the economy. This makes it more attractive for service-sector firms to shift to production processes that are relatively more unskilled labor-intensive, and rely less on improving the marginal physical product of their preexisting labor force. As a result, productivity growth in the American service sector lags that in Europe.

6. The European country where the outcomes in terms of wage and productivity changes are most like those in the United States is the United Kingdom − but it is also the European country whose firms have been globalized most extensively and for the longest period.

If this analysis is correct, then the most important effect of increasing trade openness on the position of skilled and unskilled labor within the advanced capitalist states is not conventional factor price equalization operating through goods markets, but rather the effects on investment patterns that are induced by the changes in the trade regime. Foreign direct investment in the less developed countries by firms in developed countries is neither sufficient nor necessary to generate such effects, though it can contribute to them. (In the 1980s the United States was a net *recipient* of foreign direct investment [Bhagwati 1995: 46].) More fundamental is that both native and foreign investors can now invest in labor-intensive manufacturing in low-wage economies, secure in the knowledge that political barriers to their exports to the developed world have been largely removed.

The practical consequences of this development have been explored by Feenstra and Hanson (1996), who find that nonproduction workers' share of the total wage bill in the United States is an increasing function of the extent of outsourcing broadly defined; however, the results vary greatly across industries. Overall, rising outsourcing explains about 15 percent of the increase in the share of the total wage bill going to nonproduction labor.

THE POLITICS OF TRADE LIBERALIZATION IN THE ADVANCED CAPITALIST STATES

The notion that one can generalize about trade liberalization for countries with as different a set of trade policies (and policy histories) as Japan, western Europe, and North America is hardly unproblematic; nevertheless, there are some obvious cross-national similarities that should be noted.

First, the advanced capitalist states have tended to add or shed protection together. In the post-1945 era, this covariation has been heavily influenced by explicit multilateral bargaining conducted under GATT; however, the fundamentally reciprocal nature of trade barrier reductions antedates the GATT by centuries (Conybeare [1986], for example, has identified tit-for-tat bargaining on trade barriers as far back as the Hansa League of the fourteenth century). Reducing one's own trade barriers is, from a political standpoint, nearly always a concession to foreigners (because producer interests nearly always trump the interests of final consumers), and in order for it to be politically feasible corresponding concessions from foreigners must be secured.

Second, the advanced capitalist states have tended to liberalize trade with each other much more quickly and thoroughly than they have liberalized trade with the less developed countries (LDCs). There are a number of reasons for this. Until recently the most important political barrier to liberalizing trade with the less developed world was the lack of interest on the part of LDCs in granting reciprocal concessions; since the LDCs demanded market access but were generally unwilling to grant it, the developed countries had little incentive to bargain with them. (Trade preferences for less developed countries, such as the American Generalized System of Preferences and the Caribbean Basin Initiative, or the European Yaounde and Lome conventions, are generally designed so that only metropole import merchants derive any substantial benefit from their existence [Langhammer and Sapir 1987].) Even if they had been more willing to offer reciprocal concessions, the smaller size of individual LDC markets and the presence in developed countries of sizable and politically potent sectors that are directly competitive with LDC production (e.g., textiles, sugar) would make agreement difficult. Goods exported from LDCs have historically been "commodities" in the business school sense of that term: they tend not to be differentiated products, and their market penetration often rests on simple cost advantages rather than on any qualitative feature of the good. While a firm producing a bundle of differentiated products may conclude that more open trade is tolerable because the business it loses at home in one product line will be balanced by the business it gains abroad in another, "commodity" producers are quite unlikely to experience such mixed results – if they are in the developed world, they are (with the exception of some mining and agricultural goods, mostly from North America) unequivocal losers. Because compensating the losers in the developed world is politically, fiscally, and administratively difficult,[7] they tend to resist liberalization strenuously and often successfully.

A more subtle reason for the relative lack of mutual barrier reduction between north and south is that important interests in the north actually benefited from southern protectionist policies for a considerable period. During the 1940s and 1950s, when protectionist forces in the north were strong enough to resist any openings to LDC exports, northern business interests that stood to gain from LDC economic development championed import substituting industrialization (ISI) as a second-best strategy for these countries. For the Republican Eisenhower administration, championing ISI achieved the best of both worlds politically: southern countries' domestic expansion would gratify internationally oriented business, while the lack of southern exports would avoid conflicts with import-competing

---

[7] It is politically difficult because the winners don't want to make side payments if they don't have to, and because it is difficult to disguise the side payments as something other than what they really are: a bribe to a politically influential group to induce it to accept an outcome that ostensibly is in the public interest but is costly to the group. It is fiscally difficult because the industries in question (particularly textiles) can be quite large; even if trade adjustment assistance (in the American sense) is not given to the industry, the disemployment in that industry will have serious consequences for unemployment insurance funds, social security and family maintenance funds, and tax revenues in the affected communities. Because such industries are spatially concentrated, the effects are unlikely to be diffuse enough to be gracefully absorbed (and concealed) by the economy as a whole. It is administratively difficult because of moral hazard problems: as has long been recognized by opponents of adjustment assistance, the very existence of such a program discourages timely exit, and there is an incentive to exaggerate the adverse impacts of imports on one's fortunes. Deciding how much of an industry's misfortune is due to imports, and how much is due to other causes, is a perennial difficulty in administrative proceedings designed to provide remedies to injury from imports.

sectors that formed the backbone of the Republican Party of the 1950s. Once ISI regimes were established, internationally oriented firms could benefit either by providing producers' goods to the expanding industrial sectors of these economies, or else by taking advantage of the trade barriers erected by ISI to invest directly in these countries and extract the rents provided by those barriers (Maxfield and Nolt 1990). As protectionism in the north weakened, as the United States lost its massive comparative advantage in producers' goods, and as LDCs came to be seen more as a site for exporting rather than serving domestic markets, northern interest in ISI evaporated.[8] Unfortunately for the LDCs, their artificially maintained industrial bases – and the political forces that arose from them – would not evaporate as quickly and as easily as northern interest in maintaining them.

Another common feature of advanced states' trade policies is that they all protect important blocs of voters that lack comparative advantage, and that the size of the protected blocs is large enough to affect national electoral politics. The largest and most obvious examples of this in all three regions are to be found in textiles and agriculture. Economists are fond of pointing out that of all the various ways of using public policy to protect against the disemploying impact of imports – subsidies to wage earners, subsidies to firms, tariffs, auction quotas, ordinary quotas, and Voluntary Export Restraints – governments most often choose the methods that are the least efficient (i.e., VERs and ordinary quotas), and almost never the method that is most efficient (i.e., direct wage subsidies). Of course, from a political standpoint the very inefficiency of the policy measure commends it as a solution, since the more extensive the spillover from administering an inefficient policy, the larger the coalition that will support it. Such policies complicate trade bargaining among the advanced states, not simply because they impede adjustment, but because alteration or removal of such policies would have domestic political consequences that are quite far-reaching. The association of agriculture and the Japanese Liberal Democratic Party is perhaps the best known example of this. American officials in the 1980s who otherwise would have favored energetic attacks on Japanese agricultural protection tended to act with restraint because they valued the continuation of LDP controlled governments at least as much as they valued the reduction of Japanese agricultural protection.

A fourth commonality among the advanced states is that they all have

---

[8] The equation of "northern" with "American" interests here essentially rests on the hegemonic role that the United States played in bilateral assistance, various aid consortia, and the multilateral lending institutions until the late 1960s.

responded to the negotiated reduction in tariff barriers by relying increasingly on nontariff barriers (NTBs). Doing so makes political sense in two different ways. First, unregulated NTBs are a relatively unobtrusive substitute for highly visible and now proscribed tariff barriers; second, the selective awarding of NTBs to strategically positioned import-competing firms induces all such firms to seek relief from imports individualistically, by pursuing administrative procedures and lobbying the government, rather than forming a coalition and enacting different trade laws.

Aside from the fact that NTBs are often less efficient ways of extending protection than tariffs, their definition is obscure – just about any public policy measure that affects the price of a domestically produced good or of an import could be treated as an NTB. Because of this, the consideration of NTBs in trade negotiations inevitably internationalizes domestic policy making in all sorts of areas, including research and development spending; competition policy; labor standards, occupational safety and health and collective bargaining; and environmental and product safety regulations. Producers in each nation can seek to use regulation such as product quality standards to protect themselves from foreign imports, or else they can seek to have regulatory burdens that are imposed on themselves, such as occupational safety and health standards, extended throughout the entire trading area. Political conflict over this phenomenon has already begun in Europe over the "1992" proposals and the Treaty of Maastricht and in North America over the North American Free Trade Agreement (NAFTA). One can expect that the mechanisms created by the Uruguay Round for the new World Trade Organization to review NTBs will occasion further conflicts of this sort.

Fifth, two of three developed country regions are in or are moving into bloc trading arrangements. (Although intra–east Asia exports are becoming a greater proportion of east Asian countries' total exports [Park 1994], this is a natural result of incomes in east Asia rising more rapidly than in the rest of the world; each east Asian country is becoming a better market for the exports of other east Asian countries.) This is a long-standing feature of European trade, both east and west. For the western Europeans it had an obvious advantage in improving their bargaining strength in trade negotiations with the Americans. For the Americans, regional or "minilateral" arrangements represent a significant break from policy prior to the 1980s. From 1934 to 1981 the United States generally viewed regional trading arrangements as a second-best alternative to true multilateralism, favoring them for regions such as Latin America or western Europe partly for political (i.e., nonpecuniary) reasons. With the advent of the Reagan administration, the United States government negotiated preferential trading arrangements with the Caribbean basin, Israel, Canada, and Mexico; it has expressed interest in extending the North American free trade area to encompass Latin America.

The one core country that has so far stood aloof from regional arrangements – Japan – is also the one that is deriving the greatest benefits from the existing trading system. It has already been suggested that the European Union (EU) is at least in part a defensive response to the "Japanese challenge" (Sandholtz and Zysman 1989); NAFTA can be viewed in a similar light. However, casual observation suggests that these two regional groupings embody rather different coping strategies. Compare the divergences in endowments in the two trading areas: although the long-term ratio of West German to Portuguese gross domestic product per capita is about the same as that between the United States and Mexico, the Mexican population as a percent of total NAFTA population is far greater than Portuguese population as a proportion of the EU (adding to Portugal the population of other relatively poor European countries does not change the picture very much). Labor market effects in the United States therefore ought to be greater from NAFTA than comparable effects in Europe from the expansion and deepening of the EU.

While the EU is commonly rationalized partly in terms of providing an opportunity for European firms to achieve optimal scale, and partly as a way to increase competition in national markets,[9] the United States is already a large market and it has been closely linked with Canada, even before their 1988 bilateral trade agreement. Thus, NAFTA is much less about optimal scale for American firms, or the benefits of Mexican competition for American manufacturing, than it is about lowering labor costs for American firms, providing Mexico with export earnings to pay off its debt, and holding down the cost of food and clothing to American consumers. The last point, of course, is also of interest to employers: just as manufacturers in nineteenth-century Britain supported the abolition of the Corn Laws to give their employees a cheap loaf and lower the wage cost of subsistence, so too do American employers benefit from lower trade barriers on mass consumption items.

Sixth, all have or are modifying their political system to make it more

---

[9] The potentially contradictory nature of these arguments has been noted by Richard Baldwin (1990): "optimal scale" arguments imply increasing returns in an industry, and hence oligopoly profits, while "increased competition" implies deconcentrating an industry by using trade policy to create the functional equivalent of entry.

difficult for protectionist coalitions to prevail. These attempts can be viewed as attempts by internationally oriented forces in these political systems to "lock in" national policies of increasing openness.

1. *Enlarging* the geographic size of the decision-making jurisdictions on trade, as in western Europe, probably works to the advantage of free traders, though the existing theory that seeks to justify this contention (Rogowski 1987; Magee, Brock, and Young 1989: 98–99) is not very convincing.[10]
2. Changing legislative procedures so that trade bills are not subject to floor amendment (part of the so-called fast-track procedure adopted in

[10] Brock, Magee, and Young argue that the larger the district, the more likely producer interests will dominate over consumer interests. They ground this argument on the assumption that disorganized consumers will actually contribute *less* per capita as the district enlarges, so that total consumer expenditures on elections will remain constant. Producer expenditures will not fall per capita, so their campaign expenditures will rise as the size of the district rises.

The trouble with this as an explanation for the postulated relationship between district size and free-trade policy is that the producers could just as easily be import-competing as exporting; then the mechanism postulated by Magee, Brock, and Young would lead to the exact opposite result. They attempt to avoid this difficulty by arguing that in the United States the import-competing industries are relatively "small" compared to the exporting ones, so that they become the analogue to consumers. Aside from a lack of empirical data on firm size versus comparative advantage, the possibility that small firms might be better organized into trade associations than large firms (likely in the U.S. context) is not considered.

Rogowski argues that politicians in large districts are more "insulated" from societal pressures, primarily because large districts are presumed to contain more interests than small ones, and on any given vote some "small" interest can be ignored. Implicitly, they then are freer to vote for "public interest" positions such as free trade. But if large districts and small districts are equally competitive, with pressures in both driving the size of the winning coalition down to minimum winning, then it is difficult to see how a representative of a large district is any more free to ignore interest group demands than one in a small district, assuming that the "small" interest in question is part of the winning coalition, and the winning coalition is a minimum winning one. Since it is not obvious why large districts would be systematically more likely to be uncompetitive than small districts (indeed, the opposite would seem more likely), the puzzle remains.

One possible solution: the fewer the interests, the more easily they can collude among themselves to present a united front to politicians. (Of course, at the limit, the number of interests equals one and there is no collusion problem.) In districts with large numbers of interests, politicians, particularly if they have agenda control, can influence which interests join which coalitions. They could conceivably reshuffle their own support coalition if changing circumstances impelled them to deprive some former supporter of favorable policies, and then seek new bases of support among former opponents or fence-sitters. In such a situation the relatively larger interests may be privileged in the sense that they are essential to more winning coalitions than the small interests are.

Although this explains why a member in a larger district may be more "insulated," it does not explain why the member uses her insulation to vote for freer trade.

the United States in the 1970s) precludes the possibility of using a series of amendments to peel off in succession different groups of supporters. If every legislator wants protection for her own district's output commodity, but free trade in all other commodities, and can be persuaded to vote for free trade in all commodities if all others forgo any protection, then a "clean" free-trade bill can be viewed as a cooperative solution to an n-person game among the bill's supporters. Protectionist amendments covering even a single commodity can affect the stability of that coalition by triggering further defections from the support for a "clean" bill. The process could end in the disintegration of the winning coalition. Conversely, if protection is granted administratively, so that legislative coalitions are not necessary for the most politically important import-competing industries to acquire protection, then a protectionist legislative coalition can be more easily prevented from ever forming. The increasing popularity of VERs is in part due to this logic.

Changes in the Japanese political system are difficult to assess, as this process still seems to have a way to go before it has run its course. However, it is clear that a restructuring of the party system that makes it possible for a ruling party (or ruling coalition of parties) not to include important protectionist elements and to adopt a more "neoliberal" set of economic policies will inhibit protectionism to the extent that such a coalition can maintain itself in office. Electoral reforms that abolish the combination of multimember districts and single nontransferable votes will undercut tendencies for ruling party factions to compete with one another in distributing policy favors to small slices of a given constituency (Cox and Rosenbluth 1993), and so render members of the Diet less responsive to local demands for protection and more responsive to national-level policy concerns; this is particularly likely if campaign finance is highly centralized.

A change in the way that trade agreements are negotiated may alter the domestic political cleavage structure on trade measures in all the advanced states. Both NAFTA and the Uruguay Round bundled foreign investment codes with trade regulations for the first time. In the case of NAFTA this bundling produced a striking alteration in the cleavage structure on trade in the United States. Whereas the common pattern on trade legislation heretofore had been for labor and capital within the same industry to lobby as a team either for or against a given trade bill (Magee 1980), the pattern of support and opposition to NAFTA displayed a much sharper cleavage between factors than previously had been witnessed (Commins 1993). This is due to two circumstances: (1) the weakness of organized labor in sectors that benefit from liberalization; (2) the possibility of relocation to Mexico for owners of firms that are disadvantaged by trade liberalization. The latter causes a divergence in interest between the owners, who can relocate their businesses, and their former workers, who face very high relocation costs.

Finally, the success or failure of earlier attempts to negotiate the removal of trade barriers affects the composition of interests that are active in seeking future changes in trade policy. If an import-competing industry receives protection sufficient to raise rates of return above the market rate, new entrants will be attracted, and the resources of the industry that can be devoted to political action will be augmented; the removal of protection will have the opposite effect. This suggests that changes in trade policy tend to be self-reinforcing, as the changes in agents' asset portfolios as a result of a change in trade policy then induce a change in their political activity intended to enhance the returns to those portfolios (Cassing and Hillman 1986).

CONCLUSIONS AND CAUTIONARY NOTES

It is apparent that the effects of greater trade openness are multifaceted. In the advanced capitalist countries, greater openness will generally advantage owners of capital and workers with skills, while disadvantaging those with few or no skills. However, the rate at which wages for unskilled workers converge globally is unlikely to be greater than the rate at which they have historically converged within the United States or the European Union.

If the analysis in the second section is correct, trade openness is most usefully considered in conjunction with foreign direct investment. Trade openness certainly facilitates such investment, by making it possible for firms to unbundle production processes and distribute the components to local markets that are optimal for each stage of production. It is possible that the most pronounced effects of openness on workers in the advanced economies are the ones mediated by foreign direct investment, rather than the ones associated with changes in goods prices along the traditional Stolper-Samuelson lines. While capital in Europe and Japan has hitherto been more "national" than in the United States, the convergence of wages among these countries suggests that the effect of high wages in pushing firms in these countries into global production strategies will henceforth be felt strongly in all of them. Continued global trade openness, coupled with political stability and neoliberal economic policies in the less developed world, make this strategy appear highly feasible in the near future.

While the third section suggests that there are significant commonalities in the policy responses of developed countries, it is apparent that these responses often involve discrimination (in the form of trading blocs) and the maintenance or addition of protection. In neither case is there a neat and simple pattern of results: while greater openness has costs, it also has benefits; while it provides a new constraint, it also creates a new opportunity. Policy responses in the aggregate have endorsed continued openness, but free-trade purists still find plenty of discrimination and protection to complain about – and some of their objects of complaint are not holdovers from a bygone era but rather fairly recent policy development (such as the explosion in popularity of VERs in the 1980s).

It is well to remember that, although trade is now quite open (in terms of the ratio of exports and imports to national income), the world economy is still not as open in all respects as that which existed before 1914. In particular, movements of labor and long-term capital are less important in the current economy than they were eighty years ago. It is also wise to recall that the openness of the pre-1914 period was indeed reversible, and that it took about sixty years for trade openness to attain the level that it had attained prior to World War I. Openness to labor and long-term capital flows still has not recovered completely.

The implications are important. First, as open as the system currently is, it could well become substantially *more* open if capital and labor flows are accommodated; second, there is no reason to assume that the attained openness is irreversible. Developments in European monetary integration in the past two years amply illustrate the dangers of ignoring the latter point. Theories that attempt to explain monetary integration as a one-way process (e.g., Eichengreen and Frieden 1993) focus on long-run changes in interest and endowments but are unable to address the policy reverses of the past twenty years.

Another cautionary note concerns the tendency to attribute *too much or too many* changes in advanced capitalist states to openness or "interdependence" (Garrett and Lange [1991] succinctly review this literature). The problem here is that the period since 1973 has been one of slower growth in addition to being one of greater openness, and that many of the changes in policy attributable to "interdependence" could be driven by low growth rates: slow growth would lead to increases in unemployment or declines in wages, to fiscal stringency as revenue (or at least revenue growth) declines and some unemployment-related expenditures actually grow, and to public policies to increase the rate of investment, partly by improving rates of return on capital. The world economy steadily became more open over the entire post–World War II period, but all of the literature cited by Garrett and Lange as arguing that interdependence is problematic for social democracy was written beginning in the 1980s. As others in this volume have noted, social democratic parties in Europe have long advocated free-trade policies. It is not an open goods market per se that is threatening for them, but rather the combination of the open goods market with slow growth and the increased international mobility of capital.

The economic impacts of increasing openness discussed in the first section could generate a variety of responses by governments and private interests. Aside from a simple refusal to open further, or even a reversal of present levels of openness, there are other possibilities that might mitigate some of the negative effects of more openness while preserving its gains. Some of the limitations on the freedom of maneuver of governments in macroeconomic policy could be circumvented by active policy coordination by these governments. The more export-dependent an economy, the more dependent it is on growth in demand in foreign markets. Governments thus acquire a stake in the economic decisions of other governments. Political parties and labor unions concomitantly acquire an interest in internationalizing their activities and coordinating their behavior with foreign partners. Developments on this front are obviously at an embryonic state, but it is equally obvious that as long as an open system is maintained, the incentives at least to begin to cooperate transnationally will continue to be present.

Within the developed countries, a general decline in the economic fortunes of unskilled labor is quite likely. Because of the low probability that recent changes in the trade regime will be easily or quickly reversed, a standard "welfare" measure for these people – trade protection – is less and less politically feasible. Whereas before these countries could count on the general spillover (or "trickle-down") effects of economic growth delivering at least some benefits to even the unskilled, the effects of the restructuring of economies now under way are likely to swamp whatever benefits accrue to this portion of the population through economic growth. Either a variety of nontrade related policy measures will need to be adopted to reverse the decline in fortunes of this group, or else these societies will continue to experience widening social division between those who benefit from the emerging global production system and those who do not.

The political evolution of nation-states over the period 1918–1973 was a story that was often told with very little reference to events beyond national boundaries. With respect to the history from the nineteenth century to the last part of the twentieth, that nationalist interlude now stands out as anomalous, even though the social scientific literature produced during that period still exercises a considerable influence over how scholars think about social processes. It is clear that we can no longer think of nations as closed systems. It is only slightly less clear that doing so, even for the previous era, is fundamentally misleading.

2

THE INTERNATIONALIZATION OF CAPITAL

Beth A. Simmons

The internationalization and integration of capital markets has been the most significant change in the political economy of the industrialized countries over the past three decades. From the Great Depression to the Bretton Woods period, capital markets developed largely within national boundaries. Yet the past three decades have witnessed historically unprecedented growth in cross-border capital movements that have surpassed those of the late nineteenth century, often thought of as a golden age of international finance. Moreover, since World War II, the integration of capital markets has been far more rapid and complete among the industrialized countries than has the integration of markets for goods and services. No other area of the economy has been so thoroughly internationalized as swiftly as have capital markets since the 1970s.

The consequences of such rapid and fundamental change have begun to unfold in a number of countries. More highly integrated capital markets may erode governments' ability to use monetary and even fiscal policies to stimulate the economy. At the same time, newly liberalized capital markets and the growth in foreign investment opportunities may alter the balance of power between relatively immobile labor and capital with a credible "exit option," potentially with significant consequences for domestic institutions and policy outcomes.

The purpose of this essay is to describe the recent internationalization of capital, and to explore the implications for the industrialized countries of the Organization for Economic Cooperation and Development (OECD).

The first section describes capital controls under the Bretton Woods regime and their subsequent liberalization. Bretton Woods endorsed capital controls, but these were relaxed in the 1970s and virtually eliminated in the 1980s and 1990s in most OECD countries. The second section describes the increase in transnational capital movements, and the third reviews the evidence of capital market integration since the 1960s. The fourth section explores the consequences of more integrated capital markets on national politics and policy making, and the final section offers conclusions.

THE POST–BRETTON WOODS LIBERALIZATION OF CAPITAL CONTROLS

Ever since international capital markets collapsed in the early 1930s, governments of the advanced industrialized countries have used capital controls as a key tool of economic policy. In the face of collapsing financial markets and downward spiraling trade, capital controls were employed primarily to try to stabilize currencies and prevent capital flight. Harsh controls were put into place in a number of countries, notably Germany and Japan, for which intervention in capital markets soon became connected to the goal of allocating capital according to national objectives. In other countries, such as Czechoslovakia, controls initially designed to prevent capital flight and balance-of-payments crises were gradually lifted over the course of the decade. The Gold Bloc countries (France, Netherlands, Switzerland, and Belgium) placed few restrictions on capital flows during this period (League of Nations 1938). In the United States, capital controls were favored by the Treasury Department as a way to control the inflationary effects of vast inflows from Europe, but this proposal was ultimately defeated by more liberal thinkers touting sterilization of these inflows rather than their prohibition (Helleiner 1994). In Britain, foreign loans were scrutinized in the 1930s for their effects on domestic British industry (Cairncross and Eichengreen 1983).

After World War II, however, a clear and distinctive justification for maintaining capital controls was articulated in both Britain and the United States: they could be used by governments to manage the domestic economy. Capital controls were defended by White, the primary American negotiator at Bretton Woods, as giving governments much greater control over monetary and tax policy (Horsefield 1969). According to Keynes, capital controls were essential to autonomous management of the economy: "the whole management of the domestic economy depends upon being free to have the appropriate rate of interest without reference to the rates pre-

vailing elsewhere in the world. Capital control is a corollary to this"
(quoted by Heillener 1994: 34). And in describing the Bretton Woods
agreement before the British Parliament, John Maynard Keynes defended
capital controls as an accepted norm of the new international monetary
system:

> Not merely as a feature of the transition but as a permanent arrangement
> the plan accords to every government the explicit right to control all
> capital movements. What used to be heresy is now endorsed as orthodox.
> . . . It follows that our right to control the domestic capital market is
> secured on firmer foundations than ever before, and is formally accepted
> as a proper part of agreed international agreements. (as quoted by Good-
> man and Pauly 1993: n. 5)

Thus, after World War II, a tight matrix of capital controls was continued in many countries of the OECD, and these were viewed not only as
an instrument of exchange rate stabilization, but as a means to secure full
employment and other national economic priorities. To be sure, Americans,
flush with funds to invest, were not and had never been as enamored of
controls as were deficit-plagued Europeans at this time (Epstein and Schor
1992). Nonetheless, capital controls were legitimized by Article VI of the
Bretton Woods agreement, which allowed members to regulate international capital movements, as long as these did not restrict payments for
current external transactions. Even the OECD's 1961 Code of Liberalization of Capital Movements endorsed freer markets subject to the right of
the cooperating states themselves to determine when conditions were sufficiently "severe" to warrant a departure from this principle (Lamfalussy
1981). Far from ensconcing principles of capital market liberalization parallel to those in the postwar institution for trade, the Bretton Woods
agreement condoned capital controls not only for short-term management
of balance-of-payments crises, but also for purposes of domestic economic
management.

Virtually every government – surplus and deficit – took action at one
time or another to shield its economy from undesired capital movements,
though some had constructed much tighter and more enduring barriers
than others. Recent research suggests that from the 1950s to the 1970s,
governments of the left tended to restrict international financial flows more
frequently than those of the right. Right-wing governments did not hesitate to do so, however, in economies with less competitive business firms
(Quinn and Inclan 1995). Decision makers in countries plagued by high
inflation rates, high government deficits, and high current-account deficits
also tended to implement a more intense system of controls (Lemmen and
Eijffinger 1995). Overall, controls were typically used as a tool to shield

the domestic economy and prevent the kind of capital flight that might be expected under inflationary conditions.

The most common restrictions limited capital-account convertibility by placing limits on the possession and availability of foreign exchange. Quantitative restrictions were another measure, typically involving limitations on the external asset and liability positions of domestic financial institutions (the evidence on the internationalization of these assets is discussed later). Quantitative restrictions were also at times placed on the domestic operations of foreign banks, as well as on resident firms' and individuals' foreign portfolio assets, real estate holdings, and direct investments (Mathieson and Rojas-Suarez 1994).

Another form of control on the movement of capital was the use of dual or multiple exchange rate systems involving distinct rates for commercial and financial transactions. Typically, the commercial exchange rate was controlled by the authorities, while the financial rate was allowed to float (as will be discussed, floating rates have tended to contribute to capital market segmentation by injecting uncertainty regarding future exchange rate fluctuations into the decision to invest). Dual exchange rates required a detailed set of rules to distinguish capital from current transactions. They also necessitated establishing oversight over residents' foreign exchange transactions and nonresidents' domestic currency transactions, making this approach to controlling international capital movements one of the most burdensome to administer and enforce (Mathieson and Rojas-Suarez 1994). To varying degrees, separate exchange rates for some kinds of capital transactions or invisibles were maintained in Italy between 1972 and 1982, France between 1970 and 1974, the Netherlands from 1971 to 1973, Ireland until 1978, the United Kingdom until 1979, and Belgium as late as 1990 (IMF, various years).

Among the OECD countries, Japan has perhaps made the greatest use of capital controls, largely for purposes of managing the exchange rate and international payments. Through the Foreign Exchange and Trade Control Law of 1949, the Japanese government prohibited capital transactions and restricted licenses for financial institutions engaged in international business. There were also informal controls, such as administrative guidance of the foreign-exchange positions of Japanese banks (Henning 1994). German authorities, opposed to controls in principle, tried to control the inflow of capital, which threatened inflation by increasing the liquidity in the banking system and expanding the money supply. They tried to do this largely through ceilings on overall net flows through the banking system, prohibitions of or negative interest rates on nonresidents' deposits, and bans on further deposits. So did Switzerland, Netherlands, and Belgium in the waning years of Bretton Woods. In 1966, France passed a law that gave the government the right to control foreign-exchange transactions, and oversee the liquidation of foreign funds in France and French funds overseas. Italy tightened controls in 1973 when expansionary policies led to fiscal imbalances and current-account deficits.

The United States also resorted to capital controls in the 1960s and early 1970s, though these were somewhat halfhearted and often porous in comparison to those in Japan and Europe (Henning 1994). For example, under balance-of-payments pressure, in 1963 the United States imposed the Interest Equalization Tax (IET) on U.S. residents' purchases of foreign stocks and bonds, and two years later the tax was extended to long-term bank loans. In 1965, the United States instituted a "voluntary" program aimed at protecting the balance of payments by limiting the acquisition of foreign assets by U.S. banks and nonbanks. Three years later, the United States began to regulate the outflow of foreign direct investment.

But for a number of reasons, capital controls were significantly reduced over the course of the 1970s. For one thing, despite (or perhaps because of) national regulation, offshore markets grew significantly free from government intervention. Increasingly over the course of the 1960s, national regulations and controls coexisted alongside a growing pool of largely unregulated international capital. Though the Eurodollar market began as a short-term money market, the influx of U.S. banks and multinational corporations seeking relief from national restrictions transformed it into a full-fledged international capital market serving the needs that had previously been met in New York. Despite the widespread desire in western Europe to control speculative capital movements, multilateral cooperation to do so failed in the early 1970s, due to opposition from the United States and a growing realization that effective controls would indeed have to be draconian.[1]

Meanwhile, the growth in private international financial activity jeopardized the system of fixed exchange rates. Their collapse between 1971 and 1973 changed the calculus on which capital controls were premised. Willing to float their currencies, countries could, in theory, enjoy the benefits of efficient international capital allocation while retaining a high degree of monetary policy autonomy (Haberler 1945, 1954; Friedman 1953; Johnson 1974) – a rationale that had the most appeal for the relatively insulated United States. In the American view, a more liberal international financial system would preserve U.S. policy autonomy in the long run: the dollar would still be the world's reserve currency, American

---

[1] Report of the Committee of 20 established by the board of governors of the IMF in 1972.

financial markets – the most competitive in the world – would remain preeminent, and U.S. current-account deficits could be financed by foreign investors.

In 1974, the United States dismantled the web of controls that had built up since 1963. Once the United States unilaterally lifted controls, other countries felt competitive pressures to do the same. Canada and the Netherlands, for example, lifted controls in the same year. Germany and Switzerland reduced capital controls but up to 1979 continued to regulate transactions to head off currency appreciation. Britain significantly liberalized exchange controls on capital movements beginning in 1977, and removed existing exchange controls of all kinds in October 1979. Japan relaxed controls over the course of the 1970s, and by 1980, these were formalized in the Foreign Exchange and Control Law that made all external transactions free unless otherwise specified (Eken 1984; Rosenbluth 1989: 57). France removed capital controls as a prelude to entering the European Community's single market in financial services in 1986 and had fairly completed the task by 1990; Italy did not begin to eliminate capital controls until 1987 and did not complete the task until 1992.

Figure 2.1 graphs the repeal of nine institutional indicators of capital controls for fifteen OECD countries between 1967 and 1993. The vertical axis is a count of the average number of nine different types of controls (listed in Figure 2.1) in place in each country by year.

Clearly, there have been steep reductions in these types of capital market interference. It should be noted, however, that this composite measure does not reflect various tax and taxlike incentives that even the most liberal states have devised to channel international capital flows. By this composite measure, the United States and Germany had no capital controls between 1967 and 1990, despite the pervasiveness of tax incentives in the 1960s and early 1970s that had tremendous effects on investment decisions. Nonetheless, the repeal of policies that interfere with cross-border capital movements has been substantial, taking only a slight upturn with the final breakdown in fixed exchange rates in 1973, and during the steep hike in world interest rates in 1981. Notably, there was no return to capital controls with the European Monetary System (EMS) crisis in 1992–1993. Most of the major markets were completely unfettered by capital controls by the early 1990s.

The dynamics that led to such drastic relaxation in capital controls over the past two decades are increasingly under study. Early popular accounts stressed the role of technological innovation. The financial services industry has been revolutionized by technological innovations that affect communications, the speed of computations, and the ability to conclude

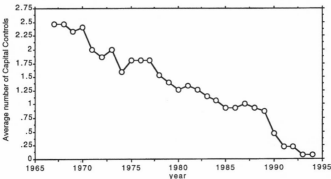

Figure 2.1. Average number of capital controls (of a total of nine measures for fifteen OECD countries, 1967–1993. Included controls: (1) *restrictions on capital account* (refers exclusively to resident-owned funds); (2) *bilateral payments with members* of the International Monetary Fund (considered a highly illiberal way to settle payments and in effect posed a barrier to the movement of capital); (3) *bilateral payments with nonmembers*; (4) *deposit restrictions* (typically a quantitative restriction on the external liability and asset positions of domestic financial institutions); and (5) *dual exchange rate regime* (separate exchange rates for some or all capital transactions and/or some or all invisibles). The following constituted limitations on current-account transactions, and are included because current-account transactions can be used to partially evade restrictions on capital transactions by overinvoicing imports and underinvoicing exports (allowing capital to exit): (6) *advance import deposits*; (7) *import surcharge*; (8) *restrictions on current transactions*; and (9) *surrender of export proceeds*. (SOURCES: All data are from the International Monetary Fund, *Annual Report on Exchange Arrangements and Exchange Restrictions*, Washington, D.C., various years. Computer readable copies of 1–4 were originally supplied to me by Geoffrey Garrett; computer readable copies of 6–9 were coded and supplied by Gian Marie Milesi-Ferretti; and 5 was hand-entered by the author from *Annual Report on Exchange Arrangements and Exchange Restrictions*, various years.)

international transactions instantaneously. Technological advances that make international transactions instantaneous and inexpensive in effect raise the cost of trying to seal off the national economy from global capital markets (Bryant 1987; Wriston 1988; McKenzie and Lee 1991; O'Brien 1992). More economically and politically nuanced renditions have stressed the element of competitive liberalization, by which lifting controls in one country creates pressures to liberalize elsewhere (Frankel 1992; Frieden 1989; Kenen 1985; Porter 1990; Moses 1994). For example, controls may disadvantage domestically based multinational firms whose foreign competitors are able to invest and borrow globally at will. Goodman and Pauly (1993) argue that by 1984, when capital markets were rapidly developing elsewhere, the competitiveness of both French industry and finance was seen to be seriously undermined by capital controls. Political pressure from internationally oriented firms provides the mechanism linking liberalizing moves in other countries with similar policies elsewhere.

To be sure, there are also a number of reasons states may have begun to favor deregulation and the lifting of capital controls on domestic policy grounds. In the cases of the United States, France, and Japan in the 1980s, for instance, liberalization of financial markets and capital controls may at least partially be related to the needs of governments to tap internal or external sources of funds to finance growing public debts (Eken 1984; Feldman 1986; Cerny 1989). Others have stressed that the policy of maintaining or lifting capital controls is a highly political – even partisan – policy choice. Some political economists have argued that the propensity to use or to eliminate capital controls is the outcome of class conflict in which market discipline is marshaled to constrain the inflationary demands of labor and the profligacy of leftist governments (Notermans 1993). Gerald Epstein and Juliet Schor (1992) have argued that the propensity to employ capital controls reflects the relative balance of power between labor and capital. Where the former has greater political influence, controls are more likely. Thus, they argue, controls have been dismantled not because they are ineffective, but because of the relative shift in political power among groups. Domestic ideology is also cited as a factor. The spread of neoclassical ideas most clearly embodied in the policies of Reagan and Thatcher provided a clear framework for eliminating controls. As one scholar has written, "Liberalization and deregulation were, after all, the catchwords of the decade" (Moses 1984; see also Plender 1988; Pauly 1988). This view attributes the decision to lift controls to convergence around the tenets of neoclassical economics.

Obviously, technological, competitive, political, and ideological explanations are not competitive, but rather are highly complementary explanations for the decision to facilitate capital-market integration. The next section examines the extent of actual capital movements over the past three decades and the evidence of increased integration across markets.

TRANSNATIONAL CAPITAL MOVEMENTS: THE EVIDENCE

Transnational capital movements have reflected the broad contours of government policy toward capital controls this century. From a historical high before World War I, international capital markets recovered somewhat during the 1920s and then virtually shut down during the Great Depression through World War II (Stallings 1987). The past three decades can be thought of as a *reemergence* of international capital, since by a number of measures, capital markets were as integrated and money flowed as readily across borders during the height of the nineteenth-century gold standard as it has in recent years. By the last quarter of the nineteenth century, for example, Italy, India, and Denmark owed more than 30 percent of their gross national product (GNP) to foreigners – a ratio that approximates that of the largest developing country debtors in the 1980s (Zevin 1992: 47). On the creditor's side, during the height of the gold standard Britain had invested some 153 percent and France 97 percent of their respective GNPs overseas. No creditor today comes anywhere near these figures. The stock of world gross foreign direct investment was approximately 49 percent of the total GNP of the five largest nations in 1914, and it was about 50 percent of the five largest nations in 1989 (Pollins 1993). Before World War I, government bond yields, and business cycle correlations among the major markets between 1876 and 1914 were apparently as correlated as they have been in the 1980s – another indicator that these markets were comparatively integrated (Zevin 1992).

A few preliminary points should be made about the reintegration of capital markets in recent years. First, the most important burst of transnational flows among the OECD countries took place in the early to mid-1980s and largely reflected the tremendous financing needs of the U.S. current-account deficit. Figure 2.2 shows that transactions in international capital movements within the OECD (measured here as the total absolute value of net changes in assets and liabilities of foreign direct and portfolio investment) bear a strong mirror-image resemblance to the U.S. current-account deficit (all figures are standardized by GNP).

Apparently, as was the case with the OPEC surplus of the 1970s, one of the major stimulants of the increased volume of capital across borders was the presence of tremendous current-account imbalances in the system. Yet despite the reduction of the U.S. deficit, international capital flows have continued, evidence that once internationalized, firms and investors do not readily retreat from their global vantage.

Second, and relatedly, the "internationalization" of capital in the

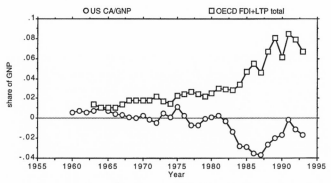

Figure 2.2. Relationship between the United States current-account deficit and the absolute value of total net flows of foreign direct and portfolio investment of OECD countries. (SOURCES: Foreign direct investment is calculated from *Balances of Payments of OECD Countries.* Portfolio investment is calculated from *Balances of Payments of OECD Countries,* supplemented by IMF, *Balance of Payments Statistics Yearbook,* detailed transactions tables: portfolio outflows are calculated from lines 53 (government bonds); 56 (corporate bonds); and 59 (corporate equities); and portfolio inflows are calculated from lines 55 (government bonds), 58 (corporate bonds), and 61 (corporate equities). Total net flows are calculated as the absolute value of the sum of these inward and outward flows. U.S. current-account deficit is from IMF, *Balance of Payments Statistics Yearbook.*)

1980s was largely an investment orgy among the wealthy, and only recently and fitfully has extended to developing countries. While the absolute value of investment in developing countries doubled over the course of the 1980s, their *share* of global foreign direct investment fell from 25 to 19 percent, largely as the result of very favorable investment opportunities in the United States (OECD 1992c: 11)[2] Even more than has been the case with foreign direct investment, the explosion of portfolio investment largely reflects transactions among advanced capitalist countries; portfolio

---

[2] In addition, ten developing countries outside Europe accounted for three-quarters of total FDI over the course of the decade: Singapore (12 percent), Brazil (12 percent), Mexico (11 percent), China (10 percent), Hong Kong (7 percent), Malaysia (6 percent), Egypt (6 percent), Argentina (4 percent), Thailand (3 percent), and Colombia (3 percent) (United Nations 1991). The increasingly "north-north" nature of much FDI is an important distinguishing feature of the current period compared with circumstances in the first golden age of the nineteenth century, when FDI tended to flow from the creditor countries of western Europe (United Kingdom, France, and, somewhat later, Germany) to Latin America, Russia, the United States, and "regions of new settlement" (Australia, New Zealand, and Canada) (Pollins 1993).

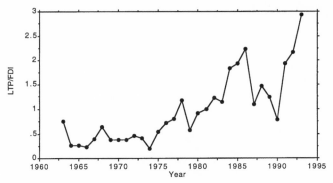

Figure 2.3. Ratio of long-term portfolio investment to foreign direct investment for the OECD, 1963–1993. (SOURCES: See Figure 2.2.)

investment in all but a few developing countries has remained rather limited. The capitalization of developing countries' stock markets stagnated at 6 percent of those of the advanced industrialized economies throughout the 1980s (Sobel 1995; Turner 1991: 52). International bond issues of developed countries were valued at $96.8 billion in 1984 and $207 billion in 1990. Developing countries' bond issues totaled $3.8 billion in 1984, but they did surge to $59.4 billion in 1993 before the Mexican crisis (IMF 1995). These investments are heavily concentrated in a few emerging markets: approximately 70 percent of non-OECD bond issues were those of Hong Kong, Singapore, South Korea, Taiwan, Indonesia, Malaysia, and Thailand (Turner 1991).

Third, within the advanced industrialized countries, there has been an important shift in the relative importance of portfolio and foreign direct investment. The former has grown far faster than the latter recently (Figure 2.3). In the 1970s, net portfolio inflows and outflows were perhaps half again as large as foreign direct investment; by the 1990s they were 2.5 times as large for the OECD as a whole – a development that has enhanced the perception if not the reality that governments are facing increasingly volatile economic forces that need not make for the most efficient allocation of resources and over which they have little control.

Finally, country-by-country evidence suggests that there are still noticeable differences among countries with respect to their reliance on foreign capital relative to their total economy. There are also some differences in the extent to which national interest rates have become correlated with those prevailing internationally, though these have narrowed significantly over time and are heavily influenced by exchange rate volatility. This leaves room to argue that it is possible, though undoubtedly, increasingly costly, to resist the waves of capital-market liberalization that have been sweeping most markets of the OECD.

FOREIGN DIRECT INVESTMENT

During the Bretton Woods period, foreign direct investment (FDI) was the most common form of international capital movement for most OECD countries. In fact, during the decade of the 1960s, every OECD country save three – Belgium, Canada, and the Netherlands – had larger total FDI transactions than any other category of international capital transaction. During the 1960s and early 1970s, American multinational firms invested heavily in Europe, but this trend was moderated in the 1970s and then reversed drastically as U.S. current-account deficits grew in the early 1980s. As a result, foreign shares of U.S. assets, employment, and production held by U.S. affiliates of foreign firms nearly trebled between 1977 and the late 1980s (Graham and Krugman 1989). All of the most highly industrialized European countries became net exporters of FDI in the 1980s.[3] Sweden had the most precipitous shift toward net export status in the late 1980s, with *net* overseas direct investment in 1990 totaling more than 5 percent of GNP.

Figure 2.4 gives some impression of the openness to FDI of several OECD countries from the early 1960s to the present. This figure charts total FDI transactions – net inflows (liabilities) and net outflows (assets) – relative to GNP each year.

In most cases these flows began to grow significantly around 1985. Thus, many advanced industrialized countries became increasingly subject to FDI inflows and outflows relative to their total productive capacity (as well as a share of their domestic capital formation)[4] in the mid-1980s. There are some exceptions, to be sure. Japan, for example, has come to rival the United States and United Kingdom as one of the leading sources of FDI, yet net inflows have not grown appreciably (Figure 2.4a). For obvious reasons the developing regions of Europe (Spain, Portugal, Ireland, Iceland, and Greece) have imported far more direct investment capital than they export (Figure 2.4b). The ratio of FDI to GNP has been highly variable for a number of countries (Australia, Canada, Norway, Switzerland; not pictured here), though the reasons for this pattern certainly vary across cases. France, Belgium, and to a lesser extent the Netherlands most

---

[3] Spain and Portugal increasingly imported foreign direct capital investment during the 1980s, though net imports decreased in Ireland.

[4] OECD 1992c: 11.

a. United States, United Kingdom and Japan:

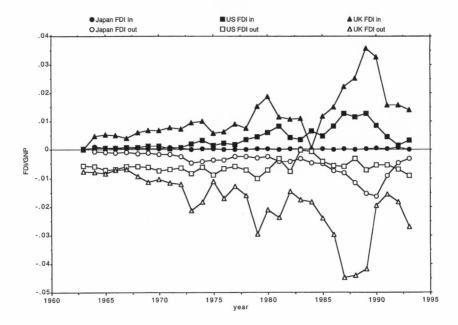

b. Spain, Portugal, Ireland:

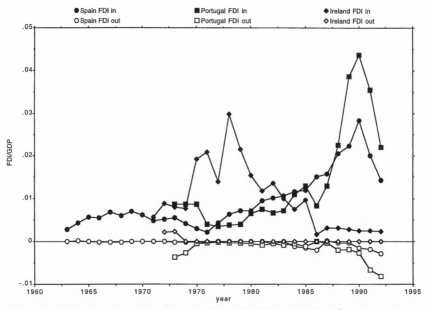

Figure 2.4. Foreign direct investment inflows (liabilities) and outflows (assets), as a percentage of GNP, 1963–1993.

c: France, Belgium, Netherlands:

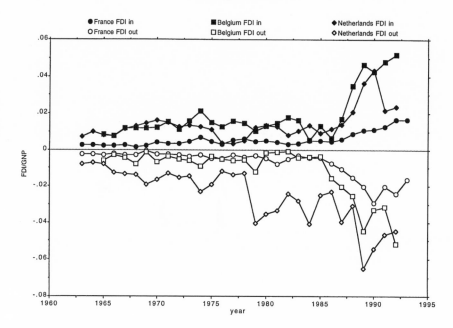

closely typify the OECD pattern over the course of the past three decades (Figure 2.4c): while Belgium and the Netherlands are overall far more open to FDI, these countries all show a marked increase in both net imports and net exports between 1985 and 1990. In each case, although there was some evidence that these movements were beginning to moderate by the beginning of the 1990s, they have since recovered. Virtually all restrictions on the outward movement of FDI have been removed in OECD countries, and inward investments face only sectoral restrictions (rail and road transport, and public utilities, for example; OECD 1992c: 11).

The kinds of direct investments made over the course of the past decade have evolved as well. Traditional investments in raw materials and manufacturing are an ever smaller portion of the share of FDI in the OECD. Foreign investors are increasingly looking to service and high-technology sectors for investment opportunities. One of the most distinguishing features of the 1980s was the fact that most members of the OECD for the first time came to authorize foreign banks to establish branches on their soil (OECD 1992c: 37). And relatively fewer foreign investors are willing to start from scratch: mergers, acquisitions, and strategic alliances account for a growing share of total investment, as firms seek to penetrate markets and tap new sources of technology cheaply and quickly (OECD 1992c: 11, 36).[5] This last trend may provide one explanation for the recent burst of FDI in many OECD countries: having liberalized their trade over the course of the past two decades, the international competition stimulates a constant search for new technology and know-how so essential to the ability to compete in global markets (Cowhey and Aronson 1993).

THE INTERNATIONALIZATION OF THE BANKING SECTOR

The internationalization of the accounts of national deposit banks provides further evidence of the internationalization of finance. Figure 2.5 shows that there has been a tremendous and, until recently, unrelenting increase in foreign assets and liabilities of national deposit banks relative to total GNP.

The decision of the United States to lift regulations on international capital flows led to a huge increase in the external claims of U.S. banks from $26.8 billion to $203 billion from 1973 to 1980. Yet the United States lags far behind the OECD average when standardized by GNP. Belgium, the Netherlands, the United Kingdom, and most especially Switzerland are best known for their highly internationalized banking sectors. These countries are the only four that are obviously above the OECD average (Figure 2.5a), but even in France and Austria, countries known for government intervention in finance for purposes of industrial and macro-economic policy making (Zysman 1983; Kurzer 1993), deposit banks have increased their international business in real terms and have kept up with the regional average. The Scandinavian deposit banks have made the most dramatic changes over time. From rather insulated beginnings these banks are increasingly accepting foreign deposits and lending to foreign borrowers (Figure 2.5b). Once again, the deposit banks of Greece and Portugal reflect the developing status of these regions: though international activity of all kinds is up, they increasingly accept more deposits (liabilities) than they make loans (assets) (not pictured here). Banks in OECD countries with the least international business relative to the size of their national economy tend to lie outside of Europe – in North America or Down Under (Figure 2.5c).

The comparative statistical evidence is fairly clear that production and banking are increasingly aimed at and depend on international markets.

[5] This is despite the fact that some governments (e.g., Sweden, Canada, and Belgium) are more likely to require authorization for foreign acquisitions than greenfield investments.

The fact that these trends are *real* – these measures of internationalization and openness persist when standardized by GNP – suggests that the economic and hence the political visibility of these more highly internationalized firms has truly increased over time. These firms are likely to continue to demand open markets, further entrenching liberal policy choices to date (Goodman and Pauly 1993; Scharpf 1991: 248).

PORTFOLIO INVESTMENT

Portfolio investment (stocks, bonds, and bank loans) have grown much more rapidly than has direct foreign investment, and tends to be much more liquid and, as a result, more volatile. Beginning around 1974, but accelerating again in the mid-1980s, net changes in portfolio inflows totaled about 3 percent of GNP per year in the OECD, but for some countries were much more.

Figure 2.6 plots total inward and outward flows standardized once again by GNP. Since portfolio investment is highly volatile, we might expect it to be highly responsive to the institutional environment, and this does seem to be the case, especially for the Scandinavian countries (Figure 2.6a). Norway's 1974 capital control liberalization coincided closely in time with that of the United States, and led to a tremendous increase in inward flows. Sweden is another case in point. Until mid-1989, Sweden imposed tight restrictions on foreign investment by domestic institutional investors. The large acquisition of foreign assets that year indicates they lost little time in starting to diversify: their holdings of foreign securities as a percent of total security holdings jumped from 4 to 10 percent between 1989 and 1990 (Lindenius 1990). The phaseout of Britain's capital controls in 1979 opened the way for massive increases in these flows in the 1980s (Figure 2.6b). For France, flows seem to have been stimulated slightly by liberalization in the United Kingdom, and even more so by France's own program of liberalization prior to the unification of the European market in 1992. Italy's 1987 reforms were followed almost immediately by unprecedented two-way flows of portfolio investment. With the exception of Greece, long-term portfolio flows increased drastically in the European periphery from the mid-1980s (Figure 2.6c). The removal of capital controls in the United Kingdom (1979) seems to have preceded large jumps in international portfolio flows even in countries such as Ireland that made no major changes in their own controls over the period.

What these graphs do not reveal is that the *composition* of portfolio investment has undergone some change over the course of the past decade and a half with a strong dip in bank lending between 1981 and 1986.

a: Belgium, Netherlands, United Kingdom, Switzerland:

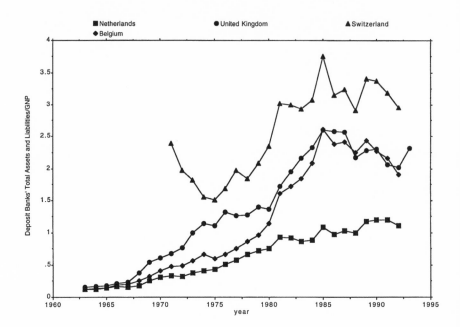

b: Sweden Norway, Denmark, Finland:

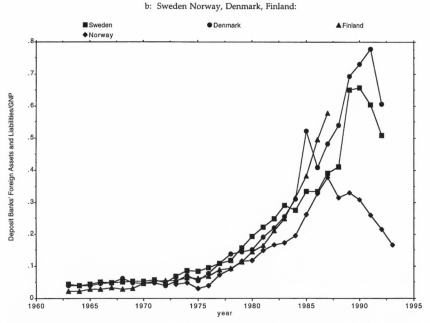

Figure 2.5. Assets and liabilities of deposit banks relative to GNP, 1963–1993.
(SOURCES: Deposit Banks' Foreign Assets and Liabilities: IMF,
International Financial Statistics Year Book [World Tables], various years.)

c: The United States, Canada, Australia, and New Zealand:

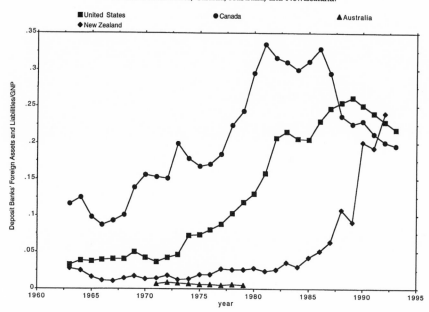

During the debt crisis international lending fell so steeply that it was very nearly overtaken by bond financing. "Securitization" and "disintermediation" were largely the result of negative interest rates in the late 1970s and the fallout of the debt crisis, and have spawned a number of new financial instruments and innovations that have greatly increased the flexibility of borrowers and lenders and deepened secondary markets that in turn render securities markets more liquid (Cerny 1993). Bank lending has since recovered, however, and now accounts for about three-quarters of international finance reported by the Bank for International Settlements (BIS) (Turner 1991).

A host of institutional innovations has contributed to the dramatic increase in portfolio investment, especially in securities. Variable-rate bonds, convertibles, futures, options, and swaps have allowed securities to be tailored to the needs of borrowers and investors, contributing to the volume of portfolio borrowing, especially for sovereign governments and large multinational corporations (Cerny 1993: 63–64; Cosh, Hughes, and Singh 1992). These instruments have been designed primarily to cope with the risks of flexible exchange rates and volatile interest rates. They are designed to increase the marketability and reduce the risk of foreign investment, and their volume attests to their perceived usefulness in this

a: Sweden, Norway, Finland, and Denmark:

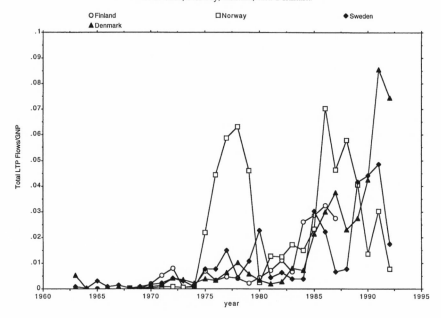

b: Germany, France, United Kingdom, Italy:

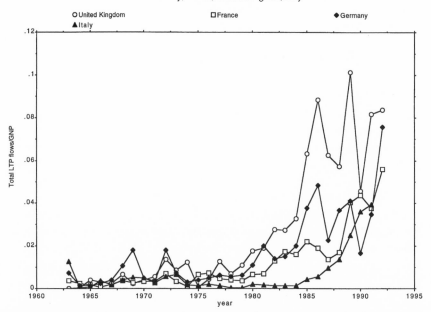

Figure 2.6. Total long-term portfolio investment flows (government bonds, corporate bonds, and equities) as a percentage of GNP, 1963–1993. (SOURCES: See Figure 2.2.)

c: Spain, Portugal, Greece, and Ireland:

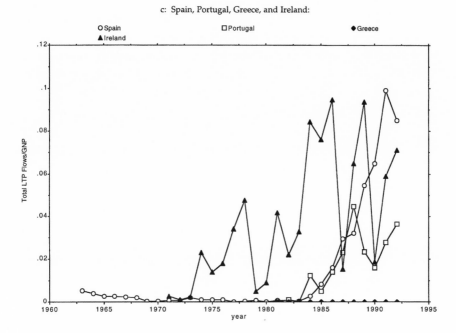

regard: futures contracts of various descriptions have increased from about $200 million in 1975 to about $440 billion in 1986, at the height of volatility in exchange rates and the dark days of the debt crisis. Various options contracts grew from virtually nothing to about $239 billion over the same period (Levich 1987). The BIS now estimates the annual turnover in all derivatives contracts – defined as financial agreements that derive their value from the performance of other assets, interest or currency exchange rates, or indexes – to have tripled in value from $3.4 trillion in 1990 to over $10.6 trillion in 1995.

The liberalization of securities markets has meant that major corporations can now gain access to New York, London, and other international financial centers nearly as readily as to their home markets.[6] The end of fixed commissions, the spread of foreign membership on national stock exchanges, the advent of automated computer quotation, and the Intermarket Trading System are recent examples of institutional innovations that have internationalized and liberalized the world's major securities markets over the past decade or so (Sobel 1994; French and Pterba 1990). As barriers to overseas participation in securities markets have been lifted,

---

[6] However, differing accounting standards, for example, continue to contribute to the fragmentation of equity markets (Simmons 1997).

there has been a perceptible rise in foreign participation relative to domestic participation on the major exchanges. In New York, the share of foreign listings nearly doubled between 1980 and 1990 (from about 2.4 to 5.4 percent); the corresponding figures for the London stock exchange were 12.5 and 21.6 percent. By this measure, internationalization of the Tokyo stock exchange was most dramatic: foreign listings went from about 1 percent to about 7 percent of all listings over the decade, though *volume* of trade in foreign securities on the Tokyo exchange remained fairly small (Sobel 1994).

CAPITAL MARKET INTEGRATION: EVIDENCE OF CONVERGENCE

Despite the dramatic increase in international movements of capital, it is risky to consider the integration of capital markets in terms of volumes alone. It should be possible to point to other measures of market integration that have followed the period of liberalization. Were capital perfectly mobile internationally, a shortfall in national savings should be easily made up by borrowing on international capital markets at the going world interest rate. If so, then investment should no longer depend on national savings rates, since international capital pools are easily tapped to finance current investment needs. Martin Feldstein and Charles Horioka were the first to investigate the relationship between national savings and investment rates over time, and found, much to the surprise of the integrationists, that changes in countries' rates of national savings had very large effects on their rate of investment (Feldstein and Horioka 1980). Further studies in the 1980s found little evidence of heightened integration by this measure before and after 1973, when the most important controls were lifted (Feldstein 1983; Penati and Dooley 1984; Dooley, Frankel, and Mathieson 1987; Feldstein and Bachetta 1989).[7] Indeed, some findings seem to suggest that savings and investment rates were much less related during the nineteenth-century gold standard than they have been in recent years – potentially providing further evidence that capital markets had been at least as highly integrated in the past as they are at present (Bayoumi 1990). Nonetheless, smaller countries have been found to have a lower correlation between savings and investment ratios than do large countries, perhaps reflective of their greater openness to international capital movements (Murphy 1984). But even in the case of the United States, recent research

---

[7] For a good review of the literature, see Tesar (1991).

suggests that the stable relationship between savings and investment had begun to break down in the second half of the 1980s (Frankel 1991). The deficits documented graphically above drew in capital in unprecedented quantities, freeing the country as never before from the constraint of domestic savings.

A second test of capital market integration is convergence of interest rates across markets. If capital is highly mobile internationally, then interest rates should be determined in world markets; there should be very little room for divergence across countries. Moreover, markets could theoretically be highly integrated by this measure, even if international capital movements are small, since among integrated markets, asset prices often adjust in *anticipation* of capital flows that *otherwise* would occur (Machlup, Salant, and Tarshis 1972). Markets can in theory adjust to new equilibrium levels without flows of arbitrage funds. So an additional measure of the integration of capital markets is to ask, To what extent do we see price convergence across these markets?

Some studies of the major economies do reveal evidence suggestive of increasingly highly correlated returns to capital across markets. By the early 1980s, U.S. and Eurobond yields were substantially the same. However, by the end of the decade it became increasingly clear that one could not speak of interest rate convergence without serious qualifications. Money market returns for five large industrialized countries (the United States, United Kingdom, Germany, Japan, and Canada) appeared to have been tighter in the late 1960s than for most of the 1980s, despite the reduction in legal barriers and the increased flow in capital across borders. Furthermore, the response of foreign interest rates to those of the United States seemed to be smaller in the 1980s than in the 1960s and 1970s, which some took as evidence that interest rate movements could not easily be characterized by convergence (Kasman and Pigott 1988). Research has turned up further anomalies: while the most open of the advanced industrialized economies certainly seem to have interest rates that are more highly correlated than those of closed developing countries, it is difficult to explain, on the basis of capital-market liberalization, why it was in the 1980s that France's interest rates – at a time when France still had stringent capital controls – seemed more highly correlated with world rates than those of Switzerland, Japan, and the Netherlands, major countries that, by that time, were known to be virtually free of capital controls (Frankel 1991).

A first cut at resolving the inconsistency between theory and evidence must single out exchange rate volatility as a prime explanation for variations in the pattern of interest rate convergence. Floating exchange rates among the G-5 subjected interest rates in those countries to crosscutting pressures: converging pressures due to market integration, but diverging pressures as a result of exchange rate fluctuations. In studies where efforts were made to separate the *exchange* premia (expectations of variability in exchange rates) from the *country* premia (including transactions costs, discriminatory tax policies, and capital controls), the results seem to suggest that the former continue to pull rates apart, while the latter influences have been virtually eliminated as a cause of interest rate divergence (Frankel 1991; Bayoumi and Rose 1993). Institutional barriers to the free movement of capital are no longer the main reason for market segmentation. Yet full integration continues to be hampered by currency volatility.

This is graphically illustrated by a plot of the yearly standard deviations of three different interest rates across countries between 1964 and 1993 (Figure 2.7). Government bills and bonds, and even money market rates were characterized by lower standard deviations before the breakdown of Bretton Wood's stable exchange rate regime than they have been since. The big jump in variance in all three markets is precisely between 1973 and 1974, when it became clear that flexible rates would prevail. Bond rates, for which evidence is available for a large number of OECD countries from the 1960s, show significant convergence with the establishment of the European Monetary System of relatively stable exchange rates in the early 1980s. Money markets also appeared to be on their way to convergence before the disruptions in the European Monetary System (EMS) in 1992. T-bill yields appear to continue to diverge, although this could be explained by the composition of the countries in the sample, two of which are non-European. Overall, price convergence is highly sensitive to expectations of exchange rate fluctuations, which have diminished within Europe but not across regions. The continuing divergence might also be explained by the fact that the purpose of much of this investment is to balance and diversify investment portfolios, the consequences of which need not be price convergence at all (Osler 1991).[8]

Another way to examine integration across capital markets is to look at correlations in interest rate *change*. Once again, these correlations can be affected by exchange rate expectations, and are ideally modeled as relationships of covered interest rate parity among national currencies.[9] Rather

[8] This argument rests on the intuition that if investors are primarily motivated to diversify their portfolios, there is no reason to expect investment to go strictly to jurisdictions with the highest risk-adjusted returns, and thus no reason to observe convergence of these returns.

[9] This is defined as the domestic interest rate (i$) minus the foreign interest rate (i*) plus any forward premium or discount (fp). The forward premium or discount is defined as

than perform these detailed calculations, Table 2.1 provides evidence on correlations in uncovered interest rate changes across markets comparing two relatively stable exchange rate regimes within Europe, before the breakdown of Bretton Woods (1965–1973) and the contemporary EMS (1983–1993). While this is not a definitive test of capital market integration, this approach controls for the worst exchange rate volatility by excluding the 1970s and limiting the observations to Europe. Table 2.1 provides correlations of eleven European countries' bond yields with those of the United Kingdom and Germany. The results overwhelmingly indicate heightened price change correlations with the major markets under the EMS compared with the earlier fixed exchange rate period. In the case of correlations with bond rates in Britain, only one European country for which data were available, Ireland, failed to demonstrate stronger price change correlations in the more recent period. Correlations with German bond yields were stronger under the EMS for eight countries; only the Scandinavian markets – already fairly highly correlated with interest rate changes in Germany during the 1960s – show no signs of price sensitivity. Sweden and Norway did maintain significant capital controls into the 1980s, which might explain their patterns. Overall, while this is not a perfect test of capital market integration, comparing two periods of relatively stable exchange rates in Europe roughly controls for exchange rate volatility, and lends support to the argument that changes in interest rates in Europe increasingly move together.

A review of the extent to which international capital markets are linked would not be complete without an examination of equities markets, since equities make up a significant and growing portion of international portfolio flows. If equity markets are highly internationalized, one would

---

the difference between, for example, the dollar price of a unit of foreign currency on the forward market less the dollar price of a unit of foreign currency on the spot market, scaled by the spot price of foreign currency:

$$i\$ - (fp + i^*) = 0$$

where

$$fp = \frac{[\text{forward \$/foreign currency} - \text{spot \$/foreign currency}]}{\text{spot \$/foreign currency}}$$

The data demands for making this calculation are very large. Forward exchange rates are difficult to find for many of the currencies represented in this sample for the 1960s. Furthermore, it is crucial to find interest rates that are quoted for exactly the same trading day as the exchange rate quotation, rather than period averages. However, end of period interest rates are not available in the IMF's *International Financial Statistics* for most market rates; rather they are averaged for the period as a whole, which would render the calculation of covered interest parity highly suspect.

a: Standard Deviation, Government Bonds, 17 Countries*

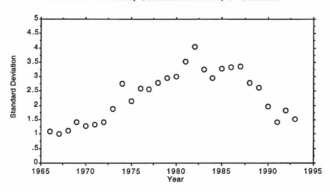

b: Standard Deviation, Government Bills, 5 Countries**

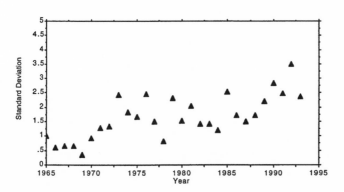

c: Standard Deviation, Money Market Rates, 6 Countries***

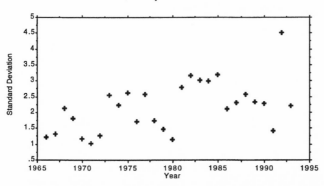

Figure 2.7. Yearly standard deviations of three different measures of interest rates, 1964–1993, various countries. * = Australia, Austria, Belgium, Canada, Denmark, Japan, France, Germany, Ireland, Italy, Netherlands, New Zealand, Norway, Sweden, Switzerland, United Kingdom, United States; ** = Belgium, Canada, Sweden, United Kingdom, United States; *** = Belgium, France, Japan, Germany, Netherlands, Sweden. (SOURCE: IMF, *International Financial Statistics,* various years.)

Table 2.1. *Correlations between yearly changes in government bond rates for twelve European countries with comparable rate changes in the United Kingdom and Germany, Bretton Woods versus the EMS*

	Correlations with changes in the United Kingdom		Correlations with changes in Germany	
	1965–1973	1983–1993	1965–1973	1983–1993
Austria	.202	.810	.290	.896
Belgium	.090	.765	.593	.791
Denmark	−.049	.444	.684	.606
France	.397	.596	.289	.801
Germany	.136	.859	—	—
Ireland	.775	.474	.417	.622
Italy	−.361	.470	.535	.680
Netherlands	.369	.812	.745	.985
Norway	−.672	.161	.460	.073
Sweden	.160	.675	.639	.566
Switzerland	−.011	.913	.525	.909
United Kingdom	—	—	.136	.859

Source: IMF, *International Financial Statistics Yearbook* (various issues).

expect strong correlations in price movements and in expected rates of return across stock markets. The stock market crash of October 1987, with its repercussions in major markets around the globe, epitomized the notion that these markets are in fact strongly linked (von Furstenberg and Jeon 1989; Hamao, Masulis, and Ng 1990; King and Wadhwani 1990). There has been some increased sensitivity in price movements between London, New York, and Tokyo in recent years, though the evidence seems to be strongest for increased common movement in expected returns between London and New York, with little evidence of such movements on the German and Tokyo markets (Bekaert and Hodrick 1992; Jeon and von Furstenberg 1990; Goodhart 1988; Fischer and Palasvirta 1990). Moreover, it is difficult to tell whether these are markets of truly interchangeable assets, or if they are in fact still highly segmented markets responding to common external shocks. If one judges by continued differences in transaction costs across markets (Japanese commissions begin at 1.2 percent while those in London are about .2 percent; a seat on the Tokyo stock exchange costs between $8 and $16 million, while a seat on the New York Stock Exchange goes for perhaps a bit over a half a million; Sobel 1994: 331), an interpretation of continued segmentation may at this point still be warranted.

POLITICS AND POLICY IN A WORLD OF INTERNATIONAL CAPITAL MOBILITY

By virtually every measure considered – the removal of institutional barriers, the flow of capital itself, the growing correlation of interest rate changes across national markets – financial markets are more integrated now than they have been at any point since the nineteenth century. Capital controls have been disassembled across the OECD, beginning with the United States in 1974, Britain in 1979, and most of Europe by 1992. As quantitative restrictions on external deposits have been lifted, the assets of domestic banks across Europe have become more highly internationalized. The U.S. deficit and the announcement of the Single European Act in 1985 sparked foreign direct investment across continents and within Europe, stimulating further internationalization of production. Even more striking has been the relative rise in portfolio investment, which is typically much more liquid and therefore potentially more volatile than direct investment. The integration of capital markets is evidenced by the increased positive correlation in national interest rate movements compared with that during the Bretton Woods period, although country-specific risks continue to explain divergent interest rate levels.

The consequences of capital-market integration for politics within Europe and the rest of the OECD countries are potentially profound. Consider first their impact on the strategies available to multinational firms (Hall, this volume). As barriers have been removed to the transnational movement of direct investment, these firms' options have broadened, and some scholars have argued that this has been at the expense of both labor and governmental authority. The existence of an ever more credible exit option has arguably increased direct investors' ability to influence tax policy (Frenkel, Razin, and Sadka 1991; Gordon and Mackie-Mason 1995), regulatory policy (McKenzie and Lee 1991; Kane 1987), and employment policy (Kurzer 1993) as jurisdictions vie for productive investments and workers increasingly compete with foreign labor. However, little empirical evidence has to date been adduced to support such claims. Quantitative as well as case studies cast doubt on the proposition that capital market integration greatly reduces governments' ability to tax capital (Quinn 1997; Hallerberg 1996). Similarly, case studies of regulatory reform frequently fail to turn up evidence that capital mobility has unleashed a regulatory "race to the bottom" (Vogel 1996). Moreover, not all firms can be expected to be affected in the same way by the removal of barriers to exit. Asset specificity may be important in firms' strategies (Frieden 1991; Maxfield 1997). Those with investments specific to a given domestic market are likely to lobby harder to influence the national regulatory environment or rules of the labor market, while firms with low asset specificity may relocate to less restrictive foreign arenas (Murphy and Oye 1994).

Some observers have also argued that the availability of an ever broader array of highly liquid investment options has undercut long-term investment. Multinational firms, it is argued, increasingly find it tempting to invest in liquid assets that are more flexible and potentially more profitable, at least in the short term, than productive investment (Crotty 1989). Kurzer argues that this has led to further disintegration of business-labor pacts and has undermined working-class solidarity and class voting, due to social democratic governments' inability credibly to oversee the negotiation of centralized wage bargains (Kurzer 1993). As long as financial investments are potentially liquid, convertible, and mobile, tripartism can be expected to be difficult to sustain, constituting a fundamental impact on institutions of economic management and social concertation that were developed in a radically different international environment (Moses 1994).

Even more significant is the potential macroeconomic impact of the recent integration of capital markets, and most especially markets for portfolio capital. Highly liquid capital gives rise to trade-offs among three broad policy aims: governments are generally not able to achieve capital mobility, monetary autonomy, and a fixed exchange rate simultaneously (Mundell 1960, 1962, 1963, 1968). Expansionary monetary policy may be able to stimulate real economic demand where capital mobility was *low* (it could reduce domestic real interest rates without real exchange rate changes or reserve losses), but where capital was able to move abroad, domestic interest rates would be forced to match those prevailing in the region or the rest of the world. Attempts at stimulation would merely lead to capital flight. Nor could monetary policy effectively be used to damp down economic activity and keep inflation under control where capital was highly mobile internationally: attempts to raise interest rates attract capital, thus stimulating demand and expanding the monetary base. In effect, interest rates are determined in world markets, and are no longer available for policy (or political) manipulation. As a result, capital mobility poses an unavoidable trade-off between fixed exchange rates and monetary policy autonomy, as a number of scholars have argued (Goodman 1992; Andrews 1994; Cohen 1993; Webb 1991). National autonomy can be had only at the price of currency instability; an exchange rate target can only be maintained, over time, at the cost of loss of control over interest rates. Smaller countries highly dependent on access to international capital markets have increasingly opted to resolve the trade-off in favor of open capital markets and exchange rate stability. In larger more insular economies, such as the

United States, capital mobility has given rise to opposed coalitions: those who placed more value on exchange rate stability (those oriented toward the international economy) and those who place more value on low interest rates (nontraded goods sector) (Frieden 1991).

For the smaller open economies, integrated capital markets can also impact the ability to use fiscal policy to stimulate economic growth. Capital mobility forces governments to pay the going world rate to finance their borrowing. If global interest rates are very high, as they were for the first half of the 1980s, fiscal policy is effectively stymied as a policy instrument, since the staggering costs of financing such debt poses a serious budget constraint. Under conditions of very high world interest rates, therefore, Keynesian coordination of the economy may be "blocked" as Fritz Scharpf and others have argued, though this critique is somewhat less telling as interest rates have fallen in the 1990s.

But even under relatively low interest rates, capital mobility may make it more difficult for governments easily to manipulate the fiscal policy lever. International capital mobility makes accessible a much bigger pool from which to borrow, but holders of this capital may demand more stringent standards of macroeconomic performance than did captive domestic lenders. The liberation of once captive national capital suggests that increasingly, democratic governments have to sell their policies not only to electorates, but to international investors, who are usually presumed to be leery of public sector growth (Moses 1994). Even successful externally financed fiscal expansions can cause problems in small open economies. Foreign borrowing can lead to a real appreciation of the currency, causing overvaluation and pressure on the traded goods sector (for the case of Sweden, see Moses 1994).

Empirical work is beginning to confirm the expectation that highly mobile capital may place limits on the ability of governments to choose not only an autonomous monetary policy but an expansionary fiscal policy as well. There is some evidence that, controlling for other effects such as the business cycle, capital mobility (measured institutionally as the removal of capital controls) is associated with lower levels of government spending, and smaller budget deficits. Garrett (1995a) argues, however, that partisan differences continue to remain with respect to the uses of fiscal policy at the highest levels of "internationalization" (combined capital mobility and trade openness): left-labor power is associated with higher spending and deficits under conditions of high internationalization. Overall, while it is not *impossible* to use fiscal policy to manage economic growth (notably through supply-side policies; Garrett and Lange 1991), the strategies appear to have become more limited and the price of expansionary fiscal policy to have become higher (Garrett 1995a).

Table 2.2 presents some suggestive evidence of a fiscal constraint. Using the budget balance as a proportion of GNP as the dependent variable, it reports the result of a time-series panel analysis of the effects of portfolio flows of capital on fifteen countries' budget position, controlling for the business cycle (unemployment), party complexion of the government, and degree of trade dependence (imports plus exports as a proportion of GNP). Country dummies were also included but not reported. The results show that, as portfolio investment has increased, there has been a substantial tendency for the budget balance to improve, controlling for these other factors. Strikingly, the opposite is true with respect to trade integration: the strong negative coefficient indicates that high levels of openness are quite consistent with budgets in deficit. This provides some evidence that the movement of highly liquid capital across borders is associated with a degree of fiscal restraint when party, business cycle, and country-specific factors are taken into account. Trade integration has apparently been more consistent with the use of budgetary deficits across the OECD (Katzenstein 1985) and with public-sector growth generally (Rodrick, 1997) than may prove to be the case with highly mobile portfolio capital.

This constraint on fiscal policy has implications for policy within the advanced industrialized countries, and a number of these are explored in this volume. If budgets are to be cut, expenditures associated with the welfare state offer the potential for savings. The finding of Stephens, Huber, and Ray (this volume) that there have been not only important reductions in various aspects of welfare benefits, but also a striking decline in partisan effects, is consonant with – though not shown to be linked to – the convergence in fiscal policies one might expect from the integration of international capital markets. The changes they have revealed in cuts in the welfare state exhibit some parallels, at least at the extremes, with changes in policy with respect to capital-market integration: Britain has most thoroughly liberalized its financial integration and disassembled the welfare state; Norway has most strenuously resisted both.

The loss of fiscal policy autonomy is also the starting point for Kitschelt's analysis (this volume) of the dilemmas facing social democratic parties: if they advocate expansionary policies, they fail to win elections; if they adopt moderate macroeconomic policies and produce macroeconomic outcomes favored by international bondholders (low inflation), they are punished by their core constituency. Though much more work needs to be done to link capital-market integration with the electoral difficulties of

Table 2.2 *The influence of portfolio investment flows on budget balance for fifteen OECD countries, 1965–1993, coefficients (standard errors)*

	Dependent variable: Government budget balance
Total long-term portfolio flows	.251[a] (.101)
Trade/GNP	−.146[a] (.025)
Cabinet partisanship	−.005 (.004)
Unemployment	−.003[a] (.001)
d.f.	354
Adj. R^2	.485
S.E.R	.03

[a]Country dummies are included but not reported here.
Sources: Long-term portfolio flows: See Figure 2.2. Trade (Imports + Exports)/GNP: OECD. Unemployment rate: OECD. Cabinet Partisanship: Garrett (1995a).

social democratic parties, these results suggest a link is not entirely far-fetched.

Tightening fiscal constraints also has implications for the future of unions and the institutions of corporatism themselves. Streeck and Schmitter (1991) have argued that without the ability to manage demand, governments have little need for union cooperation and unions have little incentive to organize collectively. As a result, fiscal austerity makes it more difficult to get the wage-restraint-for-policy-concessions bargain. The data contained in Golden, Wallerstein, and Lange (this volume) might provide an opportunity to more systematically assess the impact of fiscal constraints implied by highly mobile capital on the fortunes of European unions.

CONCLUSION

The liberalization of capital markets has changed the context of economic policy making in significant ways for a number of countries over the past several years. Two facts are certain: there has been a strong move away from capital controls, especially since the collapse of the Bretton Woods system, and there has subsequently been a burst in the movement of capital across borders in the form of foreign direct and portfolio investment among the countries of the OECD. The politics of liberalization has differed by country, but once the process was set in train in the early to mid-1970s, external competitive pressures have encouraged one country after another to reduce barriers to international capital movements. By most accounts, the prime demanders of change have been multinational corporations concerned that they would be at a disadvantage vis-à-vis competitors who could freely borrow and lend in global markets. Governments interested in accessing international capital markets themselves have been willing to oblige. Recently, the pressures (or prospects) of European Union membership have added an important external institutional dimension to the decision to lift controls on capital.

The liberalization of capital controls has facilitated a large real increase in the volume of capital movements among the OECD countries. Much of this reflects the financing needs of the U.S. balance-of-payments deficit in the mid-1980s, but these movements continue despite reduction of imbalances in the 1990s. The reasons are myriad. Foreign direct investment continues to be driven by the need to access technology, marketing networks, and newly liberalizing service industries in foreign markets. Portfolio investment surges whenever there are new opportunities to diversify portfolios internationally, as the case of Sweden in the 1990s suggests.

Yet it is possible to exaggerate the extent of the "revolution" in international market integration over the past twenty years. For one thing, the extent of monetary independence enjoyed in the 1960s should not be overdrawn. For several countries, for example, Denmark, the Netherlands, and Ireland, interest rate movements were highly correlated to those in foreign markets in the 1960s. And the variance in interest rates across markets has not tightened unambiguously over the past thirty years, which is what we should expect if capital mobility had robbed countries of all monetary independence. Part of this can be explained by persisting exchange risks and specific country risks. But some of the persistent difference in interest rates across markets is due to the fact that governments are still interfering "successfully" with the free movement of capital internationally (Epstein and Schor 1992: 146). Despite widespread evasion, capital controls (e.g., those in Finland, Norway, and, to a lesser extent, Italy in the past decade) have been effective enough to permit interest rates in some countries to diverge from those prevailing elsewhere. Where the increasingly costly choice is made to preserve monetary autonomy through the use of such controls, interest rates tend to display a somewhat more independent course.

Capital-market liberalization is likely to be more difficult for the institutions of social democracy to digest than was trade liberalization of earlier decades. International capital markets react much more quickly than do international trade markets to changes in macroeconomic policies, making it difficult to plan and implement compensatory strategies that have been the hallmark of trade adjustment in many of the smaller social democracies (Katzenstein 1985). The size of capital flows makes them far more difficult to manage than trade flows. The daily volume of trading on foreign exchange markets typically exceeds the combined foreign reserve of leading central banks, and swamps by far the value of global trade. Only in rare instances do trade adjustments have economy-wide consequences. Typically, they involve sectorally limited adjustments, to which it is relatively easy to design a compensatory policy response. Capital-market openness can permit external shocks to ripple throughout the national economy in the form of interest rate fluctuations. In short, while institutions within many OECD countries have coped well with trade openness by responding flexibly as protectionist barriers were peeled away in succeeding GATT rounds, integrated capital markets pose a new set of policy dilemmas, some of which appear to strike at the very core of the social bargain that in many countries produced unprecedented growth in the 1960s and adapted to the external shocks of the 1970s.

International capital mobility has been a significant concern to analysts of politics and policy, largely because of the fact that an unprecedented period of economic growth and stability took place under conditions of relatively *closed* national capital markets. The unprecedented period of growth, high employment, and low inflation from the 1950s through the 1960s rested on a number of conditions, but among the most important of these were a system of fixed exchange rates and the adoption of a new array of government policies that generated a belief that cyclical fluctuations could be controlled by demand management. Along with conditions in the labor markets that encouraged wage restraint, and often under the leadership of highly stable social democratic governments, the 1950s and 1960s delivered rapid growth in living standards, a prolonged period of full employment, and a very sharp decrease in the incidence of individual economic risk (Boltho 1982).

The internationalization of capital markets potentially challenges each of these conditions, but research that might more fully inform an understanding of these relationships is in its infancy. Specifically, more attention needs to be given to issues of causation. Is capital-market integration the cause or a consequence of a shift in the relative political clout of capital and labor? Does capital market integration explain the apparent convergence on particular policy instruments, or is this the result of some underlying common shift toward neoclassical economic ideas that have had a parallel impact on liberalization? What are the mechanisms through which the internationalization of capital can be expected to have its hypothesized political effects? The evidence presented here suggests that there is a good degree of variation both across countries and over time that might be exploited to untangle some of these issues. The answers to these questions will address not only scholarly debates in international and comparative politics, but also some of the most significant policy issues of the decade.

3

THE MAKING OF A POLITY: THE STRUGGLE OVER EUROPEAN INTEGRATION

Liesbet Hooghe and Gary Marks

European integration over the past decade has been a polity-creating as well as a market-deepening process. First, and most obviously, the Single European Act (1986) and the Maastricht Treaty (1993) are part of a process of market integration in which a wide variety of nontariff barriers have been reduced or eliminated. Second, perhaps less obviously, these institutional reforms have led to a single, though diverse, polity – a system of multilevel governance that encompasses a variety of authoritative institutions at supranational, national, and subnational levels of decision making.

Our point of departure is that economic developments during the past two decades – internationalization of markets for goods and especially capital, decline of traditional industry and industrial employment, pressures toward flexible specialized production, decentralization of industrial relations, declining international competitiveness, and high levels of long-term unemployment – have led to fundamental reorganization of political authority in western Europe.

The failure of Keynesian economic policy over the past two decades

We would like to thank Sven Bislev, Stephen George, Michael Keating, Peter Lange, Andrea Lenschow, Andy Moravcsik, Philippe Schmitter, Helen Wallace; participants of the University of North Carolina political science, University of Toronto political science, and European University Institute discussion groups; the 25th Workshops of the European Consortium for Political Science (Bern, February 1997); and two anonymous reviewers for comments and suggestions. A draft of this chapter was presented at the APSA Meeting in Chicago, September 1995.

was not simply the failure of a particular set of macroeconomic policies, but the failure of a mode of policy making that was distinctly national. Neocorporatist class compromises and consensual incomes policies that underpinned Keynesian economic policy in many advanced capitalist societies in the postwar decades involved national bargains among interests aggregated at the national level. The perceived failures of those policies led to a debate about the efficacy of the national state. The search for alternative policies went in several directions, but common among them was a belief that the national state could no longer serve as the privileged architect of economic prosperity. The Single European Act institutionalized a double shift of decision making away from national states – to the market and to the European level. This is the point of departure for European integration in the 1980s and 1990s.

The point of departure, but not the destination. The deepening of the market did not determine how the market was to be governed. That was – and is – subject to an intense and highly politicized struggle among national government leaders, Commissioners and high-level European Commission administrators, judges in the European Court of Justice, party representatives in national parliaments and the European Parliament, alongside a variety of social movements and interest groups.

The redesign of authoritative decision making in the European Union (EU) is closely linked to a broadening of participation. EU decision making has become a conscious political struggle among coalitions of political actors having distinctly different conceptions of how Europe should be configured politically. At stake are not only particular policy or institutional outcomes, but grand issues of political architecture. What are the guiding constitutional principles for the allocation of competencies within the European polity? How should authoritative decisions be made? What role should direct democracy have in the process? What should be the relationship between market and state?

We argue that these big questions have generated a structure of contestation that cannot be reduced to differences among national states about distributing Pareto benefits among themselves or lowering transaction costs or enforcing interstate agreements. European integration, we believe, is an irreducibly political, as well as an economic, process. In this chapter, we come to grips with the interests and ideas of those engaged in EU decision making. The next section sets out our analytic scheme. The following section analyzes the deepening of the Euro-polity following the launch of the internal market program. In the final sections of this chapter we describe the political projects that now underlie contention in the European Union.

THE MAKING OF A POLITY

The development of a Euro-polity has gone hand in hand with fundamental change in decision making. First, decision making has become politicized. The roots of this go back to the mid-1960s and the end of the Monnet era of technocratic bargaining. Monnet's method of mutual accommodation and piecemeal problem solving, which were codified in neofunctionalism (Haas 1958; Schmitter 1969), was trumped by basic conflict over decision making. Today, as in the period dominated by Charles de Gaulle, the general premises of European integration are contested. But, as the competencies of the EU have grown, so contention has spread into most areas of political-economic decision making, including the role of the state in the economy and the organization of monetary and fiscal policy.

Second, and more recently, the scope of political participation in the EU has widened. Even as EU decision making became more contested in the mid-1960s, it was still an elitist affair, dominated by a few national and supranational leaders (Wallace 1983; Wallace 1996). This has changed decisively from the mid-1980s as diverse groups have mobilized directly at the European level and as national leaders have sought to legitimize the process through parliamentary debates and referenda.

Tables 3.1 and 3.2 and Figure 3.1 formalize these distinctions in dichotomous ideal types. They can be useful as long as one remembers that the types – technocratic-elitist, politicized-elitist, and participatory-politicized – describe extreme points along continua, and that, correspondingly, the periods we delineate fit the types imperfectly. The changes in question can be summarized as follows.

Contention over Sovereignty

The accretion of authoritative competencies at the European level has raised the issue of national sovereignty in ever more transparent fashion. Notwithstanding claims by some scholars that national sovereignty is undiluted or even strengthened in the process of European integration (Hoffmann 1982; Milward 1992; Moravcsik 1993, 1994), many Europeans believe that recent shifts in decision making threaten the sovereignty of member states. The simplest way to conceptualize this source of politicization is to say that, at some threshold, incremental transfers of competencies have systemic implications for the structuration of authority. The classic neofunctionalist strategy of integration by stealth (i.e., on the merits of particular proposals without emphasizing their wider implications for sovereignty) has been undermined by its very success. Proposals for further integration are now evaluated in terms of their systemic implications as well as their policy effects.

Table 3.1. *Decision-making style*

	Technocratic decision making	Politicized decision making
Goals	Basic policy goals are *shared* among key actors	Basic policy goals are *contested* among key actors
Means	Means for achieving policy goals involve *scientific-rational* methods	Means for achieving policy goals involve basic *political* choices
Issue linkages	Issues are dealt with in *compartmentalized* policy arenas	Issues are dealt with in *interconnected* policy arenas

Table 3.2. *Actor involvement*

	Elitist	Participatory
Number	*Small number* of social groups mobilized politically	*Large number* of social groups mobilized politically
Boundaries	Boundary rules for participation are *elite determined*	Boundary rules for participation are *contested*
Group pressures	Decision makers are *insulated* from group pressures	Decision makers are *vulnerable* to group pressures

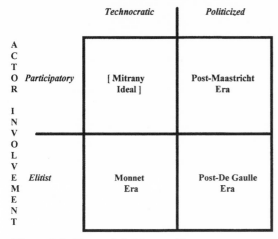

Figure 3.1. *Types of decision making*

A corollary of this is that EU decision making has become less technocratic and more contentious. Fewer decisions are resolved by rational-scientific methods, by ascertaining the most efficient means to given ends, while more decisions involve political contention concerning fundamental goals of European integration. We argue here that this politicization was triggered by the internal market program and accompanying institutional reforms.

Interest Group Mobilization

As the scope and depth of integration have increased, and as the stakes of European decisions have correspondingly been raised, an ever wider variety of groups has been drawn into the EU (Mazey and Richardson 1993a, 1993b; McLaughlin and Greenwood 1995; Fligstein and McNichol 1996). Groups that now participate directly in Brussels include private corporations, sectoral, national, and transnational associations, public interest groups, regional and local governments – in short, a range of interest groups without parallel in any European capital. Such mobilization has created new linkages between European political actors and domestic or transnational constituencies and it has intensified political pressures on elites to regulate economic activity and provide benefits to strategic constituencies.

Elite Vulnerability

Political elites have become more vulnerable to generalized public pressure (Niedermayer and Sinnott 1995; van der Eijk, Franklin, et al. 1995). The most transparent source of such pressure (in addition to the developments just discussed) has been the activation of mass publics in contentious referenda that followed the Maastricht Accord of December 1991 (Franklin, Marsh, and McLaren 1994). No longer can one conceive of decision making about basic institutional rules of the EU as insulated from public opinion, for even where referenda are not imminent constraints, politicians are induced by public scrutiny to act as if they were. Decision making at the European level is no longer divorced from the hurly-burly of the domestic political scene.

PROJECTS

A consequence of the deepening of the Euro-polity is that, as several observers have stressed, the EU has been "domesticated." Neither key institutional reforms, nor everyday policy making resemble conventional foreign-policy making among national governments. Both are subject to pressures that have palpable domestic political repercussions. In short, politics in the EU is more like that found *within* national states than *among* them.

In the remainder of this chapter, we analyze the implications and substantive character of politicization in the EU. We attempt to show that politics in the EU is structured in ways that are predictable. Our analysis seeks to move beyond studies that depict European decision making as a "primeval soup" (Richardson 1996) or as conforming to the indeterminacy of a "garbage can model" (Kingdon 1984; March and Olsen 1989; Peters 1992). We conceive European politics as an interplay among a limited number of overarching political designs or "projects," rather than a flow of discrete decisions. These projects are coherent, comprehensive packages of institutional reforms around which broad coalitions of political actors at the European, national, and subnational level have formed.

Two projects in particular (described in subsequent sections of this chapter) have been at center stage in the debate about the emerging European polity since the 1980s.

The *neoliberal project* attempts to insulate markets from political interference by combining European-wide market integration with minimal European regulation. The neoliberal project rejects democratic institutions at the European level capable of regulating the market, but seeks instead to generate competition among national governments in providing regulatory climates that mobile factors of production find attractive.

The *project for regulated capitalism* proposes a variety of market-enhancing and market-supporting legislation to create a social democratic dimension to European governance. This project attempts to deepen the European Union and increase its capacity for regulation, by among other things, upgrading the European Parliament, promoting the mobilization of particular social groups, and reforming institutions to make legislation easier (e.g., by introducing qualified majority rule in the Council of Ministers).

These projects share some basic features. First, they have an intellectual rationale. They make fundamental claims about how the European polity currently operates and how it should be organized. Second (and correspondingly), these projects provide a political line on almost all issues on the European table. They are recipes for analysis and for action that reach into most crevices of the EU polity. Finally, these projects motivate broad-based political coalitions. They are not merely intellectual constructs, but potent plans of action that, more than any others, have shaped contention in the EU since the mid-1980s.

DIMENSIONS OF CONTESTATION

While there are many alternative institutional designs on offer, it appears to us that neoliberalism and regulated capitalism have been the most politically salient. They define a fundamental cleavage in the EU. We hypothesize that these projects are located in an emerging two-dimensional political space: the first dimension ranging from social democracy to market liberalism; the second ranging from nationalism to supranationalism. We represent these hypotheses in Figure 3.2.

If Figure 3.2 reminds the reader of two-dimensional cleavage structures that are hypothesized for domestic European polities, this is our intention, for we contend that the EU has developed into a polity that can be analyzed with concepts that have been applied to other European polities (e.g., Lipset and Rokkan 1967; Kitschelt 1994b). This extends the idea that the EU is a single, territorially diverse European polity encompassing subnational, national, and supranational actors who pursue their goals across multiple arenas (Hooghe 1996a; Jachtenfuchs and Kohler-Koch 1995; Jeffrey 1996; Leibfried and Pierson 1995; Marks 1993; Marks, Hooghe, Blank 1996; Risse-Kappen 1996; Sandholtz 1996; Scharpf 1994; Wallace 1994; see Anderson 1995 and Caporaso 1996 for an overview of current conceptualizations of the EU).

As one would expect, when national actors step into the European arena they bring with them ideological convictions from their respective national arenas. This is evident in the horizontal axis of Figure 3.2, which represents a key dimension of contestation – concerning economic equality and the role of the state – imported into the EU from national polities.

Alongside this left versus right dimension, we hypothesize a distinctively European dimension of contestation: nationalism versus supranationalism, which depicts conflict about the role of the national state as the supreme arbiter of political, economic, and cultural life (Hix, forthcoming; Hix and Lord 1996). At one extreme are those who wish to preserve or strengthen the national state; at the other extreme are those who wish to press for ever closer European union and believe that national identities can coexist with an overarching supranational (European) identity.

We conceptualize these dimensions as orthogonal. However, attitudes along these dimensions appear to be constrained by the political affinity between leftist orientations and supranationalism and between right-wing support and nationalism. We hypothesize the emergence of a cleavage ranging from center-left supranationalists who support regulated capitalism to rightist nationalists who support neoliberalism. This is the dotted line in Figure 3.2.

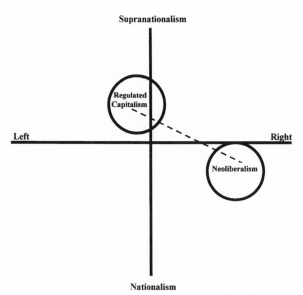

Figure 3.2. Dimensions of contestation in the European Union

As in any territorially diverse polity, the structure of contestation varies from region to region. Moreover, while the cleavage represented in Figure 3.2 is the dominant way of combining these dimensions, it does not encompass all actors. As we will note, one finds, for example, left-leaning nationalists in the Danish Social Democratic Party and right-leaning supranationalists among German Christian Democrats.[1]

This way of conceptualizing contention in the EU will be rejected by those who view European integration as a game among national governments. Our view is based on the following propositions: first, as we have argued at length elsewhere, subnational and supranational actors participate alongside national governments in EU policy making; second, territory is only one, among several, bases for interest intermediation in the EU.

Territorial identity (and, in particular, nationality) is important, but it is not all-important, as a source of individual preferences with respect to EU institutions and policy. To understand contention in the EU, it is not enough to analyze differences between, say, the British and Germans, or

---

[1] This topic demands sustained empirical analysis that goes beyond the scope of this chapter. Our hypotheses here are supported by information from interviews conducted by one of the authors with some 140 A1 and A2 Commission officials (Hooghe 1997), and by other, less systematic, evidence.

even among territorially defined groups within these countries. Political coalitions are also formed among groups sharing particular views (e.g., with regard to the environment or the role of women) or among groups with some particular economic function or socioeconomic characteristic (e.g., financial capitalists, organized workers). To the extent that political coalitions in the EU crosscut territory (i.e., pit groups in the same territory against one another), so one may speak of the "making" of a European polity that is something more than an aggregation of constituent national polities.

European integration is an experiment in creating a polity among extraordinarily diverse publics. Domestic patterns of contention, in particular, the left-right cleavage, are projected into the EU. But at the same time, European integration has come to influence contention within individual countries. As more authoritative decisions are made in the EU, and as domestic groups mobilize to affect those decisions, so European integration has come to feature in domestic contention among – and within – political parties.

How can one explain the making of this polity? In the next section we take up this question from a historical-analytical perspective, focusing on a cascade of changes in political mobilization and contention that followed the institutional reforms of the Single European Act.

POLITICIZED-PARTICIPATORY DECISION MAKING

While the European Union was first politicized as a consequence of President de Gaulle's empty-seat strategy of 1965, the period from the mid-1980s is a watershed in the political development of the EU, for it ushered in an era of more intense public scrutiny, more extensive interest group mobilization, and less insulated elite decision making. The period beginning with the Single European Act (SEA) created the conditions for *politicized-participatory* decision making in the EU, increasing the stakes of political conflict, broadening the scope of authoritative decision making, opening new avenues for group influence, and creating incentives for a quantum increase in political mobilization.

CONTENDING CONCEPTIONS OF THE INTERNAL MARKET

The success of the market program provoked an intense debate about how the market should be organized politically, and this conflict has shaped

European politics during the subsequent decade. Market liberalization was supported by a broad coalition of governments, parties, and interest groups with widely different orientations (Bornschier and Fielder 1995; Cameron 1992; Sandholtz and Zysman 1989; Cowles 1995). As the reforms took shape, these differences began to crystallize in contending conceptions of capitalism in Europe. The market program – a goal shared by many in 1985 – became a point of departure for contending political agendas.

For actors with a neoliberal outlook, market liberalization was a necessary step in limiting European integration to an economic enterprise dominated by insulated government elites. Neoliberals were strongest in the British Conservative government, led by Margaret Thatcher, and within international capital. Without a British veto the French Socialist and German Christian Democratic governments would have created more extensive European competencies in areas such as industrial policy and telecommunications (Cameron 1992; Moravcsik 1991; Sandholtz and Zysman 1989).

But there were other, very different, conceptions of the market program. Some actors conceived of the SEA as a jumping-off point for regulating capital at the European level. This view was put forward most strongly by Jacques Delors, then president of the European Commission. Rather than waiting for the intended and unintended effects of market reform to wend their way through diverse spillovers to government preference formation, à la neofunctionalist theory (Haas 1958; Schmitter 1969; George 1996 [1985]; Burley and Mattli 1993), Delors and his supporters conceived of the market program as an opportunity to orchestrate *strategic* spillovers. Their goal was to create "organized space" at the European level, regulating European capitalism in line with European Social-Democratic and Christian-Democratic traditions.[2]

In short, the market program was the beginning, rather than the conclusion, of debate about the institutional configuration of the European polity. The key to the political success of the market program was its ambiguity – the fact that it was all things to all actors – but once in place the broad coalition that underpinned it was bound to fall apart.

---

[2] This language is reminiscent to that of two French initiatives in the early 1980s. In 1981, the French Socialist government proposed to create "un espace social européen," an anti-unemployment program through fiscal stimulation. Two years later, it suggested "un espace industriel européen" aimed at supporting the technology industry (Moravcsik 1991). While these initiatives were last-minute French attempts to extrapolate traditional Keynesianism to the European level, Delors's ideas on "espace organisé" were more compatible with the prevailing paradigm of market competition. For Delors's views on future state-society relations in France and Europe, see Delors (1992).

DECISIONAL REFORMS

The market program was accompanied by two institutional reforms that have been key ingredients in the broadening of participation in the EU.

First, the SEA increased the power of the European Parliament by making internal market legislation subject to the cooperation procedure. As authoritative competencies were transferred to the EU, so pressures intensified for the replication of liberal democracy at the European level. Several national leaders pressed the normative argument that the EU would have a severe democratic deficit if it were the exclusive domain of an unelected Commission and an indirectly elected Council of Ministers. Parliamentary reform, which was extended under the Maastricht Treaty, has transformed the EU's legislative process from Council-dominated decision making into complex interinstitutional bargaining among the Council, Parliament, and Commission (Dehousse and Majone 1994; Nugent 1994; Peterson 1995). One effect of this has been to enhance the agenda-setting power of the Commission and the European Parliament (Tsebelis 1994, 1995), which have historically been keen to expand the EU agenda. Another has been to multiply the opportunities for group access to the EU beyond that provided by national governments in the Council of Ministers (Marks and McAdam 1996; Greenwood, Grote, and Ronit 1992; Kohler-Koch 1994).

Second, qualified majority voting in the Council of Ministers was introduced for a variety of policy areas connected with the internal market and was later extended to several other areas under the Maastricht Treaty. The original justification for lowering the barriers to legislation in the European Community was fear that recalcitrant governments (the Papandreou government particularly) would hold up market opening to extract side payments from promarket governments (Cameron 1992; Moravcsik 1991). However, the scope of a qualified majority turned out to be difficult to constrain as a variety of issues arose, particularly in social policy and the environment, which involved market restraints (Pierson 1996b). Qualified majority voting in the Council offered the prospect of short-circuiting the national veto and opened up new opportunities for positive legislation (Pollack 1995).

ACTOR RESPONSE

One of the original justifications for creating a single market and shifting decision making to the European level was that it would impede the efforts of interest groups, or in Mancur Olson's words "distributional coalitions," to gain rents by instituting nontariff barriers in their respective countries (Olson 1982). Some governmental leaders seemed to relish the prospect of shifting decision making to intergovenmental negotiation at the European level, beyond the reach of social and labor interests entrenched in their respective domestic polities. However, this expectation did not take into account the dynamic (and, in large part, unintended) consequences of institutional change.

In contrast to earlier economic integration, which affected mainly farmers, the food industry, and the steel and coal industry, the internal market program affected a wide range of public and private actors across many economic sectors. The years since the Single European Act have seen a rapid increase in the number and range of interests that have mobilized directly at the European level. The number of interest groups operating in Brussels was estimated to be in the range of 3,000 by 1990, having increased from around 600 in 1986 (Andersen and Eliassen 1993). Studies in individual policy areas from the chemical industry to the environment reveal a more finely grained, but consistent, picture (Grant 1993). The phenomenon of interest mobilization at the European level encompasses subnational governments (Jeffrey 1996) as well as functional and public interest groups. A survey of subnational mobilization in the EU documents the dramatic increase in the number of city, local, and regional governments represented in Brussels from 1 in 1985, to 15 in 1988, 54 in 1993, and 70 in 1994 and around 100 in 1996 (Marks, Salk, Ray, and Nielsen 1996).

As the stakes of EU policy making have grown for societal interests, and as political opportunities for influence have increased, so the EU has become a magnet for interest group activity that was formerly focused exclusively within national states. At the same time, some groups redefined their goals. Many trade unions, for example, abandoned their opposition to EU regulation in industrial relations and company law, as union leaders came to realize that national governments were less and less capable of protecting labor standards from the downward pressure of regime competition. Most trade unions now support expansion of EU competence in industrial relations and social policy. An experienced trade unionist, now a senior official in the European Commission, summarized the change in July 1996:

> They [trade unions] were very proud about having social affairs as a unanimity issue [in the European Community or Union], and then they realized that this unanimity was exactly the reason why there was no progress. At first, they were afraid of deregulation or a lowering of social security. It took them some ten to fifteen years to learn that it was just

the opposite – that they couldn't make any progress as long as there is at least one [national government] which objects. And now they have begun to realize that national sovereignty is becoming more and more an empty notion, at least as far as economic policy is concerned.

The SEA and the changes in behavior it induced were a watershed in the making of a European polity: the scope of authoritative decision making was enlarged, democratic institutions were empowered, new opportunities for group influence were created, new sets of actors were pulled into the process.

A polity is an arena for contention about authoritative allocation of values. In the EU this contention has been far-reaching because the stakes are so high and the rules of the game are in flux. The debate is not only about the level or type of industrial, social, fiscal, or monetary policy – though these are debated fiercely – but is centered on how authoritative decisions should be made. Institutional architecture is intimately connected with policy outcomes. The contention that underlies European integration concerns nothing less than the question of how Europe should be organized politically.

In the following sections we describe two projects that drive this contention.

THE NEOLIBERAL PROJECT

Neoliberals conceive the internal market reform as a means to insulate markets from political interference by combining a European-wide market under selective supranational surveillance with intergovernmental decision making vested in sovereign national governments. The idea is to create a mismatch between economic activity, which is European-wide, and political authority, which for most purposes remains segmented among national governments (Streeck 1992b, 1995, 1996b; Streeck and Schmitter 1991; Schmidt 1994a). By placing market competition under supranational surveillance, neoliberals wish to constrain national barriers to trade. By resisting the creation of a supranational Euro-polity, neoliberals minimize the capacity for European-wide regulation of economic activity.

The competition that neoliberals have in mind is not simply among firms or workers, but among governments. A vital consequence of the mismatch between market competition (which is EU-wide) and political authority (vested in national governments) is that it creates the conditions for competition among national governments to provide the most favorable conditions for mobile factors of production, namely, mobile capital. By reducing the costs of relocation, market integration makes it easier for mobile factors of production to move to the country of choice, and so penalizes governments that do not arrange their political economies to suit mobile capital by, for example, minimizing corporate taxes and market regulation (Schmidt 1994a; Streeck 1992b; Scharpf 1996a). While workers may also move in response to regime competition, cultural and language barriers make them far less willing to do so.

Finally, the neoliberal project limits the ability of social groups, such as labor unions and environmental movements, to pressure governments into regulation. The idea is to shift policy making from domestic arenas, where it is influenced by historically entrenched social groups and popularly elected legislatures, to international fora dominated by national governments (for a theoretical justification, see Olson 1982). This is the "intergovernmental" conception of decision making in the EU. Instead of making national governments outmoded, the neoliberal agenda for European integration privileges national governments as the sole intermediary between domestic politics and European bargaining. National governments frame the agenda and negotiate the big decisions; domestic actors watch on the sidelines and hope to effect outcomes indirectly through their respective governments (Moravcsik 1993, 1994).

SUPPORT

The neoliberal project is a minority project. The first and most forceful champion of neoliberalism has been the British Conservative Party, particularly under the leadership of Prime Minister Thatcher in the 1980s (Whiteley, Seyd, Richardson, and Bissell 1994; King and Wood, this volume) and, after a brief period of moderation from 1990 to 1992, continuing with Prime Minister John Major. However, neoliberalism has broad roots among strategically placed political and economic elites. These include leaders of British and European multinational companies, industrial associations (including a majority of members of UNICE, the major umbrella association for European industry), financial interests (e.g., within central banks and international finance), pressure groups (including the Bruges group), think tanks, probusiness strands in the German CDU-CSU and FDP, other liberal and conservative parties on the continent, and opinion leaders (e.g., the *Economist*).

Neoliberal ideas have also gained ground in the Commission. Under the presidency of Jacques Delors, the Commission was deeply riven by ideological conflict between its president and right-wingers, led by Sir Leon Brittan, originally Commissioner for competition and then for external trade. With Brittan's appointment in 1988, Margaret Thatcher planted a "liberal crusader" in the heart of the community "who would fight not only national-level intervention, but also EU-level industrial policy" (Ross 1995a). As George Ross observes, "if Delors wanted to 'organize' a European industrial space, Brittan, standing atop long-standing Commission prerogatives, wanted quite as much to 'open' this same space" (Ross 1995a: 176).

The neoliberal agenda, or parts of it, have gained support in several directorate-generals of the Commission (DGs), particularly those implementing the internal market such as the powerful directorate-general for competition (DG IV). The market liberal activism of DG IV has several sources, but a major factor was the recruitment of enthusiastic market supporters during the 1980s, which coincided with the higher profile for competition policy during the internal market exercise (McGowan and Wilks 1995; Wilks 1992). The shift, which was generalized to some other DGs during the early 1990s, was consolidated by the changeover from Delors to Jacques Santer as President of the European Commission (Wallace and Young 1996; Majone 1994). As a senior official in a market-oriented DG put it in July 1995: "There is no question that the balance has changed, and that there is much greater emphasis on greater [market] opportunities rather than giving out money."

Neoliberals have skillfully combined economic internationalism and political nationalism in an effort to create national governance and international market competition. They have linked their cause to nationalism to block the development of a Euro-polity capable of regulating the European economy. In the United Kingdom, France, Germany, and the Benelux, the strongest objections to the Maastricht Accord were made by extreme nationalists in the British Conservative Party, the French National Front, the German Christian Social Union and Republicaner, or the Belgian Vlaams Blok. Only in the Scandinavian countries has Euroskepticism been as significant on the left as on the right.

Like nationalists, neoliberals argue that positive market regulation is illegitimate because the European Union lacks meaningful democratic institutions that can justify tampering with markets. National states are the only legitimate democratic channels for public expression. Yet, unlike nationalists, neoliberals have goals that stretch beyond defending the sovereignty of national states. They have sought to limit the capacity of any political actor – including national states themselves – to regulate economic activity.

Nationalists and neoliberals have opposed more powers for the European Parliament, though their opposition has different roots. Nationalists oppose the European Parliament because it challenges the monopoly of national parliaments in expressing the popular will. Neoliberals reject a stronger European Parliament because it is likely to be sympathetic to economic regulation, certainly more so than either the Council of Ministers or the European Court of Justice. For neoliberals, the European Parliament provides an opportunity for special interests to gain preferential legislation (Olson 1982); for nationalists, it usurps legitimate parliamentary authority.

INSTITUTIONAL TERRAIN

Neoliberals have the considerable advantage that, in most respects, they favor the status quo. The reduction of market barriers is the one area where neoliberals have sought radical change, but here they were part of a broad coalition that included Christian democrats in national governing coalitions, big business, and the European Commission. Neoliberals have fewer allies in their rejection of positive regulation and their opposition to deepening the Euro-polity, but these are stances against change. This is a powerful strategic position in a polity where unanimity among member state governments is necessary for basic institutional change, and where qualified majorities of around 70 percent in the Council of Ministers are usually required for positive regulation.

This high threshold has helped the U.K. government impede European social policy, environment policy, industrial relations regulations, and industrial policy. The Thatcher and Major governments have also limited decisional reform, including the extension of qualified majority voting. During the SEA negotiations, French and German leaders proposed qualified majority voting in the Council on a range of policies, including the internal market, environment, social policy, and research and technology, while the British, supported by the Danish and Greek governments, favored a limited and informal norm. In the end, Thatcher was able to confine a qualified majority to the internal market (Moravcsik 1991).

Unanimity has tilted the playing field in favor of neoliberals, but it has occasionally hurt them. Southern European governments managed to institute and extend a sizable redistributional cohesion policy for the EU when they threatened to veto the SEA and the Maastricht Treaty. Unanimity is a double-edged sword, for it not only makes innovation difficult, but makes it tough to eradicate existing regulation. Now that an extensive cohesion policy is in place, neoliberals have an uphill fight to eliminate it.

Neoliberals have benefited from the fact that EU decision rules make it more difficult to regulate markets than eliminate market barriers (Scharpf 1996a). Positive market regulation demands agreement on some set of minimum standards for all member states, and attempts to set such standards usually take the form of legislation. Such regulation must therefore negotiate the EU's labyrinthine legislative process. In contrast, negative market regulation stipulates only the conditions under which market barriers are, or are not, justified, and once the general principle is laid out it may be adjudicated by a court or regulatory body. Applying the principle (Article 36, Rome Treaty) that market barriers are justified only under certain limited circumstances, the European Court of Justice has developed extensive powers vis-à-vis member states to sweep away national restraints on trade and distortions of competition (Meunier-Aitsahalia 1993; Burley and Mattli 1993; Weiler 1991). The competition directorate in the European Commission has steadily built up its powers (Wilks 1992; McGowan and Wilks 1995). Fritz Scharpf (1996a) has made the point that there is an in-built institutional asymmetry in the European treaties favoring market deepening to market correcting.

Neoliberals have struggled from a strategically powerful position to shape the European Union, but they have been only partially successful. As Philippe Schmitter points out: "The notion that the Single European Act of 1985–1986 had definitively opted for a narrowly 'liberal' conception has been denied by subsequent developments" (Schmitter 1996b). Without a doubt, the European Union would look very different today were it not for the neoliberal project and Prime Minister Thatcher's determination in pressing it. But market liberals have had to contend with powerful actors committed to very different goals, and these actors, as we will discuss, have also shaped the European Union.

REGULATED CAPITALISM

A variety of groups view market integration as merely the first step in a more ambitious project: regulated capitalism. Their goal is to create a European liberal democracy capable of regulating markets, redistributing resources, and shaping partnership among public and private actors. The most influential advocate of this project was Jacques Delors, who served as President of the European Commission during the critical decade from the beginning of 1985 to the end of 1994. Delors was not a systematic thinker, but his characterization of *espace organisé* (organized space), based on his writings and speeches (Delors 1992; Ross 1995a, 1995b; see also Grant 1994), forms the core of the project for regulated capitalism.

Positive Regulation

A defining feature of the project is its friendliness to markets and its opposition to state control or ownership. When they speak of market reform, supporters of regulated capitalism argue for market-enhancing or market-supporting – rather than market-replacing or even market-correcting – policies. They do not quarrel with the notion that markets, not governments, should allocate investment. But they contend that markets work more efficiently if political actors provide collective goods including transport and communications infrastructure, information networks, work force skills, and research and development. There is, they argue, a role for positive as well as negative regulation, and in a variety of policy fields, such regulation is best achieved at the European level.

This involves a shift from demand-side to supply-side economics. Proponents of regulated capitalism claim that the capacity to provide certain collective goods is a decisive advantage in international economic competition under conditions of flexible specialization. It separates producers competing in mass-production industries on the basis of cheap labor, low taxes, and loose environmental and social standards from producers competing in high-value-added industries on the basis of quality, style, and technology (Soskice, this volume).

Partnership

Proponents of regulated capitalism have campaigned for voluntary cooperation among groups that are affected by, or who contribute to, a particular policy. With varying degrees of success, they have proposed a "social dialogue" among representatives of labor and capital in social policy; "social partnership" among affected interests, particularly consumers and producers, in environmental policy; and "partnership" among the European Commission, national ministries, and regional authorities in cohesion policy.

Like positive regulation, the policy is justified on pragmatic grounds. An inclusive strategy is likely to generate less social conflict than an exclusive strategy and should be easier to implement. Such a strategy is also likely to be better informed than an exclusive strategy because it brings affected interests into the decision-making process.

Social Solidarity

Proponents of regulated capitalism stress policies that empower those who are less well off to compete more effectively in the market. Examples of such policies are structural policies designed to increase the potential for indigenous economic growth in poorer regions and employment policies to bring unemployed youth and the long-term unemployed into the labor market. These policies can be justified in ethical terms but – like partnership – they may also be viewed as paths to increasing economic productivity.

These principles have been at the core of several reforms, including an extensive structural policy for poorer regions, a growing commitment to a European environment policy, European-wide infrastructure in transport, telecommunications, and information technology, and a variety of less ambitious measures in research and development, education, health and safety, consumer protection, and rural development.

Central to regulated capitalism is deepening democracy in the European Union (Schmitter 1996b; Wiener 1994). The core argument is straightforward: if important decisions are being made in the European Union that directly affect European citizens, those decisions should be subject to liberal democratic scrutiny and legitimation. Indirect representation through national governments is not sufficient; a system of direct and effective parliamentary representation should be established. With respect to citizenship rights, proponents of regulated capitalism argue that transnational labor mobility, facilitated by the internal market, should not negate democratic participation in an EU citizen's new country of residence. At the heart of this project is the demand to extend basic principles of liberal democracy to the European Union, that is, to create a "Citizen's Europe."

Support for democratization of the EU is reinforced by the expectation that this will intensify popular pressures for positive regulation. In a Citizen's Europe, Europeans would have full citizenship rights and the opportunity to press demands for welfare and market regulation through political parties, interest groups, and movements as they do in national polities.

SUPPORT

The project for regulated capitalism marshals the common ground in the competition between reformist social democracy and moderate Christian democracy (Ross 1995a; Grant 1994). Following social democracy, regulated capitalism involves class compromise; following Christian democracy, it involves subsidiarity.

Most center-left parties in Europe have come to support the project. German, Austrian, Italian, and Spanish social democrats have been solidly in favor. The left has been split in Britain, Sweden, Denmark, and Greece.

Danish and Greek socialists, in particular, have opposed regulated capitalism at the European level on nationalist grounds. Majority support was forthcoming in Britain and Sweden only after the traumatic realization by many on the left that national Keynesianism is a dead end. While left nationalists point to the EU's democratic deficit, the corrosive effects of regime competition, and the prospect that European identity will never be sufficient to sustain a European welfare state, supporters of the project for regulated capitalism argue that in a globalized economy, a European approach is more feasible than a national one.

There is selective support for regulated capitalism among Christian democratic parties, particularly in countries where separate neoliberal and/or nationalist parties represent opposing views. Strong support comes from Christian democratic parties in Benelux countries and Austria. While there are divisions among German Christian Democrats and growing pressures for neoliberal reforms, Chancellor Helmut Kohl has typically advocated regulated capitalism. Kohl was instrumental in ensuring the Social Protocol against Prime Minister Major's veto in the Maastricht negotiations; he has consistently campaigned for a stronger European Parliament; and, during the renegotiations of cohesion policy in 1988 and 1993, Kohl supported increased spending for poorer regions.

The coalition for regulated capitalism is weaker than the sum of its parts because it is extraordinarily heterogeneous. National institutional variations underpin different constellations of interest. For example, social democrats in southern Europe are cross-pressured on the issue of introducing regulations (e.g., minimum-wage regulation) that diminish their competitive advantage vis-à-vis central and northern European countries (Lange 1993). Even where competitive advantage is not at stake, institutional differences can impede reform. It is difficult to create winning coalitions for regulations that apply to heterogeneous institutions that are costly to change (Scharpf 1996b; Majone 1995).

The loose coalition of Social and Christian Democrats is flanked by unionists at the European (ETUC) and national levels. But organized labor is not nearly as influential at the European level as it has been in most member countries. In contrast to multinational firms that have adapted smoothly to the Euro-polity, organized labor has had greater difficulty, partly because unions are deeply embedded in distinctly national institutions (Marks and McAdam 1996). Transnational collective bargaining arrangements have not been created, and there is little prospect of the emergence of neocorporatism at the European level (for national developments, see Golden, Wallerstein, and Lange, this volume). Furthermore, unions have been weakened by the internationalization of economic activity, a development that was accelerated by the single-market program (Frieden 1991; Streeck 1992b; Streeck and Schmitter 1991; Tilly 1994).

In addition to labor, regulated capitalism has backing from diverse groups, including environmentalists (e.g., the Worldwide Life Fund and the European Environmental Bureau, an umbrella organization of about 160 environmental groups), most green parties (including the German Grüne after its turnaround on European integration), and a variety of social movements (Marks and McAdam 1996).

Supranational actors, particularly in the European Commission and Parliament, have been responsive to this agenda. Jacques Delors and leaders of the Commission were the dynamo behind *espace organisé* from the mid-1980s to the mid-1990s, though as noted, they were opposed within, as well as outside, the Commission by market liberals. However, Commission officials tend to be significantly more supranationalist than other groups of actors, and while contention among Commission officials has intensified since the mid-1990s, they have been an important source of support.[3]

The European Parliament has been responsive to popular pressures for positive market regulation, particularly from social movements such as Greenpeace. The proregulated capitalism orientation of the Parliament has been reinforced since 1989 by the fact that social democrats in combination with Greens and other left-wing or centrist members have formed a majority (Ladrech 1993; Bardi 1994).

Support for elements of regulated capitalism has sometimes come from less obvious corners, such as the European Round Table, representing large multinational firms, which in its 1983 memorandum argued for infrastructural programs and EU-sponsored collaboration in research and development. The European Round Table campaigned for a European-wide infrastructure program, "Missing Links," the forerunner of the European Union's Trans-European Networks (Cowles 1995). In the eyes of some of its members, the European Round Table is a " 'Christian-Democratic/Social Democratic group' that does not share the ideology of Thatcherite capitalists" (Cowles 1995, quoting from an interview with a member of the Round Table). However, even though the Round Table called for a role for the European Union in industrial policy, there seems to be little evidence of support for the Social Dialogue, social rights, or environmental protection. In December 1993, for example, the Round Table proposed the

---

[3] See Hooghe (1997). Asked whether the Commission should help to preserve organized space in Europe, 46.3 percent of senior officials gave unconditional support and another 37.5 percent gave qualified support. The finding is based on data from 140 taped interviews and 106 mail questionnaires (from A1 and A2 officials in the Commission), conducted between July 1995 and May 1997.

creation of a European Competitiveness Council comprising industry, government, and science representatives, but excluding labor (Cowles 1995). This is a direct challenge to the Social Dialogue. Over the past decade backing for regulated capitalism within industry has weakened as competitive pressures have increased as a result of globalization and market liberalization.

INSTITUTIONAL TERRAIN

The achievements of the coalition for regulated capitalism seem unimpressive by comparison with current social regulation in central and northern European states. There are no functional equivalents at the European level to existing welfare states, national systems of cooperative economic governance, national systems of industrial relations, or industrial policies. Moreover, there are no indications that such distinctly national systems of positive regulation will be replicated at the European level in the foreseeable future.

One does not have to search far to explain this. Research on neocorporatism and class compromise has identified a variety of requisites for their existence, including strong working-class political organization (in particular, durable social democratic participation in government), cohesive working-class economic organization (in particular, well-organized and centralized union federations), and coherent employers' organization (Schmitter 1981; Cameron 1984; Marks 1986; Esping-Andersen 1990; Hall and Soskice, this volume). None of these are present in the EU, nor are they likely to arise in the future. The government of the EU is fragmented; social democrats are weakly represented in the Council of Ministers; neither trade unions nor employers are centralized at the European level. But most proponents of regulated capitalism do not strive to replicate national welfare or industrial regulation at the European level. Rather they seek more politically and institutionally feasible reforms.

UNANIMITY

It is important to realize that the institutional terrain is not entirely unfavorable to proponents of regulated capitalism. In the first place, unanimity, which is the decision rule in the Council of Ministers for major institutional change and for major policy initiatives, is double-edged. Earlier, we noted that unanimity raises the highest decisional barrier against change – the assent of each and every participant. But by doing so, unanimity opens the door to package deals crafted to benefit each national government.

Neoliberals have had to accept reforms involving positive regulation and redistribution in exchange for the assent of all national governments to liberalization. One of the products has been cohesion policy, a centerpiece of European regulated capitalism (Hooghe 1996b; Marks 1993, 1996).

Moreover, the force of unanimity is eroded if actors whose preferences are blocked have the credible alternative of creating an alternative regime. Here, again, the force of unanimity is less than one might think. Individual governments can get derogations that exclude particular countries from rules that apply to all others. Neoliberals see merit in this because it institutionalizes regime competition between countries that join and those that do not. The existence of different rules in different parts of the EU (in Euro-jargon, "variable geometry") should constrain the willingness of any single group of governments to impose regulations on capital for fear of losing investment (Streeck 1996b). But variable geometry does not necessarily lead to a race to the bottom, to low-tax, low-welfare, relatively unregulated economies. Where regulatory reforms may arguably increase economic efficiency, variable geometry provides more space for regulatory innovation (Scharpf 1996b). National governments may forge ahead with particular integrative measures, such as social policy or monetary union, despite opposition from nationalists or neoliberals. Because the Major government excluded the United Kingdom from the Social Protocol annexed to the Maastricht Treaty, it was possible for remaining governments to enact a Works Council Directive mandating certain types of companies to consult with workers on job reductions, new working practices, and the introduction of new technology (Rhodes 1993; Leibfried and Pierson 1995). Even though the Major government did not sign up, most major British multinationals (e.g., Marks and Spencer) have since introduced consultative works councils in their British plants to preserve uniformity in the company across the EU (Leibfried and Pierson 1996), and after the 1997 elections, the incoming Labour government signed the Protocol, which was promptly incorporated into the Treaty of Amsterdam.

QUALIFIED MAJORITY

More important yet, unanimity has been swept aside in favor of qualified majority voting in the Council of Ministers on an increasing number of issue areas. As noted, qualified majority voting was originally adopted to facilitate market-opening legislation. But it has been extended to policy areas only indirectly related to the market, including environmental policy and social policy. This allows proregulation coalitions of governments to preempt a race to the bottom.

Some regulations do not have to be supported by multilevel coalitions of national governments and supranational actors, but can be imposed by individual governments acting alone. Under Article 36 of the Treaty of Rome (which remains in force), a country may maintain high product standards if they are justified by considerations of health, safety, the environment, or consumer protection, even if they serve as a barrier to trade. This allows producers in high-regulation countries to export to low-regulation countries while protecting their own markets (Sbragia 1996; Scharpf 1996b).

Evidence of a race to the bottom is mixed even for regulations concerning the process of production (e.g., working conditions) where Article 36 does not apply. One reason for this is that national governments have demonstrated a greater capacity than expected to maintain regulations even when they appear to put domestic producers at a cost disadvantage (Scharpf 1996b; Vogel 1996). It is not obvious how governments will act when there are trade-offs between social or environmental values and national income. It depends on how such values are translated into political costs and benefits for constituencies that affect a government's popularity.

Finally, it is worth stressing that positive regulation need not be economically inefficient. Scharpf has argued that regulation may serve as a certificate of superior product quality that is rewarded by the market – for example, because a regulation may provide consumers assurance against health, safety, or financial risks or because it induces industry to increase productivity (Scharpf 1996b). Under certain conditions one may envisage a race to the top, rather than a race to the bottom (Scharpf 1996b). Economists disagree about whether raising environmental standards hinders or promotes economic growth. The economic costs and benefits of EU involvement in vocational training, human resources, and research and development are contested, and certain business interests in low-regulation countries support initiatives in these areas.

SUPRANATIONAL ACTORS

The creation of European social citizenship has been spurred mainly by decisions of the European Court of Justice (ECJ) applying the four freedoms (for goods, capital, services, and labor) at the core of the internal market (Leibfried and Pierson 1995, 1996). Since the mid-1980s the ECJ has compelled member countries to gradually open their national welfare systems to nonnational EU employees and to allow consumers to shop out of state for welfare services. The Court has stopped short of creating welfare state access for any EU citizen, but it has induced an "incremental, rights-based 'homogenization' of social policy" among member states (Leibfried and Pierson 1995).

While the Court's contributions to European regulated capitalism were largely unintended side effects of liberalization, the Commission under Jacques Delors wished actively to craft regulated capitalism in Europe. Its strategy was to formulate a series of package deals between member state governments to transform the internal market into a polity with extensive authority and effective policy instruments (Ross 1993, 1995a; Grant 1994). Where there were disagreements on major reforms, the Commission proposed side payments in the direction of regulated capitalism (e.g., cohesion policy) to buy off recalcitrant governments. Each package deal was shaped with an eye to the next round where further integrative measures would be proposed – an approach described by Delors as a "Russian Dolls" strategy (Ross 1995a, 1995b).

The first round of this strategy was the budgetary package of 1988 (Delors I), which set financial priorities for the period 1989–1993. The multiannual budgetary approach, which itself was a novelty, provided a framework for the Commission to cobble together a package to every government's liking while laying the foundation for an EU role in cohesion policy, research and development, information technology and telecommunications infrastructure, and the environment. The most important step was the doubling of funding for less developed regions, so that by 1993 almost 30 percent of the EU budget was spent on regional redistribution. This sizable resource base became the foundation for an integrated European cohesion policy exhibiting the three key features of regulated capitalism: extensive positive regulation shaped by EU actors; multilevel partnership among the Commission, national ministries, and subnational authorities; and significant redistribution from rich to poor. The main beneficiaries – Spain, Greece, Portugal, and Ireland – initially received the equivalent of 2 to 4 percent of their GDP, an amount comparable to the postwar Marshall Plan. The second Delors budgetary package (1992) increased cohesion funding to 141 billion Ecu (at 1992 prices) for the period 1994–1999. By 1999, Ireland, Greece, and Portugal will each receive more than 5 percent of their GDP from cohesion funding (Hooghe 1996a).

The next step was to insert employment policy as a Russian Doll within the European Monetary Union (EMU). While EMU would shift an important competence to the European level, Delors and his collaborators were just as interested in the potential for the EU to play a subsequent role in combating unemployment and sustaining welfare. Its 1993 White Paper, *Growth, Competitiveness and Employment*, propelled employment onto the European agenda. After some prodding by trade unions, socialist party leaders, and parts of the Commission administration (mainly DG V, social affairs), this plan was taken up by the Santer Commission. Social democrats, in and out of national governments, have pressed the Commission to campaign for a formal EU commitment to combat unemployment as a counterweight to EMU. As a result of these efforts some provisions on employment were incorporated in the 1997 Treaty of Amsterdam.

The third element of the Delors strategy was the attempt to establish a "People's" Europe based on a Social Charter setting out thirty basic social rights, mostly for workers, accompanied by specific proposals for social policy harmonization and, crucial for Delors, "Social Dialogue" between workers and employers. At Maastricht, eleven of the twelve national governments (with the Major government opting out) agreed to make the Charter legally binding (Lange 1993). For proponents of a full-fledged European welfare state, the Social Charter and Social Protocol seem much ado about nothing, while neoliberals adamantly oppose it (Lange 1993; Rhodes 1993; Ross 1993; Leibfried and Pierson 1996; Streeck 1996b). Ambitions for a European social dimension are far from realized in welfare policy or industrial relations, though the EU plays a growing role in these areas (Leibfried and Pierson 1995, 1996; Cram 1997).

The Commission does not have to change the treaty base of the EU to build regulated capitalism. It has consistently anchored new competencies in preestablished institutions. The structural funds administrations have sheltered new policies in environment, vocational training, employment-creating infrastructural investment, cooperation in new technologies, research and development, and the promotion of social partnership (Hooghe 1996b). The Court of Auditors estimated in 1992 that the structural funds administrations provide an umbrella for nearly three-quarters of total spending on the environment (Sbragia 1993b).[4] One consequence of this is that the principle of partnership that is established in cohesion policy has been exported to the EU's environmental policy.

In their national arenas, Social Democrats have had to give ground on several aspects of the postwar social contract, including employment, welfare, and participation of unions in macroeconomic policy making. While the project for regulated capitalism is far from replicating these at the European level, it has laid the foundation for an alternative to market

---

[4] These are estimates for 1991 (Court of Auditors, Official Journal C245, September 23, 1992; drawn from Sbragia 1993b). Therefore, they do not include the expenditures under the cohesion fund, created at Maastricht, which spends about 40–50 percent of its annual budget of around 2 billion ECU on environmental infrastructure.

liberalism based on positive regulation of market activity, economic redistribution, the extension of liberal democracy to the European level, and collaboration among public and private actors. The ten-year presidency of Jacques Delors in the European Commission laid the basis for this project, just as Prime Minister Thatcher was pivotal for neoliberalism. At this point in time (May 1997) we cannot predict the outcome of this struggle. What we can say is that the European Union is shaped by an ongoing clash of interests and ideas – ideas and interests that have jelled into contending conceptions of governance.

CONCLUSION

The collapse of national Keynesianism in a context of poor economic performance and declining international competitiveness led to a reorganization of the European political economy. That reorganization had to come to terms with two of the most fundamental issues of political life: the structuration of political authority and the scope of authoritative decision making in the economy. The European Union continues to serve as a means for achieving narrow collective goods, but these larger questions are never far from view. European political economy is being shaped by an intense debate that has mobilized leaders, political parties, interest groups, social movements, and, on occasion, the wider public. Segmented bargaining among policy elites still takes place in some policy areas, but it is no longer insulated from the struggle about how to organize and rule Europe.

This struggle is neither a random conflict of interests, nor a reflection of functional pressures. It is structured along two dimensions: a left-right dimension ranging from social democracy to market liberalism; and a national-supranational dimension ranging from support for the restoration of national state autonomy to support for further European integration.

Broad, multilevel coalitions are oriented to two projects combining orientations along these dimensions: a neoliberal project and a project for regulated capitalism. At stake in this conflict are not only domestic issues of political economy, but the political architecture of Europe. Neither project is hegemonic.

Whether Europeans will continue "the process of creating an ever closer union" (Article A of the Maastricht Treaty) has become a matter of the widest public discourse. European integration has become a high-profile issue in domestic politics capable of rocking governments, jeopardizing party cohesion, and spurring new party-political movements. In this context, leaders of national governments are constrained more than ever to behave, not as defenders of institutional interests, but as party-political leaders concerned with their bases of political support, party cohesion, and fighting elections. In this politicized climate, political actors without the benefit of democratic legitimacy – above all, the European Commission – are particularly vulnerable. Something new has been added to the struggle between ideological projects concerning the European political economy: a contest for endorsement by the public (Cameron 1995; Schmitter 1996a, 1996b).

A strong implication of our analysis is that there is no irreversible logic to European integration. The link between economic integration and polity creation is humanly contrived; it involves contending political projects. We reject the presumption that such projects, or the outcome of their struggle, is merely a political "superstructure" that reflects an economic logic having to do with reducing transaction costs or reaping joint gains. The sheer fact that cross-border transactions are increasing within Europe does not mean that further political integration will be the outcome. To understand European integration one must understand its irreducible political character. One must systematically analyze the clash of multilevel coalitions of governments, supranational actors, transnational and domestic interests. The Euro-polity is not a by-product of functional requirements or the pursuit of narrow economic interest; on the contrary, it is shaped by deep disagreements among political actors about how to organize political life in Europe.

PART II

THE DYNAMICS OF DOMESTIC POLITICAL ECONOMIES

4

DIVERGENT PRODUCTION REGIMES: COORDINATED AND UNCOORDINATED MARKET ECONOMIES IN THE 1980s AND 1990s

David Soskice

The systematic analysis of advanced capitalist economies has had two main focuses. One has been the *welfare state:* this owes much to the work of Esping-Andersen in distinguishing three welfare state patterns in advanced economies (Esping-Andersen, this volume; Stephens, Huber, and Ray this volume). His distinctions have been widely accepted. There is less agreement in the analysis of the other main focus – and the focus of this chapter – *production regimes;*[1] Hall (this volume) relates the discussion in this chapter to other approaches, notably of Sabel and of Hollingsworth and Streeck. The concluding section of this book sketches links between the classification of production regimes advanced here and that of welfare states (Kitschelt, Marks, and Stephens, this volume).

By a production regime is meant the organization of production through markets and market-related institutions. It analyzes the ways in which the microagents of capitalist systems – companies, customers, employees, owners of capital – organize and structure their interrelationships,

---

[1] This is the term used by Hollingsworth, Schmitter, and Streeck (1994). Hollingsworth and Boyer (1997) is a useful collection, in particular the chapters by the editors.

within a framework of incentives and constraints or "rules of the game"[2] set by a range of market-related institutions within which the microagents are embedded. These framework incentives and constraints are sometimes summarized as the "institutional framework" of the production side of the economy. The most important of the institutions contributing to the institutional framework are the *financial system*, the *industrial relations system*, the *education and training system*, and the *intercompany system* (the latter governing relations between companies – competition policy, technology transfer, standard setting, and so on).[3] The institutional framework, in the argument of this chapter, is seen as primarily defined at the national level, despite regional, sectoral, and other variations.[4] Thus the phrase "national institutional framework of incentives and constraints" will sometimes be employed.

The analysis of production regimes thus casts light on how differences across economies in the configurations of these institutions might explain differences in micro behavior – from skill acquisition of employees, for example, through relations between owners and managers of companies, and relations between companies and their suppliers, to the production, development, and innovation strategies that the average company can successfully pursue. Applied to the explanation of export behavior, the comparative production regime approach therefore argues for a theory of "comparative *institutional* advantage." The focus of the chapter is, *statically*, on the modus operandi of production regimes in advanced capitalist economies since the early 1980s.[5]

The analysis of production regimes also seeks to understand how the "rules of the game" embodied in the four systems get set and changed over

---

[2] Different writers use different terms, "rules of the game" being that employed by North (1990). Aoki refers to implicit and explicit rules of the game and their enforcement characteristics (Aoki 1994).

[3] They are important from the relational perspective of this chapter, which stresses relations between companies and their owners, their employees, and their suppliers. In this respect the chapter is influenced by the economic approaches of Aoki (1994) and of Kitschelt (1991a), and by the comparative industrial sociology of the Aix school (Maurice, Sellier, and Silvestre 1986; and Sorge and Warner 1987).

[4] Thus the chapter follows comparative political economic institutionalists in attributing importance to *national* institutional patterns: notably Hall (1986), Katzenstein (1985), Zysman (1983). In this respect it parallels comparative industrial sociologists, especially Maurice, Sellier, and Silvestre (1986), Sorge and Warner (1987), and Streeck (1991); also see recent developments in the *regulation* school, by Boyer (1995), and by economists comparing the United States and Japan, inspired by Aoki (1994).

[5] This (rough) choice of date reflects a period in which substantial primary and secondary research has now been carried out: this includes notably the massive pool of qualitative data in Michael Porter's *Competitive Advantage of Nations* (1990).

time: this may involve the changing power resources and interests of collective actors, including the state. *Dynamically*, the chapter seeks to analyze how and why production regimes have changed between the 1960s and the present. In particular it asks why systems of industrial relations have profoundly lost influence in certain economies but not in others. In answering this question, the chapter argues that it is paradoxically in those advanced economies in which business has been strongly organized that industrial relations systems have remained important; and we need to look to the capacity, power, and interests of business in those economies to explain the phenomenon. By contrast, where business has not been well organized – and, we will argue, has not had the capacity to build or maintain institutional structures needed to incorporate effective employee representative bodies – governments have seen or come to realize the need for a reduction, sometimes dramatic, in the influence of unions.

PATTERNS OF PRODUCTION REGIMES

This section shows how the production regimes of most advanced economies at the end of the 1980s and in the first half of the 1990s fall into one of two main patterns.[6] The first, which we refer to as business-coordinated market economies or CMEs, includes most northern European economies (such as Germany, Sweden, Switzerland) and in a different variant Japan and South Korea.[7] In these economies there is considerable nonmarket coordination directly and indirectly between companies, with the state playing a framework-setting role; and in all these economies, in one form or another, labor remains "incorporated." The second main pattern, uncoordinated or liberal market economies (LMEs), consists of the Anglo-Saxon economies and Ireland. Here, there is little nonmarket coordination between companies;[8] labor has been progressively excluded, and the state plays an arm's length role.

---

[6] The chapter considers neither newly industrializing countries, nor the transformational economies of eastern Europe, nor the less developed European economies of Spain, Portugal, Greece, and Turkey. This division of production regimes appears in Soskice (1990) and Albert (1991).

[7] Italy is a complex case, with northern and central Italy having many similarities with the CME pattern. The Italian case is analyzed most persuasively by Regini (1994, 1995); its complexities are well brought out by Locke (1995). In this chapter, it will be treated as a northern European type CME.

[8] A third, quite different pattern is that of France; this is only discussed briefly in this chapter. France has a pattern of its own which we will call a "state-business-elite coordinated-market economy": this third pattern is more in the course of transition and uncertainty than the other two. Again according to our general approach, this pattern is

MEASURES OF BUSINESS COORDINATION

Behind this classification, and central to the dynamic analysis of this chapter, is a basic theoretical position (to be set out in the section on the
dynamics of production regimes): namely, the most important determinant
of the different forms that production regimes have taken in the 1980s and
1990s lies in underlying and generally long-standing differences in the
nature of coordination between companies. In the present subsection, some
data are presented on patterns of business coordination in different economies, roughly at the start of our period. This coordinating capacity of
businesses in the late 1970s and early 1980s is the key explanatory variable
of the chapter: as will be argued later, operating through its reaction to
the key exogenous shifts – liberalization and technology paradigm change
– that separate the 1980s from the 1960s, business coordinating capacity
has influenced the feasibility of different production regimes and has
molded the power and interest of business as a political actor in the shaping and reshaping of regimes in the 1980s and 1990s.

Coordination among business, outside of competitive market interactions, can take many forms within an economy. One way of measuring
potential coordination is to look at noncompetitive links between companies. These forms are not always easily comparable across economies; for
instance, membership of the president's club in a Japanese horizontal Keiretsu has no analogy in western Europe, and interlocking directorships –
where the same person sits on the board of more than one company – are
unimportant in Japan, where the Japanese board system works differently.
A considerable amount of research has been carried out on the links between Japanese companies within the same Keiretsu grouping: the high
degree of coordination within financial Keiretsu groups is discussed by
Gerlach.[9] A particularly good data set on interlocking directorships covers
the United Kingdom, the United States (LMEs), and a number of northern
European economies (CMEs) in the late 1970s. This is shown in Table 4.1.
It can be seen from the first column, which measures the density of a core
group of interlocked companies, that all except the United Kingdom and

differentiated from the others by the nature of business coordination. Here much of
business coordination takes place through the networks of the elite of business leaders
whose careers have interpenetrated public and private sectors and which include senior
civil servants. Thus, in this type of coordination the state may be directly involved with
individual companies. Companies can coordinate their activities, that is to say, but not
independently of the state: the state is not at arm's length from individual companies.
Here, as in LMEs, labor has been progressively excluded. Much of this argument has been
developed by Hancke (1997), a synthesis is in Hancke and Soskice (1996a).

[9] See Gerlach (1989).

Table 4.1. *Measures of business coordination*

	Density of core, where core exists	H-index (index of concentration)	Employers' wage coordination
Austria	0.84	0.20	3
Belgium	0.72	0.30	2
Switzerland	0.79	0.16	3
Germany	0.74	0.21	3
Italy	0.67	0.11	1
Netherlands	0.56	0.21	2
Finland	0.59	0.19	3
United States	—	0.05	1
United Kingdom	—	0.07	1

Sources: The first two columns from Stokman, Ziegler, et al. (1985); this relates to estimates of interlocking directorships in large companies in the late 1970s. The third column is from Layard, Nikell, and Jackman (1991) and relates to the 1970s and 1980s.

the United States have a high density; no core group existed in the United Kingdom and the United States on which to calculate density. These calculations are confirmed by the Herfindahl index in the second column, which provides a broader measure of concentration of interlocks.[10]

An alternative, complementary way of assessing coordination is to look directly at business associational activity. The third column shows data from Layard, Nickell, and Jackman (1991) on the degree of employer coordination in wage determination, which covers a longer period and is more strongly based on expert assessment.[11] For the degree of wage coordination in the other LME economies for which they provide estimates, the figures of Layard, Nickell, and Jackman are: Australia, 1; New Zealand, 1; Canada, 1; Ireland, 1; for the other CMEs: Denmark, 3; Japan, 2; Finland, 3; Norway, 3; Sweden, 3. (Overall wage coordination is estimated by the OECD separately for 1980 and 1994, as is shown in Table 4.4; the OECD does not provide a breakdown between employer and union coordination.)

Katzenstein (1985) gives assessments of business associational activity in a number of – in our classification – small CMEs in Europe for the

[10] For an updated version which confirms similar results in the early 1990s for a comparison between Germany and the United Kingdom, see Windolf and Beyer (1996).

[11] Some of it by the present author.

period roughly of the late 1970s and early 1980s, consistent with the view of significant business coordination in CMEs. See also Marin (1983) for a description of how the Austrian Chamber of Commerce acts as a "guiding, directive business actor."

COORDINATED MARKET ECONOMIES

This pattern involves close coordination between companies, with the state being able to negotiate with companies collectively the framework in which individual companies operate.

The CME pattern has two variants, one relating to northern Europe and the other to Japan and South Korea. Again, the distinguishing feature of each variant lies in the different underlying ways in which coordination between businesses takes place. In the northern European variety (which Albert [1991] refers to as Rhennish) the most fundamental patterns of business coordination take place within the industrial sector or branch. This variety will be called "industry-coordinated economies." Such economies permit industry-defined unions, technology transfer and diffusion within the industry, technical norm setting within the industry, as well as training of engineers and other high-level specialists within an industry technology framework, and industry-based development of vocational training standards. In the other basic variety (Albert's "Nippon" capitalism), the more intense coordination between companies is within the group of companies, within vertical and horizontal Keiretsu in Japan and Chaebols in Korea: in these economies coordination between large companies in the same industry is more restrained, reflecting in fact strong industry-based competition particularly between large companies. Thus in these "group-coordinated economies," we find company-based unions, technology diffusion and development within the group of companies, technical standard setting within the group, and vocational training as a company-based and not an industry-based phenomenon. This chapter will concentrate on industry-coordinated economies.

The institutional frameworks in the CMEs (both industry- and group-coordinated) tend to encourage the development of long-term cooperative relations, between one company and another, between companies and employees, and between companies and their owners. Their institutional frameworks share the following characteristics:

1. financial systems that allow *long-term financing* of companies;
2. industrial relations systems in which unions play an important part

and which allow *cooperative industrial relations* within the company and coordinated wage bargaining across companies;

3. education and training systems that encourage *serious initial vocational training* of young people, and in which organized business and/or individual companies are closely involved;

4. intercompany systems that enable substantial *technology and standard setting cooperation* to take place between companies.

Industry-Coordinated Economies

The preceding characteristics relate to both industry-and group-coordinated economies. In Table 4.2, the institutional framework of industry-coordinated economies in the 1980s and early 1990s is set out more specifically, and here the importance of *sectoral* is evident. Training and technology transfer (and the related standard setting of training requirements and of technical product standards) take place within primarily industry-based organizations. The same is true of industrial relations. Monitoring in the system of corporate governance uses suppliers, customers, associations, and research institutes with close industry links. Business and employer associations and industry unions (and in some cases chambers of industry, commerce, handwork and/or labor) are key actors. Employee representative bodies in companies have close links with industry unions; top managers have close links with business and employer associations.

This is not, however, a purely sectoral system of coordination. In each industry-coordinated economy, the sectoral coordination is tied to a greater or lesser degree into a *national framework*. Vocational training and employee representation are normally the objects of framework legislation, with the aim of cross-sectoral uniformity of practices, and are supported by labor courts and expert standing committees, with strong associational activity in both.[12] In most economies (not Italy) the government plays a role in setting a framework for technology transfer, through research institutes and higher education; again the business associations at the national level are involved with sectoral organizations in policy making (though, nowadays the unions play a much less significant part). Wage setting is coordinated by unions and employer associations across sectors (in each country, including Italy and also Sweden and Denmark – despite the breakup of national bargains). There is a great deal of exchange of information across sectors through the corporate governance system, with banks playing a key

---

[12] Italy is an exception on vocational training.

Table 4.2. *Institutional framework of industry-coordinated economies*

Industrial relations
(a) Wage determination: Formally or informally coordinated industry-level deter-
    mination important. Formal or informal coordination across key industries.
    Employer associations and industry unions play major role.[a]
(b) In-company industrial relations: Employee-elected bodies play significant role
    in company decision making; in all cases these have links to outside industry
    unions, though less strong in the Netherlands and in Switzerland outside
    engineering and chemicals. In all cases, employee representatives have de
    facto power either directly or through recourse to arbitration. In addition,
    representation on supervisory boards (with exception of Belgium and Italy).[b]

Education and training
(a) Postcompulsory vocational training strong, reasonable status, with close in-
    volvement of industry organizations and unions; either dual apprenticeship
    (Germany, Austria, Switzerland); or vocational colleges (Sweden; though some
    of these are being set up by large companies); or both (the Netherlands, Den-
    mark). General higher education more limited.
(b) Strong industry technology linkages in engineering training at Fachhoch-
    schule level; with close professional association involvement.
(c) Substantial doctoral programs in basic sciences and engineering, with close
    links with large companies.

Company financing
(a) Publicly quoted companies generally have stable shareholder systems, with
    banks playing delegated monitor role, and using network monitoring from
    suppliers, customers, research institutes, business associations, etc. Hostile
    takeovers difficult.
(b) Smaller companies rely on bank finance also using network-reputation moni-
    toring.
(c) These (essentially industry-based) monitoring devices contribute to bank un-
    willingness to finance investment in radically new technologies.

*Rules governing intercompany relationships (technology transfer, standard setting, competi-
    tion policy)*
(a) University departments and research institutes with close links to business in
    established technologies; business associations usually play important role.[c]
(b) Consensus-based standard setting within industries and subindustries; again
    business associational activity strong.[d]
(c) Strong requirement for open competition in export markets; but some avoid-
    ance of head-on competition within relevant subbranch of industry.
(d) Business association plays role in relational contract disputes and framework
    rule setting.

role. And the neocorporatist recent past of these economies is far from dead: there is, within limits, a representational monopoly of interest groups and a framework in policy making to allow for that role.

Finally, there are strong *interlocking complementarities* between different parts of the institutional framework. Each system depends on the other systems to function effectively. A starting point is the conditions for an effective system of initial vocational training in company-specific and industry technology skills in which companies make serious investments: This requires long-term finance, since the return on the investment is a long-term one; coordinated wage setting, to minimize the risk of poaching; cooperative company-level industrial relations, to ensure cooperation from highly skilled and hence powerful employees; and cooperation between companies in technology transfer and standard setting, to develop agreed industry technologies, which form the basis for skill development and certification. Long-term finance requires the ability on the part of owners (or their delegated monitors) to have good information about the potential performance of companies and their competences; in a world of substantial industry technology skills, banks do not have the expertise to monitor companies directly, so close relations between companies, business associations, and research institutions are needed.[13] Cooperative industrial relations within companies requires that companies can credibly commit to long-term relations with employees, which in turn requires long-term finance; it also requires highly skilled employees whom companies will be

---

[13] Industry-coordinated economies differ in this respect from group-coordinated economies. In group-coordinated economies banks have greater expertise and assume more direct monitoring functions.

Notes to Table 4.2 *(cont.)*

---

[a]Soskice (1990a), IDS (1996), Golden, Lange, and Wallerstein (this volume). In the latest OECD classification of wage-bargaining systems by degree of coordination, all the CMEs in the sample score high: Austria, Germany, and Japan score 3; Norway and Italy, 2.5; Denmark, Finland, and Switzerland, 2+; and Belgium, the Netherlands, and Sweden, 2. By contrast all the LMEs in the sample score less than 2.
[b]IDS (1996) for Austria, Belgium, the Netherlands, Denmark, Germany, Italy, Sweden, and Switzerland. Least formalized in Italy: "In large to medium sized companies works councils play an active role and cannot in practice be circumvented" (p. 196).
[c]See Lutz (1993) and Soskice (forthcoming) for Germany; and Nelson (1993) for the United Kingdom, Sweden, United States, and Denmark.
[d]See Hancke and Soskice (1996) and Herrigel (1993) for Germany.

concerned not to lose.[14] Each element of the institutional framework thus reinforces the others. Note that this is neither a functionalist argument (different frameworks coexist), nor does it rule out change. But it gives a partial reason for there being only a limited number of possible constellations of institutional frameworks.

UNCOORDINATED MARKET ECONOMIES

The second main pattern, which is found in the Anglo-Saxon economies and Ireland, will be referred to as uncoordinated or liberal market economies (LMEs). Here companies have little capacity to coordinate their activities collectively. Their inability to act collectively means that they cannot combine to negotiate discretionary framework solutions with the state. The state, with all its panoply of actions from legislation to quasi-public agencies, is seldom able to change the institutional framework in which companies operate in ways that cannot be enforced in the courts. Thus the liberal market economy state – like the coordinated-market economy state – is at arm's length from the individual company; but, unlike the CME state, it cannot work out frameworks with business collectively. The institutional framework, emphasizing market deregulation, favors shorter-term and more competitive relations:

1. financial systems that impose relatively *short-term horizons* on companies, but at the same time *allow high risk taking*;
2. industrial relations systems in *deregulated labor markets* that discourage effective employee representation within companies – hence weak unions – but which facilitate unilateral control by top management;
3. education and training systems which *emphasize general education*, discourage long-term initial vocational training, but encourage subsequent bit-by-bit skill acquisition, especially for those with sufficient general education;
4. intercompany systems that impose *strong competition requirements* and hence limit possible cooperation between companies.

More detail is shown in Table 4.3. In LMEs the *lack of coordinating capacity* among companies is reflected in education and initial training, which is carried on outside the company, without serious company involvement;

---

[14] A fuller analysis (Soskice, forthcoming a) shows how the different institutional features fit together and reinforce each other.

Table 4.3. *Institutional framework of uncoordinated market economies*

Industrial relations system

(a) Wage bargaining: Largely company based and uncoordinated (U.S., U.K., Canada, N.Z.). Australia has moved away from coordination toward company determination.[a] Ireland, however, is an exception in having had centralized bargaining since 1987.

(b) In-company industrial relations: No legal or collective bargaining provision for workplace employee representation in private sector.[b] Role of unions within workplaces in 1990s very limited.

Education and training systems

(a) Postcompulsory secondary-education vocational training of lower-level workers weak, low status, with limited company involvement (true of all LMEs mentioned, despite attempts at change in 1980s in most). Postcompulsory general education strong, with higher education for more than 50% of age group in U.S. and Canada to 30% in U.K.

(b) Training of engineers not closely linked to specific industry technologies.

(c) Substantial doctoral programs in basic sciences and engineering, without close company linkages (strongest overwhelmingly in U.S.; also the U.K., Canada).

System governing intercompany relations

(a) Strong anticollusion policies.

(b) Limited framework for dealing with problems of relational contracting.

(c) Limited institutional framework for technology diffusion.

(d) Market-based standard setting.

System of company financing and corporate governance

Legal frameworks permitting hostile takeovers for publicly quoted companies, i.e., absence of stable shareholder arrangements. High-risk capital markets available.

---

[a]See the section on institutional frameworks for OECD classifications of degree of wage-bargaining coordination, which does not include Ireland; all the other LMEs have low coordination scores for the latest period (1994): the United States, United Kingdom, New Zealand, and Canada all score 1; Australia, 1.5. All the CMEs in the sample score 2 or more. OECD (1997).

[b]See IDS (1996) for the United Kingdom and Ireland.

standard setting and technology transfer, which take place largely through the market; the absence of long-term stable cross-shareholding agreements, and hence of protective long-term financial frameworks for companies, because of the difficulty of stable agreements between companies; and the unwillingness of companies to give substantial power to employee representatives because of, inter alia, the lack of powerful employer associations to come to their aid in disputes.

As with CMEs, the institutional framework is *national*. The main features of the framework sketched out in Table 4.3 are underpinned by national legislation.

Also as with the CME framework there are *strong complementarities* between different components: shorter-term finance requires companies to be able to move quickly out of old and into new activities, hence requiring low-cost hiring and firing; and also the capacity to attract those with appropriate skills, which requires no constraint on wage setting. Because of the need to move more frequently, young people are less prepared to engage in deep vocational training but want instead more general academic education so they can acquire skills when necessary. The need for companies to move quickly also makes costly any constraints on decision making from effective employee representation. And quick movement reduces the ability to commit to cooperative relations with other companies in technology transfer.

The next two sections look at the effects of these different institutional frameworks on micro- and macroeconomic performances respectively.

INSTITUTIONAL FRAMEWORKS AND MICROECONOMIC PERFORMANCE: COMPANY ORGANIZATION AND COMPANY STRATEGIES

What effect do these different frameworks have on the strategies companies adopt? In this section we describe some of the main differences in *microeconomic performance* – in terms of company behavior – between the liberal market economies and the industry-coordinated market economies. The main dependent variable of the section will be some major differences in the pattern of product market innovation strategies. And the main concern of the section will be to show how the differences in institutional frameworks discussed in the preceding section may explain in part the product strategy differences.

As far as the relative competitiveness of company strategies are concerned, the major empirical work by Michael Porter, *The Competitive Advantage of Nations*, published in 1990 and based on statistics and interviews from 1985 on provides a great deal of relevant material for eight economies (Porter 1990). The United States and United Kingdom are included as examples (in our terms) of liberal market economies, and Germany, Sweden, and Switzerland as examples of industry-coordinated market economies; it also includes Italy. The focus is on the first five economies, which are clear examples, with bracketed references to Italy.

DIFFERENCES IN PRODUCT MARKET AND INNOVATION STRATEGIES

Germany, Sweden, and Switzerland, as examples of industry-coordinated market economies, have had various characteristics in common that are opposite to those of the United Kingdom and the United States, on the basis of Porter's work. In the following discussion, references to qualitative assessments from Porter will be cited parenthetically in text (e.g., reference to Germany on p. 356 will be indicated by G: 356).

Germany, Sweden, and Switzerland have tended to produce relatively complex products, involving complex production processes and after-sales service, in well-established industries, with close customer links (G: 356, 367, 371; Swe: 331, 343, 345, 348–349; Swi: 318). These are products referred to by Streeck (1991) as *diversified quality products* (DQP). They are typically products that depend on skilled and experienced employees on whom responsibility can be devolved. By contrast, the United Kingdom and the United States have not been successful in these areas (UK: 494; US: 519). These differences can also be shown quantitatively by means of Porter's use of the SITC trade classification of industries, permitting analysis of up to a five-digit level; for each of his economies he takes the industries in 1985 with a larger export share than the country's aggregate export share, and inter alia divides these industries up into four groups, one of which is "machinery" and another "services." Numbers of "internationally competitive" machinery industries by country include:[15]

Germany	46
Switzerland	35
Sweden	28
(Italy	45)
United Kingdom	18
United States	17

The successful provision of services internationally shows the reverse picture. Many of these internationally competitive services involve the in-

[15] The classification of machinery industries in the United Kingdom is incorrect, since, for instance, "custom software" has been included as a machinery industry; we reclassified the U.K. industries so they were consistent with classifications in the other economies.

dividual skills of highly trained and mobile professionals (e.g., management consultancy; advertising and related media services; international banking, including investment banking, derivatives, etc.; tax consultancies; architectural and engineering consultancies; auctioneering). Other services involve the management of large, complex tightly coupled systems (airlines, large software houses, large entertainments systems), which require top management to be able to impose rapid changes through large organizations.[16] (Other examples in industry of large complex systems especially where the technology is changing rapidly, in which the United States and United Kingdom also have comparative advantage, are telecommunications systems, defense systems, and aircraft production.) Numbers of "internationally competitive" service industries include:[17]

Germany	7
Switzerland	14
Sweden	9
(Italy	5)
United Kingdom	27
United States	44

Germany, Sweden, and Switzerland are economies in which new industries are not easily developed, in contrast to the U.S. and U.K. economies. Comparing Germany with the United States, Porter writes: "As strong as Germany is overall in research, it cannot match the US in inventiveness in new industries . . . Germany is the undisputed leader in improving and upgrading technology in fields in which its industry is established, but there are weaknesses in newer fields such as electronics, biotechnology and new materials." These differences are mirrored by lack of formation of new companies in Germany, Sweden, and Switzerland, again in contrast to circumstances in the United States and United Kingdom (G: 377; Swe: 351; Swi: 327; UK: 507; US: 527, 530).

Why might differences in institutional frameworks – as they evolved through the 1980s – have induced differences in company product and innovation strategies? The argument uses the general approach of the new economics of organization (Milgrom and Roberts 1992) and owes much to

---

[16] See Lehrer (1996) for the example of British Airways versus Lufthansa.

[17] Based on my calculations following Porter's cross-country classification of internationally competitive industries. Note that these figures should be treated with some caution as there were some classificatory problems with the U.K. data.

Kitschelt's seminal analysis (Kitschelt 1991). For related approaches in the management literature, see Ebster-Grosz and Pugh (1996).

DIVERSIFIED QUALITY PRODUCTS

We look first at the product market strategies whose relational problems are solved by CME-type institutional frameworks but not by LME-types. The broad relational requirements for DQP development and production strategies are that the company have long-standing cooperative relations with skilled manual employees, technicians, and engineers, as well as with suppliers, and that the company's employees and suppliers have access to the latest developments in industry technology (Kern and Schumann 1984; Streeck 1991).

More precisely, the company needs first *skilled employees* with industry-technology skills as well as company-specific product knowledge skills; and it requires them to work in ways (especially autonomous group environments) that are costly for management to monitor and impossible to explicate contractually. Moreover, because problem-solving knowledge is held by employees, it is seldom practical for managers to have unilateral control over decisions: efficiency requires a more consensus-based approach to decision making.[18] These factors put employees in principle into a strong bargaining position: contracts – relating performance to management requirements – cannot be used to enforce appropriate behavior legally, both because monitoring is not easy and because decision making is consensus-based; companies cannot threaten to fire employees because of the cost of training new employees in company-specific skills that take time to acquire; and, in any case, employees with industry-technology skills can get employment elsewhere. They are in a position, in Williamson's language, to "hold-up" the company (Williamson 1985).

In addition to the problems of *work organization* are those of skill acquisition. Skill acquisition raises problems for both employees and companies. Employees have to invest early in their career in the acquisition of industry-technology and company-specific skills. These commit them, at least partially, to a particular occupation and company. Thus they must be sure ex ante that the system of wage determination, employment security, and skill certification make this a safe strategy; and that the training itself is of appropriate quality. Skilled workers need governance institutions, first, to guarantee that the industry-technology skills that they are taught

---

[18] See Aghion and Tirole (1994) for a seminal approach to formalization of this argument.

provide secure employment and conditions – notably, through some guarantee that their skills will be acceptable to other employers, because these types of companies can never guarantee their long-term existence in the face of major technological change and/or product demand change; and, second, to ensure that implicit long-term agreements with the company are carried out, despite the inside-information advantage which the company has. Acquisition of industry technology skills integrated with company-specific skills is also problematic for companies. For it requires involvement by companies in investment in and carrying out of initial training of employees, which combines industry-technology understanding with company-specific knowledge of organization, of processes, and of products. Hence, companies need advice and – in order to guarantee the quality of training to potential trainees – monitoring; the problem here is that this exposes the company to external institutions which it can trust with access to inside information. Companies need in addition assurance that the industry technology skills will be valuable to the company. And they further need assurance that the employees they train will not be poached.

CMEs provide an industrial relations system that guarantees cooperative behavior of skilled employees to employers, and which guarantees to employees that employers are pursuing strategies (research and development, training, etc.) consistent with employee stability as far as product market developments allow. In the industry-coordinated CMEs, the system consists of a combination of effective works councils (or other employee representational bodies) within the company, linked to industry unions outside it, capable of giving advice to works councils but also of disciplining them; and industry-based employer associations that cooperate in providing expertise on vocational training with unions, and to which companies can turn in case of problems with works councils or unions. In addition, coordinated wage setting provides a stability to wage developments across companies that makes poaching of skilled employees less easy than in a deregulated labor market.

The company needs, second, to be able to develop relational contracts with *other companies* in the industry for joint development, modification, and customization of components and machines; and to take part in technological and technical exchanges with horizontal companies in the industry. This requires that there are governance institutions available to cope with problems that arise in relational contracts (e.g., as a result of one side being able to "hold up" the other), and capable of managing the necessary information flows between companies – ensuring that companies make "fair" contributions to the flows and guaranteeing to the companies that the inside information acquired in the process will not be misused.

These linkages are developed and managed by business associations, with banks and professional engineering associations playing a part. Business associations also help to develop contractual forms when problems over relational contracts arise, as well as helping to provide arbitration facilities.

The company needs finally some assurance of long-term finance from its *owners*. But the value of the company at any point in time can only be evaluated by inside information. Moreover, the best picture of the company comes from both the company and the other companies and business associations with whom it has relational contracts. In industry-coordinated CMEs the institutional framework allows for relatively "cooperative" behavior between companies, even when they may appear to be horizontal competitors in the same industry. Companies in many industries tend to differentiate their products, and not to compete too strongly for each other's customers; this enables cooperation to take place. And it enables reasonably objective reputations to be built about the effectiveness of companies and their technical and market competences. Owners of companies (and banks as delegated monitors) are thus able to assess the position of companies.

RADICAL INNOVATION

A range of product market strategies was identified as competitive in liberal market economies: highly innovative products (often in purely intellectual patented form) developed in venture capital financed start-ups in new high-technology areas and in the still highly innovative larger new technology companies that absorbed start-ups or into which start-ups developed; complex systemic products (telecom systems, defense systems, large software systems) that require engineers and managers to work together in tightly coupled organizations, usually involving rapid rates of innovation in and development of new products; and the analogues of these activities in the service sector, from innovative activities in law, banking, tax, and management consulting, all requiring individual cleverness and risk taking, through complex system-based products, such as airlines, entertainment systems, standardized hotel chains, and large advertising houses.

There are three requirements common to these product market strategies. First, the possibility of strong and effective control by top management, sometimes referred to as "unilateral control," is necessary since these strategies require companies to reposition themselves rapidly externally and to reorganize themselves internally. External repositioning may permit the development of radically new products (true of all the previously mentioned areas). Internal reorganization by top management is also critical. In the fast-moving, competitive world of complex systems, companies need to be able to buy into new technologies and to adapt quickly to new standards and, consequently, to hire those with appropriate new skills – especially in technologies which are changing rapidly and unpredictably (in services such as investment banking as much as in new high technology). With complex systems it is difficult to negotiate such absorptions quickly, since many different parts of a system have to fit precisely together at the same time. Thus effective unilateral management control is critical. An institutional condition for this is the absence of institutional constraints on management decision making, such as codetermination.

Second, companies need the institutional freedom to buy and sell subsidiaries. This means an active and open market in corporate governance, in which owners of companies are not constrained by stable shareholder agreements.

Third, in order to be able to hire and give necessary incentives to those with skills in new areas that the companies cannot develop themselves, deregulated labor markets, which allow companies to hire and fire at low cost and which enable companies to set rewards at appropriate levels, are needed.

MULTINATIONALS

How do multinational companies (MNCs) fit into these institutional frameworks? MNCs pursue many different approaches in their locational, supplier, and alliance strategies. Among other reasons for their strategies is the ability to gain comparative institutional advantage. Thus the three largest German banks have located investment banking activities in London; and the three largest chemical companies have located biotechnology activities in the United States. Making use of comparative institutional advantage is not the only motivation behind MNC locational strategies; MNCs may wish to produce close to their product markets, and they may want to take advantage of cost differences. But comparative institutional advantages are important in locational decision making, and they weaken the argument that MNCs bring pressure to bear on governments to deregulate.

INSTITUTIONAL FRAMEWORKS AND MACROECONOMIC PERFORMANCE

The leitmotif of this chapter – it will be brought out even more clearly in the subsequent and final section, which seeks to explain how and why institutional frameworks have changed since the 1960s and 1970s – is that world market liberalization and technological change have forced attention to the micro-institutional conditions within which companies operate. From that perspective, what is of interest is that economies in which business was well organized at the start of the period have maintained – albeit reshaped – relatively coordinated institutional frameworks, in which unions continue to play an important role; and those in which business was not well organized have moved toward substantially deregulated frameworks from which unions have been more and more excluded.

The more traditional concern of political economy, by contrast, has been to evaluate institutional arrangements in different advanced economies in terms of macroeconomic performance. Much of the impact of the corporatism literature stemmed from the favorable macroeconomic outcomes of the more corporatist economies in the 1960s and 1970s. Since our CMEs are mostly descendants of corporatist economies – absent peak-level bargaining, social contracts, and the like – it is natural to ask about the relative macroeconomic performance of CMEs and LMEs. As shown in Table 4.4, the OECD (1997) has calculated for 1980 and 1994 a measure of coordination in wage bargaining. These scores update and supplement those in Soskice (1990b) and Layard, Nickell, and Jackman (1991) and Golden, Wallerstein, and Lange (this volume).

The straightforward comparison of OECD standardized unemployment rates is useful as an antidote to the idea that deregulated labor markets are more effective at producing low unemployment than are more regulated ones. In fact CMEs have on average slightly lower unemployment rates than LMEs. But actual unemployment rates are misleading as a measure of equilibrium (or long-term sustainable) unemployment rates in open economies. In the longer term unemployment is constrained by current-account equilibrium (Layard, Nickell, and Jackman 1991; Carlin and Soskice 1990; Soskice 1990b); in the short to medium term, economies can allow demand to expand, with excess demand absorbed in current account deficit. Countries that restrain demand (such as Germany) run in effect at higher than equilibrium unemployment, and in consequence may show current-account surpluses. A crude way of correcting actual unemployment data is therefore to subtract current-account surpluses as a percentage of GDP from actual

Table 4.4 *Coordination and macroeconomic performance*

	OECD coordination score 1994 (1980 in brackets)		Unemployment rate 1986–1994	Unemployment rate *minus* current account as % of GDP, 1986–1994
Austria	3	(3)	3.6	3.7
Germany (West)	3	(3)	7.0	5.1
Japan	3	(3)	2.5	−0.3
Norway	2.5	(2.5)	4.5	4.5
Italy	2.5	(1.5)	11.5	12.1
Denmark	2+	(2.5)	9.9	9.7
Switzerland	2+	(2+)	1.8	−3.5
Finland	2+	(2+)	8.8	11.5
Sweden	2	(2.5)	3.6	4.7
Netherlands	2	(2)	8.4	5.7
Avg (coord)			6.2	5.3
Australia	1.5	(2+)	8.5	13.0
New Zealand	1	(1.5)	7.4	10.2
Canada	1	(1)	9.5	13.1
United Kingdom	1	(1.5)	8.7	10.7
United States	1	(1)	6.3	8.4
Avg (uncoord)			8.0	11.1

unemployment rates.[19] This correction (the "alternative" measure) is provided by the OECD in Table 4.4. The data suggest that much of the low unemployment performance of the LMEs in the 1986–1994 period is due to excess demand and therefore in the long run is unsustainable; the deflationary policies of the Bundesbank, however, had the opposite effect in northern Europe for the economies that stayed within the exchange rate mechanism of the European Monetary System (EMS). On this basis, equilibrium unemployment performance of the CMEs looks significantly better than that of the LMEs in this period.

If these statistics are taken at face value, there are several possible explanations:

---

[19] If productivity and labor force are both zero, a unit decline in the unemployment rate is approximately equal to a 1 percent increase in GDP. A 1 percent rise in GDP reduces the current account by the ratio of exports to GDP, say by 0.3 units, if exports are exogenous and imports proportional to GDP. On these assumptions the "alternative" measure is a conservative correction.

1. The standard explanation is that wage bargainers in coordinated systems set wages with a concern to maintain international cost competitiveness, to keep inflation at or below world market trends. This is set out and confirmed econometrically in Layard, Nickell, and Jackman (1991); moreover, instead of the crude correction here embodied in the "alternative" performance index, Layard, Nickell, and Jackman solve explicitly for current-account equilibrium. In essence a rational expectations approach is posited, that is, a joint process among the key decision makers of forward-looking outcome forecasting. Hall (1994) discusses how central banks can be part of this process.

2. The education and training systems of LMEs have been uniformly unsuccessful in the 1980s and at least early 1990s in the education and/or vocational training of children in the bottom part of their age cohort, perhaps concerning up to 25 percent of young people. Initial vocational training has become a "low esteem" route in Australia, the United Kingdom, the United States, Canada, and Ireland (with no information on New Zealand).[20] And education systems fail to provide necessary "social" skills to enable disadvantaged young people to enter the labor market except maybe at wages too low to give any incentive to work on a regular basis.[21] By contrast, the training systems of the CMEs provide for both basic competences and for clear bridges into employment for most young people (with the exception of Italy). There is a sharply higher unemployment rate among the low-skilled (OECD 1997); so economies less capable of educating and training young people will be likely to have higher unemployment, other things being equal.

3. Even though LME labor markets are deregulated, there may be higher frictional unemployment than in CMEs because job tenure is less long.

Despite the statistics and these possible explanations, however, there is much disagreement in this area. One disagreement concerns mechanisms of employment creation, in particular the role of *wage dispersion*. Because of deregulated labor markets, there was greater wage dispersion in LMEs than CMEs in the 1980s. It is commonly argued, usually with reference to the

[20] See the OECD presentation for 1994 Final Conference on VOTEC program for the United Kingdom, United States, Ireland, Australia; and Ashton, Maguire, and Sung (1991) on Canada.

[21] See Finegold and Soskice (1988). They argue that the absence of effective vocational training institutions at the bottom end of the labor market can lead to a "low skills equilibrium."

United States, that low wages promote employment growth. If so, LMEs have a mechanism that CMEs do not have for creating employment. There is in fact considerable econometric dispute about the effectiveness of wage dispersion in creating employment: cross-country studies suggest that wage dispersion *is* positively associated with employment growth (Glyn 1995, Iversen and Wren 1997). But studies of changes in the minimum wage show insignificant employment effects (Card and Krueger 1995; Machin and Manning 1994).

A second disagreement involves *aggregate demand and equilibrium unemployment*. The external balance adjustment to actual unemployment data in Table 4.4 is designed to get rid of aggregate demand effects and hence get a clearer picture of equilibrium unemployment. In a striking argument, Iversen (1995) suggests that low unemployment supported by high aggregate demand policies may be inconsistent with employer coordination unless employers are prepared to accept compressed wage differentials; this is because low unemployment and high aggregate demand increase the bargaining power of unions representing low-paid workers, enabling them to bargain for greater equality of wage outcomes. Once employers cease to be prepared to accept compression, then aggregate demand must be sufficiently deflationary to reduce the bargaining power of pro-compression unions. If this plausible argument is correct, then it may account for some of the high unemployment in northern Europe (a slightly different variant of the argument is developed for Germany in Carlin and Soskice 1997). In that case, fully purging actual unemployment of aggregate demand effects to uncover equilibrium unemployment may be incorrect.

Clear-cut conclusions about the macroeconomic performance of these different institutional frameworks therefore cannot yet be drawn with confidence. What Table 4.4 shows, nonetheless, is that it is wrong to write off the macroeconomic capability of coordinated systems.

THE DYNAMICS OF PRODUCTION REGIMES

CHANGES AND EVOLUTIONS IN INSTITUTIONAL FRAMEWORKS

There are important elements of continuity in institutional frameworks when the 1960s–1970s are compared with the present. That is to say, the American, Japanese, or German institutional frameworks of the earlier period are clear enough ancestors of the current corresponding institutional frameworks. Despite that, both institutional frameworks and the strategic choices of microeconomic agents have changed greatly over the period.

Most obviously, all advanced economies have accepted or embraced a high measure of openness in international markets for goods, services, and capital. In consequence, institutional frameworks have increased considerably in the flexibility they allow individual microeconomic agents, in particular companies and owners of capital, in the organization of their affairs. This section will not seek to explain these changes, but rather take them as given.

The explicanda of the section are threefold:

1. Why is there more than one pattern of advanced capitalism? This is the remarkable feature of advanced capitalism in the 1990s: despite liberalization of international markets, the predicted convergence to a single institutional framework form has not taken place. Even those who argue that convergence is happening, only very slowly, must explain why convergence is so slow. Why then have different patterns of capitalism persisted, albeit with many changes, over the past two decades?

Of particular importance among the changes in the institutional frameworks have been changes in industrial relations systems. Far from the predicted *uniform* convergence to a single (deregulated) framework with marginalization of unions, the changes in industrial relations systems have contributed to a *bifurcated* convergence of most institutional frameworks on one or the other of the two models of advanced capitalism set out earlier; the LME-type model or the CME-type model. Two different shifts have taken place: one relating to those economies which have become LMEs, the other to some of those which have become CMEs.

2a. Most economies in which business was weakly organized at the start of the period (i.e., those which have become LMEs) had had, up to the 1980s, more or less extensively regulated industrial relations systems, relatively powerful union movements, and functioning apprenticeship systems – at least for a minority of young males in the private sector. By the early 1990s labor markets in these economies have become substantially deregulated outside the public sector, with weak unions, particularly inside companies, and decimated apprenticeship systems. The main force behind change was government (both of the right in the United Kingdom and of the left in New Zealand).

Quite different evolutions have taken place in economies in which business was strongly organized at the start of the period.

2b. (i) In almost all economies in which business was strongly organized (i.e., those economies which have become CMEs), unions have remained of importance, particularly as concerns participation in decision making inside companies; wage setting has remained coordinated; and initial vocational training, with links to companies, has remained strong.

However, within this group of economies there were initially two models, the Scandinavian Social Democratic and the Germanic, of the way in which wage setting and related macroeconomic policy making worked. The Scandinavian "centralized egalitarian" (or CE) model, was characterized by egalitarian, centralized wage-setting procedures; this had the effect of compressing wage differentials and hence gave limited freedom to companies to develop internal pay-based career incentives. This contrasts with the Germanic or "flexibly coordinated" model, in which average wage increases are coordinated across industries but in which companies retain considerable room for maneuver, and in which there is a hard currency monetary regime.

2b. (ii) Within economies in which business was initially well organized, there has been a convergence on the flexibly coordinated CME model. This reflects major and conflictual episodes in the 1980s over change in institutional frameworks: (a) Sweden and Denmark (and also Italy) switched from centralized egalitarian (CE) to flexibly coordinated (CME) systems over this period. (b) The German government attempted unsuccessfully to push the German institutional framework in a deregulated direction in the early 1980s. The main force behind change in (a) and resistance to change in (b) was organized business.

(There are partial exceptions: Ireland has redeveloped a system of centralized wage bargaining since 1987 – though unions remain weak and excluded from companies; Australia has moved more slowly toward deregulation than New Zealand or the United Kingdom, and the union leadership has been strategically involved in, rather than marginalized from, this evolution; the Netherlands has deregulated part-time work, though in a controlled way; and vocational training is still much more limited in northern and central Italy than in northern Europe. In most respects these four countries conform to the general arguments of the chapter, but further work is needed to understand the respects in which they do not.)

EXPLAINING CHANGE

This subsection attempts a unified explanation of these changes. It looks first at what were the critical exogenous shifts that precipitated the need to change institutional frameworks; then, at the coordinating capacity of business needed for different institutional frameworks; and, finally, at the political bargaining game between business, unions, and government over the development of institutional frameworks.

Exogenous Shifts

We take as exogenous, first, the *liberalization of external markets.* More or less common to all advanced economies, tariffs have been reduced to very low levels, and other forms of protectionism and subsidy have become much harder; companies are free to locate where they wish; and financial and exchange markets are open. (The uniform liberalization of these markets contrasts – as the earlier description of CME and LME institutional frameworks implies – with de facto lack of liberalization and openness in labor markets, in training markets, in the market for corporate control, and in research and development markets.) The effect on governments of this "external" liberalization has been to increase their dependence on the private sector to deliver good economic performance: this is both because governments can no longer protect domestic companies, and because Keynesian policies have been made less easy by the openness of financial markets. The effect on companies has been to require them to compete in export markets without government assistance, and to allow them to relocate if they wish to.

The second exogenous change has been the *technological paradigmatic shift* as a result of the microprocessor. This technological change, comparable with the development of steam and of electricity, has led since the 1970s to a new and wide set of different production and development strategies for companies. Some of these key strategies were discussed in the section on institutional frameworks and include differentiated quality production, complex systems, financial Fordism, and radical innovation. Of central importance to the argument of this chapter, hierarchical Fordist-type production of goods and services, became as a result uncompetitive as a possible product market strategy – short of access to subsidies or other protectionist measures.

It was also argued that different strategies have been facilitated by different institutional frameworks; that, while DQP strategies have needed a CME-type framework, the others have been facilitated by an LME-type framework. The joint effect of these factors common to advanced economies – external liberalization and technological paradigm shift – has been, at the level of the *company*, to adopt product market strategies that are profitable in world markets without government assistance, frequently renouncing classical Fordist methods in consequence. These product market strategies have had to be consistent with the institutional frameworks of the countries in which they located the activity. At the level of *collective actors* in each economy (government, business, unions), it has been necessary to bargain out, with a great or lesser degree of conflict, the reshaping of institutional frameworks.

Feasibility of Institutional Frameworks and Business Coordinating Capacity

The way in which business is organized – its coordinating capacity – plays a central role in the operation of institutional frameworks. Strong coordinating capacity is necessary for the CME-type framework; without business coordinating capacity, government attempts to create such a framework will not succeed. That is the topic here. The argument is presented that government cannot create business coordinating capacity (though it may be able to destroy it); it takes typically decades to grow. Then it is suggested that the underlying interests of business negotiators and those of the businesses they represent are in part determined by the preexisting pattern and degree of business coordinating capacity. The meta game of bargaining out the reshaping of institutional frameworks thus depends critically upon prior business coordinating capacity.

CME-type frameworks permit actors to engage in long-term relationships in which two or more parties behave cooperatively together in the absence of strong monitoring systems. To be effective, companies have to accept three conditions, each of which they will be reluctant to accept in the absence of a sufficiently powerful system of business organization, which they can trust to represent their collective and individual interests.

First, companies have to be prepared to engage in the *transfer of information* about their technological and skill requirements and competences, if technology transfer and the vocational training are to function effectively. In practical terms companies cannot easily pin down contractually or otherwise how information gets used. They are unlikely to trust public agencies with potentially sensitive information, and public agencies have limited means of acquiring it without consent. Strong business associations, with a reputation for defending the interests of their members, are necessary for this system to work.

Second, the institutional framework has to protect companies from the adverse consequences (some form of "holdup") of making *investments in co-specific assets*. The two most obvious examples are relations between a supplier and a final producer, especially of uneven size; and a company and its employee representation body. In both cases, the development and deepening of a relationship puts power into the hands of the other partner. This is particularly so with the industrial relations field: companies will only be prepared to give unions or works councils an effective position with access to internal company information and hence a real position of potential power within the company, if the company is quite convinced that in the last resort – in the case of serious problems with the union or works council – there exists an employer association strong enough and sufficiently prepared to resolve the problem.[22] Companies are not prepared to trust governments or public agencies to do this, because their interests are different. Again, transactions costs typically rule out explicit contractual arrangements governing such relationships.

Third, the institutional framework is engaged continuously in *complex standard setting, rule setting, and sanctioning* behavior. The individual company, if it is to take advantage of a CME-type framework, will have to make location-specific investments; thus it cannot costlessly move in response to new rules that affect it adversely. Moreover, companies need to be sure that these rules and standards are generally acceptable and imposable: otherwise investments contingent on them may be unprofitable. Thus the company needs to feel it is effectively represented in these discussions; and that other companies are engaged in a similar way. This again shows the need for powerful business and employer bodies and close relations with companies that permit company involvement in rule setting and company acceptance and understanding of rules that get adopted.

Finally, engagement in the research, development, and negotiating involved in standard and rule setting, in giving advice to and getting information from companies, requires a shared body of expertise linking experts in companies to those in research institutions and those in business associations. The shared (common knowledge) expertise is procedural and precedent-based as much as substantive. It is through this "expert community" that information flows and changes are coordinated.

These problems do not arise to the same degree in LME-type frameworks, so that extra-market business coordinating capacity is not required.

---

[22] Note that companies cannot be forced ex ante into accepting powerful works councils against their wishes, since they can always relocate abroad.

The Difficulty of Building Coordinating Capacity

By contrast to the work of political or institutional constructionists, such as Sabel (1993, 1995a, 1995b, 1995c), it is argued here that effective business coordinating capacity cannot generally be built "spontaneously" to service an institutional framework in the ways required in the previous paragraphs. There are three reasons.[23] First, effective business coordinating capacity requires that companies have confidence in their ability to solve the problems discussed previously (inside information transfer, holdup, and fairness). For companies to have confidence in an effective system of representation, negotiation, and development and diffusion of expertise in a complex issue area requires that the system have already built up a reputation with individual companies for carrying out these functions effectively. This takes long periods of time because companies have to see how it works, or they have to accept from other companies who have experienced it that it works effectively. Second, effective business coordinating capacity requires the ability to sanction companies. This in turn requires that companies be engaged in long-term relational contracts with other companies, from which they derive benefit, and from which they can be excluded. This therefore presupposes the existence of long-term close ties between companies. Third, the building up of the common shared understandings of procedures, built on precedents, committees, decision rules, and shared bodies of technical knowledge and procedures concerning research, development, information transfer, and diffusion – the creation in sum of expert communities across associations, research institutions, and companies – can only take place over long periods. For these reasons, then, the capacity to engage in business coordination of any complexity may take a considerable period of time to develop. (To this there is one qualification. While business coordinating capacity may take years to build up, it can be destroyed or self-destruct over much shorter periods. It relies integrally on the desire and need of companies to continue: the example of the area comprising the former East Germany shows how an institutional framework without company involvement may have little effect. And it is possible that it could be run down by strong anticooperation competition legislation forbidding certain types of contacts between companies.)

The Interests of Business

Neither rational choice nor historical institutionalism can justify the view that business has been uniformly in favor of deregulation along LME-

---

[23] This argument is set out in more detail in Soskice (1997b).

type lines in the post-1970s world.[24] Where business has functioned as an effective collective actor, the "interests" of business need to be sought in the interests of policy makers within the business community potentially constrained by their ability to carry member companies with them. Leading policy makers in business associations are normally senior members of companies; their interest is therefore to create or maintain an institutional environment in which they can pursue their careers, utilizing their existing technical and business expertise and reinforcing their existing networks – so long as world market conditions permit them to do so. In the northern European business world, the interests of business policy makers will normally be to promote a long-run cooperative institutional framework for companies: this maintains their high status, their security, and their networks and uses their expertise, which is often a combination of high technical competence and the ability to develop consensus solutions. (By contrast, this would not be in the interest of a business community run by finance people whose expertise lay in hostile takeovers.) Thus rational choice reinforces a historical institutionalist approach.

What order of preference do business associations with industry-coordinating capacity have over a CME framework (with flexibly coordinated wage bargaining), a centralized egalitarian (or CE) framework, and an LME deregulated framework? In the section on institutional frameworks it was argued that both CME and LME frameworks were consistent with international competitiveness, though in different types of markets and with differently organized companies. Thus it is clear that in organized industry-coordinated business communities, a CME framework will be preferred to an LME framework, since both are "world-market" compatible, and the CME framework maximizes the utility of senior business people.

In an industry-coordinated world, a CME framework will be preferred to a CE framework, since the former gives companies more potential control over in-company wage structures and hence enables companies to develop company loyalty. The critical question is the choice between a CE and an LME framework. It is assumed in this chapter that in the post-Fordist world a deregulated LME framework is preferred to the CE framework. This is because a CE framework is not seen as consistent with success in world markets for companies wishing to pursue high-quality incremental innovation or DQP type strategies;

---

[24] This view drives the argument in Kurzer (1993) that business has been in a powerful position in the 1980s in Belgium and the Netherlands and has used this power to push through a deregulationist agenda.

these strategies demand company loyalty and the preparedness to invest in company-specific skills.[25]

The Politics of Changing Institutional Frameworks

How institutional frameworks have actually evolved between the 1970s and 1980s is a matter of politics, with varying results across countries and time, including sharp conflict, explicit governmental intervention, bargaining between collective actors, and so on. The two, quite different, outcomes – in (Anglo-Saxon) economies in which business was uncoordinated a more or less uniform shift to deregulated LME-type institutional frameworks, and in economies in which business was coordinated along industrial lines to CME-type frameworks with flexibly coordinated rather than centralized egalitarian wage-setting systems – have been the consequence of two quite different political processes, reflecting different power balances between business and government and different sets of business interests. The theorization owes much to the work of Casper,[26] Hancke,[27] Iversen, King, Mares,[28] Pontusson, Swenson, Thelen,[29] and Wood.

In LME-type frameworks,[30] in economies in which business was unorganized, the move toward relatively deregulated labor, research and development, corporate governance markets, and product markets has been fundamentally driven by two factors: the infeasibility of other institutional frameworks, and the need of governments of all political colors for a well-functioning private economy. Among collective actors, governments have led this process, while individual companies have reinforced it at the microeconomic level. Because of its weak organization, business has not acted collectively in a decisive way; while business has been generally strongly supportive of the move to deregulation, governments have been able to ignore attempted opposition such as that of the Confederation of British Industries (CBI) in the United Kingdom in the early 1980s.

In each of the Anglo-Saxon economies, the preexisting institutional framework gave unions a strong position, at least in important parts of

---

[25] Iversen (1996) and Pontusson and Swenson (1996).

[26] Casper (1996) has developed a compelling microeconomic analysis of the role of business associations in institutional framework change.

[27] Hancke shows the leading role of large companies in France, and the pattern of coordination between them and the state, in the restructuring of industry, finance, company-supplier relations, and industrial relations. His ideas are summarized in Hancke and Soskice (1996a).

[28] Mares (forthcoming) has worked on the role of business in the development of unemployment benefits in the 1920s in Germany.

[29] Thelen (1991, 1994).

[30] The account here owes much to King and Wood (this volume).

industry. The critical conflict has thus been between governments and unions. In simplified form this can be thought of as a game in which the government moves first, "choosing" an institutional framework, which unions can then accept or attempt to reject.

The most important constraint on governments has been the infeasibility of developing a CME-type framework – because of the lack of business coordinating capacity. Thus the government chooses between a deregulated LME framework and maintaining the status quo. The unions then accept or attempt to reject the choice.

The critical point is that unions will not be able to reject successfully a deregulated framework. Unions cannot take successful action against companies because, if companies are to remain competitive in the absence of protection, they will only accept unions that in effect make no demands upon them. They can reject union demands because they have the option of relocating elsewhere. Nor can unions take successful action against governments, because governments of the right and left have to rely on the private sector for economic performance: in the United Kingdom and the United States deregulation was promoted primarily by right-wing governments, but in New Zealand the driving force was a Labor government; and in both the United Kingdom and the United States, the Labour Party and the Democrats respectively have come round to accept strongly deregulated frameworks.

Why has a CME-type framework prevailed in economies in which business was well organized at the start of the period with employee representatives (almost always close to unions) playing an important role within the company, and with unions actively engaged with employer associations outside? Why has centralized egalitarian wage bargaining given way to a more flexible but coordinated form? Why has organized business played an important and sometimes central role in promoting these processes, successfully opposing a Social Democratic government and much of the union movement in Sweden that wished to preserve centralized egalitarianism,[31] and successfully opposing in Germany a Christian Democratic government, which wanted greater deregulation of labor markets?[32]

Two separate games have been played in these economies.[33] In the

---

[31] See Pontusson and Swenson (1996). [32] See Wood (1996).

[33] The analytic approach of Mares (forthcoming) albeit on German employers in the 1920s, has been of great help in this section, both because of the parallels that were afforded by her insights into the leading role of employers in the development of aspects of the German welfare state, and because of her theoretical analysis of strategic behavior; see Mares (forthcoming). Discussions with Hall, Mares, Iversen, and Wood have been important in developing the argument here.

"Swedish" game, organized business in the advanced sector allied with skilled workers' unions in the same sector against the government and the rest of the union movement. Pontusson and Swenson (1996) argue in their seminal article that the overturning of the centralized egalitarian system of wage bargaining in Sweden and its replacement by coordinated bargaining that gave more flexibility to employers was the result of a *cross-class alliance*. By this they mean that the skilled unions shared the preference ordering of the advanced-sector employers and that their joint support of change was necessary. By contrast, it is argued here that – while there was indeed such an alliance – the powerful, key actors were the employers, and skilled unions would have gone along with employers even had they preferred a CE to a CME framework. The reasoning can be summarized in the following game. In move 1, suppose that *employers* propose a CME framework and that, in move 2, *unions* can respond either by cooperating with such a framework or by refusing to cooperate and insisting on the maintenance of the CE system. If unions refuse to cooperate, then, in move 3, *employers* either back down or they choose a deregulated system. Employers can always de facto impose a deregulated system by refusing to cooperate with a CE (or a CME) framework – since both CE and CME frameworks depend on company cooperation. Thus, so long as business as a collective actor prefers the deregulated LME system to a CE system (as is assumed in the subsection on the interests of business), employers will respond to sustained refusal to cooperate with a CME framework by moving to a deregulated system and unions will be powerless to prevent this; therefore, to come back to move 2, unions will cooperate with a CME framework.

In the "German" game, the German government attempted partial deregulation of labor markets in the mid-1980s. Here the work of Wood (1996) is central empirically and analytically. As discussed earlier, in an industry-coordinated system business prefers a CME framework to an LME framework. Business as a collective actor has been strongly placed to resist governmental attempts to deregulate in ways it has not wanted. This is because collective business is necessary for the effective operation of technology transfer and vocational training; hence it can threaten to withdraw cooperation from key institutions. Note that this is a qualified power of resistance to deregulation: if a government wanted to move *fully* to an LME-type deregulated framework, it would be impervious to such threats since it would accept that under deregulation vocational training and technology transfer would function through markets. Collective business might still be able to resist government desires for full deregulation – but that would then depend upon a potential blocking role of collective business in the operation of the executive and legislative system.[34]

CONCLUSION: COMPANIES, NATIONAL INSTITUTIONAL FRAMEWORKS, AND GLOBAL MARKETS

This chapter has examined how national institutional frameworks have been reshaped in an age of globalization, and how companies have structured their product – and in addition in the case of multinationals their locational – strategies in response.[35] The chapter has taken as a starting point the acceptance of the liberalization of major international markets by all advanced economies: the elimination of restrictions on international trade in goods and services and on the movement of financial and physical capital. For this reason little attention has been paid to the European Union: to the extent to which it has been effective over the past decade, its effectiveness has been in these international markets. What has been of interest in the reshaping of national institutional frameworks has been in other markets. The regulations, formal and informal, governing these other markets (the labor market with its complex of rules relating to industrial relations; research and development markets including standard setting, technology transfer institutions, and competition policy; the largely state-dominated areas of education and training; and, above all, the market for corporate governance) have not converged on a simple, single liberal regime. On the contrary, moves toward deregulation of these domestic markets have only occurred strongly in the Anglo-Saxon economies. In the business-coordinated economies of northern Europe and in Japan, industrial relations have remained well established, as have vocational training systems, and the provision of long-term capital. This agrees to a large extent with the results of the chapters in this volume by Golden, Wallerstein, and Lange on collective bargaining and by Stephens, Huber, and Ray on the welfare state.

Why these differences? The argument is *not* that some countries have more resolutely resisted globalization than others. To the contrary, we

---

[34] Wood's general argument therefore goes against Streeck's view that the German system operates because unions are powerful enough to impose labor market regulation, in particular high costs of dismissal; see Streeck (1991).

[35] There is a set of related issues of across-country company strategy, concerning research joint ventures, alliances, and supplier networks. Here also we suggest that companies make use of national institutional advantages rather than arbitraging them away.

argue that the most powerful actors in the coordinated economies have been formal or informal business representatives. Among these representatives or influencing them have been leading multinationals, those often most concerned with global pressures. Paradoxical though it may initially seem, the thesis of the chapter is that organized business has sought not deregulation but reregulation in order to face up most effectively to global markets. The reason for this has been the need of businesses to preserve for their companies long-term financial frameworks, cooperative skilled work forces, and research networks in order to remain competitive in world markets where such resources give them a comparative advantage. At the level of the individual rationality of company leaders, who play a major part in formulating the policies of organized business, their individual advantage can be seen in terms of promoting those changes which are able to maintain the stability of their high-status careers. Thus thoroughgoing deregulation, generally believed to imply greater risk of closure and hostile takeover, is not a rational choice for business if alternative regulatory systems can provide international competitiveness with greater security for preexisting top managers.

In the Anglo-Saxon economies in which business was not organized so effectively, this lack of business coordination meant that the institutional capacity necessary for reregulation along similar lines was missing, as was political power. In these liberal market economies, governments – both left and right – were forced or chose to implement wide-ranging deregulation as the only available framework in which companies could remain or become internationally competitive.

5

THE POLITICAL ECONOMY OF EUROPE IN AN ERA OF INTERDEPENDENCE

Peter A. Hall

The study of comparative political economy is at a crossroads. The conceptual foundations for the field were laid during the late 1960s and early 1970s just as the "golden age" of postwar capitalism was peaking. However, the industrialized economies have experienced dramatic changes during the past two decades. Are the concepts on which we have long relied still adequate for organizing our understanding of the political economy? How might they be extended or revised to explain economic and political developments today?

The object of this chapter is to provide some tentative answers to these questions with special reference to western Europe. In the first section, I identify the conceptual approaches represented in the "first" and "second" waves of work that laid the groundwork for the field. Building on the insights of this literature, I then attempt to develop a conceptual framework for analyzing the changes taking place in contemporary political economies. In the third section, I use this framework to identify the most central developments in the political economies of Europe during the

Preliminary work on this chapter was done while the author was a fellow at the Center for Advanced Study in the Behavioral Sciences with support from the National Science Foundation. I am grateful to the participants in the project on "European Political Economy and Institutional Analysis" and especially to its codirectors, David Soskice and Suzanne Berger, for many helpful discussions of these issues. For specific comments, I would like to thank Barry Eichengreen, Gøsta Esping-Andersen, Torben Iversen, Robert Keohane, Peter Lange, Cathie Martin, Hideo Otake, Marino Regini, and Michael Wallerstein.

1980s and 1990s. Finally, I explore how we might use such a framework to understand the adjustment paths that firms and nations are now following.

In general, the field of comparative political economy concentrates on two central issues: how to explain patterns of economic performance and policy across nations. To such questions, economics has long supplied a variety of answers that figure with growing prominence in the literature of political economy. What distinguishes the work of political economists, however, is an insistence that such outcomes cannot be explained without reference to variables that might be considered "political" in the broadest sense of the term. These variables include institutions, whether economic, social, or political; sociopolitical coalitions; and, in some cases, national or subnational cultures.

Institutional variables have been especially prominent in these analyses. Thus, the pace of change in recent decades presents special problems. A field long focused on the way in which institutions produce regularities of behavior must now come to grips with problems of change rather than of continuity. The later sections of the chapter seek an analysis capable of doing so. I turn first, however, to the intellectual evolution of the field, focusing on studies with direct bearing on western Europe.[1]

THE FOUNDATIONS: FOUR CONCEPTUAL APPROACHES

I begin by identifying four conceptual approaches that initially became prominent in the 1960s and 1970s. They are not mutually exclusive. They influenced each other and several scholars have contributed to more than one. However, each approach is distinctive in important respects, and the differences among them reveal issues of continuing significance for the field. I label these the approaches of national policy styles, neocorporatism, neoinstitutionalism, and the organization of production.

ANALYSES BASED ON NATIONAL POLICY STYLES

Although there were comparative works about political economy as early as the eighteenth century, the contemporary field might well date from the

---

[1] In an essay of this length, I can provide only telegraphic references to large literatures. For other reviews with slightly different emphases, see Alt and Crystal 1983 and Thelen 1995.

magisterial work of Andrew Shonfield. *Modern Capitalism* (1969) reflects the temper of its times. Writing at the height of the Keynesian era, Shonfield attributed the unparalleled rates of growth then reached by the industrialized nations to the development of a "mixed economy" and activist forms of economic management, epitomized in French planning.

Quaint though this posture may now seem, Shonfield went on to provide an account of the differences in the economic policy making among the industrialized nations that remains one of the most insightful ever produced. I identify Shonfield as the progenitor of a "national policy styles" approach because his analysis associates variations in economic policies and performance with diffuse differences in the orientation of policy makers, linked to the history and culture of each nation.

Following Shonfield, a number of other analysts have also explained the economic policy making or performance of the European nations in terms of this sort of national policy style (Richardson and Jordan 1978; Hayward 1976; Blank 1978). Although the organization of the political economy figures prominently in some of these analyses, the more basic causal factor seems to be differences in the attitudes or orientations of the relevant political and economic actors, with roots deep in national history.

The great advantage of such analyses is that they are able to capture a range of attitudinal variables, often cultural in character, that have especially broad effects across the political economy. They gain force from the fact that they can account for differences in action in terms of the world views and meanings that the actors themselves associate with their actions.

The principal limitations of such analyses derive from the status of their independent variables. In many cases, it is difficult to define the causal variables in terms that are clearly independent from the outcomes they explain; and the very complexity of the policy styles on which they focus makes it difficult to parse these orientations into portable variables whose effects can be observed systematically across other national settings. Broadly speaking, the quasi-cultural character of these analyses carries both strengths and weaknesses.

NEOCORPORATIST ANALYSES

The second conceptual approach with great influence in European political economy was one organized around the concept of "neocorporatism." Just as Shonfield and others were inspired by the heady economic growth of the 1960s, neocorporatist analysis became popular during the 1970s when the European economies were locked in a struggle against rising rates of inflation and unemployment. One of the great advantages of this perspective was its capacity to explain why some nations seemed to be able to control inflation or unemployment more effectively than others.[2]

In general, this approach draws a distinction between nations whose political economy can be said to be more neocorporatist and those that are less so in order to assess the impact of neocorporatist arrangments on a variety of economic and political outcomes. Neocorporatism is generally defined as a process of social or economic policy making in which considerable influence over the formulation or implementation of policy is devolved onto the organized representatives of producer groups, often by means of peak-level bargaining about wage settlements. The organizational prerequisite for neocorporatism in its classical form is the presence of highly centralized and concentrated producer groups; and nations are generally classified as more or less neocorporatist according to either the prevalence of peak-level bargaining or the presence of such centralized organizations (cf. Schmitter and Lehmbruch 1978; Lehmbruch and Schmitter 1982; Goldthorpe 1984).

Neocorporatist analyses made several distinctive contributions to the study of comparative political economy. First, they linked specific economic outcomes to organizational, as opposed to attitudinal, variables, thereby focusing our attention on the organization of the political economy. Second, they gave special prominence to the organization of the trade-union movement. Third, they emphasized the importance of negotiations at the most centralized level of the political economy. These became the principal variables in most studies of European political economy during the 1970s and early 1980s.

In addition, the neocorporatist approach opened up many other useful lines of inquiry. Scholars seeking to explain how neocorporatism originated produced more general theories to explain the organization of the political economy (Cameron 1978; Katzenstein 1985; Rothstein 1992). Others began to elaborate the role of the state in the maintenance of neocorporatist systems (Lange 1984; Pizzorno 1978; Panitch 1980).

Over time, some significant amendments have been made to the basic postulates of the neocorporatist approach. Some scholars suggest that the relationship between economic performance and the centralization of the trade-union movement is not monotonic. That is to say, economic performance at both extremes, when the trade unions are highly centralized or highly fragmented, may be superior to performance when the union move-

---

[2] Even earlier formulations of the concept of neocorporatism reflect efforts to describe the growing role of producer groups in the formulation and implementation of economic policy. See especially Beer (1965), Schmitter (1974), and Winkler (1974).

ment is moderately concentrated (Calmfors and Driffil 1988; cf. Soskice 1990a). Others have argued that neocorporatist arrangements work well only when social democratic parties are in power. Thus, superior economic performance is secured when social democratic governments are joined to centralized trade unions or when conservative parties preside over weak union movements (Garrett and Lange 1989; Alvarez, Garrett, and Lange 1991). These analyses indicate that there are important interaction effects between the character or objectives of the governing party and the organization of the political economy (cf. Schmidt 1982).

NEOINSTITUTIONALIST ANALYSES

From this body of work, a third conceptual aproach was developed during the 1980s. Like neocorporatist analysis, it also suggested that variations in economic policy and performance are affected by the organization of the political economy. However, it extended our conception of the relevant organizational variables well beyond the organization of labor to include the organization of the state and of capital. As such, many of these analyses are associated with the broader movement in political science toward a "new institutionalism" (cf. Evans, Skocpol, and Rueschemeyer 1985; Steinmo, Thelan, and Longstreth 1992).

Proponents of this approach argued that the institutions structuring the flow of funds to industry affect both the behavior of firms and the options available to public policy makers (Zysman, 1984; Hall, 1986). In addition, they pointed out that the structure of the state can affect the kinds of policies it will try to implement with resulting effects on economic performance. The relative independence of the central bank, for instance, is said to affect both the posture of monetary policy, the level of coordination between fiscal and monetary policy, and the character of wage bargaining (Scharpf 1987, 1988). In more recent years, a large literature on central-bank independence has appeared (Goodman 1992; Cukierman 1992).

The work of the neoinstitutionalists made three significant contributions to the study of comparative political economy. First, it expanded our conception of the range of organizational variables that might be said to affect policy and performance. Second, it drew special attention to the impact of the financial system on firm behavior, economic policy, and economic performance. Third, these analyses emphasized the importance of modeling interaction effects between the multiple institutional features of the political economy (cf. Scharpf 1988; Hall 1994).

THE ORGANIZATION OF PRODUCTION

The 1970s and early 1980s also saw the development of a fourth body of literature, which I will label analyses oriented toward the "organization of production" because much of it was inspired by research into the sociology of work. What unites this literature is its overarching interest in exploring how the organization of production contributes to economic performance and how it changes.

The starting point for most such analyses is the contention that the rapid growth of the 1960s was made possible by the development of a Fordist system of production based on the use of semiskilled labor to produce high volumes of standardized commodities. They argue that this system of production was underpinned by two broader social conditions that served to reduce the uncertainties facing high-volume producers, namely, the presence of Keynesian policies designed to ensure high levels of aggregate demand and industrial relations systems that secured labor peace through regularized collective bargaining (Aglietta 1982; Boyer and Mistral 1978; Noel 1987; Marglin and Schor 1990; Howell 1992).

What inspired these analysts, however, was the observation that the basis for Fordism seemed to have broken down by the 1970s. Several found that many of the firms weathering the economic storms of the 1970s best were those, often small in size, that utilized high technology and skilled labor to produce relatively small volumes of more specialized commodities. They labeled such forms of production "flexible specialization" or "diversified quality production" and found that an increasing number of firms were reorganizing their production practices to gain such flexibility (Piore and Sabel 1984; Streeck 1991).

The fundamental contribution of this literature has been to draw our attention to the impact of firm organization, interfirm linkages, and work organization on the performance of the economy. It suggests that developments at the microlevel of the firm bearing on its relations with suppliers, competitors, public authorities, and the work force are at least as important to economic performance as variation in the macrolevel structures of the political economy. In addition, many of these analysts argued that social and institutional conditions at the regional level may affect firm performance as much as, if not more than, institutions at the national level (Herrigel 1995).

THE SECOND WAVE: FOUR
CONTEMPORARY APPROACHES

In one way or another, the developments of the 1980s and 1990s in Europe have challenged all four of the conceptual approaches to comparative political economy outlined here. Scholars have responded by trying to adapt the insights of these earlier approaches to emerging conditions. Their efforts have produced four prominent lines of analysis rooted in older approaches but with some distinctive perspectives on current developments.

SECTORAL GOVERNANCE MECHANISMS

The first of these literatures has strong roots in neocorporatist analysis. As scholars inspired by neocorporatist theory began to look more closely at the way in which producers were organized, they discovered significant variation in employer and union organization at the sectoral level. In addition, many found active bargaining and the devolution of public resources or authority at the sectoral level. This phenomenon was soon labeled "mesocorporatism" and a number of scholars began to examine its impact on sectoral behavior (cf. Cawson 1985; Wilks and Wright 1987). Others began to categorize the sectoral-level relationships among firms in terms of more general "governance regimes" with a view to establishing their impact on firm behavior and economic performance (Campbell, Hollingsworth, and Hindberg 1991; Hollingsworth, Schmitter, and Streeck 1994; Hollingsworth and Boyer 1997; Schmitter 1990).

The literature on sectoral governance mechanisms makes several contributions to the study of comparative political economy. First, it reaffirms that the relationship among firms in a single industry can rarely be described simply in terms of standard notions of market competition. Not only does each market have a specific institutional configuration, the firms in it also often have a variety of relationships with each other that extend well beyond competition to forms of cooperation in such activities as wage regulation, training, technology transfer, and political lobbying. Second, these studies show that public policy, at the national, regional, or local level, can have a significant impact on industrial relationships. Finally, they indicate that this web of relationships, linking firms to other firms, to the labor movement, and to the state can have a significant impact on the nature and success of the strategies that firms pursue.

The principal dilemma still confronting those with this approach is to specify precisely which variables in these sectoral relationships have the most impact on corporate strategy and economic outcomes. Having use-

fully expanded our conceptions of interfirm relations beyond those traditionally associated with market competition, these analysts are still refining
the more sociological conceptions of interfirm relationships they have devised.

DECENTRALIZED COORDINATION

A second strand in the current literature builds directly on earlier studies
of flexible specialization but takes its inspiration from the changes in firm
strategy and structure now occurring in Europe. This perspective breaks
with approaches that emphasize the impact of institutional structures on
behavior to suggest that such structures are more elastic than many think.
On this view, it is not structure that determines strategy, but strategy that
will ultimately determine structure (cf. Chandler 1962, 1974). Similarly,
where others stress the relevance of long-standing institutional frameworks
to national adjustment paths, this line of analysis implies that such frameworks are largely crumbling. Its proponents stress the radical openness of
adjustment paths in Europe and elsewhere (Sabel and Zeitlin 1997). They
emphasize the multiplicity of experiments that are taking place at the firm
level in Europe. Faced with new challenges, European businessmen are said
to be adopting a wide variety of strategies often at odds with the long-
standing practices of their sector or nation. Out of this welter of experiments, new modes of production and economic organization, as yet
unknown, are expected to emerge.

The first theme in this literature is "decentralization." It argues that
the developments most relevant to the future shape of the European economy are taking place in a highly decentralized fashion – and deliberately
so, as many firms utilize subcontractors or smaller units to experiment
with alternative ways of industrial organization. The challenge facing these
firms is not simply to allow a range of experiments to proceed but to find
ways to monitor the results enough to learn systematically from what has
been tried. Thus, what we are seeing is not simply experimentation but
the development of new monitoring and learning systems in European
industry (Sabel 1996).

The second theme of this literature is "coordination." Its contributors
argue that the essential task facing firms is to find effective ways of coordinating the many activities necessary to production and sales. In the current conjuncture, they contend, many organizational forms traditionally
used for this purpose are being modified. In the efflorescence of subcontracting, new forms of shop floor organization, and new management practices, they see potential for radical change in the basic ways firms do

business that is significant enough to affect the overall performance of the European economies (Sabel 1992; Sabel and Zeitlin 1997).

This approach has many strengths. More than any other, it can accommodate the possibility that the economies of Europe may be in the midst of a radical transformation. Its focus on processes emerging within individual firms keeps the analysis close to some of the central developments in the economy. And its stress on the capacity of managers to learn and change the institutions within which they work reflects a fine appreciation for the potential of human creativity and the processes of "creative destruction" long said to characterize capitalism (cf. Schumpeter 1976 [1942]). Its emphasis on the importance of coordination to firm success provides a heuristic with useful points of tangency to the literature on principal-agent relationships, monitoring, and collective action.

The principal limitation of the work derives from the radical indeterminism that is at the heart of many of its analyses. While recognizing the diversities that characterize current experimentation, it offers few predictions about the forms of firm or interfirm organization that are likely to emerge or about how these will affect economic performance. It tells us much about the character of the current flux in Europe but little about what may issue from it. Nonetheless, in time, such assessments may be developed, and this work directs us to processes that should not be ignored.

VARIETIES OF CAPITALISM

A third approach prominent in contemporary inquiry concentrates on what might be termed varieties of capitalism. Here, the unit of analysis is the nation-state, as in the neocorporatist and neoinstitutionalist accounts from which this approach emerges. The emerging literature on varieties of capitalism is marked by its focus on the way in which multiple institutional frameworks in the political economy of a nation interact to produce unique types of outcomes. The claim is that there are distinctive "varieties of capitalism" each characterized by a specific constellation of organizational structures (Albert 1991; Soskice 1990b, 1991).

One of the most sophisticated of these analyses (Soskice 1990b, 1991, 1993) distinguishes between "coordinated market economies" (Germany, Japan, Sweden, Norway, Switzerland, Austria, Japan) and "liberal market economies" (Britain, the United States, Ireland, Canada, Australia). In coordinated market economies (CMEs), employers have a dense network of associations for coordinating their actions on wages, training programs, research, and other matters. Firm relations with the labor force tend to be structured around long-term employment relations, and their relations with suppliers of financial capital tend to be such as to provide them with sources of long-term or "patient" capital.

By contrast, in liberal market economies (LMEs), employers lack representative organizations with sufficient centralized power to coordinate their actions. Firms tend to rely on short-term employment contracts that make layoffs relatively easy, and the structure of financial markets is such that their supply of capital tends to depend on short-term profitability.

The argument is that distinctive organizational constellations such as these conduce toward some kinds of firm behavior and militate against others. For instance, when faced with an appreciation in the exchange rate that raises the price of their products in foreign markets, the firms in a CME are more likely to lower their prices and tolerate lower profits in order to retain market share rather than lay off workers because the structure of the labor market makes layoffs difficult and their access to patient capital renders a low-profit strategy more viable. By contrast, faced with stringent demands for profitability from financial markets and the ability to lay off labor readily, firms in an LME are more likely to let prices rise and accept a declining market share in order to preserve profitability (Knetter 1989).

Similarly, analysts working along these lines argue that the organization of the political economy makes certain kinds of collective action that might not otherwise be feasible more likely. One principal example lies in the sphere of manpower training. In LMEs, there are few employer organizations capable of mounting effective training programs and ensuring employer adherence to them, and firms face disincentives to provide generalized training to their own workers, since the latter can readily take their new skills to another firm. In CMEs, by contrast, employer organizations often have the resources and authority to operate training programs to which their members must contribute and to enforce employment regimes that make it unprofitable for workers to leave one firm in order to sell their skills to another. The result is what Finegold and Soskice (1988) term a "low skill equilibrium" in some nations and a "high skill equilibrium" in others.

This is a highly promising line of inquiry. In the first instance, it developed as a revised version of neocorporatist analysis built on the observation that wage coordination could be effected by employers' organizations as well as by trade unions (Soskice 1990a). However, further work has pushed these analyses much further so that, drawing on game theory and the new economics of organization, they can now explain how various features of the organizational structure of the economy can affect a wide range of outcomes including wage coordination, the character of technical innovation, vocational training, and policy reform, as well as overall economic performance (Soskice 1994).

The central dilemma facing such models, however, is how to generalize the analysis to a wide range of national cases. Initially, these studies turned on a comparison between Japan or Germany and Britain or the United States. Some interesting work is now being done to explore the differences between Japan and Germany, whose political economies seem to accomplish the same tasks in slightly different ways (Soskice 1994). There are many hybrid cases, however, including those of France and Italy, which do not fall clearly into the categories generated by current models.

The very emphasis of these models on interaction effects has made it difficult to isolate the impact of each independent variable given the limited development of equation systems modeling their full effects and the small sample (of OECD nations) against which they can usually be tested (cf. Franzese 1994; Milgrom and Roberts 1995). As a result, there is still an implicit emphasis in this literature on a few ideal-typical countries and the analysis is only slowly being applied to a wider range of nations. Nonetheless, it has generated an important set of propositions of wide potential applicability.

COALITION THEORIES IN A CONTEXT OF INTERDEPENDENCE

Finally, a fourth approach oriented primarily toward the explanation of economic policy has emerged with growing force in recent years. It is embodied in theories that see policy as a response to the changing interests and demands of social or political coalitions. The approach has a venerable history in political science, but it received new life during the 1980s, when Peter Gourevitch (1986) argued that economic policies are primarily a response to coalitions representing distinctive economic sectors *and* that those coalitions form and reform in response to changes in the international economy that shift the underlying interests of their members. His point was that changes in the international economy make the formation of political coalitions behind new policies possible.

In recent years, other scholars have begun to explore more deeply precisely how changes in the international economy alter the interests of key economic actors. Rogowski (1990) argues that trade liberalization shifts the comparative advantage of a nation, in familiar Samuelson-Stolper fashion, so as to favor the most plentiful factor among land, labor, and capital. Frieden (1991) carries this analysis further to argue, first, that changes in international financial regimes also affect the interests of key economic sectors and, second, that asset specificity will condition the impact of such changes on the interests of a firm or sector by determining their capacity to respond. The premise is that changes in the international economy will shift the domestic coalitions pressing for one economic policy or another.

There is an emerging debate between analyses such as these, which suggest that changes in the international economy affect policy and politics primarily by shifting the interests and demands of economic sectors or producer groups, and others which imply that the political effects of changes in the international economy may come primarily by way of their impact on the electorate as a whole. The latter put more emphasis on the constraints that international integration places on the capacity of policy makers to expand the economy and on the effects of internationally induced economic fluctuations on voters (cf. Garrett 1996).

To date, the principal limitation of such analyses lies in the difficulty they have specifying precisely how such changes in the complexion of sectoral interests will translate into changes in policies. They have a robust theory about the determination of interests but a relatively anemic theory of politics. Their great value, however, lies in their capacity to explain change, as opposed to continuity, in the economy and especially change inspired by international economic developments. Moreover, although institutions do not figure prominently in such analyses, the latter have real potential for showing how the political will necessary to shift institutional structures can be assembled.

TOWARD A DYNAMIC MODEL OF THE POLITICAL ECONOMY

NEW PERSPECTIVES

There are some striking respects in which the analyses in this "second wave" of literature move beyond the frameworks developed by their predecessors.

First, the political economists of the 1970s and early 1980s focused much of their attention on trade unions, and the organization of the labor movement remains an important variable. More recent work, however, has drawn our attention to the equally crucial role that employers and employer organizations play in the political economy (Swenson 1989, 1991; Fulcher 1991; Soskice 1990b). Some have found that employers were the principal actors in the establishment or dismantling of neocorporatist arrangements. Others have argued that employers can act to coordinate wage bargaining or vocational training with or without trade-union cooperation.

Thus, after years of neglect, more attention is now being paid to the role of employer organization in the political economy (cf. Thelen 1995).

Second, much of the recent literature places the firm at the center of the analysis. In the past, most political economists concentrated on explaining government behavior or aggregate economic performance. Firms were something of a residual, despite their centrality to a capitalist economy. Today, many more studies see firm behavior as one of the central variables to be explained. Given that we live in an era when successful economic performance depends heavily on the capacity of firms to adjust to a changing environment, this is highly appropriate.

Third, a decade ago the literature in comparative political economy was split between analyses that emphasized the impact of national-level variables on the economy and those that located the crucial variables at the regional or sectoral levels of the economy. There is still debate about the relative importance of each of these levels. However, recent analyses transcend this debate by exploring how institutions at the national level interact with those at the regional or sectoral level. For instance, some have shown that the impact of national trade unions is deeply conditioned by the character of labor relations at the local level (Thelen 1991, 1995; Locke, 1994). Others suggest that the effect of a national policy depends heavily on institutional arrangements at the regional level (Levy 1994). This effort to integrate national-level variables with regional- or sectoral-level variables into a single analysis is an important step forward.

Similarly, the "varieties of capitalism" literature, in particular, has drawn our attention to the importance of interaction effects among key institutional variables in the political economy. Earlier studies often attributed economic outcomes to a single institutional variable, such as the centralization of the trade-union movement or the independence of the central bank. However, more recent work shows that the combined effect of such institutions is often more important than their independent effects. For instance, some suggest that important macroeconomic outcomes are conditioned by the way in which central-bank independence interacts with labor market organization (Franzese 1994; Iversen 1998; Hall 1994). Others show how key dimensions of firm behavior are conditioned not by the organization of the labor market or financial market alone but by the interaction of the two (Soskice 1991, 1993).

TOWARD A SYNTHETIC MODEL

Where might the field go from here? One approach would be to emphasize the explicit or implicit debates among partisans of each approach in this second wave of literature. Much can be learned from such controversies.

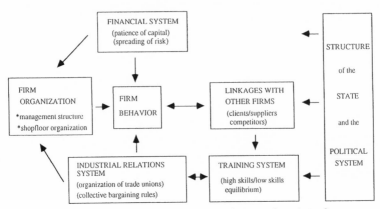

Figure 5.1. Principal institutional relationships in the political economy

However, we can also build on these insights to construct a more general model of the political economy that represents some advance on older conceptions. We need such models if we are to explain cross-national differences in economic policy or performance, and, at the current conjuncture, there is a special need for models capable of explaining the processes of change (as well as continuity) seen in the political economies of the industrialized world today. What might a model that builds on the recent literature look like?

To begin with, we can specify a model with two levels, one nested inside the other. The recent literature suggests that, at the first level, it would be useful to employ a model of the political economy that is centered on firm behavior. Moreover, we should recognize that a variety of institutional relationships matter to firm behavior. The most important of these seem to be: those associated with the structure of the financial system, the industrial relations system, the vocational training system, interfirm relations, and the organization of the firm itself. Firm behavior, in turn, has a significant impact on economic performance.

Figure 5.1 presents a diagram of the relevant institutional relationships. Implicit in it is the notion that the firm is generally influenced by several such relationships; rarely does only one determine its actions.

To take such an approach is clearly to side with the neoinstitutionalists and "varieties of capitalism" analysts who argue that a firm's behavior is deeply conditioned by its institutional environment. It implies that firm "strategy" is more often conditioned by the institutional "structures" in its environment than the other way around, although this is not meant to preclude the possibility that managerial initiatives can alter at least some

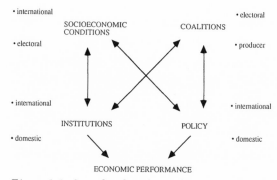

Figure 5.2. Second-order relationships in the political economy

of the relevant institutional structures over time. The premise is that many of the actions a firm takes will depend on the actions of others in the economy, as in a classic coordination game, and that all of these actions will depend, in turn, on the institutional settings in which the actors are embedded. The analysis emphasizes the degree to which the endeavors of firms and economic actors more generally entail significant coordination problems to which institutions supply the solutions by means of the monitoring, enforcement, and signaling mechanisms they supply (cf. Soskice 1991, 1993).

It is this network of institutionalized relationships surrounding the firm that accounts for many of the continuities we see across political economies over time. However, as recent events in Europe clearly demonstrate, these relationships are not always stable. Their stability depends significantly on a set of factors represented here by the second level of the model, presented in Figure 5.2. In particular, this level reflects the extent to which the institutional structures of the economy depend on variables that are broadly political in nature.

Three factors in particular appear to be important to the overall stability of the political economy. The first is the character of public policy. For instance, the operation of a specific financial or industrial relations system may be underwritten by a variety of legal arrangements essential to its functioning (cf. Streeck 1992a). The power of a trade union or the capabilities of an employers' network may be dependent on the presence of crucial social or industrial policies. The viability of neocorporatist bargaining may depend on the presence of specific economic policies (cf. Scharpf 1988; Lange 1984). Although we still have much to learn about precisely which institutional arrangements depend on which policies, there often seems to be a close relationship between the two (cf. Iversen 1998).

Second, both the economic policies and institutional arrangements of a nation are usually dependent on the presence of social or political coalitions willing to support them. This has long been one of the central insights of the coalition literature. For instance, many argue that centralized wage bargaining depends on the presence of cross-class coalitions linking employers in the export sector to those in sheltered sectors (cf. Swenson 1989). Two broad kinds of coalitions are relevant here: electoral coalitions, which influence the government through the ballot box, and producer group coalitions, which operate, often albeit not exclusively, outside electoral politics. The relationship between policies and coalitions may also be reciprocal. That is to say, the presence of specific policies (or institutional arrangements) may be crucial to the continued mobilization of a social coalition. It has been argued, for instance, that a variety of social policies are instrumental to the maintenance of a cross-class coalition behind social democracy (cf. Martin 1979; Esping-Andersen 1985; Rothstein 1992).

Finally, despite their internal resilience, institutions, like social coalitions and economic policies, also depend on the presence of specific socioeconomic conditions that may shift exogenously as a result of domestic or international developments (cf. Pontusson and Swenson 1996). Thus, the prolonged stagflation and intensified international integration of the 1970s and 1980s put severe strain on the institutional arrangements of some nations and led many to experiment with new policies or institutions (cf. Lindberg and Maier 1985; Hall 1986; Berger and Dore 1996).

The key point is that there are really two levels of determination in the political economy. At the first level, portrayed in Figure 5.1, a given set of national, regional, or sectoral institutions tends to create equilibrium forms of firm behavior. These institutions do so by providing a set of sanctions and incentives that lead firms toward some strategies and away from others, with systematic consequences for economic performance. Given their status as collective rules and understandings, these institutional arrangements tend to persist because any single firm lacks the incentive or means to alter them.

However, as Figure 5.2 suggests, the continued existence and smooth operation of such institutions also depend on a broader set of factors that include the presence of specific public policies, social coalitions, and socioeconomic conditions. We see interaction effects at this second – and more political – level of determination, as developments in one of these spheres induce or reinforce changes in the others (cf. Eichengreen 1993, 1994).

Of course, this remains a very general model. It is really constituted from a series of hypotheses, many of which remain largely untested. As such, it is meant primarily to organize these hypotheses and to specify a set of causal arrows as the starting point for further inquiry.

THE CHANGING POLITICAL ECONOMIES OF EUROPE

One of the advantages of such a model is that it can organize our understanding of the changes that have taken place in the political economies of Europe over the past two decades. These have been decades of substantial, and often baffling, change, whose outlines are only now becoming clear. In what follows, I outline the principal developments of this period, with a view to suggesting how they reflect some of the causal processes specified in this model.

SOCIOECONOMIC DEVELOPMENTS

The base point for any such analysis must be the "golden age" running for roughly thirty years, from the 1950s to the 1970s, in which western Europe experienced virtually continuous economic growth. That period saw the development of relatively stable institutions and patterns of policy in the European nations (Marglin and Schor 1990; Armstrong et al. 1991; Graham and Seldon 1990; Hall 1986). Since 1974, however, five key developments have unsettled these patterns.

First, rates of inflation began to accelerate in the 1970s to levels unprecedented since the war. At the same time, rates of economic growth dropped significantly and have remained low ever since. The corollary has been levels of unemployment that are high relative to those of the preceding thirty years. This "stagflation" provided the backdrop for much of what was to follow (cf. Salant 1977; Marglin and Schor 1990).

Second, the volume of trade has increased dramatically during the last twenty years both in absolute terms and relative to the growth in GDP. Imports as a share of real GNP, which generally ranged between 10 and 16 percent in the industrialized world after 1914, increased to almost 22 percent in the 1973–1987 period, rising 65 percent faster than domestic demand between 1972 and 1991 (McKeown 1991; Milner and Keohane, 1996). As a result, most European economies have become much more dependent on trade and sensitive to international economic fluctuations than they once were.

Third, the international integration of financial markets accelerated dramatically during the 1970s and 1980s. The volume of funds raised on international capital markets rose from about $20 billion in 1972 to $450 billion in 1986 (Cosh, Hughes, and Singh 1992: 23). The stock of international debt, which had been 5 percent of the GNP of the industrial nations in 1973, reached 25 percent by 1989 (Frieden 1991: 428). The capacity of firms to raise and transfer funds across borders rose exponentially.

Fourth, the character and sectoral composition of employment has shifted considerably in recent years. Employment in the traditional sectors of agriculture and manufacturing declined, while employment in the service sector and public sector expanded in most nations (Esping-Andersen, this volume). Intensified competition from the developing world also began to shift the demand for labor away from the unskilled toward those with substantial skill levels (Wood 1994). The result has been some fundamental recomposition in the character of employment, the wage structure, and trade-union membership.

Fifth, the past twenty years have seen a global revolution in the organization of work and production, inspired most prominently by two developments: the technological innovations that brought microprocessors into an increasing number of work environments and the popularity of Japanese models of production. Inspired by these developments and a more general need to adjust to changing world markets, a growing number of firms have begun to reorganize their corporate structures, shop floor relations, and linkages with clients or suppliers so as to secure greater flexibility in production, better quality control, lower costs, and more returns from learning-by-doing. Such innovations have been spread rapidly by the pressure of competition in global markets (Matzner and Streeck 1991: Sabel 1991; Regini 1994).

The problem of understanding how these five sets of developments have affected national political economies is one of the principal challenges facing the field today. In preliminary terms at least, some of their effects on public policy and social coalitions are visible.

ECONOMIC POLICY

The patterns of economic policy pursued by many European nations in the "golden age" disintegrated during the 1980s and 1990s. Although a complex set of forces, many of them political, contributed to these changes in policy, some were inspired, in the first instance at least, by the socioeconomic developments enumerated here. Changes can be observed in both macroeconomic and industrial policy.

For thirty years after the war, many European governments relied on fiscal policy, marked by alterations in the public-sector deficit, to moderate unemployment. In so doing, they were following a familiar Keynesian prescription. However, they turned away from this in the 1980s for several reasons. First, higher trade flows reduced the economic stimulus that a deficit could produce because more of the spending it generated leaked away into imports. Second, higher levels of inflation led many governments to worry that a fiscal stimulus would accelerate inflation and depreciate the exchange rate. As greater international financial flows increased speculative pressure on exchange rates, such fears were increasingly justified. Finally, and perhaps of greatest importance, the fiscal efforts to stimulate national economies in the second half of the 1970s failed to secure higher rates of growth over the medium term. The Keynesian consensus dissolved.

In its place, many European nations embraced a more deflationary fiscal stance. Fiscal and monetary policy, once oriented toward unemployment, was now targeted primarily on inflation, which dictated a less active fiscal policy and monetary policy oriented toward the maintenance of a relatively high exchange rate. In the hope of sustaining stable exchange rates, several European nations banded together in 1979 to fix their exchange rate parities in the European Monetary System (Ludlow 1992). This monetary regime generated policy with a deflationary bias, as governments sought to defend their exchange rate parity against a growing mass of internationally mobile capital (Blanchard and Muet 1993).

No longer willing or able to use macroeconomic instruments to reduce unemployment, the European governments turned toward supply-side policies for this purpose (cf. Boix 1997). However, here too, their arsenal was depleted. The industrial policies on which many governments had traditionally relied were rendered less effective by socioeconomic developments. Public subsidies to industry proved too expensive for many governments in an era when slow rates of growth meant lower government revenues and defense of the exchange rate demanded smaller public-sector deficits (Berger 1981). For similar reasons, many governments began to question the value of nationalized industries, whose capitalization had become increasingly expensive.

Seeking an alternative, most European governments began to emphasize three other kinds of programs: manpower policy, technology policy, and deregulation. Manpower policy was seen as a direct response to unemployment and to the demands of firms for a more highly skilled work force in the face of intensified international competition (cf. Boix 1997). Technology policy was seen as a means to strengthen the firms most likely to succeed on international markets; and government spending for research and development in the European Community doubled during the 1980s.

The principal emphasis of supply-side policy during the 1980s and 1990s, however, was on "deregulation" and "privatization." This stance reflected a more general retreat from interventionist policies in favor of the reinforcement of market mechanisms, which was inspired by a complex set of factors. Governments that had been happy to take political credit for economic growth during the 1960s and 1970s sought ways to shift responsibility for the economic sacrifices involved in restructuring during the 1980s onto the market. In the face of prolonged recession, the interventionist policies of the 1970s were also seen as unsuccessful, and market-oriented policies offered an alternative to governments seeking alternatives.

The privatization of nationalized enterprise proved attractive because it cut government spending and enhanced public revenue (Vickers and Wright 1989). The deregulation of financial markets was a logical response to the increase in international flows of capital. Once firms secured access to international capital, governments that sought to influence firm behavior via the regulation of domestic financial flows could no longer do so effectively; and many believed that the removal of exchange controls and deregulation of domestic capital markets would enhance their firms' access to finance. Thus, the privatization of public enterprise and the deregulation of financial markets became the flagship initiatives marking the embrace of the market in Europe.

The international reflection of this "movement toward the market" was the Single Market initiative taken by the European Community in 1985. Although complexly determined, it was inspired by the general enthusiasm for market mechanisms surging through Europe at the time. By strengthening the authority of European community institutions to demand deregulation, this measure greatly reinforced state capacities to deregulate in such sectors as telecommunications and financial services. Over time, it gave many firms a vested interest in international expansion and transnational financial flows, and it provided many governments with a rationale for reducing their labor market regulations so as to attract investment. It transferred responsibility for a good deal of industrial policy to the Community, effectively precluding the return of many national industrial policies; and, within a decade, it greatly intensified the magnitude of international economic integration in Europe.

SOCIAL COALITIONS

The socioeconomic developments of the 1980s and 1990s also disturbed many of the social coalitions underpinning traditional economic policies and institutions in Europe. There have been significant changes at several levels.

At the most basic level, the implicit class compromise between capital and labor, on which many postwar institutions were based, was eroded by a series of developments that shifted the balance of power from labor to capital, thereby encouraging an "employers' offensive" to dismantle some of these institutions and raising the specter of a "workers' backlash" that could eventually result in intensified social conflict (cf. Lipset 1964a; Stephens 1979; Kesselman and Krieger 1986).

Three factors converged in the early 1980s to enhance the power of employers and their associations at the expense of organizations representing labor. First, in many nations, high and persistent levels of unemployment weakened the bargaining position of workers vis-à-vis employers. Second, higher levels of trade and financial integration meant that employers could threaten to move production abroad if workers did not accede to demands for lower wages or more flexible working conditions. Finally, the 1992 initiative of the European Community set in motion a process of competitive deregulation, in which member nations were pressured to scale back social policies and deregulate labor markets to the advantage of employers (Streeck 1996; Lange 1993).

Of course, labor was further weakened by the economic policies of the 1980s. Deflationary macroeconomic policies and fixed exchange rate policies tended to sap union strength by raising the unemployment rate. Deregulation and the privatization of national enterprise accelerated the breakup of previously powerful enclaves of workers in traditional industrial sectors. The sharp declines in union membership, especially in the private sector, that some nations witnessed during the 1980s provide one measure of this shift in the balance of class power.

However, the economic developments of the 1980s did not simply shift the balance of power between classes. They also intensified conflicts of interest between particular subgroups within these classes. The most prominent of these is the conflict of interest between those in the tradable-goods sectors of the economy (whether workers or employers) and those in the sectors sheltered from foreign competition.

Higher levels of trade and financial integration have intensified this cleavage in several ways. First, international integration has increased the size of the tradables sector and its weight in many kinds of negotiations. Second, more intense international competition has put pressure on many producers of tradable goods (whether export-producing or import-competing) to seek layoffs, wage concessions, and the reorganization of production. Third, it has enhanced the propensity of such producers to threaten to move production abroad.

Arrayed against those in the tradables sector is a growing pool of workers in nontraded services and the public sector. The expansion of the service sector and public sector in recent decades has fueled this conflict. Today, public sector employees represent a growing proportion of unionized workers and substantial portions of the population derive much of their income from public policy rather than traded production.

There are many issues on which these groups find themselves in conflict. Faced with international competition, workers in the tradables sector of the economy feel more pressure to moderate wages and reorganize production, while those in the sheltered sectors are still inclined toward militant resistance. Employers in the tradables sector often come under greater pressure to "up-skill" and reorganize work in ways that favor substantial wage differentials, while those in the sheltered sector may be more amenable to wage leveling (Pontusson and Swenson 1996). As Frieden (1991) has shown, the two groups are also likely to take different positions on two of the most prominent issues on the policy agenda: the level of the exchange rate and the nature of the exchange rate regime.

The rising salience of this cleavage has begun to "disorganize" long-standing alliances and erode traditional compromises in many arenas, ranging from those coordinating wage bargaining or vocational training to those in which electoral coalitions are mobilized. The result has been rising tension and some reconfiguration in the basic institutional arrangements around which the political economies of Europe are organized.

To date, these developments have had their most pronounced effects on collective bargaining systems. Conflict between representatives of the tradable and sheltered sectors can be observed within national confederations of labor and employers in Europe. In Sweden, for instance, solidaristic wage bargaining has broken down in the face of a revolt from metalworking employers in the export sector, who sought higher wage differentials than the sheltered sectors of the economy were willing to concede (Pontusson and Swenson 1996; Iversen 1995). Similar tensions threaten the German industrial relations system (Franzese 1994). In many nations, the result has been a shift in the locus of collective bargaining away from peak-level negotiation toward sectoral-level or firm-centered bargaining, sometimes associated with new forms of microcorporatism (Streeck 1984; Howell 1992; Lange, Wallerstein, and Golden 1995).

In sum, the past two decades have seen major developments in precisely the kinds of variables on which the stability of the institutions organizing the political economy depend. In many cases, changes in policy have responded to and reinforced socioeconomic developments. Accompanying these changes have been coalitional shifts both among producer groups and in the electoral arena.

UNDERSTANDING ADJUSTMENT PATHS

Behind the evolution of the field of comparative political economy, then, we can see an evolution in the real economic challenges that the industrialized nations confront. In many respects, the intellectual development of the field mirrors these challenges.

During the 1950s and 1960s, a variety of forces converged to make it relatively easy for the industrialized economies to secure high rates of growth and employment (cf. Denison 1967; Boltho 1982; Armstrong et al. 1991). As a result, the principal problem confronting them was one of maintaining high levels of demand and of allocating scarce resources so as to ensure adequate supply – precisely the kind of problem that Keynesian policies and industrial planning were designed to address. Not surprisingly, the analyses of the 1960s, such as that of Shonfield (1969), concentrated on the determinants of such policies.

During the 1970s, however, the main challenge facing the industrialized nations changed. Attention became fixed on the rate of inflation, which rose dramatically in the period, and on the incomes policies and neocorporatist agreements designed to address it. Thus, it is on such issues that political economists writing in the 1970s focused.

Today, the principal challenge facing the industrialized nations again seems to have changed. How best to define that challenge is an issue with substantial implications both for the economic world and for the field of comparative political economy.

I would like to suggest that the best way to define the principal economic challenge of the current era is as a problem of adjustment. Of course, some problems associated with adjustment are omnipresent. We can think in terms of three kinds of adjustment problems. The first might be described as "cyclical adjustment" – that is, the adjustment of the economy to the kinds of fluctuations that recur at frequent intervals. The second entails "sectoral adjustment," by which I mean the transfer of resources from sectors that are proving less viable or competitive to those where a comparative advantage can be exploited. Both of these are problems that the industrialized economies have confronted for many years, although international integration currently exacerbates them.

The third kind of adjustment is more unusual and especially prominent today. This is the problem of "structural adjustment," by which I mean adjustment to new ways of organizing productive activity so as to take advantage of technological innovation and more flexible ways of organizing work and economic transactions. From time to time, all nations confront such issues, but three developments have rendered the problem of structural adjustment especially acute today.

First, something like a "fourth industrial revolution" has generated technological advances in telecommunications and microprocessors that make many new kinds of business practices possible and threaten to render obsolete firms that do not adopt such techniques rapidly. Second and linked to this, we are seeing a revolution in the organization of production, based on team production methods, just-in-time inventory systems, new forms of subcontracting, and the like, which entail many changes in intra-firm and interfirm relations. Again, firms that fail to adjust run the risk of losing out to their competitors.

A third and equally important development is the acceleration of international economic integration. On the one hand, international markets are a powerful force for change. Exposure to them vastly increases the competitive pressure on firms to respond to product or process innovation in the sector. On the other hand, opening national markets also alters the comparative advantage of a nation and the firms within it, in ways that demand structural adjustment. To the extent that comparative advantage is not simply given by factor endowments but created by the institutional frameworks that cultivate human capital, provide social infrastructure, and organize exchange, the adjustment challenge becomes a national and a political one: how to devise national institutions that will maximize the comparative advantage of the country (Rogowski 1990; Zysman and Tyson 1983; Zysman 1996).

These developments suggest that what political economists should be most interested in today are the capacities for structural adjustment and the adjustment paths displayed by various sectors, firms, and nations. Hitherto, most studies in comparative political economy have sought to explain cross-national differences in economic performance of the sort measured by variables such as the rate of growth, inflation, or unemployment. The latter remain important objects of study, but to them we should add a new set of dependent variables designed to capture adjustment paths and capacities to adjust.

As yet we have few ways of specifying or measuring adjustment paths and capacities. At the economic level, we might begin by focusing more attention on indicators that measure rates of change and relationships associated with adjustment, in comparative or cross-national terms, such as the national income elasticity of employment or the rate of change in world market share of key products over time. Similar indicators at the firm and sectoral level could give us a valuable sense of the way in which different firms or sectors adjust to similar shocks (cf. Schettkatt 1992). In an era of change, such measures might be better indicators of long-term economic performance than the conventional economic aggregates. However, we need not think of adjustment paths in purely economic terms. In response to multiple challenges, the European nations are gradually altering their economic or social policies and the institutional structures of their political economies. As a result, they can be said to be following particular "policy paths" and "institutional adjustment paths." In many cases, this is an overtly political process and thus a prime subject for the scrutiny of comparative political economists.

The model I have outlined here has several implications for what these adjustment paths might look like and for how they should be understood. In particular, it implies that the existing institutional structure of the political economy will affect the kinds of adjustments most likely to be made to it or to policy. The institutional starting point from which reforms are made is likely to condition the shape of those reforms. From this, it follows that those who expect changes in the international economy to engender a homogenous response across nations, leading ultimately to a convergence in their institutional structures, are probably mistaken. The past two decades have seen some common policy trends sweep across Europe, testimony to the impact of international influences, but closer inspection also reveals that many countries have responded to them rather differently (Berger and Dore 1996; King and Wood, this volume; Soskice 1993).

Figure 5.3 shows how we might use a model of the sort developed here to understand policy paths or institutional adjustment paths. It suggests that socioeconomic developments at the international or domestic level will tend to rearrange the social coalitions that divide the electorate or producer groups by shifting their underlying material interests. However, the extent of that rearrangement and its impact on policy or on the organization of the political economy will be affected by the institutional structure of both the political economy and the polity.

There are three general respects in which the institutional structure of the political economy, diagramed in Figure 5.1, might affect the response to socioeconomic developments in such a way as to generate distinctive adjustment paths. First, there is a "power dimension" to institutional impact. The structure of the polity and political economy distribute power in such a way as to give privileged representation to some sets of interests over others. Some polities, for instance, concentrate power in a small elite; others diffuse it more widely among a range of veto groups (Katzenstein 1987; Immergut 1992). The institutional structure of some nations gives particular producer groups considerable influence over decision making in

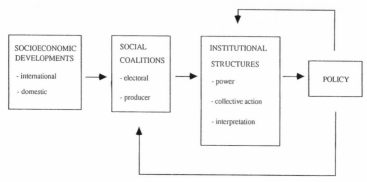

Figure 5.3. Process of change in the political economy

key economic spheres, while others confer more weight on consumers or workers.

Second, there is a "collective action" dimension to institutional impact. The successful implementation of many kinds of policies, institutional reforms, and firm strategies depends not simply on the promulgation of edicts but on securing the active cooperation of other economic actors. In short, many such changes pose classic coordination problems, whose resolution depends on the presence of institutions to provide the monitoring, enforcement, information, or deliberative capacity necessary to ensure that the behavior of the relevant actors will be coordinated (cf. Ostrom 1990; Hardin 1982). In their absence, it can be difficult to implement effective changes in policy or institutional structure.

Finally, there is an "interpretive dimension" to the impact of institutions. The institutions indicated in Figure 5.1 provide a set of sanctions and incentives that lead toward some patterns of firm strategy and away from others. Over time, both firms and policy makers become accustomed to those strategies and develop operating procedures that are congruent with them. Firms and policy makers are clearly capable of innovation, especially on a small scale. At the margin, however, familiarity with one set of institutionally induced strategies may well affect the range of potential innovations they will canvass or endorse.

We can already see each of these dimensions in operation in the policy paths adopted by a variety of European nations during the 1980s. Although many of these countries came under pressure to deregulate basic sectors and privatize public enterprise, they did so at varying rates of speed and levels of extensiveness. It was easier for Britain to proceed faster and more extensively than Germany at least in part because the structure of its political system concentrates power in the political executive, while Germany provides much more power over such matters to producer groups. Moreover, German producers were more likely to oppose such reforms because they militated against the kind of corporate behavior toward which the institutional structures of the German political economy accustomed them. By contrast, British firms had long been accustomed to corporate strategies that meshed well with the deregulatory policies of the Thatcher government (cf. Wood 1997).

The collective action dimension of institutional impact is nicely illustrated by the outcome of French efforts to improve vocational training and regional economic development in the 1980s. In each case, they hoped to duplicate German successes. In both of these spheres, however, the implementation of policy was highly dependent on the resolution of coordination problems at the local or sectoral level; and the success of French policy seems to have been greatly limited by the absence of institutional networks at these levels capable of resolving such problems (Maurice et al. 1986; Levy 1994; Hancke and Soskice 1996; Culpepper 1996). In some cases, governments can create new institutional structures to support new policies, but this is a costly process and governments tend to be able to create only certain kinds of institutions, such as public agencies. Thus, the policy paths that nations can pursue successfully will often be affected by the existing structure of their political economy.

In more general terms, we can expect the institutional structures of the polity and political economy to have an impact on adjustment paths at several levels. Most fundamentally, they should affect adjustment in firm strategies. Under competitive pressure, firms frequently seek to adjust their strategies; and in some cases, they can do so quite radically without outside support. Where the success of such shifts in strategy depends on the cooperation of other economic actors, however, the direction they take is likely to be conditioned by the institutional infrastructure available to generate such cooperation.

As noted earlier, the institutional configuration of the political economy is also likely to affect the way in which governments will adjust their economic and social policies. It can generate distinctive policy paths by conditioning both the kind of pressure for reform that a government feels and the government's capacity to implement various kinds of reforms.

Finally, it is likely that the institutional structures of the political economy themselves follow distinctive adjustment paths based on their institutional starting point. In some cases, institutional reform may be initiated or underpinned by changes in public policy which, as noted, will be conditioned by existing institutions.

In other cases, changes to these structures may take place largely independent of government intervention by means of agreement among the relevant producers. Here too, however, the character of existing institutions is likely to have a major impact on the adjustment path. In particular it will affect the degree to which the relevant producers have the "strategic capacity" to deliberate together and agree on institutional reform as well as new collective strategies. We need to know much more than we currently do about the conditions that confer such strategic capacities. However, they are likely to be greater when producers are highly organized at the regional, sectoral, or national levels.

CONCLUSION

In recent years, the pace of change in European political economies has posed serious dilemmas for those who study it. Amid the patchwork of change and continuity on the continent, it can be difficult to distinguish passing fashions from movements of long-term significance. Many of these developments have unsettled the portraits once drawn of the political economy. It is again a challenge to find analytical terms adequate to describe and explain the central differences and similarities across nations. In particular, these developments call for models capable of explaining how change takes place within the political economy and the directions in which it moves.

In this chapter, I have tried to outline such a model. My objective has been to integrate the insights present in various parts of the literature into a framework that provides some common ground for diverse analyses. I have tried to situate this framework within the context of the literature of political economy since the 1960s and to relate it to developments in Europe over the past two decades. I believe there is value in this kind of synthetic enterprise.

As all will recognize, the analysis presented here is no more than a way station en route to further inquiry. The model is pitched at a relatively general level and many of the causal connections in it are hypotheses that merit more detailed specification and further investigation. There are enough substantive contentions here to generate disagreement, but, in general, this analysis is designed to specify the relevant questions rather than to provide complete answers to them.

Nonetheless, the perspective developed here has some important implications for European political economy. It suggests that we need a more firm-centered approach to the political economy. It argues that nations and the firms within them are likely to follow distinctive adjustment paths that will be conditioned by the institutional structures of the political economy. It contends that increasing international interdependence and a fourth industrial revolution have inspired the most important changes taking place in Europe. However, it suggests that interdependence is unlikely to lead to the levels of convergence that many expect.

I have resisted the temptation to try to specify which kinds of political economies and corresponding adjustment paths are likely to be most successful. This is an important issue. However, the first task is to specify such adjustment paths more fully; and it is quite plausible that there may be more than one route to success, each applicable to different nations.

What this analysis does suggest is that successful adjustment will require not only the investment in "human capital" that is rightly popular today, but also investment in "social capital" understood as the institutional infrastructure that makes fruitful coordination among firms and other economic actors possible.[3] There is growing evidence that the success of many new policies or firm strategies will depend heavily on the presence of a supportive institutional infrastructure, itself ultimately dependent on public policy. We are used to thinking about the impact of policies in terms of their immediate objectives. But, as Levy (1994) has shown, some of the most significant consequences of a particular line of policy may lie in the kind of social organization it fosters or destroys in the long term.

---

[3] On "social capital," see Coleman (1990); Putnam (1992); and Sabel (1991, 1992). Note that my use of the term associates social capital quite closely with the presence of institutions while some of these analysts associate it more closely with values.

6

THE WELFARE STATE IN HARD TIMES

John D. Stephens, Evelyne Huber, and Leonard Ray

It is by now a widely accepted view that the sea changes in advanced capitalist economies of the past two decades, above all the increasing internationalization of these economies, have constricted the policy options of the governments of these societies (e.g., see Scharpf 1991). Economic internationalization is assumed strongly to favor market solutions and thus to be particularly unfavorable to policies traditionally promoted by social democracy and organized labor. In the case of social policy, trade unions and social democratic parties expressed fears that steps to further economic integration, such as the Europe 1992 initiative or North American Free Trade Agreement (NAFTA), would result in pressures to reduce welfare state provisions to the lowest common denominator. Indeed, significant rollbacks in provisions in countries as different as Denmark and New Zealand have been linked to the impact of changes in the international econ-

The authors would like to thank Claus Offe, Jonathon Moses, John Myles, Duane Swank, and Kees van Kersbergen for comments on earlier drafts of this chapter. The data analyzed in the first section of this article were collected by a project in progress on "The Welfare State in Comparative Perspective: Determinants, Program Characteristics, and Outcomes" directed by Evelyne Huber, John Stephens, and Charles Ragin. This project is supported by the Institute for Research in the Social Sciences and the Department of Political Science, University of North Carolina, the Center for Urban Affairs and Policy Research at Northwestern University, and the National Science Foundation (Grant # SES 9108716). We thank IRSS, the Department, CUAPR, and NSF for financial support. We also thank Tom Cusack for making data, including the public employment data analyzed here, available to us. We would also like to thank the Swedish Collegium for Advanced Study in the Social Sciences for support while the revisions on this chapter were done, and our colleagues there for comments. In addition, we owe thanks for comments to participants in seminars at the universities of Stockholm, Bergen, and Trondheim.

omy and these countries' integration into it (Marklund 1988; Castles 1996). By contrast, Garrett and Lange (1991) have argued that the constriction of political choice has been overstated and that in expenditure policies in particular there are still significant differences between governments of the left and right. Similarly, Moene and Wallerstein (1993a) argue that, although many aspects of the Norwegian and Swedish social democratic models have suffered in the new economic environment, the social policy provisions appear to be highly resistant to change.

In this chapter, we examine the politics of social policy in the contemporary era. We focus on two questions. First, to what extent has there been a rollback of welfare state entitlements in the past two decades? Second, to what extent have the partisan differences on social policy that characterized the immediate postwar decades been reduced or even eliminated? Once we have answered these questions, we can then begin to suggest some causes of these developments. We draw on two bodies of empirical evidence: (1) cross-national data on a variety of measures of social expenditure and on public employment, and (2) case studies of recent developments in about half of the universe of countries included in the quantitative analyses. These case studies allow us to bring the quantitative analysis up to date as important events in many of the cases occur after the last data points (1985 to 1988). They also allow us to uncover some causal links between economic and political developments and the social policy outcomes.

CHANGES IN THE POLITICS OF SOCIAL POLICY

There is little question that the advanced political economies did go through a sea change in recent decades, which can be conveniently dated as beginning with the breakup of the Bretton Woods system of fixed but flexible exchange rates in 1971 and the Organization of Petroleum Exporting Countries (OPEC) oil price increase of 1973. The sea change was produced by these events combined with a series of long-term secular changes: increasing internationalization of trade; internationalization and multinationalization of capital; internationalization and deregulation of financial, capital, and currency markets; the decline of the industrial and rise of the service sector; and the decline of "Fordist" assembly line, semiskilled manufacture and rise of "flexible specialization" and skill differentiated manufacture. These trends have been hypothesized to have fundamentally changed the politics of social policy.

The internationalization of trade resulting from reduction of tariff and nontariff trade barriers and reduction of transport costs has been held to have a direct effect on social policy as the "social wage" adds to total labor costs, thus making labor in countries with high social wages uncompetitive.[1] The large increases in unemployment experienced by almost all advanced capitalist societies since the early 1970s have been linked to welfare state cutbacks because increases in unemployment make any given set of welfare state entitlements more expensive and reduce the number of people contributing to the system. The increases in unemployment in turn have been linked to the changes in the international economy through a variety of mechanisms. Countercyclical demand management is now more difficult than thirty years ago. Due to the leakage of demand, increasing trade dependence makes fiscal policy less effective. Due to the internationalization and deregulation of financial markets, nations can no longer control both interest rates and exchange rates. Not only have national interest rates converged as a result, but in addition they have converged on a much higher level than in the 1950s and 1960s for a variety of reasons, including the increased national debts of countries around the world and, in Europe, the leading position of the conservative Bundesbank in setting policy. These developments have also made supply-side policies based on cheap and rationed credit aimed at creating investment and thus employment, such as those pursued by the social democratic governments, much more difficult if not impossible (Huber and Stephens 1998).

Increasing mobility of the factors of production has been hypothesized to increase "tax competition," pressure toward homogenization of tax rates, primarily by reduction of tax rates in the countries with high tax rates, and thus lead to downward pressure on social expenditure. An additional crucial factor that has had a direct depressing effect on social policy and an indirect one via increased unemployment is the lower growth in GDP and in productivity. The literature cites further reasons for social policy rollback and/or declining partisan differences in policy not connected to changes in the international economy. The most frequently mentioned one is the growing demographic burden. As the population ages, pension and health care programs become more expensive at any given set of entitlements. Thus, taxes must be increased or cuts must be made in these or other social programs.

A rarely cited but certainly important reason for the slowing of the expansion of the most generous welfare states, such as the Dutch or Scandinavian ones, is that they had "grown to limits," to borrow the title of

---

[1] For an extensive review of the impact of changes in the international and domestic economy on social policy, see Swank 1993.

Flora's (1986) comparative study. These welfare states were comprehensive, covering all major program areas, and in each program coverage was universal or near universal, replacement rates in transfer programs were very high, and, in the case of the Scandinavian countries, publicly provided services enjoyed a near monopoly in their sector. As a result, tax burdens were extremely high.

In the arguments laid out here, there was a straightforward connection between the developments outlined and welfare state retrenchment or, at least, slowed expansion. These same developments have been hypothesized to reduce partisan differences in governmental policy because they constrain the policy latitude of any government. However, the literature on the question of partisan differences in the current era is more nuanced. The most common position, laid out here, assumes that the agenda of parties of the left will be most constrained because it involved substituting "politics for markets" while these trends, especially internationalization of the economies, push in the opposite direction. By contrast, Garrett and Lange (1991) argued that, while there has been a narrowing of macroeconomic policy choices, there are still marked partisan differences in social expenditure policies. The overall policy agenda has moved to the right but there are still significant partisan differences. Others have suggested that the multiclass Christian democratic parties find it less difficult to abandon Keynesian full-employment, welfare state policies than the working-class, trade-union-based social democratic parties. In this case, one might hypothesize increased partisan differences.

We have argued (Huber and Stephens 1993b; Stephens 1996), as has Pierson (1996), that the politics of welfare state retrenchment is different from that of welfare state expansion. Once instituted, social policies develop support bases in addition to those groups that supported their original enactment.[2] The broad social coalitions supporting the welfare state status quo prevent centrist and even right-wing parties from implementing, or even advocating, significant cuts in entitlements. Thus, to the extent that economic difficulties mean the agenda in most countries is not expansion but rather retrenchment, one should expect narrower partisan differences than in the past. The narrowing of differences is a result of constraints both on the right and the left.

The effect of these increasing international constraints outlined here is mediated in part by ideology or, more narrowly, beliefs about what policies can achieve a given goal under present conditions. These beliefs could, of

---

[2] Even in the United States, broad-based entitlement programs enjoy wide popularity (Marmor, Mashaw, and Harvey 1990: 134).

course, be wrong, or, at least, alternative policies which did not involve retrenchment might be equally effective. Given this importance of beliefs about the consequences of different policies, one must assume that the rise in the international hegemony of neoliberal economics contributed to the tendency of retrenchment in state expenditures and direct involvement in social policy.

THE QUANTITATIVE ANALYSIS

THE DATA

The quantitative data analyzed here are drawn primarily from a data set assembled by the project, "The Welfare State in Comparative Perspective," directed by Evelyne Huber, Charles Ragin, and John Stephens. The data set is pooled annual data for the eighteen advanced capitalist countries that have been democracies since World War II. For the purposes of the analysis here we divide the data set into three periods and examine differences in change in welfare state effort across the nations during the three periods.[3] The data set covers the period 1945–1989, but for most of the dependent variables to be analyzed here the first data points are circa 1958. Many of the indicators of "welfare effort" are measures of government expenditure or revenue expressed as a percentage of GDP (expenditure, revenue, consumption, benefits, and transfers in Table 6.1). The pension measure divides public pension expenditure as a percentage of GDP by the percentage of the population over sixty-five to yield a measure of pension benefits per aged person. In our analyses of the pooled data of the determinants of levels of expenditure to date, we have found the primary partisan determinants of expenditure to be governance by social democratic and Christian democratic parties.[4] Partisan effects varied across the indicators in a systematic fashion, as hypothesized by recent work on welfare state regimes (Esping-Andersen 1990; also see van Kersbergen 1995). Social democratic welfare states are service heavy and thus social democracy is more strongly

---

[3] Though this had the disadvantage of the loss of data points and thus degrees of freedom, we judge this method to be better than the alternatives. See Stephens, Huber, and Ray (1995) for a more extended discussion of this and other methodological questions. That paper is an earlier, considerably longer version of this chapter.

[4] For the analyses of transfer payments, social benefits expenditure, and revenue, see Huber, Ragin, and Stephens (1993); for pensions, see Huber and Stephens (1993a); for health care, government civilian consumption, and public employment, see Huber and Stephens (1996b). An updated version of the quantitative analysis in this chapter will appear in a book now in progress by Huber and Stephens. It confirms this analysis.

Table 6.1. *Levels of and mean annual change in welfare effort indicators by welfare state regime type*

	Levels				Annual change		
	1958	1972	1979	1986	Pre-71	Interim	Post-79
Expenditure (public expenditure as a percentage of GDP)							
Christian democratic	31	37	46	49	.62	1.10	.29
Liberal	29	30	36	40	.45	.65	.19
Social democratic	28	40	51	52	.96	1.34	.08
Revenue (total taxes as a percentage of GDP)							
Christian democratic	29	36	41	44	.49	.65	.33
Liberal	25	28	30	36	.29	.15	.38
Social democratic	30	44	48	53	.97	.53	.52
Consumption (government civilian consumption as a percentage of GDP)							
Christian democratic	9	12	14	15	.25	.28	.02
Liberal	9	12	14	15	.25	.26	.03
Social democratic	11	16	20	20	.39	.45	.12
Benefits (social security benefits as a percentage of GDP)							
Christian democratic	11	15	20	21	.29	.66	.19
Liberal	6	10	13	14	.27	.46	.15
Social democratic	10	17	23	26	.50	.77	.50
Transfers (transfer payments as a percentage of GDP)							
Christian democratic	10	13	17	19	.30	.50	.18
Liberal	6	8	11	12	.14	.38	.09
Social democratic	7	12	15	16	.34	.43	.18
Pensions (public pension benefits as a percentage of GDP divided by the aged population)							
Christian democratic	30	43	56	64	.93	1.86	1.14
Liberal	14	28	43	47	1.00	2.14	.57
Social democratic	24	46	54	66	1.57	1.14	1.71
Health care (civilian public expenditure as a percentage of total health expenditures)							
Christian democratic	63[a]	77	80	77	1.27	.42	−.41
Liberal	58	64	72	72	1.01	.62	−.09
Social democratic	72	80	85	84	.71	.65	−.13
Public employment (public employment as a percentage of the working-age population)							
Christian democratic	6[b]	7	8	9	.16	.19	.05
Liberal	7	9	10	10	.19	.18	.03
Social democratic	7	11	16	18	.46	.65	.35

[a]The figures for health care are for 1960.
[b]The figures for public employment are for 1962.

related to measures that include services (revenue, expenditure, and government civilian consumption). Christian democratic welfare states are "transfer states" (Kohl 1981: 314) and thus Christian democracy is more strongly related to the transfers and pensions. Both social democracy and Christian democracy are strongly related to the International Labor Office (ILO) social security benefits measure, which combines all transfers and some social service spending (mainly health care).

Following Kim (1990), our measure of public health effort is public health expenditure as a percentage of total health expenditure, which is, as hypothesized, most strongly related to social democracy. We also analyze total public civilian employment as a percentage of the working-age population and, for a more restricted set of countries – all those for which the data are available in the Welfare State Exit Entry Project (WEEP) data set (Cusack, Noterman, and Rein 1989) – public employment in health, education, and welfare also as a percentage of the working-age population. Both of these measures tap the public service intensity of the welfare state and thus are strongly related to social democracy.

Most quantitative studies of welfare states have found party cabinet share rather than parliamentary seats or votes to be the most powerful political determinant of social policy outcomes. We operationalize leftist cabinet share in the following fashion: we give a score of 1 for each year when the left is in government alone; in the case of coalition governments, we score a fraction calculated by dividing the left's seats in parliament by all governing parties' seats. It has been argued that this operationalization overlooks the long-term political hegemony of a political bloc. For example, it is not surprising that the Swedish bourgeois governments of the 1970s deviated little from the social democrats in the area of social policy given the hegemonic position of social democracy and the trade unions in Swedish society. An alternative emphasizing long-term hegemony is to cumulate the cabinet shares from 1945 to the period in question following our previous analysis (Huber, Ragin, and Stephens 1993). This operationalization might be subject to the opposite error, overestimation of long-term effects. After some experimentation with alternatives that combined long-term and short-term effects, we settled on running the whole analysis with both the cumulative and current cabinet share variables.[5] We present

---

[5] Following Garrett and Lange (1991), indices of leftist political power were constructed, as well as comparable indices to measure Christian democracy (see Stephens, Huber, and Ray 1995). Since the results with the cumulative and current cabinet indices generally displayed the greatest dissimilarities, we report these in the text.

the results with the current cabinet share variables and note significant deviations with the results for cumulative cabinet share where they exist.

Two control variables were included in the analysis: change in demographic burden and the level of the dependent variable at the outset of the period in question. Change in demographic burden is measured as the mean annual change in the unemployment rate plus the mean annual change in the percentage of the population over age sixty-five. The initial level of each dependent variable is the level of that variable for the first year of the period in question. The reasons for inclusion of the change in demographic burden variables in the regressions on the expenditure-dependent variables should be clear: increases in unemployment and increases in the aged population will push up expenditure for unemployment compensation, pensions, and health care unless entitlements are cut. We entered the level of expenditure at the outset of the period also to control for the ceiling effect referred to earlier. We expected the effect on the health care variable to be especially strong since this is one of the core social programs that was already fully developed in the advanced welfare states by the mid-1970s.

Recent work by Cusack and Garrett (1994) on the determinants of government spending and by Mjøset (1986) on the impact of the changing international environment on Scandinavian political economies has argued that the 1970s and 1980s were distinctly different in terms of the policies governments followed to deal with the domestic and international economies. Mjøset notes that the 1970s was a period of policy "fumbling" in which governments largely attempted to deal with the crisis with the old methods. In the 1980s, governments began to realize that the game had fundamentally changed and adjusted policy accordingly. Following these leads, we analyzed the expenditure data by dividing it into three periods rather than the conventional two. The first period stretches from the beginning of our data in the mid- to late 1950s to the breakup of the Bretton Woods system in 1971. The second period extends until the second oil shock of 1979 and the third from there to the end of our data circa 1986 to 1988.

RESULTS

Table 6.1 displays the level of expenditure and taxes (parts A through E), the level of pension benefits, public share of health expenditure (part G), and level of public employment (part H) for the beginning and end of the three periods, as well as the mean annual change during the period. The countries are grouped according to the type of welfare state following Esping-Andersen's typology though not necessarily his classification for all of the individual countries.[6] The general pattern for expenditure is relatively clear: the mean annual increase in almost all of the expenditure measures is higher for the 1970s than for the "golden age" and then lower for the 1980s than for either of the two earlier periods. While there are a number of individual country exceptions to this rule, once the countries are aggregated to the level of welfare state regime type, all groups follow this pattern.

By contrast, the mean annual change in revenue follows a different and less clear-cut pattern. However, if we compare the mean annual change in revenue to the mean annual change in expenditure, a much clearer pattern emerges. A comparison of the mean annual changes indicates that expenditure is increasing much faster in the 1970s in all regime types, whereas in the 1980s average annual increases in revenue exceeded those of expenditure in all three regime types.

Taken together these patterns of the development of revenue and expenditure support not only the general hypothesis that the three periods were distinct, but also that the Scandinavian pattern found by Mjøset (1986) may be a general one. Governments first responded to the economic difficulties by following traditional formulas that entailed maintaining or increasing entitlements and expenditure in an effort to fight recession and unemployment and mitigate their social consequences. After a decade of "fumbling," government after government regardless of political color embarked on new policies, which often involved reining in the increase in expenditure and increasing revenue.

With regard to the 1970s, the increases in pension benefits, public share of health care, and public employment shown in Table 6.1 all indicate that the continued increase in all measures of social expenditure shown in the table was not simply an artifact of increasing burdens on the welfare state caused by adverse economic conditions and demographic change. This is also confirmed by an examination of the graphs of replacement rates and coverage for pensions, sick pay, and unemployment compensation based on data collected by the Social Citizenship Indicators Project (SCIP) at the University of Stockholm (Palme 1990; Kangas 1991; Carroll 1994).

---

[6] Here nations are grouped as follows: social democratic = Austria, Denmark, Finland, Sweden, Norway; liberal = Australia, Canada, Japan, New Zealand, United Kingdom, United States; Christian democratic = Belgium, France, West Germany, Ireland, Italy, Netherlands, Switzerland.

Though there are some cases of cutbacks after 1975, in most cases, entitlements were improving in this period, in some cases dramatically.[7]

While the expenditure data do indicate that fiscal policy was more austere in the 1980s and the growth in all categories of expenditure was lower than a decade earlier, it does not tell us to what extent, if at all, there was real retrenchment, with rollbacks in welfare state benefits. Making such an assessment is a matter of weighing the extent to which the more modest increases in expenditure failed to keep up with more rapid increases in recipient groups such as the aged and unemployed. Moreover, as our discussion of Sweden in our case studies will show, it was possible even to reduce expenditure and increase entitlements by a combination of public-sector economies, exchange rate policies, and economic revival.

Here we have a number of pieces of evidence that bear directly on the question of cutbacks in the 1980s. First, the pension benefits data in Table 6.1 do not show a cutback in the 1980s, which is significant given that they control for the growth of the aged population. However, they are subject to two sources of error. First, the maturation of pension systems pushes up expenditure without legislative changes; thus current cutbacks due to, say, changes in indexation, may be masked by automatic increases legislated in the past. Second, the use of early pensions to combat unemployment would drive up our figures on pension spending per person over sixty-five, as those going into early pension would not be included in the divisor.

A second and more conclusive piece of evidence is our data on the development of public share of health care expenditure. The health care figures show a different pattern than the expenditure as a percent of GDP variables (see Table 6.1). The 1970s already exhibit a lower average annual increase in the public share than the earlier period and the public share actually declines in the 1980s. All but four cases exhibit such a decline, and in at least four cases the decline in the public share is quite significant. Since OECD data on coverage indicate very few decreases in coverage (OECD 1990:143–145), these declines must be explained primarily by increased copayments and exit from the public system due to decreased services, long queues, and poor-quality services.

A third piece of evidence comes from the data on civilian public em-

---

[7] In the case of both our figures for pension benefits and Palme's (1990) replacement rates from the SCIP data, the increases are sufficiently large that we feel certain that the increases would hold even if the factors we discuss for the case of pension benefits in the 1980s were taken into account.

ployment (Table 6.1) and from the WEEP data (Cusack, Notermans, and Rein 1989: 478). As one can see from Table 6.1, the social democratic welfare states experienced a significant increase even in the 1980s, whereas in the other two groups civilian public employment was essentially stable after increasing moderately in the previous two periods. Examination of the figures for the individual countries for the period 1979–1988 confirms this general picture. Only the United Kingdom experienced a drop in the percentage of the working-age population in civilian public employment and there the decrease was quite small. The other countries experienced increases in civilian public employment but, save the Nordic countries, of less than 1 percent over the whole period. The Nordic pattern is singular: civilian public employment increased more than 2 percent from 1979 to 1988 in all four countries. The WEEP data on the percentage of the working-age population in public health, education, and welfare employment from 1975 to 1985 confirm the overall pattern we found with the civilian public employment data.

A fourth piece of evidence comes from the graphs on replacement rates and coverage in unemployment insurance, sick pay, and pensions from the SCIP project (Kangas 1991; Palme 1990; Carroll 1994). Though one has to make do with no more than rough inferences from published graphs, one can make the following assessments. Coverage for pensions, sickness, and unemployment showed few declines of over roughly 5 percent up to 1985; there were more fluctuations visible than clear trends. Declines in replacement rates of approximately 5 percent or more were confined to five countries; the other countries had not lowered replacement rates significantly by 1985. Australia and Belgium lowered replacement rates for unemployment and sickness between 1975 and 1985, the Netherlands did so between 1980 and 1985. Denmark lowered unemployment replacement rates quite dramatically between 1975 and 1985; Hagen (1992) indicates an even more dramatic decline than the graphs, over 20 percent. The other dramatic decline of this order of magnitude occurred in the United Kingdom between 1975 and 1985 in replacement rates for sickness and unemployment.

Regressions on the political variables of the expenditure and revenue variables are shown in Tables 6.2 and 6.3. The general pattern of strong partisan effects in the golden age followed by attenuated partisan effects in the 1970s and then very little partisan differences in the 1980s is striking. Though all coefficients for the political variables in the 1980s are insignificant, it is worth noting that all the coefficients for Christian democracy are negative, while one sees a mix of negative and positive coefficients for social democracy. For the variables listed in Table 6.2, regressions with

Table 6.2. *Summaries of regressions of welfare effort indicators on political variables*

	Pre-70	1970s	Post-79
Change in expenditure			
Social democracy	.772	.654	−.528
	(4.26)	(3.33)	(−2.30)
Christian democracy	.144	.315	−.074
	(.79)	(1.60)	(−.323)
Adjusted R²	.50	.39	.17
Change in consumption			
Social democracy	.361	.668	.096
	(1.47)	(3.56)	(.37)
Christian democracy	−.072	−.119	−.081
	(.29)	(−.63)	(−.31)
Adjusted R²	.03	.41	−.11
Change in revenue			
Social democracy	.790	.317	−0.54
	(4.75)	(1.61)	(−.231)
Christian democracy	.051	.618	−.450
	(.30)	(3.13)	(−1.93)
Adjusted R²	.56	.35	.09
Change in benefits			
Social democracy	.793	.387	.225
	(4.68)	(1.67)	(.95)
Christian democracy	.189	−.198	−.326
	(1.11)	(−.86)	(−1.40)
Adjusted R²	.54	.10	.07
Change in transfers			
Social democracy	.534	.358	−.129
	(2.51)	(1.60)	(1.52)
Christian democracy	.423	.415	−.282
	(1.99)	(1.85)	(−1.14)
Adjusted R²	.27	.16	−.03
Change in pensions			
Social democracy	.526	−.060	−.013
	(2.34)	(−.24)	(−.05)
Christian democracy	−.025	−.219	.086
	(−.11)	(−.86)	(.33)
Adjusted R²	.19	−.08	−.12

Note: For an explanation of the variables, see Table 6.1. Reported coefficients are standardized. T values are given in parentheses. T values for significance at .05 level: two-tailed test, |T|>2.15, one-tailed test, |T|>1.76, for significance at .10 level: two-tailed test, |T|>1.76, one-tailed test, |T|>1.36.

Table 6.3. *Summaries of regressions of welfare effort indicators on political variables with and without control variables*

	Public share of health care costs			Public employment		
	Pre-71	1970s	Post-79	Pre-71	1970s	Post-79
Social democracy	−.164 (.64)	−.147 (−.65)	.198 (.84)	.773 (5.82)	.584 (2.25)	.468 (1.95)
Christian democracy	.222 (.87)	−.564 (−2.48)	−.393 (−1.68)	−.440 (−3.31)	−.08 (−.36)	−.192 (−.80)
Adjusted R²	−.05	.20	.13	.75	.28	.20
Social democracy	.317 (1.23)	−.209 (−.87)	.388 (1.38)	.877 (4.75)	.433 (2.15)	.153 (.67)
Christian democracy	.283 (1.23)	−.373 (−1.78)	−.458 (−2.29)	−.462 (−2.65)	.171 (.80)	.060 (.27)
Demographic burden	.078 (.27)	−.615 (−2.81)	.072 (.27)	−.125 (−.79)	.038 (.20)	−.326 (−1.50)
Initial level of the dependent variable	−.757 (−2.77)	.270 (1.07)	−.652 (−2.20)	−.102 (−.51)	.631 (2.99)	.546 (2.37)
Adjusted R²	.39	.41	.36	.73	.53	.47

Notes: Health care: public percentage of total health care expenditure. Public employment: civilian government employment as a percent of the working-age population. For significance of T values, see Table 6.2.

controls for initial level of expenditure or revenue (not shown) did not change this picture. The demographic burden effects were positive as hypothesized but modest, only in a few cases significant. Nor were the hypothesized ceiling effects strong.

The health care data (public percentage of total health care expenditure) and public employment data show a somewhat different pattern. For both dependent variables, the control variables are significant for various of the time periods, so we have presented regressions with and without the control variables in Table 6.3. For health care, the regressions show quite strong initial-level effects for the first period, which is not surprising as this was an early area of program innovation in the advanced welfare states. The final period shows a significant negative coefficient for Christian democracy and a positive one for social democracy. This pattern is yet stronger for the regression with cumulative cabinet as the independent variable when the two control variables are present (for Christian democracy, $\beta = -.46$, $t = -2.3$; for social democracy, $\beta = .39$, $t = 1.4$). In the case of public employment, one finds moderately strong and significant effects for social democracy in the 1970s and 1980s, though in the latter period the effect disappears when the control variables are present. By contrast, in this case, we do get somewhat different results with cumulative cabinet as the independent variable: the regression shows significant social democratic effects with the controls present and insignificant coefficients for the control variables.

We can pursue this point a bit further in the pooled data. In Table 6.2, the coefficient for left cabinet in the regression of changes in government civilian consumption in the 1980s was near significance. In their analysis of pooled data, Cusack and Garrett (1994) did find a significant effect of left-labor power (a variable that combines indicators of cabinet composition, union density, and union centralization) during the 1980s on changes in government civilian consumption. This dependent variable was the only social policy indicator on which significant political effects appeared in their analysis. Cusack and Garrett (1994) interpret this finding to indicate that investments in human capital remained an important component of the social democratic model in the 1980s. Based on the public employment data and particularly the data of public social service employment as well as our case studies, we offer the following somewhat different, but not contradictory, interpretation. The relationships between social democratic governance and both government civilian consumption and public employment in the data are largely produced by the growth of public social services. The data presented here indicate that this may be a Scandinavian phenomenon and this is confirmed by Cusack and Rein's

(1991) data on public social service employment for a larger group of countries including Austria and Finland for 1985.

The Austrian case explains why controls for initial level eliminated the significant effects of social democracy as shown in Table 6.3, as Austria has the highest score for current social democratic cabinet in the early 1980s but low scores for both level of public employment and for public employment expansion. Likewise it explains why the cumulative cabinet regressions showed a stronger social democratic effect, as Austria ranks behind Denmark, Sweden, and Norway on this measure. We would argue that the Austrian pattern is an outgrowth of the fact that the Austrian welfare state is a product of a Christian democratic–social democratic compromise and, indeed, Austria displays the continental pattern of both low public social service employment and low levels of female labor force participation, in sharp contrast to Scandinavia on both accounts. In the absence of policies explicitly supporting traditional family patterns such as those found in Catholic countries, in Scandinavia a reinforcing cycle was introduced in which the full employment policies of the golden age brought women into the labor force and this in turn led to demands for supportive services, such as day care, and supportive transfer programs, such as parental leave (Huber and Stephens 1996b). Once enacted, these policies in turn enabled more women to enter the labor force which, again in turn, led to further demands for expansion of supportive policies and to more generalized demands for greater gender equality. This pattern was also reinforced by the greater reluctance of the Scandinavian countries to permit employers to recruit foreign labor, which was clearly a product of the influence of unions on the shaping and administration of labor market policy. The centrality of gender equality and mobilization of women into the labor force in the expansion of public social service employment can also be seen in the fact that the one area of social insurance that all four Nordic countries expanded vigorously in the 1980s was parental leave (Hagen 1992: 143–148). Indeed, this was even true of Denmark, despite the onset of the employment crisis in the mid-1970s and initiation of cuts in other welfare state programs.

There is no doubt that these developments have resulted in a Scandinavian welfare state pattern of investment in youth and thus in human capital rather than expenditure on the aged, as in the case of the continental welfare states. Thus, while it does have the productivist profile that Cusack and Garrett's interpretation indicates, this was more an unintended byproduct of labor recruitment and gender equality policies than an intentional part of a policy to promote international competitiveness.

Nevertheless, though our analysis does demonstrate strong partisan differences with regard to expansion of public social services, the overall pattern is one of a sharp narrowing of political differences in the 1980s. Our hypothesis is that this was a result of a shift of the political agenda: once it was realized that the game had fundamentally changed as a result of the sea changes in the world economy, governments found themselves with dramatically fewer options. Above all, vigorous expansion of entitlements was off the agenda. This contributed to shifting the politics of social policy to defending entitlements.

CASE STUDIES

THE SOCIAL DEMOCRATIC WELFARE STATES OF SCANDINAVIA

By almost all measures, the Scandinavian welfare states are among the most generous and, as Mitchell (1991) and Korpi and Palme (1994) have shown, they effect the greatest redistribution of income. These welfare states most closely approximate the institutional (Titmuss 1974; Palme 1990) or social democratic model (Esping-Andersen 1990). They provide basic security to all regardless of income level through citizenship benefits (via guaranteed minimums and universal or near universal coverage) and income security (high replacement rates) in case of sickness, unemployment, work injury, and retirement for even well-off white-collar workers. They are also comprehensive: they cover all major programs, are service intensive, and are statist in that the state is responsible for providing services and administering the transfer programs. Finally, they are characterized by very high female labor force participation and thus a high ratio of people working and contributing to the system to those not working and dependent on it.

Thus, the commonplace assumption would be that these very generous welfare states should experience the greatest downward pressure as a result of economic hard times and increased international competition. Indeed, entitlements have been cut in three of the countries and it is arguable that Norway would have suffered the same fate were it not for North Sea oil. Following our analysis elsewhere (Huber and Stephens 1997; Stephens 1996), we argue that, taken as a whole, welfare state entitlements have made little if any direct contribution to the current economic problems of the Scandinavian countries. Arguably, many of them, such as active labor market policies, education, day care, and other investments in human capital and labor force mobilization, actually result in competitive advantages. Rather, we argue that the Scandinavian growth and employment model, which was so successful during the golden age of postwar capitalism up to the mid-1970s in holding unemployment in the range of 1 to 3 percent and producing world record high levels of labor force participation, is much less effective in the contemporary world. This, in turn, makes welfare state entitlements that were affordable in the past no longer affordable.

Since it is the economic-employment policies that are less effective, it is necessary to outline them briefly.[8] The central goals of the Nordic economic model were full employment and rapid economic growth based on rapid technological change. Fiscal policies were moderately countercyclical and backed up by occasional devaluations. The core of the long-term growth-employment policy, however, and this cannot be overemphasized, was supply side. The supply-side policies extended well beyond the usual general supply-side policies, such as education, infrastructure, cheap credit policies, generalized support for research and development, and active labor market policy, to selective policies, such as credit policies favoring industrial borrowers over consumers and speculators, regional policies, and subsidies or subsidized credit to selected industries. Interest rates were kept low through credit rationing and through public sector surpluses. Accordingly, fiscal policy was generally austere: these countries usually ran budget surpluses. The demand side of the Scandinavian growth-employment models was only partly internally generated; it was also a result of demand for exports created by the vigorous postwar growth in the core advanced capitalist economies of North America and Europe.

Denmark deviates from the Scandinavian model in that it lacks the supply-side component. It is no accident that the employment crisis began almost immediately at the end of the golden age after the first oil shock with unemployment climbing into the double digits by 1975. The economic difficulties and particularly the rise in unemployment made existing entitlements increasingly expensive. Successive Danish governments have responded with significant welfare state cuts which have nonetheless only prevented social security benefit expenditure and total government expenditure from rising as fast as they otherwise would have. A variety of measures have been employed in this effort: increases in the selectivity of benefits, introduction of income testing, modifications of indexing, temporary deindexation, increases in qualifying conditions, and introduction of waiting days (Hagen 1992: 154; Marklund 1988: 31–35; Nørby Johansen 1986:362–363). Among the Scandinavian countries, Denmark is the

---

[8] This characterization leans heavily on Mjøset 1986, 1987 and Andersson, Kosonen, and Vartiainen 1993. Note that our description fits Denmark much less well. By contrast, the Austrian growth model is quite similar to that of Finland, Norway, and Sweden (Huber and Stephens 1997).

strongest case for continued partisan differences as most of the cuts were made by the governments of 1983 to 1993 which included the Conservative and now neoliberal Liberal Party.

In Norway, Sweden, and Finland, the dramatic increases in unemployment came in the late 1980s and early 1990s as Norwegian and Swedish unemployment neared or reached double digits and Finnish unemployment hit 20 percent. Three factors contributed to this development. First, the simultaneous rise in international interest rates and internationalization of financial markets made it impossible for these countries to maintain low interest rates and made it more difficult to privilege borrowing by industry over other consumers of credit. Second, governments in all three countries of different political colorings made an identical series of decisions on the timing of financial deregulation, income tax changes, and exchange rate policy which had strong procyclical effects, contributing to the overheating of the economy in the late 1980s and aggravating the crash of the 1990s. Third, all three countries followed policies that enabled them to bridge the employment crisis of the 1970s and 1980s: in Sweden and Norway, the expansion of public employment; in Norway, sheltered employment in public enterprises; and in Finland, the expansion of Soviet trade (Huber and Stephens 1996a). For different reasons, these policies had been exhausted by the end of the 1980s in each case.

In all three countries, significant rollbacks were resisted until it appeared that it was impossible to return to the previous low levels of unemployment. At that point, replacement rates were cut, waiting days introduced, qualifying conditions increased, and services cut. While many of these changes are still under discussion, it is clear that the depth of the cuts reflects the depth of the employment crisis, with Finland cutting the most and Norway very little. Though the recency of the events makes any long-term predictions impossible, there is indication that the political coloring of governments has (or would have) made a modest difference in Sweden, very little in Finland. Let us be clear: by international standards, these are still and will continue to be very generous welfare states. Despite the introduction of waiting days and probable cuts of replacement rates in unemployment, work injury, sick pay, and parental leave from 90 to 100 percent to about 75 percent (as in the case of Sweden), they still fit the institutional model.

THE LIBERAL WELFARE STATES: THE ANTIPODES AND BRITAIN

Castles and Mitchell (1990) argue that Esping-Andersen's division of welfare states into "three worlds" is misleading. The Antipodes fit uneasily into the liberal world as they have provided much more effective social protection than other liberal welfare states but, as Castles (1985) has pointed out, "by other means" – through the system of wage regulation. In the past decade, however, this system of wage regulation has been significantly altered if not entirely dismantled (Castles, Gerritsen, and Vowles 1996), with the result that the Antipodes have converged on the liberal model. In terms of social policy proper however, the changes were modest in Australia and were designed to compensate low-income families for the changes in the labor market. In New Zealand, the changes were modest until the advent of the National government in 1990.

Castles argues that though the Australasian welfare state is residualist, relying heavily on means-tested benefits, this has to be seen in the context of the historically developed wage regulation system, labor market conditions, and the position of the two countries in the world economy. In the systems of compulsory arbitration and conciliation, labor courts make binding decisions on wage claims and these are automatically extended to all workers and employers in the industry in question, whether organized or not. In their formative years, prolabor forces and individuals had great influence on these court decisions and they awarded what was termed a "fair wage," which in practice was defined as sufficient for a decent standard of living for the (male) breadwinner and his family. This system was later extended to sick pay. Combined with widespread home ownership, which lessened the need for high income replacement rates in pensions, and, in the postwar period, with extremely low unemployment and high per capita income, a residual welfare state was all that was needed for the working classes to enjoy a high level of security and comfortable standard of living.

These high wages were made possible by high levels of tariff protection and, in New Zealand, import licensing for domestic industry which in turn was made possible by the countries' reliance on primary product exports. Thus, the historic political economy of the welfare state was an almost mirror image to the Nordic welfare states: in the latter case, it was based on the interests of workers in competitive export industries whereas in the former, it was based on the interests of workers in internationally uncompetitive, protected domestic industry. It is little surprise, then, that a combination of the changes in the international economy described earlier, along with adverse movement of relative prices of their export products, put the Antipodean models of welfare state and wage regulation under much more stress than in the case of the Nordic welfare states despite the much greater generosity of the latter (Shirley 1993: 6; Castles,

Gerritsen, and Vowles 1996). The raw material exports no longer yielded the foreign exchange earnings necessary to sustain a protected manufacturing sector, which forced an economic opening.

The changes in the international and domestic economy pushed unemployment to double-digit rates in both countries, which in itself undermined the social protection provided by the old model. Newly elected Labor governments in the early 1980s introduced a far reaching program of deregulation of the domestic economy and of increased economic openness. As a result, real wages have fallen significantly in both countries. However, in the areas of labor market regulation and social welfare, Castles (1996; Castles and Shirley 1996) contends the two countries parted ways. In New Zealand, Labor cut the pension system that provided for a generous retirement age of sixty but stopped short of major inroads into the system. The National government elected in 1990 went much further, essentially dismantling the whole system of wage regulation and making major cuts in the welfare state, such as transforming the national health service into a means-tested regime, totally abolishing the universal child benefit, and cutting real benefits for virtually all classes of beneficiaries. By contrast, in Australia, the Labor government, which was returned to office for an unprecedented four consecutive terms, concluded an agreement with the trade unions that preserved elements of the wage regulatory system in a manner that protected workers in low-wage industries and attempted to reconstruct the social safety net to cushion those hardest hit by liberalization and changes in the wage regulation system.

In Britain, the general elections of 1979 brought to power the Conservative Party, with an explicit neoliberal agenda arguing, as a 1979 White Paper put it, "public expenditure is at the heart of Britain's economic difficulties" (Lister 1991: 91). The privatization cure was applied to social policy as well as to public enterprises. Housing is the most obvious and successful example of this, with about one-fifth of public housing being sold to occupants at prices well below their market value. Public pensions were also slated for privatization. Thatcher weakened the indexation of the basic pensions, causing the replacement rate of this plan to decline by about 20 percent by 1988 (Pierson 1994); or, between 1980 and 1993 the basic pension fell from 30 to 19 percent of net average weekly earnings for men (Danish National Institute of Social Research 1994). A proposal to phase out the state-run supplementary pensions (SERPS) ran into significant opposition both from the left and the business community, which balked at the cost of paying current pensions under SERPS while saving for future ones under new private plans. SERPS survived the initial onslaught, but, by 1996, piecemeal cuts had gutted the program. Plans to privatize the National Health Service through mandatory private insurance were far less successful. With private insurance premiums increasing at four times the rate of inflation, privatization would have cost a fortune (Pierson 1994). This cost, combined with public support for the National Health Service prevented any radical changes in health care.

The Conservatives also altered the structure of social security benefits, reducing the levels of universal entitlements and increasing the importance of means-tested benefits. The deepest cuts were, perhaps surprisingly, in universal programs, which were attacked as ill-targeted and wasteful. Maternity and death grants were simply abolished. The universal flat-rate Child Benefit was cut by 9 percent in 1980, and increases were postponed allowing the real value of the payment to fall by 26 percent between 1979 and 1993 (Lister 1991: 99). Universal unemployment benefits were also not immune from cuts despite their contributory financing and "insurance" nature. Taxation of unemployment benefits was introduced, earnings-related supplements were abolished as of 1982 and basic benefits were allowed to fall. As the SCIP data show, replacement rates in unemployment insurance and sick pay were cut from around 60 percent in 1975 to half that a decade later (Kangas 1991; Carroll 1994).

The number of individuals on means-tested assistance increased in direct response to the cuts in universal benefits. The proportion of Social Security expenditure subject to means testing has increased from 15 percent in 1979 to 25 percent in 1993 according to Sainsbury (1992) and Pierson (1994), or to 34 percent in 1993–1994 according to a different calculation (Danish National Institute of Social Research 1994). Other changes in the disability program and sickness benefits reinforced the trend toward tightening of eligibility rules and a reduction of government responsibility. In early 1995 more stringent medical tests were introduced to qualify for disability benefits. In sick pay, the first six months are now to be borne in full by all but the smaller employers, and there are plans for a complete withdrawal of government from the areas of sick pay and industrial accident insurance.

The Conservative Party, then, has been quite successful in its drive to cut the welfare state, with the National Health Service as the only major example where it did not meet with substantial success. The basic structure of social spending has also been shifted away from the Beveridge ideal toward a more thoroughly residualist model.

GERMANY, THE NETHERLANDS, AND FRANCE

The German,[9] Dutch, and French welfare states belong to the Catholic-conservative category. They have a variety of programs for different occupational groups, and they are generous in transfer payments but weak in the provision of services. They all have comparatively low female labor force participation rates, 56–59 percent in 1993, and comparatively very weak active labor market policies.[10] Accordingly, not only were they poorly equipped to handle the decrease in economic growth and the increase in unemployment, but the way in which they did handle these problems put great strain on their welfare state efforts and induced cutbacks in a wide variety of benefits.

Germany and the Netherlands are more typical examples of the Catholic-conservative category in that they have been based on the male bread-winner model and have been relying on the family for essential care for children and the elderly to an even greater extent than France. For instance, France has public day care in contrast to Germany and the Netherlands, and it has the highest public health, education, and welfare employment in the Christian democratic category. Politically, of course, Catholic parties were much more important in shaping the German and Dutch welfare states. Accordingly, we discuss France separately.

In both Germany and the Netherlands coalition governments led by social democratic parties expanded welfare state entitlements and expenditures up to the mid-1970s. In 1975 unemployment in both countries reached 4 percent and economic growth slowed significantly. These changes led to first efforts to contain rising welfare state expenditures. In both countries, economic conditions worsened in the 1980s, governmental power shifted to the right, and cutbacks were intensified. Unemployment reached a level of 8 percent in 1983 and stayed there until 1988 in Germany, and in the Netherlands it fluctuated between 14 and 11 percent in this period.

In fact, unemployment figures only tell part of the story. In Germany as well as the Netherlands, many older workers went into early retirement, and in the Netherlands many claimed disability pensions. As a result, the

---

[9] "Germany" and "German" in this section refer to the Federal Republic of Germany. Reunification imposed a major burden on the German welfare state and forced changes beyond those necessitated by the changes in the international and national economies.

[10] The ratio of passive labor market expenditures (i.e., on income replacement and early retirement) to active ones (i.e., on employment services, training, measures for special groups, etc.) was 2.68 in the Netherlands, compared with .43 in Sweden, for instance (de Beus and van Kersbergen 1994).

labor force participation rate of male workers between sixty and sixty-four
years of age fell from around 70 percent in 1973 to 22 percent in 1991 in
the Netherlands (Hemerijck and Kloosterman 1994); in Germany this rate
was at 31.5 percent in 1986 (Hinrichs 1991). Governments in both countries intensified efforts to contain the costs resulting from the increase in
claimants; they reduced benefits, increased contributions, and stiffened
eligibility criteria and enforcement provisions for a wide variety of programs. However, all these changes left the essential principles of the existing programs intact; they were aimed at putting these programs on a
sounder financial base and at curbing abuses of the programs. Only in 1993
did a Dutch Parliamentary Committee in which all parties were represented issue a report that looked at the totality of social programs and
make proposals for significant changes aimed at increasing labor market
participation.

In the Netherlands the post-1982 Lubbers government severed the
link between public-sector wages and welfare benefits and private-sector
wage development and embarked upon a series of cutbacks (Hemerijck and
Kloosterman 1994). In 1984–1986 pensions and family allowances were
frozen; in 1984 unemployment and disability benefits were cut by 3 percent and the next year the replacement rate in these programs was lowered
from 80 to 70 percent; in addition, the length of the benefit period for
disability and unemployment was reduced, which meant that recipients
had to shift to social assistance where benefits were lower (Sainsbury 1992;
Cox 1993: 178–183). In 1985 the government launched a major attempt
to reduce fraud and abuse in the social assistance and disability programs.
Abuses in the disability program to relieve unemployment were rampant
because the criteria were lenient and both employers and unions had a
strong interest in shifting older and less productive workers more or less
painlessly out of the labor force in this way (Cox 1994). In the 1990s
similar types of changes were continued and had the cumulative effect of
reducing benefits in part substantially.[11] One could also detect a gradual
shift toward increased employer responsibility (and thus an increased role
for private insurance), more emphasis on household-income testing, and
greater reliance on flat-rate rather than earnings-related benefits.

The German Social Democratic–Liberal government began to curtail
expenditures in 1977 by changing indexation rules and the calculation
formula for pensions, raising contribution rates for pensions and user fees
for prescriptions, reducing some health insurance benefits and promoting

---

[11] The information in this and the next paragraph is taken from Danish National Institute
of Social Research (1994).

concerted corporatist action to control health expenditures, and tightening controls on recipients of unemployment benefits. The post-1982 Christian Democratic–Liberal government then pursued similar types of changes but of a greater magnitude. It introduced individual contributions of pensioners to sickness insurance and of recipients of cash sickness benefits to pension and unemployment insurance, tightened elegibility conditions for unemployment benefits and for full invalidity pensions, increased copayments for medical services and prescriptions, reduced unemployment benefits in a variety of ways, reduced benefits levels for social assistance, and weakened entitlements to social assistance in favor of stronger administrative discretion. Several of these measures meant significant cuts in benefits;[12] in general, pensions were less affected than unemployment compensation. Adjustments in pension policy are essentially a corporatist affair, decided by a group of experts representing the major institutions, and accepted without major dissent (Hinrichs 1991). This was also true of the pension reform of 1988, which phased out early retirement plans, changed indexing from gross wages to net wages (i.e., gross wages minus taxes and social security contributions), fixed federal subsidies at 19 percent, and phased out the practice of revaluating contributions from very low income earners that had de facto functioned as a minimum pension plan.

Other areas are more controversial; for instance, the harsh austerity program in social assistance and social services pursued by the government in 1993 met with considerable opposition. Up to that point, social assistance benefits had actually increased (Alber 1996). Unemployment replacement rates and duration were cut further in the 1990s, down to 60 or 67 percent of net wages for unemployment insurance and 53 or 57 percent for unemployment assistance respectively for people without or with children; unemployment assistance was restricted to one year, after which recipients became dependent on income-tested, locally monitored social assistance.[13]

The results of these efforts were a containment of the increases in general public expenditures and in transfer payments. The obvious reason why expenditures did not fall, despite significant cutbacks, is the rise in the number of claimants of benefits. The social rights graphs for these two countries in the period 1975–1985 show a general pattern of stagnation or

---

[12] For instance, the requirement that recipients of cash sickness benefits contribute to pension and unemployment insurance meant a reduction of these cash benefits by 11.5 percent (Alber 1986: 268), a rather substantial reduction.

[13] The only innovations in social policy in the 1990s (as opposed to cutbacks in existing programs) have come in response to rulings by the Constitutional Court, or in response to significant new social problems, or as temporary measures to deal with the extraordinary economic situation (see Danish National Institute of Social Research 1994).

slight declines. One can guess that these graphs would show stronger declines if they were available for 1990. The most serious restrictions were not imposed until after the changes in governments in 1982, and many of them did not yet have a highly visible impact by 1985.

Unlike Germany and the Netherlands, France was governed by the right throughout the 1970s, with a leftist government taking power in the early 1980s. Nonetheless, the general trajectory of social policy since 1970 is quite similar to that in the other two nations. In the mid-1970s Conservative president Giscard d'Estaing, and his prime minister Jacques Chirac responded to the first oil shock with reflationary policies that greatly increased social expenditure. Although these increases were slowed under the austerity policies of Giscard's second prime minister, the percentage of GDP spent on social security increased by .86 percent annually from 1973 to 1981.

The elections of 1981 were followed by a spike in benefit levels as part of the new Socialist government's policy of Keynesian reflation. Minimum pensions, family allowances, and housing allowances were all increased significantly. This reflationary policy coincided with worldwide recession resulting in record trade deficits. The Socialists reacted with a series of devaluations and a policy of austerity. Taxes were increased, and many benefit levels were reduced, eligibility rules were tightened, and expensive early retirement schemes were eliminated. The net impact of reflation and austerity was to slow the increase in the percentage of GDP allocated to social spending to an annual rate of .51 percent.

Since 1983, social policy in France has focused on two objectives, coping with unemployment through work sharing and subsidies, and containing the persistent deficits of the Social Security system through tax increases and benefit cuts. Socialist innovation in social policy was restricted to anti-unemployment measures. Holidays were extended, the retirement age was reduced, and early retirement was encouraged (until this became too expensive). Youth training programs were greatly expanded, and part-time jobs for unemployed young adults were created in the public and nonprofit sectors.

The legislative elections of 1986 brought the center right back into government. While privatizing many state industries, the Gaullist government dropped plans to privatize Social Security. Social policy innovation was limited to an increase in subsidies to firms hiring the long-term unemployed. Chronic deficits of the Social Security funds were addressed with a series of new taxes, the government refusing to heed its own commission of experts and reduce pension benefits.

The return of the Socialists in 1988 saw two initiatives in social policy.

The fiscal base of Social Security was augmented with a small but controversial tax on unearned income. A means-tested minimum income was
created for individuals who had fallen between the cracks of the French
welfare system, particularly the long-term unemployed.

The center right returned to government in 1993 promising to reduce
taxes and Social Security contributions. These cuts were abandoned in the
face of persistent deficits. Fiscal crisis was averted by reducing pensions for
the weakly unionized private sector in 1993. In May 1995 Jacques Chirac
was elected president after promising increased social spending and reduced taxes. Faced with "calamitous" public finances, and with the strict
Maastricht deficit criteria, his prime minister, Alan Juppé, delivered
tax increases and broad expenditure cuts instead. A series of massive
demonstrations and public-sector strikes in December 1995 forced
the government to retreat on plans to cut public pensions and education
spending.

Major structural reforms of the Social Security system survived the
social unrest relatively unscathed. A constitutional amendment has given
parliament the right to set spending caps for the main social insurance
programs. The fiscal burden of Social Security is being progressively shifted
from payroll taxes (blamed for persistent unemployment) toward broad-
based income taxes. In 1997 a universal residence-based right to health
coverage will be introduced. In institutional terms, the architecture of
health coverage is shifting from the existing corporatist insurance model
with a state run safety net toward the social democratic model of tax-
financed universal coverage.

CONCLUSION

The quantitative data analysis tells two clear stories, which are in large
part supported but nuanced by the case studies. First, the quantitative
analyses of the expenditure and revenue data indicate relatively moderate
rollbacks only. Strictly speaking, we see no declines but the mean annual
increase in almost all of the expenditure measures is lower for the 1980s
than after a decade of actually being higher than in the golden age. Since
we know that need increased greatly, we interpret this as indicating moderate cutbacks in entitlements. Like the expenditure data, our pension data
as well as the SCIP graphs on pensions do not indicate any rollbacks in
pensions. However, two factors might be covering up actual cuts in entitlements. First, the maturation of pension benefits pushes up expenditure
without legislative changes. Second, the use of early pensions would drive

up our figures on pension spending per person over sixty-five, as those going into early pension would not be included in the divisor.

An important feature of the first story told by the quantitative analyses was that expenditure was increasing much faster than revenue in the 1970s in all three regime types, whereas in the 1980s average annual increases in revenue exceeded those of expenditure in all regime types. It appears that the first response of governments to the crisis was to follow traditional Keynesian formulas, increasing expenditure in an effort to fight recession and unemployment and mitigate their social consequences. In the 1980s, governments of different partisan composition embarked on new policies, which often involved reining in the increase in expenditure and increasing revenue.

However, if we look at the data on public share of health expenditure, on total public employment, and on public employment in health, education, and welfare, as well as the social rights graphs, we can see some cases where significant rollbacks were already introduced in the last decade covered by the data, 1975 to 1985. Italy significantly cut the public share of health expenditure. The United States and Canada cut public health, education, and welfare employment slightly. Australia, Belgium, Denmark, the Netherlands, and the United Kingdom all made significant cuts in replacement rates for sickness and unemployment benefits. Taken together, then, the data indicate that, by the 1980s, the politics of social policy had essentially become a matter of defending, or cutting, entitlements, not expanding them. The exception to this pattern is the Nordic expansion of public social service employment and parental leave.

The second story told by the data was that the golden age, the 1970s, and the 1980s were distinctive with regard to partisan effects on social policy. The strong partisan effects that characterized the golden age declined in the 1970s, and the 1980s witnessed a further marked attenuation of partisan differences. The decline in partisan influences was more marked for Christian democracy than social democracy. This result provides support for the view that it was easier for the multiclass Christian democratic than for the labor-based social democratic parties to abandon Keynesian full-employment welfare state policies. There was one clear exception; our results for public employment and Cusack and Garrett's (1994) for government civilian consumption did demonstrate continued effects of left party strength on nontransfer elements of the welfare state. Examination of data on public social services from a more limited group of countries (Cusack, Noterman, and Rein 1989; Cusack and Rein 1991) indicates that this is primarily tapping a partisan effect on the expansion of public social services and that this was a Nordic phenomenon.

Our case studies confirm that in most countries there were few really major cutbacks that went into effect before the mid-1980s; the exceptions are the United Kingdom, Denmark, and the Netherlands. Strenuous efforts to curtail expenditures did not come until the 1980s and early 1990s, when rising levels of unemployment caused sharply increasing expenditures under existing entitlements and let the number of contributors to social insurance schemes decline. Most countries had instituted some economizing measures in the 1970s, such as delays in adjustments to inflation, changes in the rules for indexing, and increases in contributions and in user fees. In the 1980s such measures were almost universally intensified, additional measures such as increased waiting days for benefits were introduced, and entitlements themselves came under scrutiny. Significantly, as late as the late 1980s, Norway, Sweden, and Finland, all of whom had avoided the unemployment crises characteristic of the rest of the case studies, had not only not cut programs, they had increased entitlements. As noted, the most significant increases were in parental insurance and public social services.

In general, pension systems remained the best protected parts of the welfare state. Changes in indexing and in calculation formulas led to some decreases in real pensions in virtually all countries, and early pension programs were phased out in some. However, with the notable exception of the United Kingdom, no significant and clearly visible lowering of replacement rates was imposed. The major cutbacks in entitlement programs came in sickness pay, disability pensions, and unemployment compensation.

Overall, then, by the late 1980s and early 1990s a picture of widespread cuts emerges, in some cases at least of considerable magnitude. However, this picture has to be qualified from two points of view. First, outside of the United Kingdom and New Zealand, there were very few cases in any country where benefits in the mid-1990s were more than marginally lower than they had been in 1970. Second, the basic institutional features of the different welfare states were preserved. In only two of our cases could one speak of a basic transformation of the welfare state pattern that had been shaped during the golden age. The United Kingdom and New Zealand have moved from a system that provided basic income security based on citizenship in the direction of an essentially residualist system. One must be careful with this assessment, though; small to moderate cuts, changes in indexing, small shifts toward more means testing, and the like may over the long run erode the foundations of existing welfare state regimes and transform them in the direction of residual regimes.

The case studies demonstrate that partisan differences in public stance and rhetoric were much larger than differences in actual policy outcomes, though there were also a few cases of substantial differences in policy outcomes. In two cases, New Zealand and Britain, significantly the two clear cases of system shift in welfare state regime, there are important partisan differences in the extent to which the parties favored cuts and were able to act on their preferences. These two countries also share single-member, first-past-the-post electoral systems, centralized government with no veto points for interest groups, and dominance of the right by a single secular conservative party, arguably a set of characteristics that encourage that outcome. In other cases, it is more difficult to know to what extent opposition parties would translate their publicly articulated dissent from the incumbent government's social policy into actual policy if they were in government themselves. What is clear, though, is that there is a constraint on the implementation of radical changes and cuts in social security. There are constraints on the social democrats as well, as any government finds it exceedingly difficult to raise taxes when there is little or no income growth and therefore increased taxes would lower people's nominal as well as real income.

If we return to the initial discussion of underlying reasons for the changes in social policy, we can say that our analyses suggest a diversity of reasons. In three cases, the United Kingdom, the United States, and New Zealand, we can speak of clearly ideologically driven cuts. Even though rising unemployment due to increased exposure to trade of the previously heavily protected economy of New Zealand certainly played a role, the cuts went way beyond what would have been warranted by the fiscal problems of social insurance in general and the programs that were cut in particular. In the United States the pressures of the rising budget deficit were used to justify the cutbacks, but one has to remember that the Reagan administration at the same time cut taxes substantially. Finally, in the United Kingdom the big jump in unemployment occurred after 1979, that is, after Thatcher's agenda of cutbacks had been set.

In the remaining countries, unemployment and declining labor force participation arguably were the driving force behind the cuts, but only in Australia was increased trade exposure a major reason for rising unemployment. As in New Zealand, Australia's industry had been protected from import competition and once trade policy was liberalized, the less efficient sectors of that industry came under pressure to rationalize and shed labor. The European countries had already had a high degree of trade openness during the golden age, and thus they were more affected by a combination of general trends underlying rising unemployment, such as rising world-wide interest rates and lower growth, and country-specific factors.

What do these developments suggest for the future of the welfare state in the next decade or so? One of the most important implications of our analysis is that governments are acutely aware of the fact that they cannot run the budget deficits that they ran in the 1970s. As noted, raising taxes in a situation of no or slow growth is politically very difficult, which means that the dominant mode of adjustment has been through cuts. It is important to point out, though, that we are dealing with a political constraint here, not an inexorable economic constraint. Societies still have political choices regarding the types of welfare states they want to maintain, though these choices are more constrained than in the golden age.

7

POSTWAR TRADE-UNION ORGANIZATION AND INDUSTRIAL RELATIONS IN TWELVE COUNTRIES

Miriam A. Golden, Michael Wallerstein, and Peter Lange

Ten years ago, when the volume *Order and Conflict in Contemporary Capitalism* (Goldthorpe 1984) was published, conventional academic wisdom regarding the future of trade unions and corporatism in western Europe was optimistic. As numerous contributors to that earlier volume emphasized, systems of industrial relations involving encompassing unions, in which authority was concentrated in either a small number of large industrial unions or in national confederations, had performed remarkably well in the decade after the first oil price shock of 1973. Most contributors to the Goldthorpe volume shared the view articulated by Peter Lange (1984) that unions could be thought of as playing an *n*-person prisoner's dilemma in which decentralized action among organizations resulted in

The data reported here were collected as part of a project funded by the National Science Foundation entitled "Union Centralization among Advanced Industrial Societies." Data collection and research assistance were provided by Allyson Benton, Bronwyn Dylla, David Ellison, Miongsei Kang, Preston Keat, Bernadette Kilroy, Danise Kimball, Amie Kreppel, Brian Lawson, Sydney Mintzer, Jonathan Moses, Stephen Newhouse, and Carolyn Wong at UCLA and Torben Iversen, Brian Loynd, Jessica Rouleau, and Lyle Scruggs at Duke University. The graphics were produced by Allyson Benton, Pia Kaiser, and Stephen Newhouse. Financial support came from the National Science Foundation, SES-9309391 and SES-9108485 to UCLA and SES-9110228 and SBR-9309414 to Duke University. Additional support came from UCLA's Institute of Industrial Relations and the Committee on Research of the Academic Senate, as well as from the Center for German and European Studies at the University of California at Berkeley.

collectively suboptimal outcomes. Unions would accept greater wage restraint collectively, the argument went, but not willingly concede acting
individually. The prisoner's dilemma analogy suggested that the more encompassing the union movement, the greater the concentration among
unions, and the more centralized the authority of the peak associations, the
more likely it was that the collectively optimal cooperative solution could
be obtained. David Cameron (1984), among others, provided support for
this view with evidence showing that corporatism was associated with wage
restraint and low strike rates, as well as with lower inflation and less
unemployment than in noncorporatist OECD countries.

The concern with how the organizational features of trade unionism
affect economic performance and the optimism about the relative merits of
corporatism were premised on an important if often inexplicit assumption:
that unions themselves would remain effective agents for the promotion of
the economic interests of workers. More specifically, it was typically assumed that in the advanced industrial economies, unions would continue
to represent a source of wage pressure which, if not controlled through
political-organizational means, could threaten macroeconomic performance. The powerful and centralized unions characteristic of corporatism
were seen as one end of a continuum, while the other was characterized by
countries in which a relatively small subset of workers was strongly unionized and likely to remain so while the remainder of the work force was
exposed to market forces with relatively little institutional protection. Labor militancy, whether overtly on show or successfully controlled by astute
union leaders, was expected to be a permanent feature in the former group
of countries, buttressed by the full-employment economy believed characteristic of advanced capitalism, while organized workers in the latter group
would also retain market power.

Today, trade unions and corporatist bargaining arrangements appear
much less durable than they did ten years ago. A series of stylized facts
fuels this suspicion. There is a general perception that unions are suffering
from declining membership and influence (Visser 1992). Instead of supporting centralized bargaining, employers aggressively promote the decentralization of wage setting to the level of the firm or even the individual
employee (Katz 1993). Unions have become less unified and more fragmented as workers have grown increasingly heterogeneous in their interests
and identities (Locke and Thelen 1995). Such changes are commonly believed to be occurring across the advanced countries, marking a presumed
crisis of trade unionism and of corporatist bargaining institutions. As a
result, today unions in OECD countries are viewed as either weak and
decentralized, with little power to affect wages and conditions in the labor

market, or as stronger but declining in power and whose ability to affect economic outcomes has been restricted primarily to the firm, industry, and/ or regional levels. Almost no one argues that unions retain the strength and cohesion they often exhibited a few decades ago.

Two explanations for the decline in unions over the past decade dominate current thinking. The first emphasizes the impact of changes in technology in altering workplace relations and occupational structures in ways that are detrimental to the unity of union movements. Gudmund Hernes (1991) and Karl Moene and Michael Wallerstein (1993b), for example, argue that the proliferation of small and highly specialized groups of workers with extraordinary market power has resulted in greater fragmentation and decentralization of unions in the Nordic countries, where collective bargaining used to be especially encompassing and centralized. Wolfgang Streeck (1993) and Jonas Pontusson and Peter Swenson (1996) emphasize the decentralizing effect of the widespread adoption of new production technologies, technologies that place a premium on product differentiation and rapid responses to changes in consumer demand. Peter Lange, Michael Wallerstein, and Miriam Golden (1995) and Geoffrey Garrett and Christopher Way (1995) have pointed to the destabilizing impact of the growing weight of public sector workers in the union movement.

The second main explanation of union decline concerns the impact of increased economic integration, or what has come more generally to be termed "globalization." Melvin Reder and Lloyd Ulman (1993) argue that economic integration has eroded the ability of unions to raise wages above the level that would exist in the absence of unions. As long as unions' ability to "take wages out of competition" stops at national borders while product markets have expanded to include the entire European Union, the room for union-negotiated wage increases is sharply reduced. Such union weakness is only exacerbated by the growth in capital mobility and increasing potential for firms to "exit," or to threaten to "exit," if union demands threaten their competitiveness and profits. Likewise, Dani Rodrik (1996: 2) stresses that because globalization has led to an increased substitutability of unskilled labor, "globalization makes it difficult to sustain the post-war bargain under which workers would receive continued improvements in pay and benefits in return for labor peace and loyalty." In contrast to this view but also in a context of globalization, Wolfgang Streeck and Philippe Schmitter (1991) emphasize the declining room for discretionary macroeconomic policies on the part of national governments in an integrated Europe. Without the ability to manage demand, Schmitter and Streeck argue, governments have little need for union cooperation and unions have little incentive to organize collectively in order to be able to deliver wage restraint for policy concessions. Finally, Timothy McKeown (this volume), echoing the perspective adopted by Rodrik, argues that increasing levels of international trade in the advanced industrial economies have weakened the market power of less skilled workers while potentially increasing that of their more skilled counterparts, a transformation that is bound to affect the largest industrial unions, whose membership largely comprises the less skilled.[1]

What is striking about both these lines of interpretation of union decline is that they imply a *widespread* and *permanent* weakening of unions. The decline of trade unions and corporatist bargaining institutions is viewed as a product of deep and irreversible transformations of the social structures of the advanced industrial economies and of their positioning in the international economy. Globalization, for instance, has become the latest in a series of supposedly impersonal and uncontrollable forces sweeping the advanced countries (and indeed the less developed nations as well) whose effects can only be borne but not circumvented or even very greatly controlled. The requirements for successful economic competition in a new global economy are believed to be largely incompatible with strong and cohesive unions and with centralized collective bargaining.

If this is the case, then we should see exactly what many observers claim is occurring: a process of convergence underway among industrial relations systems of the OECD countries toward the noncorporatist end of the continuum. Yet this view encounters a basic problem: some prominent industrial relations specialists argue that what is most striking in European industrial relations today is the divergence of national experiences and the absence of a general pattern of union decline (Hyman 1994; Traxler 1994, 1995).

Such divergent views about the simple facts of the situation mean that before we can begin to compare the relative explanatory power of different putative causes of union decline and fragmentation and their impact on the conditions that permitted corporatist practices, we need better data on how much has really changed in industrial relations in the past ten years. To date, almost all discussions have been largely anecdotal. The primary purpose of this chapter is to present more systematic information on the extent to which the organizational strength of unions and employers' associations may have actually changed in the past decade.

We summarize data concerning twelve countries: Austria, Britain,

---

[1] The impact of trade with the Third World on the demand for unskilled and semiskilled labor in Europe and North America is subject to a vigorous debate. See Freeman 1995; Richardson 1995, and Wood 1995 for three views.

Canada, Denmark, Finland, France, Germany, Italy, Japan, Norway, Sweden, and the United States. This group includes the most and least corporatist countries in the OECD, as well as the countries with the largest populations.[2] We chart changes in these countries along four dimensions, each of which has often been considered a condition for union strength and corporatist bargaining. First, we summarize changes in union *density*, or the share of the work force belonging to unions. Second, we investigate the extent of union *coverage*, or the share of the work force covered by a union agreement. Third, we present data on changes in union *concentration*, both between union confederations and within union confederations. Fourth, we compare the *authority* held by different levels of union and employer organizations. Finally, we summarize our findings and discuss what can be inferred regarding the nature and sources of change in the institutions of industrial relations and the implications of such changes for future union strength and bargaining practices.

UNION DENSITY

Union density – the proportion of eligible employees who become union members – is usually taken as the first and perhaps most fundamental measure of union strength. This is easily justified. Only in very unusual circumstances is union density an unimportant indicator of the ability of organized labor to attract mass support and of its potential to mobilize workers for industrial action.[3] Trends in density are therefore usually considered significant indicators of the state of trade unionism more generally.

Reinforcing the dominant and relatively pessimistic interpretation of contemporary unionism, Jelle Visser, the OECD's foremost authority on union density (Visser 1989, 1990, 1991), describes recent trends by noting that "in fourteen of the eighteen countries [considered] unionization levels fell in the 1980s" (Visser 1992: 18). Visser's analysis shows that only in Sweden, Finland, Norway, and Canada did aggregate union density rates remain stable or increase between 1980 and 1989. While Visser is careful to note the continuing diversity of unionization rates and trends among countries, his interpretation of the recent period resonates with the more

---

[2] See Golden and Wallerstein 1996 and Wallerstein, Golden, and Lange 1997 for additional data not presented here.

[3] In countries such as Italy and France, where membership is not obligatory and rival union confederations exist, rates of strike participation and rates of participation in elections for union representatives may surpass membership rates by very large amounts, making the latter weaker proxies for union strength than elsewhere.

general sense of union crisis that is often encountered in the comparative literature.

While it is certainly true that in most OECD countries trade unions have not experienced recent growth, examining only the 1980s leads to conclusions that may be unwarranted. In Table 7.1, we present union density rates for our twelve countries since 1950 in five-year intervals. By extending the time span from one to four decades, a more nuanced and qualified interpretation of changes in membership levels emerges. Over the longer postwar period, union density in most of the countries studied has increased and then fallen back, but usually to a level still above that where it began in 1950.[4]

Comparing density rates in 1989 with those that obtained in 1950, we can group countries into two classes: those in which density has increased or remained stable, and those where it has fallen, which we define as a decline of more than 10 percent off the original 1950 value. Over the forty-year period, most of the countries we examine (seven of the twelve) exhibit either stable or increasing rates of union density.[5] Quite substantial increases have occurred in Denmark, Finland, Norway, and Sweden. Perhaps not surprisingly, as Bo Rothstein's work alerted us (1992), three of these are countries in which trade unions control unemployment funds.[6] Although officially employees who suffer job loss need not be union members to receive unemployment insurance, in these countries access to unemployment funds is facilitated by union membership. In only five of the twelve countries – Austria, France, Italy, Japan, and the United States – has density undergone a decline over the postwar era, taking the 1989 value against that from 1950.

As frequently observed in the literature, decline has indeed been more widespread if we examine trends only since 1980. Seven of our twelve countries experienced declines of greater than 10 percent between 1980 and 1989. Undoubtedly decline has multiple causes, including vast ongoing occupational shifts from industry to tertiary employment, where unions typically have more difficulty enrolling members. Indeed, as we will note in greater detail, unionization has recently tended to increase only in those

---

[4] This generalization is not true of Finland or Sweden, where density rose throughout the period, nor is it true of Japan, where it has declined since 1950. The other nine countries experienced increases, and then more recent declines in union membership.

[5] We class Germany and the United Kingdom as cases of stability, since density declined less than 10 percent in both countries (from 34 to 31 percent in Germany and from 41 to 38 percent in the United Kingdom).

[6] A fourth country where unions control unemployment funds is Belgium, which also had high and stable union density throughout the 1980s.

Table 7.1. *Net union density at five-year intervals (1950–1989) and unadjusted coverage (1990) for twelve countries (percentages)*

	Net density									Unadjusted coverage, 1990
	1950	1955	1960	1965	1970	1975	1980	1985	1989	
Austria	57.51	58.39	57.38	56.43	54.86	51.04	50.35	48.43	45.52	71
Canada	32.77	36.09	27.59	25.58	29.05	31.81	33.16	32.83	32.70	38
Denmark	53.30	54.68	60.10	61.32	60.16	68.19	76.34	78.50	74.39	74[c]
Finland	31.47	31.12	32.67	37.62	51.93	65.92	70.35	69.00	71.94	95
France	30.88	19.95	19.57	19.71	21.55	21.61	17.56	15.19	10.15	92[c]
Germany	34.17	34.72	35.01	33.52	32.95	34.61	34.33	32.08	30.77	76
Italy	40.27	33.10	23.05	23.36	33.37	43.57	44.13	36.23	33.53	83
Japan	36.47[a]	35.59	31.34	34.60	34.49	33.61	30.28	27.79	25.36	21[d]
Norway	44.26	46.42	57.66	57.31	55.56	51.47	55.74	54.10	53.84	75[e]
Sweden	66.66	68.62	70.08	64.92	66.18	72.85	78.01	81.26	82.89	83
United Kingdom	40.59	40.90	40.70	40.63	44.65	47.58	48.61	40.47	38.26[b]	47
United States	28.38	31.20	29.35	26.95	25.85	23.11	20.24	17.22	14.76	18

[a] Data from 1953.
[b] Data from 1988.
[c] Data from 1985.
[d] Data from 1989.
[e] Data from 1992.

few countries – found especially in Scandinavia – where union movements have been unusually successful in recruiting white-collar workers. In addition, however, in countries where unions do not administer unemployment insurance, density rates have tended to track labor market conditions, albeit with a lag (see Western 1993 and 1997). By this reasoning, part of the decline that we observe in density rates in the 1980s is a function of sustained weak demand for labor, a view also supported by the analysis undertaken by Peter Lange and Lyle Scruggs (1996). If this is correct, density rates can be expected to recover, at least in part, when and if unemployment rates decline significantly in Europe.[7]

It is worth noting explicitly that the best-known cases of union decline, including the United States, are not representative of more general trends across the countries we study. The United States, like France and Japan, has exhibited a secular decline in membership rates over many decades, a decline clearly independent of fluctuations in the business cycle and short-term changes in labor market conditions. In the United States, as in France and Japan, density rates have dropped steadily over the past decades even when unemployment rates have improved. There is, moreover, evidence for the United States that density is responding at least as much to changes in national public policy as to labor market conditions (Goldfield 1987). But the evidence for our twelve countries shows that trends in unionization rates in the United States should not be taken as representative of trends elsewhere.

Overall, the data on union density suggest three conclusions. First, substantial differences in density trends characterize our twelve countries. There is no uniform pattern of decline even in the period since 1980, even if it is the most common trend since then. Second, even among union movements that have experienced declining density in the past decade, decline, when seen in a longer temporal perspective, often becomes more clearly short-term and hence somewhat less striking. Most countries in our sample have experienced increases and more recently declines in density. If the first did not herald a permanent strengthening of labor movements, neither may the second indicate their permanent weakening. Rather than decrying purported union decline, perhaps we should be looking for the systematic cross-national causes of fluctuations in union membership. Third, density rates, far from converging across countries, remain vastly different and this difference has increased dramatically since 1950. In 1989, density ranged from 15 percent to 83 percent (in the United States

---

[7] For a review of the causes of persistent unemployment in Europe, see Alogoskoufis et al. (1995).

and in Sweden, respectively), whereas density rates in 1950 ranged only from 28 percent to 66 percent (again, in the same two countries). Despite all the recent attention to common technological changes, occupational shifts, and globalization, labor movements in advanced countries are becoming more dissimilar in their abilities to attract members, not more alike.

UNION COVERAGE

Coverage rates refer to the proportion of employees who are covered by collectively bargained contracts.[8] Because many employees who are not union members are nonetheless covered by collectively bargained agreements, the degree of union coverage is a more accurate measure of the extent to which unions affect wage levels in the economy than is the rate of union membership. Substantial declines in union coverage would indicate an erosion of the ability of trade unions to influence wage levels. Stable and high coverage, by contrast, suggests that unions continue to have an important role in wage setting despite whatever declines in membership may have occurred in recent years. Coverage rates have rarely been used as measures of union strength, however, because comparative data have been almost entirely unavailable. Now, Franz Traxler (1994, 1996) has compiled and made available data on collective bargaining coverage rates among selected OECD countries. In Table 7.1, we present figures on coverage for our twelve countries in 1990.

In the 17 countries Traxler examines (of which the twelve studied here are a subset), coverage was (with the exception of the Japanese case) always at least as extensive as unionization, and often a good deal more so (see Traxler 1994; 173, chart 5.1), as observation of the data reported in Table 7.1 corroborates. The latter phenomenon occurs in a variety of ways. In some cases, firms are legally required to pay a collectively bargained wage to all employees, regardless of their union status. In other cases, employers' associations mandate that the firms affiliated with them pay collectively bargained wages to all employees. And in remaining cases, finally, governments may extend the collective agreement to entire industries, for instance, by ministerial decree.

As a result of these various measures, which vary considerably country

---

[8] Although we are really interested in collectively bargained wage contracts, the available data refer only to collectively bargained contracts generally. While some of these probably do not set wages, undoubtedly most do.

by country, coverage in 1990 was very high (greater than 70 percent) in eight of the twelve countries studied here. In the remaining four – Canada, Japan, the United Kingdom, and the United States – unionization rates are modest and extension mechanisms nonexistent. Only this specific combination of variables produces low coverage. All of the continental European countries that we study are, by contrast, characterized by either high union density, extension mechanisms, or both.

We know few studies that have tracked coverage over time. In a recent paper, Simon Milner (1995) presents data that he compiled on union coverage in Britain between 1895 and 1990. Over the course of the twentieth century, Milner finds that coverage has increased from below 10 percent in 1900 to a peak of 73 percent in 1973. For the recent period, Milner finds significant change in the extent of coverage in Britain. Whereas coverage increased in the early 1970s, it declined slightly in the latter part of the decade and then slipped precipitously in the 1980s, falling to its latest estimate of only 47 percent in 1990. This is, indeed, a dramatic and major decline in the extent to which collectively bargained wages are paid to British employees.

Are British findings generalizable? Traxler (1994: 185), surveying existing data on seven of our countries (and four that we do not cover) for the decade from 1980 to 1990, argues that they are not. The decline in coverage in Britain is the most extreme instance of decline that he finds, and decline itself, he shows, has been limited to only a handful of the countries investigated. Coverage rates in the 1980s remained largely stable in Canada, Finland, and Germany, increased in France, and declined in the United States, Japan, and Great Britain. Moreover, the decline in Japan was relatively modest (from 28 to 23 percent). As a result, it seems unlikely that there has been a widespread or general collapse in the ability of unions to negotiate wages for large numbers of nonunion employees.

We can also investigate the relationship between coverage and density visually in order to obtain more information to assess whether union strength is generally declining. Figure 7.1 presents a scatterplot showing the relationship between the degree of unionization in a country in 1989 and its degree of bargaining coverage the next year. Traxler himself, working with a larger sample of countries, found that "there is only a modest positive correlation ($r = 0.41$) between the two rates" (1994: 174). Nevertheless, as inspection of the scatterplot reveals, the relationship between density and coverage is quite clearly positive, especially if one removes the deviant French case. As density rises, so too does coverage. The line that we have fitted shows this quite well.

More careful review of the scatterplot reveals that the variance of cov-

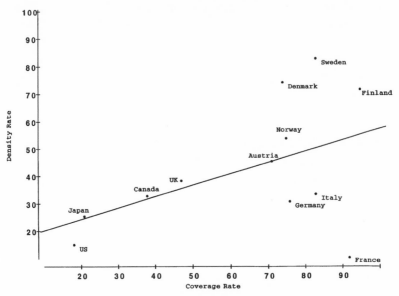

Figure 7.1. Net density versus unadjusted coverage in twelve countries (c. 1990)

erage rates is much greater at low levels of union density than at high levels. Low levels of union membership (say, 40 percent or less) correspond to extremely variable levels of coverage, levels that range from under 20 percent (the U.S. case) to more than 90 percent (the French case, where unionization in 1989 was only 10 percent but coverage an astonishing 92 percent). Low unionization is thus entirely indeterminate in its relation to coverage. However, once union membership exceeds a certain threshold – about 40 percent – coverage rates are uniformly greater than 70 percent.[9]

Particularly striking is the uniformly high level of union coverage in Europe, especially on the continent, and despite the diversity of union density rates. Although more than half of European workers do not belong to unions, relatively few workers on the continent are not covered by a union-negotiated collective agreement, at least among the countries for which we have data. Across Europe, four out of five workers receive wages that reflect the outcome of a process of collective bargaining. In North America and Japan, by contrast, the wages and salaries of most employees are determined in competitive labor markets.

How do these data reflect on the issues of union crisis, its generalizability and its likely duration? While the absence of long-term longitudinal

---

[9] There are only two countries (Germany and France) with density rates below this threshold where coverage exceeds 60 percent.

data do not allow us to examine trends for the entire postwar era, the high rates of coverage that obtain in continental Europe speak against the union crisis hypothesis. Even in 1990, all of the continental countries on which we present data boasted coverage rates above 70 percent. These figures indicate that unions continue to bargain over the wages of most wage and salary earners in continental Europe. This is not to say that unions today bargain as effectively on behalf of their workers as they did earlier, but it does mean that their institutional role in the bargaining process remains largely intact and that they often continue to be able to take a large portion of wages "out of competition."

UNION MONOPOLY AND CONCENTRATION

Many see signs of union decline in aspects of union organization other than membership and the coverage afforded by union contracts. Even if collective bargaining still covers 80 percent of the work force on the continent in western Europe, unions are seen as less unified and therefore less influential than they used to be. The dominant argument in the literature is that unions across the OECD countries have experienced a loss of internal cohesion. Richard Hyman (1994: 11) characterizes the prevalent view: "A further aspect of changing union effectiveness and representativeness concerns the balance between unity and division: the inter- and intra-union dynamics of solidarity and sectionalism. It is a familiar argument that European trade unions in harder political and economic times have displayed a loss of cohesion at best, or at worst have been riven by internecine conflicts."

In this section, we investigate changes in concentration, or the extent to which single organizations of workers organize potential constituents. Concentration indicates the ability of a small number of actors to dominate decision making. In principle, the smaller the number of actors, the easier it is to prevent free riding and therefore to obtain collectively optimal outcomes (Golden 1993).

We distinguish two dimensions of concentration. The first, *interconfederal* concentration, refers to the number of actors and their relative size at the confederal level. We measure interconfederal concentration by the number of peak-level union confederations and the distribution of union members among them. As a summary measure, we also provide figures on the proportion of total union members enrolled in any of the major confederations, where major is defined as any confederation with at least 5 percent of total union membership in at least one year between 1950 and 1989.

Table 7.2. *Interconfederal concentration at five-year intervals (1950–1989) for twelve countries (percentages)*

	1950	1955	1960	1965	1970	1975	1980	1985	1989
Group 1									
Denmark									
LO	84.48	81.98	81.51	78.82	78.37	67.28	69.56	69.72	67.95
FTF	—	10.55	11.84	12.56	13.65	14.92	15.44	15.40	15.40
AC	—	—	—	—	—	3.13	3.88	3.69	4.84
Total	84.48	92.53	93.35	91.38	92.02	85.33	88.88	88.81	88.19
Finland									
SAK/FFC	70.38	66.42	48.83	39.71	68.71	65.80	62.68	59.14	58.55[a]
TVK/TOC	18.12	16.56	23.69	23.61	22.28	21.00	19.72	21.02	19.57
SAJ	—	—	11.43	16.89	—	—	—	—	—
Akava	—	—	—	—	4.48	9.30	9.85	11.99	13.28
STTK	—	—	—	—	2.89	6.20	7.00	7.30	7.75
Total	88.50	82.98	83.96	80.21	90.99	86.80	82.40	80.16	99.15
France									
CGT	75.50	61.83	54.40	49.14	47.70	44.00	37.02	31.19	n.a.
FO	9.07	13.71	15.43	16.30	17.39	16.49	19.71	24.75	n.a.
CFTC	8.68	13.04	16.28	2.40	2.25	2.32	3.11	4.15	n.a.
CFDT	—	—	—	16.16	17.22	19.01	19.77	20.35	n.a.
Total	93.24	88.57	86.11	88.13	87.94	86.45	84.97	86.67	n.a.
Italy									
CGIL	88.99	85.53	75.45	70.03	56.32	54.55	52.43	53.42	52.54
CISL	22.82	27.37	38.68	40.42	34.60	34.66	34.88	34.35	35.32
UIL	n.a.	n.a.	n.a.	n.a.	n.a.	n.a.	15.35	15.20	15.04
Total	111.81[b]	112.9[b]	114.13[b]	110.45[b]	90.92	89.21	102.67[b]	102.96[b]	102.89[b]
Norway									
LO	100.00	100.00	81.93	80.92	78.29	75.23	71.30	67.47	65.00
AF	—	—	—	—	—	8.16	9.80	12.01	16.76
YS	—	—	—	—	—	—	9.27	11.19	14.82
Total	100.00	100.00	81.93	80.92	78.29	83.39	90.36	90.66	96.58
Sweden									
LO	79.00	77.23	75.86	71.61	65.98	62.90	61.00	60.27	58.63
TCO	16.80	18.83	20.10	23.34	28.26	31.20	29.91	32.04	33.03
SACO/SACO-SR	1.43	2.38	2.92	3.96	4.52	5.41	6.45	7.47	8.34
Total	97.22	98.43	98.87	98.91	98.75	99.51	97.36	99.78	100.00
Group 2									
Austria									
OeGB	100.00	100.00	100.00	100.00	100.00	100.00	100.00	100.00	100.00
Germany									
DGB	90.93	84.05	80.54	79.67	81.35	82.10	81.72	80.70	81.56
DBB[c]	2.00	7.12	8.21	8.52	8.74	8.10	8.51	8.32	8.23
DAG[c]	5.13	5.79	5.69	5.76	5.59	5.24	5.13	5.24	5.22
CGB	n.a.	n.a.	2.53	2.71[d]	2.36	2.50	2.99	3.21	3.16
Total	98.06	96.96	96.96	96.66	98.05	97.95	98.35	97.47	98.18
UK									
TUC	84.87	83.23	82.65	84.95	84.11	85.06	94.02	91.08	85.93[e]

Table 7.2. *(continued)*

	1950	1955	1960	1965	1970	1975	1980	1985	1989
Group 3									
Canada									
TLC/CLC	37.78	38.03	76.96	74.34	75.11	70.86	66.79	56.83	56.58
CCL	24.84	22.87	—	—	—	—	—	—	—
CTCC/CNTU	6.59	6.32	6.98	9.45	9.54	6.02	5.37	5.66	5.23
Total	69.21	67.21	76.96	74.34	75.11	70.86	66.79	56.83	61.81
Japan									
JCTU/Sohyo	47.88	49.21	48.88	41.88	36.90	36.32	36.79	35.15	31.95
Rengo	—	—	—	—	—	—	—	—	44.53
JTUC/Domei	—	9.93	12.06	16.35	17.75	18.00	17.48	17.40	—
Churitsuroren	—	—	—	9.69	12.06	10.88	10.98	12.54	—
Zenroren	—	—	—	—	—	—	—	—	—
Total	47.88	49.21	48.88	41.88	36.90	36.32	36.79	35.15	76.49
United States									
AFL/AFL-CIO	57.68	60.36	75.93	79.86	71.60	73.56	68.99	77.12	79.93
CIO	24.78	25.97	—	—	—	—	—	—	—
Total	82.46	86.33	75.93	79.86	71.60	73.56	68.99	77.13	79.93

Notes: n.a. = not available. — = not applicable.
[a]Finnish data for 1989 are from 1988.
[b]See data appendix for a discussion of why Italian totals exceed 100%.
[c]Data from 1951.
[d]Data from 1964.
[e]British data for 1989 are from 1988.

The second dimension of concentration, *intraconfederal* concentration, refers to the number of actors and their relative size within each confederation. Our indicators of intraconfederal concentration are the number of affiliated national unions and the share of members belonging to the largest affiliate and the largest three affiliates. In many cases, measures of interconfederal and intraconfederal concentration have changed in opposite directions over the four decades on which we have data.

As regards interconfederal concentration, our countries divide into three groups, as illustrated by the data reported in Table 7.2. In six of the twelve countries, interconfederal concentration has clearly declined over the postwar period. This is true of Norway, Sweden, Denmark, Finland, France, and Italy. In the four Nordic countries, the confederations are divided along essentially occupational lines. In all four, the main blue-collar confederation has lost ground relative to confederations of white-collar and professional workers. To some extent, this reflects changes in the composition of the labor force. More importantly, the change reflects the sharp increase in union membership among white-collar and professional workers that has occurred in these countries. In France and Italy, the decline of interconfederal concentration is linked to the political decline of the Communist parties of those two countries. In both cases, the relative size of the Communist-allied union confederation has declined throughout the postwar period.

In the second group of countries, comprising Austria, Germany, and the United Kingdom, interconfederal concentration has not changed very much in the past forty years. In Austria, the main confederation's monopoly status is enshrined in law. No other confederation enjoys legal recognition. As in Austria, little change in interconfederal concentration has occurred in the United Kingdom, where the Trades Union Congress (TUC) remains the country's predominant peak association for labor. In Germany, the share of union members in the largest confederation has fallen since 1950, but the decline is small and was arrested part way through the period. No decline in the German confederation's organizational cohesiveness has been observed since 1970.

Finally, there is a third set of countries, comprising the United States, Canada, and Japan, in which interconfederal concentration has increased over the forty years thanks to mergers of rival confederations. In both the United States and Canada, mergers of rival confederations occurred early in the postwar period. Since then, interconfederal concentration has followed divergent paths in the two countries, with membership in unions outside the main confederation declining modestly in the United States but increasing in Canada. In Japan, the merger of rival confederations is quite recent.

There appears to be a relationship between union density and changes in interconfederal concentration. The country in which a merger of rival confederations has occurred in recent years – Japan – is one where union membership has fallen significantly as a share of the labor force.[10] In contrast, in the three countries in our sample where density has increased over time – Denmark, Finland, and Sweden – interconfederal concentration has fallen as the share of membership organized by the largest confederation has declined relative to the whole organized work force. Density has been increasing in these countries as new confederations have successfully enrolled previously unorganized groups of workers. Indeed, the emergence of new, occupationally specific union confederations has probably enhanced the ability of the union movement generally to organize such workers.

[10] The Netherlands is another example of a country where rival confederations have merged and union membership had declined significantly. See Wallerstein, Golden, and Lange 1997, for additional information.

They appear more likely to join an organization tailored to their needs than a general confederation of both blue- and white-collar employees.

In contrast to the diversity of trends we observe in interconfederal concentration, there is a widespread tendency toward increased intraconfederal concentration among the countries in our sample, as illustrated by the data presented in Table 7.3[11] The number of unions affiliated with the main confederation has declined significantly since 1950 in Great Britain and the United States, as well as in the four Nordic countries of Norway, Denmark, Sweden, and Finland. The largest decline in the number of affiliates, measured as a percentage of the number of affiliates in 1950 or 1970, occurred in Great Britain. In 1950, the main British confederation had 186 affiliates, whereas four decades later, it had only 76. Another dramatic case is Denmark, which, like Britain, has historically housed a large number of craft unions. There unions in the main confederation have recently reorganized into five bargaining units. In Germany and Austria, the number of affiliates remains unchanged while the concentration of members in the largest affiliates has increased slightly. Declines in the number of affiliates can also be observed in Italy, although we have data only since 1975. The only countries of our twelve whose major confederations have witnessed increases in the number of affiliated unions since 1950 are Canada (although here the number has been falling since about 1970) and Japan.

Our other measures of intraconfederal concentration – the share of membership held by the largest single and largest three affiliates – likewise show a general tendency to increase across almost all of our countries. Unions have rationalized their organizations by reducing their number of affiliates and concentrating more members in their largest affiliates in all countries except where the number of affiliates was already small at the beginning of the postwar period.

Overall, our data show a common tendency toward greater concentration within confederations but divergent trends with regard to concentration among union confederations. The latter seems systematically related to changes in union density. Where density has fallen, there has been a tendency for concentration to increase, as unions have responded to membership losses with mergers. Where density has risen, there has been a tendency for concentration to decline, as the growth of new members has occurred largely outside the traditionally dominant union organizations. Indeed, we suspect that the ability of organized labor to cope successfully

---

[11] We have been unable to obtain affiliate figures for France; hence Table 7.3 offers data on the other eleven countries only.

Table 7.3. *Intraconfederal concentration (1950–1990) for eleven countries (percentages)*

Country and confederation	1950			1955			1960		
	Number of affiliates	% in largest affiliate	% in largest 3 affiliates	Number of affiliates	% in largest affiliate	% in largest 3 affiliates	Number of affiliates	% in largest affiliate	% in largest 3 affiliates
Austria									
OeGB	16	15.7	39.8	16	17.5	43.6	16	18.3	46.1
Canada									
TLC/CLC	80	8.1	20.0	88	9.1	22.6	107	7.3	18.6
CCL	27	19.9	47.2	27	16.6	42.6	—	—	—
Denmark									
LO	57	36.7	52.5	54	36.1	53.8	53	32.9	55.0
Finland									
SAK	38	16.7	34.6	39	15.1	35.5	25	16.8	46.2
TVK	31	29.2	57.1	23	31.3	67.7	26	28.0	57.2
Germany									
DGB	16	24.8	48.8	16	27.2	51.0	16	28.9	52.4
Italy									
CGIL	n.a.	22.1	45.9	n.a.	23.4	45.3	n.a.	22.7	40.9
CISL	n.a.	21.9	46.5	n.a.	16.6	32.0	n.a.	14.8	28.2
UIL	n.a.	n.a.	n.a.	n.a.	n.a.	n.a.	n.a.	n.a.	n.a.
Japan									
JCTU/Sohyo	32	19.7	47.1	37	18.8	46.2	57	15.8	40.0
Rengo	—	—	—	—	—	—	—	—	—
JTUC/Domei	—	—	—	14	49.3	93.3	23	44.2	82.0
Norway									
LO	39	11.0	31.1	43	11.0	30.8	41	12.7	32.0
AF	n.a.	n.a.	n.a.	n.a.	n.a.	n.a.	n.a.	n.a.	n.a.
YS	n.a.	n.a.	n.a.	n.a.	n.a.	n.a.	n.a.	n.a.	n.a.
Sweden									
LO	44	17.2	32.7	44	17.6	34.6	44	19.2	36.9
TCO	43	22.0	40.9	42	24.5	43.5	37	27.2	46.4
United Kingdom									
TUC	186	15.9	35.2	183	15.3	35.2	183	15.3	35.9
United States									
AFL/AFL-CIO	108	12.8	27.0	137	12.4	29.5	136	7.9	19.9

Notes: n.a. = not available; — = not applicable.

with the occupational shifts away from employment in industry and toward the tertiary sector depends heavily on organizational specialization and hence proliferation.

This latter phenomenon suggests that unions may be caught in a dilemma. The share of the work force in the traditional core of the union

Table 7.3. *(continued)*

1965			1970			1975		
Number of affiliates	% in largest affiliate	% in largest 3 affiliates	Number of affiliates	% in largest affiliate	% in largest 3 affiliates	Number of affiliates	% in largest affiliate	% in largest 3 affiliates
16	18.7	48.4	16	18.6	48.6	16	18.9	48.7
110	9.3	23.1	110	9.2	24.9	113	9.7	25.5
—	—	—	—	—	—	—	—	—
50	30.8	56.5	45	28.7	56.0	40	27.3	55.1
24	24.7	54.2	31	16.2	39.0	28	16.4	38.4
29	25.2	51.2	29	17.6	42.0	23	18.4	40.3
16	30.6	53.7	16	33.1	56.6	16	34.7	57.8
n.a.	15.8	36.6	n.a.	15.3	38.8	24	13.7	37.8
n.a.	12.1	29.3	n.a.	14.2	33.7	41	14.4	33.3
n.a.	n.a.	n.a.	n.a.	n.a.	n.a.	n.a.		
63	18.7	39.0	63	20.9	40.3	64	25.9	46.9
—	—	—	—	—	—			
22	31.6	52.6	26	26.6	47.7	28	22.2	46.4
40	13.6	33.4	35	15.1	36.6	35	16.4	40.0
n.a.	n.a.	n.a.	n.a.	n.a.	n.a.	32	22.5	49.2
n.a.	n.a.	n.a.	n.a.	n.a.	n.a.	n.a.	n.a.	n.a.
38	21.2	41.9	29	22.0	46.3	25	23.7	50.7
32	30.2	48.7	23	28.9	49.0	24	27.7	49.8
172	16.3	36.7	150	16.3	36.9	111	17.9	38.1
130	8.3	19.7	123	6.8	17.8	112	7.4	18.7

movement – blue-collar workers in manufacturing, transportation, mining, and construction – is declining. Those union movements to have responded successfully in organizing the growing share of the work force in white-collar and professional occupations have experienced splits along occupational lines. This is what has occurred in the four Nordic countries. White-collar and professional workers there exhibit a preference to join

Table 7.3 *(continued)*

Country and confederation	1980 Number of affiliates	1980 % in largest affiliate	1980 % in largest 3 affiliates	1985 Number of affiliates	1985 % in largest affiliate	1985 % in largest 3 affiliates	1990 Number of affiliates	1990 % in largest affiliate	1990 % in largest 3 affiliates
Austria									
OeGB	15	20.4	48.7	15	20.8	49.3	15	20.5	49.1
Canada									
TLC/CLC	91	11.0	28.2	96	14.0	34.1	90	16.0	35.9
CCL	—	—	—	—	—	—	—	—	—
Denmark									
LO	33	25.0	56.7	31	22.6	54.7	30	22.7	54.6
Finland									
SAK	29	15.2	40.4	28	17.0	41.1	24	18.8	42.8
TVK	19	21.1	48.6	15	18.4	51.2	15	22.3	50.9
Germany									
DGB	17	33.8	56.7	17	33.1	56.8	16	34.4	58.6
Italy									
CGIL	22	13.0	35.3	19	9.9	27.6	18	8.7	24.5
CISL	38	13.1	31.0	17	10.2	25.4	21	7.2	20.0
UIL	32	11.1	30.0	29	9.2	26.8	29	8.2	24.0
Japan									
JCTU/Sohyo	50	27.6	49.6	50	29.0	51.6	—	—	—
Rengo							81	13.9	32.9
JTUC/Domei	31	21.3	44.5	32	22.8	46.4	—	—	—
Norway									
LO	33	19.2	48.4	34	21.8	49.8	29	25.4	61.6
AF	32	21.8	49.5	36	22.4	49.7	40	19.7	49.8
YS	15	23.9	54.6	15	23.0	56.1	17	18.6	52.5
Sweden									
LO	25	24.2	54.9	24	28.0	57.5	23	28.5	57.8
TCO	21	28.3	54.6	21	23.9	49.3	21	23.7	48.1
United Kingdom									
TUC	109	17.1	35.1	91	15.1	33.9	76	15.1	33.8
United States									
AFL/AFL-CIO	105	7.6	21.2	96	7.6	22.6	89	n.a.	n.a.

their own distinctive confederations rather than those traditionally dominated by blue-collar workers. Conversely, those unions that have preserved
their unity across occupational lines have generally suffered declines in union
density.[12] The main German confederation has been unique in suc-

---

[12] This is very similar to the electoral dilemma faced by socialist parties in western Europe
described by Przeworski and Sprague (1986).

cessfully preventing a significant decline in union density while nonetheless maintaining its dominant organizational position within the German union movement. Not surprisingly, Germany is also exceptional in its degree of stability in the manufacturing work force as a share of the total labor force; that is, occupational shifts have not been as important there as elsewhere.

AUTHORITY IN UNIONS AND EMPLOYERS' ORGANIZATIONS

The authority of different levels of organization – national, industry, and local – in wage negotiations and industrial conflict is a central component of every measure of corporatism. Moreover, the changing roles of union confederations, national unions, and shop floor organizations in collective bargaining and industrial conflicts are central elements of the current debate over the degree to which traditional patterns of industrial relations have been shattered and wage-setting processes decentralized. In this section, we examine the authority of union confederations and national industrial unions, as well as the autonomy of shop floor bodies. We also investigate the authority of peak business associations and national affiliates over their member enterprises.

We distinguish statutory authority from participation in wage determination or the predominant level of wage setting. Statutory authority refers to what lower levels of union organization can or cannot do without the permission of the central confederation as specified in the confederation's constitution or, in a few cases, national law. Participation in wage setting refers to the activities of the confederation during wage negotiations. While the extent of confederal participation in wage setting can change with every bargaining round, statutory authority only changes when the organization's statutes are revised. In this chapter, we present data only on statutory authority, although elsewhere we also investigate the involvement of central confederations in wage setting (see Wallerstein and Golden, forthcoming; Wallerstein, Golden, and Lange, 1997; and Golden and Wallerstein 1996).

Our assessment of the authority of the central confederations and the industry-level union and employer organizations rests on the rules as specified in organizational statutes for a number of related reasons. First, it is simply easier to gather hard evidence of constitutional change than of informal changes of processes and relations among various levels. Fewer inevitably arbitrary judgment calls are required. Second, statutory authority may have a larger impact than is readily visible. If actors in a subordinate position restrict their activities to those that higher levels will not veto, the higher levels may effectively delimit the actions of lower levels even though an actual veto is never observed. However, the gulf between formal and actual authority can be particularly wide at the enterprise level. Where actual practice differs from formal authority at the enterprise level, we report what we believe to be customary practice. Third, many of the more informal changes that occur in authority relations are better captured by our data on confederal involvement in private sector collective bargaining, presented in Golden and Wallerstein (1996) and Wallerstein, Golden, and Lange (1997).

We examine the statutory authority of actors at three levels of union organizations: the peak confederal level, a major national union (typically the leading metalworking or engineering union), and the shop floor organization.[13] As regards national unions, it proved difficult to collect information on how national unions function generally, and we have therefore almost always used the country's national metalworking or engineering federation as emblematic of national trade unionism more generally. This is not because we necessarily believe that these unions are "average," but instead because they often play a pattern-setting role, thereby influencing wage growth throughout the labor force. For the same reason, the metalworkers' or engineers' union is typically the most frequently studied and about which, therefore, most information is publicly available.

Our index of union authority is meant to assess the extent to which each of the three levels wields authority in wage bargaining vis-à-vis the other two. Thus, we have been principally concerned with the extent to which each level maintains independent resources – its own strike fund, its own authority to sign collective agreements, independence in calling and settling disputes – and the degree to which each level controls the selection of officers or influences the wage bargaining of other levels. As a rule, a positive answer indicates a greater degree of authority or autonomy for the level in question, and a negative answer, the reverse.[14]

---

[13] In general, we report on shop floor union organization. However, in Austria and Germany, where works councils are both more important than shop floor union organization and where the former are effectively if informally dominated by the latter, we report on works councils instead.

    In some countries, regional unionism may also play an important role in collective bargaining (this is true, for instance, of Germany, where bargaining is almost all regional in scope), but it is generally so difficult to collect data on regional union organizations that we have omitted this level entirely. For the German case, we have merged the national and regional levels for coding purposes.

[14] A negative answer to the question of whether shop stewards cannot be dismissed or replaced from above indicates that they *can* so be, whereas a positive response indicates shop steward autonomy in this matter.

We have collected parallel data on employers' organizations. The hypothesis that employers have been systematically attacking centralized bargaining and attempting to push collective bargaining down to lower levels could be verified with evidence of devolution of authority within employers' organizations. For employers, we have distinguished only the peaklevel confederation and the national (i.e., sectoral) employers' organizations, since it hardly makes sense to assess the authority of the firm in a freemarket context. At the national level, we have considered the metalworking or engineering sector as representative, as we did for organized labor.

Our results for unions and employers' associations are presented in Tables 7.4 and 7.5 respectively. Among union movements, the data show that most are characterized by shared governance; that is, there are relatively few unions in which a single level exercises uncontested authority. In particular, shop floor union bodies in all the countries considered except the United States and Canada enjoy some notable degree of autonomy in decision making, and thus some potential for independent action.[15]

With this qualification, we can still classify the twelve cases according to the authority of different levels. Peak-level union confederations in Austria, Norway, and Sweden, as well as in Finland until 1971 and Italy until 1968, are the only major confederations in our twelve countries to enjoy very significant statutory authority over lower levels. Not surprisingly, Austria, Norway, and Sweden (and to a lesser extent Finland) are considered classically corporatist cases. The other extreme is found in Japan and to a slightly lesser extent in Italy after 1969, where neither national nor confederal bodies exercise significant authority over shop floor union agents. Canada, Denmark, Finland after 1971, France, Germany, the United Kingdom, and the United States, finally, are all cases where national unions seem to exercise the greatest authority, authority that is, as we have noted, shared with shop floor bodies in all cases except the North American.

Among employers' organizations, the data reported in Table 7.5 show that the peak level exercised substantial authority over national affiliates in

---

[15] It is interesting that shop floor autonomy is lowest in the two countries where collective bargaining is traditionally considered among the most decentralized. This may be less paradoxical than it appears, however, if we consider that higher levels of union organization may require much more authority over enterprise union representatives than where bargaining is more often located at the level of the enterprise itself. Without such authority, superordinate levels would be in danger of allowing bargaining outcomes to occur that they could not control. Where, by contrast, bargaining occurs at higher or on multiple levels, shop floor union representatives can enjoy greater autonomy because their ability to affect outcomes is intrinsically less.

Table 7.4. *Statutory authority in major union confederations and their metalworking affiliates (1950–1992) for twelve countries*

	Austria	Canada	Denmark	Finland 1950–71	Finland 1972–92	F
Peak-level confederation	OeGB	CLC	LO	SAK	SAK	A
Appoints leaders of lower levels	Yes	No	No	No	No	N
Signs own wage agreement	No	No	No	Yes	Yes	N
Has own strike fund	Yes	No	No	Yes	No	N
Veto power over wage agreements signed by affiliates	Yes	No	No	Yes	No	N
Participates in demand formulation and/or bargaining of lower levels	Yes	No	Yes	Yes	No	N
Veto power over strikes by affiliates	Yes	No	Yes	Yes	No	N
National metalworkers, auto workers, or engineers	Metall	CAW/USA	Metall	Metall	Metall	A
Appoints leaders of local or shop stewards	No	No	No	No	No	n
Signs wage agreement without countersignature from above	No	Yes	Yes	Yes	Yes	Y
Can initiate strike action without approval from above	No	Yes	Yes	No	Yes	Y
Has own strike funds	No	Yes	Yes	Yes	Yes	n
Veto power over wage agreements signed by locals	No	Yes	No	Yes	Yes	n
Participates in demand formulation and/or bargaining by lower levels	No	Yes	No	Yes	Yes	n
Veto power over strikes by lower levels	Yes	Yes	Yes	Yes	Yes	n
Shop stewards or work councillors in metalworking	Metall[a]	CAW/USA	Metall	[b]	[b]	[b]
Recognized by union and/or legal statute	Yes	Yes	Yes	Yes	Yes	Y
Are elected rather than appointed from above	Yes	Yes	Yes	Yes	Yes	Y
Cannot be dismissed or replaced from above	Yes	No	No	Yes	Yes	n
Right to strike without approval from above	No	No	No	No	No	Y
Automatically receive strike funds or control own	No	No	No	No	No	N
Right to negotiate local or enterprise wage agreements	Yes	No	Yes	Yes	Yes	Y
Right to bargain without external officials present	Yes	No	Yes	No	No	Y
Sign wage agreements without countersignature from above	Yes	No	Yes	Yes	Yes	Y
Participate in wage bargaining delegation of higher levels	Yes	Yes	No	No	No	n

Note: n.a. = not available.

[a]Information concerns shop stewards generally, but probably also extends to those in metalworking industries.

[b]Information concerns works councillors.

Table 7.4. *(continued)*

Germany	Italy 1950–68	Italy 1969–92	Japan	Norway	Sweden	United Kingdom	United States
DGB	All	All	All	LO	LO	TUC	AFL-CIO
No	Yes	Yes	No	No	No	No	No
No	Yes	No	No	Yes	Yes	No	No
No	No	No	No	Yes	Yes	No	No
No	Yes	No	No	Yes	No	No	No
No	Yes	Yes	No	Yes	Yes	No	No
No		No	No	Yes	Yes	No	No
IG-Metall	All	All	IMF-JC	Felles.	Metall	AUEW/CSEU	UAW/USA
No	n.a.	No	No	No	No	No/Yes	Yes/No
Yes	No	Yes	No	Yes	Yes	No/Yes	Yes
Yes	n.a.	Yes	Yes	No	No	Yes/Yes	Yes
Yes	No	No	No	Yes	Yes	Yes/No	Yes
No	n.a.	No	No	No	Yes	No/Yes	Yes
No	n.a.	Yes	Yes	Yes	Yes	Yes/—	Yes
Yes	n.a.	No	No	Yes	Yes	Yes/No	Yes
IG-Metall[a]	[b]	All	[b]	[b]	[b]	Engineering	UAW/USA
Yes	No	Yes	Yes	Yes	Yes	Yes	Yes
Yes	No	Yes	Yes	Yes	Yes	Yes	Yes
Yes	No	No	Yes	Yes	Yes	No	No
No	n.a.	Yes	Yes	No	No	No	No
No	No	No	Yes	No	No	No	Yes
Yes	No	Yes	Yes	Yes	Yes	Yes	No
Yes	No	Yes	Yes	Yes	Yes	Yes	No
Yes	No	Yes	Yes	Yes	Yes	No	No
No	No	Yes	n.a.	No	No	No	Yes

Table 7.5. *Statutory authority in central employer organizations and their metalworking affiliates (1950–1990) for ten countries*

Employers' organizations	Austria	Denmark	Finland	France
Peak-level confederation	BWK	DA	STK	ONPF
Appoints officials of lower levels	No	No	No	No
Signs own wage agreement	No	No	Yes	No
Has own strike funds	No	Yes	Yes	No
Veto power over wage agreements signed by affiliates	No	Yes	No	No
Participates in demand formulation and/or bargaining of lower levels	Yes	Yes	Yes	No
Veto power over lockouts by affiliates	No	Yes	Yes	No
Metalworking or engineering industry federation	All	Unknown	FIMET	UMM
Signs wage agreement without countersignature from above	Yes	n.a.	Yes	Yes
Can initiate lockout without permission from above	Yes	n.a.	No	Yes
Has own strike funds	Some	n.a.	Yes	Yes
Veto power over wage agreements signed by members	No	n.a.	No	No
Participates in demand formulation and/or bargaining at lower levels	No	n.a.	No	No
Veto power over lockouts by members	Yes	n.a.	Yes	No

Notes: Data on Austria reflect industry-level employers' associations, not metalworking in particular. n.a. = not available. — = not applicable.
[a]1950–1962/1963–1992.
[b]1971+.
[c]1950–1989/1990–1992.
[d]1950–1988/1989+.

Table 7.5. *(continued)*

Germany	Italy	Japan	Norway	Sweden	United Kingdom
BDA	Confindustria[a]	Nikkeiren	NAF/NHO	SAF[c]	CBI
No	n.a./No	No	No	No/No	No
No	n.a./No	No	Yes	Yes/No	No
No	n.a./No	No	Yes	Yes/Yes	No
No	Yes/No	No	Yes	Yes/Yes	No
Yes	n.a./Yes	Yes	Yes	Yes/Yes	No
No	n.a./No	No	Yes	Yes/Yes	No
All	Federmeccanica[b]	None	TBL	VF	EEF[d]
Yes	n.a.	—	Yes	Yes	Yes/No
Yes	n.a.	—	No	No	Yes/n.a.
Yes	No	—	No	Yes	Yes/No
No	No	—	No	Yes	No/No
No	Yes	—	Yes	Yes	No/No
Yes	No	—	Yes	Yes	Yes/No

Denmark, Finland, Italy until 1962 (although the lack of complete information must temper this assessment somewhat), Norway, and Sweden until 1990. Peak-level organizations in Austria, France, Germany, post-1963 Italy, Japan, and the United Kingdom held very little authority over affiliates. In Canada and the United States, finally, employers are not organized into peak-level associations, and these countries are thus absent from the table.

These data suggest two interesting conclusions. First, the extent of authority over lower levels enjoyed by the central organizations of labor and of business in any particular country can be quite different. For instance, the classically corporatist countries of Austria, Denmark, Germany, Norway, Sweden, and Finland exhibit high levels of statutory authority on either the employers' or the union side, but not necessarily both. This is somewhat surprising, given that one might have expected the two kinds of organizations to mirror each other organizationally in order to be equally effective in coordinating collective bargaining.

One reason they do not, we suspect, speaks to our second conclusion. There is simply much less of a relationship than might have been anticipated between the extent to which central organizations exercise statutory authority over lower levels and the extent to which they actively intervene in and control the practice of collective bargaining from year to year. Indeed, substantial discrepancies often obtain, as we detail elsewhere (Wallerstein, Golden, and Lange, 1997). In Austria, for instance, the central organization of labor exercises relatively significant authority over lower levels, but collective bargaining nonetheless occurs exclusively at the industry level. The Finnish central confederation, by contrast, exercises little statutory authority over its affiliates but nonetheless bargains regularly on their behalf. In France, likewise, the central confederations enjoy almost no statutory authority, but their role in collective bargaining has been very extensive thanks to numerous important agreements they have signed regulating benefits and working conditions.

It is surprising that statutory authority and the extent of central intervention in wage setting do not necessarily coincide. The economic effects of these two different ways of centralizing industrial relations may be more or less equivalent, although that remains an empirical question deserving further research. Nonetheless, it would not necessarily be accurate to infer that central organizations directly intervene in collective bargaining just because they exercise a high degree of statutory authority, just as it would be inaccurate to infer that they enjoy significant authority on paper just because they play important roles in the bargaining process. These two indicators do not necessarily go together, implying that collecting separate data on each may be required to assess the effects of centralization more generally on economic outcomes.

Our data on statutory authority thus show large variations among countries. However, there is almost no variation over time. In most countries, the authority relations that were established after World War II (if not earlier) endure even today. The major exceptions on the union side are Italy and Finland, which witnessed changes in union authority relations in the 1960s and 1970s. In Italy, these entailed a decentralization of confederal authority, and the concomitant empowerment of shop floor union organizations. In Finland, whereas the statutory changes also weakened the authority of the main confederation, the national industrial unions were the main beneficiaries rather than shop floor organizations. Moreover, the Finnish changes were part of the process of unifying rival confederations and establishing a centralized system of wage negotiations that would serve as a national framework for subsequent industry-level agreements. The only other exceptions to the general pattern of little change is the weakening of the authority of the British engineering federation of employers in the late 1980s and of the Swedish employers' confederation in 1982 and again in 1990, when the organization's peak bargaining unit was dismantled.

The general absence of change in patterns of internal authority in trade unions and employers' organizations in the postwar period is quite remarkable. If there is a crisis of unions, they are certainly not responding by undertaking significant statutory changes, or by adapting union statutes to the powerful external economic forces presumably at work. Authority relations also show little reflection of the changes in inter- and intraconfederal concentration discussed earlier. Employers, moreover, are generally not following the lead offered by British and Swedish organizations and devolving authority to lower levels, thereby rendering peak-level offices relatively ineffective and forcing unions to adjust accordingly.

Of course, as we have already suggested, these findings may tell us little about changes underway in collective bargaining. At least in some countries, notably Sweden and Britain, bargaining became significantly less centralized in the 1980s. While this is confirmed by the shifts in authority relations undertaken by employers over their affiliates, we suspect that in other countries, bargaining may devolve substantially even in the absence of statutory alterations.[16] Suffice it to say here, however, that diversity in formal authority remains as great as it has been historically and few changes are to be noted. This, in turn, means that in unions in which the formal authority of the center was considerable in the past, it remains so today.

CONCLUSION

In this chapter, we have examined changes in industrial relations along the dimensions of union membership; union coverage; concentration, both in-

---

[16] In Italy, for instance, a dramatic decline in the level of central intervention in collective bargaining occurred just at the end of our data set (in 1992), when the country's wage indexation system was dismantled. This is not reflected, to the best of our knowledge, in changes in the extent of statutory authority on either the employers' or union side, however.

terconfederal and intraconfederal; and statutory authority, both for employers and for unions. Our main findings are summarized here.

Union membership as a share of the work force has declined in most
countries in our sample since 1980, in some cases dramatically. Nevertheless, this trend must be qualified in two ways. First, in the countries where
the unions provide unemployment insurance – Denmark, Sweden, and
Finland – union density continued to increase in the 1980s. Second, the
trend of declining membership disappears in some countries if one begins
with a baseline of 1950 or 1970 rather than 1980. A long-term decline in
union membership over most of the postwar period is true in only a minority of countries, albeit a minority that contains a majority of the work
force of our sample.

In Great Britain, Japan, and the United States, the coverage of collective agreements appears to have declined as union membership has declined. In continental Europe, by contrast, coverage remains high and
stable. In spite of the decline in union membership, almost all western
European workers, outside of Britain, work for wages that were negotiated
by a trade union.

Two trends are evident with regard to interconfederal concentration.
Among the Nordic countries, which have some of the highest rates of
union density in the world, interconfederal concentration has declined as
the growth of unions has occurred largely outside the traditional, blue-
collar, socialist confederations. Among some of the countries with the
greatest decline in union membership, such as Japan, interconfederal concentration has increased as previously rival confederations have united.
With regard to intraconfederal concentration, there is a nearly universal
trend to reducing the number of affiliates except in cases where this number was already quite low.

The lack of change in statutory authority in most countries is quite
notable. By and large, the statutory authority established during the interwar years or immediately after World War II has remained unchanged,
even, in some countries, in spite of big changes in the organizational
structure of the confederations or the practice of wage negotiations. Moreover, the few changes that did occur in the postwar period in trade unions
were concentrated in the 1960s and early 1970s. There has been little
change in authority relations in response to the more recent demands for
greater decentralization that has come from employers in some, albeit not
all, countries, even among employers' associations themselves.

Overall, there are more diversity and fewer common trends occurring
across the OECD nations than most scholars have assumed. Some features
of union movements in some countries have remained largely unchanged,

whereas others have changed but not in predictably similar ways. Thus, our data support the view that industrial relations institutions and trade unions have by and large proved quite resilient in the face of considerable domestic and international economic pressures in the past two decades. In only two of the twelve countries we investigate, Britain and the United States, is there broad and conclusive evidence of a dramatic decline in the influence of unions: secular declines in membership, a sharp falloff in coverage, and efforts to merge unions in order to respond to growing weakness. These are the only countries where organized labor exhibits decline along multiple indicators. And in these countries, we suspect that government policy and politics played at least as important a role as the market in promoting such catastrophic collapse.

Were the proponents of the union crisis hypothesis correct, we might expect to have seen substantial changes in authority relations within both labor movements and employers' organizations within the past decade. With the decentralization of bargaining purportedly underway, one would have expected that employers' organizations would have devolved authority to lower levels. We have found no evidence to support this claim, however, except in Britain and Sweden.

These findings do not appear consistent with arguments that changes in domestic sociooccupational structures or in international economic relationships are (already) creating a crisis in trade unions across the advanced industrial countries. Yet the conclusion that unions have proved more resilient than commonly believed may be premature. There are three possible lines of argument supporting such skepticism.

First, our categories may be too crude to pick up the relevant changes underway; that is, perhaps beneath the surface of seeming institutional resilience as measured by the cross-national indicators we have gathered, extensive de facto changes have been occurring in the interactions among levels of unions and employers' organizations over wage bargaining.

Second and related, we have not included direct measures of the centralization of wage setting in this chapter. The level of collective bargaining can change even when the statutory authority of the different organizations remains constant. Thus, perhaps the formal resilience of the institutional trappings of centralization hides substantial bargaining decentralization. Sweden is the most visible illustration of such a possibility. There, a clear decentralization of wage setting has occurred since 1983 with no change in the statutory authority of the union confederation (although changes have occurred in the statutory authority of the employers' confederation). Yet we know from other work that significant changes in the actual practice of wage setting is far from universal. Sweden and Britain, in this regard, represent exceptions rather than the rule (Golden and Wallerstein 1996; Wallerstein, Golden, and Lange 1997).

Finally, it is possible that the changes anticipated have yet to come. While we cannot exclude such a possibility, we nonetheless remain impressed by the relative absence of change in trade-union organization and industrial relations systems despite more than two decades of apparent pressures for such changes. This suggests that possibly the pressures working against trade unions and preexisting patterns of collective bargaining have been overstated.

Underlying each of these doubts about our preliminary conclusions is a more general criticism: that what is being measured does not indicate the extent of union strength, the ability of unions effectively to promote the interests of their members and workers more generally, or the current and future state of corporatist practices. In other words, skeptics would argue that beneath the surface of relative stability on some of the dimensions we examine and relative divergence on others, there is actually a convergence toward unions that are weaker, more divided, and more decentralized. Obviously, we cannot counter such skepticism with data, for we do not have it, nor do they. Nonetheless, some concluding observations can be offered.

First, the lack of a uniform pattern of union decline by virtually any available measure causes us to be skeptical of *all* general explanations for *why* unions are declining. General explanations seem to explain too much. Only in terms of recent membership trends is union decline widespread, and here the evidence points as much to mass unemployment as to domestic and international structural changes as the underlying cause (Western 1993, 1997).

Second, on all other dimensions that we examine, significant change is limited to a minority of countries. Only the United States and the United Kingdom have witnessed union decline along multiple dimensions. These two cases both point to the importance of government policy. The United States and the United Kingdom are the only countries in our sample where conservative governments actively encouraged employers to engage in a frontal attack on union power. The rapidity of union decline in these two countries is a stark reminder of the vulnerability of unions to political attack, but it says little about the vulnerability of unions to occupational change or international economic transformations.

This brings us to our final point. In the majority of the countries we have studied, unions have retained most of the *institutionally based* capacities for the defense of worker interests that they had prior to the 1980s. Indications of union weakness, such as declining union density since 1980, must be weighed against indications of continuing union strength, such as the high levels of union coverage in continental Europe. The continued authority of central confederations, where they enjoyed such authority earlier, is more evident in the data than a trend toward greater decentralization, except in Sweden and Britain. The current weakness of unions appears, in most countries, to be more a product of sustained unemployment (and occasional political assault) than an instance of institutional decay.

If there is little evidence of institutional change in most countries, that may be because existing institutions have important benefits for employers and governments as well as for unions. Interpretations stressing the apparent weakening of organized labor and trade unionism rest on the implicit assumption that existing institutional arrangements embody union successes, successes that had been gained at the expense of and in opposition to employers. Such a view underlies the widespread belief that employers would dismantle corporatist institutions as soon as possible – that is, once the economic tide turned against labor. But what if these very institutions – including those providing high coverage, relatively cohesive union organization, and relatively strong central authority – embody compromises between labor and capital, compromises from which both parties benefit? If this is so, then it is much less surprising that industrial relations systems have been weathering the economic turmoil of the post – oil-shock decades with such little substantial change.

DATA SOURCES

TABLE 7.1: NET UNION DENSITY

Except for Japan, membership data refer to union members who are neither retired nor self-employed. Data for Japan formally refer to total union membership (i.e., they include retired and self-employed). However, there should be no difference between net and total Japanese union membership, since the retired and self-employed are not allowed to join unions there.

All data were drawn from Jelle Visser, "Trade Union Membership Database" (unpublished data base, Department of Sociology, University of Amsterdam, 1992), heretofore referred to as the 1992 Visser data base. We are grateful to Visser for having made the data available to us, and for allowing us to reprint it here.

The deflator used in constructing the figures is the dependent labor force, also drawn from the Visser data base. Visser's data, in turn, were largely drawn from the OECD.

TABLES 7.2 AND 7.3: INTERCONFEDERAL AND INTRACONFEDERAL CONCENTRATION

Data on membership in individual union confederations and their affiliates were collected from individual country sources. Most confederations do not make separate figures available on the number of retired members, and membership in individual confederations therefore includes pensioners (except for organizations that do not allow persons who retire to maintain their membership). For Table 7.2, the deflator used is thus total union membership (i.e., membership including retired and self-employed members), drawn from the 1992 Visser data base. (Note that the deflator is thus not identical to the membership data reported in Table 7.1.)

We have included in our analyses of interconfederal concentration only those confederations on which it proved possible to collect relatively complete and accurate annual data. As a result, the table omits specifically listing very tiny confederations (those with less than 5 percent of total union membership in at least one year) as well as membership in unions unaffiliated with any confederation. The difference between the proportion of union members in the major confederations that are listed by name and total union membership thus reflects membership in very minor confederations and unaffiliated unions.

Sources for figures on individual confederations and their affiliates are listed below by country.

Austria

ÖGB *Tätigkeitsbericht* and the *Wirtschafts-und Sozialstatistisches Taschenbuch*.

Canada

Confederal membership for the period 1960–1990 from David J. Arrowsmith, *Canada's Trade Unions: An Information Manual* (Kingston, Ontario: Industrial Relations Centre, Queen's University, 1992). For 1950–1955, data were drawn from Bureau of Labour Information, *Directory of Labour Organizations in Canada* (Canada: Minister of Supply and Services, various years), which was also the source for all data on affiliates.

Denmark

Statistisk årbog, various years. Data on unaffiliated white-collar unions are not included in the official statistics until 1975. In addition, the number of affiliates of the Danish LO does not include affiliates too small to be listed in the statistical yearbook (affiliates with less than 300 or 500 members, depending on the year).

Finland

Suomenon tilastollinen vuosikirja, various years. In the schism that led to the formation of the rival SAJ from 1960–1969, some SAK affiliates left the SAK to join the SAJ while other affiliates split in two. The data in Table 7.3 refer to the SAK alone.

France

Confederal membership from Jelle Visser, *European Trade Unions in Figures* (Deventer, Netherlands: Kluwer Law and Taxation Publishers, 1989).

Germany

Statistisches Jahrbuch, and for 1950, from Walter Müller-Jentsch, *Basisdaten der industriellen Beziehungen* (Frankfurt am Main: Campus, 1989). The *Statistisches Jahrbuch*, as of 1956, notes explicitly that it does not include all professional organizations. As of 1991, figures include both East and West Germany, since the *Statistisches Jahrbuch* does not provide disaggregated figures. We have assumed that DHV figures are included in those for the CGB as of 1959. Data for the CGB for 1959–1985 are from Visser, *European Trade Unions in Figures*, for 1986–1987 from Müller-Jentsch, *Basisdaten der industriellen Beziehungen*; 1988–1992 from the *Statistisches Jahrbuch*. Data for the DAG and DBB in 1950 from Visser, *European Trade Unions in Figures*. The data are actually from 1951 (there are no 1950 figures available). The CGB figure for 1965 is likewise from 1964. Data on the DHV for 1950–1952 from Visser, *European Trade Unions in Figures*, and for 1953–1958 from the *Statistisches Jahrbuch*. Data for the DGB and its affiliates for 1950 from Müller-Jentsch, *Basisdaten der industriellen Beziehungen*.

Italy

Confederal figures for the CGIL, CISL, and UIL for 1950–1976 from Guido Romagnoli, ed., *La sindacalizzazione tra ideologia e pratica: il caso italiano 1950/1970*, vol. 2 (Rome: Edizione Lavoro, 1990). Data on membership in the UIL is unavailable until 1977. Confederal figures for the period 1977–1990 from CESOS, *Le relazione sindacale in Italia* (Rome: Edizione Lavoro, various years). Membership in CISL affiliates for 1970 from Romagnoli 1990, tables 3.1–3.12. Membership in CISL affiliates and number of affiliates for 1975 and 1980 courtesy of CISL, Rome. Membership in CGIL affiliates for 1970 and 1975 from Romagnoli 1990, tables 3.1–3.12. Membership in CGIL affiliates and number of affiliates for 1980 from Dipartimento Organizzazione della Cgil Nazionale, *CGIL anni '80: l'evoluzione delle strutture organizzative* (Rome: Editrice Sindacale Italiana, 1981), pp. 386–387. Affiliate data for the UIL for 1980 from UIL, Servizio Organizzazione. Data on affiliates for all confederations for 1985 from CESOS, *Le relazione sindacali in Italia: rapporto 1985/86* (Rome: Edizione Lavoro, 1987).

Japan

Data on affiliates in 1970 from *Japan Labor Bulletin* ("Directory of Major Trade Unions in Japan"), various years. All other membership figures, including affiliate data prior to 1970, are drawn from the *Year Book of Labour Statistics*, various years.

There is a break in the series for total union membership as of 1953, when figures first include members who are not likewise affiliated with a "unit" union. Prior to 1953, this type of "direct affiliation" was not included in the statistics.

Norway

Statistisk årbok, various years.

Sweden

Statistisk årsbok, för Sverige, various years.

United Kingdom

Membership in the TUC, number of affiliates, and membership in affiliates from the *Report of the Annual Trades Union Congress* (London: TUC, various years).

United States

Figures for the AFL, the CIO, and the AFL-CIO from 1950 through 1983 are from Leo Troy and Neil Sheflin, *U.S. Union Sourcebook: Membership, Finances, Structure, Directory* (West Orange, N.J.: Industrial Relations and Information Services, 1985). Data covering later years are from the *Directory of U.S. Labor Organizations*.

TABLES 7.4 AND 7.5: STATUTORY AUTHORITY IN UNIONS AND EMPLOYERS' ORGANIZATIONS

The data presented in these tables were compiled from a series of country code books assembled by the authors. The information was gathered initially by research assistants, who consulted available secondary sources in both English and the country language, as well as through questionnaires sent to union and employer organizations. The actual coding was undertaken by the authors. Code books are available from the authors upon request.

FIGURE 7.1: UNION COVERAGE AND DENSITY

Except for Italy, all data on unadjusted coverage rates are from Franz Traxler, "Collective Bargaining: Levels and Coverage," in OECD, *Employment Outlook*, July 1994 (Paris: OECD), 167–194, or Franz Traxler, "Collective Bargaining and Industrial Change; A Case of Disorganization? A Comparative Analysis of 18 OECD Countries," paper presented at the 1996 annual meeting of the American Political Science Association, San Francisco, August 29–September 1. In cases where Traxler provides different figures in 1996 from those published in 1994, we used the later figures.

To calculate the Italian unadjusted coverage rate, we took the size of the total work force and subtracted the self-employed, the unemployed, and managerial personnel, using government figures available in Pietro Ichino, *Il lavoro e il mercato. Per un diritto del lavoro maggiorenne* (Milan: Mondadori: 1996), 14. This resulted in a figure that represented the number of regularly and irregularly employed wage and salary workers. Given Italy's extension laws, we assumed that all regularly employed dependent wage and salary earners were covered by collective agreements. The coverage rate is thus the percentage of regularly and irregularly employed who are covered by agreements.

Traxler distinguishes what he calls the unadjusted and the adjusted coverage rates. The unadjusted coverage rate is the proportion of employees covered by a collective agreement in relation to the total number of employees in a country, regardless of whether they enjoy bargaining rights. The adjusted coverage rate takes as the deflator only those employees who legally enjoy the right to bargain. In most cases where there is a difference, it is because public employees (or certain groups of them) are legally prohibited from collective bargaining. We have chosen to work with the unadjusted coverage rate because it more nearly captures the extent to which collective agreements regulate the terms of employment throughout the economy. Laws prohibiting collective bargaining are, like laws extending agreements to firms and employees even when they fail to subscribe to such agreements, endogenous to the concept of coverage.

The data on density are the same as those reported for 1989 in Table 7.1.

8

SOCIAL DEMOCRATIC LABOR MARKET INSTITUTIONS: A RETROSPECTIVE ANALYSIS

Karl Ove Moene and Michael Wallerstein

The golden age of social democracy in western Europe in terms of both political prominence and economic performance might be dated as beginning in 1966, when the social democrats entered government in West Germany for the first time since 1930, and ending in 1974–1975, with the first serious slump of the postwar period. The high point of social democracy in terms of its academic reputation, however, was just beginning in 1974. During the 1960s and early 1970s, all of western Europe experienced steady growth and low levels of unemployment. Only after the first oil shock did dramatic cross-national differences in macroeconomic performance appear. In comparison to the steady rise of unemployment within the European Community in the late 1970s and 1980s, the maintenance of full employment in the European Free Trade Association (EFTA) countries – Norway, Sweden, Finland, Austria, and Switzerland – was striking. If Switzerland is removed from the list of good performers on the

We thank Gøsta Esping-Andersen, Peter Lange, John Stephens, Frederik Wulfsberg, and an anonymous reviewer for their comments. An earlier paper covering many of the same topics was presented at the conference on "The Politics and Political Economy of Contemporary Capitalism," University of North Carolina at Chapel Hill, September 9–11, 1994, and later published as "How Social Democracy Worked: Labor Market Institutions," in *Politics and Society* 23 (1995): 185–211. Financial support from the Norwegian Council of Research is gratefully acknowledged.

grounds that the Swiss maintained full employment by expelling guest workers, the correlation between any reasonable measure of social democratic strength and macroeconomic permanence was almost perfect.[1] If one adds the impressive achievements in terms of comprehensive social insurance and, in Norway and Sweden, the extraordinary reduction of wage inequalities, the academic respect that social democracy enjoyed is easy to understand.

By the end of the 1980s, however, it was clear that a general retreat from social democratic policies and institutions had occurred throughout northern Europe. In Sweden, twenty-seven consecutive years of centralized bargaining came to an end in 1983 when a separate agreement was signed in the metalworking sector (Lange, Golden, and Wallerstein, this volume). Deregulation of housing and financial markets was promoted by socialist as well as bourgeois governments. The most dramatic change, however, was the rise of unemployment. Since 1988 in Norway and 1990 in Sweden and Finland, unemployment rates have risen sharply. In Sweden and Finland, the decline of production and employment in the early 1990s was worse than the decline that occurred during the 1930s (Rødseth 1994).[2] There is no longer any difference between average unemployment in the Nordic countries and unemployment in the rest of Europe.

Albert Hirschman once proposed what he called a fundamental theorem of social science that "as soon as a social phenomenon has been fully explained by a variety of converging approaches and is therefore understood in its majestic inevitability and perhaps even performance, it vanishes" (1979: 98). Similarly, it seems that just as scholars were beginning to appreciate and understand how social democratic institutions worked in the Nordic countries, social democracy was beginning to vanish. Nevertheless, even if social democracy is in decline in practice, the social democratic goals of reducing inequality and insecurity while promoting growth and employment remain politically salient. While the collapse of the political consensus in support of social democratic institutions and policies in the Nordic countries reveals a fragility that was not evident during social democracy's golden age, it may also blind us to the earlier successes the policies enjoyed.

In this chapter we address the performance of the labor market institutions and policies that made Nordic social democracy distinctive. In

---

[1] Switzerland experienced the greatest decline in employment in western Europe in the late 1970s and early 1980s (Rowthorn 1992).

[2] Because of active labor market policies and unemployment insurance, the economic hardship caused by the rise of unemployment in the 1990s is much less than in the 1930s.

particular we discuss centralized wage-setting, the egalitarian wage policy known as solidaristic bargaining, active labor market policies, and full employment. In each case, we attempt to describe how the policy worked and offer an explanation of the policy's decline.

It should be noted that our discussion of the decline of social democracy is limited in two ways. First, we only discuss social democratic labor market institutions. Social democracy, conceived here as a particular set of policies and institutions, was much broader than the labor market. In particular, we do not discuss the character of welfare policies in the Nordic countries, although such policies are proving to be the most durable policies implemented by social democratic governments.[3]

Second, our discussion is focused on the central policies and institutions adopted in the Nordic countries. In fact, only Norway and Sweden adopted all of the policies we discuss. Other countries commonly called social democratic adopted some but not all. Denmark was as committed to an egalitarian wage policy as Norway and Sweden, but not to full employment. Finland and Austria were broadly similar to Norway and Sweden in terms of centralized wage setting (or, in the Austrian case, central control over wage setting) and maintenance of full employment, but dissimilar in terms of wage equality. Moreover, most continental western European countries have centralized wage setting and an egalitarian wage distribution in comparison with Great Britain or the United States. In addition, unemployment is a major economic problem in Europe as a whole. Thus, the discussion of wage compression and the persistence of high unemployment apply to most countries in western Europe.

CENTRALIZED WAGE SETTING

Industrial relations in the Nordic countries are often given the label of "corporatist." But corporatism is a particularly bad choice of word to describe the Nordic system of centralized wage setting, since corporatism has connotations of anticompetitive practices and trade protection, not to mention fascism. Even pro-union books like Richard Freeman and James Medoff's *What Do Unions Do?* presume that the exercise of monopoly power is one of the main functions of unions.[4] Most economists think

---

[3] On the difficulties of the welfare state in the Nordic countries, see Stephens, Huber, and Ray, this volume.

[4] *What Do Unions Do?* is pro-union because Freeman and Medoff argue that the exercise of monopoly power is not the only thing unions do. In particular, Freeman and Medoff

that, in the long run, the rents that exist in the absence of monopoly power are relatively small. A union can only raise the average wage significantly if the firm has some monopoly power, if the union is able to raise the wages paid by all producers in the industry, or if the unionized firms obtain some form of government protection against producers with lower labor costs.

Yet, the Nordic variety of corporatism was associated not with protectionism and monopolistic pricing, but with free trade and the subsequent need to remain competitive. In Norway, Sweden, and Denmark, the leading proponents of the centralization of private sector wage bargaining at the national level were not the unions but the employers for the straightforward reason that centralization helped restrain wage growth. This is not to say that the unions were irrelevant. The centralization of bargaining remained limited in Denmark relative to Norway and Sweden because the single largest union, the union of unskilled and semiskilled workers, refused to give up its autonomy (Due, Madsen, Jensen, and Peterson, 1994). Centralized bargaining required support from both sides to succeed.

The common understanding of why centralization at the national level promotes wage restraint is in terms of a collective action problem among unions. The general theoretical argument is that there are important externalities in wage setting whereby the wage gains for one group of workers lower the welfare of other groups of workers. In the words of an influential OECD report from the 1970s: "unless wage bargaining is highly centralized, individual unions can rationally hope that an improvement in their real wages can be achieved at the expense of profits and hence employment elsewhere in the economy" (1977: 159). The externalities may be due to the effect of wage increases on consumer prices (Calmfors and Driffill 1988), on the cost of complementary inputs in production (Wallerstein 1990), or on the likelihood that unemployed workers can find new jobs (Layard, Nickell, and Jackman 1991). A bargaining system that enables such externalities to be internalized by the wage setters, the argument goes, will result in lower wages and higher employment.[5]

argue that unions also allow workers to express their preferences in the labor market in a manner that is superior, in some instances, to the way that preferences are revealed in workers' choice of jobs.

[5] Some scholars who accept the presence of externalities in wage setting in an economy with many unions regard centralized bargaining at the national level as a second best arrangement, with purely plant-level bargaining or a nonunion labor market being the first best. Thus, Calmfors and Driffill (1988) argue that the relationship between centralization and macroeconomic performance is U-shaped since, in their view, very decentral-

The externality most closely associated with the initial steps in the establishment of centralized bargaining in the Nordic countries in the 1930s and 1940s, however, was none of these possibilities but rather the spillover of wages from the nontraded-goods sector to the traded-goods sector, as the historical investigations of Peter Swenson (1989, 1991) have revealed. In both Norway and Sweden, the effect of centralization was to limit the influence of militant unions in the nontraded sector, primarily construction workers in the 1930s, and allow the wages of all to be governed by the ability to pay of employers in industries exposed to international competition.[6] Construction workers were the target in both Sweden and Norway because they were highly paid, militant, and sheltered from foreign competition. When foreign demand collapsed in the 1930s, metalworkers accepted large wage reductions in order to stem the decline of employment. Construction workers came under less pressure, in part because of government policy. In both Norway and Sweden, social democratic governments responded to the crisis by increasing government spending on housing. Since construction workers were employed in the export sector as well as in home construction, higher construction wages raised labor costs in the export sector. The more construction workers were paid, the more metalworkers had to reduce their wages in order to maintain employment. Moreover, the ability of construction workers to win large wage increases undermined the ability of both employers and the union leadership in the metalworking sector to convince their members that wage reductions were really necessary.

Wage costs average around 20 percent of the costs of production at the level of the firm. Yet, workers typically receive 70–80 percent of national income. The discrepancy between those two figures gives a good indication of the extent to which the cost of nonlabor inputs for one firm represents wage payments in another firm. Both workers and employers in the traded-goods sector share an interest in restraining the growth of the costs of nontraded inputs, which necessitated obtaining some control over wage growth in sheltered industries. At its inception, the centralization of bargaining was driven by a cross-class alliance in which the union movement cooperated with employers to establish an institutional arrangement whereby those workers who were directly subject to international compe-

ized unions have little capacity to raise wages above their competitive level. See Moene, Wallerstein, and Hoel 1993, for a review of the literature on the impact of different bargaining systems on economic performance.

[6] The best account of the centralization of bargaining in Norway is Bjørgum 1985.

tition set the pace of wage increases for the entire economy. Far from being the product of a protected economy, centralized bargaining at the national level was a product of an exceptionally high degree of trade openness and trade dependence.[7]

This argument seemingly conflicts with the temporal correlation between growing economic integration and pressures for greater decentralization of wage setting in the 1980s, most evident in Sweden and Denmark among the Nordic countries. The assertion that trade dependence has increased over the postwar period is ambiguous, however. While trade is everywhere expanding as a share of national output, the work force in the traded goods sector is declining as a share of national employment. In Norway, for example, half of the value of the goods produced are exported and half of the goods consumed are imported. Yet, only 20 percent of the work force is employed in firms that face international competition (Hernes 1991).

In the Nordic countries, almost all of the growth of employment since the mid-1970s has been in welfare service provision in the public sector (Esping-Andersen, this volume). This shift in employment has changed the composition of the unions. In Sweden in 1975, 65 percent of union members were in the private sector, 35 percent in the public sector. By 1990, the public sector unions had grown to 45 percent of total union membership (Kjellberg 1992: 103). The Norwegian pattern is similar. From 35 percent of union members in 1970, the public-sector unions had grown to close to half of union membership by 1985 (Visser 1989: 180–182). In 1970, to illustrate the same point another way, the largest union in all of the Nordic countries except Denmark was the metalworkers.[8] By 1990, the largest union in all three was the union of municipal employees. In the private sector as well, unions in the service sector have growth relative to unions in manufacturing.

This shift in the composition of union membership is not universal in Europe. In West Germany, for example, two-thirds of union members worked in the private sector in 1970, and two-thirds worked in the private sector in 1985 (Visser 1989: 100–102). Even more striking is the fact that membership in IG Metall was 33 percent of total German union member-

---

[7] The dominance of the traded-goods sector in determining the rate of wage growth, and hence the rate of price growth, for the entire economy became one of the central assumptions of the Aukrust model of inflation that was used in both Norway and Sweden for macroeconomic planning. See Aukrust 1977 for a description.

[8] The Danish case doesn't fit well since unions are organized largely on a craft basis. The largest union throughout the postwar period is the union of unskilled and semiskilled workers, which has members in both the traded and nontraded goods sector.

ship in 1970 and 34 percent of total union membership in 1990 (Golden, Wallerstein, and Lange, this volume). The decline of the relative size of the Nordic unions in manufacturing reflects the changing composition of employment in the Nordic countries documented by Esping-Andersen (this volume).

Unions are political organizations where numbers count. As public-sector unions have grown in relative size, their influence within the central confederations has inevitably increased.[9] With large numbers of members who are low-paid and who are female – these two categories overlap to a considerable extent – the public-sector unions have been strong advocates of reducing wage differentials. Moreover, public-sector employees are not constrained by competition in output markets, either at home or abroad. Where centralized bargaining once allowed workers and employers in manufacturing to determine the aggregate level of wage growth, the public-sector unions were increasingly driving wage growth by the 1970s and 1980s. Moreover, with the loss of a private-sector wage premium, private-sector employers had difficulty competing with the public sector for workers, in part because the public sector offered greater employment security. Originally established to attenuate wage rivalries and establish workers in the traded-goods sector as the wage leaders, centralized bargaining eventually turned into a battleground with wage leadership up for grabs in each bargaining round. This brings us to the topic of solidaristic bargaining.

EGALITARIAN WAGE POLICIES

Even where unions are strong, unions have little impact on the distribution of income between wages and profits. The need to maintain adequate profitability of private investment and employment insures that the share of profit in national income is not dramatically reduced. This does not mean, however, that unions are without influence on the distribution of income. Unions potentially have a large impact on the distribution of income among wage earners. In general, there is a close association between centralized bargaining and wage compression (Moene and Wallerstein 1996). Wage dispersion is greatest in countries like the United States where the share of the labor force covered by a collective agreement is small. Countries with industry-level bargaining, such as Germany, have a more com-

---

[9] See Garrett and Way 1994, for further examination of the impact of the relative decline of unions in the traded goods sector in northern Europe.

pressed wage scale than countries such as Great Britain where plant-level bargaining is more important. Countries with centralized wage setting for the private sector as a whole have the most compressed wage scales of all.

In Norway, Sweden, Denmark, and, in the early postwar period, the Netherlands, the national union confederations pursued an ambitious egalitarian wage policy called "solidaristic bargaining." The solidaristic bargaining policy called for the equalization of workers' pretax income by eliminating or reducing wage differentials between plants in the same industry, between industries, between regions, and ultimately between occupations. "Equal pay for equal work" is a common demand of unions, easily explained by unions' desire to reduce managerial discretion and competition among low-wage employers. Solidaristic bargaining was unique in extending the principal of "equal pay for equal work" from one industry to the entire economy, and then moving beyond the demand for "equal pay for equal work" toward the goal of "equal pay for all work."[10]

The egalitarian wage policy was remarkably effective. In Sweden between 1970, when comprehensive wage data on individuals began to be collected, and 1983, when the system of centralized bargaining collapsed, the variance of the log of hourly wage among private-sector blue-collar workers declined by over 50 percent (Hibbs and Locking 1991). That dramatic decrease does not include the equally prominent reduction of the wage differential between blue-collar and white-collar workers. Hibbs and Locking estimate that a similar decline occurred during the 1960s as well, implying that the variance of log hourly wages in 1983 was only one-quarter of what it was in 1960. Similar longitudinal data are not available for Norway but the pattern appears the same. According to survey data reported by Kalleberg and Colbjørnsen (1990), wage inequality in 1980 as measured by the coefficient of variation (standard deviation divided by the mean) of log earnings was even lower in Norway than in Sweden. Industry-level wage data reported by Freeman (1988) indicate that Norway, Denmark, and Sweden have lower interindustry wage differentials than other OECD countries.

The most common view today is that such wage equality creates severe problems with the allocation of labor and workers' productivity. Too much solidaristic bargaining and too little connection between work performed and wages received became a prominent and persistent complaint of Swedish employers during the 1970s and 1980s (Myrdal 1991). The reduced sensitivity of wages to either the performance of the firm or to local con-

---

[10] See Pontusson and Swenson 1995 for a description of changes in the goals of solidaristic bargaining over the postwar period.

ditions in the labor market that results from imposing a common wage at the industry or sectoral level is often blamed for the persistence of European unemployment. Comparisons are frequently made between the impressive growth of private-sector employment in the United States during the 1980s and the stagnation of private-sector employment in Europe. By preventing the decline of wages at the bottom of the wage distribution, the restriction of wage differentials is viewed as blocking American-style employment growth.

It is usually assumed that the Scandinavian unions fought for reduced wage differentials out of an ideological commitment to equality, while employers resisted giving up their ability to use wage differentials as an incentive and recruitment device. In fact, the original arguments made on behalf of solidaristic bargaining when the policy was first proposed in 1951 by two Swedish union economists, Gösta Rehn and Rudolf Meidner, concerned macroeconomic stability and efficiency, not equality (Rehn 1952). Even more surprising, the goal of equalizing wages among firms and among industries had the implicit support of the Swedish Employers' Association (Swenson 1992a).

Both Rehn and Meidner's argument for the efficiency of solidaristic bargaining and the initial support of employers for such a policy can be explained by comparing local and industry-level bargaining in a growth model with embodied (exogenous) technical change. Implicitly, Rehn and Meidner followed Schumpeter (and Marx), in attributing the dynamic of capitalist economies to what Schumpeter (1976 [1942]) called the "process of creative destruction" in which existing productive units are incessantly being dissolved as new units are inaugurated. Industries expand by building new plants and contract by scrapping obsolete ones. Entering firms introduce new techniques that drive the least efficient of the existing firms out of the market. When new techniques are embodied in new plant and equipment, technical progress entails continual turnover of plants and firms.

To take the simplest case, consider an industry in which the price of output is fixed in world markets, employment is proportional to the number of plants in operation, and the productivity of each plant is determined by the date it was built.[11] Newer plants are more productive than older ones, but building new plants is costly so older plants are not immediately replaced. The key decisions made by firms, in this context, are when to build new plants and when to scrap older ones.

---

[11] See Moene and Wallerstein 1997 for the details of the mathematical analysis that is summarized in this section.

Once the plants are built, investment costs are sunk. Firms will keep plants in operation as long as revenues exceed operating costs. Thus, the age of the oldest plant in operation is determined by the condition that it just breaks even. The number of firms in operation is determined by the real product wage, that is, the nominal wage divided by the price of output. At a lower real product wage, more firms earn enough to cover their wage costs and fewer plants are shut down.

Figure 8.1 illustrates the dispersion of plants according to their productivity in the case in which the rate of productivity growth is constant over time. Plants are arrayed from youngest to oldest, with revenue per plant drawn as the declining exponential curve. If r is the common wage paid in all plants, the intersection of the horizontal line at the level of r and the revenue curve determines the age at which employers would close a plant. Thus θ^L, in Figure 8.1, is the age of the oldest plant in operation when firms pay r per worker.

Plants younger than θ earn positive profits. Firms will open new plants as long as the expected present value of profits earned over the plant's operating life exceeds the initial investment costs. Assuming that the cost of new plants increases as more are ordered at the same time (i.e., the supply curve of new plants is rising), the number of new plants that are built each period is determined by the condition that the present value of the future profit stream of the last plant built equals the cost of construction and equipment.

With decentralized bargaining, workers in each plant bargain separately. In a pure system of local bargaining, wage contracts do not extend beyond the individual firm or plant. Even when local wage bargaining takes place within a frame agreement negotiated at a higher level, the outcome is equivalent to purely local bargaining if local bargainers are free to call strikes or lockouts when bargaining reaches an impasse (Moene, Wallerstein, and Hoel 1993a: 100–103). As long as employment at the plant level is determined by the capital equipment installed, union members will want the highest wage possible subject to the constraint that the plant is not closed. According to standard bargaining theory, the outcome of local negotiations under the specified assumptions is a wage that is a fraction, say α where $0 < \alpha < 1$, of the plant's revenues per worker, provided the fraction of the plant's revenues exceeds what workers could earn elsewhere. In any bargaining system, workers must be offered at least as much as they can earn elsewhere or firms will be unable to fill vacancies.

If the industry is small enough relative to the aggregate labor market such that industry-level employment does not affect wages in other indus-

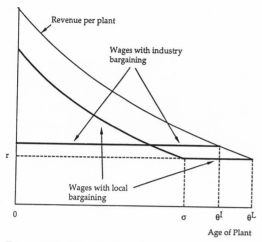

Figure 8.1. Distribution of wages across plants with local and industry bargaining

tries, the distribution of wages with decentralized bargaining can be drawn as indicated in Figure 8.1. Let the value of the expected wage that workers could obtain in employment elsewhere, or workers' outside option, be indicated by r. Then, wages with decentralized bargaining will be a share of the plants' revenues as shown in Figure 8.1 as long as that share exceeds r, which occurs in plants that are younger than the age σ. Plants older than σ but younger than θ^L pay workers their outside option.

The time path of wages in a single plant with local bargaining is illustrated in Figure 8.2. The upper horizontal line represents the revenues earned by a plant of a given vintage. If workers' outside option rises with the average level of productivity in the economy, the outside option will be an exponentially rising curve as drawn. As long as the wage exceeds workers' outside option, the wage in each plant is constant over time since the negotiated wage depends on the price, which is constant by assumption, and productivity, which is determined by the date the plant was built. As the plant grows older and the outside option rises, the gap between the union wage and workers' outside option falls. Eventually, at $t = \sigma$ in Figure 8.2, the outside option becomes binding and the wage increases with r.

Since the wage with local bargaining equals the outside option after the period $t = \sigma$, the exit decision is to scrap the plant when the value added per worker equals the outside option wage. Accordingly, the life-span of plants with local bargaining is independent of the unions' share of

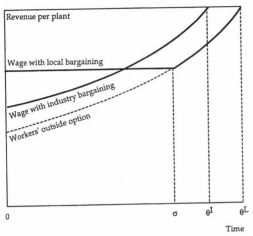

Figure 8.2. Time path of wages with local and industry bargaining

the plant's revenue. All plants pay a wage equal to workers' outside option once they get sufficiently old, regardless of the bargaining power of the local union.

Although decentralized bargaining does not affect firms' exit decision, entry is discouraged. A higher union share lowers the market value of new plants since profits are reduced when the plant is relatively young. A lower value of new plants leads to fewer entrants. As the number of plants that are constructed each period declines, so does the industry's output and employment.

With sunk costs of investment, the union is able to appropriate some of the quasi rents (the difference between the plant's revenue and workers' outside option) earned by the firm. Anticipation of the union's future bargaining strength causes firms to reduce investment, which lowers aggregate employment. But once a plant is built, both the employer and the local union have a common interest in maximizing the quasi rents to be shared over the plant's lifetime. Thus, if the outside option is fixed, the operating life of existing plants remains unchanged whatever the share of the quasi rents received by workers.

We represent industry-level bargaining as setting a uniform wage for all plants in the industry. This assumption exaggerates the impact of industry-level bargaining, since, in most bargaining systems where wages are set at the industry level or higher, local organizations are regularly able to obtain supplements to the centrally negotiated wage at the plant level. Unions and firms, however, are typically forbidden to engage in strikes or lockouts once the central agreement is signed. These restrictions on permissible forms of industrial conflict limit the extent to which local bargainers can obtain increases above the central agreement, and allow central bargainers to anticipate subsequent local wage increases when setting the central wage (Moene, Wallerstein, and Hoel 1993: 100–103; Hibbs and Locking 1991; Rødseth and Holden 1990). To simplify the presentation, we assume that the control of the central negotiators is absolute.

We maintain our assumption that the union seeks to maximize the wage received by its members, now subject to the constraint that the wage is uniform throughout the industry.[12] Again applying standard bargaining theory, the outcome of the labor negotiations with industry-level bargaining is a wage equal to the share α of the average revenue per worker in the industry as a whole (rather than the revenues earned in the plant where the worker is employed). As before, the wage paid must be greater than or equal to workers' outside option, or employers will be unable to attract labor.

By assumption, industry-level bargaining imposes a uniform wage in all plants, as illustrated in Figure 8.1. As Figure 8.1 indicates, an increase in the uniform wage forces older plants out of the market, shortening the average life of plants in operation. In addition, a higher wage reduces investment in new plants. Thus, the effect of a wage increase through industry-level bargaining is to increase average productivity but reduce employment and output.

The time path of the wage with industry-level bargaining is illustrated in Figure 8.2. Since the average productivity of the industry increases continually over time, as new plants are opened and old ones are closed, so does the wage with industry-level bargaining. As Figure 8.2 illustrates, the industry wage and workers' outside options both grow with the rate of productivity growth. Within our stylized description, local bargaining produces a wage in each plant that is constant over time (until the plant becomes so old that workers receive the outside option), while wages in different plants vary according to the plant's productivity. With industry-level bargaining, wages are uniform across plants but rising over time at the same rate as productivity growth.

The two bargaining systems differ in terms of the average productivity of the industry, aggregate employment (and output), aggregate profits, and average wages. Decentralized wage setting allows wages in the oldest

---

[12] We maintain the assumption that the union seeks to maximize the wage received by union members in order to isolate the impact of industry-level bargaining holding union bargaining goals constant. Our argument would only be strengthened if we used the more realistic assumption that central bargainers care about employment as well as wages.

plants to fall to workers' reservation wage. With industry-level bargaining, wages everywhere may be held above the reservation wage, forcing marginal plants out of operation. As long as the centrally bargained wage is greater than workers' outside option, industry-level bargaining reduces the average age of plants ($\theta^I < \theta^L$) and raises average productivity.

An increase in productivity that merely reflects a decline in employment and output is not an improvement, however. Whether or not industry-level bargaining increases efficiency depends on how industry-level bargaining affects the entry of new plants. In our model, industry-level bargaining has two, counteracting effects on entry. On the one hand, entry is encouraged since industry-level bargaining holds wages down in the newest, most productive plants. On the other hand, entry is discouraged by the anticipation that wages will rise independently of the plant's (stagnant) productivity, and will eventually exceed what wages would be with decentralized bargaining. Which of these two effects dominates depends on the value of α, as illustrated in Figure 8.3.

Figure 8.3 illustrates the present value of a new plant as a function of α. For sufficiently low levels of α, workers receive their outside option and collective bargaining has no economic effects. Let α_0^L be the highest level of α such that local bargaining has no effect on wages and let α_0^I, be the same for industry-level bargaining. Since, α_0^L is determined by equating workers' outside option with α times the productivity of the most productive plant, while α_0^I is determined by equating workers' outside option with α times average productivity in the industry, it is clear that $\alpha_0^L < \alpha_0^I$ as shown in Figure 8.3. For $\alpha \leq \alpha_0^L$, α does not affect the wage or the value of new plants with either bargaining system. For $\alpha_0^L < \alpha \leq \alpha_0^I$, α affects wages only if bargaining is decentralized. For $\alpha > \alpha_0^I$, the market value of new plants is a declining function of α with either local or industry-level bargaining.

The value of new plants goes to zero as α goes to one in both bargaining systems. Because the threshold wage share is lower with decentralized bargaining, however, there is a range of values of α where decentralized bargaining depresses the value of new plants (and thus lowers investment) more than centralized bargaining. Thus, if α is such that the wage with industry-level bargaining is not much above workers' outside options, industry-level bargaining raises the market value of new plants relative to local bargaining. Since the number of new plants built is an increasing function of the market value of new plants, entry is greater with industry-level bargaining when α is sufficiently low ($\alpha < \alpha^*$ in Figure 8.3).

Whatever the bargaining system, firms invest until the value of a new plant equals its cost. Changes in the bargaining system, however, can alter

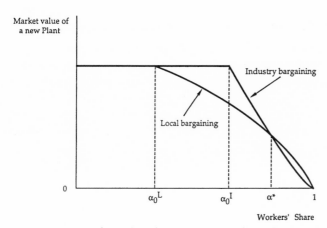

Figure 8.3. Market value of a new plant with local and industry-level bargaining

the market value of existing plants and thereby affect employers' wealth. Whether or not employers would prefer industry-level bargaining or local bargaining depends, in general, on both the value of α and the age of the plant. If α is sufficiently low such that collective bargaining only raises wages with decentralized bargaining, the market value of newer plants is higher with industry-level bargaining, and the value of older plants is no lower. If, at the other extreme, α is sufficiently high that even owners of newly built plants prefer local bargaining ($\alpha > \alpha^*$ in Figure 8.3), employers are unanimous in preferring decentralized bargaining. When α is greater than α_0^I but less than α^* in Figure 8.3, there is some vintage (which depends on α) such that owners of newer plants prefer industry-level bargaining while owners of older plants prefer local bargaining. The closer is α to α_0^I, the larger the proportion of plants whose value would be increased with industry-level bargaining.

Thus, the answer to the question of whether or not centralized bargaining is more efficient than decentralized bargaining, in the sense of raising productivity, employment, and output simultaneously, depends on the value of α. There are not many studies of the union wage differential in western Europe, partly because in many industries almost all workers are covered by union contracts. Given the low unemployment that existed in Norway, Sweden, Finland, and Austria until very recently, the difference between the wages set in the central or industry-level agreement cannot have been significantly higher than the level that would have existed without unions. Therefore, α close to α_0^I in Figure 8.3 is the relevant case in northern Europe for most of the postwar period. According to our model,

Rehn and Meidner's belief in the efficiency of a union wage policy that reduced wage differences among plants is valid provided unions exercise sufficient wage restraint.

The potential benefits of wage compression that have been discussed so far apply to all countries with industry-level bargaining, a group that includes most of western Europe apart from Great Britain. The Nordic countries went further and centralized wage setting at the level of the private sector as a whole. However, the same reasoning on the elimination of wage differences among plants within an industry can be applied to the elimination of wage differentials between industries. With industry-level bargaining, wages will differ by industry in accordance with industry-level differences in productivity or profitability. Solidaristic bargaining, applied over the national economy, limits the ability of the most efficient industries to pay a wage premium and prevents the least efficient industries from staying in business by lowering wages. In fact, the elimination of wage differentials between industries can be understood as a subsidy for new industries and a tax on older ones (Agell and Lommerud 1993). The result of nationwide solidaristic bargaining is to force older industries to shut down while encouraging the growth of new industries. The consequence is a national economy composed of more modern industries than would be the case with less centralized bargaining.

In our discussion so far, wage differentials occur with local wage setting because workers are able to obtain a share of the productivity differences between plants. A purely competitive labor market – that is, a labor market in which all workers received their outside option – would result in uniform wages for homogeneous workers doing equal work. Indeed, one way to understand the potential efficiency gains from solidaristic bargaining is that the reduction of plant-specific rent sharing may create a labor market that more closely approximates the competitive model than the wage differentials that result from decentralized bargaining. Yet, wage dispersion among workers with similar training requirements may occur for more than one reason in a decentralized system. Some sources of wage inequality are, in a deeper sense, egalitarian. If jobs differ in nonpecuniary ways that matter to workers, employers who offer less desirable employment must pay compensating wage differentials to attract labor. Other sources of wage inequality, however, do present potential trade-offs between efficiency and equality.

Suppose workers differ in terms of quality, and that some positions are more sensitive to the quality of workers hired than others. One simple way to model this is to assume that the output of a position depends on a measure of workers' quality multiplied by a measure of the productivity of the capital stock. Thus, in our vintage capital model, the newest plants get more benefit from hiring the highest-quality labor than older plants. In competitive equilibrium, employers bid for workers of different quality with the result that the most modern plants end up paying higher wages to attract the best workers. In Moene and Wallerstein (1997), we show that the competitive wage differentials are (a) efficient, in the sense of maximizing the present value of net national income, and (b) unequal, in the sense that the wage differential exceeds the underlying quality differential among workers. To be precise, we prove that $w_H^D/w_L^D > q_H/q_L$ where w_H^D is the wage received by a worker with quality q_H and w_L^D is the wage received by a worker with quality q_L with $q_H > q_L$ when wage setting is decentralized.

Solidaristic bargaining might be interpreted as setting a "fair" wage distribution where wage differentials are allowed to exist only to the extent that they reflect quality differentials, or $w_H^I/w_L^I = q_H/q_L$, where w_H^I and w_L^I represents the wages for high- and low-skilled workers with centralized bargaining at the industry or national level. In this case, we prove (Moene and Wallerstein 1997) that, if the wage schedule is kept low enough to maintain full employment, solidaristic bargaining results in "excess profits" in the sense that profits are higher than in the purely competitive equilibrium. It follows that investment is also higher than in the purely competitive equilibrium. Indeed, if the market interest rate is taken to be the appropriate social discount rate, investment is excessive when wages are low enough to maintain full employment in the sense that the present value of the benefits of investment at the margin is less than the cost of forgone consumption.

The consideration of heterogeneous workers highlights one of the difficulties of sustaining a policy that combines full employment with the compression of wage differentials. The policy generates high profits for firms, which makes it difficult for union leaders to sell wage restraint to their members. With solidaristic bargaining, higher-quality workers are in excess demand. Holding wages below market clearing levels for a prolonged period of time is apt to lead to wildcat strikes directed at both employers and the union leadership, which is what happened across western Europe in the late 1960s and early 1970s (Soskice 1978). In Sweden, the problem of "excess profits" in the early 1970s led Rudolf Meidner to draft a plan in which a fixed share of profits would be turned into equity shares and deposited in union-controlled wage-earner funds.[13] The Meidner

---

[13] See Esping-Andersen 1985 for a good but, with 20-20 hindsight, overly optimistic account of the Meidner plan in Denmark. Neither the Norwegian nor the Finnish unions showed much interest in wage-earner funds.

plan turned out to be a political disaster. The idea of workers' collective ownership provoked intense opposition from employers and managers without generating enthusiasm among workers. Moreover, opposition to the wage-earner funds led employers to attack the economic and, therefore, political influence that the Swedish Trade Union Confederation (LO) exercised via centralized wage-setting.

A deeper reason why Swedish employers turned from supporters to opponents of solidaristic bargaining in the 1970s and 1980s can be found in the work of Hibbs and Locking (1995). In the late 1960s and early 1970s, the goals of solidaristic bargaining shifted. In the characterization of Hibbs and Locking, the policy evolved from pursuing the goal of "equal pay for equal work" to aiming for "equal pay for all work" (1995: 8–9). In part the shift reflected the growing strength of the public-sector unions with many low-wage members mentioned earlier. The shift also reflected a growing demand for gender equality as women's participation in the work force increased dramatically. In part, however, the shift also occurred in response to demands from the metalworkers union, which, with an average wage that was not low, received little from a policy that equalized interindustry differentials but who nevertheless had a large number of low-paid members (Pontusson and Swenson 1995). For all of these reasons, the centralized agreements after 1969 began to compress significantly wage differentials between jobs within plants. Hibbs and Locking (1995) estimate that between 1964 and 1972, when solidaristic bargaining primarily eliminated interplant and interindustry wage differentials, the policy of wage compression raised industrial output and labor productivity in Sweden by between 8 and 14 percent. After 1972, however, Hibbs and Locking find that productivity began to decline. By the late 1970s, the previous productivity gains had been lost and, by the early 1980s, Swedish productivity was lower than if solidaristic bargaining had never been adopted according to Hibbs and Locking's calculations.

Why the reduction of wage differentials within plants caused productivity growth to fall in Sweden is not clear. Employers blamed their inability to use wages as a reward for performance (Myrdal 1991). Edin and Topel (1995) argue that the decline in the return to education and skill acquisition caused the supply of skilled workers to shrink. Another possibility, suggested by the increase in conflict between unions over relative wages in the 1980s (Hernes 1991; Moene and Wallerstein 1993b), is that the compression of traditional wage differentials generated such resistance from higher-wage workers that productivity suffered. Whatever the causes, the decline in Swedish productivity growth, both relative to the past in Sweden and relative to other European countries in the late 1970s and

1980s, was significant. Since both profits and wage growth depend, ultimately, on productivity growth, the negative effect of wage compression within plants found by Hibbs and Locking, if correct, suggests a compelling explanation for why the policy was abandoned.

In the decade following the breakup of centralized bargaining in Sweden in 1983, wage inequality, as measured by the ratio of the wages received at the ninth and first decile of the wage distribution, increased by 9 percent.[14] Although smaller than the increase in wage inequality during the same period in the United States (23 percent) or the United Kingdom (14 percent), the rise of wage dispersion in Sweden was the largest in northern Europe. In other countries in north and central Europe, however, the dispersion of wages did not change significantly between the early 1980s and 1995. In Austria, Denmark, and the Netherlands, wage inequality remained constant or increased very slightly during the 1980s and early 1990s. In Norway, Finland, Belgium, and Germany, wage inequality declined from the early 1980s to 1995. In part, the relative stability of the wage distribution is due to the incremental nature of change in relative wages. More importantly, the stability of the wage distribution in northern Europe apart from Sweden reflects the continuity of collective bargaining institutions (Golden, Wallerstein, and Lange, this volume).

ACTIVE LABOR MARKET POLICIES

Perhaps the most widely admired innovation of the Swedish social democrats was the set of policies known as active labor market policies. There are four main components: placement services, training courses, wage subsidies for employers who hire workers who have been unemployed for more than a specified period of time, and temporary public employment, mostly in construction and caring services (Layard, Nickell, and Jackman 1991). As Swenson's (1989) account makes clear, the development of the active labor market policies in the late 1950s and early 1960s in Sweden was one of the by-products of the earlier adoption of solidaristic bargaining. A wage policy that increased the rate of entry of new plants and shortened the lifespan of older plants created a need for labor market policies that increased the ability of workers to move from the positions that were being destroyed to the positions that were being created.

---

[14] Even after a decade of rising wage dispersion, the Swedish wage scale in 1995 remained more egalitarian than in any other OECD country except Norway. The figures for wage dispersion in the text are from OECD 1996a: 61–62.

In the 1970s and 1980s, various active labor market policies were adopted by many countries in western Europe, but the Swedish commitment was still far above the rest. In 1987, expenditures in active labor market policies per unemployed person as a share of output per person was 35 percent in Sweden, roughly 10 percent in Norway, Finland, Austria, and Germany, and around 5 percent in other OECD countries (Layard, Nickell, and Jackman 1991: 51). Put another way, in 1987 Sweden spent 1 percent of GDP on active labor market policies when open unemployment (unemployed workers not placed in training programs or subsidized work) was less than 2 percent. In the rest of Europe, unemployment was four times as high on average, and spending in active labor market policies only one half as much. Yet because open unemployment was so low, Swedish expenditures on active labor market programs and passive unemployment benefits together were close to the European average (Layard, Nickell, and Jackman 1991: 479). Thus, Layard, Nickell, and Jackman (1991) argue that Swedish active labor market policies are self-financing. The active labor market policies have the advantage of providing retraining, keeping workers in the labor market, and avoiding the deterioration of skills. So far, Sweden, along with the other Nordic countries, has avoided the problem discussed by Esping-Andersen (this volume) of the emergence of a large group of workers in a state of seemingly permanent unemployment.

Nevertheless, like all other aspects of social democracy, the active labor market policies have come under academic attack in recent years.[15] The evidence from studies of the benefits of training programs is mixed. It is difficult to estimate the impact of participating in active labor market policies on the likelihood of finding employment and on future wages because the workers selected to participate are not a random sample of the unemployment population. Subsidized job creation may encourage municipalities to replace nonsubsidized jobs with subsidized jobs. Finally, it is argued that by making unemployment less painful for workers, active labor market policies reduce the threat of unemployment and increase union militancy (Calmfors 1994).

Few, if any, of the recent critics argue that replacing the entire set of active labor market policies with passive unemployment benefits would be superior, although some advocate reducing expenditures or targeting the programs to the long-term unemployed. The real dilemma of active labor

---

[15] See Calmfors 1993, 1994 for surveys of the empirical Swedish literature on active labor market policies. For studies of the Norwegian policies, see Raaum, Torp, and Goldstein 1995 and Raaum and Wulfsberg 1995.

market policy today is that the system falls apart under conditions of high unemployment. The level of expenditures per unemployed person that was supportable when unemployment was 3 percent is no longer supportable when total unemployment (including participants in active labor market programs) jumps to 12 percent, as it did in Sweden in the early 1990s. Even apart from their cost, active labor market policies cease to function well when unemployment rises sufficiently high. The Swedish policy was both tough, in that workers who refused to accept training or employment lost their unemployment benefits relatively quickly, and generous, in that all workers were guaranteed at least a temporary job after their benefits expired. With mass unemployment, neither toughness nor generosity can be sustained. How can the authorities insist that workers accept employment upon completion of their training if there are no jobs for them to take? Instead of being a step toward finding a new job, entering a training program becomes a way to renew one's eligibility for another period of unemployment benefits. With no jobs available to graduates of training programs, neither the students nor the staff have much reason to take the training seriously. Paying people to go to school or to work for the municipality may be better than paying them to sit at home, but it is no answer to mass unemployment.

FULL EMPLOYMENT

The single most important objective of the labor market policies followed by social democratic governments in the postwar period was the maintenance of full employment. Like the Democratic Party in the United States, the social democratic parties in northern Europe came to power near the peak of unemployment during the Great Depression and established a long-lasting parliamentary majority by presiding over an economic recovery and the achievement of full employment. Throughout the postwar period, social democrats successfully appealed for votes on the basis of their record as guardians of full employment.

In the 1960s, full employment was achieved throughout western Europe. In most of western Europe, however, the era of full employment ended abruptly in the mid-1970s. By the 1980s, the average rate of unemployment in the eight members of the European Community since 1973 exceeded 10 percent. In contrast, the average unemployment rate in the five continental members of the European Free Trade Association (EFTA) – Austria, Finland, Norway, Sweden, and Switzerland – remained below 3 percent. In the 1982–1988 period, every European Community country had an unemployment rate above the highest level of unemployment found in an EFTA country.

In the early 1990s, the difference between the Nordic social democracies and the rest of Europe in terms of unemployment disappeared. In Norway, unemployment rose from below 2 percent in 1987 to over 6 percent by 1993. In Sweden the rise in unemployment came later but faster. In 1990, unemployment in Sweden was still below 2 percent. By 1992 Swedish unemployment had risen above 5 percent. In 1993 the Swedish unemployment rate reached 8.5 percent. Unemployment in Finland rose from 3.5 percent in 1990 to 15 percent by the end of 1992. Moreover, standard unemployment figures do not include the participants in active labor market policies. Including workers enrolled in active labor market programs would increase unemployment by around 50 percent. In the mid-1990s, the Nordic economies are recovering rapidly, but unemployment is falling slowly. No forecasters expect unemployment to fall to the low levels that were common before the recent crisis.

Two factors are generally credited for the superior performance of the social democracies of northern and central Europe in terms of unemployment and job creation until the 1990s: centralized bargaining and the active labor market policies (discussed in the preceding sections). As Calmfors (1993) notes, neither factor provides a sufficient explanation. Even when the participants in active labor market policies are added to the openly unemployed, unemployment was still extraordinarily low by international standards. There were not enough workers in the active labor market policies before the arrival of mass unemployment for these policies to account for the difference between the Nordic countries and the rest of western Europe (Edin and Topel 1995). While centralized wage setting at the national level contributed to the restraint of wage growth under conditions of full employment, in none of the Nordic countries was nominal wage restraint sufficient to prevent unemployment. All of the Nordic countries relied on periodic devaluations during the late 1970s and early 1980s to maintain international competitiveness.

That leaves a third factor: the social democratic macroeconomics policy commitment to the maintenance of full employment (Therborn 1986; Calmfors 1993; Rødseth 1997). Yet this explanation, too, is insufficient. The rise in unemployment in the Nordic countries in the 1990s can be explained in standard macroeconomics terms (Calmfors 1993; Stephens 1994; King 1994; Martin 1996; Rødseth 1997). In all three countries, the deregulation of credit markets and strong foreign demand resulted in a boom in employment, investment, and asset prices during the mid-1980s.

Rapidly rising housing prices and easy credit encouraged a dramatic increase in private-sector borrowing. When the boom ended and asset prices began to fall, private-sector saving increased rapidly as households struggled to reduce their accumulated debt. The result was a sharp decline in private domestic consumption that coincided with a decline in foreign markets as all of western Europe entered into a recession. The decline in the demand for Finnish exports was particularly severe, due to the collapse of the Soviet market for Finnish products. In addition, governments in all three Nordic countries kept interest rates high to defend exchange rates that had been fixed to the ECU until the system of fixed exchange rates in the European Union collapsed in the fall of 1992. The consequent decline in aggregate demand resulted in a sharp rise in unemployment.

What a standard macroeconomic account cannot easily explain is the failure of the Nordic economies to return to the low levels of unemployment that had been common prior to the crisis when the Nordic governments adopted more expansionary policies after 1992. In this, unemployment in the Nordic economies in the 1990s displayed the same tendency to remain stuck at high levels that unemployment in other European economies had exhibited earlier in the 1980s. A number of explanations for the persistence of both full employment and high unemployment have been suggested, including the insider-outsider model (Gottfries and Horn 1987; Blanchard and Summers 1987; Lindbeck and Snower 1988), the decline in the employability of the long-term unemployed (Layard, Nickell, and Jackman 1991), or a shortage of capital (Soskice and Carlin 1989; Malinvaud 1980). In this section, we offer a different explanation, and provide some evidence that it provides a plausible account of changes in unemployment in the Nordic countries.[16]

Conditions of general labor scarcity induce adaptations on the part of employers that help maintain low levels of unemployment. In particular, when filling vacancies and keeping workers is difficult, employers adapt by hoarding labor. Even if current conditions would warrant a reduction in the work force, employers may keep their entire work force employed if demand is expected to increase in the future and if workers are sufficiently difficult to replace. It is widely recognized that raising the cost of laying off workers inhibits firms from hiring. Less appreciated is the reverse point: the greater the cost of filling vacancies, the fewer workers firms will lay off.

Consider two simplified types of employment policies. A "flexible em-

---

[16] See Moene and Wallerstein 1995b and Moene, Nymoen, and Wallerstein 1995, 1997 for the full elaboration of the underlying theoretical model and econometric tests.

ployment policy" is the policy of hiring when production is profitable and laying off when production is unprofitable. By following a flexible employment policy, firms avoid losses when the price of output is below variable costs but firms may pay a price in terms of forgone profits during the time it takes to fill positions once the price of output rises sufficiently to make production profitable again. The alternative employment policy could be called a "fixed employment policy." This is the policy of hoarding labor when demand is low in order to have a full work force available immediately when demand rises again.

Which employment policy is better in terms of the present value of the firms' current and future profits depends on the wage and on the properties of the stochastic process that describes future prices. The shorter the likely period of time before the price increases enough so that production is profitable, and the higher the profits that are expected once the price increases, the more likely firms are to hoard labor when the price is low. Which employment policy is better from employers' point of view also depends on the ease with which vacancies can be filled. Clearly, if vacancies could be filled immediately at no cost, a flexible employment policy would be the profit-maximizing choice. If the cost of filling vacancies is sufficiently high, however, firms may increase their long-term profits by hoarding labor during periods of low demand, provided demand is expected to rise in the future.

This can be illustrated by a simple model where we allow the price of output to fluctuate between a high and a low level. The revenue of the firm depends on both the price it can obtain for its output and its productivity. Assume that the only variable costs are labor costs. If labor costs exceed revenues even when the price is high, the firm would close. If labor costs are less than revenues even when the price is low, the firm would never have layoffs. The interesting case, therefore, is when labor costs are lower than revenues when the price is high but higher than revenues when the price is low.

Let there be a constant probability that the price will fall within a given unit of time when the price is high. In addition, assume there is a fixed probability that the price will rise within a given unit of time when the price is low. Starting out in a situation when the price is low, Figure 8.4 illustrates the present value of expected future profits with both flexible employment and fixed employment strategies as functions of the cost of filling vacancies. The variable μ, on the horizontal axis, is a measure of the speed with which firms can fill vacancies. The probability that a vacancy will be filled within a time interval Δ is $\mu\Delta$. Alternatively, $1/\mu$ is the average length of time it takes a firm to fill a vacancy. Firms that follow a

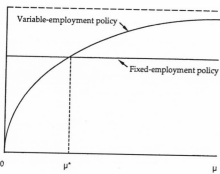

Figure 8.4. Value of a position when the price is low as a function of the ease of filling future vacancies

fixed employment policy do not lay off, so their long-run profits are independent of μ. In contrast, the market value of firms that follow a flexible employment policy rises with μ since the more quickly vacancies are filled, the more quickly flexible employment firms can start production when the price rises.

If $\mu = 0$, vacancies remain unfilled forever. In this case, the fixed-employment strategy is superior, provided the wage is low enough relative to the price distribution such that production is profitable in the long run. If μ is sufficiently large, however, the flexible employment strategy is superior from the firm's point of view since, as $\mu \to \infty$, the variable employment policy approaches the best of all possible worlds for employers if they can lay off workers whenever the price is low and immediately fill vacancies when the price rises again. In general, the fixed-employment strategy is superior from employers' point of view whenever μ is less than a critical value, μ^*, which depends on the price distribution, the plant's productivity, and the wage.

From a single firm's point of view, the likelihood of finding a suitable worker within a given time period is exogenous, at least if the firm's wage offers are constrained by an industry-level wage agreement. But, in aggregate, the likelihood of filling a vacancy depends, in part, on other firms' choices of employment policy. Assume, for illustrative purposes, that the price distribution is independent for each firm. Thus, at each moment of time, a roughly constant share of firms faces a low price. For a given wage and price distribution, the number of unemployed workers rises with the number of firms that follow flexible employment policies. As long as the probability of filling a vacancy rises with the number of unemployed, then μ rises with the number of firms that follow flexible employment policies.

The more firms follow flexible employment policies, the higher the long-run profits of firms following flexible employment policies. If, instead, most firms follow fixed employment policies, the number of unemployed is lower and the time it takes to fill a vacancy is longer. This, in turn, lowers the long-run profits in firms following flexible employment policies.

The simultaneity of firms' choice of employment policies and the probability of filling positions can produce two locally stable equilibria: one where unemployment is high and firms follow a flexible employment strategy (since vacancies are easily filled) and the other where unemployment is low and firms follow a fixed employment strategy (since workers are hard to replace). Since the opportunity cost of an unfilled vacancy increases with productivity of the firm, a fixed employment strategy is more likely to maximize profits the more productive the firm. Thus for each level of μ, there corresponds a critical level of productivity such that firms will follow a fixed employment policy if the firm has higher productivity than the threshold and a flexible employment policy if the productivity is lower. Firms hoard labor in the most productive positions, but hire and fire as demand fluctuates in less productive positions.

Let β represent the share of firms that follow a flexible employment policy in period t. If all firms were alike, β_t would be either zero or one. When firms differ with respect to productivity, however, β_t depends positively on the threshold level of productivity below which firms choose flexible employment. This threshold depends positively on the probability of filling a vacancy, μ, since the easier it is to fill vacancies, the higher the level of productivity that is required to make labor-hoarding profitable. In addition, the ease of filling vacancies, μ, depends on the employment strategies of firms in the previous period. The higher the share of firms that followed a flexible employment policy in the previous period, β_{t-1}, the larger the inherited pool of unemployed relative to the number of vacancies. Taking these two effects together, we can describe the share of firms that choose flexible employment as an increasing function of the share of firms that chose flexible employment in the previous period, denoted by $F(\beta_{t-1})$. The evolution of employment strategies over time is then given by $\beta_t = F(\beta_{t-1})$, which is illustrated in Figure 8.5 for the distribution of productivity among plants derived in the section on egalitarian wage policies.[17]

[17] Let $G(b)$ denote the cumulative density function of plant-level productivity b. The model of the section on egalitarian wage policies implies that the distribution of plants is uniform in the log of productivity, or $G(b) = (1/\gamma\theta)[\ln b - \ln b_{max} + \gamma\theta]$, where γ is the

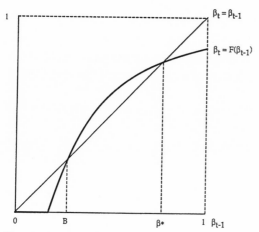

Figure 8.5. Equilibria in the labor market

When $F(\beta_{t-1})$ is below the 45 degree line in Figure 8.5, $\beta_t < \beta_{t-1}$ and β declines over time. The level of β increases when $F(\beta_{t-1})$ is above the 45 degree line. Possible steady-state solutions must satisfy $\beta = F(\beta)$. In Figure 8.5 there are three steady-state equilibria at 0, B, and β^*. The equilibria at 0 and β^* are both locally stable in the sense that small perturbations lead to reactions that return to the initial equilibrium. It is also possible that only one equilibrium will exist. A sufficiently large shift in the $\beta = F(\cdot)$ curve, either up or down, can reduce the number of equilibria to one. An increase in the wage, for example, shifts the $\beta = F(\cdot)$ curve upward since flexible employment strategies become relatively more profitable than fixed employment strategies. Increases in average prices and in the likelihood of an upswing shift the $\beta = F(\cdot)$ curve downward since the fixed employment strategy becomes relatively more profitable the higher the expected level of demand.

In an environment of labor scarcity, firms that offer workers long-term employment contracts may earn higher profits than firms that use layoffs to reduce costs when the price falls. Thus, labor scarcity may lead firms to adopt a no-layoff policy. In contrast, in an environment with a large pool

rate of growth of productivity, θ is the age of the oldest plant in operation, and b_{max} is the productivity of the newest, most productive plant. For each μ, there is a critical productivity level, b^*, such that firms follow a fixed employment policy if $b \geq b^*$ and a flexible employment policy if $b < b^*$. Then $\beta = G(b^*)$ is the share of firms that follow a flexible employment policy. Since b^* is a positive function of μ and μ is a positive function of β_{t-1}, we have $\beta_t = G[b^*(\mu(\beta_{t-1}))] \equiv F(\beta_{t-1})$ as shown in Figure 8.5.

of unemployed workers, companies that act quickly to reduce costs through layoffs may earn higher profits than firms that offer long-term employment guarantees. Note that the high unemployment equilibrium does not necessarily imply that all workers are threatened with layoffs when the price is low. Even in the high unemployment equilibrium, firms continue to hoard labor in the most productive positions. What changes, in the shift from the low-unemployment to the high-unemployment equilibrium, is the fraction of the work force that has secure employment.

The difficulty of filling vacancies because other firms are hoarding labor is a friction in the labor market, a friction that was prominent in Norway, Sweden, and, to a lesser extent, Finland until recently. But the effects of such friction are not unambiguously harmful. On the one hand, there may be productivity losses from a lower turnover of labor. In a world in which some price declines are permanent, labor hoarding may slow the necessary transfer of capital and labor to other sectors. On the other hand, there may be productivity gains since workers who are protected from layoffs have greater incentives to acquire and develop firm-specific skills and knowledge.

With multiple equilibria in the labor market, as illustrated in Figure 8.5, the effect of a change in demand on unemployment may be discontinuous. If the labor market is initially at the low-unemployment equilibrium, a small shift downward in the price distribution will not increase unemployment. But a larger decline in prices may shift the $\beta = F(\cdot)$ curve up sufficiently far that the low-unemployment equilibrium ceases to exist. In this case, the labor market would move more quickly to the equilibrium at β^*. Moreover, a subsequent recovery in which the price distribution returned to its original position would not, by itself, move the labor market back to the low-unemployment equilibrium. The equilibrium would remain at $\beta,^*$ and unemployment would remain high.

Elsewhere (Moene, Nymoen, and Wallerstein 1995, 1997) we provide some estimates of the importance of the decline of labor market friction in the rise of unemployment in the Norwegian manufacturing sector. The increase in the ease of filling vacancies that occurred with the increase in unemployment in Norway between 1989 and 1990 was sufficient to explain a short-run decline in employment of 3 percent and a long-run response, including lagged effects, of a decline of 12 percent, holding other variables like aggregate demand, wage costs, and export prices fixed. In order to offset a negative shock of that magnitude, the real exchange rate would have had to depreciate by 40 percent, or the wage share would have had to have been reduced by 33 percent.

High unemployment induces changes in behavior that inhibit the recovery of full employment. As discussed in the previous section, active labor market policies lose effectiveness when there are no jobs available for those who complete training programs. Employers who have no trouble filling vacancies hesitate less in letting employees go when demand is temporarily low. Once lost, full employment is difficult to regain.

CONCLUSION

Social democratic labor market institutions worked reasonably well for a long period of time. To a significant extent, the socialist goals of equality and security of income were attained without disrupting the functioning of capitalist economies. Moreover, core social democratic policies, such as centralized bargaining and active labor market policies, benefited and received support from employers as well as organized workers.

By the 1990s, however, all aspects of the social democratic labor market policy are under intellectual and political attack (Lindbeck 1994). The egalitarian wage scale associated with centralized bargaining is charged with cutting the connection between effort and reward and with reducing workers' incentives to acquire skills. Active labor market policies are accused of driving unemployment higher, by reducing the pain of being unemployed. Generous welfare policies are accused of reducing the ability of the European economies to adjust to external shocks (Ljungqvist and Sargent 1995).

Underlying the attacks on social democratic policies in the Nordic countries in the 1980s and 1990s are disappointing economic growth and the emergence of high unemployment. Our reading of the evidence is that both the earlier advocates and the current critics overstate the impact of social democratic labor market policies on macroeconomic performance. Both centralized bargaining and active labor market policies can help, but neither is sufficient to prevent unemployment from rising when aggregate demand falls.

Consider the contrast between wage bargaining and unemployment in Sweden and Norway in the 1980s and 1990s. In the early 1980s, the Swedish social democrats maintained a very low level of unemployment with large devaluations in cooperation with the unions who agreed not to seek compensatory wage increases. After the decentralization of bargaining in 1983, however, securing wage restraint via a centralized agreement became substantially more difficult. In the second half of the 1980s, Swedish labor costs were rising significantly faster than in the rest of Europe and most economists thought another devaluation would just trigger faster wage increases (Calmfors 1993). When the Swedish social democratic government tried to head off the coming crisis with an emergency package of a wage and price freeze and a strike ban in the winter of 1990, the government was defeated by a coalition of both the right and left and forced to resign.

In many respects the situation in Norway in the mid-1980s was similar to that in Sweden. The Norwegian economy was overheated with wage increases that resulted in a significant loss of competitiveness. In contrast to Sweden, however, the Norwegian employers and main blue-collar confederation accepted a return to centralized wage agreements in 1988, backed by a parliamentary act that set limits on local bargaining and extended the terms of the contract to the entire work force. Econometric estimates indicate that the central agreements and government intervention reduced wage growth by between 4 and 8 percent (Rødseth 1997: 180). The partial wage freeze was not enough to prevent the rise in unemployment. Our estimates indicate that the wage share would have had to be reduced by 33 percent to prevent an increase in unemployment. No wage-setting system can deliver wage cuts of that magnitude. But the increase in unemployment in Norway was less than in Sweden.

With regard to economic growth, the econometric work of Hibbs and Locking (1995) suggests that wage leveling as ambitious as in Sweden in the early 1980s did lower productivity. Yet, the model presented in the section on egalitarian wage policies and Hibbs and Locking's estimates suggest that a more moderate degree of wage leveling can increase productivity. In fact, the determinants of productivity growth are insufficiently understood to make any strong claims regarding the impact of social democratic labor market policies on long-term economic growth.

Where social democratic policies have clearly succeeded is in reducing inequality, insecurity, and poverty. Equality per se may or may not be an important goal, but the elimination of extreme poverty is an important achievement. In addition, the provision of comprehensive insurance against the risks of life through labor market and welfare policies is an important benefit that must be included in a comprehensive assessment of the success or failure of the social democratic model.

9

THE DECLINING SIGNIFICANCE OF MALE WORKERS: TRADE-UNION RESPONSES TO CHANGING LABOR MARKETS

Jytte Klausen

INTRODUCTION

In the past two decades two concurrent sociological changes have redefined the working class in many advanced industrialized countries. The first is the mobilization of women as workers. The second is the contraction of the manufacturing sector and the concomitant rise of the service sector. The combined effect of these changes has been to shrink the blue-collar working class of male breadwinners, which postwar trade unionism and social democracy took as its core constituency. In place of a homogenized male and blue-collar, unionized working class, unions are now facing a constituency consisting of a heterogeneous group of part-time, flex-time, and full-time workers comprising increasingly women and service-sector workers, mostly male post-Fordist industrial workers adapted to the computer revolution, and the remnants of traditional constituencies of male industrial workers and workers in crafts-oriented skilled occupations. With

I am grateful to two reviewers, and to Rianne Mahon, Miriam Golden, Gary Marks, Stephen Silvia, Peter Lange, Jonas Pontusson, and John D. Stephens for comments.

sociological diversity comes also diversity of interests and often increased
conflict over strategy, aims, and style of interest representation.

This chapter examines some aspects of union responses to the changing
composition of labor markets. The question of how unions have adjusted
to growing diversity is linked to some core issues about the transformation
of social democracy. The social democratic axiom that the individual rises
with his or her group can only be true if the labor movement is inclusive
enough to represent disadvantaged groups, among them women. In addition, the close relationship between union and party is what in the past
has defined social democracy, but if the unions are increasingly divided
among themselves, this relationship inevitably suffers, to the detriment of
both. Adjustment has involved both organizational and political reap-
praisal, often both at the same time. The long-running debate over voting
rules and trade-union representation within the British Labour Party is an
example of the interdependence between political and organizational adjustment. In this case, curtailing trade-union control over the party has
been seen as central to the party's capacity to appeal to groups in the
electorate that regard the trade unions with mistrust. Trade-union reform
is central to overcoming friction between party and unions.

GENDER AND POSTINDUSTRIALISM: THE
NEW WORKING CLASS

Gender issues have been particularly important to trade-union adjustment
for several reasons. The steady increase in the numbers of women working
represents an issue in itself, putting pressures on unions to put more
women on boards and to organize women. Lack of organization among new
occupational groups depresses union membership in relation to the working population and inevitably raises long-term questions about the role of
unions in society. The conflict potential grows when gender issues coincide
with other cleavage lines within the union constituency. Gender bias often
overlaps with important cleavages within the union constituency: service
versus manufacturing sector, private versus public, and in Scandinavia also
sheltered industries versus export sectors. Union stances on matters of wage
policy, social policy, and economic integration are affected by how unions
respond to gender issues. Contentious issues are pay parity and quotas for
the representation of women in unions and labor parties. Less obvious
issues are European integration and economic adjustment to internationalization. Broadly speaking, gender is linked to almost every important political issue facing social democratic trade unions and parties today (Jenson,
Hagen, and Reddy 1988; Jenson and Mahon 1993).

The aim here is not to explain the causes of gender segregation in labor markets, but it is important to note that much of feminist scholarship on this topic presumes the cause of segregation to be "rooted in the sexual division of labor" and labor market policy to be reproducing cultural presumptions about gender roles (Hagen and Jenson 1988: 9). Unions are seen as biased against women and instrumental in confining women to "work ghettos." Progress for women has been linked to improved representation of women within trade-union and party hierarchies and policies aiming to reduce gender-based pay inequity and job opportunity. The conversion of traditional female-centered familial obligations into public services providing paid employment for women is also frequently seen as essential (Hernes 1987; Jenson and Mahon 1993).

Institutionalist perspectives give less weight to the reproduction of cultural gender bias as an explanation of gender bias in labor markets and emphasize instead the coincidence of the mobilization of women as workers and the concentration of job growth to the service sectors. The absorption of women in the public service sector in Scandinavia is the result of deliberate welfare state policies, which mostly aimed to benefit women. Policies have intended and unintended consequences, and gender rigidities are due to both. Whatever the cause of bias, however, trade unions are faced with a bifurcated class of male and female wage earners working in different economic contexts and with different welfare interests.

Postindustrialist theory presumes that economic development has wrought changes in the character of work that have had wide cultural and psychological implications. It paints a picture of the disappearing, so-called Fordist, manual worker in work clothes smeared with grease, who has been displaced by a post-Fordist employee in casual clothes using tools directed by computers. The change in working conditions is presumed to have been accompanied by a change in consciousness from that of a "worker" to that of a "technician," making the new industrial worker less susceptible to traditional invocations of class-based union appeals (Piore and Sabel 1984; Lipietz 1987). We cannot link aggregate data for the shifts in the relative balance between occupations and industries to changes in working conditions, nor to changes in life-styles and attitudes.

A note on terminology is in order. When Esping-Andersen and others speak of a "postindustrial class structure," they refer to the rise of service-sector jobs and to the transformation, through the microchip revolution, of manufacturing work to a new kind of postindustrial production stripped of the attributes normally associated with the industrial blue-collar worker (Esping-Andersen 1993a). The comparison has to be framed in traditional sectoral terms as one between industrial workers, counting Fordist blue-collar workers with their computerized post-Fordist counterparts, and service-sector workers.

METHOD AND CASE SELECTION

The cases included in the study (Sweden, Denmark, Great Britain, the Federal Republic of Germany, and Austria) are all examples of unified labor movements, and I use this term in the traditional social democratic fashion to indicate the combined movement of trade unions and labor or social democratic parties. Communist or Christian democratic confederations and unions similarly have to adjust to sociological changes, but their distinct histories and ties introduce an ideology component in the comparison that I would rather avoid. The five cases discussed here share a tradition of close relations between unions and parties, and the political constraints of "responsible" unionism (Przeworski and Sprague 1986).

That does not mean that the dynamic of the comparative argument rests on a similar-case scenario because, while we approximately control for ideological variation, the five labor movements vary in other key respects. British labor has never conformed to the corporatist mold that the other four used to sustain social coordination in the postwar years, for example. Of the five, only the Swedish Social Democrats have held government power nearly continuously. (In 1976–1982, they were in opposition.) The political composition of governments has shaped welfare state trajectories – Christian democratic or social democratic – which in turn have shaped the relative distribution of job growth between public- and private-sector service occupations (Esping-Andersen 1990, 1993a, van Kersbergen, this volume). The Scandinavian emphasis upon institutional delivery of services has opened up public-sector occupations to women on a large scale in care professions, while women elsewhere have been channeled into private-sector service occupations. The public-private distinction has important implications for trade-union mobilization, and it is reasonable to expect it to be highly salient to trade-union strategies. Hence, the case selection permits us to draw inferences about the causal importance of institutional variables – ranging from control of government to welfare state regimes – for union strategies and responses to sociological change.

In order to link sociological change in general and the rise in the numbers of working women in particular to policy conflict, I looked for suitable sources to establish the salience of conflict independently from the sociological description. The contents of a sample of national confederation and trade-union journals, newspapers, and magazines from all five countries were examined, most covering the years from 1980 through the early

1990s. A set of clearly identifiable clusters of policy conflicts related to gender issues and the sociological implications of industrial restructuring emerged from the content analysis.[1] In some cases, it was possible to trace particular issues from inception and initial mobilization to the responses of union elites. Policy conflicts are inherently unique in nature, shaped by contingent historical and political contexts. Yet all conflicts involved either adjustment to rising numbers of women in the labor force and their insertion into the labor movement, or conflicts between industrial and postindustrial trades. The key issues were (1) part-time work and flexible hours, (2) pay equity, (3) representation of women, (4) the welfare state, and (5) foreign trade and economic policy.

The argument proceeds in three steps, combining historical and cross-national perspectives. The first part aims to simplify the comparison by providing past-and-present profiles of the configuration of labor markets and trade unions in two base-line years roughly twenty years apart, from the 1970s to the 1990s. The argument proceeds with a discussion of the issue areas identified as central points of contention on the basis of trade-union journals and papers, and how unions have reacted to them. The final section discusses union-party relations and how we can explain cross-national variations in the capacities of unions and parties to change. Before we turn to the evidence, we need to reflect on the links between sociological change and interest mobilization.

GROUP CONFLICT AND POLITICAL ACTION

The nexus between labor market stratification and trade-union politics is a complicated one linking first-order causal variables to second-order causation. A feedback loop exists between labor market stratification and policy, in the sense that a hallmark of postwar union policies has been to use union power to ease conflicts between trades and occupational groups. While the national economies furnish a fundamental structuration of labor markets, policy decisions – ranging from industrial policies protecting the manufacturing sector to decisions to let immigrants supplement tight la-

---

[1] A total of twenty-eight union papers was examined. In addition, various congress protocols and more theoretical journals published by unions were also consulted. The sample included papers from the national confederations, as well as from unions considered representative of postindustrial, predominantly male occupations, white-collar service-sector unions organizing in predominantly female occupations, and "old" industrial, blue-collar occupations. A full list and description can be obtained from the author.

bor markets in the 1960s or to admit women to work – and trade-union rules regarding part-time work also shape who works and in which occupations.

A recent study of trade-union politics in the 1990s suggested that one of the differences between the "golden age" of welfare state capitalism and today is that then most intraclass conflict stemmed from friction between the rank and file and union elites, while now conflicts are predominantly between groups of labor (Golden 1992). This change can be traced to general large-scale shifts in the economy and the context for collective bargaining. Wage restraining policies in the 1960s and 1970s sought to keep wages down in order to avoid fueling inflation. Such policies were often, rightly or wrongly, perceived by trade-union activists and the rank and file to have kept wages below those that could have been obtained by means of wage militancy (Soskice 1978). The shift to an emphasis on fiscal austerity in place of income policy may have eased some of the conflict between union leaders and activists. On the other hand, wage restraint was thought to be in the interest of wage earners because it helps balance employment concerns and other macroeconomic stabilization goals with wage earners' interests in higher wages, shifting the focus from nominal wage gains to higher real wages. If so, discontentment with the unions' ability to produce material gains is unlikely to have been at the core of past conflicts within the unions. (For evidence and a review of the literature, see Lange and Garrett 1985.) An alternative explanation is that friction arose, both then and today, from distributional conflicts between trades and occupational groups. What has changed is who the groups are. The rising numbers of working women have added political clout to a group that in the past often found itself isolated by small numbers and weak job control, in competitive collective bargaining and within the labor movement (Karlsson 1996).

One new conflict that has received attention concerns the divergent interest of wage earners working in the market sector exposed to import competition or dependent upon export markets and those working in sheltered sectors (Frieden 1991). Labor groups organizing in either will have different interests on a broad range of policy issues, from trade policy to social policies. At the heart of the conflict lies a difference with respect to the character of the Phillips curve trade-off between wages and employment. In the sheltered industries, particularly the public sector, market competition does not swiftly punish excessive wage gains beyond those justified by increases in productivity by means of decreasing demand. A much publicized attack in 1986 by the general secretary of the Swedish metalworkers' union on the high salaries of public employees, which precipitated the breakup of centralized bargaining, can be seen as an illustration of this cleavage (Swenson 1992b: 52). In the Scandinavian countries, it adds to the potential conflict material that gender segregation makes one group (exposed, private sector) predominantly male and the other predominantly female (public sector).

Rapid sociological change and enhanced international competition represent a potential source of political and organizational conflict between trades and occupations because the new realities of the labor market are not reflected accurately in the alignment of organization power within the unions and in union goals and strategies. We may expect that groups who in the past held a powerful position within the unions, and now see their advantage diminished by economic and sociological change, may resist change and use their organizational power as a bulwark against change. The mismatch problem between union strategies and the political and social realities of labor markets poses a particular problem for social democratic and labor parties, who have used unions to mobilize electoral support and organizational capacities. The party will in that situation see itself as hemmed in by the unions, and prevented from reaching an important new constituency. Hence, union strategies become a matter of keen concern to parties. Unions engaged in a rearguard defense of previously gained benefits, on the other hand, will fight the party's reorientation, which may even be seen as a betrayal of principle.

LABOR MARKET STRATIFICATION AND TRADE-UNION MOBILIZATION: THE 1970s AND 1990s COMPARED

Since the statistical material leaves us no choice but to define the character of work in terms of sectoral employment, industrial work has been defined as employment in mining, manufacturing, construction, and electricity, gas, and water.[2] It is fair to presume that these four groups include what we in the past would have called blue-collar occupations, both in the Fordist types of occupations and what we now call post-Fordist. They also include mostly private-sector workers, except in the utilities sector, which in some countries still is overwhelmingly government run. The classification system collapses transportation, storage, and communications industries into one group, which blends white-collar and blue-collar occupations

---

[2] Survey methods use the international standard trade classification system (ISIC). Groups included are ISIC 2, 3, 4, and 5. ISIC 1, agriculture, has been excluded.

and the private and the public sectors. It has been excluded from the comparison, together with agriculture. Postindustrial service-sector employment encompasses employment in three sectors: wholesale and retail trade, and restaurants and hotels; financing, insurance, real estate, and business services; and community, social, and personnel services. This group mixes public- and private-sector occupations, but expanding welfare state employment shows up in the last of the three.

GENDER-SEGREGATED LABOR MARKETS

The analysis yields a picture of striking changes. Table 9.1 shows the changes in the distribution of industrial and service-sector workers by gender between 1970 and 1993. The first column shows the increasing importance of women in the labor force over the past twenty-three years. It also shows marked cross-country differences. In Sweden, women now are a majority. In 1993, 115,000 more women than men were labor market active. This is a striking development that reflects numerous other changes, which will be spelled out in the following. Austria and the Federal Republic of Germany have also seen a rise in the numbers of working women, but to a lesser extent than the other countries. The table shows a higher proportion of working women in Britain than in Denmark. This is likely the result of measurement bias due to difference in base figure. If we recalculate the British figure for women's share in the labor market on the same basis as the Danish (and Austrian) figures, we find that women here constitute 42.0 percent of total civilian employment, less than in Denmark. Austrian and Danish labor force statistics unfortunately do not permit comparison on gender segregation.

The ubiquitous decline that took place in industrial employment in Scandinavia and Britain is remarkable (Table 9.1). Between 1970 and 1993, Sweden lost 500,000 industrial jobs or 35 percent of all industrial jobs; Britain lost 5 million industrial jobs, 50 percent of all industrial jobs. In contrast, Austria and Germany have retained industrial near dominance. The industrial sector declined the least in Austria, the most in Britain. Decline has not affected men's control on jobs; roughly two-thirds of all industrial jobs were occupied by men twenty-five years ago and are so still today. Service-sector expansion has advanced the furthest in Scandinavia and in Great Britain, with the difference that in Scandinavia growth has been particularly strong in social services and the public sector whereas in Britain much of the growth took place in the predominantly private-sector service occupations. The degree of gender segregation is high, although not as high as in industrial occupations. Still, the service sector is predom-

Table 9.1. *Industrial and service-sector employment by gender, 1970 and 1993, as percentage of all wage earners and salaried employees*

	Women's share of total employment[a]	Industrial employment share of total[b]	Men's share of industrial employment	Service employment, share of total[c]	Women's share of service employment
Sweden					
1970	40.8	41.0	79.5	48.7	62.4
1993	51.6	25.8	76.7	65.6	65.3
Denmark					
1970	38.6[d]	36.8	n.a.	38.5	n.a.
1993	47.1[d]	27.2	n.a.	62.5	n.a.
United Kingdom					
1970	37.7	46.6	74.4	43.8	54.4
1993	49.3	25.7	72.5	67.0	60.3
Austria					
1970	38.7[d]	50.6	n.a.	25.2	n.a.
1993	41.7[d]	39.1	n.a.	51.9	n.a.
Germany					
1970	34.7	55.8	74.2	42.9[e]	46.5[e]
1993	43.6	39.2	74.0	53.8	57.8

[a]Share of all wage earners and salaried employees, excluding armed services, including the unemployed.
[b]Mining and quarrying; manufacturing; electricity, gas and water; and construction (ISIC 2, 3, 4, and 5). Transportation, storage, and communication (ISIC 7) not included.
[c]Wholesale and retail trade, and restaurants and hotels; financing, insurance, real estate, and business services; community, social and personal services (ISIC 6, 8 and 9).
[d]Based on total civilian employment, includes self-employed.
[e]Includes ISIC 7; transport, storage, and communications.
Source: OECD, *Labour Force Statistics,* 1970–1990, and 1974–1994 (Paris, 1992 and 1996).

inantly providing jobs for women, and gender segregation has increased as more jobs were added.[3] Table 9.1 provides a picture of increasing gender-based labor market rigidities. The loss of industrial jobs has been matched by service-sector expansion. Only Great Britain experienced an overall loss

---

[3] A six-country comparative study by Esping-Andersen and others found women's share of public- and private-sector service jobs to be close to 70 percent, except in Germany (Esping-Andersen 1993a: 43).

of jobs in the period, corresponding to about 5 percent of the total labor market. It is disappointing but not surprising that women have been unsuccessful in making significant inroads in male-dominated industrial occupations during a period of decline. It is puzzling that men have not been able to take advantage of job growth in the postindustrial sector to a greater degree.

The result of these changes is a radical transformation of the working class in the past twenty-three years. In 1993, 40 percent of all British wage earners were women employed in female-dominated, service-sector occupations; in Sweden, 43 percent were. In comparison, only roughly 19 percent of all wage-earners in the two countries were men employed in industrial occupations. If we go back to 1970, male industrial workers accounted for close to 35 percent of all wage earners and female service-sector workers for little more than a quarter. The picture is somewhat different in Germany and Austria. In 1993, some 30 percent of all German wage earners were men in industrial occupations and women in service-sector jobs accounted for another 30 percent.[4] These are important transnational variations that help us understand the divergent policy responses of labor in the five countries. This brings us to the question of the role of labor market institutions in shaping stratification.

PATTERNS OF UNION MOBILIZATION

Although few countries have unions organizing exclusively on the basis of gender (Denmark does), highly gender-segregated labor markets are mirrored by unions depending on historically evolved patterns of organizing. Ironically, more working women may well increase gender segregation within and between unions. The high organization rates among women and among service workers have made Scandinavia a distinct model of pervasive unionism seemingly unaffected by recessionary labor markets (Golden, Wallerstein, and Lange, this volume; OECD 1991, chap. 4). In Sweden, women are now more likely to be union members than men in occupations organized by the LO unions. In addition, women dominate the white-collar unions. Forty percent of all union members are public-sector employees, and in the white-collar confederation, TCO, women constitute more than 50 percent of the membership.[5] In other countries, union organizing has historically often been weak in female-dominated occupa-

---

[4] Calculated on the basis of sources used for Table 9.1. Comparable figures are not available for Denmark and Austria.
[5] *Statistisk Arsbog för Sverige 1992*, table 214.

tions and in the service sector. The organization of gender bias across unions shapes the dynamic of political conflict over gender issues by making it into an occupational issue and, hence, also shaping the possible remedies available. If, in the face of industrial decline, unions react by protecting the interests of the core constituencies and fail to mobilize new members among new occupations, the long-term prospects for unions are, if not bleak, then quite different from the inclusive model of trade unionism held up as a goal in the past.

The long-term decline of manufacturing unions has been the greatest in the United Kingdom. Compared with their high point, manufacturing unions have lost about 2.5 million members, close to 50 percent of their members. British unions have made up for some of the loss by organizing more workers in the public sector, where employees now are more likely to be unionized than in the market sector. Table 9.2 shows changes between 1970 and 1988 in unionization levels by sector and gender in the five countries discussed.

Women employed in service-sector jobs have been the most important source of new union members in both Scandinavia and in Great Britain. German women are less inclined to organize, but the unions have still seen an increase in membership in the 1980s. In Austria, union density declined 10 to 14 percentage points across all sectors of the economy, the biggest loss of union members in any of the countries discussed here in this period. (Still, British long-term losses in union members exceed those of Austria.) The loss was concentrated in the market sector and among men. Table 9.2. gives us cause to speculate about the effect of heightened international competition for trade-union mobilization.

FOREIGN COMPETITION AND TRADE EXPOSURE

Differences with respect to the economic importance of exposure to foreign competition represent another source of conflict between groups of labor. The most sheltered sector of all is of course the government sector. Here workers need not worry about foreign competition when they bargain for wages. Although the public sector historically has been more resistant to unionization than the private sector has, the increased importance of trade exposure may make it comparatively easy for unions to mobilize workers in protected industries, for example, during periods of high unemployment and recession. Since the occupational definitions in the previous tables do not well reflect the public-private distinction, union memberships as a share of all employment in the public and the private – or market – sectors

Table 9.2. *Union members as percentage of all employees, 1970 and 1988*

	Labor force[a]		Public sector		Market sector		Female		Male	
	1970	1988	1970	1988	1970	1988	1970	1988	1970	1988
Sweden	67.7	85.3	n.a.	81.3	n.a.	81.3	53.7	88.3	77.4	82.4
Denmark	60.0	73.2	67.5	70.0	56.7	72.0	36.2	71.6[b]	74.7	78.0[b]
Austria	59.8	45.7	77.7	56.9	54.6	41.2	44.6	36.7[b]	72.8	56.8[b]
Germany	33.0	33.8	61.0	44.9	26.9	29.9	15.3	21.6	42.4	82.4
United Kingdom[c]	44.8	41.5	60.2	55.4	40.1	37.8	29.1	33.3	54.2	44.0

[a]Share of employed labor force.
[b]1985.
[c]The decline in overall British union density is probably underestimated in Table 9.1. The 1991 Labour Force Survey reported a density rate of 38 percent.
Source: OECD (1991), ch. 4.

are included in Table 9.2. Indeed, unionization is often higher in the public sector than in the private sector (e.g., in Austria, Germany, and the United Kingdom).

The question of trade exposure is linked to a related issue, which it is possible only to hint at in the context of this chapter, namely changes in collective bargaining institutions since the 1970s (see Moene and Wallerstein, this volume). In three of the countries discussed here, Austria, Denmark, and Sweden, confederational control over collective bargaining has been weakened – most dramatically in Sweden perhaps, where employers have dismantled the national bargaining apparatus – and wage disparities increased (Ahrne and Clement 1992; Katz 1993; Guger and Polt 1994). German wage bargaining institutions have remained largely intact in the West but show some strain, both from the incorporation of East Germany into the existing industrial relations framework and from the opposition of small- and medium-sized employers to reductions in weekly working hours (Silvia 1996). In Great Britain, collective bargaining has become decentralized to the point of fragmentation. British employers increasingly bargain directly with unions rather than through confederations or multiemployer bargaining (Walsh 1993; Edwards et al. 1992; Marsh 1992). The British case is an example of a possible trajectory of change that increasingly limits union capacity to engage in meaningful collective bargaining outside the public sector.[6]

INTRACLASS CONFLICT IN POSTINDUSTRIALISM

Our analysis of trade-union journals yielded clusters of contentious issues related to the accommodation of women and to postindustrial and post-Fordist occupations, but a few methodological reflections are in order before we proceed to link sociological change to policy change. We cannot distinguish between the influences of cyclical and structural causes of enhanced friction in the analysis of contemporaneous events. Hence, what looks like a significant shift in policy may in fact be a transient phenomenon, and vice versa.[7] We have two tools to help us distinguish between

---

[6] By one estimate, wages are determined by collective bargaining in only 40 percent of all British establishments with more than 25 employees (OECD 1994b: 181). France is another example of weak private-sector unionism. As little as 8 out of every 100 workers in the private sector are represented by unions (OECD 1991: 114).

[7] Declining trade-union membership is one example of coinciding cyclical and structural change. A 1980 study, for example, found that rising unemployment explains 44 percent of the decline in union membership, if the four countries where union memberships continued to climb irrespective of increasing unemployment – Belgium, Denmark, Fin-

temporary shifts and more fundamental change, in the present case. The first is that the rise in female labor force participation has been ubiquitous for twenty-five years or more, which suggests we are not looking at a transient phenomenon. Nor is it likely that an economic revival will restore lost industrial occupations. Second, the severity and pervasiveness of conflict also serve as a guide. Structurally based cleavages can be distinguished by their generalized and repeated manifestation in a broad range of policy disagreements, more so than conflicts induced by cyclical swings.

PART-TIME WORK AND JOBS FOR WOMEN

In a comparative perspective, a clear link emerges between women's labor market participation rates. The availability of part-time work boosts women's work force participation. The more women who work, the higher the incidence of part-time work and the more gender-segregated labor markets tend to be. Part-time work is a women's issue because women tend to work part-time. Between 1973 and 1995, the incidence of part-time work rose from 10–15 percent of total employment to close to 25 percent in Scandinavia and in Great Britain. (In the Netherlands, it represents more than a third of all jobs.) In Austria and Germany, part-time work has increased, despite policies hostile to part-time work, but it represents only 13–15 percent of total employment. In all countries, women occupy between 80 and 90 percent of all part-time jobs (OECD 1996a: 192). The apparent conclusion is that not permitting part-time work discourages women from working. It is somewhat ironic that part-time work so clearly emerges as a causal variable explaining levels of female work force participation, if we consider the history of opposition to part-time work as exploitative that informed both union opposition to part-time work and early feminist efforts in favor of a universal six-hour day.[8] But it appears that women prefer part-time work and flexible working hours to full-time work, even if they have a choice.[9]

land, and Sweden – were excluded from the comparison (OECD 1991: 106). Does that mean that unions will regain their losses if unemployment declines? It may, but on the other hand it may not. The Insider-Outsider theorem suggests that temporary shock may have long-term effects on wages and employment because of the changes in actors' orientations that are caused by the original shock (Lindbeck and Snower 1988: 241)

[8] The Swedish Social Democratic women's organization faced defeat on the issue when it was redefined as a family policy issue at the 1975 party congress (Karlsson 1996:288).
[9] Commission of the European Community (1993a): suppl. 3, 40; Commission of the European Communities (1993b): 158–160. For a survey indicating membership preferences contrary to union policies in this respect, see Kvindeligt Fagblad 2 (February 1994): 20–21.

In Scandinavia, women with young children continue to work (and work as much as married women) but close to 40 percent of women work part-time or reduced-time.[10] Close to 45 percent of British women work part-time. In Germany and Austria, only a third of all working women work part-time. Not coincidentally, the proportion of women who work is lower than in the other countries and trade-union policy has aimed to disallow part-time work. In addition, Christian democratic welfare state policies have continued to reinforce the male breadwinner focus of golden age wage policy and discouraged women from working (van Kersbergen, this volume). We are faced with two distinct approaches to the question of working women: one that discourages women from working by disallowing part-time work and emphasizing family care, another that allows part-time work and, in the Scandinavian countries at least, provides welfare state services sustaining women's participation in the labor market.[11] Union policies with respect to part-time work are clearly important for women. They are also important for unions, but in a less obvious way.

The official positions of the German, the Austrian, and the Scandinavian union confederations were for a long time the same. They opposed part-time work, fearing that it would undermine union control of working conditions. Nevertheless, part-time work has increased. Swedish unions changed their views first, accepting part-time work, and moved to ensure that part-timers were included under the union umbrella. Danish unions have dealt with the problem by officially opposing part-time work but in reality accepting it. British unions have had no coherent response, but some unions have moved aggressively to organize part-timers. German and Austrian unions have continued to resist part-time work.[12] Union opposition to part-time work has had unintended consequences because it impairs the capacity of trade unions to organize women and to represent women who work part-time. Unions have generally preferred to bargain for

[10] The distribution of actual working hours between men and women is similar in Denmark and Sweden. Fathers with young children work about forty-two hours per week on average, mothers about thirty-four hours (1988 and 1989 figures). For Danish figures, see *Ligestillingsrådets årsrapport* (Annual report of the Equal Opportunity Council) (1991): 221. For Swedish figures see *Statistisk årsbok för Sverige 1992*, table 188.

[11] Eighty percent of British working women work in female-dominated occupations, and 82 percent work in services. Within the European Union, Denmark and Britain have the highest incidence of gender-based occupational segregation (Commission of the European Communities 1993a: 35; Humphries and Rubery 1988). Austria has both the lowest participation rates of women in the work force, and the lowest incidence of part-time work (*ÖGB* February 24, 1994, 11 and March 31, 4).

[12] *Solidarität. Die Illustrierte des ÖGB* 757 (May 1994): 3–4. Verzetnitsch has been adamantly opposed to part-time work, declaring that, "Flexible Arbeitzeiten sind Alltag" (Flexible working hours are full-time work).

overall reductions in working hours, with the result that men get to work less, but working women still have few choices about how to combine work and family. In Austria, for example, male industrial workers successfully bargained for a thirty-five-hour work week, while white-collar workers who are also predominantly women still work forty-hour weeks.

Part-time work is concentrated in female-dominated occupations, like clerical and service occupations. Unions organizing in predominantly female service-sector industries have had little choice (despite the official position of national confederations) but to accept it. By extending union contracts to the part-time area and reducing wage competition (particularly on benefits) between part-time and full-time workers, some unions have done well among women. Responding to fierce competition among unions for membership, some British unions have been organizing very aggressively among women part-timers (e.g., NALGO, COHSE, TGWU, and Usdaw). Confederational structure turns out to be an important variable in this context. The decentralized character of British confederational structure has enabled British unions to be more responsive to the interests of women in this respect than the centralized Austrian and German confederations, which have remained dominated by the old industrial unions.

PAY EQUITY AND WAGE POLICY

In Scandinavia, pay equity between men and women increased in the 1980s and is comparatively high due to a gender-neutral pay equity policy ("solidaristic" wage policy) aiming at wage compression across industries and skills. Wage compression benefited women because it raised the pay of low-wage sectors relative to that of the high-wage sectors. One study estimated the earnings of unskilled women to be 90 percent of those of unskilled men (Persson 1990). Pay equity is particularly pronounced in the public sector. A 1982 Swedish survey found an earnings ratio of 1.7:1 between lawyers and nurses, for example, but with changes in the collective bargaining system wage differentials are increasing apparently with the consequence that gender-based pay equity also is rising again (Hibbs 1990; Hibbs and Locking 1996; Björklund 1990; Smith 1992; Rubery and Fagan 1994; Rosenfeld and Kalleberg 1990; Persson 1990). In Britain, in contrast, gender-based pay inequity is high. A study by the Equal Opportunities Unit of the European Commission (DG-V) found pay inequity between men and women to be higher in Britain than in any other European Union member state (Eurostat 1992: 118–119). Similarly, the 1992 earnings of Austrian women workers were only 65 percent of those of men.

Pay inequity is even more marked among salaried employees where women make only 61 percent of what men do, (*ÖGB*, February 24, 1994, 11).

In highly segregated labor markets, equal pay policies targeting pay differences between occupations help women by eliminating pay inequity in general. Once occupational equity ceases to be a primary objective for wage policy, gender inequity can only be remedied by means of gender-based policies. This dilemma currently marks Swedish wage policy, which now has shifted to the creation of redistributive pools for improving women's wages ("kvinno-potts").

Gender-based labor market inequality does not end with differences in pay but extends into benefits and social policy. Women are almost universally overrepresented among the unemployed, receive less than men in unemployment compensation, and receive considerably less than men in retirement benefits. Future inequality is guaranteed by the underpayment of women's contributions to retirement funds, particularly when contributions are tied to employment.[13] Feminists have been more inclined to demand a prominent place for equal pay regulation in wage policy and statutory regulation than trade unions have. This is not a new position that is informed by opposition to women's demands (it may be that too) but rather an expression of a principled opposition to government regulation of union affairs and collective bargaining in particular. Certain hallowed aspects of postwar union wage policy – for example, the emphasis on productivity improvement as a determinant of wages – conflicts with pay equity goals. Rather than linking pay inequities to the underlying differences in labor markets between trades and industries, feminists have tended to see labor market rigidities with respect to gender-based pay equity as caused by gender bias, "the historical legacy of social attitudes towards different forms of work" (Rubery and Fagan 1994: 285). Yet there are important obstacles to effective policy making in this respect. As long as women work in low-skill occupations and in services where there are real limits to productivity increases, economic constraints exist on how far pay equity can be taken. Pay differences are not simply socially constructed valuations but reflect differences in employer capacities to pay. There is no universal agreement on this issue. Rubery and Fagan argue, for example, that linking pay to productivity and skills imposes "a further burden on women in their struggle for equal pay" (286).

[13] *WSI-Materialen* 25 (May 1990). Figures for 1989 showed that the average difference in various retirement benefits and disability pay was 1:2.6 for female and male workers and 1:2.1 for female and male salaried employees.

QUOTAS FOR WOMEN

Although Scandinavian women have done well in national parliamentary elections and within the political parties, the trade unions have been slow to change (Haavio-Mannila 1985). Women constitute 49 percent of the Danish LO's members but only 10 percent of the leadership (LO, October 15, 1992, 6–7). Despite a decade of action plans and the work of a special equal opportunity committee, little progress has been made. The Swedish Social Democrats have moved further than any others in making special provisions for the representation of women within the labor movement to a point where the women's movement has become integrated with the labor movement. Nearly all Austrian white-collar employees are organized in one union affiliated with the national confederation, the ÖGB. This union is now the largest of the unions within the confederation but its clout has not improved the organization rate among women, nor changed trade-union policies with respect to women's issues. Union densities in service-sector occupations are relatively high but only 36.7 percent of all working women are union members.

In the highly centralized ÖGB and the less centralized but conservative-dominated DGB, change has barely been put on the agenda. The result has been that women remain marginalized within the unions. The TUC, DGB, and ÖGB have clung to a traditional socialist (and Communist) paradigm of "special" representation for women, through separate women's organizations and designated women representatives (*Frauenvorsitzenden*) appointed from above to be responsible for women's issues.

In Sweden, a carefully orchestrated campaign ensued prior to the implementation of a quota rule guaranteeing women half the seats on party boards and electoral tickets. "Soffan," a.k.a. Ann-Sofie Hermansson, an automobile worker at Volvo and rising star in the Swedish labor movement, regularly appeared in the labor press attacking the male dominance in the unions and the party. "We have created our own class society within the labor movement," she declared. After a grass-roots challenge to the party elite at the 1990 party congress, the leadership decided to invite the women in by the 1993 congress. The 1991 election loss likely influenced the decision. The 1993 congress gave women a promise of 50 percent of all party positions and a majority in the party leadership. The generational implications of the change were dramatic. Men with thirty years' tenure on the committee were made to retire.[14] The new executive

---

[14] One of the men with long tenure who was unseated declared, "I am proud to lead the menfolks' retreat." He declared, in the tradition of bombastic congress statements,

committee consisted only of appointees who were less than sixty years old.

The German SPD, the British Labour Party, and the Danish Social Democratic Party have all discussed quota arrangements for women but none of the accepted proposals have been as radical as that of the Swedish SAP. The SPD has agreed that women should have no less than 40 percent of all party offices and to apply quotas also to candidate lists in parliamentary elections. In the United Kingdom, majority elections are considered an obstacle to affirmative action and to the implementation of quotas. Affirmative action has for that reason been linked to the difficult question of changing to proportional representation (Lovenduski and Norris 1994; Loesche and Walter 1992).

Trade-union confederations and many trade unions have continued to oppose quotas guaranteeing women equitable representation in union councils or executive boards, in the leadership of social democratic parties, and on corporatist boards and agencies. In the context of party leadership positions and outside boards (e.g., corporatist oversight of policy making), increased representation for women in practice mostly implies less representation for unions. Within the trade unions, the issue has also assumed a generational dimension. The recruitment of women to leadership positions here often implies that men who have moved up through the ranks and waited their turn be passed over. The sanctity of union autonomy is the standard argument against effective equal opportunity rules.

WELFARE ISSUES

There is a great deal of evidence that women's work experiences and the conflict between work and motherhood strongly shape women's political views. Scandinavian women favor stronger state action, both in terms of economic regulation and welfare state expansion, than men do. They also opposed European integration and policy coordination more often than men. The difference in views is even more marked among younger women. Working women with low skills were particularly opposed to European integration and favored strong state action more than others. Moreover, the gap between men's and women's political views increased between 1977 and 1989 (Togeby 1994). The feedback loop between policies encouraging

"Women power in Europe will change Europe for the better." See "Med Soffan mot mansväldet," *SIA. Skogsindustriarbetera Facket* 1 (January 20, 1994): 19, and *AiP. Aktuel i Politik, Fackpressen* 35 (September 3, 1993): 2, and 38 (September 24, 1993): 14 and 35.

women to work and women's support for trade unions and the left is illustrated by the reversal of the gender gap in Austria and Germany, where women's unionization rates are lower and voting patterns distinctly more conservative. German women are more inclined to vote for the conservative CDU/CSU alliance, whereas in Scandinavia women have moved to the left of men (Kolinsky 1993: 118). The possibility that the difference is partly a question of lagged development is high, since younger women are less conservative than older women and more supportive of the SPD and a welfare state agenda.

Women's role as chief caretakers within the family is an issue that often stimulates contradictory policies and political strategy. The Scandinavian Social Democrats have appealed to women as a low-wage partner and as women in need of gender-abating social policies by means of a range of compensatory policies tied both to the labor market and the welfare state (Ruggie 1984; Lewis and Aström 1992; Jenson and Mahon 1993). By offering child care and parental leave arrangements, the welfare state has aimed to encourage women to work and to make it easier to combine the "caring" role with work. These policies have clearly benefited women's economic status, work participation rates, and increased women's support of both unions and the Social Democrats. They have still been met with disapproval by some feminist scholars who see the welfare state as reproducing gender bias in labor markets and in the family, because they accept that women are the primary caregivers in the family (Spakes 1989; Elman 1993).

The distinctly familialist policies of Austrian trade unions and the Austrian welfare state provide a sharp contrast. Austria also emerges as the most conservative example of a preserved Fordist appeal. A significant decline in trade-union membership figures (see Table 9.2) has done nothing to deter the unions from continuing with a commitment to traditional "productionist" policies and ignoring or opposing things that would help women. The unions want investment policies favoring traditional "productive" employment but oppose what have become known as flexible working conditions. A 1994 speech on union goals, by Fritz Verzetnitsch, the president of the ÖGB, referred to women only in the context of a demand for higher minimum wages. Union publications rarely discuss women and women's interests, except to oppose part-time work. Generally favorable toward European Union membership, the unions demanded exemption from its liberal rules. One example that received particularly heated press was that they permit women to work nights, which Austrian unions opposed strongly.[15]

[15] See note 12.

The German unions have been more inclined to try to appeal to women as a special group with special interests. The emphasis has been on special "women's issues" and symbolic action but not aimed to change core union policies. The declaration of the International Women's Day, March 8, as *FrauenStreikTag* (Women's Strike Day) is an example of how activism can be used to deflect energy from substantive change. Two white-collar unions, the HBV (Gewerkschaft Handel, Banken und Versicherung), which has a 70 percent female membership, and the ÖTV (Gewerkschaft Öffentliche Dienste, Transport, Verkehr) cooperated to make March 8 a special action day for what they called "imaginative" protests on women's issues. They suggested that women should refuse to make the usual coffee for birthday celebrations and not shop for the boss that day. Women might also bring their small children to work and demand that employers provide child care or that men assume more responsibility for housework (*ÖTV-magazin*, February 1994, 6). It was suggested by skeptics that money trouble and declining membership were among the reasons for this new activism on the part of the HBV, which competes with an independent union, DAG (Deutsche Angestelltengewerkschaft) for members. (HBV is affiliated with the national blue-collar confederation, the DGB.)

"Imaginative" protests do not help women unless they lead to real changes in policy, and that was more difficult. When activists argued that the high unemployment among women in the East should be listed as a special grievance together with a demand that more public works schemes be created, the demand was cut out in the end by union leaders.[16] It appears that the unions agreed to let the women activists "have" March 8, but were not willing to make real policy changes. The action day coincided with the final contract negotiations between employers and the two largest unions, I G Metall and ÖTV. No provisions in the contract agreement targeted women, nor was improvement of low-pay occupations made a special priority.[17] Even the symbolic attempts to give more attention to women ran into opposition from the very top. When the DGB prepared to march under the slogan *Frau geht vor* (Woman First) at the 1993 May Day demonstrations, the president of I G Metall vetoed it and the slogan was dropped. The I G Metall also prevented an article on the controversy written by a member of the DGB's women's department from appearing

---

[16] In the DDR, 80 percent of women worked in the late 1980s, representing 49.5 percent of the work force. With unification, many lost their jobs and the supportive services that sustained the high work participation rates of women; see Commission of the European Communities (1993b): 51; Erler (1988).

[17] *ÖTV-magazin* (March 1994): 4; *LederEcho. Zeitung der Gewerkschaft Leder* (January–February 1994): 14 and (April 1994): 3.

in the January 1993 issue of the confederation's journal, *Quelle* (Silvia 1998: 106).

How typical was it for unions to respond to the rising demands and needs of women by means of symbolic or evasive action? It will take a broader study than the present one to determine the larger patterns of union responses across countries and trades, but another example of awkward union reaction suggests that it has not been an atypical response pattern. It was provided by the general secretary John Edmonds of the British union GMB (General, Municipal, and Boilermaking and Allied Trades Union) in an interview with a magazine published by the predominantly female white-collar section of the union. Reflecting on Labour's loss in the 1992 parliamentary election, Edmonds said, "Looking back I still cannot understand why we allowed Labour's campaign to be so macho." He continued, "We did not mention those symbolic issues that would have convinced women that Labour was the party for them. Like removing VAT from women's sanitary products – a small reform that would have demonstrated that Labour really understands."[18] It was a bizarre expression of sensitivity but Edmonds has tried hard to reorient his union.

The instinctive response on the part of the unions has often been to define women as a weak partner in need of protection, rather than as a group of wage earners with specific demands, which unions may use to mobilize women organizationally and politically. This response hides self-interested behavior on the part of still male-dominated unions. The Austrian unions are a prime example. Political conflicts among different groups in the Social Democratic constituency (and on the left wing in general) have increasingly assumed the guise of cultural conflicts for reasons having to do with the divagating self-understandings of different groups of wage earners, particularly contrasted against those of "old" unionized labor (Kitschelt 1994a: 298). The quota issue has been linked to other organizational reforms aiming at modernizing trade unions and social democratic parties. The protracted conflict within the British Labour Party illustrates this thesis amply. Often portrayed as a conflict between "modernizers" and "traditionalists," policy reform within the Labour Party has been inextricably linked to reform of the ties between party and labor unions. It appeared in the context of constitutional change in the British Labour Party and the adoption of the "One Man, One Vote" (OMOV) proposal at the 1993 party conference, which aimed to reduce union control over the party. Reform debates brought repeated threats on the part of the tradi-

---

[18] See *Access: The Magazine for White Collar Staff* (Summer 1992): 13–14.

tionalist camp, such as Arthur Scargill from NUM (mineworkers) and Tony Benn, that they would support the creation of a splinter party.[19]

Some British unions supported reform, particularly the smaller and medium-sized unions that were tired of being dominated by the bigger unions within party organs and white-collar unions, such as NUPE (public employees), COHSE (health workers), USDAW (shop workers), but also AEEU (engineers). Bill Morris from the large TGWU (white- and blue-collar) opposed reform. Edmonds, whose unfortunate definition of woman-friendly policy was discussed already, had originally favored reform but later changed his stance.[20] The latter's vacillations can be interpreted as an attempt to satisfy both "old" and "new" labor groups within his union. The notable presence of Swedish traditionalists, who similarly responded to woman-friendly reforms with threats to create a new party, is further evidence of the universal quality of these debates.[21]

ECONOMIC POLICY AND EUROPEAN INTEGRATION

Intraclass cleavages were expected to cause conflicts over welfare state generosity. In stylized form, the conflict would look more or less the following way: while women have a strong interest in gender-abating policies, men working in the competitive market sector will resent increased welfare spending and be opposed to the generous welfare state. The latter would be inclined to think of public-sector workers as spoiled, and prefer fiscal restraint combined with economic policies attuned to concerns about national competitiveness. The former in contrast will prefer to erect protective barriers against the insidious influence of international competition and traditional Keynesian countercyclical policies boosting public consumption.

The stylized picture of intraclass conflicts based on gender issues and sectoral variation in exposure to international trade outlined earlier holds up only partly. In fact, trade-union support for the welfare state remains strong. The dichotomy between "old" and "new" labor often fails to describe the cleavage lines accurately. In Denmark, a union (Kvindeligt Arbejderforbund) that organizes close to 100,000 women working predominantly in the public sector or in low-pay service-sector jobs has been doggedly opposed to European integration and to any changes in a

---

[19] *Guardian*, June 19, 1993, 11, and *Tribune*, April 8, 1994, 12.
[20] *Guardian*, June 29, 1993, 24; Lovenduski and Norris 1994.
[21] *AiP. Aktuel i Politik, Fackpressen* 3 (July 30, 1993): 3.

traditional left-Keynesian welfare state program. Another union that has been sticking to old policies is the general workers' union (SID). The union has opposed bargaining centralization from the confederational level and the creation of new bargaining cartels.

Another Danish union, the metalworkers' union, *Metal*, does not share the fears of European integration of the female-dominated unions. It organizes predominantly male workers in the competitive market sector where employment has declined significantly in the past decades, but its policy views are distinctly post-Fordist. In fact, it is impossible to tell how many of its members are working in Fordist occupations compared to post-Fordist occupations. Bargaining decentralization has been welcomed by this union and it now self-consciously regards itself as freed from the old constraints of skills classifications. (British and Danish trade unions are the only union systems that have continued to organize predominantly on the basis of skills and retained the character of craft unions.) It has declared skills "irrelevant," and the union organizes skilled metalworkers and white-collar technicians side-by-side.[22] Politically, the union is centrist and its outlook is that of a professional association. Women are welcome, though few, and members are urged to improve themselves, for example, by learning languages. A survey of relative wage gains found women members within *Metal* to have benefited in particular from the decentralization of contract bargaining.

Metal stands out as an example of a union that has successfully bridged the gap between Fordist and post-Fordist production. Always fairly centrist with respect to economic policy issues, it has now embraced European integration and stressed the need to compete internationally. It supports the elimination of subsidies to shipyards and has taken a leadership role in supporting liberalization in international contexts. Together with employers, it participates in the formulation of European Union standardization directives. Complaints from members published in the membership journal that new standards were published only in English were refuted with the argument that language knowledge was a comparative advantage in international trade and a Danish engineer should be able to understand technical directions in English. Not surprisingly, this union has also declared the class struggle over and stresses the need for cooperation between employers and unions.

---

[22] An internal 1992 white paper boasted that, "The new 'blacksmith' still gets grease on the fingers every once in a while, but he (she) uses the screen and keyboard more often than the hammer." *Metal. Dansk Metalarbejderforbund*, November 1992, 6.

The British ISTC (Iron and Steel Trade Confederation) renders a sharp contrast to the trade liberalism of the Danish *Metal*. The ISTC favors protectionism, voted the opposite way of the Danish union on the issue of reducing subsidies, and supports a "Buy British" campaign aimed at limiting imports of steel, metal, and engineering products.[23] The ISTC also continues to regard the class struggle as important. *Metal* is a Fordist union turned post-Fordist, whereas ISTC is a Fordist union caught, at least for now, in a declining industry. The difference illustrates that variation in skill levels (by the ISTC's own account, the skill level of its membership compares unfavorably with that of sister unions in other countries) and industry performance are important for the capacity of a trade union to make the transition from Fordist to post-Fordist occupations. Ultimately, employer strategies play an important role in shaping trade-union prospects.

The survey of trade-union journals produced only few temperate protests against the high costs of the welfare state. To the extent there is a conflict, it takes the form of contention over public-sector wage demands and industrial action in the public sector. Public-sector unions couch their demands for pay raises in cautious terms, calling, for example, for "defense of the service level," and stress consumer interests in a well-functioning public sector. Sometimes, pay increases for public-sector workers have been marketed to other unions on consumptionist grounds: higher pay for public-sector workers increases demand and hence jobs for private-sector workers. The arguments barely sidestep the source of friction, namely that higher public-sector pay means higher taxes.

Even if contention over wage policy runs high, general support for the generous welfare state is still high. Surprisingly, the Danish *Metal*, the paradigm of the post-Fordist union, did not protest publicly about high taxes. The union has its reasons. First, chances are that the male post-Fordist metal worker is married to a postindustrial service-sector worker employed by the government. Second, one of the most criticized aspects of the Danish welfare state concerns the extremely generous unemployment compensation rules. Attempts at reform have changed very little, permitting the unemployed to stack as much as seven years of various kinds of support. Generous support helps the union shed members who are unable to make the shift from the wrench to the keyboard. Additionally, the union

---

[23] *Phoenix, The Iron and Steel Trade Confederation* 25 (November 1993): 3–4. At its 1993 annual conference, the union featured about 130 male speakers and only 1 female speaker.

remains in favor of some demand stimulation and thinks that deflation can be taken too far.[24]

Intellectuals and party elites may be trying to rethink the welfare state but the union rank and file still supports it as it was. At the 1993 Congress of the Swedish Social Democratic Party, which otherwise successfully promoted reform, the party leadership's new economic platform was voted down because it suggested that welfare state cuts were needed. It was felt that Social Democrats had no business campaigning against the welfare state.[25]

If there is a consensus position on the issue of the welfare state, there is none on European integration. Although their opposition is based on different concerns, European integration is an issue that unites "old" and "new" labor. Danish women who depended upon the welfare state either for services, benefits, or for their jobs are opposed. Male workers in low-productivity industries, such as Swedish forestry and fishery workers, and British steelworkers and miners, are at best lukewarm. The British unions would like to take the Social Charter, because it offers protections that they currently do not have, but want to do away with economic policy coordination; some Danish unions may take the Single Market, because they work in industries dependent upon access to foreign markets, but most would like to cut out social policy coordination, which is seen as a threat to existing generous policies. The Social Charter may make European integration look attractive to British women but it offers little to Danish women who have relied on national systems of wage regulation and responsive social policies for protection. The leader of a predominantly female union organizing housekeeping workers working mostly in the public sector expressed the reasons for her opposition by asking, "How can you strike against an EU directive?"[26]

German and Austrian unions favor European integration with few reservations. German discussions barely touch upon political union, which is considered a nonissue since most Germans fully expect German interests will dominate the union. In the British, Danish, and Swedish debates, political and monetary union produce more internal conflict than any other issue, apart perhaps from constitutional reforms that would reduce union control over the party.

---

[24] Metal, Dansk Metalarbejderforbund, May 21, 1992, 18–19, and June 24, 1994, 5.

[25] AiP. Aktuel i Politik, 38 (September 24, 1993): 20 and 9.

[26] The union is Husligt Arbejderforbund (Houseworkers' Union), which organizes cleaning personnel, cafeteria workers, and the like; see LO-Bladet 22 (November 19, 1992): 5.

CONCLUSION

The success of the Scandinavian Social Democrats in mobilizing women as trade-union members and loyal voters through special policies sustaining a compromise between women's work and family obligations is put in sharp contrast by Austrian and German policies discouraging women from working (Vogelheim 1988; Esping-Andersen 1993). In Austria, Denmark, and Sweden, national-level wage negotiations were of key importance to the creation of positive feedback between welfare state policies, Keynesian economic policies, and the accommodation of union interests within the corporatist framework, but not all groups of labor benefited equally. For that reason some groups are happier to see such negotiations go than others and the shift to decentralization has different implications in different countries (Swenson 1989; Pontusson and Swenson 1996). In Austria, women have no stake in centralized bargaining because they never benefited from it; in Sweden and Denmark, they did. The political response to decentralization will consequently also vary in these countries.

A broad picture of adjustment trajectories over the past twenty-some years emerges, which has involved one or more of the following reforms: (1) increased reliance on appeals to women as a special interest group and source of organizational and political rejuvenation (Sweden, Denmark, Britain, and increasingly also Germany); (2) reforms aiming to curtail the influence of the trade union in the party aiming to give the party greater autonomy, but with the corollary that the unions' ties to the party also are eased (Great Britain and Sweden); (3) increased political feebleness (Germany and Austria) or broad shifts to the center (Denmark and Britain). The more sweeping the changes, the better the party has done, illustrated by the Swedish Social Democrats and the Labour Party.

In Sweden, the party took the lead in shaping policies more inclusive of women. The new party elite has promised to take on the unions next.[27] The party's activism illustrates some important differences between parties and trade unions with respect to their susceptibility to gender issues. There are important strategic reasons for this. Unions represent the interests of

---

[27] After changing party rules to guarantee women 50 percent of leadership positions, the LO's equal-opportunity delegate said, "It is among the women that you find renewal and diversity. Therefore, the unions and the labor movement will have to let us in. And, as we have said, we will concede to half of the leadership positions." The last remark refers to the fact that women now constitute a majority of the LO's membership; see *AiP. Aktuel i Politik* 50 (December 17, 1993): 6.

existing members over those of potential members; parties concerned about winning elections target the marginal voter first, the core voter second. What prevents unions from adopting short strategic horizons, as when they decide to treat the rise of a nonunionized female population of service workers as a threat rather than an opportunity? Aside from the financial implications associated with declining memberships, declining unionization rates may ultimately be of greater concern to parties relying on the capacity of unions to mobilize voters than to unions themselves. The precise construction of union-party ties plays an important role here. In Sweden, the union-party exchange has for historical reasons tilted in favor of party control. In Britain, the unions have controlled the party through the bloc vote and through their dominant position in the National Executive Committee, which made constitutional reform a principal objective. Confederational structures similarly play a role. In Germany and Austria, the predominance of industrial unions that organize white-collar workers with blue-collar workers has sustained male industrial dominance within labor and worked to marginalize women. In contrast, the decentralized character of British unionism made it possible for particular unions to strike out on their own and organize women.

The radical transformation of the working class in the past twenty years has been a source of trade-union decline but also one of rejuvenation. In Sweden, Denmark, and Great Britain, public-sector workers and women have become main sources of union mobilization. Although the adjustment to post-Fordism has hit certain unions hard, leaving some trades behind to face extinction the way spinners and weavers once faced it, this particular cleavage assumes less political importance than the gender-based cleavages associated with the expansion of the service sector and public sector, in part because the numbers are smaller and the shedding of labor is ameliorated by the welfare state. In Britain, the ability of unions to represent workers in the private sector has been compromised, but not so in the two other countries. In Austria and the Federal Republic of Germany, no comparable reorientation of union efforts has taken place. This fact raises questions about the capacity of unions to represent new occupational groups and women in particular.

Two aspects of economic policy stand out as issues around which deep conflict based on intraclass cleavages revolve. One is international trade policy, the other wage policy. Wage policy has come under considerable strain from the divergent interests of private-sector and public-sector workers, so much so that central coordination and the associated need for confederational authority may be outright detrimental to union cohesion. This is only a problem in countries where central coordination has taken place in the past – Austria, Sweden, and Denmark. From a functionalist perspective, decentralization is an appropriate response to diversity and heightened group conflict. Unions derive distinct advantages from being freed of some of the responsibility for adjusting wage claims to other political and economic priorities. But from the perspective of economic policy, change in this respect raises important questions regarding the future role of trade unions in the regulation of capitalist economies. Encompassing trade unions generally are assumed to be more sensitive to macroeconomic priorities than unconstrained unionism (Olson 1982; Flanagan, Moene, and Wallerstein 1993; Moene and Wallerstein, this volume). I refer the readers to other discussions of the direction of wage policy in this collection. Even though confederational authority has given way, other mechanisms for restricting wage militancy are in place (Hibbs and Locking 1996). Pay equity is one of the more elusive and unresolved issues. As long as women predominantly are concentrated in industries where the link between productivity increases and wages is weak, women will depend on redistribution between sectors and classes for enhanced income. That makes pay equity a matter of high politics.

There are two groups of labor who will almost inevitably be opposed to integration and trade liberalism, although with varying degrees of intensity, because they want to hold on to social and economic protectionism which they, rightly or wrongly, see as threatened by European integration. This cleavage cuts across other cleavages, as is illustrated by the shared opposition of Scandinavian child care workers and British steelworkers. For the women, the issue becomes intensified by the coincidence of gender-based and sectoral cleavages reinforcing the conflict potential: as low-pay workers they are dependent on national wage coordination and as women they are dependent on the welfare state for their jobs. The Swedish Social Democrats returned to power in 1982 with a program for a "Third Way" that eschewed privatization and fiscal austerity (Mjøset 1996). Although the program failed, and the government later turned to austerity measures and social cuts, it still suggests a path for bridging the varying interests of workers in sheltered sectors and those in exposed industries. The Swedish example is particularly interesting because it worked (Mahon 1995).[28] The Swedish Social Democrats found a road back to power by articulating a new wage-earner feminism.

[28] A November 1993 election survey confirmed that the image overhaul almost immediately produced the desired results. It found support for the Social Democrats to be increasing in the two white-collar confederations, TCO and SACO. Gains were especially strong among younger people and women; See *AiP. Aktuel i Politik* 51 (December 23, 1993): 16.

The relative success of labor in Scandinavia and to a lesser extent Britain in mobilizing women has been a source of new organizational strength but also a source of new conflict. By including women in the left bloc, new incompatibilities arise that leftist economic policy must address, in particular the balancing of gender-abating policies and welfare state expansion against policies protective of economic openness and the competitiveness of export industries.

PART III

POLITICAL ECONOMY AND DEMOCRATIC COMPETITION

10

POLITICS WITHOUT CLASS? POSTINDUSTRIAL CLEAVAGES IN EUROPE AND AMERICA

Gøsta Esping-Andersen

Many claim that postindustrial politics is becoming classless. The erosion of materialist and collectivist values favors new social movements, "libertarian," ecological, or neopopulist parties at the expense of traditional laborist or Christian democratic mass politics. Socialist parties seem particularly vulnerable given their identification with a now vanishing working class. Political success today, it appears, means cultivating a diversified appeal or, alternatively, opting for a particular niche.

This scenario is said to be driven by vast structural changes, such as the declining salience of the capital-labor conflict, accelerated social differentiation, women's economic independence, and educational and job upgrading. In heterogeneous and highly mobile societies, the meaning of class should disappear altogether, and the working class, once the flagship of redistributive collectivism, will be destined to conduct a rearguard defense of past victories. New disadvantaged strata, such as contingent workers, single mothers, long-term unemployed, and welfare dependents, appear too amorphous to coagulate into a viable collective force. The post-

I would like to thank José-Ramon Montero, Herbert Kitschelt, and John Stephens for their generous comments on earlier drafts of this paper. Alas, I have not been capable of incorporating all their suggestions. I would especially like to thank Søren Holmberg for data on the 1994 Swedish electoral survey.

war "Fordist" politics were designed around the life conditions of a proto-typical standard (male) worker who is now in the minority Postindustrial politics, in contrast, will mirror a society of highly differentiated working lives and families.

How credible is this portrait? Manual workers are obviously declining, and jobs, skills, and occupations are steadily being upgraded. Similarly, the revolution of family structure and women's economic position is be-yond doubt. There is also much to be said for the optimistic scenario of a professionalized, meritocratic postindustrial society as depicted by Bell (1976) and, most recently, by Clark and Lipset (1991).

There is, however, a chorus of pessimists who see deep new social divisions arising from the ashes of the old class divide. Some emphasize the polarization of incomes; others, a cleavage between the postindustrial "knowledge" strata and an army of low-skilled, marginal workers. Still others, particularly in Europe, identify a new insider-outsider divide be-tween a shrinking, largely male, core of secure and privileged employed, and a mass of more or less chronically unemployed and marginalized pop-ulations (for the United States, see Kuttner 1983; Harrison and Bluestone 1988; Levy 1988; Burtless 1990; and Jencks and Peterson 1992; for Eu-rope, see Rodgers and Rodgers 1989; Brown and Scase 1991; Engbersen, Schuyt, Timmer, and van Waarden 1993; and Esping-Andersen 1993a).

We should be cautious in believing that such trends create class struc-ture. Classes have no meaning if, as with Schumpeter's (1964: 126) omnibus, they are "always full, but always of different people." Hence, inequalities do not generate classes unless they are accompanied by entrapment and social closure, unless the losers become a priori condemned to inferior life chances. The meaningful debate, then, is between those who claim that class politics will disappear because life chances are no longer systematically linked to class, and those who believe that new class divisions are emerging because postindustrial society is creating a new set of systematic losers.

The empirical problem we face is that society is in the midst of a great but incomplete metamorphosis. We may therefore identify sweeping po-litical dealignments without knowing where they take us. They reflect perhaps the demise of the old class order without giving a clear picture of a new, stable political order. A conclusive adjudication between the two alternative scenarios must clearly have to await the passage of time. What, in the meanwhile, is possible is to reexamine the evidence in a Popperian spirit; that is, to question the credibility of vying interpretations. This I shall do by means of comparative analysis. Most of the debate today is couched in terms of an assumed universality of change. I shall suggest that societies are heading in very different directions.

Just as today, the reigning models of postwar class politics also stressed universals at the expense of differences. Concepts such as the "democratic class struggle" (Lipset 1960, 1964a), the "frozen cleavage structures" (Lipset and Rokkan 1967b), and the "waning of oppositions" (Kircheimer 1957) were analytically powerful insofar as they captured a common thrust behind postwar political change. But as cross-national evidence accumulated, the claims seemed less universal. Nations embedded their particular "democratic class struggle" in very different institutional arrangements, and this meant that similar structural impulses produced more variety than grand theory would permit.

Today, all nations experience the universal thrust of economic globalization, industrial decline, and tertiarization. Such vast forces are filtered through national institutional structures, primarily the welfare state and industrial relations, and thus come to produce very different employment patterns and distributional outcomes. Postindustrial development is haunted by the kinds of arrangements that nations adopted in the "Fordist" era. Our analyses must accordingly begin a half century ago.

There are clearly losers and winners everywhere, but their configuration varies. I shall suggest that there are three distinct cleavage trends under way. Europe's strong welfare states and trade unions have helped sustain equality; in contrast, the weakness of both threatens to polarize seriously the American (and British) distributional structure. Scandinavia's welfare-state-driven service expansion has, so far, prevented employment marginalization but at the price of a heavily gendered, sectoral employment cleavage. Continental western Europe, and maybe Italy in particular, is producing an ever deeper divide between a privileged employed core and a swelling mass of excluded and possibly marginalized outsider strata.

The emergence of novel cleavages is a possibility because the postindustrial omnibus fails to unload many of its passengers. Across Europe we witness the spread of new, and rather ominous, class labels to depict the "outsiders" and losers. In Denmark, the distinction between an A-team (the winners), B-team (the losers), and now even a C-team (the thoroughly marginalized) is now part of everyday vocabulary. The Germans speak of the two-thirds society; the British, like Americans, have a new underclass; France has become a "société à deux vitesses." "Outsiders" that rely on social benefits are often identified as a distinct substratum of the slow-track class. Hence, the French "RMIstes" and "SMICs," and the Dutch "uitkeeringstrekkers" (benefit drawers).[1]

---

[1] RMI is the French acronym for social assistance while SMIC stands for the legislated minimum pay. Even French electoral surveys appear now to have embraced the new class

Do such protoclasses become political actors? I shall suggest that, yes, a new divide between the "A" and "B" teams does appear to be evolving, but only at the margin. Its significance fades in comparison to two more powerful – and apparently paradoxical – trends. The first is that conventional national political alignments remain surprisingly stable, notwithstanding the whirlwind of structural change. The second is that new cleavages around marginalized outsiders seem acute in only one group of nations – those in western Europe. Their absence in Scandinavia and North America is easily explained. However, their lack of articulation either in terms of class labeling or in the form of distinct "outsider politics" in Italy and Spain is somewhat of a puzzle when we recognize that nowhere else is the degree of measurable employment exclusion so extreme.

The chapter is organized in three parts. We first revisit the consolidation of the postwar "democratic class struggle" since this forms a necessary backdrop for understanding the diversity of contemporary trends. The second part interprets ongoing structural changes. And the third attempts to link structural and political-electoral trends.

THE DEMOCRATIC CLASS STRUGGLE REVISITED

The postwar pluralist model was credible as long as there was middle-class growth and a good chance of upward mobility: working-class children moved into white-collar jobs, and workers attained middle-class living standards.

Few postwar writers denied that the factory worker was still a factory worker, or that politics still spoke the language of class. Traditional cleavage structures were, indeed, frozen. Hence, the essence of Lipset's (1960, 1964a) "democratic class struggle" was not that class did not matter, but that it had lost its political bite because the conflict-producing *correlates* of class had disappeared: workers now enjoyed job security, high pay, and income protection across the entire life cycle; their offspring were not only likely to earn more than their parents, but also to experience upward class mobility. Life-style differences narrowed with mass home ownership and universal pension entitlements. Full employment and prosperity produced the affluent worker in Europe, the "middle class" in America (Myles and

---

language. A large proportion of French voters, for example, are in a self-declared "underprivileged" class, distinct from the standard notion of the "classes populaire" (Goldey 1993: 310).

Turegun 1994). For the average manufacturing worker in general, and for the unskilled worker in particular, the world seemed a much better place to live.

The vanishing correlates of class were intimately connected to trade unionism and the welfare state. Differences in both meant that the profile of correlates came to vary cross-nationally. America's more residual unionism and social policy helped create labor market dualisms, whereas Europe's highly elaborate welfare states and full-employment policies, combined with broad unionization and comprehensive interest representation, resulted in much greater homogeneity and equality of life chances, not only within the working class, but also between classes.[2] Put differently, in Europe (especially in Scandinavia) emerged a universalization of the Fordist life cycle.

Postwar European class politics came to be based not on pluralism, but on encompassing systems of class and interest representation within the framework of neocorporatist consultation and intermediation.[3] This helped reproduce classes as the principal collective actors, in particular in countries with strong social democracy, such as Austria and Scandinavia. But this does not necessarily imply that the less corporatist countries were more pluralist in the American sense; instead, they were dirigiste, as in France; pillarized, as in the Netherlands; clientelistic, as in Italy; or dictatorial, as in Spain.

Also, the European welfare states helped reproduce collectivist solidarities. The status-demarcated European social insurance tradition reproduces narrower, occupationally based communities, but also the conventional male breadwinner family model, thus stifling the "feminization" of the employment structure. Female employment and services in most of continental Europe remain far below American or Scandinavian levels. As we shall see, the emerging insider-outsider cleavage across continental Europe is very much a consequence of these welfare state attributes.

The universalistic "peoples home" welfare states of Scandinavia, in contrast, sought quite successfully to cultivate a broad solidarity of all wage earners and to universalize female employment. Thus was created the two-

---

[2] This has been widely documented in stratification, poverty, and income distribution research (Erikson and Aaberg 1985; Palmer 1988; Mitchell 1991; Smeeding, O'Higgins, and Rainwater 1990). Comparative data also point to a considerably greater degree of interclass equality in Scandinavia compared with the situation in the rest of Europe, mainly due to Scandinavia's much more universalistic and egalitarian welfare states (Mitchell 1991; Erikson 1990). Freeman (1993) shows that Europe's stronger welfare states and trade-union systems have helped prevent the degree of rising wage inequality that has occurred in the United States over the past decade.

[3] For an overview, see Goldthorpe (1984); Streeck (1992); and Regini (1992).

career family norm and a huge infrastructure of social services that, in its own right, constitutes a formidable occupational hierarchy. Here, welfare states' accent on employment maximization has not only helped avert insider-outsider cleavages but has, as I shall argue, also made women into independent class actors.

Neither of these two portraits captures well the British case, which, in western Europe, is unique (at least so far) in its deliberate or implicit strategy of scaling back the social wage and of recommodifying labor, both via welfare state reforms and trade-union erosion. In terms of employment and earnings trends, the British situation resembles more closely the American with sharply rising income inequalities, a "declining middle," and a growing share of "lousy jobs" (Gotschalk 1993; Freeman 1993; Esping-Andersen 1993a).

FROM HIGH INDUSTRIALISM TO POSTINDUSTRIALIZATION

Nations' solutions to "deindustrialization" determine how new social strata are formed. It is on this basis that nationally specific models of postindustrial stratification can be identified.

In terms of employment, most of the advanced economies reached the pinnacle of industrial mass production in the 1960s. The backside of the coin was massive deruralization. In Germany, primary-sector employment dropped from 32 percent of the labor force in 1930 to 9 percent in 1960; in the United States, from 25 to 8 percent. In Italy and Spain, deruralization came later, but was equally rapid. Italian agricultural employment dropped from 32 percent of total in 1959 to 21 percent in 1968, and 7 percent in 1993 (Paci 1973; CENSIS 1995).[4]

The success of the "democratic class struggle" hinged on the economy's spectacular ability to absorb the huge masses of "deruralized," largely unskilled workers. This was in most countries a success for two reasons. One, labor supply growth was slow because of the small 1930s cohorts and housewifery. Two, factory and construction job growth was buoyant. As a consequence, males could count on high-paid, secure employment which, in turn, permitted women to adopt the full-time house-

---

[4] Both Italy and Spain face the unique problem that deruralization and deindustrialization have coincided. This means that the huge numbers of basically unqualified rural workers could not easily be absorbed in well-paid factory jobs – hence, an added unskilled labor force surplus.

wife role. Still, toward the 1960s women's activity rates began to rise in tandem with the growth of sales, clerical, and service jobs. The employment contours of the democratic class struggle differed to the extent that Europe became considerably more "industrial," the United States more "distributional." At its peak, around the 1960s, the German, British, and Scandinavian manual working class accounted for roughly 40–42 percent of the labor force, compared with only 34 percent in the United States.[5]

Full employment and strong unions helped narrow intraclass differentials in terms of pay and job security. Thus was born the "standard worker." Europe's centralized bargaining systems and broader coverage under collective agreements assured a, comparatively speaking, extraordinary degree of status homogenization, mainly of benefit to the unskilled worker. In the United States, too, earnings inequalities and poverty declined, but as data on earnings differentials suggest, there remained a stratum of low-paid workers in the "secondary" economy. In Europe around 1970, the *lowest*-paid quintile of workers earned roughly 65–70 percent of the median, compared to only 41 percent in the United States.[6]

In essence, the postwar middle-class myth gained credibility because of affluence and the homogenization of living standards. It was far less a reality as far as class mobility was concerned. Indeed, Lipset and Bendix (1992: 165) cite data from the 1950s that show that 80 percent of American workers spent their entire career in manual employment. Most mobility was therefore "positional" rather than "class" – either *between* manual jobs, or movement into white-collar jobs by working class offspring (or wives). And, as more recent findings demonstrate, the lion's share of intergenerational upward mobility has been due to changes in occupational structure rather than greater openness (Erikson and Goldthorpe 1992).

This is the setting within which "postindustrial" employment transformation has unfolded. Just like deruralization in the 1940s and 1950s, deindustrialization now creates massive labor redundancies. But, this time

---

[5] Delayed deruralization in Italy meant also that the industrial working class proper remained smaller. At the height of Italian industrialism, say 1971, industrial workers accounted for only 34 percent (Paci 1973: 310). If not indicated otherwise, the data presented here derive from a cross-national employment data bank developed at the European University Institute. For a discussion, see Esping-Andersen 1993.

[6] The data discussed in the text derive from OECD (1993a: table 5.2) and refer to male wage earners only. The uniformity of European wage profiles is brought out by the rather narrow variance between countries. The most extreme egalitarian was the Netherlands (with 78 percent of median pay), and the most inegalitarian, France (with 61 percent). Note that both these cases are outliers and that virtually all other nations hover closely around 70 percent.

around it is accompanied by a huge growth in youth and female labor supply. The outcome now depends on the dynamics of services, which, in turn, are influenced by collective bargaining and welfare state structure.

"Postindustrial" occupational change favors skilled and professional jobs at the expense of unskilled jobs, servicing occupations over manual production jobs. Table 10.1 divides the working-age population, circa mid-1980s, into an "industrial," a "postindustrial," and an "outsider" stratum.[7] We confront three prototypical countries: Germany (West) exemplifies a best-case version of European "jobless growth," mainly because of slow service employment expansion; Sweden, the Scandinavian welfare state services-led model of employment change; and the United States, the deregulated, market-driven road to a service economy.

There is certainly some convergence: farming has virtually disappeared; manual jobs decline; and professional-technical occupations are a driving force in the emerging labor market. In the postwar decades, managerial, clerical, and sales occupations constituted the major source of middle-class growth, but they are now stagnant. Hence, upward class mobility in postindustrial societies depends very much on whether the skilled and professional service occupations grow. Full employment, on the other hand, depends on the growth of routine, less qualified service jobs.

A truly ideal postindustrial scenario would combine a slim but highly skilled industrial labor force with a largely professionalized servicing work force in a full-employment setting. This ideal is nowhere in sight. In Germany, so often depicted as the epitome of skill upgrading (see, e.g., Kern and Schumann 1984), skilled manual workers actually decline faster than the unskilled. But, then, Germany depicts the most "deproletarianized" service economy. But this is principally the result of sluggish job growth, due, on the one hand, to feeble public services growth and, on the other hand, to high wage costs, which suppress private-sector service growth. As a consequence, Germany provides no substantial employment outlet for either laid-off manual workers or less qualified women. Instead, both these groups have been managed primarily through labor reduction strategies: early retirement or unemployment for industrial workers; discouragement of female careers. Germany's favorable job-structure comes at the expense of employment exclusion.[8]

---

[7] Note that the occupational strata are measured in terms of percentage of the active labor force; the not-employed as a percent of the total active age population (ages sixteen to sixty-five).

[8] Germany scores systematically "worse" on all outsider indices. Had we instead examined Italy or Spain, arguably the two countries in Europe with the deepest insider-outsider divide, the rates of exclusion would have been dramatically higher. To cite some examples: the Italian not-employed rate is 46 percent; the long-term unemployed are 68 percent of total; and the monthly outflow rate from unemployment is only 4 percent.

Table 10.1. *Occupational distribution and the outsider population in the 1980s: Percentage change (in parentheses), 1960–1980s*

	Germany 1985	Sweden 1985	United States 1988
Primary sector occupations[a]	5.2 (−64)	4.4 (−68)	3.1 (−52)
Industrial society			
Unskilled manual	16.5 (−0)	12.4 (−42)	14.4 (−33)
Skilled manual	17.3 (−32)	15.2 (−18)	8.7 (−34)
Clerical and sales	29.6 (+30)	18.6 (+16)	28.3 (+21)
Managers[b]	4.5 (+36)	4.0 (−15)	9.1 (+17)
Total	67.9 (−0)	50.2 (−18)	60.4 (−8)
Servicing society			
Unskilled service	4.5 (−48)	16.9 (+78)	11.7 (−0)
Skilled service	5.0 (+194)	4.4 (−0)	6.6 (+57)
Professional-technical	17.3 (+121)	21.9 (+89)	18.1 (+56)
Total	26.8 (+47)	43.2 (+70)	36.4 (+31)
Outsider society			
Not employed	35.2	16.7	29.5
Long-term unemployment[c]	46.3	5.0	5.6
Probability of transition out of unemployment[d]	30.0	14.2	37.3

[a]Includes farmers, fishermen, and related occupations.
[b]Includes also self-employed (non-professional).
[c]As a percentage of all unemployed (1990).
[d]Monthly average outflow rate from unemployed, 1991 (in percent).
Sources: Recomputations from Esping-Andersen (1993a: tables 2.3 and 2.4); and OECD (1992b, 1994a).

In contrast, Sweden conforms to the industrial skill-upgrading thesis but suffers from strong skill (but not earnings) polarization in the service occupations. Sweden's capacity to raise female employment rates to world record levels is closely related to the huge numbers of (often low-skilled) public-sector jobs. And Sweden's formidable investment in retraining and active manpower programs has, until very recently, helped recycle redundant industrial workers into more qualified jobs. The combination of these two factors has helped avoid the growth of labor market outsiders, be it in the form of early retirees, mass unemployment, or discouraged women.[9]

---

[9] Overall female participation rates in Sweden and Denmark are around 80 percent, for women both with and without small children. This is double the rate in southern Europe

What stands out in the American trajectory is its greater skill polarization in both industry and services. Comparatively speaking, the U.S. economy remains biased toward unqualified jobs. Deindustrialization has reduced manual employment equally between the skilled and unskilled. But relatively low (and declining) wages have helped sustain the employment chances of the less skilled. Of course, our data disguise the fact that, in *absolute* terms, the number of net new jobs has risen phenomenally. Hence, the huge growth in women's employment, high levels of immigration, and the relocation of redundant industrial workers were made possible by massive growth in the volume of jobs.

The juxtaposition between Germany's more favorable skill mix and the large share of unskilled servicing jobs in both Sweden and the United States highlights a fundamental dilemma: today, a major employment expansion requires heavy growth in consumer and social services, both a reservoir of large masses of low-skilled jobs – hence a seeming trade-off between either joblessness or a mass of inferior jobs (Esping-Andersen 1993a). Of course, the "correlates" of inferior jobs matter. In Sweden, they are almost exclusively well paid and secure welfare state jobs; indeed, private-sector "Macjobs" are virtually nonexistent. In the United States, such jobs are mainly in the private sector, are typically poorly paid, and provide little job security – they are easy-entry jobs at the car wash, restaurant, or cleaners. In Sweden, the female concentration is extreme (about 80 percent), while American low-end service jobs tend to be ethnically (mainly Hispanic) rather than gender-biased.

A key point in the end-of-class argument is that postindustrial trends break up the traditionally homogeneous and collective experience of employment, thus promoting individualization and differentiation. In part, this is ascribed to the shift toward smaller-scale production units, a process that is obvious in the services, but also clearly present in manufacturing (OECD 1995b). And, in part, it is ascribed to a rise in educational attainment and a decline in peoples' employment stability over the life course.

Considerable differentiation is happening also because the leaner industrial working class is undergoing a combined process of upgrading and of "peripheralization." Manufacturing, once the bedrock of the industrial class divide, is rapidly becoming "deworkerized." Nonmanual occupations now account for a third of the total manufacturing labor force, and the

and 30 percentage points higher than in Germany. About 45 percent are part-time, although this is declining. In contrast to most other countries (except Italy), women's careers are life-long. The upshot is that the dual-career, double-earner family has become the norm.

tasks of production workers are increasingly concentrated on service and maintenance activities. In brief, the homogenizing effect of concentrated masses of manual workers is likely to weaken.

Equally important are the attributes of the growing service economy where, almost by definition, small-scale production units predominate, where Taylorist management and hierarchies are only marginally possible. Here the relations of production are predominantly between producer and client.

There is also evidence that suggests a destandardization of the life cycle. The stable "once a worker, always a worker" phenomenon is in sharp decline: careers are increasingly nonlinear. The risk of (long-term or repeated) unemployment has spiraled. The orthodox sequencing of school, work, and retirement for males, or school and housewifery for women, is crumbling. Education and retraining are now becoming a typical feature *during* peoples' working careers, as are also job and career shifts (Carroll and Mayer 1986; Mayer 1993). The differentiation of life courses is empirically documented for some countries, like Germany (Brose 1989; Berger, Steinmuller, and Sopp 1993; Mayer 1993), and Britain (Gershuny 1991).

The argument that class inheritance is declining, and that education is a source of class disarticulation is, however, not convincing. As Erikson and Goldthorpe (1992) show, the intergenerational transmission of father's class has remained basically stable (see also Cobalti and Schizzerotto 1994). It is of course true that the average level of schooling has risen everywhere. Yet, this alone does not automatically translate into greater life chance equalities. Indeed, the most systematic cross-national study so far shows that the impact of class background on educational attainment remains as stable as always (Shavit and Blossfeld 1993). Hence, a key source of class reproduction remains largely unchanged and this, indeed, may account for the sustained importance of class inheritance found in the Erikson and Goldthorpe study.

If mounting employment differentiation cannot be denied, its influence on collective behavior is less evident. We simply lack data. It is almost certain to promote greater heterogeneity within the "great" social classes as we know them, but it may also engender new collectivities and new divisions. It has, for example, been argued that specific phases in the modern life cycle will promote distinct collective interests, "chronopolitics" as Hernes (1987) calls it (see also Mayer 1993). The retired are an often cited "new class" with particularistic interests. It is also dubious whether the rise of service occupations generally, and professionalization in particular, will simply promote class disarticulation. In many countries, professionals are highly organized in peak national associations, such as the

SACO in Sweden, or in traditional corporative entities, such as in Italy and France. There is, in fact, good reason to suspect that postindustrial society will promote class closure at the elite level, if for no other reason than that access to privileged professional positions requires, virtually by definition, higher education. If, as research suggests, class inheritance persists with regard to educational attainment, class mobility into the new elites may very well become quite closed (Shavit and Blossfeld 1993; Gershuny 1993; Schizzerotto 1993).

At the other end of the pole, social differentiation is said to produce both exclusion and new strata of marginalized contingent workers. What, precisely, does this mean? Table 10.2 presents some rough indicators of both.

Youth (long-term) unemployment should constitute a particularly sensitive measure of labor market exclusion. The incidence of long-term youth unemployment (not shown in Table 10.2) is two to three times higher in Germany, France, and Italy than in either Scandinavia or the United States.[10] Italy epitomizes the insider-outsider labor market problem. Its overall unemployment rate hovers between 10 and 12 percent, almost all of which is concentrated among youth and women (and mainly in the Mezzogiorno). Thus, the adult male unemployment rate is below 5 percent but roughly 30 percent among young (under twenty-five) males, and more than 40 percent among young females (my calculations are based on the 1993 Italian Labor Force Sample Survey).

There are, in other words, indications that exclusion is hardening in the "outsider" societies, especially because exclusion tends to concentrate within households. European Community data show that the likelihood of wives being unemployed when the husband is unemployed doubles or even triples in most countries. The percentage of households with *two or more unemployed* is 15 percent in Germany, 22 percent in France, and 27 percent in Italy, but only 6 percent in Denmark.

The B-team of outsiders is, however, unlikely to crystallize into one distinct class. It is difficult to imagine an alliance of housewives, early

---

[10] The incidence of long-term unemployment in the fifteen to twenty-four age group (1990) is 4.8 percent in Sweden and 5.6 percent in the United States. In comparison, the rate is 38.3 in France and 71.1 in Italy. Germany has low overall youth unemployment, but a high incidence of long-term unemployment (46.3) (OECD 1992b). Note that an almost identical pattern emerges if we instead examine long-term unemployment among adults. Engbersen, Schuyt, Timmer, and van Waarden (1993: 30) provide an especially telling profile of Dutch unemployment. While the overall rate of unemployment declined from 1984 to 1990, the rate of hard-core unemployment (more than four years) more than doubled. A similar hardening of unemployment has been shown for Italy (Pugliese 1993).

Table 10.2. *Labor force marginalization and atypical employment*

	Youth unemployment 1991[a]	Temporary employment 1991[b]	Nonagricultural self-employment[c]	
			1975	1990
Denmark	—	11.9	9.6	7.2
Sweden	6.5	—	4.4	7.0
United States	12.9	—	6.9	7.6
France	19.5	10.2	11.1	10.3
Germany	5.6	9.5	9.0	7.7
Netherlands	10.5	7.7	9.2	7.8
Italy[d]	30.8	5.4	18.9	22.3
Spain[d]	31.1	32.2	15.7	21.0
United Kingdom	13.5	5.3	7.2	11.6

[a]Unemployment rate among workers aged twenty-five and younger.
[b]As a percentage of dependent employment.
[c]Excludes nonpaid family workers.
[d]Data on self-employment refer to 1979 instead of 1975.
Sources: OECD 1992b, 1993a.

retirees, excluded youth, and a variety of groups with a more or less irregular connection to the labor market. The various members of the slow-track population are certainly likely to perceive ongoing change in terms of ever rising relative deprivations. But if this is to find collective expression, the more probable scenario is social closure within distinctive subcategories, such as the SMICs or the unemployed.[11]

The postindustrial pessimists also point to a B-team of workers with inferior forms of employment such as contingent, temporary, or involuntary part-time workers. There is a similar reemergence of nonagricultural self-employment (often franchise workers). The upshot is the emergence of a class of peripheralized workers (Rodgers and Rodgers 1989).

Empirically, these trends are ambiguous. See Table 10.2. Temporary and casual workers have grown significantly only in France and Spain. Except for Spain, their share is hardly ever above 10 percent, which is what it was a decade earlier. They are concentrated in areas such as hotels and

[11] Ultee et al.'s research suggests, for example, the emergence of closed "unemployment careers," not only for individuals but for households as a whole (Ultee, Dessens, and Jansen 1988). Engbersen et al.'s (1993) and Pugliese's (1993) studies of the unemployed also indicate the formation of a distinct substratum of marginalized hard-core unemployed.

catering and involve primarily those same groups that tend to suffer most from labor market exclusion, women and youth (OECD 1993a). Other data point to a more dramatic scenario. Thus, French labor force survey data show that between 1982 and 1988, a little more than one million full-time, permanent contract jobs were lost while nonstandard employment grew by one million – half of which was part-time jobs (Maurau 1993: 366). Standing (1993: 433), citing employer confederation data, suggests that the number of workers on temporary contracts across the entire European Community has been growing by 15–20 percent annually since 1980. This is about ten times the overall rate of employment growth. Casey (1991) insists that we should expect nonstandard employment to grow much more in the 1990s.[12]

In Europe, a polarization between core and periphery workers may exist, but it is not clear enough to warrant generalizations. There *are* indications that the periphery work force coincides with the outsider population in terms of being heavily youth, female, and low-skilled. Indeed, there is a huge degree of mobility back and forth between these two statuses, suggesting that B-teams may very well be undergoing social closure. Whether they do so will depend on mobility chances from unemployment, precarious employment, or low incomes into regular permanent positions. Long-term entrapment in unemployment is clearly related to "exclusion." The mean duration is fourteen months in Germany and, indeed, thirty-nine months in Italy compared with a modest three to four months in Sweden and the United States (Esping-Andersen 1996). As regards precarious employment, Buechteman's (1993) findings for Germany suggest that chances for improvement are very good, while Bentolila and Dolado's (1994: 72) study of Spain paints a decidedly pessimistic portrait of a low-paid, chronically precarious class of marginal workers. If, then, there are signs that Schumpeter's omnibus fails to unload its passengers in Europe, there are also signs that America's superior performance in terms of unemployment entrapment is matched by an inferior capacity to guarantee escape from poverty. Duncan et al. (1995) show that the percent of families

---

[12] Official statistics may seriously undercount precarious jobs, especially in countries like Italy. Available studies do confirm a very widespread degree of black market employment which, virtually by definition, is "precarious" and void of any social rights. Irregular jobs in Italy grew at twice the rate of regular jobs during the 1980s. In Italy there is also a huge class (one to two million) of outworkers, principally women, but its size appears stable (Dallago 1990: 54–65). The combined size of temporary, casual, and outwork labor is estimated at circa five million, but many of these are multiple job-holders, pensioners, or persons officially unemployed. If, as Dallago (1990: 104) suggests, almost 30 percent of the unemployed really work, it is unlikely that such "outsiders" will become a distinct class.

who are poor three years in a row is 14 percent in the United States, compared with only 1.5 percent in Germany and France (Alsace-Lorraine) and 0.4 percent in the Netherlands.

Self-employment may be one new form of contingent employment. It has grown sharply in Britain (Feur 1991), but also in those very same nations with jobless growth, such as Italy and Spain. OECD (1992b: 175ff.) suggests that self-employment is particularly likely to grow in economies with strong job security provisions (for the "insiders"), and also that self-employment is a prevalent coping strategy among unemployed or laid-off males.

THE CORRELATES OF OCCUPATIONAL TRANSFORMATION

To Lipset and his postwar contemporaries, income was a key indicator of the declining correlates of class. The European nations may, like the United States, be undergoing massive structural changes but these are, so far, unaccompanied by changes in the distribution of household income or poverty rates. Except in Britain, strong unions and welfare states have upheld earnings and income guarantees (Freeman 1993). Indeed, earnings differentials in Germany have actually narrowed during the 1980s, and a sharp rise in poverty, such as has been found in the United States, has not been registered in Europe. In fact, all evidence points to a very stable profile of earnings and household incomes (OECD 1993a; Gotschalk 1993).

The stability of income distribution combined with very different patterns of structural change in Europe can best be explained by systems of institutional regulation. The Nordic countries' emphasis on employment maximization has safeguarded against marginalization, be it in terms of labor force exclusion or second-grade employment.[13] In addition, women have become fully incorporated in lifelong careers and are increasingly class actors in their own right as their economic dependence on the male partner diminishes.

Female "class attainment" in Scandinavia is, however, unfolding in an unusually segregated form within the welfare state hierarchy. Even though a large proportion of female employment is in bottom-level service jobs,

---

[13] Note, however, that even in the strongest welfare societies, a certain growth of marginalization has been registered. Ingerslev and Pedersen (1996) show for Denmark a 43 percent rise in the population stuck in semipermanent underemployment from 1990 to 1994. Still, this apparently dramatic trend involves a (so far) very small stratum.

educational opportunities and the dynamics of mobility within the welfare state hierarchy have by and large guaranteed good career-mobility opportunities. Thus, in Scandinavia (so far) the huge bottom-end service stratum is not synonymous with a class divide because its occupants are well paid, secure, and often upwardly mobile.[14] Still, for the exact same reasons, the Nordic model is nurturing a gender-sector axis with males concentrated in the more productive private sector and women in the less productive public sector. This is becoming a genuinely conflictual cleavage around which opposing collective interests and identities find articulation. Thus, the focal point of wage conflicts has shifted to the relative claims of the two sectors. As we shall see, a female public-sector "alliance" against a male private-sector "coalition" appears also to spill over into electoral behavior.

This contrasts sharply with trends in continental Europe where the contours of a divide between the "ins" and "outs," an A-team and B-team, are most apparent. To a degree, the cleavage is, as in Scandinavia, gendered. But, overall, it seems much more complex since it is overlaid by equally salient characteristics, above all youth (of either sex), being unskilled, and being a guestworker. In Scandinavia there is an element of homogeneity in the emerging postindustrial cleavage since it pits one sector and sex against another; in continental European countries, the B-team is much more likely to be internally divided. More importantly, in the "familialistic" Mediterranean countries, the B-team often disappears within the family in the form of unemployed youth continuing to live with their parents.

THE END OF CLASS POLITICS?

Lipset and Rokkan's (1967b) "frozen cleavage structure" varied in content across Europe so that, in many polities, the basic class cleavage was overlaid – and perhaps even drowned – by religious, ethnic, linguistic, or regional cleavages. The weight of some cross-cutting cleavages has clearly diminished, while in others it has grown (Rose 1974; Lane and Ersson 1991; Harrop and Miller 1987). Nonetheless, in some countries – Italy being a prime example – social class was never a major predictor of party choice. This should be kept in mind in any discussion of the erosion of class politics.

---

[14] This is clear from the results of panel data analyses of Denmark for the period 1980–1988 which, incidentally, was a time of relative stagnation and considerable unemployment (Esping-Andersen, Rohwer, and Sorensen 1994).

Those who insist that classes are "dead" emphasize, in part, the decay of traditional class organizations and parties and the surge of new-issue movements (e.g., the Greens) and, in part, the decline in class voting. The political death of class, it is typically held, accelerated in the 1970s and 1980s. At first glance, this view looks credible. Lipset (1991) and Clark, Lipset, and Rempel (1993: 312) point to the uniformly declining Alford index of class voting, and to the eroding support for socialist or left parties together with the shift in favor of postmaterialist parties.

There is considerable evidence in favor of such a view. Inglehart (1990a), for example, points to a steady generational rise in postmaterial values, and postmaterialists are more likely to support new movements. Similarly, Kitschelt (1990) argues the emergence (and consolidation) of left-libertarian parties that cater to specific strata, such as public-sector professionals and intellectuals. However, this kind of narrower "social strata voting" remains quite modest everywhere (5–6 percent of the electorate), and in some countries the traditional labor parties (such as the Swedish Social Democrats, the French Socialists, or the Italian PDS) have managed quite successfully to incorporate new postmaterial issues (and the rising postindustrial electorates) without any apparent loss of conventional class support. The Danish Socialist Peoples' party is the only case, according to Kitschelt's data, with a substantial left-libertarian following (about 14 percent of the electorate), but then this party, like its Italian or Spanish counterparts, the Rifondazione Comunista, and the Izquierda Unida, respectively, is a delicate amalgam of 1960s new left forces and old-style workerist socialism, dedicated to the defense of past privileges. Indeed, workers account for a large share of its votes.

From a 1990s perspective, left-libertarian politics appear less dynamic than do rightist politics. On one side we see the emergence of xenophobic, protofascist parties like the Republikaner in Germany, the Front National in France, the Centrumsdemocraten in the Netherlands, and the Vlaams Blok in Belgium. They may, as Inglehart (1990b) suggests, constitute the diagonal opposite to the libertarian left. On the other side, we find populist-liberalistic-rightist (and antiauthoritarian) protest parties like the Progress parties in Denmark and Norway, or the Italian Lega Nord. The sudden rise of the authoritarian protofascist right coincides with social exclusion, poverty, and mass unemployment; this is not the case for the populist protest movements.

Much has been said of the "end of social democracy," and, drawing on select cases (such as Britain) or elections (such as the recent French elections), there is some support for the view that traditional working-class parties (and trade unions) face considerable problems in maintaining their classical political hold in northern Europe.[15] And those that have emerged in southern Europe seem only vaguely, if at all, socialist. Still, it is long-run trends that matter and here the data paint a picture of stability rather than death. Substantial trade-union membership decline has occurred only in Britain. As to politics, the average strength of the European socialist parties from 1985 to 1992 is identical to that of the late 1960s to early 1970s, arguably the golden era of social democracy (Merkel 1993). Again, Britain is the only real exception.

Of course, electoral stability alone does not disprove the "death of socialism" thesis if nothing but the name remains of the labor parties. To Lipset (1991), they have irrevocably rid themselves of their ideological and material legacy. Few, and least of all socialist politicians, would dispute the fact that contemporary socialist parties – from Sweden to Spain – are in a state of programmatic floundering. There is probably not a single socialist party today that remains dedicated to the socialization of industry, and there are many that ardently advocate privatization. It is also evident that their steady electoral performance, in light of working-class decline, is due to a rise in "middle-class" support.[16] Indeed, it is evident that they are caught in a severe tension between preserving loyalty to traditional working-class causes and defending the position of the new strata of social losers. Such tensions are only aggravated by the fact that the conventional worker enjoys a menu of privileges and securities that, on one hand, are erstwhile labor movement achievements and, on the other hand, are obstacles to the social integration of the new "outsiders."

However, representational contradictions and programmatic paralysis cannot be equated with ideological death. Otherwise we would have had to bury the Scandinavian socialist parties already in the 1930s, the German SPD and the Austrian Social Democrats (SPÖ) in the 1950s, and the French socialists and Italian Communists in the 1970s. As exemplified by the European-wide Socialist Party working group on "Social Justice," and now also the program revision committee (chaired by Filippe Gonzales) of the Socialist International, it is clear that socialist party elites are energetically engaged in a reformulation, not burial, of the egalitarian promise (for an overview, see Gillespie and Paterson 1993; and Miliband 1994). In brief, it is difficult to draw conclusions on matters pertaining to the substantive content of contemporary labor parties precisely because, as in the

[15] See Visser (1992) for a most recent analysis of trade-union decline.
[16] In the following, I shall make use of a rather crude "working class," "middle class" dichotomy, mainly for want of more detailed occupational information regarding party support. By and large, the former refers to the traditional blue-collar workers while the latter combines the conventional white-collar employee with the new professions.

1930s, they are wrapped in the fog of rapid transformation, the outcome of which may not be clear for years to come. Clearly, much will hinge on trends in class voting.

Here, one thing appears clear. Those labor parties least capable of ridding themselves of their orthodox workerist image tend to fare worst. As we have seen, occupational change upgrades manual workers all the while that it condemns them to minority status. As British research shows, the massive working-class defections from the Labour Party in the past are connected to its failure to modernize programmatically (Crewe 1991; Kitschelt 1994a). But a resurgence (including a return of disaffected workers), such as we currently see in British Labour, can happen if the party manages to turn its back on old-style workerism.

There may, however, also exist a trade-off. Socialist parties that abandon their workerist image may, like the Italian Party of the Democratic left (PDS), provoke an exodus to the left (the Rifondazione), especially if the traditional working class sees its erstwhile "Fordist" political gains, such as job security or pension rights, threatened.

When we examine class voting trends in greater detail, there is little evidence to suggest that conventional political cleavages are dead. Instead, they are being overlaid by new kinds of "class" politics: the frozen cleavage structure may be thawing at the edges. In the traditional social democratic stronghold of Scandinavia, class was always the dominant determinant of party choice. Recent data indicate that this has changed only moderately (Björklund 1991; Andersen 1992; Gilliam and Holmberg 1990). In Sweden, the percentage of workers voting left has been a constant two-thirds from 1968 to 1988. The Danish and Norwegian social democratic parties may have suffered working-class defections, but they went mainly to their socialist peoples party rivals on the left. Social democracy's capacity to maintain its aggregate voter share is based on growing white-collar support, especially from women in public-sector jobs. Indeed, since it is likely that lower-level female white-collar workers are married to working-class men, the social democratic parties' loss of working-class allegiance may be purely epiphenomenal (Björklund 1991: figure 2; Andersen 1992: 93).

The *general* trend across Europe shows a similar profile of rather stable class voting (Dohring 1990; Lane and Ersson 1991; Kitschelt 1994a).[17] Kitschelt (1994a) shows that, from the mid-1970s to the mid-1980s, working-class support for the left rose in Belgium and Germany, was stable in Italy, declined marginally in the Netherlands, and declined somewhat

---

[17] As is well known, some European socialist parties, such as the French, have traditionally been middle-class parties.

more in France. The picture looks somewhat less stable when we disaggregate the "left" and segments of the social classes. Indeed, several trends suggest the emergence of new class (or intraclass) cleavages superimposed upon the traditional – and still operative – class divide.

The rise in white-collar salaried-employee support for the left in Scandinavia is quite bifurcated between a female, public-sector social democratic camp, and a male, private-sector camp harboring anti-public-sector attitudes that tend to favor the right. In Sweden, public- and private-sector employee support for socialist parties was similar in the mid-1970s (50 and 48 percent, respectively); by 1991 had emerged a gap of 10 percentage points (Gilliam and Holmberg 1990; Björklund 1991). The sector gap has become even wider in Denmark. From an identical 40 percent support for social democracy in 1971, the socialist share among private-sector employees had fallen to 33 percent, but risen to 59 percent among public employees in 1990: from a differential of zero to 26 percentage points! The difference becomes even more extreme when we control for sex (Andersen 1992: 96–100). Thus, where social democracy was once the voice of the male working class, it is now becoming the party of the (largely female) "welfare state classes." The other side of this intraclass realignment is the right-wing drift of private-sector *males*, in large part to the anti-welfare-statist and vaguely xenophobic-populist Progress Party. In both Denmark and Norway, it is quite overrepresented by private-sector, manual working-class male voters, while its support from public employees is truly marginal (Andersen 1992: 104; Björklund 1991: figure 2).[18] Scandinavia, then, depicts stable, traditional class voting overlaid by a new "welfare state" cleavage (Andersen 1992; Korpi 1993).[19]

Turning to continental Europe, the old, especially religious, cleavages have waned while, as Dohring's (1990: 31–88), Merkel's (1993: 81), and Kitschelt's (1994a) overviews show, working-class support for traditional left (and conservative) parties is virtually unchanged since the 1970s, be it in Holland, Germany, France, or Italy. And, white-collar support for the socialists has shown a modest growth over the past decades.

Realignment is somewhat more visible at the disaggregated level. In contrast to Scandinavia, the new alternative left parties on the continent

---

[18] It is important to note, however, that Danish Progress Party voters do not advocate a rollback of social benefits (Andersen 1992). Put simply, they like pensions but not social workers.

[19] Andersen (1992: 93) shows that left-party support has fallen somewhat among workers (from 82 percent in 1964 to 71 percent in 1990) and has risen among nonmanual wage earners (from 41 to 48 percent). Korpi (1993: 6) shows essentially the same trend for Sweden from 1956 to 1988.

draw their strength almost entirely from the "postindustrial winners": younger, educated, middle-class voters. Thus, in Germany (1987 data), the educated "middle class" was about three times more likely to support the Greens than were workers.

A perhaps more profound intraclass change involves the losers in the labor market. In Scandinavia (and Britain), unemployed or marginalized workers show no tendency to shift party allegiance (Björklund 1992; Harrop and Miller 1987). Indeed, workers who support the Danish and Norwegian Progress parties are decidedly not marginalized, nor – despite the parties' antiimmigration stance – are they concentrated in high-immigration communities (Andersen 1992; Andersen and Björklund 1990). In brief, a political divide between the A-team and B-team has failed to materialize in Scandinavia.

But, continental Europe, with the notable exception of Italy and Spain, displays exactly such tendencies. Thus, recent data for France, Germany, the Netherlands, and Belgium point to a possible new polarization in which the losers increasingly favor the protofascist, xenophobic right. For Germany, Kolinsky (1992: 70–79) suggests that the Republikaner Party draws its following from the "losers of modernization," the bottom third of the "Two-Thirds" society. According to Feist and Liepelt's data (1990: 99–106) those without risk of job loss vote almost equally for the CDU and the SPD (46 and 43 percent, respectively), while employees in threatened jobs are more than twice as likely to support the SPD (64 percent compared with 28 percent for the CDU). The pendulum swings, however, among those who actually *experience* marginalization (unemployment). With 21 percent prepared to vote for the extreme right, this group is four times as likely to support the extreme right as is the population average. Similar evidence is available for France where Jean Le Pen's Front National finds its strength among young, unemployed, low-level working-class males in high-immigration areas (Hainsworth 1992a: 44–48). Those who are self-declared "underprivileged" have, between 1988 and 1993, moved sharply to the Front National. Thus, 20 percent of the "underprivileged" support the FN, which exceeds their support for the Socialist Party (14 percent) *and* the Communists (16 percent). The voting pattern among the "Classes Populaire," that is, stable working class, is exactly the opposite (Goldey 1993). The profile of right-wing extremism is virtually the same in the Netherlands and Belgium. The Dutch Centrumsdemocraten is most powerful in poor, high-immigration areas of the main industrial cities (Husbands 1992a: 115–120). The Belgian Vlaams Blok has become the single largest party in Antwerp and succeeded, indeed, in winning more than 10 percent of the aggregate Flemish vote in 1991. Husbands (1992b:

139–141) indicates that its supporters are similar to the profile of French, German, and Dutch ultrarightists.

The puzzle is southern Europe where labor market exclusion is unusually heavy, while new class labels and a new politics of the marginalized hardly exist. The best, if somewhat speculative, answer has to do with the strength of the family. Unlike in most of Europe, a young unemployed person does not stand naked in the marketplace but is firmly integrated in a broader family system, both for welfare needs and for occasional employment.[20] Youth may be unemployed but are not socially excluded. Their politics are thus more likely to be allied to familial political interests. And in this case, family interests most probably coincide with the preservation of parties dedicated to job security and high pensions.

In Italy, of course, the neofascist MSI (now the Alleanza Nazionale) has existed since the war and, together with the Lega Nord, could be seen as the voice of protest. But neither party has much in common with the New Right north of the Alps. To be sure, both espouse antiimmigration policies, but this is far from being their defining characteristic. The MSI/ AN is above all a nationalist law-and-order party that appeals to traditionalism, a strong unified state, and a continuation of Christian Democracy's earlier practice of "assistentialism" in the Mezzogiorno. The Lega is, in many respects, a Latin version of the Nordic Progress parties with its blend of hyperliberalist, antibureaucratic, and antitax, petit bourgeois ideology, coupled with federalist aims (Mannheimer 1993; Sidoti 1993). The Lega may articulate a "politics of anger," but this is the anger of the well-to-do, not of a new lumpen proletariat.

CONCLUSION

The Clark-Lipset thesis rests on shaky ground even if it correctly points to greater individualization and, with it, an erosion of the compact workerist *Weltanschaung*. The problem with the "death of class" thesis is that it too uncritically equates the contemporary flux with a steady disarticulation of class. With marginal exceptions, the working-class vote is as left as it always was. And, by and large, the social democrats have compensated for the shrinking working class by gaining among the growing white-collar

---

[20] In Italy and Spain, 80–90 percent of young unemployed live with their parents. This compares with about 20 percent in Germany, Belgium, and France, and less than 10 percent in Denmark (OECD 1995b: table 1.18).

strata. Hence, the long-run electoral support for most European socialist parties, if this is what they still are, remains stable.

There is less stability when we examine nuances. On hindsight, the amazing durability of the social democratic and Christian democratic mass parties lay in their capacity to secure working-class welfare in the era of high industrialism. Their fate, today, is closely related to how they simultaneously manage working-class decline and the rise of new strata.

Being in control of government, the Scandinavian social democrats were uniquely placed to expand public employment while minimizing marginalization. In so doing, they inadvertently nurtured a potential public- and private-sector cleavage with strong gender undertones. They averted, at least so far, heavy marginalization and the rise of a new underclass.

The continental European strategy of managing structural change through labor reductions has, in contrast, created a wholly different interest constellation: on one side, a huge population of retirees whose welfare depends on erstwhile "Fordist" politics; on the other side, a similarly huge population of outsiders. The new marginalized strata, especially the unskilled and young, are sinking behind, not catching up. Indeed, their fathers' high earnings and job security have become prime obstacles to their own chances of achievement. But they will see this very differently, depending on family structure. Latent insider-outsider conflicts are emerging in France, Germany, and the Low Countries, but not in Italy or Spain. In the latter countries, in fact, unemployed sons have a vested interest in safeguarding their fathers' pension rights.

The new marginalized groups certainly do not make up a coherent and homogeneous stratum, and their social articulation differs substantially from country to country. Still, there is clear evidence that this is where the new right finds its strength, and this is where antiimmigrant xenophobic ideologies have a receptive clientele.

In summary, the weight of the evidence leads to a double rejection of the more radical "end of class" formulations. The first is, paradoxically, that Lipset's "democratic class struggle" remains in large part well and alive. Trade unions remain the principal mechanism for economic interest intermediation; they have in many countries been extraordinarily successful in organizing also the new postindustrial strata. Traditional patterns of class politics are equally persistent.

The second rejection refers to emerging new cleavage patterns, in particular the public- and private-sector employment cleavage in Scandinavia, and the A-team and B-team cleavage in the European Economic Community countries. These new divisions *may* be producing new protoclasses. The coincidence of labor market marginalization and right-wing extremism in many European nations has closer affinities to the class conflicts of prewar Europe than to any image of a classless postindustrial society. If the opportunity structure for youth, women, and the unskilled remains as blocked as it is today in much of Europe, we are more likely to see a rebirth of Disraeli's Two Nations than a pluralist haven.

11

EUROPEAN SOCIAL DEMOCRACY BETWEEN POLITICAL ECONOMY AND ELECTORAL COMPETITION

Herbert Kitschelt

In the 1980s and 1990s, social democratic parties have experienced unprecedented difficulties in choosing and implementing economic policies. At the same time, they have found it harder to frame electoral appeals in an increasingly complex environment of party competition. The pressure to make choices in innovative ways, in turn, has generated strains in social democratic party organizations and has affected the loyalty of party members and activists. Explaining the diverse trajectories of European social democratic parties in these decades requires a substantive and a theoretical departure from conventional accounts of social democratic success that worked well for the post–World War II era labeled by some contributions to this volume the "golden age" of social democracy.

In substantive terms, if social democracy has the fundamental objective of moderating wage earners' exposure to market risks (due to sickness, old age, unemployment) and engineering significant income redistribution toward the less fortunate in society, while promoting economic growth, then the strategic opportunities for such policies have dramatically changed since the 1950s and 1960s. In those decades, high postwar economic growth rates, a stable proportion of the population in retirement, national controls over financial markets, and the absence of competition from newly industrializing countries allowed social democrats to expand the welfare state and create full employment while maintaining balanced budgets.

From the transition decade of the 1970s onward into the 1980s and 1990s, opportunities for conventional social democratic growth and social security policies have deteriorated. Now social democrats find themselves in an environment of lower per capita growth, an aging population calling upon massive social-insurance-covered health and pension entitlements, open capital markets, new foreign industrial competitors, and new political concerns with the domestic quality of life, multiculturalism, and participatory democratic procedures that constrain the favorite social democratic problem solving techniques – economic growth and centralized administrative governance of a culturally homogeneous population. I argue in this chapter that the altered socioeconomic and cultural environment generates dilemmas of social democratic political-economic choice at the level of government policy. The political-economic dilemma is intrinsically linked to two other dilemmas of political choice, the struggle for votes in the electoral arena and the mobilization of support for electoral and political economic strategies inside social democratic parties. The way social democrats address the political economic alternatives depends on the answers they provide for their electoral and organizational dilemmas. Conversely, political economic choices reduce or intensify electoral and organizational dilemmas.

In theoretical terms, the study of social democratic party strategy calls for a bridge across the familiar divide between students of comparative political economy and parties and elections. Political economists typically assume that social democratic policy preferences are exogenous and stable so that economic policy variance among social democratic governments depends entirely on the political web of interest intermediation and state capabilities in conjunction with economic conditions. Political economists rarely, however, consider varying social democratic policy objectives in the context of changing conditions of electoral competition that derive from new voter demands and strategic stances of their competitors and are mediated by intraparty coalitions.[1] Conversely, political scientists analyzing the electoral and organizational fortunes of social democratic parties have typically shunned the opportunity to place the parties' strategic choices and electoral coalitions within changing political-economic conditions and institutions.

This chapter analyzes social democratic strategic dilemmas in order to make a modest effort to link political economic concerns to the dynamics of party systems and party organization in advanced capitalist democracies. It builds on previous publications (Kitschelt 1994a, 1995) that emphasized the *limitations* of accounting for parties' electoral fortunes in terms of po-

---

[1] For a critique of this blind spot, see Keech (1995: ch. 4).

litical economics alone. In this chapter, however, I examine the *interdepend-ence* of political economy and electoral party politics. More as an illustration than a proof, I apply this theoretical framework to account for social democratic electoral and government fortunes in the first half of the 1990s.

POLITICAL ECONOMY AND PARTY COMPETITION

In simple political-economic models of electoral business cycles and partisan politics, politicians do not choose strategic appeals and policies. Electoral business cycle theories assume opportunistic politicians in an ideology-free world and naive voters with converging objectives.[2] Little evidence, however, confirms the predictions of political business cycle theory (cf. Lewis-Beck 1988: ch. 6). In models of partisan government economic control, both the early simple models (Hibbs 1977; Castles 1982), as well as later rational-expectations variants that predict transitory partisan effects of economic policy in the immediate aftermath of electoral victories (cf. Alesina, Cohen, and Roubini 1993; Alesina and Rosenthal 1995), postulate fixed government party preferences. They do not explain variance in parties' programmatic appeals in terms of the exigencies of electoral competition.[3]

This limitation also besets more sophisticated institutionalist political-economy models that account for economic strategies in terms of the inter-action effects between partisan government and systems of interest intermediation (beginning with Lange and Garrett 1985 and Scharpf 1991). Because such models conceive partisanship in terms of exogenously fixed "leftist" or "rightist" party programs, rather than party leaders' variable strategic choices coping with changing voter demands and competitor strategies, they do not sufficiently explore the diversity of political-economic strategies pursued by the same leftist parties at different points in time. The strategic calculus of party politicians, predicated on voter preferences and strategic stances of competitors, is not an integrated component of partisan political-economy models.

The literature on electoral partisan politics suffers from the reverse

---

[2] Cf. Nordhaus (1975). As a critique, see Alesina and Rosenthal (1995: ch. 7), Alt and Chrystal (1983: ch. 5), and Keech (1995: ch. 3).

[3] Potentially, the "divided government" literature promises some comparative leverage (cf. Alesina and Rosenthal 1995: ch. 10), but that has been exploited more in the parties, coalitions, and elections literature, quite divorced from political-economy concerns (e.g. Strom 1990).

one-sidedness. It ignores political-economic institutions and processes, but focuses on sociological accounts of voter preferences that are then fed into various models of party competition.[4] Studies of electoral dealignment and realignment, for example, devote much attention to the changing role of class and social structure for voters' political preferences, but ignore political-economic developments such as the expansion of welfare states, changing patterns of collective bargaining, or increasing international exposure of domestic economies vis-à-vis world market competition as powerful forces affecting political demands (cf. Dalton, Flanagan, and Beck 1984; Crewe and Denver 1985; Franklin et al. 1992). But patterns of competition and government formation over time shape political-economic features, such as comprehensive welfare states in open economies. Such features, in turn, generate conditions for the lasting electoral success or failure of certain political parties.[5] Recognizing these linkages, Przeworski's (1985) account of social democratic parties' electoral fortunes makes an effort to combine institutional analysis and political economy in the study of electoral party performance, but it remains sociologically too rigidly focused on class formation in early twentieth-century capitalism and institutionally too narrowly concerned with class compromises emerging in the aftermath of World War II to be useful for the analysis of social democratic strategic dilemmas and electoral politics in advanced capitalist democracies.[6]

In electoral studies, the only literature to offer a bridge to political economy deals with the short-term effects of economic performance on retrospective and prospective economic voting. But while perceived or expected economic performance undoubtedly has *some* effect on parties' electoral support, the nature and magnitude of this effect and its cross-national variance are not well understood (cf. Paldam 1981; Lewis-Beck 1988: ch. 1). Moreover, electoral voting studies never model parties' strategic appeals as an explanatory variable that intervenes in voters' retrospective or prospective assessment of the economy and the partisan inferences they draw from it.[7] Several studies have linked the magnitude of changes in party

---

[4] Such models postulate spatial, directional, or issue based competition among vote- or office-maximizing parties.

[5] Esping-Andersen (1990) and Katzenstein (1985) make efforts to account for this linkage from the electoral and the political-economy side.

[6] For a theoretical critique, see Burowoy (1989). Sainsbury (1990) and Kitschelt (1993) present evidence contradicting Przeworski's claims.

[7] Alesina and Rosenthal (1995) argue that sophisticated voters discount parties' strategic stances. Hence, parties have never an incentive to change their reputation through new voter appeals. MacKuen, Erikson, and Stimson (1992) examine how voters employ economic data on the past to generate prospective economic judgments, but also here partisan appeals play no role.

support due to retrospective economic voting to institutions of party competition that facilitate or impede voters' attribution of economic outcomes to political parties, such as the presence and form of coalition governments (cf. Lewis-Beck 1988: ch. 7; Powell and Whitten 1993). In a similar vein, political-economic institutions, such as collective bargaining systems and welfare states, may affect the intensity of economic voting.[8]

My sketchy review of the literature at the interstices between political economy and party competition motivates a research agenda that exceeds this chapter, but gives it a reference point and direction. The interaction between parties' choice of strategic stances in the arena of intraparty debate and interparty electoral competition for voters, on the one hand, and the institutional conditions and material consequences of economic policy making for growth, employment, and income equality, on the other, provide many opportunities for innovative comparative analysis.

SOCIAL DEMOCRATIC STRATEGIES BETWEEN ELECTORAL COMPETITION AND POLITICAL ECONOMY: MULTIPLE TRADE-OFFS

Social democratic party strategies and outcomes can be analyzed in terms of three interconnected dilemmas. The first is the *political-economic dilemma* that those economic policy strategies which have allowed social democrats in the 1980s and 1990s to gain government office in the short run contribute to serious electoral losses and eventual defeat of left-dominated cabinets in the longer run. Closely related is the second, the *electoral dilemma* that winning or preserving government office often may involve sacrificing vote shares, yielding a trade-off between strategic objectives that occur in multiparty systems with at least four relevant competitors. The third is the *organizational dilemma* between a party's commitment to an internal organization that facilitates strategic flexibility and responsiveness to changing "tastes" in the electorate and an organization that captures a loyal "core electorate." Organizational flexibility is beneficial for vote- or office-seeking politicians in the short run, but introduces an element of strategic volatility that may hurt a party's reputation for policy consistency in the long

---

[8] For a rationale and a tentative test, see Kitschelt (1994a: 109–110). Where pluralist systems of collective bargaining and weak welfare states prevail, voters engage in more retrospective voting, because they are more vulnerable to market developments than under conditions of corporatist collective bargaining and strong welfare states.

run. Moreover, it may allow to ascend into the party's dominant coalition politicians who pursue policy objectives which are neither vote nor office maximizing.

The three dilemmas are interdependent. Social democrats accept political-economic strategies risking significant long-term electoral losses, particularly among their core electorates, *only* when they are also prepared to resolve the electoral dilemma in favor of an emphasis on government office rather than vote seeking. This preference, in turn, depends on an internal commitment to cope with the organizational dilemma by favoring organizational flexibility at the risk of strategic volatility, together with a loss of reputation and entrenchment in a core constituency.

THE POLITICAL-ECONOMIC DILEMMA

In contemporary capitalism, the strong demand for highly skilled employees to operate flexible production systems and sophisticated business, financial, and cultural services has contributed to wage differentiation and job polarization (cf. Kern and Schumann 1984; Piore and Sabel 1984). At the same time, international capital-market integration and new industrial competitors offering lower unit production costs for all but industries relying on the highest-skill employees make it more attractive for many firms and sectors exposed to foreign competition to move production facilities away from advanced industrial countries. These tendencies contribute to occupational, firm-level, and sectoral conflicts of interests inside the capitalist core countries that undermine the capacity of unions to homogenize labor interests vis-à-vis employers and, as a consequence, the ability of social democratic politicians to appeal to workers and employees as a homogeneous electoral constituency.

Employees in exposed sectors competing with lower-cost foreign producers develop an interest in limiting production costs, including the "social wage" and taxation that finance the welfare state and public services, while employees in the domestically sheltered sectors, particularly the public sector, see no reason to restrain their demands. Moreover, in open economies with few capital controls, social democratic governments cannot resort to expansionary demand-side fiscal policies to boost employment and growth, because such policies would fuel imports, inflation, and ultimately the out-migration of further industries. In the 1950s and 1960s, social democratic governments had the capacity to resort to Keynesian expansionary fiscal policies of deficit spending, but sustained economic growth relieved them from resorting to such measures and focused their attention instead on "supply-side" policies of economic modernization and labor requalification; beginning with the oil shocks in the 1970s, most social democratic governments have felt a need for expansionary fiscal policies, but discovered that in the changing political-economic environment it has become increasingly difficult to employ them successfully.[9]

Against this political-economic backdrop, social democrats cannot hope to avoid economic policies of market liberalization that increase the international competitiveness of domestic economic sectors by reducing the costs of factor inputs and making their combination more efficient. What still distinguishes them from conservative parties is the search for policy formulas that makes economic liberalization less painful for the most vulnerable constituencies in society than the policies their competitors are likely to choose. Social democrats search for a different balance between equity and efficiency and present themselves as better political managers of capitalism, because their commitment to comprehensive social policies, job retraining and education, advanced infrastructure, and industrial modernization builds on the insight that sometimes a judicious use of nonmarket arrangements assists a productive economy more than an ideological zeal to assert the rules of the marketplace in all matters of economic governance.

Nevertheless, social democrats cannot avoid revising their conventional commitment to a mixed economy with significant public enterprise in favor of more market liberalization. At this point, they run into the political-economic dilemma of social democratic governance. On the one hand, social democratic efforts to deny the need for liberalization have relegated social democrats to the opposition benches, no matter how bad the economy performs under sitting conservative governments. This occurs either because they lose voters who doubt the parties' credibility, or they lose potential coalition partners because centrist parties demand market liberalization. On the other hand, where social democrats embrace economic liberalization and stabilization programs, either as opposition or governing parties, they initially broaden their electoral support or their range of potential coalition partners, particularly if they control the median voter. Once in office and committed to a policy of market liberalization, however, they follow a trajectory of gradual and often accelerating electoral decline. In fact, a robust predictor of electoral decline for social democratic government parties in Austria, Belgium, France, Germany, Italy, the Netherlands, Sweden, or Spain in the 1970s and particularly in the 1980s is their success in reducing inflation, a result of austerity policies and market lib-

---

[9] Sweden is an exception. Here currency depreciation served as a functional equivalent to expansionary fiscal policies in the 1980s and 1990s.

eralization. Changes in unemployment levels, by contrast, appear not to affect their electoral fortunes.[10]

> Dilemma 1: Either social democratic parties stay or are pushed into the opposition because they signal aversion to economic liberalization policies. Or social democrats embrace such policies, lead governments, but then experience precipitous electoral decline, once in office and pursuing liberalization strategies.

It is worth noting that conservative governments are not exposed to an equivalent dilemma. Changes of their electoral support appear to be unaffected by unemployment, inflation, and economic growth in the 1970s and 1980s. What is the micrologic underlying this uniquely social democratic dilemma? Faced with austerity policies, handed down by a social democratic government, many of its core supporters who expect a defense of the welfare state and short-term job creation rather than expenditure cutbacks and market liberalization abstain from voting or support more leftist parties, including the parties of the libertarian left. This pattern of defections becomes more common because the 1970s and 1980s witnessed the increasing salience of noneconomic issue dimensions – ecology, feminism, disarmament, multiculturalism – on which social democrats could embrace new libertarian demands only at the cost of alienating core voters. As a consequence, *social democratic electoral losses usually do not significantly benefit "bourgeois" parties, although they may prompt a defection of coalition partners and a loss of social democratic bargaining power over government formation.* Little direct symmetric economic voting takes place in the sense that voters, disappointed with social democratic governments' economic performance, would transfer their vote to the "bourgeois" parties.[11]

Why do some social democratic parties grit their teeth and persevere with austerity policies, while others abandon the market liberalizing program or never endorse it in the first place? Reasons for differences in social democratic strategies may lie in conditions of the electoral marketplace, imposing smaller or greater losses of voters and bargaining power on social democratic parties if they embrace market liberalization, and in the parties' internal patterns of interest mobilization and decision making. Whether or

---

[10] For a model specification of the statistical estimates, see Kitschelt (1994a: 109–110).

[11] This is consistent with Bartolini and Mair's (1990) finding that net electoral volatility is increasingly within ideological blocs, not across them. Left-libertarian parties have a commitment to market-correcting economic policies and thus tend to be close to the leftist bloc.

not parties accept the political-economic dilemma and commit themselves to austerity thus depends to a considerable extent on the ways they address the *electoral dilemma* and the *organizational dilemma*.

THE ELECTORAL DILEMMA

Sociological and political-economic changes in advanced capitalism create a dominant dimension of salient electoral preferences and interparty competition that runs from left-libertarian politics, at one pole, to right-authoritarian politics, at the other (Kitschelt 1994a: ch. 1).[12] Left-libertarians endorse an encompassing welfare state and economic equality, while simultaneously calling for a politically participatory and culturally tolerant, individualist society. Right-authoritarians favor a residual welfare state and a broad scope of market competition, combined with hierarchical political deference structures and conformity with traditional moral values that emphasize the paternalist family, ethnocultural homogeneity, and the bindingness of collective norms.

An interaction of sectoral and occupational self-interests in the current political economy with cultural preferences shaped by voters' education, occupational task structures, gender, and consumption styles creates the distribution of political preferences over this dimension. Left-libertarians tend to be highly educated and overproportionally female individuals in client-interactive jobs employed in economic sectors sheltered from international market competition. There is no group more committed to left-libertarian politics than young educated women in public personal-service jobs (education, social counseling, health care). At the other extreme of right-authoritarian politics, male, less educated individuals who are self-employed or work in private industry and perform simple manual or clerical tasks are overrepresented. There are many political positions between these extremes. Moreover, some are removed from what is today's main axis of political division, such as the shrinking manual labor force with nonmarket, but more authoritarian inclinations[13] or the growing electorate of highly educated private sector managers and self-employed professionals with promarket libertarian orientations.[14]

With the changing long-term salience structure of political preferences

---

[12] Comparative evidence for this argument is discussed in Kitschelt (1995).

[13] The theme of "working-class authoritarianism" goes back to Lipset (1981 [1961]) and has generated research up to the present (cf. Middentorp 1993).

[14] For a further discussion and refinement of authoritarian-libertarian political preferences, see Altemeyer (1988). Knutsen (1995) maintains that the religious divide is a further political dimension that is only partly captured by the authoritarian-libertarian divide.

and the shrinking old social democratic core electorate that is leftist on economics, but not particularly libertarian on culture, and the consequential need to attract new constituencies, social democrats are compelled to consider (1) whether and how much to embrace market liberalism and (2) whether and how much to adopt political and cultural libertarianism. More market liberal positions would particularly appeal to private-sector employees, especially in the internationally exposed sectors, but meet resistance from traditional core electorates in the public sector and sheltered private-sector industries. Adopting culturally more libertarian positions would help social democrats to attract younger and well-educated public- and private-sector voters, but precipitate an attrition of older less educated blue-collar workers and simple clerical employees who would become available to new rightist parties with strongly authoritarian appeals, no matter whether these also attract small-business people with promarket appeals.

Social democrats are thus caught up in a system of electoral trade-offs quite unlike those postulated by Przeworski (1985). How they will make strategic choices over programmatic appeals, and thus, by implication, how they address the political-economic dilemma as well, depend to a considerable extent *on the magnitude of electoral penalties* each strategic alternative is likely to generate. In a stripped-down model, I suggest that the number and relative strategic position of competing parties determines the relative costs of alternative social democratic electoral programmatic appeals. This is not to suggest that no other forces affect the cross-national and intertemporal diversity of social democratic party performance, such as the varying size of economic sectors,[15] short-term factors (sudden crises, scandals, political personalities, economic performance under a government), or cross-national differences in the salience of economic and noneconomic issues.[16] Nevertheless, when we examine a sufficiently large number of elections, a simple spatial model of multiparty competition with competitors located along the left-libertarian versus right-authoritarian political dimension captures the basic dilemma of social democratic party strategies and gains contours in spite of the noise of all the short-term forces that impinge on election outcomes. This model rests on four assumptions.

---

[15] I would maintain that hitherto sheltered economic sectors, such as finance, insurance, construction, telecommunication, and transportation (rail, airlines), become economically exposed and increase the pressure for economic liberalization that impinges on social democrats (cf. Kitschelt 1996).

[16] For an explanation of cross-national variance in the extent to which noneconomic libertarian-authoritarian issues matter for the competition among the major parties, see McGann and Kitschelt (1995).

1. There are at least four relevant parties in the system, one of which is a serious competitor located to the libertarian left of the social democratic party, with the other two being in the center or on the authoritarian right.
2. Competition among the parties is spatial in a single dimension and voters support the party closest to their ideal point.[17] Only minor parties may carve out niches on secondary dimensions, such as ethnicity or special interest (farmers).
3. Obstacles to the entry of new parties (electoral laws, party finance, mass-media attention) and the distribution of voters give parties an incentive to differentiate their strategic appeals, even if they are vote seeking.[18]
4. Voters cannot abstain, vote sincerely, and take the declared stances of parties at face value, without discounting them in light of some prior reputation.[19]

Given these circumstances, let I, II, III, and IV be announced party stances that range from a centrist position on the economic left-right and the libertarian-authoritarian axis (strategy I) to a pronounced left-libertarian position (strategy IV). Social democrats can choose between strategies I and II and their left-libertarian competitors between strategies III and IV. Now consider the payoff matrix of the parties' different stances in Table 11.1. The left-libertarian parties, facing competitors only on the moderate side, but not the radical side, have a simple dominant strategy if they wish to maximize their political influence. They always opt for the more moderate strategy III. In contrast, social democrats face a dilemma. Strategy II maximizes their electoral return and appeals to a vote-maximizing party, no matter what is the strategy of the left-libertarian competitor. But strategy I is attractive to an office-maximizing party, because social democrats would control the median voter, given that left-

---

[17] I am ignoring here Rabinowitz and MacDonald's (1989) directional theory of voting, which is theoretically insightful, but also relies on spatial arguments (e.g., a "zone of acceptability" within which successful parties must operate on each dimension) and yields empirical results only marginally different from strictly spatial theories of voting.
[18] Rabinowitz, MacDonald, and Listhaug (1991) demonstrate that without such assumptions and a single-peaked voter distribution around the median voter, in a spatial model no equilibria would be possible. All parties would have an incentive to adopt increasingly "centrist" positions, but then disappear in a "black hole," as more radical parties displace them from the outer flanks of the political space.
[19] These and other idealizations of simple spatial models of multiparty competition are spelled out by Shepsle (1991).

Table 11.1. *Electoral trade-offs of social democratic strategy*

	Strategic choices of left-libertarian competitors		
Strategic choices of social democrats	Intermediate III	Radical IV	Combined payoffs of SD+LL
Moderate II	42%/6%	45%/3%	48%
Centrist I	36%/15%	41%/10%	51%

libertarians could not collaborate with parties on the right-authoritarian side of the political spectrum, thus making social democrats the pivotal party in all government formation.[20] In this situation, social democrats can choose between a left-libertarian and a centrist coalition strategy and maximize their control of government and policy making, although they lose voters. The second dilemma thus can be formulated as follows:

> Dilemma 2: In the presence of a strong left-libertarian competitor, either social democrats maximize votes but fail to win the median voter and therefore have only limited bargaining power over government formation, or they maximize their bargaining power by controlling the median voter but sacrifice votes to their left-libertarian competitor.

Whether a moderate strategy delivers the pivotal voter to the social democrats also depends on the number and location of "bourgeois" parties in the center and the right-authoritarian sector of the competitive space. The electoral costs of a moderate strategy approach a maximum for social democrats if (1) the left-libertarian competitor is credible and relatively moderate (strategy III) and (2) the social democrats' road to capturing the pivotal voter is blocked by centrist "bourgeois" parties. Conversely, the moderate strategy is most attractive and least costly in the face of a weak left-libertarian party and little centrist competition.

The social democratic response to the political-economic dilemma may thus be linked to the electoral dilemma in the following way. Where social

[20] The "tipping point" for social democrats to control the median voter may be lower than 50 percent support for all parties on the left-libertarian side of the competitive dimension, provided that some parties in a highly fragmented system fall below the threshold of electoral representation.

democratic parties encounter a particularly sharp trade-off between vote- and office-maximizing strategies, such as when strong left-libertarians squeeze them from the left and centrist parties block them from the right, they will be most reluctant to embrace centrist strategies of market liberalization in order to gain the median voter by sacrificing electoral support among left-libertarians. By contrast, where the parties face little left-libertarian competition and weak centrist alternatives, they are more likely to choose the office-maximizing strategy together with a market-liberal resolution of the political-economic dilemma. Whether or not either strategic alternative occurs, however, also depends on the mechanisms of political preference articulation and aggregation inside social democratic parties and here we encounter the third dilemma.

THE PARTY ORGANIZATIONAL DILEMMA

Strategic flexibility enables social democrats to embrace more market-liberal, "centrist" positions to capture the pivot of the party system or, at other times, to adopt more libertarian stances with the objective of keeping left-libertarian parties at bay. But both moves imply a departure from the parties' strategic status quo in the post–World War II era, the smallest common denominator of which is a mixed-economy model with comprehensive welfare state and income redistribution toward the less well off. Strategic flexibility requires forceful innovators who can move the parties' mainstream toward new positions. *From the bottom up* new entrants into the party organization may push strategic innovation. Innovative new members are particularly influential, if the traditional party membership is sufficiently small so that even modest-sized new groups have considerable weight and compel party leaders to compete for their support. *From the top down*, political leaders can push strategic innovation, if they enjoy considerable autonomy from rank-and-file opinions and protection from the threat of displacement by competing leaders endorsing status quo policies. Empirically in the 1980s and 1990s, in social democratic parties innovation from below through new party entry tended to push left-libertarian ideas, whereas autonomy at the top sometimes favored left-libertarian ideas, but more often boosted market-liberalizing, centrist political appeals.

In terms of organizational structure, the two major obstacles to strategic flexibility are an inert mass-membership organization (roughly indicated by member-voter ratios of 10 percent or greater) and a leadership that is strictly accountable to a large base of intellectually immobile organizational constituents. Mass-membership parties are particularly conservative and resistant to strategic innovation where they are constructed around extensive clientelist networks penetrating the state apparatus and public industry, as in Austria, Belgium, and Italy, and increasingly in Spain, but not in Scandinavia and Germany. Yet even without clientelism, mass-membership parties often become an impediment to strategic flexibility because innovators have a hard time convincing the mass of voting members that change is needed. The uphill struggle that women, ecologists, and libertarian Christian groups encountered in the union-dominated Swedish social democrats in the late 1980s demonstrates this problem well (cf. Kitschelt 1994b). If there is a large mass organization, strategic innovation is likely only where the top leadership can isolate itself from day-to-day accountability. Rank-and-file activists have great leverage over the leadership, if local party organizations control the nomination of legislative candidates, if national party conferences take place frequently, and if the party executive leadership is divorced from the legislative leadership. An innovative leadership, by contrast, tries to centralize as much decision-making power as necessary in as few party executives as possible.

Organizational reforms that increase the innovativeness of social democratic parties from below require membership attrition in mass parties, a process accelerated by (1) the abolition of automatic party membership when joining labor unions and/or (2) the removal of material membership incentives where clientelism prevails (preferential public housing and jobs for party members, party-affiliated social insurance funds), and (3) a reduced decision-making role of territorial party sections in favor of functional committees configured around study groups, clubs, and task forces addressing particular issues. From the top down, leaders gain autonomy for innovation, if (1) they can schedule fewer party conferences (and preferably before elections), (2) they control the nomination process for parliamentary candidates, (3) executive and legislative party leadership are integrated, and (4) the party leadership loosens its ties to the labor unions, which are, on balance, a conservative force in all Western social democracies opposing their strategic opening toward libertarian sociocultural and centrist-liberalizing economic positions.[21]

In the competitive electoral environment of the 1980s and 1990s, the decline of the old "machine model" of mass-party organization benefits social democrats not just because of its operational drag on strategic flexibility, but also because of its liabilities as symbols of a bygone era. The mass party is the symbol of a "Fordist" social order in which large numbers

---

[21] This generalization does not rule out exceptions. Educators' and cultural workers' unions, for example, fight economic liberalization, but not sociocultural libertarian policies.

of individuals with more or less identical interests are "processed" through a centralized political organization that offers little opportunity for individualized participation and is primarily concerned with the broad income and economic growth policies. With the increasing differentiation of the social order and the rise of libertarian demands for individualism and participation, mass-membership parties, and particularly Austrian- or Italian-style clientelist patronage organizations governed by machine bosses who craft compromises among different party constituencies, come under public attack as symbols of an oligarchic, antidemocratic political mode of domination. The mass media now frame well-worn clientelist practices as "scandals." In some ways, the libertarian assault on the European mass-membership party displays a political thrust similar to that of the "progressive" middle-class movements in the United States that attacked the urban party machines after the turn to the twentieth century (Shefter 1994: ch. 3). By abandoning their traditional organizational form, social democrats may make a symbolic gesture to highlight the sincerity of their programmatic change in order to reach out to unorganized constituencies whose members cannot possibly conceive of participating in a traditional mass-party organization.

The greater flexibility of small-membership framework parties that are more porous to the influx of activists with new ideas and/or permit more autonomy to party leaders, however, comes at a price, namely a *greater volatility of party strategy*. Where the demise of the mass-membership party encourages innovation from below and from above, internal party conflict may intensify, if new entrants have different ideas than innovative party leaders who, at least for certain time periods, can insulate themselves from outside pressure.[22] Alternatively, small, committed ideological currents entering from below may "hijack" entire parties, including their leadership positions, and dramatically change the party's programmatic appeals in ways that serve neither vote- nor office-seeking objectives. The new dominant coalitions then may attempt to lock in their control by organizational changes that reduce leadership autonomy, a favored objective of leftist politicians in the British and Dutch labor parties in the 1970s and the first half of the 1980s.

In order to reduce strategic volatility created by ideological conflict at the grass-roots level, party leaders may attempt to insulate themselves from

---

[22] In this vein, the structure of the French Socialist Party in the 1980s facilitated organizational innovation, but also intense internal conflicts, exacerbated by the ambition to seek the party's nomination for the presidency that the French semipresidentialist system generated among the leaders of the rival intraparty currents.

challenges within the organization. As the Italian and Spanish example in the 1980s shows, however, the price for such autonomy may be material side-payments to the party apparatus that fuel patronage, clientelism, and corruption. These techniques of loyalty building, however, are likely to precipitate public scandals that shake the parties' electoral foundations.

Smaller, nimbler basic party organizations and greater leadership autonomy produce more strategic innovation, but also increase the potential for sustained intraparty conflict over strategic alternatives with the consequence of wide swings in the parties' strategic positions, if one dominant coalition replaces another. Rapid strategic change, in turn, makes it harder for parties to maintain a well-defined reputation in the electorate. Nothing is more unappealing to both sentimental party identifiers and rationally calculating voters than continuous struggle within a party's elite, amplified by conflicts with different rank-and-file sectors and currents. Rational voters prefer parties with slowly changing, predictable programmatic positions in order to calculate their payoffs from alternative party choices. Social democratic parties thus face an organizational dilemma between strategic immobility but firm reputation, and strategic flexibility but highly volatile reputation.

> Dilemma 3: Either social democratic parties adhere to mass-party organizations and accountable leadership and thus guarantee strategic continuity, but accept programmatic immobility and the increasing symbolic disadvantages of mass-party organization. Or they increase the parties' openness for innovation from below and above through organizational reforms, but run the risk that strategic flexibility translates into greater volatility of party appeals and uncertainty about the parties' positions in the electorate.

On which side of the dilemma social democrats come down depends on a party's government status and electoral performance, and here the first, second, and third dilemmas are closely intertwined. Parties typically enact profound organizational and strategic reforms in times of dire electoral straits after a long period of decline, loss of government office, or stagnation in the opposition, followed by leadership turnover (Harmel, Heo, Tan, and Janda 1995). Examples are social democratic or socialist parties in the Netherlands in the late 1960s and late 1980s, France in the early 1970s, Italy and Spain in the late 1970s, or Britain in the late 1970s and late 1980s. Efforts to engineer change after long periods of decline from a high plateau were more limited in Austria and Sweden, but have led to a reduced emphasis on mass organization and increasing leadership autonomy

(Kitschelt 1994c). In the German social democrats, leadership autonomy has lagged. This situation, combined with a halfhearted opening to new left-libertarian activists from below in the 1970s, led to an intraparty stalemate that left the party unable to choose a consistent national strategy that could revive its electoral fortunes or improve its strategic bargaining position over coalition governments until 1998.

Organizational reform enhances the chances that parties embrace new strategic stances. Most of the time, more strategic voice to new entrants into social democratic parties has enabled the parties to assimilate libertarian demands in the 1980s. This strategic stance, however, may be more helpful as a vote- than an office-maximizing resolution of the electoral dilemma, because the most left-libertarian voters and political activists have more redistributive economic policy preferences that make it harder to move a social democratic party toward the median voter and toward policies of economic liberalization. Greater leadership autonomy in socialist parties, in turn, makes it more likely that parties resolve the electoral dilemma in favor of office-seeking strategies competing for the median voter and enhancing a party's bargaining power over government office (dilemma 2). Leadership autonomy also facilitates the adoption of policies of market liberalization in the face of long-term electoral losses (dilemma 1). Once in office, however, social democratic leaders may employ the spoils of office to entrench their position and to shore up intraparty support by reviving patronage and clientelist practices. Such techniques eventually undercut strategic flexibility and accelerate electoral decline because they prompt the defection of educated, sophisticated, and typically libertarian voters who initially felt attracted to the "new" social democratic appeal.

SOCIAL DEMOCRATIC PARTIES FROM THE 1980s TO THE 1990s

This final section of the chapter is devoted to some plausibility probes of the three dilemmas characterizing social democratic strategic choices. I argue first that economic government performance, by itself, cannot explain the electoral fortunes of leftist parties in the 1990s. I then reconstruct the interaction between political economic conditions and electoral and organizational dilemmas first by focusing on the big socialist "winners" of the 1980s who became losers in the 1990s, the Spanish, Italian, and French parties, before I close with a brief sketch of the logic of strategic trade-offs in other western European countries.

POLITICAL ECONOMY AND LEFTIST PARTY PERFORMANCE FROM THE 1980s TO THE 1990s

A retrospective economic voting argument is insufficient to explain party performance if (1) voters abandoning the governing parties do not turn to the opposition party that offers an alternative economic policy and (2) if the resilience of social democrats and conservative governments to retrospective economic voting varies. Previously, I demonstrated these points for social democratic party fortunes in the 1970s and 1980s (Kitschelt 1994, ch. 3) and now extend the argument into the 1990s.

Between 1991 and 1994, four left-dominated European cabinets faced parliamentary elections. In Austria (1994) and Denmark (1994) social democrats lost votes *in spite of* reasonable economic performance. In Denmark, social democratic losses mostly benefited opposition parties further to the left and confirmed the existence of a trade-off between electoral and policy-seeking social democratic strategies evident in that country since the 1960s. Also in Austria, the "grand coalition" of SPÖ and ÖVP lost less on economic performance than on conflict about noneconomic left-libertarian and right-authoritarian issues and about the institutional structure of Austria's political economy. Here the incumbents lost heavily in favor of the Greens, a new middle-of-the-road liberal party, and the right-wing populist Freedom Party.

Left-dominated cabinets in France (1993) and Spain (1993, 1996) faced elections in recessionary economic environments, yet the French socialists lost big, while the Spanish socialists each time lost only marginally. In both instances, the electoral beneficiaries were *not* the mainline bourgeois parties. In Spain, the beneficiary was a leftist and libertarian alliance. The socialists were displaced from office in 1996 because the bourgeois parties finally consolidated around a single party and thus took full advantage of the Spanish electoral system. In France, Gaullists and Republicans gained the same electoral share of about 42 percent in 1993 they have garnered since the early 1980s, but socialist and Communist losses benefited a scattering of minor parties.

In three countries social democrats participated in governments with major nonsocialist parties and lost heavily in the ensuing elections. In Italy, socialists became the major exponent of economic stabilization policies in the 1980s and early 1990s. Here they held steady at about 14 percent in the 1992 parliamentary elections, then all but vanished from the political stage in the 1994 legislative elections. Economic performance evaluations did not play a decisive role in this political earthquake. In the Netherlands and Belgium, social democrats joined with Christian democrats in governments pursuing economic austerity policies and suffered steep declines in the elections of 1991 (Belgium) and 1993 (Netherlands). Also in these instances, beneficiaries were left-libertarian and right-authoritarian competitors, not primarily market-liberal parties criticizing the economic performance of the incumbent governments.

In three countries, bourgeois governments were up for reelection in the first half of the 1990s. In Britain, John Major's conservative government was reelected with the same vote share of about 42 percent as every preceding Tory government since 1979, regardless of the economic environment. In Germany, the Christian democratic–liberal government did survive the 1994 election with an extremely thin majority after an economic recession in the early stages of recovery. In Sweden, finally, retrospective economic voting appears to explain the 1991 and 1994 elections most unambiguously. Whereas the social democrats lost heavily as the governing party in the economic crisis of 1991, the conservative government was punished for its stabilization policies in 1994, although the economy was recovering at that time. But even in this instance, gains and losses of the relevant parties are asymmetric and thus do not conform to retrospective economic voting theory. The three main nonsocialist parties for whom economics counts – conservatives, liberals, and center party – as a bloc and, more specifically, the conservative party as the spearhead of the austerity program did *not* lose vote shares in 1994. Electoral volatility was primarily attributable to the decline of minor parties that did not primarily appeal to economic issues, such as the New Democrats and the Christian democrats.

The brief narrative shows that we need more complicated theoretical tools to account for leftist party performance than knowledge of the parties' government status and their announced or implemented economic policies. It is critical to analyze the competitive dynamic of party systems (dilemma 2) and the role of party organization as a mechanism of strategic choice (dilemma 3).

THE "WINNERS" OF THE 1980s AS "LOSERS" IN THE 1990s: SPAIN, FRANCE, AND ITALY

The micrologic of the three dilemmas is most transparent in the case of the Spanish PSOE. After gaining government office in 1982 in a deep recession, it pursued a policy of economic austerity and liberalization, which – in agreement with the political economic dilemma – led to gradual electoral decline (1986: 44.3 percent; 1989: 39.6 percent; 1993: 38.7

percent; 1996: 37.5 percent). After 1986, the socialist losses primarily benefited the United Left (Izquierda Unida, IU), consisting of former Euro-Communists, ecologists, and other social movement groups. This party surged from 4.7 percent in 1986 to 10.6 percent in 1996, attracting disenchanted workers and also the public-sector intelligentsia and counterbalancing almost all socialist electoral losses. The electoral system, consolidations of the bourgeois parties around the Popular Party, and a switch of the Catalan Party to a new coalition partner explain the government change in 1996.

Between 1986 and 1996, the PSOE leadership pursued a centrist policy that gave up electoral market share to the IU in order to preserve its pivotal position and indispensability in government formation, although this policy was increasingly challenged by traditionalist socialists in the leadership around Alfonso Guerra and a growing proportion of the rank and file who did not understand the trade-off between vote- and office-seeking strategies.[23] In part, the leadership tried to preserve its internal autonomy by tolerating the growth of socialist patronage appointments in local, regional, and national government, a practice that led to a proliferation of scandals, contributing to the party's loss of electoral support.

In the French case, the interaction between political-economic and organizational dilemmas as well as the electoral trade-off provides a crisp explanation of the socialists' rapid decline in the 1990s. After its electoral victory in 1981 on a state-interventionist, fiscally expansionary economic policy platform, the PS government made a 180-degree turn toward austerity policy in 1982–1983. In the legislative elections of 1986, the PS's electoral support declined moderately, while its erstwhile coalition partner, the Communists, suffered the brunt of voters' disappointment with the new government. After two years of a lackluster conservative government, the socialists prevailed with a centrist strategic appeal in the 1988 presidential and parliamentary elections. Five years later, the socialists lost more than half of their voters in the 1993 legislative election without benefiting the main bourgeois opposition parties. The leftist alternatives to the socialists proved unable to mop up dissatisfied populist blue-collar and left-libertarian constituencies in a single party, so that former PS voters dissipated across a spectrum of small parties that did not gain any

---

[23] I tested this hypothesis at a conference with PSOE Socialist Party secretaries and social scientists in the socialist training center of Galapagar in the summer of 1994. The participants were more or less surprised by my interpretation of their strategic dilemma in terms of a trade-off between vote- and office-seeking alternatives.

representation under the French majoritarian electoral system.[24] The fragmentation of the left also impaired the socialists' performance in the 1994 European elections and the first round of the 1995 presidential elections. The strategic problem of a fragmented left is, in part, thrust upon the socialists by a rigid, decaying Communist party but is also of their own making. Socialists engaged in a tactic of undermining newly emerging leftist and libertarian parties that attract voters alienated from the socialist's centrist appeal, but willing to see their favored parties ally with socialists in majoritarian runoff elections and government coalitions.

In other words, the French socialists solved the political-economic dilemma in favor of centrist, liberalizing policies, but could not resolve the complementary electoral dilemma in favor of an office-seeking strategy that would give up electoral market share to left-libertarian competitors in order to preserve the party's bargaining power over government formation. The reason for this failure must be sought in the party's inability to preserve the coherence and autonomy of the party leadership. A small membership always made the party quite volatile. More important, however, was the "decentering" of the party leadership around bands of political entrepreneurs who built their own personal followings in order to stake out a claim to the party's nomination for the presidential office in 1988 before Mitterrand announced he would run again and in 1995. The constitutional rules of the French political game brought about divisions in the party leadership that paralyzed the party to the extent that it ceased to exist as an effective policy-making body. The small, flexible party organization served the socialists well earlier in the 1970s and 1980s, but then contributed to a volatility and strategic uncertainty that made the party unpalatable to many voters and paralyzed its capacity to address unavoidable electoral and political economic dilemmas.

In Italy, the PSI never faced an electoral trade-off because, in view of the multiplicity of leftist and libertarian competitors (PCI, Demoproletarians, Radicals, and Greens), its best bet was a centrist policy of office seeking. This strategy prevailed under Bettino Craxi who entrenched the dominant coalition configured around him by organizational changes increasing the authority of the party leadership and abolishing the system of "currents." Why, then, did the party almost disappear in 1994 when it received only 2.2 percent of the vote? While Craxi boosted the autonomy of the party leadership, he did not abandon the PSI's mass organization, including its vast patronage network. Quite to the contrary, Craxi em-

---

[24] In addition, of course, the disintegration of the left helped the radical rightist National Front.

ployed government office to increase access to patronage resources and eventually divide up patronage control over the state apparatus and public companies between his own party and the Christian Democratic coalition partner. This strategy drove both parties into electoral ruin in a political climate in which voters increasingly rejected bribery and patronage as political operating procedures.

REBOUND OF THE LESS FORTUNATE LEFTIST PARTIES IN THE 1990s?

Several socialist parties barely held steady or declined in the 1970s and 1980s compared with their typical electoral support level in the 1970s, because they ran into serious electoral trade-offs. In these instances, party activists and leaders often do not understand the logic of such trade-offs and intuitively opt for vote-maximizing strategies. It takes a sophisticated and robust segment of the party leadership to organize an intraparty coalition around office-seeking strategies and impose it on recalcitrant rival leaders and party members.

The two longest-standing cases of sharp electoral trade-offs are the Dutch Workers' Party (Partij van de Arbeid, PvdA) and the Danish Social Democrats (SD). A comparison of these parties is particularly useful because they "solved" their dilemmas in rather different ways. In the Dutch case, the PvdA has always played against two competitors on the left side of the spectrum: first, those left-socialist parties that regrouped under the Green Progressive Accord (GPA) in the 1980s and eventually founded a single party and, second, the more pragmatic, highly libertarian, but economically quite moderate Democrats '66 (D'66). Whenever the PvdA moved to the center and abandoned left-libertarian positions, these parties would strengthen at the PvdA's expense, while the PvdA would receive only partial compensation by adding voters formerly supporting the Christian Democrats and the Liberals.

Throughout the 1970s and 1980s, the leftist sector (PvdA + D'66 + GPA) won roughly 43 percent of the vote. The Democrats' 66 typically garnered 5 to 6 percent, the GPA 3 to 4 percent. In 1986 the PvdA received 33 percent of the vote and established itself as the hegemon on the left by pursuing a decidedly left-libertarian appeal. This strategy, however, locked the party into a minority position that excluded it from government. After 1986, an increasing disaffection of the rank and file with the opposition role, a change of leadership, and a reform of party structures that strengthened the authority of the parliamentary leaders made the PvdA abandon its leftist course in favor of centrist appeals. This strategy weakened its electoral support in 1989 and particularly in 1994 after five years of coalition with the Christian Democrats. But by weakening its electoral support, the PvdA managed to strengthen its bargaining position for government office. In 1994, it gained only 24 percent of the vote, but together with the D'66's 15.5 percent, the 3.5 percent of the GPA, and the 4.5 percent of the Pensioner's Party, a new populist party upset by economic austerity policy and welfare cuts for the elderly, the leftist sector in Dutch politics amounted to 47.5 percent of the vote and no government coalition could be formed against the PvdA any more.

In Denmark, the Social Democrats engaged in a strategy to cope with the electoral dilemma different from that of the Netherlands. Here, from the late 1960s to the late 1980s the SD had given up on the strong left-libertarian sector and pursued a centrist-pivoting, office-seeking strategy. This stance allowed left-libertarian parties to grow strong, with the Socialist People's Party receiving almost 15 percent of the vote at its high point compared to the Social Democrats' 30 percent. In the late 1980s, however, under the new and more left-libertarian SD leader Sven Auken, the Social Democrats engaged in a strategic reversal that severely weakened its left-libertarian competitor while strengthening the Social Democrats in the 1991 election. But because the SD's victory came primarily at the expense of the SPP rather than by expanding its support base into the centrist sector of the Danish electorate, the Social Democrats' bargaining position did not significantly improve. Since then, Social Democratic Party strategy has been in flux. Potential bourgeois coalition partners found Auken unacceptable as the new head of government so that a more moderate Social Democratic leader formed a centrist government. The party returned to an office-maximizing strategy and lost votes primarily to more leftist alternatives in the 1994 election.

What distinguishes the Dutch PvdA and the Danish SD is the intraparty process of political debate and interest aggregation since the 1970s. In Holland, the old mass-party organization virtually collapsed in the 1960s and allowed small bands of left-libertarians to hijack the party in the early to mid-1970s. As they grew old and disappointed on the opposition benches, a strategic reversal became possible in the 1980s, which a new leadership lost no time in cementing by organizational rule changes. In contrast, in Denmark, from the early 1970s on, the mass-party organization was in a gradual process of decay (cf. Esping-Andersen 1985), but it never experienced the momentous collapse that would have permitted a strategic rupture. Moderate Social Democrats who accepted the political economic dilemma in favor of market liberalizing structural policies remained in charge. They resolved the electoral dilemma by prioritizing office-seeking, because they solved the organizational dilemma by gradually dismantling the power of traditional rank-and-file forces, but without permitting left-libertarian forces a breakthrough.

A further example of the interdependence between political-economic, electoral, and organizational dilemmas in the 1980s and 1990s is the Belgian Socialist camp. In Belgium, the Socialists are hemmed in between a rather strong left-libertarian bloc commanding 10 percent of the vote in the 1991 parliamentary election, and the centrist Christian Democrats. In the 1980s, a middle-of-the-road social democratic voter appeal to defend the welfare state and to reflate the economy improved the Socialists' electoral support at the margin, but kept them on the opposition benches. When they joined a coalition with the Christian Democrats and began to support stabilization policies to curtail Belgian public-sector deficits, the Socialists lost electoral support. What is worse, the pillarized mass-party organizational structure with strong clientelist patronage networks embroiled the party in a string of political scandals that made it increasingly unpopular with younger and more libertarian voters.

A case with particularly sharp political-economic, electoral, and organizational dilemmas is the German Social Democratic Party (SPD) which was incapable of choosing a winning strategy between losing government office in fall 1982 and the 1994 election. Although in the opposition for more than fifteen years, the party could not convincingly embrace a political-economic strategy of liberalization to capture the pivotal voter or at least to strengthen its bargaining position sufficiently to enter a government coalition at the federal level. The reason for this failure is the particularly sharp nature of the electoral trade-off and the party's inability to reform its organizational structures by increasing the autonomy of the national leadership.

On the left and libertarian side of the competitive dimension, the SPD faces the Greens and, since 1990, the East German Communist successor party, the Party of Democratic Socialism (PDS). Social democratic strategic moves to the center typically prompted considerable electoral losses to the left-libertarian political sector. With the exception of the extraordinary unification election in 1990, in West Germany the combined vote share of Greens and Social Democrats oscillated between 43 and 45 percent of the vote in 1980, 1983, 1987, and 1994. Whenever the SPD moved to the center, the vote share of the Greens expanded overproportionally and the SPD was either a net loser of votes (in 1983 and 1987) or barely made up for losses to the left-libertarian sector (in 1980 and 1994). In the extraordinary 1990 election, it appealed to left-libertarian themes and deeply cut into the Green electorate, but its luke-warm stance on German unification led to even greater losses to the center-right parties (Kitschelt 1991b).

The dynamics of SPD, Green, and PDS support suggests that only a centrist SPD strategy, taking away votes from the Christian Democratic–Liberal government, but shedding leftist voters to the Greens and PDS, may displace the incumbent Liberal-Christian Democratic government co-alition. But because the pursuit of such appeals is electorally costly from the vantage point of a vote-maximizing strategy, each time national party leaders pursued such a strategy, majorities of the party faithful interpreted the election results as defeats and removed the chancellor candidates who took on the responsibility for the party strategy, Johannes Rau in 1987 and Rudolf Scharping in 1994. Only a severe crisis of the long-term in-cumbent Christian Democratic–Liberal coalition government could enable the Social Democrats to break out of that dilemma in 1998.

To appreciate the electoral trade-off, Table 11.2 presents results of the European elections in 1989 and 1994 and of the national elections in 1990 and 1994. For each election, I also calculate the share of seats each potential coalition commanded, taking the electoral threshold of representation into account. Both the European and the national election results show that the "centrist" SPD strategies in 1994 either led to a substantial loss of electoral support or only a marginal recovery compared with results in 1990, but that the leftist parties were either victorious (in the 1994 European elec-tion) or almost victorious (in the 1994 national election) in terms of seats won in the legislature. An additional .6 percent of the vote in the October 1994 national elections would have sufficed to deprive the Kohl govern-ment of its majority in the Bundestag. Nevertheless, many SPD leaders and activists interpreted the election results as a defeat.

The SPD's internal organization explains why the party as a collective actor has had a hard time understanding the logic of electoral trade-offs in its strategic stances and producing a dominant coalition that would em-phasize office-seeking over vote-seeking strategies. On the one hand, the party's mass organization has been committed to traditionalism in work-ing-class strongholds and since the 1970s to more left-libertarian politics in the big service-oriented metropolitan areas. In contrast to the Dutch PvdA, the left-libertarians, however, never decisively prevailed over the party stalwarts. On the other hand, the national party leadership is insuf-ficiently autonomous and regionally too divided to impose a consistent strategy of pivoting and office seeking on all relevant state-level party sections. Particularly those regional party bosses who are *Land* prime min-

Table 11.2. *Election results in Germany*

	European elections		Federal elections	
	1989	1994	1990	1994
Christian Democrats	37.8	38.8	43.8	41.5
Social Democrats	37.3	32.2	33.5	36.4
Greens	8.4	10.1	5.0	7.3
Free Democrats	5.6	4.1	11.0	7.1
Republicans	7.1	3.9	2.1	1.9
Ex-Communists (PDS)	—	4.7	2.4	4.4
Rightist camp (overall vote) CDU + FDP + REP	50.7	46.8	56.9	50.5
Rightist camp (votes into seats) CDU + FDP (+ REP in 1989)	50.7	38.8	54.8	48.6
Leftist camp (overall vote) SPD + G (+ PDS in 1994)	45.7	47.0	38.5	48.1
Leftist camp (votes into seats) SPD + G (+ PDS in federal)	45.7	42.3	34.6	48.1

isters, frequently have strategic incentives to defect from the "centrist" national strategy in their own state and thus undercut a consistent national appeal. Only in 1998 has the SPD overcome this obstacle.

To complete our brief tour of important European social democratic parties, let us touch on the Austrian, British, and Swedish situation, all cases where leftist parties experienced no electoral dilemmas or only mild trade-offs between office and vote seeking so that they had clear incentives to resolve the political-economic dilemma in favor of a market-liberalizing strategy. But also in these countries, the pursuit of such strategies hinged upon the resolution of the organizational dilemma.

In Austria, the relative weakness of the left-libertarian electoral constituency made "centrist" policies both office and vote seeking. But the Austrian socialists moved rather slowly in this direction, because their large patronage-based party organization fought against the market-liberalizing strategic opening promoted by elements of the party leadership. As long as a coalition between the Austrian People's Party (OVP) and the Social Democratic Party (SPÖ) governs Austria, the populist rhetoric of the third party, the Freedom Party, against partocracy and patronage is likely to inflict serious electoral damage on the SPÖ.

In Britain's three-party system, the lack of a credible left-libertarian competitor frees the Labour Party from worrying about an electoral trade-off. Thus, the party should have had an easy time in adopting a centrist, market-liberalizing vote- and office-maximizing strategy. Instead, its organizational rules in the 1970s and early 1980s, endowing traditionalist or radical unions and militant socialist grass-roots organizations in a political-economic environment of decline with considerable power over the party leadership, prevented the electorally rational strategy from prevailing. After a sequence of bitter defeats, it took the party more than a decade to fully shed its reputation of the "loony left" by replacing its leadership twice, revamping its program thoroughly, and changing its intraorganizational decision rules sufficiently to assure voters that the party is committed to a political-economic strategy of continued market liberalization without possibility of relapse into old socialist visions.

In Sweden, finally, whatever electoral trade-off the Swedish social democrats (SAP) experienced in the 1980s is difficult to calculate because the Green Party (MP) initially was less a left-libertarian than a single-issue party attracting considerable support from bourgeois parties. Nevertheless, voter flow analysis shows that the SAP's decline from 1982 to 1985 and from 1985 to 1988 appears to have benefited primarily the libertarian Left Party (VPK) (cf. Kitschelt 1994a: 171–172). After 1988, in the midst of a deep economic recession, the SAP made a sudden, sharp turn to market liberalization by adopting a stringent economic austerity package and seeking European Union membership. Although the SAP's stark losses in the 1991 election did not benefit its left-libertarian competitor, they cannot, however, be interpreted in terms of a retrospective economic voting model because the left's losses did not convert into substantial gains of the more market-liberal right-wing parties. Instead, disappointed blue-collar constituencies and first-time voters supported a new protest party (New Democracy) with uncertain issue stances on anything but immigration. When this party after its initial success failed to elaborate a right-authoritarian programmatic profile, akin to that of the Norwegian and Danish Progress parties, but instead drowned in internal squabbles, most of its supporters returned to the SAP in the 1994 election. As the model of electoral trade-offs would predict, the SAP's decisively "centrist" economic stance in 1994 led to a loss of more leftist and libertarian voters to the VPK and the now programmatically repositioned left-libertarian Greens, both of which together received a greater share of votes in the 1994 election than at any time in the 1980s.

CONCLUSION

My chapter addresses the dual tasks of (1) providing an analytical reconstruction of social democratic strategic dilemmas after the golden age of
the post–World War II recovery by (2) weaving together models of political-economic processes and of party competition in advanced postindustrial capitalism. I tried to show that social democratic parties typically
encounter three interconnected dilemmas. First, the political-economic dilemma forces them to choose between a "centrist" programmatic appeal
conceding the need for market liberalization that allows them to boost
their electoral support initially or to participate in coalition governments
with other market-liberalizing parties, but that incurs significant electoral
losses over time. Second, social democratic parties resolve the political-
economic dilemma in favor of market liberalization only if the second,
electoral dilemma is mild. According to this dilemma, centrist programmatic appeals lead to a loss of social democratic voters to left-libertarian
parties, that may only partially be offset by an influx of centrist voters.
As a consequence, centrist strategies may rarely be vote maximizing, even
though they are office maximizing by bringing social democrats closer to
the control of the pivotal voters and making it harder to form governments without their participation. Whether or not social democratic parties bite the bullet and sacrifice votes for government office and accept
the consequences of gradual electoral decline by embracing market-
liberalizing political-economic strategies, in turn, depends on the parties'
internal organization that affects the formation of dominant coalitions.
Market-liberalizing, centrist strategies presuppose organizational flexibility. In this regard, both a mass organization, especially when it is rooted
in clientelist mechanisms, and governance structures that make leaders
strictly accountable to the party rank and file represent definite obstacles.
At the same time, however, removing the mass organization and making
leaders more autonomous may increase the parties' strategic volatility and
reduce the size of a loyal core electorate.

National and subnational political-economic, competitive, and party
organizational conditions affect the precise interaction between the three
strategic dilemmas. This chapter cannot sufficiently account for these sub-
tleties. As the stylized case studies and examples I presented may suggest,
however, a simplistic view of inevitable social democratic electoral decline
is inaccurate. It is indisputable that social democratic parties are doomed
to extinction, if they are unable to respond to the new political-economic
conditions of postindustrial capitalism after the golden age. But given
that social democratic politicians are rational, strategically reasoning

beings who fight competitors invading their electoral turf by innovative appeals, the current search for new "winning electoral formulas" on the political left may yield considerable *electoral and programmatic instability* of social democratic parties across Europe rather than uniform and progressive decline.

12

CONTEMPORARY CHRISTIAN DEMOCRACY AND THE DEMISE OF THE POLITICS OF MEDIATION

Kees van Kersbergen

This chapter starts from an intriguing observation: the historical fate of the Christian democratic parties of continental western Europe does not seem to be determined solely or linearly by the declining impact of religion on social and political attitudes. The survival of Christian democratic parties in the 1970s, their capacity to adapt to the changing conditions of the 1980s and their diverging electoral paths in the 1990s indicate that – contrary to expectations – the impact of the transformation of the religious structure on the appeal of Christian democratic parties has been neither straightforward nor immediate. The anticipated association between secularization and the decline of religiously motivated social and political movements is variable and puzzling.

The questions that govern this chapter originate from this ostensible incongruity between social structural changes and diverging political outcomes. How has Christian democracy been able to survive politically in a social context marked by mounting secularization? What kinds of social coalitions has Christian democracy fostered in the 1980s that help explain its electoral endurance? What kind of political economy have the parties attempted to nourish and to what extent has a specific set of social and

For helpful comments I would like to thank the editors, Stathis Kalyvas, Jytte Klausen, and Hanspeter Kriesi.

economic policies helped sustain their electoral appeal? Can the contemporary diverging electoral paths and governmental records of national parties, with the Italian Democrazia Cristiana (DC) (remodeled as the Partito Popolare Italiano, PPI) at the low end, the German Christlich-Demokratische Union/Christlich-Soziale Union (CDU/CSU) at the high end, and the Dutch Christen Democratisch Appèl (CDA) somewhere in between, be explained in terms of the different ways in which these parties are located in their political economies?

Secularization is a diffuse social process of which the outcomes are politically relevant for all religious parties, but also variable under different conditions and in particular contexts. It engenders a structural element of the decomposition of Christian democracy. The difficulties of the postwar Christian democratic model of welfare capitalism, social capitalism, with which the movements can be identified, are further modifying the capacity of enduring power mobilization. This is a second component of political decline. However, political parties are no passive spectators of social and economic developments but political actors that adapt their strategies to change. Within the set of structural constraints, in the context of historically unique events and facing varying patterns of party competition, Christian democratic parties make choices over strategic dilemmas that affect the extent and the timing of political decline.

The chapter analyzes secularization and the electoral performance of Christian democratic parties, the ideology, social and political alliances, and characteristic policies of Christian democracy in power; current developments in social capitalist nations; and the predicament of Christian democracy and the politics of mediation.

ELECTORAL TRENDS AND THE ENIGMA OF SECULARIZATION

Secularization refers to a broad and diffuse social process "by which sectors of society and culture are removed from the domination of religious institutions and symbols" (Berger 1990: 107). It includes the decline in church membership and church attendance. The "natural" clientele of religious parties could even be smaller than the decline of church attendance suggests, because the diminishing political significance of religion among loyal churchgoers could also be seen as an aspect of secularization.

However, secularization also represents the condensation or transference of religious morality into secular ethics and comprises a transformation of religious contents into worldly substance. Christian values are increasingly represented in secular terms. Secularization is not solely a process of religious diminution or the decreasing presence of the church in society. It also concerns a process of assimilation and translation of a religious system of values into a secular ethic. The religious idealism is adjusted to worldly affairs and interests. As a consequence, the original Christian contents of some of the central values of worldly belief systems are increasingly difficult to discern. This aspect of secularization makes the open religious influence on politics vanish and supplants it by a "diffuse moralism throughout society" (Mead 1983: 52–53). Modern Western society is still continuously shaped by its own religious heritage, but in a manner that is increasingly imperceptible. In other words, "there may not only be secularization of consciousness within the traditional religious institutions but also a continuation of more or less traditional motifs of religious consciousness outside their previous institutional contexts" (Berger 1990: 109; see Chadwick 1975; Kaufmann 1989; Martin 1978). This implies that the "natural" clientele of religious parties could in fact be larger than the decline of church attendance suggests, because of the presence and political significance of diffuse religious values among nonreligious voters. This uncertainty with respect to secularization underlies one of the central dilemmas of Christian democracy, namely whether to appeal to a Christian inspiration of political action.

Measured in terms of the frequency of church attendance the decline of religion since the 1960s has been articulate, particularly in countries where Roman Catholics constituted at least a large minority of the population. It is in these Roman Catholic countries that Christian democracy has traditionally found its core constituency among religious voters. The decomposition of Christian democracy has to a certain extent followed the pattern of secularization, but not in any linear manner.

Between 1960 and 1980 weekly (or more) church attendance as a percentage of total population declined from 55 to 30 percent in the Netherlands, from 53 to 30 percent in Italy, from 60 to 40 percent in Belgium, from 26 to 11 percent in France, and from 31 to 20 percent in Germany (Mackie and Franklin 1992: 39, table 2.1). Between 1981 and 1990 this trend partially continued as the number of core and modal church members (measured as church members attending religious services at least once a month, some of whom are also actively engaged in activities of and for the church) dropped from 40 to 29 percent in the Netherlands, from 42 to 30 percent in Belgium, from 37 to 34 in Germany, but remained roughly stable in Italy at around 50 percent (Halman and De Moor 1993: 44, table 3.1).

The electoral results of Christian democratic parties in western Europe do mirror the observed secularization trends to the extent that one can note a slight general decline in electoral appeal from a European average of 36 percent in 1970 to 35 percent in 1980 and 34 percent in 1985 (Mackie and Rose 1991; various tables). Looking at some of the cases more closely and comparing the electoral fortunes of Christian democratic parties in Germany, Italy, and the Netherlands in the postwar era (until the late 1980s), three distinct patterns can be distinguished (Mackie and Rose 1991). German Christian democracy consistently polled over 42 percent, while volatility (measured as the average sum of total votes won or lost as compared with averages in previous elections) declined. Between 1976 and 1990 the CDU/CSU on average appealed to approximately 46 percent of the voters. In Italy, the postwar pattern is one of gradual decline in electoral results and volatility. The DC won an average of approximately 36 percent of the vote in the period 1976–1990. The Dutch pattern is slightly U-shaped to the extent that after a period of electoral decline in the 1960s and early 1970s the movement recuperated between 1976 and 1990, on average polling about 31 percent of the vote.[1]

For Italy and the Netherlands, however, the picture changes dramatically at the end of the 1980s and the beginning of the 1990s (see Table 12.1). Christian democracy in the Netherlands has experienced a considerable loss of electoral appeal. The CDA lost 13.1 percent of the vote at the 1994 election and now attracts no more than 22.2 percent. Moreover, the Dutch have recently witnessed a historic political event, when in 1994, for the first time since the introduction of universal suffrage and proportional representation in 1917, coalition bargaining in the Netherlands resulted in a government in which Christian democracy does not participate. As a result, the CDA has lost its long-established political dominance. The electoral defeat of May 1994, the weakening ties between party and affiliated organizations, the ideological rapprochement of social democracy and conservative liberalism, and the consistent anti-Christian politics of the liberal democrats effectively blocked a return of a usual government dominated by the Christian democratic party.

Italian Christian democracy has been marginalized and fragmented. At the national elections of 1992 the DC already attracted a historic low 29.7 percent of votes. A full-scale electoral collapse occurred at the local elections of 1993. In the struggle to modernize, stifle the scent of corruption, attempt a radical break with the past, and maximize the chances of rebirth, Italian Christian democracy fragmented into three separate parties. At the

[1] The Catholic party is taken as the precursor of the Christian democratic party that first took part in the elections of 1977.

Table 12.1. *Electoral results of Christian democracy in Germany, the Netherlands, and Italy in the 1990s*

Country	Party	Year	Result	Difference
Germany	CDU/CSU	1990	43.8	−0.5
		1994	41.5	−2.3
Italy	DC/PPI	1992	29.7	−4.6
		1994	11.1	−18.6
		1996	6.8	−4.3
Netherlands	CDA	1989	35.3	0.7
		1994	22.2	−13.1

Sources: Bull and Newell (1995); Newell and Bull (1996); Van Holsteyn and Nie-möller (1995); Roberts (1995).

national elections of 1994 the (center-left) successor of the DC, the PPI, fell to 11.1 percent. The Center Christian Democrats (CCD) took part in the 1994 elections under the banner of Forza Italia! (FI) and managed to win thirty-two seats (= 5.1 percent) in the Camera dei Deputati through the 75 percent of seats that are allocated on a plurality basis. In 1995 the Christian Democratic Union (CDU) separated from the PPI in order to ally itself for the 1996 elections with FI and the postfascist National Alliance (AN) in the center-right Polo della Libertá (Freedom Alliance). The CCD/CDU won 5.8 percent of the list votes and 5 percent of total seats. The PPI was part of the center-left Ulivo alliance (which included Italy's former Communist Party) and won 6.8 percent of the list vote and 11 percent of total seats (see Donovan 1994b, 1995; Bull and Newell 1995; Furlong 1996; Newell and Bull 1996; Parker 1996).

In other continental European nations the electoral appeal of Christian democracy is decreasing, too. Whereas in the 1970s Belgian Christian democracy still attracted about 36 percent of the vote (see Deruette and Loeb-Mayer 1992: 363), by the 1990s its electoral support had dropped to around 25 percent. And whereas the Österreichische Volkspartei (ÖVP) consistently won 42–45 percent of the vote in the 1970s, the 1990s signify a considerable loss for Christian democracy in Austria, too (Müller and Steiniger 1994: 93). Christian democracy here scored a 32.06 percent in 1990 and a further historic low in 1995 of 28.3 percent.

By contrast, Christian democracy in Germany shows much fewer signs of decomposition (see Table 12.1). The 43.8 percent of the vote that the CDU/CSU managed to win at the first "all German" federal elections of 1990 was speculated to be 6 to 10 percent above the party's support that the polls had been anticipating before the collapse of the Communist regime in East Germany. This favorable unification effect was expected to have been played out as a postunification tax backlash, and eastern popular discontent seemed to be taking over. It was expected that a downward electoral trend was likely to be confirmed at the elections of 1994 and that the unification surplus of Christian democracy would be undone. However, this did not happen. At the elections of 1994 the CDU/CSU remained remarkably stable at 41.5 percent, losing a mere 2.3 percent of votes, turning it at present into the strongest Christian democratic party of continental western Europe (see Conradt, Kleinfeld, Romoser, and Søe 1995; Roberts 1995).

The current position of Christian democracy is difficult to explain by looking at the declining influence of religion alone, unless of course one would adopt the view that secularization suddenly *is* causing the decomposition of the parties in the 1990s, with the exception of Germany. Again, if it were the case that secularization causes the downfall of religious parties, then one should observe an unequivocal decline of these parties in the European political systems. This is not the case. But even if it were the case, then the question is why now, rather than, say, five to ten years ago. I am not arguing that secularization is unrelated to the declining electoral appeal of Christian democratic parties. However, political sociology reaches its limits here. If it is correct to assume that the declining social and political meaning of religion constrains the electoral appeal of these parties at least to some extent, why is it then that there appears to be a time lag in the effect and why does this effect vary cross-nationally? I think a more political-economy point of view can be helpful.

THE MEDIUM AND OUTCOME OF POWER MOBILIZATION

Christian democracy has historically nurtured and profited from the salient religious cleavage in western Europe. This cleavage not only changed the logic of political conflict in general by transforming and moderating the political significance of social class (Kalyvas 1996), but has also provided the terms of the distinctive manner in which the political economies of countries with a strong or dominant Christian democratic movement were constituted.

Christian democracy is a distinctive political movement that has fostered an equally characteristic political economy and a qualitatively distinctive postwar path to welfare capitalism (van Kersbergen 1995). In order to avoid conceptual misunderstanding, however, I will use the term "Christian democracy" for the vote- and office-seeking actor and the notion of "social capitalism" for the movement's alleged achievements in terms of policies and institutions (van Kersbergen 1995). This allows me to argue that roughly until the mid-1980s social capitalism has been both the medium and outcome of Christian democratic power mobilization.

IDEOLOGY

The contrast between modern Christian democracy on the one hand and political Catholicism, denominational political parties, or confessional politics on the other is highlighted by the former's emphasis on the independent lay responsibility for applying Christian principles to the realm of politics. Christian democracy has been open both to different denominations and to secular influences, and has explicitly dissociated itself from too direct an attachment to the churches (van Kersbergen and Ten Napel 1994).

The religious inspiration of Christian democratic parties has distinguished them from conservative or secular center parties, but also from liberal and social democratic parties in a number of respects. First of all, typical were distinctive political beliefs with respect to issues that concern private morality, such as divorce, abortion, and euthanasia. Second, Christian democratic parties differed from conservative parties in their social concern. Third, the consistently pro-European point of view of Christian democratic politicians has diverged considerably from other political movements and from British conservatism in particular. The social concern of Christian democratic parties is related directly to one of its main historical ancestors, social Catholicism. Even where the Protestant influence was discernible (in Germany, the Netherlands), Catholic social teaching was a prominent property of the political ideology of Christian democratic parties.

The key concept of social theory has been "subsidiarity," which derives its specific and current meaning in relation to other concepts such as "personalism," "solidarity," "pluralism," and "distributive justice." As is well known, subsidiarity was first introduced in the social encyclical *Quadragesimo Anno* (1931). Christian democrats subsequently developed this concept into an elaborate political theory of modern democratic government, which differed considerably from the ideas of their principal political rivals, notably social democracy, conservatism, and liberalism, and which has helped them to attain their characteristic status in the polities of continental Europe.

Contemporary Christian democrats have shared the conviction that each private, semiprivate, or semipublic association or institution of society performs indispensable moral, social, and economic tasks. In principle, a government should be disinclined to take over the responsibility for these tasks. Nevertheless, the principle of subsidiarity prescribed that political action was mandatory whenever "lower social organs" failed to perform their duties. Under such conditions, the state had the obligation to intervene in moral, social, and economic relations by offering temporary support with a view to restoring the sovereignty of social associations and their capacity to perform adequately in accordance with their natural function.

With respect to social and economic policy, subsidiarity functioned historically both as an encouragement of public intervention and as a justification of nonintervention or even of discontinuing previously initiated policies. In this specific sense, Christian democratic parties tended to be dynamic and historically sensitive, yet open-ended in their moral, social, and economic policies.

On the Christian democratic account, "solidarity" was primarily defined as the attempt to realize harmony between various social groups and organizations with opposed interests. The search for societal "integration" and accommodation in a plural society has characterized the social and political practice of Christian democratic parties to a large extent. The social Catholic notion of "personalism," a term recently enjoying a remarkable revitalization, particularly among Flemish Christian democrats and – together with "subsidiarity" – at the European level (see van Kersbergen and Verbeek 1994), constituted a distinctive theory of social justice, that, rather than balancing rights and duties, fundamentally underscored a moral obligation to help the "weak," "poor," "lower strata," or whoever might have been in need of help. Furthermore, social justice did not refer to the relations between individuals or citizens, but instead to the relations between social groups and organizations.

ALLIANCES

It has been the ceaseless attempt of integrating and reconciling a plurality of societal groups with possibly opposed interests that has made Christian democracy distinctive. Even within its own ranks the Christian democratic movements included various social organizations that had opposed social and political interests. As a result, the movements always needed to be flexible and, therefore, continuously attempted to retain or to increase their capacity to adapt to changing circumstances and to new wishes and demands in their venture of formulating a compromise of antagonistic interests. Christian democracy was in this sense the embodiment of societal accommodation, or at least aspired to become so. It has been peculiar to Christian democracy that the movement is necessarily internally divided into factions or established wings.

Recent empirical studies have shown the relevance of the principles of "integration," "accommodation," and "mediation" to the extent that they all emphasize the institutionalization of different social groups as recognized factions of the parties and find empirical support for the hypothesis that the electorate of Christian democracy has traditionally mirrored to a large extent the social and demographic structure of society (e.g., Lucardie and ten Napel 1994; Müller and Steiniger 1994; Broughton 1994; Donovan 1994a).

In Germany in the 1950s and 1960s, Catholics were strongly in favor of the CDU/CSU, workers tended to vote SPD (Sozialdemokratische Partei Deutschlands), and Protestants had a preference for the SPD. Among Catholics Christian democracy gained a plurality of votes from most classes and a majority from the salaried class and the farmers. On average over the various classes, Catholics were overrepresented in the Christian democratic vote and Protestants were overrepresented in the SPD vote (Linz 1967: 302). The SPD disproportionally depended on the working-class vote, whereas Christian democracy relied on the middle-class vote. However, what was crucial and should be stressed here is that Christian democracy's difficulty of attracting voters from the working class was much less critical than social democracy's inability to get proportionate middle-class support. In general, the CDU/CSU was the least class distinctive, the liberal party the most, and the SPD was somewhere is between.

Looking at the religious and occupational bases of the CDU/CSU support in the 1980s (Broughton 1994: 108, table 6.1), the general picture is one of stability. Most marked is that there seems to have been some growth among the number of non-Catholics and workers (both unionized and nonunionized) between 1980 and 1990. Comparing the social composition of the CDU/CSU electorate with SPD voters in 1986 (Pappi and Mnich 1992: 203, table 9.12), the former's appeal to Catholics, white-collar workers, the self-employed, and churchgoers stands out, while the latter's strength among Protestants, manual workers, and union members is characteristic. One interesting fact is that the difference (in percentage points) in working-class support between the CDU/CSU and the SPD has declined (Pappi and Mnich 1992: 202–203), from 15.7 percent in 1968 to 11.3 percent in 1986, whereas the difference in white-collar support has increased from 0.8 percent in 1968 to 2.6 percent. In general, patterns of class and religious voting have been relatively stable, at least until the

1980s (Pappi 1984; Padgett and Burkett 1986), but also still in the 1990s (Gobowski 1995).

Until the mid-1960s voting behavior in the Netherlands was strikingly stable. Party choice depended on religion or – if not religion – on class. Voting behavior was utterly predictable. It was "an almost faultless product of the matrix of pillarization" (Andeweg 1989: 84, my translation). Until the late 1960s the most important determinants of voting behavior were church affiliation, church attendance, and social class, whereas geographical variables, age, and sex, were unimportant (Lijphart 1974: 257). In terms of class the three major Christian parties were the least distinctive, and it is safe to conclude that the secular parties were the most class-distinctive and the Confessional parties the least. Data on the working-class vote for the 1970s clearly suggest that the social democrats were disproportionally supported by the working class, the liberals lacked substantial support of this class, and the Christian democrats were the least distinctive in this sense (Van der Eijk and Van Praag 1991: 161). If we take the Dutch case in the 1980s (Gladdish 1991: 89, table 5.5; 91, table 5.8), the CDA and the social democratic PvdA (Partij van de Arbeid) both appear as cross-class parties, but the CDA had become more class-distinctive, since a majority of CDA voters considered themselves as middle class (see Van Holsteyn and Niemöller 1995).

In Italy, Christian democracy was the least class-distinctive political party in the 1960s and 1970s, obtaining roughly equal percentages among all status groups. Although overrepresented among small farmers and underrepresented among skilled workers, the social composition of the DC electorate has always been nearer to the composition of the electorate as a whole than any other party and, for instance in 1968, no group differed by more than 3 percent from the composition of the entire electorate (Wertman 1974: 164).

Religion has been an important conditioning factor of the working-class vote in Italy. Members of the working class were most likely to vote for Christian democracy if they were embedded in the Catholic organizational infrastructure, if their religiosity expressed itself not just in a proclaimed membership but in church attendance in particular, and if they came from regions where the Catholic subculture was strongly developed (Wertman 1974: 176). Organizational ties – membership of the Catholic trade-union and other Catholic organizations – were the determining factor (see Leonardi and Wertman 1989). These patterns have remained relatively stable, and in the mid-1980s the occupational structure of the DC's electorate to a large extent still mirrored the social composition of Italian society, although small farmers were overrepresented and workers were underrepresented (Mannheimer and Sani 1987: 65–72). Working-class support for the DC was low when workers subjectively identified themselves as working class and high when workers were affiliated with the Catholic labor unions.

THE POLITICS OF MEDIATION AND SOCIAL CAPITALISM

Cross-class coalitions, both among the electorate and within the parties have distinguished Christian democratic parties to a large extent. Particularly the absence of extreme class-distinctiveness as well a high level of institutionalized acceptance of factions has been a property of European Christian democracy. The cross-class electoral appeal and the integration of various social groups within the parties as such is obviously not a guarantee for a political accommodation of interests. Nevertheless, the integration of social interests can be considered as an important procedure for building cross-class coalitions on the basis of exchange, social compensation, and maintaining relations with affiliated social organizations.

Christian democratic parties have therefore always had to search for means to conciliate conflicting interests. And it has been the "politics of mediation" – that is, the religiously inspired, ideologically condensed, institutionally rooted, and politically practiced conviction that conflicts of social interests can and must be reconciled politically in order to restore the natural and organic harmony of society – that has governed the social and economic practice of Christian democracy in the entire postwar era. Favorable economic conditions initially provided the opportunity to launch the social and economic policies that facilitated such a politics of mediation. The diverging ways in which Christian democratic movements have structured and institutionalized the representation and accommodation of interests under different historical circumstances, however, have caused a considerable amount of cross-national variation in the character, complexion, and political impact of the movements and of social capitalism.

Typically, Christian democracy has always promoted a passive or reactive type of social policy which was characterized by the readiness to moderate the harmful outcomes of the imperfect market mechanism by transferring considerable sums of money to families in need, without changing the logic of the market itself. In this sense, the movement has always looked for a feasible middle way between socialist collectivism and liberal individualism. Christian democratic reformism normally aimed at restoring the self-responsibility and self-reliance of social institutions.

Social capitalist welfare states are transfer-oriented welfare states. Comparing public expenditures on social protection as a percentage of GDP between 1960 and 1990, it is striking that Austria, Belgium, France, Germany, and the Netherlands consistently scored above average over the entire period, as did Sweden (OECD 1994b: 57–61, table 1). In 1960 and 1970, Austria, Belgium, and Germany even score more than one standard deviation above the mean and in 1970, 1980, 1985, and 1990 public expenditure in the Netherlands is significantly above average.

An unconditional commitment to full employment has never become a central element of social capitalism (see Therborn 1986). This can perhaps be illustrated by the fact that active labor market policies have never been really supported by Christian democratic parties, whereas extensive measures to compensate loss of income, of course, have. Thus, the ratio of passive to active labor market measures in 1990 (OECD 1991: 237–249) was 2.50 in Belgium, 2.21 in the Netherlands, and 3.23 in Austria. Germany (1.14), however, seemed to be much more in line with Norway's 1.16, whereas the Swedish welfare state (.42) clearly relied more strongly on active than passive labor market measures. The ratio of services to transfers in 1990, moreover, was .16 in Germany and .06 in Italy, as compared with .33 in Denmark and .29 in Sweden (Esping-Andersen 1995: 35).

Subsidiarity has found an important expression in the manner in which Christian democracy has opposed the transfer of authority and control over social and economic policies to the state. The ideal has always been privately governed but publicly financed welfare arrangements. Such institutions have become the intermediary organs between state and society in the continental welfare state. The corollary of self-government was self-responsibility. The financing of welfare activities through taxation only, as well as Beveridge-type flat-rate benefits, ran against Christian democratic philosophy. As a result of successful Christian democratic politics, the continental welfare states are strongly characterized by the principle of social insurance, status reproduction and particularism, and modest to considerable generosity of benefits. Thus, Therborn (1995: 96) shows that the patterns of European welfare states in the second half of the 1980s are clearly clustered along the dimensions of the organization, the size, and the scope of social rights of the welfare state (health care and pensions). On the one hand one finds the "medium" to "big" Nordic welfare states (Denmark, Sweden, Finland, Norway) with their state supply of services and income maintenance arrangements and universal social rights. On the other hand, there are the "medium" to "big" continental welfare states (Belgium, France, the Netherlands, Austria, West Germany) with their publicly subsidized private provision of services and benefits and particularistic social rights. The "medium" Italian welfare state is characterized by a mix of public (health care) and private (pensions) arrangements and particularist social rights.

With respect to social inequality Christian democracy promoted distinctive policies, too. An extensive redistribution of societal wealth was considered to disrupt the precarious balance between social groups and associations. Social policy, therefore, was never promoted with a view to establishing a more equal distribution of income. Related to this was the distinctive conception of justice, or, better, the peculiar theory of distributive justice. Distributive justice accords to each and every class what is its due. Yet, social policy was not to alter social status, but rather to reproduce it well into retired life. As a theory of social justice it lacked a conception of individual rights of citizens as full members of a society. In Christian democratic thought individuals are first and foremost full members of lower social organs that make up society as a whole, not citizens of the national community. Their rightful claim to assistance was therefore not an absolute right derived from their status as citizens, but from their status as members of indispensable classes and other groups.

Although the theory of private property did initially play a role in the Christian democratic tradition of social policy, the theory of the just wage (or family wage) has gradually replaced it. Christian democrats consistently supported the idea that a money income ought to be sufficient for a man and his family. Such a wage was supposed to be not only sufficient for a worker to provide for himself and for the needs of his family, but should also allow him to put something aside. This is the background of the theory of the just wage. It addressed the family as well as the propensity to save.

These ideas on the just wage have had considerable influence on the kind of social and economic policy Christian democrats tended to encourage. Social benefits for adult male employees, for instance, were to replace the family income at the level of the existing status. An unintended, yet conspicuous consequence of this was that the continental welfare states have developed rather generous benefit structures, especially with regard to families. Benefits for women, on the other hand, were either made dependent on the income of the husband or at least lower than for an adult male worker. In its extreme form, social security systems became sexually differentiated, not as the result of an implicit theory about the lesser worth of women, but stemming from the explicit theory about the natural gender role of men and women. Historically, Christian democrats have assumed women to be only marginally present on the labor market and the family to be the prime provider of care. Christian democratic social thought elaborated strong images of the division of labor according to gender: paid jobs for men, unpaid domestic labor for women.

Such images underlay many policies directed toward the traditional family and reinforced typical male and female employment careers. Generally speaking, the Christian democratic nations have distinctive patterns of female labor force participation. The discouragement of female labor force participation and the encouragement of female labor market exit are properties of Christian democratic welfare states (van Kersbergen 1995: 144). Schmidt (1993: 204–205) has recently shown that "center parties in catholic countries transform the conservative stance of catholicism in gender-related issues into public policy, such as in family policy, taxation, education, social security and care for children, the elderly and other dependents. These governments thus place priority on the maintenance of traditional patterns of gender differentiation. . . . That policy, of course, creates powerful disincentives and obstacles to the incorporation of female labour into the economy."

Typically, then, nations still characterized by below average female labor force participation in 1990 are Austria, Belgium, Germany, Italy, the Netherlands, and Switzerland as well as France and Ireland (OECD 1992a: 29, table 2.8). Many countries have come from low female participation rates in the 1960s and experienced a period of substantial increase since then. However, none of the Christian democratic nations has followed the trajectories of Australia, Canada, Denmark, Norway, New Zealand, and the United States that came from below or around average female participation rates in 1960 to above average rates in 1990.

CURRENT DEVELOPMENTS IN SOCIAL CAPITALIST NATIONS

If postwar advanced capitalist democracies have generally been characterized by economic prosperity, stable polities and relatively fixed political alignments, politically recognized systems of interest intermediation, the institutionalization of the welfare state, and international economic integration, the Christian democratic nations are no exception in these respects. However, these nations have exhibited historically specific economic and political-institutional qualities that have governed a distinctive path of postwar economic growth and modernization, that have constrained their adaptation to the economic stagnation and the crises of the 1970s and

1980s in a particular manner, and that are currently structuring a characteristic response to the globalization of the international economy and the
transformation of capitalism into what we are still compelled to call postindustrial society.

In his study of the conservative transformation of the welfare state in
the United Kingdom, Canada, the United States, and Germany, Borchert
(1995: 14–17) argues that the majority of bourgeois governments in the
1980s must be viewed as conservative governments. The justification is
that the historical process of secularization, the modernization of conservatism, and the radicalization of bourgeois politics have blurred the distinction between conservatism and Christian democracy. The position taken
here is that it is still necessary to distinguish between Christian democracy
and conservatism. As argued, secularization is a diffuse process of which
the political outcome is contingent or variable. Moreover, the modernization of conservatism has nowhere led to the absorption of the politics of
mediation and social policy as equally pivotal as in Christian democratic
politics. Finally, the radicalization of bourgeois politics is indeterminate
and in need of explanation, because the concept of "bourgeois" contrasts
with "social democratic" and therefore already assumes the similarity of
Christian democracy and conservatism (see Van Kersbergen 1994).

Christian democratic parties in power in the 1980s have opted fully
neither for the social democratic project of maintaining full employment
nor for the neoliberal market-based accommodation to changes in the international economic order. During the second half of the 1980s the Christian democratic movements in power were – as other parties – increasingly
compelled to follow policies of retrenchment and austerity, but these policies were characterized by a more or less consistent attempt to preserve
some form of social compensation for economic adjustment. Christian democrats have attempted to uphold what they view as a socially acceptable
capitalism until the limits of such policies appeared to be reached by the
early 1990s.

Generally speaking, the trend in social protection expenditure between
1980 and 1990 is one of declining growth (Italy), stabilization (the Netherlands), or modest cutback (Germany) (OECD 1994b), but certainly not
one of radical break. The major problems Christian democratic governments in Germany, Italy, and the Netherlands had to deal with in the late
1980s and early 1990s were slackening economic growth, high (long-term)
unemployment, deteriorating fiscal balances, public debt, and specific
problems in the realm of social security, particularly with respect to unemployment, disability, and pensions. However, the macroeconomic performance in these nations has diverged considerably. In terms of economic

growth, unemployment, general government deficits, and gross public debt, Germany has performed best, Italy worst, and the Netherlands somewhere in between, in effect largely in line with the electoral fortunes of the respective Christian democratic parties.

The average growth of the economy between 1987 and 1993 was about 3 percent in Germany, 2 percent in Italy, and 2.4 percent in the Netherlands. The growth of employment in Germany and Italy has been slow and below the OECD average and modest but above the OECD average in the Netherlands between 1987 and 1993. Unemployment has been particularly high in Italy (10.5 percent), moderate in Germany (5.4), and the growth of employment was not capable of generating enough jobs to temper unemployment in the Netherlands (8.1) (OECD 1994d), whereas the generous disability scheme in the latter country absorbed an additional amount of unemployment.

Unemployment has of course been a major problem for most political economies in the 1980s. Apart from the unfavorable general unemployment record of many nations on the European continent, the incidence of long-term unemployment (as a percentage of total unemployment) in 1990 in Germany (46.3 percent), Italy (71.1), and the Netherlands (48.4) is particularly striking. These figures sharply contrast with the record of such countries as Canada, Finland, and the United States (less than 7 percent in 1990, OECD 1993a). The unemployment problem has more or less continuously dominated public and political agendas, increasing the electoral predicament of Christian democratic parties in government.

In spite of the common political rhetoric of governments led by Christian democracy in the 1980s to contain the expansion of the public sector and seriously limit public-sector borrowing, long-term trends in deficit spending and public borrowing apparently are in reality difficult to turn (OECD 1994d). The political and socioeconomic context for adjustment policies, however, has diverged considerably.

The unification of East and West Germany in 1990 has had a strong impact on the public deficit and on the public debt. Government transfers and investments were raised considerably in order to facilitate the social, economic, and political integration of the new Länder. Thus, whereas the general government financial balance in Germany showed a surplus of 0.1 percent of GDP in 1989, it had already reached a deficit of −3.3 in 1993, −2.5 in 1994, and −3.5 in 1995 (provisional) (OECD 1996b). Several fiscal measures were introduced by the Kohl government to finance unification, such as the 7.5 percent tax surcharge of 1991, as well as a number of budget restraints. In the view of the Christian democratic–liberal coalition in Germany, the unification has interrupted the consolidation of budget policies, particularly because of large public (social) transfers to the East. Net transfers from the West to the East amounted to 4.4 percent of "all German" GDP (equaling 50 percent of East German GDP). These transfers mainly function as social compensation (income and consumption support) for the "shock" of integration, particularly in the form of unemployment benefits and pensions (see OECD 1993b).

In the context of slackening economic growth, lower tax returns, worsening labor market conditions (unemployment figures reached double digits by the end of 1996), the rise in social spending due to unification, and the attempt to meet the criteria for Economic and Monetary Union (EMU), the Kohl government embarked upon an unprecedented package of austerity measures. In addition to federal and state savings, strict measures in social security, particularly in pensions and health, were prepared.

In the Italian case the usual politics of social compensation has been seriously constrained by the process of European economic integration. Successive Italian governments dominated by Christian democracy have unsuccessfully struggled throughout the 1980s to reduce the large public deficits of around 10 percent of GDP and the increasing load of public debt that surpassed GDP in 1990, particularly in order to meet the requirements of the European Monetary System (EMS). The Maastricht treaty on EMU has strongly increased the pressure on Italian governments to tackle the budget deficits and the public debt (around 125 percent of GDP in 1994–1995) (Daniels 1993; Padoa and Kostoris 1996).

As a result of these increasing pressures, the capacity to uphold social compensation policies appeared to be exhausted and a search has started to find ways out of the fiscal crisis. One obvious – yet, for Italian Christian democracy, politically risky – direction was to try to diminish the huge tax evasion from which the electoral core of the DC (small business and the self-employed) traditionally profited (the tax burden is concentrated on direct taxes and employers' social security contributions, OECD 1996c: 115). Taxes and social security contributions have been increased while benefits were lowered and eligibility criteria, especially for state pensions, were tightened. Moreover, attempts have been made to increase labor market flexibility, for instance by modifying the *scala mobile* of central wage setting. Thus, the budget policy for 1994 aimed at considerable cuts in public spending, to be achieved by cuts in public investments and transfers, a decrease in state pensions and health expenditure, the suspension of automatic adjustments of benefits, an attempt to reduce overpricing in government and social security institutions, a change in the logic of costly public work contracts, and a limit on the rise of public wages (OECD 1995b: 37–39). In 1992 a pension reform was introduced that envisaged a gradual increase in the compulsory retirement age as well as an increase in contribution period. In the spring of 1995 the Dini government reached a parliamentary agreement on the reform of the generous pension system. This reform included a restriction on early retirement and benefit cuts, the outcome of which at present, however, is still uncertain (for an overview, see OECD 1996c: 50–51; Ferrera 1997).

The Dutch Christian democratic–liberal and Christian democratic–social democratic coalition governments of the 1980s and 1990s have consistently attempted to cut public spending and to bring down the public deficit, supported by cooperative collective agreements between labor and capital on wage restraint (since 1982). The deficit indeed decreased from 5.1 percent in 1990 to around 3 percent in 1993. Up until recently the absolute policy priority concerned wage moderation mainly to be achieved by a lowering of wages, taxes, and social security contributions of employers, that is, a policy aimed predominantly at the reduction of labor costs. Successive measures have been introduced to cut public spending, to lower the level of benefits, and to tighten eligibility criteria, particularly of the generous disability scheme. Social benefits and wages in the public sector were first lowered and then systematically "frozen," as was the level of the statutory minimum wage to which the lowest social benefits were linked. Nevertheless, social security spending kept rising during the 1980s. Thus, social security expenditures as a percentage of primary public expenditure have increased from 51.6 percent in 1982 (the start of the Christian democratic–liberal coalitions that ruled until 1989) to 58.4 percent in 1994 (the arrival of the liberal–social democratic coalition) (OECD 1994c: 46), mainly as a result of the growing burden of unemployment and disability benefits. Moreover, attempts were made to reform the health care system in order to cut expenses, although the inherent social democratic element of income redistribution provoked the CDA to delay its implementation.

In general, the causes of inflexible labor markets and persistent high unemployment were argued to be high labor costs, institutional, legal and contractual impediments to wage flexibility, and too generous welfare state arrangements. Successive Christian democratic governments have tried to adapt to new economic requirements and to reduce labor market rigidities, while nevertheless refusing to follow stern neoliberal policies, for instance, by allowing time and again for various forms of special social compensation, such as one-time measures to compensate loss of income of special groups, particularly the aged.

One of the main difficulties that governments dominated by Christian democracy in the Netherlands have faced beginning in the 1980s concerned the difficulty of containing the increasing claims on the welfare state. An increasing number of people are becoming dependent on the welfare state, while a decreasing number of people are contributing to the resources of the system. This has led to a severe "crisis of inactivity," exemplified by the dependency ratio: the ratio of social benefit recipients to employed persons, 45.9 percent in 1970, increased to 68.4 percent in 1980, and to 86.4 in 1985. In 1990 it was 85.6. The social democratic–liberal government continued the policy of fiscal consolidation, but shifted policy priorities gradually to the problem of inactivity, particularly by changing the balance of passive and active labor market policies in favor of the latter and by partly privatizing the social security system (sickness) (see Rigter, Van den Bosch, Van der Veen, and Hemerijck 1995; SZW 1996).

THE PREDICAMENT OF CHRISTIAN DEMOCRACY IN EUROPE: GENERAL REFLECTIONS

The extent to which Christian democratic parties have managed to uphold a specific form of welfare capitalism even under worsening economic conditions and changing structural conditions hinged upon the capacity to mobilize, preserve, and reinforce social and political coalitions and power resources that were capable of countering various forces of transformation, whether these arose from domestic social and political contexts or stemmed from transnational, "systemic" constraints.

The main reason why secularization did not have an immediate and universal negative effect on the electoral position of Christian democratic parties is that the transformation of the social structure was in fact mediated by the institutionalized social coalitions that Christian democratic parties have fostered since the 1950s and 1960s and were able to maintain to a large extent in the 1970s and 1980s. On the basis of such patterned coalitions and via its policy-oriented behavior, Christian democracy attempted to shape a postwar configuration of the political economy that had the capacity to maintain or even to reinforce the social bases of power in spite of the declining social and political impact of religion.

The increasing difficulty of defending this distinctive social and political heritage is seriously hampering the capacity of continued power mobilization. As Christian democratic politics and policies became increasingly contradictory, the parties found themselves in precarious circumstances. Crucial is the decay of what I have called the politics of mediation. It has been this feature that has stained the distinction between Christian democracy and conservatism and which has facilitated the appeal to nonreligious voters. The perennial search for an accommodation of social and political conflicts has been one of the movement's major electoral assets and determined its "natural" position in the center of the political system (van Kersbergen 1997), but it has lost its pronounced ideological significance and this is blurring the electorally favorable distinction between conservatism and Christian democracy.

The golden age of the politics of mediation has come to an end. The sources that once provided the media of exchange for social capitalist coalitions are drying up under the impact of increasing transnational pressures (globalization, European integration) and domestic changes that are both social (aging populations, individualization) and political (transformation and moderation of traditional political cleavages). The passive, corporatist, transfer-oriented political economies of Christian democratic nations increasingly fail to deliver the goods that provided the currency for the kinds of beneficial political exchanges that the parties traditionally nurtured in the attempt to mediate opposed societal interests.

Controversies over the rising costs of the welfare state rapidly intensified and these tended to make favorable positive-sum exchanges between different social groups much more demanding. Nevertheless, social and economic policies remained largely rooted institutionally in the postwar paradigm of stable, highly regulated labor markets for male breadwinners, traditional family structures, and a relatively balanced demographic structure. The new requirements of flexible labor markets, the transformation of the composition of households, demographic changes, increasing economic interdependence, and the need to adjust to the criteria of monetary union in Europe require more fundamental or radical economic and social policy innovations. The existing institutional arrangements, in the context of which social and economic policies were formulated, can no longer remain grounded on the kinds of arrangements that Christian democracy conventionally attempted to fashion.

Christian democracy's major predicament is therefore also partly an effect of the incompatibility of the social and economic realities of the 1990s and the ill-adapted institutions of continental welfare states to which the movements are politically attached. Secularization has contributed to this predicament by frustrating one of the parties' most advantageous electoral assets and by lacerating the sacred canopy of a religiously inspired social harmony.

Christian democracy's contemporary trouble is double. On the one hand, it consists of the still declining significance of religion, which contributes to the decreasing ideological importance of the politics of mediation. On the other hand, the politics of mediation is losing its potential for success in any case as the terms and goods upon which a stable accommodation of conflicts of interests could be based are increasingly becoming scarce and the conditions under which social capitalist arrangements originally arose no longer obtain.

In the 1990s the politics of mediation via the welfare state had spent its force, although to varying degrees, as the analysis of the dissimilar paths of the German, Italian, and Dutch cases indicates. The diverging electoral performances of the movements in the 1980s and 1990s were related to the differences in the nature of Christian democratic alliances and social capitalist arrangements, to historically unique events (the unification of Germany, the collapse of Italy's "first republic"), to varying patterns of party competition, and to the outcomes of strategic choices over a set of crucial dilemmas.

In those countries where Christian democratic parties primarily integrated social coalitions via highly organized and regulated institutional practices of visible political protection and tangible exchange, such as pillarization in the Netherlands and clientelism (e.g., in the health sector, see Ferrera 1995), patronage, and institutionalized corruption in Italy, the fate of Christian democracy became much more directly linked with the state of the political economies. To put it simply: the worse these political economies fared, the more precarious the position of Christian democracy became. Here electorates held Christian democracy instantly responsible for the failure of the government dominated by the party to continue to guarantee the kind of social compensation for the adjustment to the new conditions of post-Fordist capitalism that they had been accustomed to even during the 1980s. The explanation of the crisis of the Italian system of corrupt exchanges, a perverted form of mediation, is obviously more complicated than this. Yet, Della Porta (1996: 230) argues that the "difficult international economic conjuncture reduced the available resources for ambiguous earnings at the very moment when the Maastricht agreements were increasing expectations for efficiency." In nations, such as Germany, where social coalitions and social capitalist arrangements had traditionally relied much less on such visible and directly palpable social compensations, the political backlash so far has been less pronounced.

My answer to the general question of the seeming incongruity between social structural changes and diverging political outcomes is that it is not so much the transformation of the religious cleavage structure of continental western Europe, but rather the exhaustion of the postwar Christian democratic model of welfare capitalism, social capitalism, and the demise of the politics of mediation that are presently modifying the capacity of enduring power mobilization.

THE PREDICAMENT OF CHRISTIAN DEMOCRACY IN EUROPE: SPECIFIC REFLECTIONS

Contemporary Christian democracy in continental western Europe is confronted with a number of strategic, ideological, organizational, and policy-related dilemmas that affect the movement's destiny in the 1990s and beyond. Generally speaking, these dilemmas are increasingly difficult to solve under the changing social, economic, and political conditions of post-Fordist capitalism. The policy-related difficulties tend to intensify Christian democracy's strategic, organizational, and ideological predicament. Such dilemmas are, of course, not unique to Christian democracy but also afflict social democracy. Yet, because of the special nature and importance of the politics of mediation and of social capitalist arrangements, the predicament of Christian democracy is particularly intense.

The *strategic questions* primarily concern the need to construct new social, political, and governmental coalitions – at the subnational, national, and European level – without entirely breaking down traditional alliances. Of the three cases examined here, Christian democracy in Germany seems to be affected the least by electoral and coalitional dilemmas. The German political system is characterized by a remarkable degree of continuity, summarized by four "rules": "Germany can be governed only from the political center; Germany can be governed only by coalition; electoral contests are bi-polar; federal governments are re-elected" (Pulzer 1995: 144). However, the bipolar nature of German party competition does make Christian democracy's governmental capacity dependent on the small, but pivotal liberal party.

Among the many factors that are relevant for the explanation of the collapse of the Italian DC (see Pasquino and McCarthy 1993; Follini 1993; Wertman 1995), three can be singled out for their effects on the logic of party competition. The first is the end of the cold war and the almost instant transformation of Italy's Communist Party (PCI) into the Democratic Party of the Left (PDS). This altered the position of the DC as an inevitable party of government as the PDS gradually became acceptable as a potential party of government. The second factor concerns the rise and success of new parties that have reorganized the right (Berlusconi as well as the postfascists) and the regional dimension of electoral competition (the Northern League). The third factor is the introduction of a mixed proportional and majoritarian electoral system in 1993 (Donovan 1995; Parker 1996). This system forces the construction of broad, preelection alliances, has bipolarizing effects, and decreases the political space of the center. The former DC is now scattered over the main electoral alliances. The right-wing factions joined the Freedom Alliance which includes the National Alliance (postfascists) and Berlusconi's *Forza Italia!* The PPI and other former Christian Democrats (e.g., Prime Minister Prodi) have joined the PDS and other left movements in the Olive coalition which won the 1996 elections.

In the Netherlands, the strategical issue has clearly surfaced with the arrival of a coalition between social democracy, conservative liberalism, and liberal democrats. The electoral competition for the CDA has intensified both on the left and on the right. Also here Christian democracy has lost its "natural" governmental capacity now that the social democrats and conservatives no longer exclude each other as partners in government. On the right the competition with the conservatives is over the nonreligious and middle-class voters. In this struggle social policy issues are toned down to such an extent that the competition from the left becomes increasingly fierce. Comparable electoral dilemmas loom up with respect to the defense of the established rights of privileged groups, particularly farmers and the elderly. This is the background of a host of incidents that negatively affect the electoral and coalitional strength of Dutch Christian democracy.

The Dutch story is telling. Social security as a positive electoral item has increasingly lost importance in the CDA's party manifestos. In 1981 about 10 percent of the election program was devoted to positive statements on social policy. This declined to 5 percent in 1989 and to 0.2 percent in 1994 (Pennings 1995: 32). The electoral strategy of the CDA in 1994 was strongly marked by an attempt to counter the advance of conservative liberalism, exemplified by an ideological deficiency on social policy issues and a neoliberal economic rhetoric. During the third Lubbers government (social democracy and Christian democracy, 1989–1994), the CDA had already radicalized its austerity policies, but pursued a wavering strategy with respect to social policy. In 1993 the parliamentary group of the CDA, ignoring its own ministers in government, attempted to strike a deal with the conservative liberals on the reform of the disability scheme. The strategic goal was to provoke a cabinet crisis, put the blame on the social democrats, and pave the way for new elections and for a coalition with the conservative liberals. The attempt utterly failed, damaged the image of the party, and paradoxically contributed to the rapprochement of social democracy and conservative liberalism. The announcement during the 1994 campaign that no social security scheme, including public pensions and health care, would escape retrenchment was another major strategic error. It virtually annulled the remnant of the party's social image, provoked a clash between the party and the (affiliated) league of old-age pensioners, and caused the establishment of new parties for the elderly, which increased electoral competition.

The *ideological* question pertains above all to the need of modernizing the religiously inspired belief systems and of adapting these to the requirements of politics in increasingly secularized societies. Moreover, there is the difficult task of reformulating an ideology that is capable of breathing new life into the politics of mediation, while the material means for such a politics are lacking. Finally, there is the option of entirely abandoning Christian-inspired politics and transforming the parties into explicitly secular conservative political movements. However, the electoral appeal of secular conservative parties is unclear, while there is a distinct risk of losing a still existing and loyal core of religious voters.

The *organizational* issue first of all concerns the declining significance of the traditional party organization, exemplified by a loss of members and of financial means. Most political parties struggle with this issue. An additional problem for Christian democracy is the decomposition of the infrastructure of formerly affiliated social and economic associations that have traditionally facilitated the construction of consensus and payoffs via the politics of mediation. This type of organizational problem is obviously most acute in Italy where a single party has ceased to exist, but also in the Netherlands where the party has lost its position in government. In both cases, formerly affiliated organizations turn to other political actors that are willing to defend vested interests or accommodate conflicts of interests. Finally, the loss of governmental power of Christian democracy in Italy and the Netherlands severely constrains a crucial mechanism of power mobilization, namely the distribution of political favors and the control over public office. This reinforces intraparty strife among factions and hampers the maintenance of clientelistic exchange.

The *policy-related dilemma* includes the complicated if not paradoxical struggle to regulate publicly issues of private morality and the family on the basis of Christian norms and values in an unfavorable context of an individualizing and, at the same time, globalizing moral culture. The problem is the typical discrepancy between the religious and pious character of philosophical principles and the profane nature of political practice. The more definite religious principles are associated with political principles, the more difficult it is to defend policy proposals on the basis of an explicit religious ethic that is not widely shared. However, the policy dilemma comprises above all the decisive issue of finding a politically viable balance between upholding and transforming the continental welfare state regimes in an increasingly unfavorable social and economic context without provoking an immediate political backlash. Dutch and Italian

Christian democracy have failed to find such a balance. In Germany rising pressures, especially mounting unemployment figures and the difficulty of meeting the EMU-criteria, increasingly constrained the popularity of the Kohl government. A political backlash against German Christian Democracy is not excluded, particularly as the CDU has attached its political prestige to the EMU and to a solution for mass unemployment.

CONCLUSION

The decline in power of Christian democracy in western Europe has a structural and a contingent component. The cause of the structural downfall is not only found in the process of secularization, but also in the demise of the politics of mediation. Under favorable economic circumstances the Christian democratic parties pursued a strategy of social policy that was capable of generating a payoff between opposed interests and that reinforced their social and political power. However, the beneficial conditions for such a politics of mediation were disappearing in the 1980s and 1990s as the sources upon which it was based were becoming scarce. The effect of these developments became clear in the 1990s when the embedding of the politics of mediation in political institutions and social coalitions started eroding. This generated a context in which it became increasingly difficult to appeal to religious and nonreligious voters alike.

This structural context, however, cannot explain why the electoral fate of the parties diverged to such an extent, but does make plausible over which strategic, ideological, and organizational dilemmas the parties were forced to make choices and how these choices and the policy-related predicament contribute to the intensity of the dilemmas. The logic of the analysis allows for a counterfactual argument and a prediction. The counterfactual argument is that more favorable conditions would have postponed and moderated the decomposition of Christian democracy in the Netherlands and would have led to a much less dramatic collapse of Christian democracy in Italy. The prediction is that German Christian democracy will soon face a comparable predicament under the current deteriorating social and economic circumstances.

13

THE POLITICAL ECONOMY OF NEOLIBERALISM: BRITAIN AND THE UNITED STATES IN THE 1980s

Desmond King and Stewart Wood

If ever a scholarly claim for Anglo-American exceptionalism received empirical support, it was during the ascendant New Right administrations of Margaret Thatcher and Ronald Reagan. During the 1980s, these governments embarked on a systematic and comprehensive project of fiscal retrenchment, financial and labor market deregulation, and erosion of the Keynesian assumptions that had underpinned postwar economic and social policy. The ideological bases of the New Right agenda have been examined in detail, as have the policies attempted in their name (Cooper, Kornberg, and Mishler 1987; King 1987; Hoover and Plant 1988; Jordan and Ashford 1993; Marsh and Rhodes 1992; Palmer and Sawhill 1984; Palmer 1986; Campbell and Rockman 1991; Heclo and Salamon 1982). But theories of political economy have yet to be satisfactorily applied to these two cases. This chapter employs recent work in the study of the relationship between organized interests and the state to cast light on features of the policies pursued in the 1980s.

The United States and Britain were not the only two countries that swung electorally to governments espousing neoliberal principles. A bourgeois coalition government came to power in 1976 in Sweden, ending over six decades of social democratic hegemony, while in the early 1980s coalition governments with a similar ideological complexion came to power in Germany, the Netherlands, and Denmark. But the impulse toward retrenchment and deregulation under these administrations was never strong, perhaps surprisingly so given the neoliberal rhetoric that preceded their arrival in power (for the German case, see Esser 1986). In the face of common demographic, global, economic, and intellectual transformations, therefore, the pronounced neoliberal responses of American and British administrations warrant study.

The literature on these cases characterizes the neoliberal agenda as a comprehensive ideology premised on the rejection of postwar Keynesian politics, in particular the role of the state and of organized interests in economic governance. Put in these terms, the policies of the Reagan and Thatcher administrations can simply be "read off" from the tenets of the ideology that underpins them. But the task of linking policies in terms of a consistent underlying ideology has not been an easy or a satisfactory one. Typologies and characterizations have had to embrace policies that have at times promoted market-allocative mechanisms and at other times undermined them, at times lowered taxes but just as frequently raised them, and simultaneously espoused the cause of "limited government" while centralizing power in many areas to an unprecedented degree. Furthermore, explaining policies in terms of an "external" ideology ignores the ways in which policies are themselves informed by past policies, economic structures, and political expediency (Weir and Skocpol 1985). In other words, policies may, in important ways, be endogenous to the organizational, electoral, and economic context in which they are applied. The ideology-based characterization also has problems answering the question, Why did neoliberalism flourish in the United Kingdom and the United States and not in other countries? To respond by invoking a common liberal heritage based on a deep mistrust of government is to add additional questions (why now and not before? why not in other countries with similar traditions?) as well as seriously to mischaracterize the policies that were introduced.

This chapter relates the neoliberal policies of the Reagan and Thatcher administrations to distinctive organizational features of the American and British political economies. New Right neoliberalism is best understood as the result of an alliance or natural affinity between the functional requirements and organization of Anglo-American market economies, and the political goals of right-of-center parties in power. Neoliberalism lies at the interaction of an economic policy project to promote the cost competitiveness of domestic firms, and a political-strategic framework to undermine the demographic and institutional bases of electoral opponents' work.

UNCOORDINATED CAPITAL AND COST COMPETITIVENESS

Advanced industrial democracies have faced common exogenous pressures since the early 1970s. First, nations have encountered a crisis in the stability of aggregate demand. Climbing rates of unemployment were detectable in the late 1960s, but became politically and economically consequential in the early 1970s following the commodity price boom and the 1973 oil shock. As a result, the assumption of stable world markets that had underwritten economic growth since the reconstruction period of the 1940s evaporated. Second, and in defiance of conventional macroeconomic policy models based on the Phillips curve, unemployment and inflation rose simultaneously at various stages throughout the 1970s. Not only did the appearance and persistence of stagflation undermine conventional Keynesian models of economic analysis, but additionally the policy tasks of governments were transformed (Hirsch and Goldthorpe 1978; Goldthorpe 1984). Governments were no longer able easily to fine-tune macroeconomic demand to "select" an optimal location on the Phillips curve, combining moderate levels of inflation and unemployment. Third, national economies have become progressively more interdependent in two senses: national product markets are increasingly integrated as a result of the expansion of international trade; and capital mobility has accelerated since the collapse of the Bretton Woods fixed exchange rate system in 1971. The effect is an international economic system that transmits both inflationary and deflationary shocks across national borders.

These latter developments have limited the policy autonomy of national governments. The expansion of trade has meant that continued economic growth is increasingly dependent on the success of the exposed sectors of the economy. Thus, the primary task of economic management has been transformed from that of guaranteeing stable aggregate demand to promoting the competitiveness of national firms. In addition, international integration has drastically reduced the potential for governments to pursue without "punishment" autonomous fiscal and monetary policies in foreign exchange markets. Consequently, the "Keynesianism-in-one-country" approach to economic policy has proved unsustainable: that is, governments can no longer ensure full employment unilaterally (on French experience, see Machin and Wright 1985). This in turn has led to the weakening market position (and thus political power) of trade-union movements in advanced industrial democracies. These economic constraints on the pursuit of independent policy have been complemented by a widespread fiscal crisis of the welfare state. Demographic shifts and economic turbulence have undermined the accumulative capacities of postwar states. These developments have made it much harder for any state, notably those controlled by social democrats or socialists, to act as an agent of redistribution in the furtherance of aims such as equality or social rights of citizenship.

In the 1980s governments have confronted these new policy tasks with an impoverished "toolkit" of policy options. As the theoretical basis and practical possibility of sustaining high public-sector involvement have declined, governments of all partisan compositions have become harshly aware of their increased reliance upon the strategies of domestic firms for economic and political success. Yet the strategies that are available to firms are, we argue, themselves a function of the *organizational context* of supply-side governance structures, that is, the ways in which business organizes the provision and distribution of supply-side public goods required for production. The central distinction in this respect is between what David Soskice terms coordinated and uncoordinated business communities (Soskice 1990, 1990a, 1994). This organizational feature not only shapes the strategies available in domestic firms, but is associated with distinct patterns of demands and possibilities for government intervention in order to bolster competitiveness.

Coordinated market economies (CMEs) are characterized by "national capitals" with strong (i.e, high-density, high-concentration) organization of industrial representation (Chambers of Commerce, trade and industry associations, etc.), and a plethora of informal, noncontractual linkages between large and small companies, industrial groups, banking networks, and business leaders. Where these linkages exist, business has been able to overcome problems of collective action endemic to the provision of supply-side goods (such as research and development, skilled labor, industrial peace, long-term financing).[1] In consequence, business in CMEs has been able to construct complex infrastructural support systems in the areas of capital finance, education and training, wage coordination, and integrating employee representation into company management. In the 1980s this

---

[1] The consequences of this organizational capacity are multiple: "employment tenure of both managers and workers is longer in CMEs; there is more teamwork and autonomous responsibility in work organization; workers are generally more skilled and get better training within the company; managers have more technical knowledge of the company's technology, and they work across specializations; decision-making is more consensual, and there is a formalised system of employee representation within the company; companies produce higher quality goods and services, have more emphasis on in-house product development, and take investment decisions within a longer term framework; they have closer relations of a long-term nature with other companies, especially in product modification and development" (Soskice 1994: 3).

organizational capacity has become salient to business and governments alike. Technological developments (notably development of the microprocessor) have sharpened the need for both a highly skilled work force and collective resources to sustain competitiveness in higher value-added markets; concurrently firms have become more dependent on the range of services that only coordinated business can provide its members (e.g., collective knowledge of reputations, expertise in export marketing).

The implications for government of the extent of capital coordination are less profound for CMEs than for liberal market economies (LMEs). Where banks and associations of industrial representation coordinate the activities required for maintaining the supply of those goods which enable firms to compete through the development of "high skill, high quality" (e.g., in Germany or Switzerland), governments assume a configurative role, maintaining favorable environmental conditions for the autonomous activities of coordinated business. Soskice has written extensively about the characteristic product market and innovation strategies of CMEs. Yet it is an implication of this framework that LMEs are characterized by equally distinctive dynamics between firms, banks, and employer organizations, and between business and other groups. As yet, Soskice has not made these dynamics explicit. In addition, the CME-LME approach lacks an articulated political level of analysis. The need to incorporate political factors is most pressing in the case of LMEs, where the weak collective organizational and strategic capacities of business, and the consequent unavailability of "private ordering" solutions to problems of collective governance, *imply a greater role for governments in determining supply-side outcomes.*

Among the many features implied by the lack of capital coordination, four are pertinent. First, the inability of business to solve basic problems of collective action undermines any public policy effort predicated on concentration between the social actors and the state. The most notable example of this is the "corporatist" effort at coordinated wage bargaining, but the logic of policy failure stemming from the organizational incapacity of capital can be extended to a number of supply-side initiatives in the 1960s and 1970s.[2] However, whereas corporatist analyses attribute the failure of concertational policy making to the inability of elites of represen-

---

[2] Notable examples of such legislative initiatives were, in the United Kingdom, the tripartite National Economic Development Council of 1964 (NEDC and "little Neddies"), the Industrial Training Act of 1964, creating tripartite industrial training boards, and the Manpower Services Commission of 1973–1988; in the United States, a variety of programs and bodies were founded under the auspices of the Manpower Development and Training Act of 1962, and succeeded by the Comprehensive Employment and Training Act of 1973.

tative organizations to control free riding among member firms, the analysis we provide suggests a more explicit incentive based on examination of the failure of such policies. Firms embedded in uncoordinated organizational contexts, and consequently unable to provide supply-side public goods, develop product market strategies that minimize their reliance on such inputs. As a result, state-sponsored attempts to stimulate the collective provision of these goods in LMEs should be expected to meet with a mixture of indifference and outright hostility from domestic manufacturing firms (for the British case, see Wood 1997).

Second, the attitude of firms in LMEs to labor is ambivalent. At the macroeconomic level, firms reject collectivism in all its forms, particularly attempts to privilege the views of organized labor over and above the decisional autonomy of firm managements. At the microeconomic level, however, firms are eager to cooperate with plant-level unions, and to offer competitive wages to attract scarce labor, in order to tackle problems of production generated by the lack of industrial coordination. Third, firms in LMEs compete on the basis of cost rather than quality, and therefore their dominant preference regarding public policy is that government takes action to remove the obstacles that are responsible for inflating the costs of production – in particular, labor costs (this contrasts with a country such as Germany, where a legal framework enforcing high wages across industries enjoys a basic consensus among firms producing "high-skills, high-quality" products). Policies regarding the legal status of trade unions, benefit entitlements of the unemployed, social security contributions, the behavior of government-as-employer within the public sector, and taxes are thus all central to the imperative to stimulate competitiveness by reducing production costs. Fourth, the inability to control wages through corporatist bargains reduces the capacity of governments in LMEs to mitigate the trade-off between unemployment and inflation. Given the centrality of wage control to competitive strategies, containing rising costs can only be accomplished at the expense of reducing growth and employment. Governments committed to tackling inflation must be prepared to embrace the political ramifications of macroeconomic contraction.

It may be objected that one cannot account for changes merely by the need for them (the functionalist error: cf. Elster 1984). For example, the structure of capital is a relatively durable feature of British and American political economy – it is therefore, on its own, unable to account for the timing of neoliberal policies. This objection certainly points to the need for a political mechanism to establish why these policies emerged as vote winners for parties. In other words, we need to provide an interpretation of policies that not only demonstrates their functional importance for Anglo-American capitalism, but also why they were advantageous for parties seeking to return to power. One might refer to this phenomenon as an affinity between the political and economic dimensions of neoliberal public policy. The affinity can be analyzed as two distinct relationships. On the one hand, we claim that the lack of industrial coordination in the United Kingdom and the United States (coupled with exogenous economic changes in the 1970s) gives strong incentives for parties to promote neoliberal policies in order to get reelected. On the other hand, neoliberal policies adopted for specifically political ends (i.e, to increase the likelihood of reelection and to weaken political opponents) met the functional requirements of firms in an uncoordinated organizational environment. Neoliberal policies permitted a harmony of interests between parties in power seeking reelection and firms in the organizational context of Anglo-American capitalism.

The importance of the organization of capital in LMEs for government policy can also be seen during the period preceding the rise of neoliberalism. For the absence of coordination strongly implies that policies premised on forms of "corporatist collaboration" are structurally doomed in the organizational context of LMEs. Successive governments between the mid-1950s and late 1970s in both the United States and Britain attempted various "manpower policies" that fall into this category, involving increased funding to firms, industrial organizations, and local public bodies; incentive schemes designed to promote training and investment; state-sponsored efforts at industrial tripartism; and attempts to institutionalize wage control through centralized agreement between the state, business, and labor. These initiatives proved unsustainable for several reasons. With regard to negotiated wage control, for example, peak representatives of weakly organized business and labor organizations were unable to deliver their members for any negotiated agreement. Business participation in experiments such as the regional training boards and the National Economic Development Council was halfhearted – such institutional experiments were judged to incur unwelcome cost burdens and to interfere with firm-level autonomy in pricing and investment decisions. Problems of institutionalized wage control were exacerbated in the mid- to late 1970s by several factors – the weakening of the market position of unions and the individualization of the work force as unemployment rose, reductions in the growth in labor productivity throughout the industrial democracies, and increased union militancy (particularly with public-sector unions in the British case). Activist industrial policy also came up against large fiscal constraints in the aftermath of the two oil shocks.

Consequently, it is no accident that these policies were, in the 1970s,

associated with economic decline and electoral unpopularity for those responsible. Rephrased, the infeasibility of corporatist policies in LMEs generated poor economic outcomes, for which incumbent governments were
electorally punished in the late 1970s.[3] This pattern helped the opposition
conservative parties to break with the politics of Keynesian consensus
(however fragile such a consensus may have been). This argument can be
developed further. Given the structural roots of the failure of corporatist
policies in American and British capitalism, it is unsurprising that neoliberal policies found such fertile intellectual soil during the 1970s, both
within the Conservative and Republican political parties, and within industrial opinion more generally. Furthermore, exogenous developments in
trade and capital mobility undermined the feasibility of Keynesian demand
management strategies, and forced governments to focus greater attention
on the functional requirements of domestic capital to generate the economic performance required for reelection. Above all, given the requirements of firms in LMEs, this meant tackling the issue of production costs,
inflation, and the level of the tax burden borne by the private sector, and
the size of the public sector more generally. In this last area – the reduction
in size of the state and its commitments – the New Right governments
demonstrated their greatest policy innovation, conjoining an ideology of
popular capitalism with both an electoral strategy designed to win votes,
and an economic strategy aimed at stimulating the private economy. These
were measures that business organizations in both countries demanded
with increasing belligerence from the late 1970s onward (Martin 1994).[4]

[3] This is, of course, an argument for the rejection of social democratic policy efforts, rather
than an endorsement of neoliberalism per se. Nevertheless, a basic retrospective voting
model in a two-party system indicates that the "failure of incumbents" can be sufficient
reason to account for the initial electoral success of one's opponents (though not their
reelection). In the American case, for example, one need only invoke the poor record of
Carter's macroeconomic policy (part bad timing, part poor electoral politics) to account
for his rejection in 1980 in favor of Reagan. As Hibbs observes, Carter pursued the
opposite of a political business logic: "Carter tackled the unemployment issue head on,
and the administration pursued stimulative macroeconomic policies throughout 1977 and
into 1978. The policy shift succeeded in creating an election-year recession, but because
of the sluggish response of wages and prices on economic slack, the inflation rate declined
only slightly during the last two quarters of 1980 from its midyear peak. Consequently
President Carter and the Democrats went before the electorate in 1980 with the worst of
all possible situations – high inflation, increased unemployment and falling real income
and output" (Hibbs 1987: 191).

[4] In the British case, the links between government departments and large firms are entrenched. In the early Thatcher years, while "corporatist" representative associations were
shunned, links with groups such as the Employers' Engineering Federation were important factors in the deregulatory drive (Grant 1994).

To summarize the link between the organization of capital and public policy: the absence of structures of coordination between firms and employers' associations limits the sets of product market strategies available to domestic firms. This constraint in turn shapes the determinants of competitiveness in LMEs, generates a set of domestic firms' preferences regarding public policy, and renders certain "incongruent" policy initiatives infeasible. But exogenous economic developments (notably growing trade and capital interdependence rendering Keynesian full-employment strategies unviable) have weakened the power of trade unions, and increased the centrality of firms' competitiveness in economic performance. Correspondingly, governments seeking reelection are more than ever compelled to meet the needs and demands of domestic firms, and to tolerate the political costs of the policies required. Neoliberalism can be seen in part as the response of political parties of the right to the logistical imperatives of firms in LMEs in an age in which the salience of these imperatives to domestic economic performance (and thus to their chances of reelection) has itself increased.

We turn now to three policy areas – fiscal policy, labor market policy, and the initiative to redraw the public-private dichotomy – to illustrate these economic and political dynamics. The pursuit of these policies enhanced both electoral and economic imperatives. Neoliberal policies were used for political ends in two ways. First, the impact of the policies was to distribute the pain and benefits of economic adjustment in ways that secured winning political coalitions in subsequent elections. Though the manipulation of the "political business cycle" is a familiar phenomenon, there are good reasons to believe that the strong distributive consequences of neoliberal policies were only *politically* feasible in a limited set of nations. For example, the ability of the Thatcher administration to engineer excessive macroeconomic contraction in 1981 without irreparable electoral damage owes much to features of the plurality electoral system, demographic factors, and felicitous contingencies. Second, the ideology of neoliberalism was manipulated to recommend structural changes that had a more permanent impact on the international bases of political opponents' power. This second political ambition, less conventional but arguably more permanent in its electoral effects, points to a distinction between the American and British cases. While the Reagan and Thatcher administrations shared similar (but not identical) macroeconomic policy records, the record on *institutional* change contrasts sharply. This divergence stems from important differences between the two nations at the constitutional level. In all three policy areas, the impact of the constitutionally entrenched separation of powers in the United States – both at the federal level and between the federal and state levels – was to constrain the ability of the Reagan administration to enact its neoliberal agenda. In the United Kingdom, however, a constitution that reserves an exceptional amount of discretionary power to central government and does not entrench the powers of subordinate levels of government or parapublic bodies, was employed by Thatcher to bring about unprecedented levels of institutional change.

THE POLICIES OF NEOLIBERALISM

FISCAL POLICY AND THE MACROECONOMY

The United Kingdom

In Britain, the fiscal restraint was at the heart of the 1979 Conservative manifesto, though financial restraint had been in place in some form since the constraints imposed by the International Monetary Fund in 1976. The important innovation of the Conservative government, elected in May 1979, was to abandon the macroeconomic target of full employment. In its place, the reduction of inflation became the prime task, achieved by limiting public expenditure and controlling the rate of monetary growth. The argument underlying this emphasis centered on reducing the borrowing requirement of the public sector (PSBR), which would cut its claims on savings and facilitate cuts in general taxation and interest rates (which would in turn boost private enterprise and lower inflation). The economic vision of macroeconomic management thus rested on a supposed virtuous circle of public-sector cuts, lower interest rates, and low taxation, generating resumed and sustainable economic growth.

There is considerable debate about the extent to which the Thatcher administration pursued this promised economic path. The attempts at monetary control through the annual setting of money supply targets soon became prey to frequent moving of the goalposts and, by 1981, had arguably given way to a more pragmatic (and conventional) approach of interest rate management, with the exchange rate taking the place of monetary targets as the crucial guideline. Nevertheless, three striking features of the Conservatives' economic record earn attention – unemployment, taxation, and public spending.

The Conservatives presided over a dramatic rise in the unemployment rate over a seven-year period from 1.09 million in May 1979 to 1.13 million in July 1986 (the level had fallen to 2 million by March 1989). What is important about this macroeconomic contraction is not merely its size, longevity, and significance in the context of the postwar full-employment British economy, but the fact that it was as much the result of deliberate fiscal policy moves as of global recession. The midrecession fiscal tightening in the March 1981 budget (to facilitate lower interest rates without inflation) acted procyclically to lower growth and employment still further. Such a contraction can be interpreted as a response to the problems of inflationary control in LMEs.

Politically, how was it possible to sustain such historically high unemployment without electoral punishment? Part of the answer lies in the pecularities of voter sensitivity to unemployment measures compared with other issues, such as the level of inflation and taxation. Hibbs (1982) argues, for example, that right-wing parties' constituencies are less concerned with unemployment than those of the left, while there is evidence that sustained levels of high unemployment have few detrimental effects on voters' electoral preferences (Whiteley 1985). Another part of the answer in the case of the 1983 general election concerns the electoral benefits of the "Falklands factor" for the Conservative vote, though the magnitude of the effect independent of macroeconomic variables is considered by many to be negligible (for opposing positions, see Sanders, Marsh, and Ward 1987; Clarke, Mishler, and Whiteley 1992). The beneficial electoral impact of the reduction in inflation achieved during the Thatcher administrations may have more than compensated for the harmful effects of rising unemployment. Indeed, the successful control of inflation is a key aspect of the affinity between the economic and political tasks of neoliberalism: its reduction simultaneously assisted domestic industry to control production costs (bolstering their cost competitiveness) and reward core and swing constituencies of the Conservatives in the electorate.[5] Controlling inflation was central, in other words, to the coalition of increasing real wage earners that facilitated repeated Conservative electoral success.

The more general answer lies in the structure of the British electoral

---

[5] Inflation was reduced from 21.9 percent in August 1980 to 3.7 percent in May 1983. Despite a modest rise in the subsequent two years, the rate was 2.4 percent in August 1986. The effect on the annual rate of growth of average earnings was equally dramatic — from a level of 22.2 percent in the second quarter of 1980, the rate was reduced to 8.7 percent by the beginning of 1983. The issue of whether or not inflation rates have a discernible electoral impact in the United Kingdom is a controversial one. Heath and Paulson (1992) contend that inflation has no significant impact on the vote after 1974 in the United Kingdom, while every percentage point increase in the unemployment rate costs around 0.6 percent points in government support. If this is the case, the Conservative electoral victories in 1983 and 1987 (when unemployment was high) are even more remarkable, and confirm the importance of the asymmetrical spatial distribution of the vote for Labour and Conservative parties in determining the electoral result. For the view that inflation does have a role in determining electoral outcomes, see Sanders (1993).

system. The reelection of the Conservative government in 1983 with a landslide majority[6] despite its poor employment record can only be explained by an appreciation of the spatial distribution of the vote in the context of the first-past-the-post electoral system. The regional concentration of manufacturing industry (in the north, northwest and Midlands), in which the contractionary effects of Thatcher's fiscal policy were felt the hardest, meant that the electoral costs of high unemployment were disproportionately concentrated in safe Labour seats. Consequently, the harmful effects on total vote were translated into a proportionately smaller effect on total seats won. The ability of the government to bear the political costs of high unemployment was therefore in no small measure due to the properties of the electoral system in which the parties competed. But the electoral system had a more profound influence in producing the repeated Conservative victories in a second way. The single member plurality electoral system rewarded the Conservatives for the division of the Labour Party and the formation of the Social Democratic Party (SDP). The three-way electoral race robbed a potential "unified" opposition of seats, and punished especially the Alliance in 1983 and 1987 for the fact that its vote was geographically highly dispersed.

The remarkable Conservative record in controlling public expenditure was also pivotal to its economic and electoral success. Between 1980–1981 and 1989–1990, the PSBR was reduced from 5.7 to 2.8 percent of GDP. Despite this striking fall in public borrowing, however, public expenditure in the first five years of the Thatcher administration *rose* by 6.3 percent in real terms (the target set out in March 1980 was a reduction of 4 percent by this time). In part, this rise was the result of necessary expenditures induced by a recession and unemployment, but a significant amount was the result of higher than anticipated spending in defense and "law and order" categories. From 1986, the Conservatives managed to increase real levels of public spending across categories and, simultaneously, to reduce public expenditure to national income ratios of under 40 percent by 1990, the lowest figure for twenty years. Direct taxation, meanwhile, was also cut across income groups, while the overall tax burden in 1990 was roughly equal to the figure in 1978.

---

[6] The Conservatives won 397 seats to Labour's 209 (with 23 for the Liberal Alliance), whereas the popular vote was divided: Conservatives 43 percent, Labour 28 percent, and Liberal Alliance 26 percent. The exaggerated effects of the single-member plurality system (Cube's law) has declined over time in the U.K. case, but remains significant, particularly at the regional level, In the 1983 election, Conservative total vote percentage was 53.57 percent higher than the percentage scored by Labour, but the number of Conservative seats was 89.95 percent higher than Labour's total seats (Curtice and Steed 1986).

This record of public expenditure cuts can be directly traced to the imperative of low-cost competition in LMEs. Income and corporation taxes were cut; the reduction in the borrowing burden and total expenditure of the public sector freed up capital for private industry, and undoubtedly had a beneficial effect on medium- to long-run interest rates; and the dismantling of the public sector helped to promote wage moderation in the sheltered sector. But how, politically, did it prove possible to produce this fiscal miracle, to maintain high real spending in a period of recession, while eroding the PSBR and maintaining an electoral image as a party of low taxes? Several fiscal tricks are responsible. The tax revenues from North Sea oil boomed in the early 1980s (after the second oil shock), peaking at £12 billion in 1984–1985. The revenue from council house sales, beginning in 1980 and continuing throughout the decade, boosted public coffers significantly (particularly in the early 1980s)[7] Lastly, the receipts from privatization provided over £33 billion between 1979 and 1991. Due to a quirk of public expenditure counting, privatization proceeds count as negative expenditure.

It is difficult to see how such policies could have been pursued in political and constitutional systems significantly different from that of the United Kingdom. For the fiscal miracle relied on two distinctive institutional features. First, to put it more crudely, the revenue gained from the sale of state industries was made possible by the acquisition of these industries under the collectivist policies of a number of postwar British governments. The industries ranged from commanding heights industries (such as coal) to public utilities (such as electricity and telecommunications), and lame-duck industries acquired in the 1960s and 1970s when on the verge of bankruptcy. Mrs. Thatcher may well have seen her central political task as the eradication of socialism in Britain, but the fiscal revolution she pioneered was in this respect dependent on the collectivism she abhorred. Second, the twin centralizing and privatizing attacks on local governments and their spending powers were feasible because of the tepid constitutional standing of local government. The traditional powers of local government are not constitutionally entrenched in the British polity. They form a myriad of privileges and prerogatives granted by central government. The experience of the 1980s demonstrated the low political costs and high feasibility of radical attacks by central government on

---

[7] Since 1980, over 1.5 million houses have been sold to occupants, often at discounts of up to 80 percent. The fiscal profile was also aided by the savings in expenditure on future public construction and maintenance implied by the load-shedding of the state housing sector.

these powers, justified by the need to attack the sources of spiraling public expenditure.

The United States

In 1980, Ronald Reagan benefited from the disastrous macroeconomic record of his incumbent opponent Jimmy Carter, who was faced in an election year with high and rising inflation, high and rising unemployment, falling real income and output, and declining productivity. Over the next four years, Reagan engineered a macroeconomic policy geared to the electoral cycle. Inflation, as in the United Kingdom, was brought down (from 9.6 percent in 1981 to 3.7 percent in 1984). Real income growth, on the other hand was reduced from 1.3 percent in mid-1981 to 0.2 percent in the third quarter of 1982; by the election period, however, it had risen to 4.75 percent, delivering the best year for real incomes since 1964. Unemployment followed a similar trajectory. Between 1981 and the end of 1982, unemployment rose over 3 percent to reach 10.5 percent, but two years later it had fallen back to the level of 1981. Unlike the experience of Thatcher's administration in the United Kingdom, however, the deflationary policies did not come without electoral disadvantage. In the midterm elections in 1982, in midrecession and midpolitical business cycle, the Republicans lost seats in the House and the Senate. The resulting strengthening of congressional opposition was an undoubted factor in the modest record of the Reagan presidency in promoting further tax and expenditure cuts beyond the achievements of 1981.

The most radical macroeconomic policy initiative of the Reagan presidency was the Economic Recovery Tax Act (ERTA) of 1981. Influenced by supply-side economics, graphically if simplistically conveyed in the infamous Laffer curve, Reagan's attempt to enact a 30 percent across-the-board tax cut failed in 1981 but a reduction of 25 percent phased over three years was accepted by Congress and included in the act. This measure reduced the proportion of federal income from tax revenues significantly in the ensuing years. The central features of the act were an aggregate tax cut of $162 billion, consisting of a 23 percent reduction in personal income taxes, a cut in the highest marginal rate from 70 to 50 percent, lowering of capital gains tax from 28 to 20 percent, and major cuts in business taxes (largely through loosening the time period on depreciation allowance). But perhaps most importantly for the durability of these changes, tax brackets were indexed to the inflation rate to preclude "bracket creep" as a result of price rises. Hibbs (1987: 311) estimates that the highest income group received 26 percent more take-home personal income as a result of the ERTA (see also Feldstein 1995).

Further reductions in taxation were hamstrung by not only the intransigence of a Democrat-controlled Congress but the constricting effects of the budget deficit. The Tax Reform Act of 1986 exemplified the dilemmas faced by a neoliberal government in this context. The purpose of the act was to rationalize the collection of taxes by enforcing the principle that all income was to be taxed uniformly regardless of the way in which it was earned. But while this gave the reduction in personal taxation a further boost (bringing top rates down still further to 28 percent), the act "increased the tax burden borne by capital and . . . damaged the competitive position of American corporations" (Steinmo 1993: 169). Between 1985 and 1987, taxes received from businesses doubled from $60 billion to $120 billion. It seems that given the fiscal constraints imposed by the deficit, the Reagan administration accepted a higher corporate tax burden as an acceptable price to pay for lowering personal taxation (Peterson and Rom 1989: 221). Similar constraints were evidenced in the spending record of the Reagan years. The 1981 Omnibus Budget Reconciliation Act pushed through $35 billion cuts in nondefense spending (while increasing defense spending by $7 billion). Over the whole Reagan period, however, public expenditure cuts were limited. Programs for the elderly increased by $56 billion, as much as under Johnson or Carter, while the real cost of the umbrella Aid for Families with Dependent Children (AFDC) welfare program and Medicaid was only slightly lower in 1986 than in 1980. In agricultural subsidies, support rose to record levels by the end of Reagan's tenure.

The Reagan presidency faced similar opposition in its attempts to control public expenditure on the federal bureaucracy. Central to the problems Reagan faced in this area was the constitutional requirement that Congress approve budgetary changes. Severe cuts were proposed, both in staffing and appropriations. By 1984, however, Congress had stalled the cuts and in many cases had approved increased funding. Reagan underestimated the resilience of both the public lobby groups he was attempting to defund and their links to congressional representatives. Congress repeatedly refused to abolish the Legal Services Corporation, the largest body supporting public-interest litigation and a prime agent in the liberalizing of the AFDC welfare program, and even defended it from budget cuts. The courts also proved opponents of reform in their rejection of Reagan's efforts to link state reimbursements to public-interest groups for costs incurred in law enforcement.

The weak record on tax and expenditure cuts offers an illuminating comparison with the United Kingdom, and illustrates the stronger political constraints imposed by the American Constitution on the neoliberal agenda. First, the separation of powers offers ample opportunity for Congress (and the Court) to block presidential proposals. In addition, the fact that congressional elections take place at the midterm of presidential election cycles limits the ability of the president to engineer straightforward four-year macroeconomic cycles without electoral cost to his supporters in Congress. Second, the American federal state's modest involvement in public ownership and direct industrial support meant that there could be no recourse to sale of state assets (or windfall revenues from highly taxed resources such as North Sea oil, as in the United Kingdom), in order to solve the basic trade-offs and dilemmas of introducing tighter fiscal policies. Third, public expenditure in the United States occurs at both the federal and state levels, yet much of state spending is constitutionally protected from central interference. Unlike the United Kingdom, where expenditure control was effected through a political and legal attack on the powers of local government, a significant portion of total public expenditure in the United States lies beyond the reach of the federal government. Fourth, it is plausible that the spiraling deficit in the 1980s, which handicapped attempts at more thoroughgoing fiscal control, itself has its roots in the structure of the federal polity. The pork-barrel politics of Congress and the congressional committee system makes it hard to overcome problems of collective action with regard to collective goods, such as the control of public spending.

LABOR MARKET DEREGULATION

The United Kingdom

In Britain, the state has waged war corrosively against trade unions since 1979 (for the intellectual sources of this attack, see Hayek 1980; Hanson 1991; Hanson and Mather 1988). Visibly triumphant over the National Union of Miners in 1984–1985, the Conservatives' diminution of workers' rights began five years earlier, and occurred incipiently through a series of industrial relations legislation (Davies and Freedland 1993; Longstreth 1988; MacInnes 1987; Taylor 1993). Secondary picketing – the practice of workers from one plant turning up at a strike at another – was outlawed in the Employment Act 1980, while plant-level union monopolies (closed shops) have been weakened by the provision of legal redress for aggrieved parties. A series of legislative measures made union membership much more voluntarist rather than automatic consequent to certain forms of employment. Union leaders cannot now embark on strike activity without conducting a postal ballot to win agreement from their members. The government also overturned the legal immunity that unions enjoyed in the British common law, so that employers can now sue for losses under certain conditions, a sequestering option exploited by numerous employers since the 1980s. Perhaps unsurprisingly, given the weak macroeconomic position of unions in the early 1980s and the content of these measures, the number of days lost from industrial disputes has declined significantly.[8]

It is difficult to underestimate the comprehensiveness of this attack on trade unions, which were the popular scapegoat for the excesses of collectivist politics in the 1970s. The record contrasts strongly with the experience during the same period and in the same hostile macroeconomic climate of unions in northern European countries, whose (already stronger) legal standing, workplace participation rights, and membership rules have been safeguarded. As we argued, the difference is explicable in terms of the organizational context of national economies. In CMEs, strong unions form an essential part of productive strategies focusing on high-skill, high-quality export manufacturing goods. In LMEs, where competitive advantage is, on average, provided in low costs, strong unions are perceived as merely inflating costs of production. This factor is insufficient on its own to explain the timing of the legislative attack. The explanation of the latter is rooted in two factors: the opportunities offered to the Conservative government by the economic climate (i.e., high unemployment), and the specific legacy of the political and economic failure of corporatist incomes policies and industrial relations in the 1970s. But the attractiveness of this agenda for the Conservatives – and of contractionist economic policies that eliminated a section of British manufacturing – lay primarily in the political gains from attacking one of the institutional pillars of its opponents, the Labour Party. Membership in Trade Union Congress (TUC)-affiliated trade unions declined from 12.2 million in 1979 to just over 8 million by 1990 (less than the number of private shareholders). Because of the close historical links between the TUC and the Labour Party, the financial impact of this contraction on the latter has been significant. Furthermore, Garrett (1994) provides regression analysis results that suggest that voters who left a union between 1983 and 1987 are strongly disinclined to vote Labour subsequently, while the number of those who have never been union members is strongly inclined to vote Conservative.

---

[8] In 1979 and 1980 a total of over 41 million working days were lost to industrial action. The figure for 1981–1988, excluding effects of the Miners' Strike in 1984–1985, was 32.9 million.

Changes to the labor market promoting low-level flexibility have also occurred through reform of social policy. First, the rights of part-time workers and those on the fringes of the labor market have been reduced through the 1989 Employment Act: the disincentives to employers to hire part-time workers (such as their inclusion within the jurisdiction of Wages Councils) have been eroded. Most dramatically, the policy toward the unemployed has been transformed from the goal of providing security to that of generating a return to (often low-wage) work. Replacement rates have fallen sharply since 1980. Monitoring of availability to work was introduced in 1986, and has been stiffened considerably in subsequent acts. Social and welfare policy reform has been designed to effect a martinet integration of benefits programs with work or training requirements. Since 1988 unemployed workers under twenty-one have been faced with the choice of participation in youth training schemes or loss of benefits. Training has thus been transformed in part into a means of supplying firms with temporary, low-cost labor, and used as a threat of further insecurity rather than as an incentive to invest in employable skills. John Major's administration has advanced this punitive emphasis in work-welfare policy by tightening the rules making unemployed people eligible for benefits. From October 1996 a new "jobseeker's allowance" system makes the welfare contract explicit: in exchange for benefits unemployed people must participate in work schemes. Workfare has arrived.

Collectively, these policies constitute a systematic shift in labor market deregulation in British industry. The costs of this deregulation have been borne by voters who would be extremely unlikely to vote for the Conservatives anyway. The impact on electoral outcomes has therefore been marginal, while, in the case of trade-union members, there may well have been a positive impact on voters' preferences. These changes are characteristic of the political-economic dynamics of LMEs. Moreover, their feasibility is a product of the absence of legal structures, such as those of many European countries, that would have provided strong resistance to attacking the security and income of those on the fringes of the labor market.

The United States

The absence of a similarly extensive range of legislation concerning labor organization and the labor market in the United States in the 1980s is perhaps misleading. The American postwar political economy has always been a purer case of a deregulated market economy: ownership remained overwhelmingly private, macrocorporatist policies were never as seriously pursued as in Britain,[9] and the federal welfare system has never been more than a patchwork of programs designed to cater for market failures. Collectivist institutional structures were never successfully constructed in the United States. With regard to the welfare system, for example, the paramount distinction between insurance contributory-based programs and means-tested noncontributory ones has been retained since the Social Security Act of 1935, and has informed subsequent welfare legislation. Attempts to transcend the dichotomy – such as Nixon's family assistance plan or Carter's 1977 reform – foundered precisely because of the embeddedness of the demarcation (King 1996; Quadagno 1994). The regional cleavages institutionalized in New Deal welfare programs, manifest in different congress members' interests, themselves constituted an obstacle to enlarging welfare. Southerners wanted to maintain traditional forms of race relations in their states, retain control of the level of welfare benefits, and ensure that benefits did not affect the supply price of labor, while northerners sought an enlarged federal role in welfare to offset the costs of their proportionately larger welfare programs.

Nevertheless, there were a variety of tone-setting actions in the early months of the Reagan presidency that signaled to private employers the extent of permissible behavior, most notably the public support for the crushing of the air traffic controllers' union in 1981. In welfare legislation the resemblance between American and British neoliberal initiatives is striking. In 1981 the Social Security Block Grant Act encouraged states to devise their own work-welfare programs. Seven years later Congress passed the Family Support Act. The crucial component of the act was the introduction in federal policy of a work or training requirement to be discharged by recipients in exchange for the receipt of welfare payments. Each state government introduced this work element – the JOBS programs – into their welfare programs from October 1990, attempting to satisfy the stringent participation rates required to receive federal funding (Mead 1992: ch. 9). This important modification of the welfare system built on measures implemented by many of the state governments in the preceding seven years and paved the way for Clinton's elemental reform signed in August 1996. The reduction in federal aid under Reagan's New Federalism and the linkage drawn forcefully by the National Governors' Association between welfare and economic prosperity promoted the development of

---

[9] The Comprehensive Employment and Training Act of 1973 was quasi-corporatist in design, but very soon collapsed into a collection of ad hoc temporary measures (King 1995).

these programs, such as those in Massachusetts (Employment Training, ET), California (Greater Avenues to Independence, GAIN), and Georgia (Positive Employment and Community Help, PEACH). Their aim is to provide persons receiving benefits with exposure to work or training skills to facilitate their transition to full-time employment.

RESTRUCTURING THE STATE

The United Kingdom

Perhaps the most enduring dimension of the Thatcher administration has been its restructuring of the collectivist British state that emerged between 1945 and 1979. Its significance for this chapter lies in its exemplification of the affinity between the economic, political, and electoral ambitions of public policies. The Conservatives defined policies that, (a) reduced the burden of public expenditure and relieved the pressure on governments to accumulate resources (either by borrowing or raising taxes, that is, fiscal load-shedding); (b) attempted to augment Conservative votes by targeting cheap capital at lower-middle-class swing voters; and (c) attacked organizations that offered the strongest resistance to the neoliberal agenda.[10] Finally, restructuring is often a way of centralizing political power by sidelining, disarming, or regulating intermediary political institutions.

First, the government has depleted the physical assets that the postwar British state acquired. The sale of state industries, public utilities, and houses achieved multiple ends. Economically, load-shedding has reduced the fiscal burden, and thus helped to suppress public-sector pressures for higher taxation, borrowing, and interest rates. More subtly, the emasculation of the public sector has robbed future leftist governments of a substantial element of any industrial or economic policies based on social democratic economic management. It is an investment against the possibility of a return to traditional social democracy. The effect on the health of the industries concerned in the sale is hard to estimate, though in the case of some there is reason to believe that state policies preparing the industry for flotation at attractive share prices was a key financial boost to postprivatization performance. Even more controversial has been the esti-

[10] This is not meant to belittle the independent influence of political ideas in the formation of the neoliberal agenda. Our claim here is that there are good structural reasons to explain why this agenda proved appealing and politically successful in the British political economy, and that, from a rational choice perspective, conservative governments are primarily attracted to such measures by the opportunities they present to win elections and attack political opponents.

mated effect of load-shedding on the proclivity of the electorate to vote Conservative. The sales were pitched as attempts to disperse capital and to establish popular capitalism, a theme that found a significant audience among the upwardly mobile lower middle classes that allied themselves so strongly with Mrs. Thatcher. Garrett finds independent effects of popular capitalism in both the weakening of Labour support and the propensity of share and council house buyers to vote Conservative; the magnitude of these effects does not diminish over time (Garrett 1994). Additionally, the sales have eliminated a large section of the public-sector *unions* whose wage militancy caused such problems for the Labour government in the late 1970s, yet whose members have traditionally been among the most solid constituents of the Labour vote.

Second, the government has restructured government itself. The central government bureaucracy has been pruned drastically and its constitutional status redefined through the creation of independent executive agencies, whose functions and targets are stipulated in terms of contracts with central government. By the end of 1993, 60 percent of British civil servants were working in such agencies, and there are indications that they may be privatized in the future. Furthermore, the center has continuously and purposefully intervened in local government, removing layers of administration (most famously the Greater London Council and metropolitan county councils in 1986) and shifting significant areas of local responsibility from elected local authorities to unelected, centrally appointed quasi-nongovernmental organizations (quangos). Where the Conservatives have not attempted to disengage the state directly, they have introduced market mechanisms into the operations of the welfare state, notably through the division of purchasers and providers of health services and education within the National Health Service and the primary and secondary school systems respectively. Client and contractor categories have been instituted for the franchised provision of services by local government (e.g., refuse collection and road maintenance). The campaign against government itself was propelled by a popular ideology attacking bureaucratic profligacy, but undermined the institutional loci of support for political opponents.

The United States

The assault on the American regulatory system was launched in Reagan's first State of the Union Address, and consisted of two related elements. Reagan issued a series of executive orders to centralize control and oversight of agencies in the hands of the Office of Management and Budget (OMB), and appointed a Task Force on Regulatory Relief to apply cost-benefit principles to regulatory rules. These measures proved to be the most substantial deregulatory initiatives, though notably at the level of administrative reorganization rather than through enacting new legislation. Consequently, commentators have concluded that Reagan's bureaucratic reorganization was merely a temporary, stylistic change rather than a permanent reform (Harris and Milkis 1989: ch. 4). The paucity of statutory law to consolidate the deregulatory ambition was the result of a formidable series of obstacles. Congress resisted the encroachment on its autonomy in the direction and control of executive officers (guaranteed by the Administrative Procedures Act). In *Environmental Defense Fund v. Thomas* (1986), the Supreme Court came to the aid of Congress and confirmed the views that the newfound discretion of the Office of Management and Budget was "incompatible with the will of Congress and cannot be sustained as a valid exercise of the president's Article II powers" (Civil Action No. 85-1747, District Court of D.C., January 23, 1986, Slip Opinion: p. 9). Second, Congressional oversight committees forced policy reversals through constant pressure and criticism of executive interference, excessive secrecy, and inconsistency. Attempts to pass an omnibus bill to provide statutory authority for regulatory review by the executive office were foiled by jurisdictional disputes, and the further possibility of deregulation-through-legislation was eliminated after the Court limited congressional oversight measures involving the legislative veto in 1983. The congressional backlash reached its climax in 1986 with a statutory attempt to restrain the authority of the newly created Office of Information and Regulatory Affairs (OIRA).

Transferring powers from the federal to state governments was the second element of Reagan's neoliberal ambition and was intimately bound with the deregulatory drive. The Presidential Task Force reduced the regulatory burden on states to save money and improve efficiency, and through "partial preemption" programs delegated regulatory authority to the states themselves. But many states have been reluctant to use this newfound discretion, continuing their passive acceptance of federal guidelines. Increasing states' regulatory discretion soon proved not to be synonymous with deregulation; many states increased and complicated the regulatory load, leading business representatives in some states to call for Washington to preempt state laws (Foote 1984). Returning responsibility to the states for welfare, social, and local development policy excited not only the opposition of the courts (e.g., on authorization of land usage), but also, and perhaps surprisingly, of the very actors whom the proposals were designed to empower (in particular, state governors). This was in no small part due to a contradiction between the desire to grant states a larger role in intergovernmental programs, and a concurrent cutback of federal grants-in-aid to the states (Reagan 1987). An additional irony is that Reagan's encouragement of states to innovate administratively in the provision of general goods has resulted in some notable liberal as well as conservative experiments (e.g., the industrial regeneration programs in Wisconsin). The Republican agenda thus unwittingly facilitated some of the most diverse experiments in public policy and administrative management, making central political or fiscal control even more difficult.

These distinct outcomes – marginal reform in the United States, substantial restructuring in Britain – pose an analytic problem for those who conventionally couple these two countries. Many of the commonalities between the two nations derive from the lack of market coordination between firms. An additional feature shared by the two cases is electoral systems that reinforce the dominance of two-party competition, and therefore produce single-party governments unencumbered by the need to appease coalition partners. Explaining the differential ability to effect institutional design, however, requires consideration of another dimension: the constitutional differences between the two states. The configuration of political power in the United States, we contend, renders central reform of the disparate branches of government extremely difficult. In contrast, the "decisional autonomy" afforded to cabinet governments in the British system is immense.

The Madisonian design of the American Constitution is familiar and remains profound in its impact. At the federal level, the constitutional separation and sharing of powers between the presidency, a bicameral Congress, and the Supreme Court have created a system with numerous veto points for various political actors. The consequent inability to generate concerted action is multiplied by a host of companion institutions and practices – notably the weak American party system, political finance laws that decentralize campaign funding and localize political coalitions, and the congressional committee system with its accompanying practices of logrolling and pork-barreling. In addition to horizontal separation of powers the federal system of government incorporates a vertical dimension of fragmentation (and indeed some theorists talk of "three-dimensional federalism" – federal, state, and local levels: see Nathan and Doolittle 1987). The accumulated consequences of these features were exemplified in the frustration of Reagan's attempts at state withdrawal and deregulation in the early 1980s.

In contrast to the United States, the opportunity for nongovernmental actors to exercise veto power in the British political system is circumscribed. The combination of the doctrine and practice of parliamentary sovereignty (Parliament cannot be constrained by other bodies or by its predecessors) with the fusion of executive and legislative powers in parliamentary government affords a high degree of decisional autonomy to British governments. Governments have immense scope to pass bills. Strong party discipline and a long-standing (effectively) two-party system have reinforced this autonomy. In the absence of a written constitution the practice of judicial review in British courts is not one with significant political implications (although this may change with the incorporation of European law). The functions of local government have gradually been eroded or replaced by creeping central administration since the latter part of the nineteenth century. Local government has been comprehensively reorganized on more than one occasion and does not enjoy any protected constitutional status; neither do the numerous quangos that have accumulated to fulfill a range of ad hoc functions. Checks to the incentives are weak in Britain, despite the recent creation of a set of parliamentary select committees to monitor the activities of government departments.

It is hardly surprising then that Thatcher was able to bring about a wide-sweeping reform of the position of the state within British society, while Reagan's administrative fiats and rhetorical encouragement produced few lasting results. The obstacles in the American case were not simply the vetoes of other political actors: many of the institutional resources and tactics available to the British Conservatives were denied the Reagan administration because of different historical trajectories (e.g., the presence of sizable state assets that could be sold). But the comparison illustrates the neglected importance of constitutional questions in determining the bounds of political feasibility in any public policy project.

CONCLUSION

This chapter has explicated a theoretical link between the organization of capital in the United States and Britain and the neoliberalism of Reagan and Thatcher in the 1980s. Furthermore, the differential abilities of central reformers to effect far-reaching and permanent institutional changes in these two countries owes much to differences in the constitutional distribution of power. Together these two factors – the organization of business and the organization of the polity – configure (i.e., constrain and enable in different ways) the policy ambitions of central governments.

Our analysis has a number of implications for the study of the relationship between business and public policy. The first is that the consequences of organizational incapacity are as relevant to the record of public policy in the post-1979 period as they were to the failure of collectivism in the 1960s and 1970s.[11] A good example of this persisting disorganization is the poor reception of training and enterprise councils (TECs) in the United Kingdom. Despite the privileged institutional position afforded to business by central government, TECs have found little favor. Large companies complain that the demands on their resources to fund collective projects are excessive; firms complain of confusion about the ill-specified differentiation of functions between the various administrative bodies; and fierce rivalry rather than cooperation characterizes the relationship between Chambers of Commerce, TECs, and enterprise agencies (EAs). The relationship between TECs and the government departments has proved even more fraught. Government and the business representatives they have appointed to local TECs disagree on basic objectives. TEC members are wary of "rubber-stamping" government policy, and are keen to redefine themselves as agents of economic development rather than channels through which the government can pursue its strategy of reducing long-term unemployment.[12] Meanwhile, local governments, for whom TECs represent a profound enervation of traditional policy autonomy in the area of economic development, are hostile to partnerships with local business leaders.

Second, bringing capital back in should not necessarily be equated with the idea that all outcomes can be directly read off from the preferences of capital. Governments have competing imperatives other than the satisfaction of the demands of firms, however dependent they are on economic success for reelection. The LME model implies a structural link between capital's preferences and government public policies, not uninterrupted harmony. The relationship between even the Conservative government and British business is one of mutual ambivalence. The remarkably small budget of the U.K. Department of Trade and Industry (£1 billion in 1993) and the low levels of industrial subsidy per person employed (670 ECU in 1993 – the European Union average is 1,150 ECU) continues to disappoint CBI representatives. The department has been recently characterized as "essentially" regulatory, advisory, and reactive under a series of ideologically right-wing ministers. Business groups such as the CBI, and business

---

[11] Recognition of this is demonstrated by the "new" Labour Party's commitment to policies attempting to meet the problem of capital coordination (Wickham-Jones 1995).

[12] In a questionnaire survey (*Financial Times*, May 10, 1993), 63 percent of responding TEC members rated economic development as their chief priority, while only 17 percent cited the training of the unemployed. For further details, see also *Financial Times*, September 7, 1993.

leaders, regularly complained that they could find no sympathetic ear in government (Wilks 1993). Even the rhetorical alignment of the Conservatives with small business seems not to have been reciprocated.

Third, the analysis is intended as part of a more general corrective within contemporary political economy toward the study of the preferences, organization, and strategies of capital. There are good theoretical and empirical reasons to suggest that capital rather than labor should take center stage in work that attempts to explain political-economic outcomes in the 1980s and 1990s. Such an emphatic shift would be particularly welcome in the study of British politics, which for too long has been content to attribute the fragility of collectivism solely to the incapacity of organized labor.

The strategic limitations of collective actors in LMEs suggest that the state in these nations plays a crucial role in constructing regulatory environments amenable to the production strategies of domestic firms. This inference implies the need to dispense with the conventional characterization of Anglo-American states as weak in comparison to their continental counterparts. Rather, the experience of the 1980s in the two countries studied here illustrates how profound an impact government policies can have on social and economic structures. Modern political economies are characterized in multiple forms of state involvement in economic life that escape categorization into weak and strong forms. Theories of public policy should consequently address the more general question of the forms of governmental and constitutional structure that make certain types of public policy more or less flexible.

Finally, the experience of LMEs in the 1980s demonstrates the need to take more seriously the claim that there may be strong links between the needs and preferences of domestic firms and the public policies that governments produce. This chapter offers an argument about this link based on an electoral mechanism that (coupled with exogenous economic changes that altered the balance of power between capital and labor in national economies) gives strong incentives for governments to attend to the production strategies of domestic firms. An implication of this argument is that governments in LMEs are constrained to an increasing degree by market and organizational structures. This claim stands in contrast to arguments centering on the importance of partisanship in explaining differences in national policy. The argument acquires support from the compelling case of New Zealand in the 1980s, which, under a *social democratic* government, out-Thatchered the Conservatives with an array of radical deregulatory measures in economic and social policy. Of course, naive functionalism should always be treated with deep skepticism, but an account that stresses the effects of functional imperatives emanating from the economy *combined* with political mechanisms that distribute incentives to respond to these imperatives in different ways may be a defensible and fruitful means of linking politics and economics.

14

MOVEMENTS OF THE LEFT, MOVEMENTS OF THE RIGHT: PUTTING THE MOBILIZATION OF TWO NEW TYPES OF SOCIAL MOVEMENTS INTO POLITICAL CONTEXT

Hanspeter Kriesi

The upheaval of the late 1960s constitutes the background for the mobilization of what came to be the most important social movements in western Europe during the 1970s and 1980s: the so-called new social movements.[1] This cluster of social movements includes the ecology movement (with its antinuclear branch), the peace movement, the solidarity movement (solidarity with the Third World), the women's movement, the squatters' (or urban autonomous) movement, as well as various other movements mobilizing for the rights of disadvantaged minorities (such as the gay movement). On the one hand, these movements go back to the new left, the new generation of radicals who were the protagonists of the anti-authoritarian revolt of the late 1960s. On the other hand, they are an offspring of the citizens' action committees that had started to articulate

---

[1] Although these movements no longer are all that new, I shall stick to this label to characterize them because it has become so widespread and generally accepted.

more specific grievances of local or regional populations in the early 1970s. These citizens' action committees were much more pragmatic and at the same time much broader in scope than the new left proper. Thanks to their dual political roots, the new social movements have managed to achieve what the new left has never been able to do on its own – the political mobilization of masses of citizens on behalf of their emancipatory goals.

The new social movements have dominated the social movement sector in many western European countries since the end of the "golden age." More recently, another type of movement has risen that is associated not with the left but with the radical right. The movements of the radical right have mainly taken the form of new radical right-wing parties, but they also include older parties with a fascist heritage, new right intellectual circles and publishing houses, extraparliamentary organizations, and violent youth subcultures (such as the skinheads).[2] These new movements of the right have not managed to push the new social movements off the scene, but they constitute a serious challenge to everything the social movements have stood and continue to stand for.

In this chapter, I analyze the two types of movements, the new social movements of the left and the new movements of the radical right. In a first step, I discuss their structural and cultural origins. Social movements are ultimately based on social and cultural cleavages. In other words, they have their origin in broad societal transformations that oppose social groups for structural and cultural reasons. These societal transformations determine structural and cultural potentials for mobilization by social movements. However, as has been pointed out by Bartolini and Mair (1990: 216) and Kitschelt (1994a) for the study of political parties, and as the representatives of the "political process approach" (McAdam 1982) have brought to bear against more classical approaches in the field of social movement studies, "structure" and "culture" do not impinge directly on politics. Social and cultural dividing lines – societal cleavages – only result in political cleavages, if they are politicized. In a second step, I therefore discuss how some aspects of the national political context of western Eu-

[2] Given the heterogeneity of the different phenomena of right radicalism, Koopmans and Rucht (1996) do not consider them as being part of one and the same movement. In the case of Germany, which they have studied in detail, they identify the extraparliamentary neonazi organizations and the subculture of the skinheads partially linked to them as a social movement within the radical right spectrum. However, I do not think it is useful to restrict the concept of the movement in this way, even if the links between the different currents of right-wing radicalism are often only tenuous. The different currents articulate common ideas and, as Koopmans (1996b: 210) has argued elsewhere, violence (as perpetrated by the nonpartisan branch of the movement) and parties can be seen as strategic alternatives for activists and adherents.

ropean countries determine the extent to which the structural and cultural potentials are mobilized by the two types of movements.

THE POTENTIAL FOR TWO NEW TYPES OF SOCIAL MOVEMENTS

TWO NEW STRUCTURAL CONFLICTS

The profound transformation of the society's conflict structure implies a weakening of traditional cleavages that frees people from traditional ties of class, religion, and family. The result has been an unprecedented degree of individualization, but not the complete dissolution of structural and cultural bonds. Contrary to what seems to be assumed by many authors referring to the process of individualization, the weakening of traditional structures is not equivalent to a lack of structure at all. The great structural transformation has brought with it new forms of social control. Individuals now find themselves to be dependent on new kinds of structurally determined circumstances giving rise to conflicts between large groups in society. Some theorists have proposed to analyze these new conflicts in terms of processes of large-scale societal differentiation (Neidhardt and Rucht 1993). I prefer to stay closer to traditional class analysis.

One of the main forces of contemporary societal change is constituted by the new "educational revolution." In the first stage of the modernization process, the educational revolution referred to the spread of basic education. Now it concerns the spread of higher education. The new educational revolution is intimately linked to the transformation of the state (expansion of the welfare state) and the economy (tertiarization and reorganization of the production process). To some extent, the expansion of higher education constitutes a functional prerequisite for the modernization of the state and the economy: it provides the personnel to fill the newly created positions, to implement the new production regimes and to handle the newly developing technology. That is, education has become a crucial factor in the reproduction of the social structure. At the same time, it has also become a crucial factor for the social placement process. In modern societies, the family typically determines the amount of education children receive instead of supplying them with more or fewer financial resources. This "cultural capital" of education increasingly takes over the role of the classic means of production in the social placement process. This implies that the expansion of higher education is also a response to the challenges of powerful social movements of the past – the labor movement and the women's movement in particular – which have demanded an extension of individual rights to education to fulfill the aspirations of millions of people for equality of opportunities. The expansion of higher education is a pervasive phenomenon which can be observed all over the industrialized world. The term "revolution," however, may be somewhat misleading, insofar as this process is in fact a long drawn-out one that has been going on in western Europe since the early 1960s and has not yet come to an end. If this process has started before the end of the golden age, it is reaching beyond it and will develop its most conspicuous consequences only after this period has come to an end.

The expansion of higher education has a "liberalizing" effect. It induces a general shift in political value orientations toward antiauthoritarian and emancipatory claims. But the precise impact of higher education on political preferences is conditioned by the occupational placement process. Individual investment in higher education no longer automatically implies that one's career is made: on average, the return on educational investment decreases. Higher-ranking positions are in short supply, and they constitute "positional goods" in the terminology of Hirsch (1980: 76ff.), which is why there are principal limits to the return on educational investment. That is, if higher education constitutes a major resource for an individual's success in life, it is also likely to give rise to status inconsistencies. Frustrated expectations of the highly educated, in turn, give rise to mobilization potentials, as has already been pointed out by Schumpeter (1976 [1942]: 145ff.) and, more recently, by Alber (1989: 201). They may give rise to intergenerational conflicts and to political preferences favoring redistribution and state intervention.

More specifically still, if educational investment typically gives access to the new middle class, it does not guarantee individual control over one's own work. In the modern organizational society (Perrow 1989), the highly educated typically work in large-scale organizations and the degree to which they are able to control their own work depends on their control of organizational assets. This introduces a basic antagonism within the new middle class between those who control organizational assets and those whose resources are limited to individual skills and expertise not tied to the organization (Kriesi 1987, 1989, 1993). In this conflict, which traverses the new middle class, the professionals whose only resources are individual expertise and skills – the professional "specialists" – are defending themselves against the encroachments on their work autonomy by their colleagues who are primarily involved in the administration of the large private and public organizations – the "managers." To be more precise, we should introduce an additional distinction between different forms of expertise and skills, since some of them are more organization-dependent than others. The skills of administrators and technical specialists – the "technocrats" – tend to be more closely tied to the organization for whom they work than the skills of the "social and cultural specialists," which are cued to servicing the clients of the organizations.[3] As a result, the "social and cultural specialists" are most likely to defend antiauthoritarian and emancipatory political values, whereas the "managers" are most likely to defend the authority of the organization and the technical and economic imperatives of the status quo, with the "technocrats" taking a middle position. Moreover, the "managers" and "technocrats" are expected to be more bourgeois in political-economic terms, while the "social and cultural professionals" have a social-democratic orientation.

In addition to this new cleavage within the new middle class, there is a second cleavage taking shape under the impact of the structural transformations of contemporary society. This second cleavage concerns a deepening conflict between the winners of the modernization process and those who find themselves on the losing side.[4] If education has become a crucial asset in the occupational placement process, the flip side of the coin implies that those who do not obtain more than a minimal amount of education will be excluded from access to the new middle class. The poorly educated or unskilled will end up in poorly paid, often unstable job positions with no or only limited prospects for occupational mobility. If unskilled workers have been among the chief beneficiaries of the golden age, there is now ample evidence that they are becoming the main victims of economic change (Esping-Andersen, this volume). The unskilled are most directly threatened by the immigration of foreign workers from the less developed countries of the south and the east, by the newly industrializing competitors in former Third World countries – that is, the increasing trade of manufactured goods between the North and the South (Wood 1994), and by the retrenchment of the welfare state (Stephens, Huber, and Ray, this volume). Moreover, the unskilled are least equipped to deal with the globalization of the economy and the immigration of foreigners, since they

---

[3] Esping-Andersen (1993: 13) makes a similar distinction between "scientist-professionals" and "managers-administrators." While the latter are "hierarchical creatures," the former usually stand "outside of the lines of command, possess a great deal of autonomy but probably little authority over subordinates, their approach to work is task-oriented and their authority, legitimacy and collective identity are more likely to derive from the scientific standards of their chosen discipline, and not from bureaucratic office." Kitschelt's (1994a: 29) most crucial socioeconomic predictor of communitarian orientations – the distinction between client-interactive occupations and occupations that treat clients as standardized cases or manipulate objects and documents – also tries to operationalize this same distinction.

[4] This idea has already been observed by Todd (1988) for the case of France.

do not have the resources to communicate with foreigners or to understand them in a more general sense. Not having undergone the "liberalizing" effect of education, the minimally educated tend to have a rather parochial and authoritarian political orientation – they tend to be "social conservatives" in the terminology of Lipset and Raab (1978: 428–477). Lacking the resources for occupational success, they at the same time tend to be in favor of redistribution and state intervention – they tend to have a social-democratic orientation in political-economic terms. But, as Kitschelt (1995) points out, their support for the welfare state may be of the "chauvinist" type, combined with a rejection of foreigners who are felt to endanger the preservation of the social safety net for the ethnic citizens of their country.

In addition to the unskilled, the modernization process creates other categories of people ill-equipped to cope with its consequences. Among these categories have traditionally been counted the declining old middle classes – farmers, artisans, and small shopkeepers – but they may include additional groups as well. Thus, people working in declining sectors in general, those living in peripheral or declining regions or in declining neighborhoods of cities in the center often share the lot of the poorly educated. It happens that they find themselves trapped in a situation that does not allow them to adapt to social change. Their resources – professional skills, means of production, housing – are not convertible and prevent them from becoming geographically or occupationally mobile.[5] Finally, to these groups we should add those whose only resources are entitlements to the provisions of the welfare state – the pensioners, the disabled, and the long-term unemployed. Their lot depends on the vicissitudes of the financial situation of the state and on the whims of the political process. For the development of the political preferences of these groups of people, the objective difficulty is probably less decisive than their subjective expectations with respect to the future. Their fears – justified or not – determine their political orientation, which is most likely to be at the same time socially conservative and economically social-democratic.

Thus, the profound transformation of the modernization process creates two types of structural conflicts, which form the basis for political mobilization. First, a structural conflict takes shape between the new middle-class winners of the modernization process, and the heterogeneous class of losers. The basic difference between the two categories lies in the fact that the former have at their disposal sufficient amounts of convertible resources –

---

[5] I deliberately adopt here the terminology used by Kitschelt (1992), which in turn is following the conception of class introduced by Wright (1985).

mainly professional skills and expertise – which allow them to cope with the new situation, while the latter, for some reason or other, do not have such resources. Second, among the new middle-class winners of the process, there are nevertheless some who are winning more than others. This defines the second structural conflict, which is above all a conflict about the control of professional work, about individual autonomy, and, in the final analysis, about different projects of the good life in the modern society.

THEIR ARTICULATION BY TWO NEW TYPES OF SOCIAL MOVEMENTS

These two conflicts form the basis of two new political cleavages, which have given rise to the so-called new social movements, on the one hand, and to the mobilization of the movements of the radical right, on the other hand. The social and cultural professionals who tend to lose out in the conflict about the control of work constitute the core of the structural potential for the new social movements, all of which attack in one way or another the unrestricted reign of technocracy. Eurobarometer data of 1990 (Eurobarometer 34.0), which have been summarized in the first part of Table 14.1, indicate that, in various western European countries, the adherents of Green parties – parties that are typically close to the new social movements – are generally more highly educated than national averages, but do not differ significantly from the average citizen in other respects. This table reports the order of magnitude of the respective differences for six western European countries. Negligible deviations are indicated by a "0," small differences by a single plus or minus, larger ones by double pluses or minuses. More specifically, a detailed analysis of the Dutch situation confirms that it is the social and cultural specialists who are most heavily represented in the avant garde of the various movements belonging to this movement family (Kriesi 1989, 1993).

I would, of course, concede that the structurally determined conflicts of modern society cannot be reduced to this new class conflict about the control of work. This conflict is part of a larger struggle about the blueprint of modern society. As many analysts of new social movements have pointed out (Beck 1983; 1986; Brand 1987; Duyvendak 1992; Giddens 1990, 1991; Kriesi 1987; Offe 1985; Raschke 1985; Schmitt-Beck 1992; Touraine 1980), these movements have been mobilized both by new types of threats to individual autonomy exerted by corporate actors – "the colonization of the life world by systems' imperatives" of Habermas, or the "iron cage" of Weber – and by *new risks* affecting people in more or less the same way irrespective of their social position (e.g., radioactivity or

Table 14.1. *Characteristics of the supporters of green parties and radical right parties in six European countries: Percentage differences/average differences with respect to national/overall means*

Country	Level of education		Occupation		"Losers"		Left-right self-placement	n
	% up to 15 years	% 20 years+	% farmers/artisans	% unskilled	% unemployed	% expecting worse personal situation		
Green parties[a]								
Belgium	– –	+ +	–	–	0	–	–	125–133
Denmark	– –	+ +	+ +	+ +	+	–	– –	9
France	–	+	–	0	0	–	0	116–124
Germany, W	– –	+ +	0	–	0	0	– –	59–74
Germany, E	– –	+ +	–	–	–	0	– –	108
Italy	– –	+ +	–	0	0	0	–	68
Netherlands	– –	+ +	0	–	0	0	– –	62–65
All countries	(–15.7%)	(+11.6%)	(–1.9%)	(–4.6%)	(+0.1%)	(–0.3%)	(–.79)	547–577
Radical right parties[b]								
Belgium	+ +	–	–	+	+	0	0	17
Denmark	+	– –	+	+ +	0	+ +	+ +	50–53
France	0	–	–	–	+	+ +	+	41
Germany, W	+	–	+ +	+ +	+	–	+	10–11
Germany, E	+	–	+ +	+ +	–	– –	+ +	9
Italy, MSI	+	0	+ +	–	–	+	+ +	31–32
Italy, League	–		+ +		0		+	34
Netherlands	+ +	–	+ +	+ +	+ +	+ +	+ +	4
All countries	(+5.4%)	(–1.6%)	(+5.0%)	(+7.9%)	(+2.4%)	(+9.9%)	(+1.73)	162–166

Notes: Percentage differences are indicated as follows: +/– 2.0% (0); +2.1 to +10.0% (+); greater than +10.1% (++); –2.1 to –10.0% (–); greater than –10.1% (– –). For left-right self-placement, differences between averages (on the ten-point scale) are indicated in the same way: +/–0.2 (0); +0.21 to +1.0 (+); greater than +1.0 (++); –0.21 to –1.0 (–); greater than –1.0 (– –).

[a] Green parties: Ecolo, Agalev (B); De Gronne (DK); écologistes (F); Grüne/Bündnis 90 (D); Federazioni delle liste verdi (I); Groen Links (NL).

[b] Radical right parties: Vlaamse Blok (B); Fremskridtspartiet (DK); Front national (F); Republikaner, NPD (D); MSI, Northern League (I); Centrumdemocraten (NL).

Sources: Data are my own calculations on the basis of *Eurobarometer 34.0: Perceptions of the European Community, and Employment Patterns and Child Rearing, October–November 1990*.

AIDS). For the new middle class, these new threats and risks have replaced the dependence on traditional bonds and the deprivation stemming from inequality of the resource distribution. The social and cultural service professionals are generally most sensitive to these kinds of risks, but their fears and motives are shared by large numbers of educated people who have, in part at least, been sensitized by the past mobilization processes of the very same new social movements for which they form a potential at present. The appeal of the new social movements has gone far beyond the narrow circle of the social and cultural professionals, which is indicative of the broad value change that has taken place in western Europe since the late 1960s. They have attained very high levels of mobilization throughout the past two decades. Moreover, they can count on the continued existence of enormous potentials for future political campaigns (Fuchs and Rucht 1992; Kriesi 1993; Watts 1987). To cite just one example: the level of mobilization attained by the Dutch ecology movement is higher than that of all Dutch political parties taken together or of all Dutch unions (Kriesi 1993: 258). It is quite likely that not only the goals of these movements, but also their *mode* of doing politics – a participatory, issue-specific mode, oriented toward public opinion – has struck a responsive cord within the populations of the western European countries.

By contrast, I would like to suggest that the dissatisfaction of the losers of the modernization process is being mobilized by the movements of the radical right. If these movements constitute quite a heterogeneous lot, their different elements share some common orientations, which allow us to put them into the same general category. These orientations are most conspicuous in the programs of the parties of the radical right. Their main characteristic is their xenophobia or even racism, expressed in their opposition for either racist or economic reasons to the presence of immigrants in western Europe (Elbers and Fennema 1993; Hainsworth 1992b; Mitra 1988): "our own people first" is typically the slogan at the core of their programs. Even a party such as the Danish "Progress Party," which was originally, above all, mobilizing against the Danish welfare state, introduced an antiimmigration stand in its program in 1989. It is important to note that, in the conception of these parties, the immigration issue is closely linked to the central elements of the radical right's value system: nation, national identity, and ethnocentrism.

Second, these parties also have an antisystem's profile (Ignazi 1992; Elbers and Fennema 1993). Theirs is a populist appeal to the widespread resentment against the established parties and the dominant political elites. As is observed by Betz (1993: 413), they are populist in their instrumentalization of sentiments of anxiety and disenchantment as well as in their appeal to the common man and his allegedly superior common sense. They build on the widespread dissatisfaction with big business, big unions, and big government, and they connect with the strong belief of their clients in simple and ready-made solutions. All these parties seem to advocate a simple solution to the crisis of the welfare state, the problems of unemployment, housing, and law and order: "keep the foreigners out." As has been observed by Hainsworth (1992b: 10), the combination of xenophobic nationalism and a populist appeal – "national populism" – helps largely to differentiate the radical right from the moderate or traditional right.

Betz (1991, 1993) adds that their ideology also includes neoliberal elements: they are said to advocate individual achievement, a free marketplace, and a drastic reduction of the role of the state. Kitschelt (1995) points out that not all radical right-wing parties share this element, but he insists that the most successful among them – the French National Front and the Scandinavian Progress Parties – add a neoliberal element to their authoritarian, ethnocentric, or racist appeal. According to Kitschelt, this combination constitutes the "winning formula," which allows these parties to forge electoral coalitions including both their declining middle-class clientèle and the losers from the unskilled working class. However, since these elements are not shared by all the parties of this current, I do not consider it as essential for their definition. The reduction of the definitional elements to "national populism" has the additional advantage that it can cover the more violent, nonpartisan currents of the radical right, too.

Empirical evidence to substantiate the hypothesis that the new radical right is above all mobilizing the losers of the modernization process is very difficult to come by. One difficulty is that the category of "modernization losers" is, as we have seen, quite a heterogeneous one that does not correspond to any of the categories in questionnaires purported to measure social status. Another difficulty stems from the fact that the essential driving force of the radical right seems to be the subjective expectation of loss, and not the objective threat to one's own position. As has already been suggested by observers of the rise of German fascism in the early 1930s (Falter, Link, Lohmüller, de Rijke, and Schumann 1983), it was much more the fear of unemployment than the personal experience of being unemployed that incited large numbers of Germans to vote for the fascists. However, this subjective element escapes the social status categories typically used to indicate winners and losers. In addition, survey data of general samples of the population are quite fragile for the radical right, given that most of its supporters seem to refuse systematically to participate in such surveys. Just like the poor or the unemployed, supporters of the radical right are very difficult to tap with general social surveys.

In spite of these difficulties, general surveys allow some corroboration of the existence of a cleavage of the indicated type. The already mentioned Eurobarometer data of 1990 on the social-demographic composition of the adherents of radical right parties give us some indication of the expected pattern (see the lower part of Table 14.1). The relevant indicators are *level of education* (percentage of supporters having left school at fifteen or younger/percentage having left school at twenty or older or being still in school), *occupation* (percentage of supporters who are farmers/artisans/shopkeepers or unskilled workers), *unemployment* (percentage having been unemployed for a longer period during their professional career), *left-right self placement*, and, to capture the subjective element, the percentage of supporters who believe that their *personal situation* will get worse in the year to come. For each criterion, the composition of the supporters of the radical right is compared with that of the population as a whole. These figures give us a sense of the distinctiveness of the potential of the movements of the New Right. The differences generally point in the expected direction. In general, supporters of the radical right are somewhat less educated than the population as a whole, come more frequently from the declining middle classes or the unskilled working class, are more often unemployed, anticipate more frequently that their personal situation will get worse, and clearly are more to the right than the national averages.

Analogously to what I have observed for the new social movements, the appeal of the movements of the radical right extends far beyond the core of the electorate of the radical right-wing parties. With respect to xenophobic sentiments, Eurobarometer data from 1992 indicate that majorities of the Italian (67.2 percent), Belgian (57.8 percent), German (57.5 percent), French (55.8 percent), British (53.7 percent), and Dutch (50.8 percent) populations believe that there are too many immigrants from states outside the European Community living in their respective countries. These values lie generally higher (for Italy much higher) than the corresponding values for 1988. For 1993, there is little change from 1992 (Baldwin-Edwards and Schain 1994: 6). In line with my general argument, xenophobic sentiments are particularly widespread among the least educated in all the European Community countries, with the exception of Portugal and Greece:[6] those who lose out in the economic competition

---

[6] The relationship between xenophobia (measured as described in note 2) and level of formal education for the different countries varies quite a bit. It is most pronounced in the Netherlands (Gamma = −.44), in Germany (−.37), Italy (−.35), the United King-

underscore ascriptive characteristics in a compensatory fashion (Eckert and Willems 1993: 485).

Following the distinction introduced by Kerbo (1982), we can characterize the new social movements as "movements of affluence," while the movements of the new right are much more "movements of crisis." As I have argued, the new social movements are spawned by a conflict among social groups that have resources at their disposal. They articulate the interests of a particular segment of the new middle class, but their claims go beyond the immediate interests of this group and assume a universalistic character in the name of a better life for humanity as a whole (Kriesi 1987). In the terminology of Tilly (1978), they constitute "proactive" movements that articulate new claims. By contrast, "movements of crisis" mobilize social groups that experience socioeconomic decline or expect to experience such a decline in the future. They articulate particularistic claims in the name of the preservation of traditional privileges or in the defense of threatened life chances. In other words, their claims are typically of a "reactive" kind.

THE NEW SOCIAL MOVEMENTS IN CONTEXT

NATIONAL CLEAVAGE STRUCTURES

If, in the course of the 1970s, the new social movements have become major actors in movement politics, the strength of their mobilization capacity varies significantly from one country to the other as a function of their political context. Given that the new social movements articulate a new societal cleavage, it seems obvious that the continuing strength of traditional cleavages, which is reflected in the national political conflict structure, has an impact on the possibility of the new cleavage to emerge. While the structural underpinnings of the new cleavage are present in all western European countries, the relative strength of the traditional cleavages may be expected to restrict the possibilities of the mobilization based on the new cleavages in different ways. The construction of new identities is only possible when old identities fade and lose their capacity to help people to interpret the world. Distinct existing identities provide, in other words, a shield against the framing attempts of rising collective actors.

---

dom (−.33), and Denmark (−.30); it is still quite substantial in Belgium (−.25), Ireland (−.25), France (−.24), and Spain (−.24), and negligible in Luxemburg (−.17). Figures are my own calculations on the basis of *Eurobarometer* 30 (Fall 1988).

Moreover, the articulation of a new cleavage presupposes the mobilization of resources, which may not be available if political mobilization on the basis of traditional cleavages is absorbing a great deal of the time, energy, and money of the relatively small part of the population that engages in political action. Organizations engaged in traditional political conflicts may even actively prevent potential supporters of new collective actors from contributing to their mobilization. According to this line of reasoning, there exists a zero-sum relationship between the strength of traditional political cleavages and the possibility of the new social movements to articulate the new societal cleavages.

In order to capture the strength of a traditional cleavage, we have suggested distinguishing between its degree of closure and the degree of its pacification (Kriesi and Duyvendak 1995). The _degree of closure_ of a cleavage is determined by the social homogeneity and cultural distinctiveness of the respective social groups involved, as well as by the degree of their internal organization and political encapsulation. The _degree of pacification_ of a cleavage refers to its salience, to the degree to which it dominates the conflicts in the political arena. The two aspects need not coincide. For social groups to become available for the mobilization by new social movements, traditional cleavages need to lack closure and conflictuality. Closure of the traditional cleavage excludes any possibility for newcomers to mobilize the social groups involved. Lack of closure under conditions of high conflictuality constitutes a more ambiguous situation. It gives rise to a great amount of competition not only within the traditional organizational field, but also between traditional organizations and newcomers to the political scene. In this competitive space, the political organizations associated with the traditional cleavage are likely to make every attempt to impose the terms of the traditional conflict on the newly emerging conflicts in movement politics – that is, they shall try to absorb new issues and new collective actors into the traditional conflict and to thereby reduce the "space" for newcomers to the political scene. In the case of the new social movements, this competition is likely to be one-sided, since the new social movements hardly appeal to more traditional social groups at all.

In a comparative study of the mobilization of new social movements in four western European countries – France, Germany, the Netherlands, and Switzerland – we have tested this zero-sum hypothesis for the period 1975–1989 (Kriesi, Koopmans, Duyvendak, and Giugni 1995). Reviewing the structure of the four traditional political conflicts underscored by Lipset and Rokkan (1967b) – center-periphery, religious, rural-urban, and class conflicts – in the four countries, we have found that the French situation differs considerably from that of the other three countries of our study

(Kriesi and Duyvendak 1995). While the traditional cleavages lacked closure and were more or less pacified in the latter countries, they continued to be highly conflictual in France, even if they lacked closure in this country, too. With respect to the class cleavage in particular, the French situation contrasted sharply with that which obtained elsewhere. In France, the continuing competition between the two branches of the split old left – the Communists and the Socialists – has kept this cleavage alive and highly conflictual (Duyvendak 1992). We, therefore, expected the "space" for the mobilization of the new social movements, which are, as we have seen, also situated on the left, to have been particularly restricted in France, and, as a result of this lack of "space," we expected the mobilization of the new social movements in France to have been much weaker than in the other three countries.

This expectation is largely borne out by our data on protest events for the period in question. As Table 14.2 indicates, in Germany, the Netherlands, and Switzerland, the bulk of the political mobilization in the form of protest events was carried out by the new social movements. In contrast, by whatever kind of indicator we apply, the new social movements have been much weaker in France during the same period. In France, not only the class cleavage (labor movement), but also the center-periphery cleavage (regional movements), the religious cleavage (movements mobilizing around educational issues), and the rural-urban cleavage (farmers' movements) have given rise to a substantial amount of mobilization, which has served to constrain the mobilization capacity of the new social movements. The class cleavage in France alone accounts for no less than two-thirds of the number of people protesting. In fact, strikes have mobilized comparatively more people in France (participants per million inhabitants) than all the new social movements taken together in each one of the other three countries. These results confirm the notion that there exists a zero-sum relationship between the mobilization capacity of traditional cleavages and the corresponding capacity of the new social movements.

THEIR RELATIONSHIP WITH THE LEFT

The relationship between the new social movements and the left is, however, more complex than the argument has suggested so far. The proximity of the new social movements to the left has ambivalent consequences for both the new social movements and for the left. It implies that the two are not only competitors for popular support but also possible allies. Alliances between the two are, indeed, omnipresent. However, the terms of these alliances depend very much on two sets of conditions: the configuration of

Table 14.2. *Summary of the relative strength of the new social movements in four countries (percentages)*

	France	Germany	Netherlands	Switzerland
Relative number of unconventional events	36.1	73.2	65.4	61.0
Relative number of people mobilized (mobilization capacity)	24.2	79.6	72.0	64.7
Relative size of mobilization capacity (also includes strikes)	10.7	67.7	64.7	63.9
Relative size of mobilization capacity (also includes strikes and petitions/festivals)	17.3	69.9	69.1	58.8

Source: Kriesi and Duyvendak (1995).

power and the strategies of the left, and the presence or absence of the left in government.

Where the old, established left is split between Communists and Socialists as it is in France, support for the new social movements has been forthcoming only to the extent that their concerns could be reformulated in terms of the classic struggle of the labor movement. In France, the old left has been very successful in co-opting the new social movements – with fatal consequences for their further independent development, as we shall see in a moment. By contrast, a unified and pacified old left, as we find it in the other three countries, has been much more likely to support the new social movements on their own terms. In these countries, the social-democratic old left was mainly challenged – on its left – by the New Left, which was pressuring it into supporting the goals of these movements. As a result, the new and the old left *jointly* contributed to some of the new social movements' large-scale campaigns. In turn, the mobilization of the new social movements contributed to transforming the configuration of the left in these countries. Thus, the massive mobilization of the German peace movement was not only a crucial factor for the electoral breakthrough of the German Greens but also for strengthening the new left within the Social Democratic Party (SPD). In other words, in countries with a pacified old left, not only are the new social movements transformed if they conclude alliances with the left, but the left as well may be strongly affected by these alliances. In these countries, the reinforcement of the new left may well be one of the main unintended consequences these movements have had for "normal" politics.

The second aspect to be taken into consideration with respect to the relationship between the left and the new social movements is of a more short-term nature. It refers to whether the established old left is in government or not. When it is in the opposition, the old left profits from the challenges new social movements direct at the government. This is especially true of moderate challenges that are considered to be legitimate by a large part of the electorate. Moreover, since the supporters of new social movements also form a constituency of the left, the established old left will appeal to them in the framework of a general strategy designed to build as broad an electoral coalition as possible. Being in the opposition, it will, therefore, tend to facilitate the mobilization of new social movements. By contrast, if it is in government, the old left not only faces electoral constraints, but also has to face the constraints of established policies and of pressures from dominant societal forces (industry, finance, technocracy). Given these constraints, it will be much more reluctant to support the mobilization of any movement.

These considerations imply decisive changes in the political opportunities of new social movements, both when the left becomes part of the government and when it resigns from government. When the left takes power, the necessity for mobilization decreases for new social movements, because of anticipated chances of reform in their favor. At the same time, their mobilization is no longer facilitated by their most powerful ally. The net result predicted is a clear-cut decrease in the mobilization of new social movements, but not necessarily for other movements that are not dependent on the support of the left or that are not addressing demands directly to the government. Conversely, when the left resigns from government, the necessity for mobilization increases for new social movements, because the chances of reform in their favor become much more limited, while the threat that the government will implement policies which run counter to the concerns of new social movements assumes much more important proportions. Moreover, their mobilization is now likely to be facilitated by their most powerful ally. The net result to be expected in this case is a clear-cut increase in the mobilization of new social movements, but not necessarily of other movements that are not dependent on the support of the left or that are not addressing demands directly to the government.

In our study of the development of the new social movements in the four countries (Kriesi 1995: 73–80), we have been able to show that, given their dependence on the old left, the *French* new social movements collapsed when the old left abandoned them at the moment of its accession to power in 1981. By contrast, the *German* new social movements profited considerably when the left-liberal coalition lost power in 1982. In line with the expectations, other social movements were hardly affected by these changes of power. Turning to the two smaller countries, the case of the Netherlands partly confirms the general hypothesis once again. After the Social-Democrats lost power in 1977, the level of mobilization of new social movements started to increase and reached impressive peaks in the early eighties. The reaction to the change in power has not been as rapid as in France or Germany, but the general pattern conforms to our expectations. After 1985 the Dutch new social movements experienced a relatively strong decline that coincides with changes in the strategy of the Social Democrats. After their close liaison with the peace movement had proved to be a failure, the Dutch Social Democrats almost completely severed their long-term alliance with the new social movements. In 1986, they adopted a new strategy designed to regain acceptance as a coalition partner by the Christian Democrats. This aspect of the Dutch case deviates from the expected pattern and illustrates that there may be conditions under which an oppositional Social Democratic party may refrain from supporting the new social movements. Finally, in a highly decentralized, weak state such as *Switzerland*, the local or regional alliance structures may be more important for the mobilization of new social movements than those of the national political context.

THE MOVEMENTS OF THE RADICAL RIGHT IN CONTEXT

If there is a general structural potential for the new radical right, the level of its mobilization as well as the ways in which it mobilizes vary considerably from one country to the other in western Europe, depending again on specific aspects of the national political context. Before trying to account for country-specific variations, let us have a brief look at the level of mobilization of the radical right in the different countries. As far as unconventional political protest events are concerned, I have systematic information only on the four countries we have studied extensively – France, Germany, the Netherlands, and Switzerland – and, unfortunately only for the period 1975–1989. Compared with the new social movements, the movements of the radical right have been relatively insignificant everywhere throughout the period 1975–1989. The overall share of unconventional protest events accounted for by right-wing extremism during this period attained 3.8 percent in Germany, 3.3 percent in France, 0.7 percent in the Netherlands, and 0.6 percent in Switzerland. However, a substantial increase in the number of right-extremist events took place toward the end of the 1980s.

This increase was most substantial in the two larger countries, while wholly absent in the Netherlands. In the last year of the period studied, in 1989, right-wing extremism accounted for 12.3 percent of the unconventional protest events in France, for 8.3 percent in Germany, 4.2 percent in Switzerland, and none in the Netherlands. Although these data do not document the 1990s, Koopmans (1996b: 194) indicates that racist and extreme-right violence has substantially increased over the period 1988–1993 in five of the eight western European countries he investigated. It turned out to be particularly high in Germany, Switzerland, and Great Britain, relatively high in Sweden, rather low in Norway and the Netherlands, and very low in France and Denmark.

If we consider the vote for the parties of the radical right, it was – with few exceptions – also quite limited until the second half of the 1980s. Table 14.3 presents the shares of the vote obtained by the radical right-wing parties, including those with a fascist heritage, in ten western European countries during the past three decades. Italy is the only country with a stable presence of a radical right-wing party since World War II – the MSI. In all the other countries, the share of the radical right-wing vote has vacillated considerably throughout the postwar period. Looking at the past thirty years, we find some isolated successes of this type of party in the late 1960s, in Germany and the United Kingdom, and in the early 1970s, in Switzerland and Denmark. By contrast, Table 14.3 shows a general increase in the appeal of this type of party since the second half of the 1980s, an increase that closely parallels the one we have just observed for the right extremist mobilization in the form of unconventional protest events. The United Kingdom is the only exception to this general observation. The increase took place first in France, where it also appears to have been stronger than in any other country except Austria and Italy.

electoral system doesn't allow......

NATIONAL CLEAVAGE STRUCTURES

Traditional cleavages constrain the mobilization "space" for collective actors articulating new cleavages most decisively if they retain a high degree of closure. Thus, the relative resistance of the German Catholics against the mobilization of the fascist movement in the Weimar Republic can mainly be attributed to their higher degree of closure, as compared with the German Protestants (see Lepsius 1966). Mayer and Perrineau (1989: 352) illustrate the same point in explaining local differences in the success of the French National Front. Lack of closure and pacification of the traditional cleavages makes the losers of the modernization process generally available for appeals by the new radical right in Germany, Switzerland,

Table 14.3. *Share of the vote obtained in national elections by radical right-wing parties (percentages)*

	Italy	France	Austria	Switzerland	Belgium	Sweden	Denmark	Germany	Netherlands	United Kingdom
1965–70[a]	5.7	—	—	0.5	—	—	—	4.3	—	3.6
1971–75	7.4	—	—	6.6	—	—	14.8	0.6	—	3.2
1976–80	5.3	0.9	—	2.2	1.4	—	13.3	0.3	—	1.4
1981–85	6.8	0.2	—	3.8	2.2	—	6.2	0.2	0.5	1.1
1986–90	5.9	9.8	13.2	6.3	1.9	—	6.7	1.8	0.7	0.0
1991–94	19.1	12.0	22.9	10.4	6.6	6.5	6.4	1.9	2.5	0.7

Notes: Parties: Italy (MSI, Leghe); France (Front national); Austria (FPÖ, since the take-over by Haider in 1986); Switzerland (Nationale Aktion, Republikaner, Schweizer Demokraten, Autopartei, EDU, Lega dei Ticinesi); Belgium (Vlaamse Blok); Sweden (Ny Demokratie); Denmark (Progress Party); Netherlands (Centrumpartij, Centrumdemocraten); Great Britain (National Front).
[a] If there was more than one national election during the period in a given country, the average percentage share obtained by radical right-wing parties is presented.

and the Netherlands. The sharp narrowing of partisan differences in social policy as a result of the constraints faced by both parties of the left and of the right, which has been observed by Stephens, Hube, and Ray (this volume) for the 1980s, may be just one more reason for those losers who had traditionally been encapsulated by parties of the left to become available for the new radical right. In France, where the traditional cleavages lack closure, but are not pacified, the hypothesized result is enhanced competition between traditional organizations and the newcomers on the political scene. In the case of the new social movements, this competition was hypothesized to be one-sided, given their lack of interest for the mobilization concerning traditional issues. With respect to the new movements of the radical right, this presupposition no longer seems plausible, since these movements also tend to appeal to traditional clienteles: they exploit the farmers' plight, they court religious fundamentalists, they represent traditional regional claims against the political center, and their populism also appeals to working-class resentment against the rich and the powerful. In other words, in none of the four countries do we expect a restriction of the mobilization "space" of the new radical right because of the traditional cleavage structure. In the case of the new movements of the radical right, instrumentalization of unpacified traditional issues may even constitute a key to their success. In other words, the open, unpacified character of the traditional cleavages in France may have significantly contributed to the success of the French National Front. However, to what extent the "open space" can be filled in by the mobilization of the new radical right crucially depends on its relation with the established right.

THE RELATIONSHIP WITH THE ESTABLISHED RIGHT

While the new social movements are particularly dependent on the configuration of power and the strategy on the left, the movements of the radical right are particularly dependent on the configuration of power and the strategy of the right. However, the aspects that matter for the mobilization of the radical right differ to some extent from those which were essential for the mobilization of the new social movements. This is mainly a consequence of the fact that no established political actor of the right would openly facilitate the mobilization of the radical right. There has been so far a taboo on the overt facilitation of the mobilization of the radical right. Contrary to the left, which has openly supported the new social movements, the established right has so far consistently avoided facilitating openly the mobilization of the movements of the radical right.

The first aspect of the configuration of power on the right to be taken into consideration concerns the radicality of the position of the established right with respect to the crucial issues of the radical right – immigration and the general insecurity – in particular, and its radicality more generally. As has been observed by Von Beyme (1988: 15), "xenophobia does not push the rigid nationalist potential into extremist parties if Chirac, Thatcher or Kohl offer an outlet for these feelings as part of the programmes of their dominant, moderate conservative parties." Or, as Hainsworth (1992b: 11) points out, strong right-wing leaders such as de Gaulle in the 1960s, Reagan and Thatcher in the 1980s, "have soaked up the potential for radical right success via nationalism, populism, media skills and leadership style."[7] A radical established right can preempt the mobilization of the radical right. Thus, the radicalization of the Conservative Party under Margaret Thatcher since 1978 has decisively contributed to the demise of the British National Front, with a little help from the British electoral system, one might add. Conversely, a moderate position of the political forces of the established rights opens up a niche for the mobilization of the radical right. As the established parties of the right become "catchall" parties, orient themselves toward the center of the political space, and abandon a pronounced ideological position, the radical right has an opportunity to step into the vacant space and to mobilize those who no longer feel represented by the established parties of the right. From this point of view, it is significant that the German Republicans got their chance after the death of Franz-Josef Strauss in 1988.

The second aspect of importance is the strategy adopted by the actors of the established right with respect to the organizations of the radical right. Given that overt facilitation is excluded, there are two remaining strategies: instrumentalization or demarcation. These strategies need not coincide with the varying degrees of radicality of the established right's position with respect to the issues articulated by the radical right. Thus, it is conceivable that the established right makes issue-specific concessions without entering into an explicit dialogue and lets stand a coalition with the radical right. Such a combination leaves in fact very little action space to the radical right. By contrast, if the established right tries to instrumentalize the radical right, my contention is that it is bound to strengthen the radical right's mobilizing capacity: by trying to instrumentalize the extremist groups, the established right not only gives weight to its cause, but at the same time *legitimates* its leaders, organizations, and political approach and thereby indirectly reinforces its mobilizing capacity. The

---

[7] Similarly also Höhne (1990: 89).

coming to power of Hitler is probably the most significant case of an instrumentalization strategy of the established right that failed to obtain its objectives. Another case in point is the rise of the National Front in France. As has been pointed out by Mayer and Perrineau (1989: 345) and Schain (1987: 239–249), the National Front has profited from direct collaboration with the political forces of the established right in the very significant local elections in Dreux (1983), but also in certain regions in 1986, and in the Bouches-du-Rhône in 1988.

Faithful to the predominant French tendency to instrumentalize the mobilizing capacity of new collective actors in order to beat the longtime enemy in the partisan arena, the established French right has reacted to its new competitor in the same way as the established French left – with much less success, however. While the French left succeeded in absorbing and decisively weakening the thrust of the new social movements, the French right in fact invited an actor into the political game who was up to that point considered "hors jeu," as Ignazi (1989: 69) has put it. But, contrary to what Ignazi implies, it is not so much the radicalization of the established right after its defeat by the left in 1981, which caused the integration of the radical right into French politics, but its attempt to instrumentalize the radical right instead of demarcating itself quite clearly from its leaders and organizations. Later on, when the major French leaders fell back on the demarcation strategy and tried to erect a "cordon sanitaire" around the National Front, it already proved to be too late: the party had become an established participant in the game.

Next, let us consider the government participation of the established right. Given the taboo on its overt facilitation, the radical right can under no circumstances count on the support of the established right, not even when the latter is in the opposition. But if the established right is in government, the radical right can at least mobilize its populist opposition against the political elite. The opportunity to do so is particularly great, if the major parties of the right enter into a governing coalition with the left. That is, grand conditions between the parties of the moderate left and right are conducive to the mobilization of the radical right. Thus, the early success of the German neofascist NPD in the late 1960s was in large measure a reaction against the grand coalition between the Christian Democratic Union (CDU) and SPD. Once "normal" party politics was restored and the CDU and SPD were openly competing for power once again, the NPD disappeared from the scene (Smith 1982: 116).[8] Similarly, the radical

---

[8] As Kitschelt (1995) points out, the decline of the NPD was also hastened by internal organizational processes: the party underwent progressive right-wing radicalization, which went too far for most of its potential electorate.

right seizes its opportunity in the small western European countries that follow the pattern of Lijphart's (1984) "consensus democracy": the Liberal Party (FPÖ) turns against the "Lager" mentality in Austria; the Vlaamse Blok mobilizes against the complicated "pillarized" structure in Belgium; the various parties and organizations of the Swiss radical right successfully use direct democratic procedures in order to mobilize against the grand coalition that has governed the country since 1959 (Papadopoulos 1991). The Italian case can also be put into this context: the Northern League and the Alianza nazionale (formerly MSI) mobilized above all against the "partitocrazia,"[9] against the political elite in Rome, and for institutional reform. As Kitschelt (1995) points out in discussing the Austrian and Italian cases, populist antisystem mobilization of this type is able to broaden the radical right's electoral base and to attract electorates that are not genuinely moved by xenophobia and law-and-order authoritarianism. Thus, for the bulk of the league's electorate, its anticentralist and antipolitical class slogans have probably been more important than its latent xenophobia.

Let me add a final point: given that the mobilization capacity of the extreme right may be considerably enhanced when the established right is in government, preemption of the radical right may be a particularly effective counterstrategy for the established right. Being in government, the established right is able to pass tough legislation which not only shows that it has understood the grievances of the potential of the radical right, but also that it is capable of doing something about it. While this type of preemption by a governing established right prevents the radical right from mobilizing successfully, it implies, however, at the same time that the radical right obtains a considerable measure of substantive success. In other words, the radical right has a blackmailing potential, which may prove to be most successful when it mobilizes least. The detailed analysis by Koopmans (1996a) of the development of extreme right violence in Germany between 1990 and 1994 illustrates the effectiveness of government concessions to the radical right, although in this case, these concessions only intervened after a series of impressive waves of radical right violence against asylum seekers. His analysis shows that the inconclusiveness of the political debate on the problem of asylum seekers was at the origin of the wave of violence in the first place, which suggests that it could have been prevented had the tough decisions been taken earlier.

---

[9] A term used "to indicate the fusion of state, party, and economic elites in political-economic networks characterized by patronage, clientelism, and corruption" (Kitschelt 1995).

CONCLUSION

The new social movements have not brought about a fundamental change of the political and economic conditions in western Europe, but they have contributed to change on two levels – normal politics and the transformation of society – in, at first sight, less conspicuous ways. With respect to normal politics, they have put new issues on the political agenda. They have provided the recruiting ground for a new political elite, in particular for a new elite on the left. They have contributed to the transformation of the configuration of power and of established alliances in the party systems and in the systems of interest groups, above all again on the left. However, they have contributed especially to the shaping of participative, knowledgeable citizens. Just recall the early 1960s, the period before the first mobilization of the new left set in. At that time, Habermas (1961: 24) had noted the paradox that an intrinsically politically managed society was at the same time progressively depoliticized. Habermas complained that, in a society where the state increasingly intervened, citizens increasingly retired into private life, since there were not enough opportunities for them to intervene in politics. Later on, Habermas (1973) spoke about the emergence of a "privatized citizenship" (staatsbürgerlicher Privatismus) which corresponds to the emergence of increasingly invisible "bureaucratic politics" colonizing the parliamentary arena as well as the public space. While these tendencies are no doubt characteristic of the transformation of democracy in the West, the new social movements have come to provide a countervailing force to these tendencies by mobilizing increasingly educated and politically sophisticated citizens.

The great appeal of the new type of movement politics in western Europe indicates that it is here to stay. As a result of twenty years of mobilization by the new left and the new social movements, a third arena – an arena of movement politics – has come to be established alongside the traditional arenas of party and interest group politics. Movement politics have become an accepted way of doing politics and it provides an additional channel of political articulation linking the citizenry and the state – a channel that forms a complement rather than a substitute for the conventional politics in the arenas of party and interest group politics (Roth 1991). The collective actors of the new social movements have, in part at least, left the arena of movement politics in order to participate in the arena of party politics – as the Green parties have done, or in that of interest group politics – as has been the case of many organizations of the ecology movement. They have, in other words, to some extent become institutionalized. But this does not mean that they have abandoned movement politics altogether. Just as the organizations of the labor movement have continued to mobilize outside of the institutionalized channels of political articulation, those of the new social movements can be expected to continue to mobilize in the arena of movement politics, too.

If the impact on politics of the new social movements has been profound, we should not underestimate "the great significance of the social and cultural dimensions of contemporary collective action" (Melucci 1989). The new social movements have mobilized to regain control of the individuals' own actions in all walks of life. They have tried to reclaim the individuals' "right to define themselves against the criteria of identification determined by an anonymous power and systems of regulation that penetrate the area of 'internal nature' " (Melucci 1989: 61). The women's movement may have contributed more than any other movement to social and cultural change in the West by redefining the gender relations in everyday life, even if its mobilization capacity as measured by our protest events has been comparatively marginal.

As far as the movements of the radical right are concerned, I am on much less secure ground. These movements have proved to have an increased mobilizing capacity in most if not all the western European countries since the late 1980s. They have obtained some remarkable political successes thanks to the blackmailing potential they possess with regard to the established political forces on the right and on the left. The vicissitudes of their mobilizing capacity indicate that their continued existence very much depends on the appropriate policy responses of the established political elites – especially on those from the established right. However, we cannot conclude that we have above all to do with a conjunctural phenomenon. The continued success of the French National Front is proving the contrary. More generally, we should not overlook the root cause of the movements of the radical right, which is related to the fact that the present transformation of Western societies creates a significant number of losers who are faced with ever stiffer competition from immigrants and, for that matter, from the economies of the Third World countries. The discontent of the losers has been focused on the immigrants so far – as a result of the political discourse of the radical right. Its focus could change. Its intensity is bound to grow, if no new social contract is found that allows every citizen of the western European democracies to retain his or her civil, political, and social rights.

I have stressed the crucial relevance of the national political context for the mobilization of social movements in western Europe. While acknowledging the growing importance of economic internationalization and of supranational political institutions, I think we cannot escape the fact that nation-states continue to be the main actors in international relations, and that the national political context continues to constitute a crucial filter that conditions the impact of international change on domestic politics. Therefore, I believe that for some time to come most of the mobilization of social movements will continue to be "embedded" in the national political opportunity structure. National political institutions and national political coalitions will continue to shape in characteristically different ways the issues on which people mobilize, the ways in which they organize and act, and the outcomes their mobilizations are likely to have (Della Porta, Kriesi, and Rucht 1998).

PART IV

CONCLUSION

15

CONVERGENCE AND DIVERGENCE IN ADVANCED CAPITALIST DEMOCRACIES

Herbert Kitschelt, Peter Lange, Gary Marks, and John D. Stephens

Generic concepts such as market economy, capitalism, or democracy conceal as much as they reveal about the ways scarce resources and life chances are allocated in advanced industrial societies. One message the contributions to this volume bring across loud and clear is the need to pay attention to variation in institutional patterns of political and economic governance across wealthy Western countries. This is an insight that goes back at least as far as Shonfield's (1969) seminal study of the interaction between politics and economics in capitalist core countries during the decades of recovery after World War II. It is still true today.

For us, and for the contributors to this volume, however, the task of characterizing contemporary capitalism at the end of the twentieth century is more complicated than merely reaffirming cross-sectional patterns of political economic variation. Our most challenging task today is to determine how these patterns of variation, locked in through intricate pathways of industrialization and democratization, are shaped by growing global interdependence and domestic political and socioeconomic change. To what extent are capitalist countries and regions maintaining their "path-dependent" trajectories? Are there pressures toward greater institutional and policy convergence? And even if there are, are there also continuing and new sources of diversity? We want, in other words, to explore not only *how* the earlier diversity is, and is not, changing but also *causal processes* behind the emerging patterns.

In this conclusion, we draw on the contributions to this volume to offer an answer to these queries that marries continuity and change. There are undoubtedly trends toward convergence in advanced capitalism, but these do not rule out that regions and countries respond to such challenges in partially path-dependent ways. Traditional patterns of divergence are in decline. They are being modified and transformed through processes that reflect the sometimes competitive, sometimes cooperative, search among political actors within constraining institutional contexts for new solutions to old dilemmas: how to balance economic growth and income equality, how to assure political participation and government effectiveness. The result is a mix of convergence and new and old divergence.

All pathways that have been institutionalized in post–World War II capitalism exhibit signs of economic and political "disequilibrium": markets do not clear, economies grow too slowly, political conflicts sharpen and take on new, more volatile dimensions. And since leaving the "golden age" of sustained economic growth in the early 1970s, no pattern of democratic capitalism appears to have found a niche in which it has come to rest around a stable set of democratic class compromises similar to the divergent but relatively stable "postwar settlements" established in the first two postwar decades. As a consequence, our sketch of contemporary capitalist democracies does not outline some definitive picture of equilibrium institutions and policies in different countries. Rather it highlights still unstable, evolving features of partially path-dependent, partially converging trajectories, reflecting domestic institutional and policy responses to the present global political-economic conjuncture.

In order to sharpen our explanatory account, we begin with a simple model of institutional diversity among advanced capitalist democracies in the post–World War II era that draws heavily on the contributions by Soskice (Chapter 4), Golden, Wallerstein, and Lange (Chapter 7) and King and Wood (Chapter 13). Our initial account will be comparative-static and thus highlight persistence of institutional patterns more so than change. We then introduce several alternative conceptions of dynamic change in contemporary capitalism at the highly abstract level of theoretical models, settle in favor of one of the alternatives, and flesh out that model drawing on, but not confining ourselves to, the contributions to this volume.

POSTWAR PATTERNS OF VARIATION AMONG CAPITALIST DEMOCRACIES

In the "varieties of capitalism" literature, a vast range of typologies has been suggested, but we commit ourselves here to an adaptation of David Soskice's distinction between business coordinated market economies (CMEs) and liberal market economies (LMEs). In contrast to the political-economy literature of the previous decade, represented in Goldthorpe (1984), for Soskice it is not the organization of labor, but that of business which determines a country's or region's "type" of capitalism (cf. also Thelen 1994).[1] Critical to the distinction is the extent to which businesses coordinate their interactions primarily with spot-market contracts, or with mechanisms of generalized exchange or resource pooling and hierarchical coordination among firms and business associations. In coordinated market economies, employers are able to produce collective goods, such as basic research and technology, extensive human capital training systems, industrial standards, and even institutions designed to reduce uncertainties and costs of financing and investment. Little of this kind of coordinated behavior happens in LMEs.

Among CMEs, further differentiation is called for. Soskice distinguishes coordination at the industry or subindustry level (industry-coordinated market economies) in much of northwestern Europe from *keiretsu* or *chaebol*-type coordination among groups of companies across industries in Japan and Korea (group-coordinated market economies).[2] For our purposes, we will further subdivide industry-coordinated market economies into those with *national* concertation and those with primarily *sectoral* coordination. At least until the early 1980s, national concertation clearly set apart the Scandinavian countries from the primarily sectoral coordination of the "Rhine" capitalist European continent (e.g., Belgium, Switzerland, Germany). Both groups are set apart from the Anglo-Saxon world of competitive market capitalism where employers are rarely able to produce collective goods through horizontal or vertical coordination.[3]

---

[1] The focus on business rather than labor organizations helps us resolve "anomalies" in the characterization of such cases as Switzerland and Japan that evidently have weak and divided unions, but a great deal of nonmarket coordination with business, just as do some democracies with strong encompassing labor organizations. On the difficulties of labor corporatist characterizations of varieties of capitalism, see Soskice (1990a: 41–42).

[2] In our subsequent discussion, as in most of the essays in this volume, we do not extensively examine the group-coordinated market economies.

[3] As with all typologies, certain countries represent "mixed" cases and among those, France and Italy (between LME and industry-coordinated CME) are the most prominent instances.

The nationally concerted market economies are characterized by peak-level bargaining and coordination between hierarchical organizations of business and labor over issues ranging from wages and public policy to training and workplace organization. Government plays a distinct, if often indirect, role.

In the industry-coordinated market economies, the acquisition of occupational skills is effectively organized in companies or with strong company and union involvement in public schools. Unions combine workers mainly along industrial lines and play an important cooperative role in organizing working conditions within companies and in setting wage levels for the economy as a whole.[4] Both subtypes of the CMEs are to be contrasted with uncoordinated market economies in which training for lower-level workers is not undertaken by private business and is generally ineffective. Private-sector trade unions are viewed as impediments in employer decision making, have little role in coordinating their activities, and have little say in shop floor management.

Together, these divergent arrangements comprise a country's "production regime," a framework of incentives and constraints that is deeply embedded in a set of institutions that are relatively impervious to short-run political manipulation. These institutional frameworks can be seen as national/economy-wide, although with room for some sectoral variation (see Peter Hall's contribution in this volume). We are, furthermore, prepared to argue that the production regimes of different capitalist economies interact with, reinforce, and are reproduced by a variety of further organizational features and corporate actors. Following the lead of many contributors to our volume, we see an elective affinity between the types of production regime, patterns of socioeconomic inequality and protection through welfare states, and the constitution of corporate political actors in parties and interest groups.

ROOTS OF EMBEDDED DIVERSITY

A central theme of this essay is that existing, divergent "production regimes" strongly condition how national political economies are responding to the commonly felt pressures of internationalization and domestic socioeconomic change. In order to develop this argument, we need briefly to

---

[4] In the group-coordinated market economies of Japan and East Asia, initial training is handled within companies and leads to company-specific skills, and unions are organized along company lines.

review further the roots and nature of these embedded policy and institutional configurations.

From early on, liberal market economies were characterized by the absence or early abolition of guild systems (Crouch 1993) and the lack of severe sociocultural cleavages of a religious, linguistic, ethnic, or regional nature that in other systems furnished the communitarian alternatives liberalism and socialism. Historically, LMEs developed strong free-market-oriented liberal parties, and political struggle between politicians and parties in the emergent democracies became focused on distributive issues of property and income that divide occupational groups, sectors, and classes. In such a setting, the welfare state emerged as a compromise between group interests, but on liberal terms. This "residual" welfare state guaranteed citizens a means-tested minimum floor of protection from the risks of market society, but did not provide entitlement to earnings-related financial support of a particular social status and life-style.[5]

"Left" and "right" in LMEs thus became and still are primarily divided over economics. Because citizens' life chances are quite weakly buffered from the contingencies of the capitalist marketplace, the focus of the political agenda and the main lines of competition among parties was and has remained fixed on economic distributive issues, with few opportunities to politicize other institutional and cultural issues. Furthermore, more than in the other production regimes, values of individualism rather than forms of collectivism pervaded economic and political debate. In this sense, party systems reproduce a political discourse and map alternatives that closely interact with the political economic structure of LMEs and residual welfare states. The archetypical examples of LME-type capitalisms, welfare states, and party systems are Britain and, with some qualifications, the United States.

Australia and New Zealand – the Antipodes – fit less easily among the liberal market economies, although they have become much more like them in the past decade or so. Previously, while the organization of their firms, training systems, and the like resembled the liberal market model, their welfare state and especially their labor market regimes did not. They had highly regulated markets through compulsory arbitration and highly active labor courts, both of which tended to support considerable "decommodification" in the labor market and thus similar levels of social protection but by means different from those in the northern European CMEs.

---

[5] Our general argument about the relationship between production regime and welfare state is informed by Esping-Andersen (1990).

This explains, among other things, the wage dispersion figures for Australia and New Zealand in Table 15.2. This pattern was rooted in their heavy
dependence on, and strong returns from, primary exports and willingness,
in this situation, to protect uncompetitive manufacturing. In more recent
years, in the face of declining primary-sector revenues, both countries have
opted for openness and undertaken a dismantling of their systems of social
protection. This, in turn, has led to a convergence of these countries toward
the LME type (Castles 1985; Castles, Gerritsen, and Vowles 1996).

In contrast to LMEs, nationally coordinated CMEs have hegemonic
workers' parties that emerged against the backdrop of later industrialization. They also have been and remain characterized by stronger nonmarket
coordination, widespread collectivist and egalitarian principles, vertical integration in industry, and party competition in which a relatively unified
left competes with a fragmented field of nonsocialist parties originally
divided by the agrarian question. In this context, socialists could craft
alliances with nonsocialist forces, such as the representatives of agrarian
smallholders, in coalitions that committed themselves to comprehensive,
redistributive welfare states offering high levels of income replacement in
case of job loss and a wide range of direct and universally available public
services. Here, as in LMEs, political competition focused on economic
questions but with a strong commitment to collective solutions. In the
1970s and 1980s, however, the high level of economic security and the
growth of public-sector welfare services have led to an increased emphasis
on political and cultural divisions about gender, modes of political participation and cultural diversity. These divisions generated a left-libertarian
opposition to social democracy, which, however, has done little to undercut
the pivotal, hegemonic role of social democrats in the competitive party
system. The prime cases of this configuration are the Scandinavian countries, above all, Norway and Sweden and, to a lesser extent, Denmark and
Finland.

In sector-coordinated CMEs ("Rhine" capitalism), in contrast, the existence of cultural cleavages and the persistence of guild structures provided a nonsocialist and nonegalitarian but communitarian alternative to
both liberalism and socialism, yielding tripolar party systems with secular
liberals and socialists competing with religious "center" or "people's" parties. In this configuration, religion-based communitarian parties, particularly those associated with Catholicism, eventually succeeded in organizing
a class compromise on their terms by becoming pivotal actors between
market liberal and socialist camps. Rather than devising egalitarian, univ-
ersalist, redistributive, or liberal-residual welfare states, the Christian democrats built status and group-based, segmented, but encompassing welfare

states as complements to a sector-coordinated economy. In the "Rhine" capitalist cases, social democracy was weakened by cross-cutting communitarian cleavages, but nonetheless exercised significant political influence within the system. The weakening of religious cleavages since the 1960s through secularization, however, did not benefit liberal and social democratic parties, but facilitated the rise of new cultural and communitarian conflicts between authoritarian and libertarian politics. Although such divisions flourish in most advanced welfare states, they are particularly encouraged by the political legacies of a communitarian divide between Catholics and liberals.

In a highly schematic way, Table 15.1 summarizes the interlocking of institutions and corporate actors in different modes of capitalism.[6] Beyond these very general qualitative differences between types of capitalism, Table 15.2 offers a variety of indicators illustrating the diverse shapes of welfare states and systems of organizing social inequality associated with each form of capitalism. In addition to the various financial measures of welfare effort (columns 1 through 4), we especially wish to highlight the varying degree to which social policy benefits depend on previous earnings (column 5) ("commodification" stands for high dependence of benefits on earnings) across the three types of capitalism with which we are most concerned and the great variation in income inequality (columns 6 and 9) associated with and, to a large extent, resulting from such patterns of social policy and wage bargaining. Moreover, public employment in social services is high only in the national CMEs (column 7), whereas sectoral CMEs surpass other countries in terms of transfers, most of which are earnings-related (column 3). Each of the groups of countries is also associated with a different party family as dominant governing party. In the nationally coordinated economies it is social democracy (column 10); in sector-coordinated economies, Christian Democracy (column 11); and in liberal market economies, secular centrist and conservative parties not listed in the table.

As Table 15.2 indicates, the sectoral CMEs of continental Europe are closer to the national CMEs on most economic and labor market indicators (wage dispersion, union contract coverage, degree of corporatism) than to the LMEs. They differ, however, in their welfare state patterns. Though both groups have generously financed welfare states, the Christian democratic welfare states are more transfer-intensive while the social democratic welfare states are more service-intensive. The Christian democratic welfare states rank between the social democratic and the liberal groups on redistribution and decommodification. The service intensity as well as the more

---

[6] We include the group-coordinated market economies for further comparison and contrast.

Table 15.1 *Types of capitalism and political organization*

Type of capitalism	Party system formats	Organization of the class compromise
Uncoordinated liberal market capitalism	Bipolar systems, divided by an economic-distributive cleavage	Residual welfare states, many means-tested programs
National coordinated market economies (labor corporatist)	Hegemonic social democratic parties and divided nonsocialist party camp; rise of left-libertarian and right-authoritarian parties	Comprehensive, egalitarian, and redistributive welfare states; high decommodification; direct public services
Sector-coordinated market economies ("Rhine" capitalism)	Tripolar party systems: liberal, Catholic, socialist parties; emergence of strong left-libertarian and right-authoritarian parties	Employment and income-related transfer entitlements, medium decommodification, few public services
Group-coordinated Pacific basin market economies	Hegemonic "bourgeois" parties; nonideological, clientelist party competition	Residual and paternalist welfare states

generous parental leave policy of the social democratic welfare state is related to the much higher level of women's labor force participation and much higher levels of public employment in Scandinavia as compared with levels on the continent. Not only are the public-sector jobs disproportionately filled by women, but some of the social services that they provide, most obviously day care, enable women to enter the labor force. All of these contrasts are related to the political underpinnings of the two welfare state types: social democratic hegemony in Scandinavia and Christian democratic dominance but significant social democratic influence in the sectoral CMEs of the continent (Esping-Andersen 1990; Huber, Ragin, and Stephens 1993; Huber and Stephens 1996a).

The differences in histories, institutional configurations, and policies discussed here are reflected as well in some illustrative data on economic performance. In Table 15.3 we have indicated mean unemployment and growth rates for each of the countries grouped by types for four postwar periods. The first observation about these data is that in the first three periods – through 1989 – the national CMEs did on average better than the sectoral CMEs and both did substantially better on average than the

Table 15.2 *Types of capitalism (circa 1980)*

	1 SS expenditure % GDP	2 Total taxes, % GDP	3 Transfers % GDP	4 Civilian nontransfer expenditure	5 Decommod- ification index	6 Posttax transfer Gini	7 Public HEW employment	8 Female labor force	9 Wage dispersion	10 Left cabinet years	11 CD cabinet years	12 Agrarian cabinet years	13 Union density %	14 Union contract coverage	15 Corporatism
National CMEs, social democratic welfare states															
Sweden	31	56	18	45	39	.19	20	74	2.0	30	0	4	82	83	4
Norway	20	53	14	32	38	.23	15	62	2.1	28	1	1	59	75	4
Denmark	26	52	17	37	38	.24	18	71	2.1	25	0	6	70		3
Finland	17	36	9	28	29	.22	9	70		14	0	14	73	95	3
Mean	23.6	49.4	14.5	35.6	36.2	0.22	15.5	69.3	2.1	24.3	0.3	6.1	71.1	84.3	3.5
Sectoral CMEs, Christian democratic welfare states															
Germany	23	45	17	27	28	.25	4	51	2.7	11	16	0	40	76	3
Austria	21	46	19	28	31	.21	4	49	3.4	20	15	0	66	71	4
Belgium	21	43	21	28	32	.23	6	47	2.3	14	19	0	72	90	3
Netherlands	27	53	26	33	32	.27	4	35	2.2	8	22	0	38	60	4
Switzerland	13	33	13	15	30	.34	5	54		9	10	5	35	43	3
France	25	45	19	23	28	.31	7	54	3.1	3	4	0	28	92	*
Italy	20	33	14	29	24	.31	5	39	2.6	3	30	0	51		2
Mean	21.6	42.4	18.4	26.2	29.3	0.27	5.0	47.0	2.7	9.6	16.4	0.7	47.0	72.0	3.2
LMEs, residual welfare states															
Canada	13	36	10	29	22	.29	4	57	4.0	0	0	0	31	38	1
Ireland	19	39	13	36	23	.34		36		3	0	0	68		3
UK	17	40	12	28	23	.26	8	58	3.1	16	0	0	48	47	2
USA	12	31	11	17	14	.31	5	60	4.8	0	0	0	25	18	1
Australia	11	31	8	23	13	.29	7	53	2.2	7	0	0	51	80	1
New Zealand	16		15		17			45		10	0	0	59	67	1
Mean	14.8	35.3	11.5	26.6	18.8	0.30	6.0	51.5	3.5	6.0	0.0	0.0	47.1	50.0	1.5
Japan	10	28	10	22	27		3	54	2.8	0	0	0	31	21	

Notes: 1: social security expenditure, % GDP; 2: total taxes, % GDP; 3: transfer payments, % GDP; 4: civilian nontransfer expenditure, % GDP; 5: decommodification index (Esping-Andersen 1990); 6: Gini index of post direct tax, post transfer payment income distribution (Mitchell 1991); 7: public health, education, and welfare employment, % working-age population; 8: % of working-age females in the labor force; 9: 90/10 earnings ratio (Moene and Wallerstein 1996); 10: social democratic cabinet (Huber et al. 1993); 11: Christian Democratic cabinet; 12: Agrarian Party cabinet; 13: union membership, % of the labor force; 14: % of the work force covered by union contracts; 15: corporatism scale (Lehmbruch 1984).
[a] Concertation without labor.

Table 15.3. Unemployment and growth

	Unemployment				Growth			
	1960–73	1974–79	1980–89	1990–94	1960–73	1973–79	1979–89	1990–93
National CMEs, social democratic welfare states								
Sweden	1.9	1.9	2.4	5.2	3.4	1.5	1.8	-1.6
Norway	1.0	1.8	2.7	5.6	3.5	4.4	2.3	2.0
Denmark	1.4	6.0	8.1	10.9	3.6	1.6	1.8	1.0
Finland	2.0	4.6	5.1	12.3	4.5	1.8	3.2	-3.6
Mean	1.6	3.6	4.6	8.5	3.8	2.3	2.3	-.6
Sectoral CMEs, Christian democratic welfare states								
Austria	1.7	1.6	3.3	3.9	4.3	3.0	1.9	1.0
Belgium	2.2	5.7	11.3	10.7	4.4	2.1	1.9	1.2
France	2.0	4.6	9.1	10.6	4.3	2.3	1.6	.2
Germany	.8	3.4	6.7	7.8	3.7	2.5	1.7	2.1
Italy	5.3	6.3	9.3	10.6	4.6	3.2	2.4	.7
Netherlands	1.3	5.0	9.7	6.2	3.6	1.9	1.1	1.2
Switzerland	0	.4	.6	2.7	3.0	-.1	1.8	-.8
Mean	1.9	3.9	7.1	7.5	4.0	2.1	1.8	.8
LMEs, residual welfare states								
Canada	5.0	7.2	9.3	10.3	3.6	2.9	1.8	-1.0
Ireland	5.2	7.6	14.3	14.9	3.7	3.3	2.7	4.8
United Kingdom	1.9	4.2	9.5	8.4	2.6	1.5	2.2	-.3
United States	5.0	7.0	7.6	6.6	2.6	1.4	1.5	.8
Australia	2.0	5.1	7.5	9.6	3.2	1.5	1.8	.3
New Zealand	.2	.8	4.4	9.2	2.2	-.2	1.4	.6
Mean	3.2	5.3	8.8	9.8	3.0	1.7	1.9	.9
Japan	1.3	1.8	2.4	2.3	8.3	2.5	3.4	2.2

Notes: Unemployment figures are percentage of the labor force unemployed. Growth figures are percentage annual increase in GDP.
Source: OECD, various publications, 1988–95.

LMEs. Second, there are some noteworthy within-group differences – for instance, Denmark's and to a lesser extent Finland's unemployment performance deteriorates more quickly than that of Sweden and Norway, in some ways "corporatist" Austria resembles Sweden and Norway more than it does the other sectoral CMEs, Switzerland is in some ways entirely distinctive, and, as we might expect, the Antipode countries look somewhat different from the other LMEs. Nonetheless, overall for these three periods, the similarities among the countries within each group and their differences from the countries in the other groups stand out.

In the years of the 1990s for which we have data, however, the clarity of these patterns is obscured. Average performance on both unemployment and growth degenerates across all the groups, but the rise of average unemployment is particularly striking in the national CMEs. The worsening of growth is also noteworthy – with the noticeable exception of Ireland – but here the extent of changes does not appear as systematic within groups. Perhaps most interesting for our current considerations, the differences between the groups in performance narrow. There is a degree of "convergence" in direction and degree of change and in the resulting level of performance regardless of type.

These brief remarks obviously do not exhaust all the interesting observations that could be made about Tables 15.1, 15.2, and 15.3. Moreover, we mention only briefly or ignore certain anomalies, such as Austria's resemblance to national coordinated systems on some of the policy and performance indicators, despite the fact that its Christian Democratic welfare state fits the pattern of the sectorally coordinated economies. France too, though listed in our sectoral CME group, differs from others in this group in the form of economic management in the golden age (far more statist than concerted) and in the weakness of its Christian Democracy (though not in Catholic political influence).[7] Nevertheless, our analysis drives home the point that there were rather robustly patterned differences among advanced capitalist democracies, if we take 1980 as the cut for our cross section, as in Table 15.2, or the years up to 1990, as in Table 15.3.

The question is, however, Did these differences endure? What has the past decade and a half, on which the contributions to this volume focus, taught us about the durability and adaptability of different forms of capitalism in the face of the effects of globalization and domestic socioeconomic change? The data on economic performance for the 1990s in Table 15.3 suggest that there may be significant changes underway. To address these

---

[7] We should also note, though we cannot dwell on, outliers such as Japan, which would merit close attention in a detailed analysis.

issues in a more systematic and comparative manner, we move on to a dynamic analysis of capitalist political economies after the golden age.

DYNAMIC CHANGE: CONVERGENCE, DIVERGENCE, OR RECONFIGURATION OF DIVERGENCE?

Our understanding of institutional change and convergence is generally more intuitive than systematic. We think we know what we mean by convergence but in fact several alternative understandings are possible. Institutions and policies could become more alike, for instance, by becoming more like those already in existence in one country, or they could all change to some new configuration. And when we speak of convergence, do we recognize it by similarities in the direction of movement (shared trends) or by a narrowing of differences, or both? In order to make sense of how the different types of capitalism have been changing since the 1980s, we need first to consider alternative ways of thinking about the pathways and the logic of institutional change.

The most common way to conceive of capitalist development is evolutionary and functional: to presume different regional and national historical starting points and then to argue that they are subject to pressures that reward the most efficient systems and penalize the rest. Such an approach stipulates that the growing relative importance of market exchange in allocation shifts resources to the most efficient patterns of corporate organization and government institutions across regions, countries, and sectors. Less efficient configurations are either adapted or eliminated. Such models of convergence assume an open global competition not only among goods and services but also among capitalist governance structures without protected niches. Under those circumstances, one general type of political-economic organization will prove to be superior and others are condemned to oblivion.

What is "superior" is not, however, agreed upon. In fact, evolutionary convergence models come in market-liberal, mixed, and socialist stripes. Liberals assume that political interference with market allocation is inefficient and countries that interfere the least with competitive markets will prove superior to their competitors. As of late, this view has again gained the upper hand in policy circles and is enshrined in the "Washington consensus" that economic growth requires domestic and international market liberalism.[8] At the other extreme, Marxist authors have assumed that

---

[8] For a critique, see Przeworski (1995).

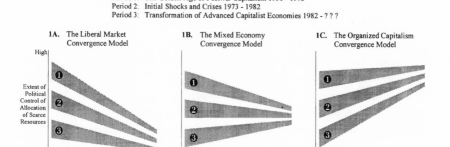

Period 1: The Golden Age of Postwar Capitalism 1950 - 1973
Period 2: Initial Shocks and Crises 1973 - 1982
Period 3: Transformation of Advanced Capitalist Economies 1982 - ? ? ?

1A. The Liberal Market Convergence Model

1B. The Mixed Economy Convergence Model

1C. The Organized Capitalism Convergence Model

Figure 15.1. Simple evolutionary models of capitalism

technical and organizational imperatives of production will make nonmarket coordination through horizontal and vertical organization superior in efficiency to market exchange. The transition to organized capitalism is a step along the pathway to a socialist economy, but imbued with a contradiction between private relations of appropriation and collective relations of production (cf. Offe 1984). Between the liberal and Marxian alternatives, proponents of "mixed" economies in the 1950s and 1960s expected the evolution of a private market economy with state intervention through Keynesian demand-side policy, social policy, and a range of microeconomic supply-side interventions to create collective goods beneficial for economic growth. Sophisticated convergence theorists of this type, such as Shonfield (1969), allow for different, but "functionally equivalent," mechanisms to provide organized coordination in individual countries or regions.[9]

The simple models are schematically illustrated by Figures 15.1A through 1C. The horizontal dimension represents the time line, the vertical dimension the degree to which the allocation of scarce resources is determined "politically," broadly understood, or via the market. The "political" dimension aggregates direct state control of the economy (i.e., the scope of state ownership of productive resources and the extent to which state actors are guided by criteria other than profitability in allocating those resources); indirect state control of the economy (i.e., the extent of state intervention in markets via subsidies, taxes, and regulations); welfare state intervention (i.e., the extent to which the state decommodifies labor and redistributes life chances); and labor market organization (i.e., the scope and intensity

---

[9] Of course, Shonfield does not predict a final convergence of all capitalist democracies on functionally equivalent organizations, although he is convinced that only countries that follow the imperatives of a mixed economy will perform well in terms of growth and full employment.

of collective versus market allocation in determining conditions of work). In each model we depict three "streams" of evolutionary adaptation that begin with different institutions and factor endowments. Type 1, the model of the initially most organized, represents political economies with centralized national coordination (e.g., Scandinavian corporatism); Type 2, the intermediate "social market" economies, that is, the decentralized form of coordinated economies via sectors (e.g., "Rhine" capitalism); and Type 3, the uncoordinated liberal market economies (e.g., Britain). Each model then depicts different anticipated pathways of adaptation over time.

The three models illustrate different types of convergence. We would argue, however, that convergence of modern political economies on a uniquely superior model of markets and collective decision-making institutions is theoretically and empirically implausible for at least five reasons. First, international competition, even in a world with falling costs of transportation and communication, remains imperfect. There are still plenty of niches and local production regimes that are sheltered from international exposure. Second, the effects of economic internationalization on domestic economies will differ depending on the prior mix of economic factors and resultant economies of scale within a particular society. As Oliver Williamson (1985) has argued, even in open competitive markets, different production systems may gravitate toward different organizational "solutions," combining diverse mixes of spot-market transactions and horizontal and vertical organization. Thus regions and entire countries generally specialize with regard to their "portfolios" of production regimes, and it is, therefore, likely that the institutional makeups of such entities will systematically vary across time and space. What is more, in light of existing institutional structures and comparative advantages, the choices of new and the updating of existing production regimes may be endogenous: countries, regions and sectors primarily pick areas of economic activity and will specialize in markets that are compatible with their existing institutional and factor endowments.

Third and relatedly, common international competitive pressures are likely to be perceived differently by actors in different institutional settings. The range of credible responses to a given set of problems will be interpreted in light of past experiences, existing problem-solving techniques, and cognitive focal points (precedents, models provided by neighbors, etc.) that are in part endogenous to the institutions that govern the actors' capacities to process information and problem-solving ideas. In other words, each set of institutions and actors has its own "bounded rationality" by means of which it comes to terms with new challenges and uncertainties. One would, therefore, expect divergence to be sustained, even in the face of similar challenges.

Fourth, the pervasiveness of international economic pressures as a source of convergence is determined by the willingness and the capacity of individual governments and regional regimes to liberalize. The level of economic internationalization is produced collectively by governments and geopolitical regimes having widely divergent preferences and institutional capacities concerning the elimination of tariff and nontariff barriers. Thus, adaptation patterns are a function not only of economic and organizational logics but of explicitly political ones as well.

Fifth, and perhaps most critically, the impact of international competition on domestic policy and institutions is refracted by the domestic status quo – that is, by the relative strength and organizational capacity of producer groups, the configuration of political parties, electoral rules, executive-legislative relations, the capacity of the bureaucracy and the administrative territorial stratification of the state (cf. Garrett and Lange 1996). Rather than treating institutions only as a "dependent variable" forced to change in light of new challenges, we must recognize that they are a critical component of the environment in which actors shape their strategies of adaptation.

These five arguments have two implications. On the one hand, a great deal of comparative research on industrial production regimes and institutions, here represented by Hall and Soskice, has found that different countries and regions do well with different production regimes.[10] There is not likely to be a uniquely satisfactorily efficient adaptation. On the other hand, even if a possible adaptation is more efficient, this does not guarantee that it will be chosen. Institutional structures may promote successful resistance to adaptation to efficient organization because such changes would have negative distributive consequences for actors with strong influence in an existing system of institutions. In other words, even if there are potential Pareto-improving reforms, these may not be undertaken because the transaction costs involved may be greater than the benefits of change for any actor or the dominant set of actors.[11] In sum, for economic, organizational, and political reasons, it is unlikely that convergence will occur around any unique production regime and related configuration of social and political policies and institutions.

In light of these considerations, is it possible to specify, in general

---

[10] For this argument, see especially Michael Porter (1990) and – based on a theoretical synthesis of organizational contingency theory and the new economic institutionalism – Kitschelt (1991a).

[11] The standard scenario for this is when technological innovation (Arthur 1994) or institutional choice (North 1990) is characterized by increasing returns to scale, which result from some combination of large fixed costs, progressive learning effects, reinforcing coordination effects, and adaptive expectations.

terms, the conditions under which we would expect the policies and institutions of the advanced capitalist societies to have grown more similar to each other? Consistent with an institutionalist approach, we would expect convergence to become more probable when, in the face of similar challenges, the relevant policy or institution is less closely tied to deeply embedded other institutions, less determined by deep-seated beliefs and when its specific features are less critical to the returns of the assets of powerful actors. More generally, where institutions are flexible, outcomes will be closer to a simple vector outcome of current power relations. Where institutions are embedded, path dependence is greater: outcomes reflect not only adaptive pressures but also the influence of power relations at the time of institutional formation (cf. Knight 1992).

A simple but elegant example of how preexisting institutional arrangements determine the effect of common exogenous challenges is the influence of the Ghent system of unemployment provision in explaining the growing divergence in levels of unionization as described by Golden, Wallerstein, and Lange in their chapter. As Rothstein (1992) has shown, the Ghent system, under which unions are responsible for the administration of unemployment insurance, creates selective incentives for union membership and helps account for high levels of union density in countries in which it is present (Sweden, Denmark, Finland, and Belgium). As a result, the rising levels of unemployment across most of the advanced industrial democracies of the past two decades have had opposite effects on union membership in countries with the Ghent system and those without. Membership has risen in the Ghent countries, declined in the others, thus increasing existing differences in union density. Different patterns of change in density, in turn, influence union strength and thus the types of adaptations that employers can either impose or bargain for in response to new conditions in the domestic and international marketplaces for their goods.

We can now return to our general models of conceptualizing change in the political economies of advanced capitalist democracies. To do so we need first to recognize that there are at least three distinct historical periods in the post–World War II development of advanced capitalist democracies. Each of these represented a distinct "environment" that posed unique challenges for the choice and adaptation of political and economic institutions. There is considerable agreement on what happened in the first two environments, but disagreement on developments that are unfolding in the current third one. The first was the golden age of reconstruction from the eve of World War II until the collapse of the Bretton Woods currency system in the early 1970s. In this period, nationally different class compromises were crafted and growth models institutionalized along the lines we have sketched in the previous section. (For periodization, see data in the chapter by Stephens, Huber, and Ray. See also Keohane and Milner 1996.)

Second, in the subsequent decade from the economic recession precipitated by the first oil crisis 1973 to the end of the second oil crisis in 1982, and including the shift to international monetary restriction, existing growth regimes were disrupted, but governments generally responded by incremental "muddling through." In practice, this meant that most of the same policy instruments, policies, and institutions that had been enlisted during the golden age to enhance economic performance were employed to fight the new ills of inflation and unemployment. The difference was that often governments attempted to overcome the new challenges by applying even stronger doses of the old cure. By the beginning of the third period in the early 1980s, such trial-and-error incrementalism had run its course. Responding to domestic and/or international pressures, many governments undertook more radical departures from established policies and practices.

The current debate within comparative politics and political economy is less about the extent of such shifts than about their direction and the mechanisms that underpin them: are they governed by a logic of convergence, driven by a growing scope and increasing depth of international competition and the search for the unique, functionally superior set of policies and institutions, or by a logic of "refracted divergence" in which some of the past patterns of diversity disappear, are replaced by new ones, reflecting institutionally mediated responses to the challenges posed by the new environment? With some simplification, these theoretical rivals are depicted in the models of Figure 15.2A and 15.2B. In both, the golden age is characterized by persistent divergence of all three types of capitalism, but also by gradual shifts toward an increasingly "organized capitalism." In other words, divergence prevailed in terms of the *level* of political allocation of scarce resources, convergence in terms of the *trend* toward greater political control over market outcomes (Shonfield 1969). In a similar vein, both models depict increased path-dependent policy experimentation in the second period. Countries with more organized capitalism, such as the national CMEs (Type 1), reinforce their efforts to organize their economies. In contrast, countries with comparatively little organization, the LMEs, begin to withdraw from state organization ("regulation") and attempt to reinsert more competitive market relations.

The disagreement between the two models involves the third period. According to the "neoliberal" model (2A), all types of capitalism are now being subjected to strong forces that yield a reassertion of market relations in areas previously dominated by nonmarket institutions (labor relations,

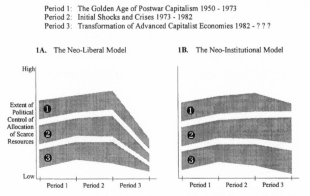

Period 1: The Golden Age of Postwar Capitalism 1950 - 1973
Period 2: Initial Shocks and Crises 1973 - 1982
Period 3: Transformation of Advanced Capitalist Economies 1982 - ? ? ?

1A. The Neo-Liberal Model   1B. The Neo-Institutional Model

Figure 15.2. Neoliberal and neoinstitutionalist models of capitalist change

finance, business associations, training, and research and development), regardless of the type of capitalism at the beginning of the period. This
neoliberal convergence model therefore ignores all or most of the sources
of institutionally rooted variation that may blunt or refract pressures toward evolutionary convergence.

The rival "neoinstitutionalist" model, which we will defend in the
remainder of this conclusion based on evidence provided by the chapters
in this volume, maintains that institutional divergence has a tendency to
persist and to reconstitute itself. We argue that there has been a clear
tendency for *national* CMEs to converge toward the sectoral CMEs, and
that the latter are being reconfigured to meet contemporary political-
economic challenges. This process of change, however, is not leading to
convergence between the coordinated and liberal market economies. The
more organized market economies remain organized, interventionist, regulatory, and socially supportive, and they continue to seek to manage
adaptation through cooperation and concertation among collective organizations and governments. The liberal market economies are becoming even
more liberal, with a weakening of social supports and an increased emphasis on individual merit and markets. Furthermore, both the emerging
CMEs and LMEs continue to be exposed to new challenges and to experiment in the face of policy and institutional failures. They remain in some
flux. This cautions against any claim to being able to identify the nature
of the ultimate "equilibria solutions" to the contemporary problems of
policy and institutional adjustment.

Our schematic diagrams concern development within the political
economy. Developments within politics proper – parties, party systems,

political behavior, social movements, and the like – covered in this volume and related works cannot be so easily depicted.[12] Nonetheless, we do find similarities between the developments in the political economy and the polity more narrowly defined. First, as we will point out, technological change has been one root cause of the long-term secular changes in both arenas. Second, the institutional continuity (e.g., in labor market institutions, in party strengths, etc.) within both spheres is impressive, especially given the magnitude of changes in the environments of these institutions. Third, the political institutions and processes, like those of the political economy, have undergone a refractive process in which similar exogenous developments lead to different outcomes depending on the differing pre-existing institutional political configurations of the countries.

SOURCES OF CONVERGENCE ACROSS DIFFERENT TYPES OF CAPITALISM

In this section and the next, we move from theoretical models of convergence and divergence and the possible mechanisms that might underlie patterns of change to look more closely at the empirical phenomena that characterize recent developments in the advanced industrial democracies. We do so drawing on evidence from the various chapters in this volume as well as other sources. We treat first the international and domestic factors that appear to create similar pressures for change.

While technological determinist thought in sociology, ranging from Marxist to "logic of industrialism" theories, now has few proponents, technology does drive many of the transformations common to the advanced industrial democracies in the past thirty years. New production technologies, and the electronic revolution in data processing and communications underlie broad changes in production systems, such as the shift to "flexible specialization." They are also the source of changes in occupational and social structures, including the decline of the proportion of the labor force engaged in farming and blue-collar manufacturing, the increase in the share of professional and white-collar employment, the decline of semi-

---

[12] Among other things, while the single dependent variable (political control of the economy) and thus the single vertical axis in our graphs was already a simplification in the case of the political economy, it would be impossible to summarize developments in the polity in neat graphic format as there is no plausible candidate for a single dependent variable.

skilled assembly line work, and the increase of differentiated skill diversified quality production work. They also promote rising levels of education
and changing demographic structures.

Beyond the changes induced by technological trends in many areas of
manufacturing and service, the exposure of a growing number of economic
sectors to international competition has also led to common pressures on
advanced capitalist democracies. Declining costs of transportation and
communication, together with the rise of newly industrializing countries
primarily in the Far East, have imposed unprecedented financial pressures
on the production and employment systems of Western advanced capitalist
countries. Although trade openness has been a mark of the post–World
War II period from its inception and, as McKeown points out, merchandise
exports from the advanced industrial countries are now not considerably
higher as a percentage of GDP than they were before World War I, the
rising competitiveness of comparatively low-wage countries in sophisticated goods is a qualitatively new development that has affected Western
countries since the beginning of the 1980s at the latest.

Finally, and probably constituting the greatest international challenge,
the growing internationalization of finance in the 1970s and 1980s has
made private capital far less "national" and far more willing to seek out
the most profitable opportunities wherever they may arise in the international economy. This has led to an overall shift in bargaining power from
labor and political parties to private capital, and within private capital
from sheltered domestic producers to international capital. As a result,
governments have come under increased pressure to institutionalize and
deepen liberal trading regimes at both a global and a regional level (see
Hooghe and Marks, this volume). Domestically, business has been more
willing and better able to challenge existing basic frameworks of industrial
relations and to seek to restructure "class compromises" to its advantage.
Taken individually, the changes in technology, trade, and money are not
entirely new, as Simmons emphasizes, but their pace and the fact that they
are occurring simultaneously is unprecedented.

The three common technological and global economic trends have
provoked changes in the occupational structure and distribution of remu-
neration in advanced industrial democracies. First, in the face of low-wage
competition, production has increasingly shifted to types of goods and
services that depend on highly trained technicians and professionals rather
than unskilled and semiskilled workers. Second, the personal-service sectors
that create and restore human capital – education, retraining, health care,
social counseling – have experienced major growth in demand and employment. Together these changes have led to an increasing centrality of white-

collar, trained, service-sector workers in the economy and polity and to pressures toward increasing income inequality between the skilled and less skilled.

The common technological and international economic changes, and their domestic consequences for the structure of jobs and pay, leave their mark on politics as well, affecting both how popular interests are articulated and the values that are expressed. A better educated population, on average, is better informed about politics and more inclined to discriminate among political representatives based on their issue positions. This, in turn, has complicated party competition and opened the way to a greater role for interest groups, social movements, and forms of direct representation. Traditional hierarchical vehicles of interest intermediation, such as milieu-based mass parties, either decline in favor of parties that mobilize voters around more specific issue packages or must change their strategic appeals and the nature of their linkages to the citizenship. At the same time, interest groups and social movements that seek their competitive advantage by promoting single issues or a narrow range of concerns become more attractive than parties that make encompassing claims.

These developments are reinforced by a differentiation of citizens' preferences. High education and growing employment in personal-sector symbol and client-processing jobs have increased the demand for libertarian, participatory institutions and cultural policies among those benefiting from the economic changes under way, but have also contributed to a backlash of authoritarian, xenophobic, and racist currents among those who are the relative losers in the restructuring of the labor force. Esping-Andersen, Kriesi, and Kitschelt throw light on different facets of these developments in their contributions. Moreover, these trends raise questions of gender in economic, social, and cultural policy arenas, although these are often, as Klausen demonstrates, mediated by the existing institutional filters of interest intermediation.

These general tendencies in citizens' political demands and involvements make democratic party politics considerably more open and competitive. The parties most likely to suffer from such developments are the large "milieu parties," whether in social democratic or Christian democratic guise, a development discussed in the contributions by van Kersbergen and Kitschelt. Even though devout Catholic voters and unionized skilled blue-collar workers may be almost as likely to vote for their milieu parties today as they were a generation ago, social change has made such voter groups a much smaller portion of the electorate and thus less critical in the electoral game. Parties cannot afford, therefore, to confine their appeal to such "regulars" with high party identification. Under certain political conditions, milieu parties can fight back by shaping new voter coalitions that include constituencies mobilized by new demands and more willing to shift their electoral support from one party to another. But such strategies involve trade-offs and strategic dilemmas that precipitate substantial changes of party systems. The patterns of party competition and political representation characteristic of the golden age, and even more the under-lying mechanisms which reproduced them, are giving way to a more fluid, less predictable, and possibly more volatile politics of representation.[13]

Altogether, then, there are powerful economic, social, and political pressures for change to which all the advanced capitalist democracies are exposed. Nevertheless, these need not lead to convergence, much less the neoliberal version of convergence theory. The neoliberal theory that com-petitive markets are superior to nonmarket institutions everywhere and under all circumstances and that they can, therefore, be expected to be chosen is, as we have sought to suggest, both simplistic and misleading. First, the supposed superiority of one political economic model ignores the diversity of existing production regimes and the implications of this diver-sity for the efficiency of particular institutional configurations and for the costs and possible benefits of change.

Second, it ignores the *politics* of political economic change. The exist-ing diversity of production regimes implies different distributions of soci-oeconomic and political power among actors with different stakes in current and possible alternative political-economic policy and institutional configurations. It also ignores that governments themselves may have dif-fering links to sectors of the population and different capacities to enact changes that, even if beneficial in the longer term, may be politically costly in the short run. In fact, implications of the recent political changes dis-cussed here are that governments may have shortened time horizons be-cause they need to pay more heed to a volatile, "dealigned," public opinion and that political conflict over changes toward a more "liberal," free-market-oriented political economic policy may become *more*, not less, in-tense because there is increasing separation between the winners and losers of the political economic changes underway. Thus, existing institutional conditions and their interaction with actors' preferences are likely to con-tinue to reproduce divergence in political economic policy and institutions even in response to similar challenges.

---

[13] To date the increasing volatility of voter preferences at the individual level has not been reflected in significantly increased fluctuation in aggregate levels of party support, espe-cially in the Catholic parties, although there have been large changes in some countries (e.g., Italy).

THE CONTINUATION AND TRANSFORMATION OF DIVERGENCE AMONG CAPITALISMS

Both economic and political arguments support the expectation of continued, if altered, divergence in political-economic policies and institutions among the advanced industrial democracies. In this section we demonstrate that this is the case, drawing both on our earlier discussion of the theoretical reasons why divergence might be expected to continue and on the chapters in this volume.

The first, and often neglected, source of divergence is the role of politics in the determination of the rate and extent to which internationalization has been affecting any individual country. As McKeown, Simmons, and Hooghe and Marks all point out, the road to economic internationalization has been paved by government decisions, and while some of these appear to have been inescapable sacrifices of national economic sovereignty, others were made to serve immediate national economic purposes. It is, in other words, misleading to conceptualize international market engagement solely as an external force shaping individual countries, for it is at the same time a construction of domestic political decisions.[14] There appears, however, to be a reinforcing causality here that sustains the illusion of the inevitability of the intensification of international market engagement. Market liberalization increases the political power of mobile, relatively abundant factors of production that press for further liberalization, and it reduces the political power of immobile, relatively scarce factors of production that are opposed to further liberalization.[15]

This logic is seen most transparently in the European Union which, as Hooghe and Marks argue, is both an emergent polity and an international market. Labor, the quintessential immobile factor of production, has little voice and less power at the European level; capital, and particularly the most mobile elements of capital, are there in force. Thus, the causal link between internationalization and liberalization is in part a product of the shift in power relations between labor and capital, and the liberalization process further reinforces that power shift. While this shift is almost certainly going on in all the advanced industrial democracies, it is not neces-

---

[14] It is, in part, because of the political determination of "openness" that the extent of internationalization in goods and capital markets varies considerably across countries and across time.

[15] Note that this is abundance-scarcity relative to other countries with which the country in question is experiencing increasing economic integration. Thus, capital is abundant in Germany relative to Portugal.

sarily doing so at the same rate or to the same extent. Furthermore, the responsiveness of governments to the winners and losers from internationalization is likely to vary over time. There is, therefore, no necessary reason to assume that the current cross-national trend toward greater openness will continue or be the same across all countries (Rodrik 1996).

If the rate and even direction of internationalization is subject to diverse pressures, there is also no reason to think that traditional mechanisms of domestic market regulation necessarily must give way to "liberal" principles. For much of the postwar period, intervention into markets by the state or unions, as practiced in Scandinavian social democratic production regimes, was consistent with efficient production and world market competitiveness. There was, therefore, no fundamental reason to abandon such institutional arrangements (Moene and Wallerstein, this volume). Likewise, the financial controls that were the prerequisite for the supply-side credit and investment policies of Nordic and Austrian social democracy were very effective in producing growth and employment (Stephens, Huber, and Ray, this volume; also see Huber and Stephens 1988; Mjøset 1986, 1987; Vartiainen 1997a, 1997b).

These experiences suggest that there is no reason to believe that free-market arrangements nowadays are clearly superior, under all domestic production conditions, to more regulated and interventionist production regimes, even though the latter may be undergoing change away from the traditional national CME, Scandinavian model. Instead, the essays in this volume suggest that while the Anglo-American LMEs may be *a* model of economic efficiency, they are not *the* model: other models of capitalist self-organization may have equal or higher capacity to produce efficient results, contingent upon the profile of industries and institutions that characterize the endowment of a region or a country.

Why is this the case? In the first place, the *resource endowments of countries and regions* vary. As a result, efficient institutions differ across sectors, regions, and countries. Whereas some economic branches and sectors are organized better by liberal market institutions, others benefit from non-market horizontal and vertical coordination. As a further consequence, different endowments may lead to variance in the pressure the joint forces of technological change, internationalization, and different patterns of citizens' political mobilization and orientation impose on strategies of domestic adaptation.[16]

---

[16] Here one could also accommodate Pontusson's (1995) argument that sometimes industrial structure by itself is a trait that accounts for varying political forms of interest organization.

Given contrasting national economic governance structures and sectoral portfolios that shape the extent to which employers invest in labor force training, therefore, one would expect that economic internationalization would have sharply contrasting effects in different types of economies. In his contribution, McKeown argues that increasing economic openness tends to equalize the return to each factor of production irrespective of territorial location, but in doing so will actually increase diversity across countries to the extent that their initial factor endowment varies. Hence, economic internationalization should reinforce, rather than moderate, differences between CMEs in which employers are induced to train their labor force and LMEs in which the labor force is on average relatively less skilled and where the distribution of skills is more bifurcated.[17] An implication of this is that the movement toward economic integration in Europe and in North America may exacerbate rather than moderate wage dispersion across the member states if divergent economic governance structures are sustained.

The preceding arguments suggest that the European CMEs as a group are extremely unlikely to converge on the Anglo-American LME pattern. Indeed, the continental sectoral CMEs have been least affected by the long-term changes and post–Bretton Woods shocks laid out earlier. By contrast, these structural changes have had major effects on Scandinavian national CMEs. As the contributions by Moene and Wallerstein and Stephens, Huber, and Ray argue, these changes, above all the changing occupational structure and the internationalization of financial markets, have been the primary root causes of the movement in these countries toward less centralized bargaining, growing wage differentials, higher equilibrium unemployment, and less decommodifying social policy, which in every case moves the Nordic countries in the direction of the sectoral CMEs.

Persistent variation in advanced capitalism also has to do with the *organization of collective labor market participants*. Golden, Wallerstein, and Lange demonstrate in their contribution the tenacity of established formal institutions of collective bargaining across a wide range of European countries. The evidence about the formal organization of labor unions and collective bargaining disproves the common wisdom that unions and their role in economic and labor market policy making are declining, although the authors cannot rule out that de facto power in wage bargaining and work conditions has declined and/or shifted to more decentralized levels in

---

[17] Note that the other side of McKeown's point, that wage dispersion should increase within countries, holds not only for the LMEs mentioned earlier but also for the Scandinavian countries since 1980, reversing a postwar trend in the latter cases.

many countries. Nevertheless, the authors' figures on union density show persistent variance across countries and no general trend over time. If anything, dispersion has increased, with high-density countries increasing unionization while low-density countries fall further behind.[18] Countries respond with different trajectories of change to apparently similar structural socioeconomic trends and international pressures.

The power of unions still constrains the capacity of business to adopt new production regimes. The presence of strong unions in the export sectors of CME economies and of generous welfare states funded in part by employer contributions makes it difficult to move toward a liberal market economy. The economic and political costs of change in the direction are almost certainly high and the benefits doubtful. As Golden, Wallerstein, and Lange show, in all of these countries coverage of labor contracts is broad, either because union density is very high, as in Scandinavia, or because union contracts are extended to the unorganized due to some combination of strong employer associations, sectoral or wider collective bargaining, or legal arrangements of the labor relations system.[19] In addition, generous welfare states also limit the development of a subpoverty-wage service sector along American lines. The lower levels of wage dispersion within manufacturing in both groups of European CMEs shown in Table 15.2 is almost certainly at least in part a product of the absence of low-wage production. As Moene and Wallerstein point out, employers as well as workers benefit from lower wage dispersion, for it promotes productivity growth.[20]

The *political actors*, particularly the parties and party systems, and the *formal political rules* that are in place in different countries also reinforce the probability of continued divergence. Numerous observers have found that parties maintain their labels – Christian democrats, social democrats, or liberals – but change their programmatic appeals and electoral coalitions that support them (Mair 1993; Kitschelt 1996). For this reason, the extent of social structural change often greatly exceeds the degree of change in party support, as indicated by Esping-Andersen, Kriesi, Kitschelt, and van

[18] See the earlier discussion of the Ghent system.
[19] See Figure 7.1 in Golden, Wallerstein, and Lange. Among the LMEs in the lower-left-hand corner of the graph, contract coverage closely follows the level of unionization, which is not true of European CMEs.
[20] As they also point out, these productivity effects only hold for the earlier type of solidaristic wage bargaining in Scandinavia (i.e., compression of interplant and interindustry wage differentials among workers with equivalent work tasks). The second type (compression of intrafirm wage differentials among workers with tasks requiring different levels of skill and education) has harmful effects. See Hibbs and Locking (1995) for empirical evidence supporting this for the Swedish case.

Kersbergen. Large changes in the class structure, especially at the level of class formation, and declines in class voting are accompanied by relative resilience of the leftist vote. Secularization has been accompanied by modest declines in the Christian democratic vote. Rising education and affluence and the growth of public-sector, symbol-, and client-processing occupations have led to the growth of postmaterialist values in all advanced capitalist societies, but the electoral strength of environmental and new leftist parties is small by comparison and varies greatly across advanced capitalist democracies. Nevertheless, new parties may make inroads, because the existing parties cannot span too diverse a set of constituencies. This process accounts for the rise of both parties of the libertarian left and parties of the authoritarian right.

The nationally unique structures of party competition help or hinder the capacity of countries to move toward liberal market economies. Particularly the absence of nonsocialist Catholic-communitarian parties and the clear-cut bipolarization of political competition around two large, relatively coherent liberal-conservative and socialist blocs has facilitated the adoption of radical market-liberal policies. As the examples of Britain, Australia, and New Zealand show, even formally leftist parties may eventually be compelled to embrace much of the market-liberal program in order to remain a viable political competitor, once conservatives set the economic policy agenda in an environment of increasing international competition. In contrast, in countries with Catholic-communitarian "center" parties and/or diverse, fragmented nonsocialist parties, it is much easier for social democrats to continue to craft policy alliances that resist a wholesale adoption of liberal market capitalism.

Going from the level of party system to that of party organization, mass-party organizations and networks of clientelism tend to constrain the strategic flexibility of parties when faced with new challenges. As Kitschelt argues, mass-party organization with an encompassing membership and accountable leaders may have helped social democratic parties in the days of frozen party cleavages and relatively immobile electorates. But in the current more turbulent context of more volatile popular preferences and new challenging parties, mass organizations impede the filtering through of new demands. Moreover, leadership accountability constrains strategic flexibility and makes parties less competitive. Thus, in Britain, a Labour Party executive stacked with leftist members could hold the parliamentary leadership hostage and compel it to pursue electorally losing appeals for close to a decade. The party did finally reform its leadership, program, and organization in the 1990s, but it took a string of consecutive electoral defeats to galvanize institutional change.

The policy malleability of competitive democracies is affected not only by parties, generally the key political actors, but also by the formal constitutional rules under which governments operate. Unitary government, the territorial concentration of power at the national level, unicameralism or weak bicameralism,[21] strong parliamentary or presidential leadership, and plurality voting systems increase the ability of the sitting government to press through reforms, either of market-liberalizing or interventionist variety. In contrast, a multiplication of veto points through federalism, strong powers of local government, strong bicameralism, weaker executive leadership, and systems of proportional representation or single-member district majority election (and hence often more fragmented party systems) impede reform (Huber, Ragin, and Stephens 1993; Garrett and Lange 1996).

In their comparison of the United Kingdom and the United States under neoliberal governments, King and Wood show that market reforms had to traverse very different political institutions with sharply contrasting degrees of centralization. The unitary character of the British polity allowed wide latitude for Prime Minister Thatcher to shape local political institutions and shift decision making from the state to the market. In contrast, the dispersion of authority in the United States, among institutions in Washington, D.C., and between Washington and the states, limited the capacity of the Reagan administration to reshape American political economy. The comparison is revealing because, as King and Wood emphasize, other aspects of these societies, including their uncoordinated market economies and the ideological orientation of these governments, were similar.

The interaction of constitutional arrangements with the partisan composition of government in producing or impeding radical market-liberalizing reform can also be seen if one extends the comparison to the Antipodes. The most radical changes, particularly in the area of social legislation, occurred in New Zealand (as in the United Kingdom). These reforms were carried out by conservative governments in political systems, which concentrated power in the government due to the absence of federalism, the limited number of veto points (strong upper house, presidential veto, unitary government, judicial review), and the existence of single-member district plurality systems which greatly overrepresent the largest party in parliamentary elections.

By contrast, in the Australian case (and in New Zealand before 1990),

---

[21] According to Lijphart's (1984) definition, bicameralism is "strong" when both chambers have equal powers and they are elected on the basis of different criteria.

a Labor government carried out extensive labor market deregulation, which, according to many social democratic analysts such as Castles (1996), was an essential adaptation to the new international economic conditions, but which greatly increased wage stratification and the proportion of sub-poverty wages in the country (see Stephens, Huber, and Ray). However, in contrast to the other two countries, the Australian government, in a compact with the unions (the "Accord"), passed compensatory social policy in an attempt to cushion the transformation. A prime example of this is the family allowance for the working poor, which not only is compatible with the development of a low-wage sector of the economy but might even encourage it by in effect subsidizing such jobs. Nonetheless, it does help cushion the impact of the change on the working poor.

In his chapter, Kriesi argues that the repertory of a new social movement reflects the particular structure of political opportunities with which it is confronted. Such opportunities are a function of the institutional structure of the state and the response of established political elites. In exploiting political opportunities, social movements adapt symbiotically with their institutional context. Kriesi observes that the sources of mobilization for movements of the left and right are common across Western societies, yet because political structures and elite responses vary across France, Germany, Switzerland, and the Netherlands, one finds concomitant variations in the strength and activities of new social movements.

Intimately linked to the types of capitalist resource endowment, the configuration of collective actors in the labor markets, and the systems of party competition is an additional force for persistent diversity in advanced capitalist democracies, that of *welfare states and social policy*. Many comparativists have demonstrated how different patterns of welfare states and social policies result from power struggles and political institutions that help or hinder the realization of redistributive economic policy objectives and the protection of the weak from the vagaries of the labor market. As King and Wood and Stephens, Huber, and Ray in this volume show, the process of institutional refraction in response to common technological and international challenges can be observed also with regard to the divergence of social, labor market, and economic policies. Most of the liberal market economies (the United Kingdom, the United States, Canada, Australia, and New Zealand) have deregulated labor markets and rolled back the welfare state (King and Wood; Stephens, Huber, and Ray). As King and Wood argue, this was an intentional attempt to compete internationally on the basis of low wage costs. It is telling in this regard that the areas of social policy that suffered the greatest rollback were precisely those in which motivation to work at low wages was at stake. Thus, replacement rates in unemployment insurance and sickness pay were cut, qualifying conditions were tightened, and, in the case of unemployment insurance and social assistance, work requirements were introduced or tightened. By contrast, pension entitlements and replacement rates suffered little. In all five countries, the "reforms" either created a dualist economy with a low-wage, low-skill, largely nonunionized sector or reinforced the preexisting dualist pattern.

As other studies of welfare state retrenchment have shown (Pierson 1994), producers and consumers of welfare state services become the strongest defenders of the status quo and the most powerful agents of resisting cutbacks, regardless of the configuration of external political actors. Thus, sedimented class relations articulate themselves in welfare states and affect trajectories of social reform. This provides another reason for the continued distinctiveness of Nordic social policy and welfare states that employ a large share of the female labor force in social services. Esping-Andersen (1990; also this volume) and Stephens, Huber, and Ray emphasize the distinctiveness of the tremendous growth of public-health, education, and welfare employment in the social democratic welfare states and its consequences on economic redistribution and political power relations. Both as producers and consumers, women have the greatest stake in such welfare states and have become their prime defenders. Their fear that European integration may lead to welfare state retrenchment is a major reason for Nordic women's hostility to European integration. The increasing recruitment of women into the Nordic welfare states has led to a reversal of their political alignment more broadly. In the early postwar period, Nordic women displayed a greater tendency to vote for the right than men, though not to the degree of women in Catholic Europe. By the mid-1970s, this gender gap had disappeared (Stephens 1976). By the early 1990s, a reverse gender gap has opened in Scandinavia, with women being more likely to vote for the left and to support the welfare state than men (Svalfors 1992; also see Hobson and Lindholm 1997).

A final reason why external technological and international pressures and domestic socioeconomic changes do not directly translate into the convergence of domestic economic and social policies and institutions has to do with the emergence of *regional defensive and offensive alliances* that may intervene and shape the emerging process of global competition. Regional economic and political alliances may intensify internal competitive openness while protecting the region from external forces. The creation of the European Economic Community in 1958 established a set of constitutional arrangements at the supranational level that later channeled innovation in response to the economic problems of the early 1980s and the demise of national Keynesianism. The European Economic Community developed in the 1960s and 1970s as a side show to economic policy making conducted by individual states. But, as Hooghe and Marks note, once the supranational framework of the European Court of Justice, the European Council, and the European Commission were in place, they were deployed in a concerted attempt to eliminate nontariff barriers to upgrade the competitiveness of European economies.

The deepening of the European Union as a market and as a policy suggests that the changes of the past two decades cannot be understood exclusively in terms of individual countries as the critical units of governance moving through time. From our institutional perspective, the emergence of these political institutions, policies, and resources at the level of the European Union should represent further spurs to divergence. They present national actors with additional options in pursuing their goals under the pressures of international and domestic change. Whether and how they will use these can be expected to differ, depending on their interests and the strategic opportunities available within the national political setting. What is certain, however, is that they expand further the repertoire of policy and institutional options available. At the same time, of course, they also assure that an option to seek to close off national markets from at least European competition becomes even less attractive (see France in mid-1980s).

CONCLUDING REMARKS: THE LIMITS OF DIVERGENCE

Figure 15.3 summarizes the variables that promote convergence and sustained and new divergence among advanced capitalist democracies. We wish to close with a few skeptical remarks about the future of each of the three models of capitalism we have dealt with. In doing so, we should recall the difficulties that surround the achievement of stable and efficient new institutions and policies and the probability that none of the models has reached a viable equilibrium. Our claim is not only that there is no unique model toward which all of the capitalist democracies are now converging. It is also that none of the three models has yet stabilized around a set of policies and institutions well adapted to a particular global market niche. We observe, instead, dynamic regional and national political economies, embedded in an imperfect global competitive context, in search of partially path-dependent adaptation, but without yet having developed efficient governance structures or even a clear sense of what these might

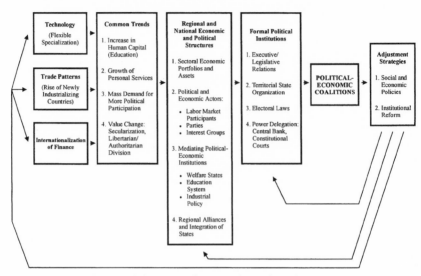

Figure 15.3. A model of change in the capitalist political economy

be. The stable political economic regimes of the golden age have been disrupted but not replaced.

Overall, the national CME type appears to have suffered the sharpest breaks with the past. Wage leveling within industries and firms arguably had reduced the incentives for students and employees to acquire new skills and seek riskier occupational environments to exercise such skills and the ability of employers to attract such skilled and educated labor when it was needed. The internationalization of finance removed policy tools that these countries had used to produce growth and employment. At the same time, the tax burden had reached such a proportion that, once the employment crisis hit, the increased cost of social provision had to be met primarily by entitlement cuts. With the end of intraindustry wage leveling, the decline in centralized wage bargaining, the rise in unemployment, and cuts, however modest, in the welfare state, the national CMEs are now moving toward the sectoral CME countries that share a number of features with national CME countries (business-labor cooperation, comprehensive welfare states, business concertation, strong unions).

However, the existing sectoral CMEs do not represent equilibrium solutions for the new international and technological challenges and are themselves changing. They too suffer from rigidities in the process of industrial and political innovation and reorganization because they rely on intricate processes of representation and negotiation among potentially conflicting groups at the level of firm, sector, region, and national polity.

Moreover, the conventional vehicles of organizing political-economic compromise in CME economies, primarily the Christian democratic parties,
find themselves under severe strains due to conflicting currents pressing for
more market liberalism or a strengthening of cooperative arrangements.
Furthermore, all this is taking place at the same time as secularization and
new libertarian political agendas are eating into one part of the electoral
support of such parties, and new nationalist movements into another part
(as well as into the constituencies of the left). Contingent upon the organization and immersion of such parties into the web of power relations,
however, their fortunes have varied dramatically, as is highlighted by the
Italian Christian Democrats and the Dutch Christian Democrats, on the
losing side, and the German Christian Democrats, on the winning or at
least electorally more stable side.

Do these difficulties of national and sectoral CMEs compel us to conclude that indeed, in the end, liberal market economies, together with
supranational regional institutions enforcing market disciplines such as the
European Union, will represent the model onto which the other regimes
will converge? The uneven economic performance and the deep political
conflicts in LME countries over the past fifteen years furnish few reasons
for earmarking this type of capitalist political economy as the uniquely
superior model. Marginal and shrinking welfare states have not significantly raised economic growth rates beyond the level achieved by sectoral
CMEs. It is also difficult to see how, in the long run, these countries can
follow their current strategy of attempting to compete in the world market
on the basis of wage cost cutting, as other countries – now the East Asian
and, tomorrow, the Southeast Asian countries – will always be able to beat
them at this game. Moreover, the sharp growth of income inequalities and
the virtual disenfranchisement of a growing "underclass" from effective
participation in the capitalist market economy and the democratic polity
impose their own tangible and intangible costs on such systems that render
them a less than attractive growth model.

Thus, we are left with three firm conclusions. First, convergence on
any unique democratic capitalist political economic model is unlikely, both
because there are strong theoretical reasons to doubt such convergence is
even functionally dictated and because path-dependent cognitive, institutional, and political factors militate against it. Second, there are no strong
empirical indications that convergence is occurring. While national and
sectoral coordinated market economies are becoming more alike, and more
like the latter, they are not becoming more like the liberal market economies. In fact, it might well be argued that the differences between these
two types have in several respects grown since the golden age and over the

past fifteen years. Finally, nowhere is the future likely to be the present. None of the democratic capitalist market economies appears to have achieved stability in the face of the disruptive pressures coming from technological change, internationalization, and domestic socioeconomic change. In this sense, we can be certain that the diversity that has characterized the entire history of capitalism will continue. Stable contours of that diversity, however, are not yet in sight.

REFERENCES

Agell, Jonas, and Kjell Erik Lommerud. 1993. "Egalitarianism and Growth." *Scandinavian Journal of Economics* 95: 559–579.

Aghion, P., and J. Tirole. 1994. Formal and Real Authority in Organizations. Nuffield College, Oxford, and IDEI, Toulouse. Mimeographed.

Aglietta, Michel. 1982. *Regulation and Crisis of Capitalism*. New York: Monthly Review Press.

Ahrne, Göran, and Wallance Clement. 1992. "A New Regime? Class Representation within the Swedish State." *Economic and Industrial Democracy* 13 (2): 455–479.

Alber, Jens. 1986. "Germany." In *Growth to Limits*, vol. 4, ed. Peter Flora. Berlin: Walter de Gruyter.

——— 1989. "Modernization, Cleavage Structures, and the Rise of Green Parties and Lists in Europe." In *New Politics in Western Europe*, ed. Ferdinand Müller-Rommel. Boulder, Colo.: Westview Press.

——— 1996. "Toward a Comparison of Recent Welfare State Developments in Germany and the United States." Paper presented to the Health Policy Seminar of the Institution for Policy Studies, Yale University, New Haven, Conn., February 5.

Albert, Michel. 1991. *Capitalisme contre capitalisme*. Paris: Seuil.

Alesina, Alberto, Gerald D. Cohen, and Nouriel Roubini. 1993. "Electoral Business Cycle in Industrial Democracies." *European Journal of Political Economy* 9: 1–23.

Alesina, Alberto, Vittorio Grilli, and Gian Maria Milesi-Ferretti. 1994. "The Political Economy of Capital Controls." In *Capital Mobility: The Impact on Consumption, Investment, and Growth*, ed. Leonardo Leiderman and Assaf Razin. Cambridge: Cambridge University Press.

Alesina, Alberto, and Howard Rosenthal. 1995. *Partisan Politics, Divided Government, and the Economy*. Cambridge: Cambridge University Press.

Alogoskoufis, George, Charles Bean, Giuseppe Bertola, Daniel Cohen, Juan Dolada, and Gilles Saint-Paul. 1995. *Unemployment: Choices for Europe*. Monitoring European Integration 5. London: Centre for Economic Policy Research.

Alt, James E., and Alec Chrystal. 1983. *Political Economics*. Berkeley: University of California Press.

Alt, James E., and Kenneth Shepsle, eds. 1990. *Perspectives on Political Economy.* Berkeley: University of California Press.

Altemeyer, Bob. 1988. *Enemies of Freedom: Understanding Right-Wing Authoritarianism.* San Francisco: Jossey-Bass.

Alvarez, Michael, Geoffrey Garrett, and Peter Lange. 1991. "Government Partisanship, Labor Organization and Macro-Economic Performance." *American Political Science Review* 85 (2): 539–556.

Andersen, Jorgen Goul. 1992. "The Decline of Class Voting Revisited." In *From Voters to Participants*, ed. Peter Gundelach and Karen Siune. Copenhagen: Politica.

Andersen, Jorgen Goul, and Tor Björklund. 1990. "Structural Changes and New Cleavages: The Progress Party in Denmark and Norway." *Acta Sociologica* 33(3): 195–217.

Andersen, Svein S., and Kjelle Eliassen, eds. 1993. *Making Policy in Europe: The Europeification of National Policy-making.* London: Sage Publications.

Anderson, Jeffrey J. 1995. "The State of the (European) Union: From the Single Market to Maastricht, from Singular Events to General Theories." *World Politics* 47: 441–465.

Andersson, Jan Otto, Pekka Kosonen, and Juhana Vartiainen. 1993. *The Finnish Model of Economic and Social Policy: From Emulation to Crash.* Åbo: Nationalekonomiska Institutionen, Åbo Akademi.

Andeweg, Rudolf Bastiaan. 1989. "De burger in de Nederlandse politiek." In *Politiek in Nederland*, ed. Rudolf Bastiaan Andeweg, Andries Hoogerwerf, and Jacobus Johannes Andrianus Thomassen. Alphen aan den Rijn: Samsom.

Andrews, David. 1994. "Capital Mobility and State Autonomy: Toward a Structural Theory of International Monetary Relations." *International Studies Quarterly* 38 (2): 193–218.

Aoki, Masahiko, 1994. "The Japanese Firm as a System of Attributes: A Survey and Research Agenda." In *The Japanese Firm: Sources of Competitive Strength*, ed. Masahiko Aoki and Ronald Dore. Oxford: Clarendon Press.

Armstrong, Philip, et al. 1991. *Capitalism since 1945.* Oxford: Basil Blackwell.

Arthur, Brian. W. 1994. *Increasing Returns and Path Dependence in the Economy.* Ann Arbor: University of Michigan Press.

Ashton, David N., Malcolm J. Maguire, and Johnny Sung. 1991. "Intermediate Level Skills: Lessons from Canada and Hong Kong." In *International Comparisons of Vocational Education and Training for Intermediate Skills*, ed. Paul Ryan. Falmer Press.

Aukrust, Odd. 1977. "Inflation in an Open Economy: A Norwegian Model." In *Worldwide Inflation: Theory and Recent Experience*, ed. Lawrence B. Krause and Walter S. Salant. Washington, D.C.: Brookings Institution.

Baldwin, Richard E. 1990. "Factor market barriers are trade barriers–gains from trade from 1992." *European Economic Review* 34: 831–845.

⸻ 1992. "Measurable Dynamic Gains from Trade." *Journal of Political Economy* 100: 162–174.

Baldwin-Edwards, Martin, and Martin A. Schain. 1994. "The Politics of Immigration: Introduction." *West European Politics* 17: 1–16.

Bank for International Settlements. Various issues. *International Banking and Financial Market Development*. Basle.

Bardi, Luciano. 1994. "Transnational Party Federations, European Parliamentary Party Groups, and the Building of Europarties." In *How Parties Organize: Change and Adaptation in Party Organizations in Western Democracies*, ed. Richard S. Katz and Peter Mair. London: Sage Publications.

Barro, Robert J., and Xavier Sala-i-Martin. 1991. "Convergence across States and Regions." *Brookings Papers on Economic Activity* 1: 107–158.

Bartolini, Stefano, and Peter Mair. 1990. *Identity, Competition, and Electoral Availability: The Stabilisation of European Electorates, 1885–1985*. Cambridge: Cambridge University Press.

Bayoumi, Tamim. 1990. "Saving-investment Correlations." *IMF Staff Papers* 37: 360–387.

Bayoumi, Tamim, and Andrew K. Rose. 1993. "Domestic Saving and Intra-National Capital Flows." *European Economic Review* 37 (2): 1197–1202.

Beck, Ulrich. 1983. "Jenseits von Klasse und Stand?" Special issue of *Soziale Welt*, 35–74.

1986. *Risikogesellschaft: Auf dem Weg in eine andere Moderne*. Frankfurt: Suhrkamp.

Beer, Samuel H. 1965. *Modern British Politics*. London: Faber.

Bekaert, Geert, and Robert J. Hodrick. 1992. "Characterizing Predictable Components in Excess Returns on Equity and Foreign Exchange Markets." *Journal of Finance* 47 (2): 467–509.

Bell, Daniel. 1973. *The Coming of Postindustrial Society: A Venture in Social Forecasting*. New York: Basic Books.

Ben-David, Dan. 1991. "Equalizing Exchange: A Study of the Effects of Trade Liberalization." National Bureau of Economic Research Working Paper no. 3761. Cambridge, Mass.

Bentolila, Samuel, and Juan Dolado. 1994. "Spanish Labor Markets." *Economic Policy* 10: 55–99.

Berger, Peter L. 1990. *The Sacred Canopy: Elements of a Sociological Theory of Religion*. New York: Doubleday.

Berger, Peter, Peter Steinmuller, and Peter Sopp. 1993. "Differentiation of Life Courses? Patterns of Labour Market Sequences in West Germany." *European Sociological Review* 1: 43–64.

Berger, Suzanne, 1981. "Lame Ducks and National Champions: Industrial Policy in the Fifth Republic." In *The Fifth Republic at Twenty*, ed. Stanley Hoffmann and William Andrews. Brockport, N.Y.: SUNY Press.

ed. 1982. *Organizing Interests in Western Europe*. Cambridge: Cambridge University Press.

Berger, Suzanne, and Ronald Dore, eds. 1996. *National Diversity and Global Capitalism*. Ithaca, N.Y.: Cornell University Press.

Betz, Hans-Georg. 1991. "Radikal rechtspopulistische Parteien in Westeuropa." *Aus Politik und Zeitgeschichte* B44/91 (25): 3–14.

1993. "The New Politics of Resentment: Radical Right-Wing Populist Parties in Western Europe." *Comparative Politics* 25: 413–427.

Bhagwati, Jagdish. 1995. "Trade and Wages: Choosing among Alternative Explanations." *Economic Policy Review* 1: 42–47.

Bjorgum, Jorunn. 1985. "LO og NAF 1899–1940." *Tidsskrift for Arbeiderbevegelsens Historie* 2: 85–114.

Björklund, Anders. 1990. "Unemployment, Labour Market Policy and Income Distribution." In *Generating Equality in the Welfare State*, ed. Inga Persson. Oslo: Norwegian University Press.

Björklund, Tor. 1991. "Public versus Private Sector." Unpublished manuscript, Institute for Social Research, Oslo.

———. 1992. "Unemployment and Party Choice in Norway." *Scandinavian Political Studies* 15: 329–352.

Blanchard, Olivier, and Pierre-Alain Muet. 1993. "Competitiveness through Disinflation: An Assessment of the French Macroeconomic Strategy." *Economic Policy* 8 (1): 11–56.

Blanchard, Olivier, and Lawrence H. Summers. 1987. "Hysteresis in Unemployment." *European Economic Review* 31: 288–295.

Blank, Stephen. 1978. "Britain: The Politics of Foreign Economic Policy, the Domestic Economy, and the Problem of Pluralistic Stagnation." In *Between Power and Plenty*, ed. Peter Katzenstein. Madison: University of Wisconsin Press.

Boix, Charles. 1997. *Political Parties, Growth and Equality*. Cambridge: Cambridge University Press.

Boltho, Andrea. 1982. *The European Economy Growth and Crisis*. Oxford: Oxford University Press.

Borchert, Jens. 1995. *Die konservative Transformation des Wohlfahrtsstaates. Großbritannien, Kanada, die USA und Deutschland im Vergleich*. Frankfurt: Campus Verlag.

Bornschier, Volker, and Nicola Fielder. 1995. "The Genesis of the Single European Act. Forces and Protagonists behind the Relaunch of the European Community in the 1980s: The Single Market." Unpublished manuscript.

Bound, John, and George Johnson. 1992. "Changes in the Structure of Wages in the 1980s: An Evaluation of Alternative Explanations." *American Economic Review* 82: 371–392.

Boyer, Robert, ed. 1986. *The Search for Labor Market Flexibility*. Oxford: Clarendon Press.

———. 1990. *The Regulation School: A Critical Introduction*. New York: Columbia University Press.

Boyer, Robert, and Jacques Mistral. 1978. *Accumulation, Inflation, Crises*. Paris: Presses Universitaires de France.

Boyer, Robert, and Yves Saillard, eds. 1995. *Theorie de la regulation: L'état des savoirs*. Paris: La Decouverte.

Brand, Karl-Werner. 1987. "Kontinuität und Diskontinuität in den neuen sozialen Bewegungen." In *Neue soziale Bewegungen in der Bundesrepublik Deutschland*, ed. Roland Roth and Dieter Rucht. Frankfurt: Campus Verlag.

Brint, Steven. 1984. "'New Class' and Cumulative Trend Explanations of the Liberal Political Attitudes of Professionals." *American Journal of Sociology* 90: 30–71.

Brose, Hans-Georg. 1989. "Coping with Instability: The Emergence of New Biographical Patterns." *Life Stories* 5: 3–26.

Broughton, David. 1994. "The CDU-CSU in Germany: Is There Any Alternative?" In *Christian Democracy in Europe: A Comparative Perspective*, ed. David Hanley. London: Pinter Publishers.

Brown, Philip, and Richard Scase. 1991. *Poor Work*. Milton Keyes: Open University Press.

Bryant, Ralph. 1987. *International Financial Mediation*. Washington, D.C.: Brookings Institution.

Buechtemann, Christoph F. 1993. "Employment Security and Deregulation: The West German Experience." In *Employment Security and Labor Market Behavior*, ed. Christoph F. Buechtemann. Ithaca, N.Y.: ILR Press.

Bull, Martin J., and James L. Newell. 1995. "Italy Changes Course? The 1994 Elections and the Victory of the Right." *Parliamentary Affairs* 48 (1): 72–99.

Bureau of the Census, U.S. Department of Commerce. 1996. *Statistical Abstract of the United States*. Washington, D.C.: U.S. Government Printing Office.

Burley-Slaughter, Anne-Marie, and Walter Mattli. 1993. "Europe before the Court: A Political Theory of Legal Integration." *International Organization* 47: 41–76.

Burowoy, Michael. 1989. "Marxism without Micro-Foundations." *Socialist Review* 19: 57–86.

Burtless, Gary, ed. 1990. *A Future of Lousy Jobs? The Changing Structure of U.S. Wages*. Washington, D.C.: Brookings Institution.

Cairncross, Alec, and Barry Eichengreen. 1983. *Sterling in Decline: The Devaluations of 1931, 1949, and 1967*. London: Basil Blackwell.

Calhoun, Craig J. 1983. "The Radicalism of Tradition: Community Strength on Venerable Disguise and Borrowed Language." *American Journal of Sociology* 88: 886–914.

Calmfors, Lars. 1993. "Lessons from the Macroeconomic Experience of Sweden." *European Journal of Political Economy* 9 (1): 25–72.

———. 1994. "Active Labour Market Policy and Unemployment: A Framework for the Analysis of Crucial Design Features." *OECD Economic Studies* 22: 7–47.

Calmfors, Lars, and John Driffill. 1978. "Centralization of Wage Bargaining." *Economic Policy* (April).

———. 1988. "Bargaining Structure, Corporatism and Macroeconomic Performance." *Economic Policy* 3: 13–61.

Cameron, David. 1978. "The Expansion of the Political Economy: A Comparative Analysis." *American Political Science Review* 72 (4): 1243–1261.

———. 1984. "Social Democracy, Corporatism, Labour Quiescence, and the Representation of Economic Interest in Advanced Capitalist Society." In *Order and Conflict in Contemporary Capitalism*, ed. John Goldthorpe. Oxford: Oxford University Press.

———. 1987. *The Colors of a Rose: On the Ambiguous Record of French Socialism*. Cambridge, Mass.: Harvard University Center for European Studies.

———. 1992. "The 1992 Initiative: Causes and Consequences." In *Europolitics: Institutions and Policymaking in the "New" European Community*, ed. Alberta M. Sbragia. Washington, D.C.: Brookings Institution.

1995. "National Interest, European Identity, and the Dilemmas of Integration: France and the Union after Maastricht." Presented at the annual meeting of the American Political Science Association, Chicago, September 1–4.

Campbell, Colin, and Bert A. Rockman, eds. 1991. *The Bush Presidency: First Appraisals.* Chatham N.J.: Chatham House Publishers.

Campbell, John L., J. Rogers Hollingsworth, and Leon N. Lindberg, eds. 1991. *Governance of the American Economy.* Cambridge: Cambridge University Press.

Caporaso, James. 1996. "The European Union and Forms of State: Westphalian, Regulatory or Post-Modern?" *Journal of Common Market Studies* 34 (1): 29–52.

Card, D., and A. Krueger. 1995. *Myth and Measurement: The New Economics of the Minimum Wage.* Princeton: Princeton University Press.

Carlin, Wendy, and David Soskice. 1990. *Macroeconomics and the Wage Bargain: A Modern Approach to Employment, Inflation and the Exchange Rate.* Oxford: Oxford University Press.

1997. "Shocks to the System: The German Political Economy under Stress." *National Institute Economic Review* 159: 57–76.

Carroll, Eero. 1994. "The Politics of Unemployment Insurance and Labor Market Policy." Paper presented at the International Sociological Association meeting, Bielefeld, Germany, July 18–23.

Carroll, Glenn R., and Karl Ulrich Mayer. 1986. "Job-Shift Patterns in the Federal Republic of Germany: The Effects of Class, Industrial Sector and Organizational Size." *American Sociological Review* 51: 323–341.

Casey, Bernard. 1991. "Survey Evidence on Trends in Non-Standard Employment." In *Farewell to Flexibility?*, ed. Anna Pollert. Oxford: Basil Blackwell.

Casper, S. 1996. "German Industrial Associations and the Diffusion of Innovative Economic Organization." *WZB Discussion Paper* FSI 96–306.

Cassing, James H., and Arye L. Hillman. 1986. "Shifting Comparative Advantage and Senescent Industry Collapse." *American Economic Review* 76: 516–523.

Cassing James H., Timothy J. McKeown, and John Ochs. 1986. "The Political Economy of the Tariff Cycle." *American Political Science Review* 80: 843–862.

Castles, Francis G., ed. 1982. *The Impact of Parties: Politics and Policies in Democratic Capitalist States.* Beverly Hills, Calif.: Sage Publications.

1985. *The Working Class and Welfare.* Sydney: Allen and Unwin.

1996. "Needs-based Strategies of Social Protection in Australia and New Zealand." In *Welfare States in Transition*, ed. Gøsta Esping-Andersen. London: Sage Publications.

Castles, Francis G., Rolf Gerritsen, and Jack Vowles, eds. 1996. *The Great Experiment: Labour Parties and the Public Transformation in Australia and New Zealand.* St. Leonards, NSW, Australia: Allen and Unwin.

Castles, Francis G., and Deborah Mitchell. 1990. "Three Worlds of Welfare Capitalism or Four?" Discussion Paper 21. Australian National University, Public Policy Program.

Castles, Francis G., and Ian Shirley. 1996. "Labour and Social Policy." In *The*

Great Experiment, ed. Francis G. Castles, Rolf Gerritsen, and Jack Vowles. Sydney: Allen and Unwin.

Cawson, Alan, ed. 1985. *Organized Interests and the State*. Beverly Hills, Calif.: Sage Publications.

CENSIS. 1995. *Rapporto sulla situazione sociale del paese, 1994*. Rome.

Cerny, Philip G. 1989. "The Little Big Bang in Paris: Financial Market Deregulation in a Dirigiste System." *Journal of European Research* 17 (2): 162–192.

——— 1993. "The Deregulation and Re-regulation of Financial Markets in a More Open World." In *Finance and World Politics: Markets, Regimes, and States in the Post Hegemonic Era*, ed. Philip Cerny. Aldershot: Edward Elgar.

Chadwick, Owen. 1975. *The Secularization of the European Mind in the Nineteenth Century*. Cambridge: Cambridge University Press.

Chandler, Alfred. 1962. *Strategy and Structure*. Cambridge, Mass.: MIT Press.

——— 1974. *The Visible Hand*. Cambridge, Mass.: Harvard University Press.

Clark, Terry, and Seymour Martin Lipset. 1991. "Are Social Classes Dying?" *International Sociology* 4: 397–410.

Clark, Terry, Seymour Martin Lipset, and Michael Rempel. 1993. "The Declining Political Significance of Class." *International Sociology* 3: 293–316.

Clarke, Harold D., William Mishler, and Paul Whiteley. 1992. "Recapturing the Falklands: Models of Conservative Popularity, 1979–1983." In *Issues and Controversies in British Electoral Behavior*, ed. David Denver and Gordon Hands. Brighton: Harvester.

Cobalti, Antonio. 1993. "La classe operaia nella societa postindustriale." *Polis* 3: 477–502.

Cobalti, Antonio, and Antonio Schizzerotto. 1994. *La mobilita sociale in Italia*. Bologna: Il Mulino.

Cohen, Benjamin J. 1993. "The Triad and the Unholy Trinity: Lessons for the Pacific Region." In *Pacific Economic Relations in the 1990s: Cooperation or Conflict?*, ed. Richard Higgot, Richard Leaver, and John Ravenhill. Boulder, Colo.: Lynne Reinner.

Cohn-Bendit, Daniel. 1980. "Dann ist der Pessimismus eben realistisch . . . Diskussion mit Daniel Cohn-Bendit u.a." In *H. Marcuse: Das Ende der Utopie. Vorträge und Diskussionen in Berlin 1967*. Frankfrut: Verlag Neue Kritik.

Coleman, William. 1990. *Foundations of Social Theory*. Cambridge, Mass.: Harvard University Press.

Commins, Margaret M. 1993. "From Security to Trade in US-Latin American Relations: Explaining Bush Administration Support for Free Trade with Mexico." Ph.D. dissertation, University of North Carolina, Chapel Hill.

Commission of the European Communities, Directorate-General for Employment, Industrial Relations, and Social Affairs. 1993a. *Social Europe*. Supplement 3. Luxembourg: Commission of the European Communities.

——— 1993b. *Employment in Europe*. COM(93) 314. Luxembourg: Commission of the European Communities.

Conradt, David P., G. R. Kleinfeld, G. K. Romoser, and C. Søe, eds. 1995. *Germany's New Politics: Parties and Issues in the 1990s*. Oxford: Berghahn Books.

Conybeare, John. 1986. "Trade Wars: A Comparative Study of Anglo-Hanse,

Franco-Italian, and Hawley-Smoot Conflicts." In *Cooperation under Anarchy*, ed. Kenneth A. Oye. Princeton, N.J.: Princeton University Press.

Cooper, Barry, Alan Kornberg, and William Mishler. 1987. *The Resurgence of Conservatism in Anglo-American Democracies*. Durham, N.C.: Duke University Press.

Cosh, Andrew D., Alan Hughes, and Ajit Singh. 1992. "Openness, Financial Innovation, Changing Patterns of Ownership, and the Structure of Financial Markets." In *Financial Openness and National Autonomy: Opportunities and Constraints*, ed. Tariq Banuri and Juliet B. Schor, 19–42. Oxford: Clarendon Press.

Cowhey, Peter F., and Jonathan D. Aronson. 1993. *Managing the World Economy: The Consequences of Corporate Alliances*. New York: Council on Foreign Relations Press.

Cowles, Maria Green. 1995. "Setting the Agenda for a New Europe: The ERT and 1992." *Journal of Common Market Studies* 33 (4): 501–526.

Cox, Gary W., and Frances Rosenbluth. 1993. "The Electoral Fortunes of Legislative Factions in Japan." *American Political Science Review* 87: 577–589.

Cox, Robert H. 1993. *The Development of the Dutch Welfare State*. Pittsburgh: University of Pittsburgh Press.

——— 1994. "Social Entitlement and the Limits of Retrenchment: Welfare Cutbacks in Denmark and the Netherlands." Paper presented at the Conference of Europeanists, Chicago, March 14–17.

Cram, Laura. 1997. *Policy-making in the EU*. London: Routledge.

Crewe, Ivor. 1988. "Has the Electorate Become More Thatcherite?" In *Thatcherism*, ed. Robert Skidelsky. London: Chatto and Windus.

——— 1991. "Labour Force Changes, Working Class Decline, and the Labour Vote." In *Labor Parties in Postindustrial Societies*, ed. Frances Fox Piven. Oxford: Polity Press.

Crewe, Ivor, Neil Day, and Anthony Fox. 1991. *The British Electorate, 1963–1987*. Cambridge: Cambridge University Press.

Crewe, Ivor, and David Denver, eds. 1985. *Electoral Change in Western European Democracies*. New York: St. Martin's Press.

Crompton, Rosemary, and Gareth Jones. 1984. *White-Collar Proletariat: Deskilling and Gender in Clerical Work*. London: Macmillan.

Crotty, James. 1989. "The Limits of Keynesian Macroeconomic Policy in the Age of the Global Marketplace." In *Instability and Change in the World Economy*, ed. Arthur Machine and William Tabb. New York: Monthly Review Press.

Crouch, Colin. 1993. *Industrial Relations and European State Traditions*. Oxford: Clarendon Press.

Crouch, Colin, and Alessandro Pizzorno, eds. 1978. *The Resurgence of Class Conflict in Western Europe since 1968*. 2 vols. New York: Holmes and Meier.

Cukierman, Alex. 1992. *Central Bank Strategy, Credibility and Independence*. Cambridge, Mass.: MIT Press.

Culpepper, Pepper. 1996. "Employers Organizations and the Politics of Vocational Training in France and Germany." Paper presented to the annual meeting of the American Political Science Association, San Francisco, August 28–September 1.

Curtice, John, and Michael Steed. 1986. "Proportionality and Exaggeration in the British Electoral System." *Electoral Studies* 5: 209–228.

Cusack, Thomas R., and Geoffrey Garrett. 1994. "International Economic Change and the Politics of Government Spending, 1962–1988." Unpublished manuscript, Stanford University.

Cusack, Thomas R., Ton Noterman, and Martin Rein. 1989. "Political-Economic Aspects of Public Employment." *European Journal of Political Research* 17: 471–500.

Cusack, Thomas R., and Martin Rein. 1991. "Social Policy and Service Employment." Wissenschaftszentrum, Berlin. Unpublished manuscript.

Dallago, Bruno. 1990. *The Hidden Economy*. Aldershot: Dartmouth.

Dalton, Russell J., Scott C. Flanagan, and Paul Allen Beck, eds. 1984. *Electoral Change in Advanced Industrial Democracies: Realignment or Dealignmemt?* Princeton, N.J.: Princeton University Press.

Dalton, Russell J., and Manfred Kuechler. 1990. *Challenging the Political Order*. Oxford: Polity Press.

Daniels, Philip. 1993. "Italy and the Maastricht Treaty." *Italian Politics: A Review* 8: 178–191.

Danish National Institute of Social Research. 1994. *Recent Trends in Cash Benefits in Europe*. Copenhagen: DNISR.

Davies, Paul, and Mark Freedland. 1993. *Labour Legislation and Public Policy*. Oxford: Oxford University Press.

de Beus, Jos, and Kees van Kersbergen. 1994. "Employment Policy Legacy and Political Party Strategy in the Netherlands." Paper presented at the Conference of Europeanists, Chicago, March 14–17.

Dehousse, Renaud, and Giándomenico Majone. 1994. "The Institutional Dynamics of European Integration: From the Single European Act to the Maastricht Treaty." In *The Construction of Europe: Essays in Honour of Emile Noël*, ed. Stephen Martin. Dordrecht: Kluwer.

Della Porta, Donatella. 1996. "The System of Corrupt Exchange in Local Government." In *The New Italian Republic: From the Fall of the Berlin Wall to Berlusconi*, ed. S. Gundle and S. Parker. London: Routledge.

Della Porta, Donatella, Hanspeter Kriesi, and Dieter Rucht, eds. 1998. *Social Movements in a Globalizing World*. London: Macmillan.

Delors, Jacques. 1992. *Our Europe: The Community and National Development*. Trans. Brian Pearce. London: Verso.

Denison, Edward Fulton. 1967. *Why Growth Rates Differ: Postwar Experience in Nine Western Countries*. Washington, D.C.: Brookings Institution.

Deruette, Serge, and Nicole Loeb-Mayer. 1992. "Belgium." In *Political Data Yearbook, 1992 (January 1991–January 1992)*, ed. Ruud Koole and Peter Mair. Special issue of *European Journal of Political Research*, 22 (4): 362–372.

Dohring, H. 1990. "Wahlen Industriearbeiter zunehmend Konservativ?" In *Wahlen und Wehler*, ed. Max Kaase and Hans-Dieter Klingemann. Opladen: Westdeutscher Verlag.

Donovan, Mark. 1994a. "Democrazia Cristiana: Party of Government." In *Christian Democracy in Europe: A Comparative Perspective*, ed. David Hanley. London: Pinter Publishers.

1994b. "The 1994 Election in Italy: Normalisation or Continuing Exceptionalism?" *West European Politics* 17 (4): 193–201.

1995. "The Politics of Electoral Reform in Italy." *International Political Science Review* 16 (1): 47–64.

Dooley, Michael, Jeffrey Frankel, and Donald Mathieson. 1987. "International Capital Mobility: What Do Saving-Investment Correlations Tell Us?" *IMF Staff Papers* 34: 503–530.

Due, Jesper, Jorgen Steen Madsen, Carsten Stroby Jensen, and Lars Kjerulff Petersen. 1994. *The Survival of the Danish Model.* Copenhagen: DJOF Publishers.

Duncan, Greg, B. Gustavsson, and R. Hauser. 1995. "Poverty and Social Assistance Dynamics in the United States, Canada, and Europe." In *Poverty, Inequality and the Future of Social Policy*, ed. Katherine McFate, Roger Lawson, and William Julius Wilson. New York: Russell Sage Foundation.

Dunleavy, Patrick, and Christopher Husbands. 1985. *British Democracy at the Crossroads.* London: Allen and Unwin.

Durlauf, Steven N., and Paul A. Johnson. 1992. "Local versus Global Convergence across National Economies." National Bureau of Economic Research Working Paper no. 3996. Cambridge, Mass.

Duyvendak, Jan-Willem. 1992. "The Power of Politics. France: New Social Movements in an Old Polity." Ph.D. dissertation, University of Amsterdam.

Duyvendak, Jan-Willem, and Marco G. Giugni. 1995. "Social Movement Types and Policy Domains." In *The Politics of New Social Movements in Western Europe: A Comparative Analysis*, ed. Hanspeter Kriesi et al. Minneapolis: University of Minnesota Press.

Ebster-Grosz, D., and D. Pugh. 1996. *Anglo-German Business Collaboration: Pitfalls and Potentials.* London: Macmillan.

Eckert, Roland, and Helmut Willems. 1993. "Fremdenfeindliche Gewalt." *Neue Justiz* 47 (11): 481–485.

Edin, Per-Anders, and Robert Topel. 1995. "Wage Policy and Restructuring: The Swedish Labor Market since 1960." In *Reforming the Welfare State*, ed. Richard B. Freeman and Robert Topel. Chicago: University of Chicago Press.

Edwards, Paul, et al. 1992. "Great Britain: Still Muddling Through." In *Industrial Relations in the New Europe*, ed. Anthony Ferner and Richard Hyman. London: Basil Blackwell.

Eichengreen, Barry. 1993. "Institutions and Economic Growth: Europe after World War II." Paper presented to the Conference on the Comparative Experience of Economic Growth in Postwar Europe, Oxford.

1994. *International Monetary Arrangements for the 21st Century.* Washington, D.C.: Brookings Institution.

Eken, Sena. 1984. "Integration of Domestic and International Financial Markets: The Japanese Experience." *IMF Staff Papers* 31 (3): 499–548.

Elbers, Frank, and Meindert Fennema. 1993. *Racistische partijen in West-Eurpa: Tussen nationale tradite en Europese samenwerking.* Leiden: Stichting Burgerschapskunde/Nederlands Centrum voor Politieke Vorming.

Elman, Amy R. 1993. "Debunking the Social Democrats and the Myth of Equality." *Women's Studies International Forum* 16 (5): 513–522.

Elsheikh, Farouk, and George Sayers Bain. 1980. "Unionization in Britain: An Interestablishment Analysis Based on Survey Data." *British Journal of Industrial Relations* 18: 169–178.

Elster, Jon. 1984. *Ulysses and the Sirens*. Cambridge: Cambridge University Press.

Elvander, Nils. 1990. "Incomes Policies in the Nordic Countries." *International Labour Review* 1: 1–21.

Employment Gazette. 1992. 9: 433–459.

Engbersen, Godfried, Kees Schuyt, Jaap Timmer, and Frans van Waarden. 1993. *Cultures of Unemployment*. Boulder, Colo.: Westview Press.

Epstein, Gerald A., and Juliet B. Schor. 1992. "Structural Determinants and Economic Effects of Capital Controls in OECD Countries." In *Financial Openness and National Autonomy: Opportunities and Constraints*, ed. Tariq Banuri and Juliet B. Schor. Oxford: Clarendon Press.

Erikson, Robert. 1990. *Welfare Trends in Scandinavian Countries*. Armonk, N.Y.: M. E. Sharpe.

Erikson, Robert, and Rune Aaberg. 1985. *Welfare in Transition*. Oxford: Clarendon Press.

Erikson, Robert, and John H. Goldthorpe. 1992. *The Constant Flux: Class Mobility in Industrial Societies*. Oxford: Clarendon Press.

Erler, Gisela A. 1988. "The German Paradox: Non-feminization of the Labor Force and Post-Industrial Social Policies." In *Feminization of the Labor Force: Paradoxes and Promises*, ed. Jane Jenson, Elisabeth Hagen, and Ceallaigh Reddy. New York: Oxford University Press.

Esping-Andersen, Gøsta. 1985. *Politics against Markets: The Social Democratic Road to Power*. Princeton, N.J.: Princeton University Press.

———. 1990. *The Three Worlds of Welfare Capitalism*. Cambridge: Polity Press.

———. 1993b. "Post-industrial Class Structures: An Analytical Framework." In *Changing Classes: Stratification and Mobility in Post-Industrial Societies*, ed. Gøsta Esping-Andersen. London: Sage Publications.

———. 1995. "The Continental European Welfare States: The Strategy of Labor Reduction and the Impending Overload of Social Insurance." Unpublished manuscript, University of Trento and Istituto Juan, March.

———. 1996. "Welfare States at the End of the Century." Background document for the OECD Conference on Beyond 2000: The New Social Policy Agenda, Paris, November.

Esping-Andersen, Gøsta, Gøtz Rohwer and Søren Leth Sørensen. 1994. "Institutions and Class Mobility: Scaling the Skill Barrier." *European Sociological Review* 10 (2): 119–133.

Esser, Josef. 1986. " 'Symbolic Privatization': The Politics of Privatisation in West Germany." *West European Politics* 11 (4): 61–73.

Ethier, Wilfred. 1986. "International Trade Theory and International Migration." *Research in Human Capital and Development: Migration, Human Capital and Development* 4: 27–74.

Eurostat. 1992. *Women in the European Community*. Luxembourg: Office for Official Publications of the European Communities.

Evans, Peter, Dietrich Rueschemeyer, and Theda Skocpol, eds. 1985. *Bringing the State Back In*. Cambridge: Cambridge University Press.

Falter, Jürgen W., Andreas Link, Jan-Bernd Lohmüller, Johann de Rijke, and Siegfried Schumann. 1993. "Arbeitslosigkeit und Nationalsozialismus." *Kölner Zeitschrift für Soziologie und Sozialpsychologie* 35: 525–554.

Feenstra, Robert C. and Gordon H. Hanson. 1996. "Foreign Investment, Outsourcing, and Relative Wages." In *The Political Economy of Trade Policy: Papers in Honor of Jagdish Bhagwati*, ed. Robert C. Feenstra, Gene M. Grossman, and Douglas A. Irwin. Cambridge, Mass: MIT Press.

Feist, Ulrich, and Klaus Liepelt. 1990. "Dynamik des Arbeitsmarkts und Wahlerverlhalten." In *Wahlen und Wehler*, ed. Max Kaase and Hans-Dieter Klingemann. Opladen: Westdeutcher Verlag.

Feldmann, Robert Alan. 1986. *Japanese Financial Markets: Deficit, Dilemmas, and Deregulation*. Cambridge, Mass.: MIT Press.

Feldstein, Martin. 1995. "The Effect of Marginal Tax Rates on Taxable Income: A Panel Study of the 1986 Reform Act." *Journal of Political Economy* 103 (3).

Feldstein, Martin, and Phillippe Bacchetta. 1983. "Domestic Savings and International Capital Movements in the Long Run and the Short Run." *European Economic Review* 21: 139–151.

1989. "National Saving and International Investment." National Bureau of Economic Research Working Paper no. 3164. Cambridge, Mass.

ed. 1994. *Reagan's Economic Record*. Chicago: University of Chicago Press.

Feldstein, Martin, and Charles Horioka. 1980. "Domestic Savings and International Capital Flows." *Economic Journal* 90: 201–220.

Ferrera, Maurizio. 1995. "La partitocrazia della saluta." *Il Mulino* 44 (361): 855–868.

1997. "The Uncertain Future of the Italian Welfare State." *West European Politics*.

Feur, Ralph. 1991. "Emerging Alternatives to Full-Time and Permanent Employment." In *Poor Work*, ed. Philip Brown and Richard Scase. Milton Keyes: Open University Press.

Finegold, David, and David Soskice. 1988. "The Failure of Training in Britain: Analysis and Prescription." *Oxford Review of Economic Policy* 4 (3): 21–53.

Fischer, K. P., and A. P. Palasvirta. 1990. "High Road to a Global Marketplace: The International Transmission of Stock Market Fluctuations." *Financial Review* 25 (3): 371–394.

Flanagan, Robert J., Karl Ove Moene, and Michael Wallerstein. 1993. *Trade Union Behavior, Pay Bargaining and Economic Performance*. Oxford: Oxford University Press.

Fligstein, Neil, and Jason McNichol. 1996. "The Institutional Terrain of the European Union." University of California, Berkeley. Unpublished manuscript.

Flora, Peter, ed. 1986. *Growth to Limits: The Western European Welfare States since World War II*. Berlin: Walter de Gruyter.

Follini, Marco. 1993. "Christian Democracy: Extreme Remedies for Extreme Problems?" *Italian Politics: A Review*, vol. 8.

Foote, Susan Bartlett. 1984. "Beyond the Politics of Federalism: An Alternative Model." *Yale Journal on Regulation* 1: 217–225.

——. 1985. *The Decline of Class Voting in Britain.* Oxford: Clarendon Press.

——. 1989. "Quantifying International Capital Mobility in the 1980s." National Bureau of Economic Research Working Paper no. 1773. Cambridge, Mass.

——. 1992. "Measuring International Capital Mobility: A Review." *AEA Papers and Proceedings* 82 (2): 197–202.

Frankel, Jeffrey. 1991. "Quantifying International Capital Mobility in the 1980s." In *National Saving and Economic Performance*, ed. D. Bernheim and J. Shoven. Chicago: University of Chicago Press.

Frankel, Jeffrey, and Steven Phillips. 1991. "The European Monetary System: Credible at Last?" National Bureau of Economic Research Working Paper no. 3819. Cambridge, Mass.

Franklin, Mark N., Tom T. Mackie, Henry Valen, et al., eds. 1992. *Electoral Change: Responses to Evolving Social and Attitudinal Structures in Western Countries.* Cambridge: Cambridge University Press.

Franklin, Mark, Michael Marsh, and Lauren McLaren. 1994. "Uncorking the Bottle: Popular Opposition to European Unification in the Wake of Maastricht." *Journal of Common Market Studies* 32 (4): 455–473.

Franzese, Robert. 1994. "Central Bank Independence, Sectoral Interest and the Wage Bargain." Harvard Center for European Studies Working Paper. Cambridge, Mass.

Freeman, Richard B. 1988. "Labour Market Institutions and Economic Performance." *Economic Policy* 3: 64–80.

——. 1993. *Working under Different Rules.* New York: Russell Sage Foundation.

——. 1995. "Are Your Wages Set in Beijing?" *Journal of Economic Perspectives* 9: 15–32.

Freeman, Richard B., and Lawrence F. Katz. 1994. *Differences and Changes in Wage Structure.* Cambridge, Mass.: National Bureau of Economic Research.

Freeman, Richard B., and James L. Medoff. 1984. *What Do Unions Do?* New York: Basic Books.

French, Kenneth, and James M. Poterba. 1990. "Japanese and US Cross-Border Common Stock Investments." *Journal of the Japanese and International Economies* 4: 476–493.

Frenkel, Jacob A., Assaf Razin, and Efraim Sadka. 1991. *International Taxation in an Integrated World.* Cambridge, Mass.: MIT Press.

Frieden, Jeffry A. 1989. *Banking on the World.* New York: Basil Blackwell.

——. 1991. "Invested Interests: The Politics of National Economic Policies in a World of Global Finance." *International Organization* 45 (4): 425–451.

Frieden, Jeffry A., and Ronald Rogowski. 1996. "The Impact of the International Economy on National Policies: An Analytical Overview." In *Internationalization and Domestic Politics*, ed. Robert Keohane and Helen Milner. Ithaca, N.Y.: Cornell University Press.

Friedman, Milton. 1953. "The Case for Flexible Exchange Rates." In *Essays in Positive Economics*, ed. Milton Friedman. Chicago: University of Chicago Press.

Fuchs, Dieter, and Dieter Rucht. 1992. "Support for New Social Movements in

Five Western European Countries." *WZB-Discussion Paper*, FS III 92–102. Berlin: Wissenschaftszentrum.

Fulcher, James. 1991. *Labour Movements, Employers, and the State: Conflict and Cooperation in Britain and Sweden*. Oxford: Clarendon Press.

Furlong, Paul. 1996. "Political Catholicism and the Strange Death of the Christian Democrats." In *The New Italian Republic: From the Fall of the Berlin Wall to Berlusconi*, ed. Stephen Gundle and Simon Parker. London: Routledge.

Gale, David. 1974. "The Trade Imbalance Story." *Journal of International Economics* 4: 119–137.

Gallie, Duncan. 1991. "Patterns of Skill Change; Upskilling, Deskilling, or the Polarization of Skills?" *Work, Employment and Society* 3: 319–351.

Garrett, Geoffrey. 1994. "Popular Capitalism: The Electoral Legacy of Thatcherism." In *Labour's Last Chance? The 1992 Election and Beyond*, ed. Anthony Heath et al. London: Dartmouth.

1995a. "Capital Mobility, Trade, and the Domestic Politics of Economic Policy." *International Organization* 49 (4): 657–687.

1995b. "The Politics of Legal Integration in the European Union." *International Organization* 49: 171–181.

1996. "Trade, Capital Mobility and the Politics of Economic Policy." In *Internationalization and Domestic Politics*, ed. Robert Keohane and Helen Milner. Ithaca, N.Y.: Cornell University Press.

Garrett, Geoffrey, and Peter Lange. 1989. "Government Partisanship and Economic Performance. When and How Does 'Who Governs' Matter." *Journal of Politics* 51.

1991. "Political Responses to Interdependence: What's Left for the Left?" *International Organization* 45 (4): 539–564.

1996. "Internationalization, Institutions, and Political Change." In *Internationalization and Domestic Politics,*, ed. Robert O. Keohane and Helen V. Milner. Cambridge: Cambridge University Press.

Garrett, Geoffrey, and Christopher Way. 1994. "The Sectoral Composition of Trade Unions, Corporatism and Economic Performance." Working Paper 1.28. Center for German and European Studies, University of California at Berkeley.

1995. "The Sectoral Composition of Trade Unions, Corporatism, and Economic Performance." In *Monetary and Fiscal Policy in an Integrated Europe*, ed. Barry Eichengreen, Jeffry Frieden, and Jürgen von Hagen. Berlin: Springer.

General Agreement on Tariffs and Trade [GATT]. 1993. *International Trade: Statistics*. Geneva: General Agreement on Tariffs and Trade.

George, Stephen. 1996 [1985]. *Politics and Policy in the European Community*. Oxford: Oxford University Press.

Gereffi, Gary, and Donald L. Wyman. 1991. *Manufacturing Miracles: Paths of Industrialization in Latin America and East Asia*. Princeton, N.J.: Princeton University Press.

Gerlach, M. 1989. "Keiretsu Organisation in the Japanese Economy." In *Politics and Productivity: How Japan's Development Strategy Works*, ed. C. Johnson, L. D'A. Tyson, and J. Zysman. Harper Business.

Gerlich, Peter. 1992. "A Farewell to Corporatism." *West European Politics* 1: 132–146.

Gershuny, Jonathan. 1991. *Changing Times: The Social Economics of Postindustrial Societies*. Report to the Rowntree Memorial. University of Bath.

———. 1993. "Postindustrial Career Structures in Britain." In *Changing Classes: Stratification and Mobility in Postindustrial Societies*, ed. Gøsta Esping-Andersen. London: Sage Publications.

Giddens, Anthony. 1990. *The Consequences of Modernity*. Cambridge: Polity Press.

———. 1991. *Modernity and Self-Identity*. Cambridge: Polity Press.

Gillespie, Richard, and William Paterson, eds. 1993. *Rethinking Social Democracy in Western Europe*. Special issue of *West European Politics*, no. 1.

Gilliam, Mikael, and Søren Holmberg. 1990. *Roett, Blatt, Groent. En Bok om 1988-aars Riksdagsval*. Stockholm: Bonniers.

Gladdish, Ken. 1991. *Governing from the Centre: Politics and Policy-Making in the Netherlands*. London: Hurst; The Hague: SDU.

Glyn, A. 1995. "Employment and Wages in Services." Oxford University. Mimeographed.

Gobowski, W. G. 1995. "Germany's General Election in 1994: Who Voted for Whom?" In *Germany's New Politics: Parties and Issues in the 1990s*, ed. David P. Conradt, Gerald R. Kleinfeld, George K. Romoser, and Christian Søe. Oxford: Berghahn Books.

Golden, Miriam. 1986. "Interest Representation, Party Systems and the State: Italy in Comparative Perspective." *Comparative Politics* 18 (3): 279–301.

———. 1992. "Conclusion: Current Trends in Trade Union Politics." In *Bargaining for Change: Union Politics in North America and Europe*, ed. Miriam Golden and Jonas Pontusson. Ithaca, N.Y.: Cornell University Press.

———. 1993. "The Dynamics of Trade Unionism and National Economic Performance." *American Political Science Review* 87 (2):439–454.

Golden, Miriam, and Michael Wallerstein. 1996. "Reinterpreting Postwar Industrial Relations: Comparative Data on Advanced Industrial Societies." Unpublished manuscript, University of California at Los Angeles and Northwestern University.

Goldey, David. 1993. "The French General Election of 1993." *Electoral Studies* 12 (4): 291–314.

Goldfield, Michael. 1987. *The Decline of Organized Labor in the United States*. Chicago: University of Chicago Press.

Goldthorpe, John H., ed. 1984. *Order and Conflict in Contemporary Capitalism*. Oxford: Clarendon Press.

Goldthorpe, John H., David Lockwood, Frank Bechhoton, and Jennifer Platt. 1968. *The Affluent Worker: Industrial Attitudes and Behavior*. Cambridge: Cambridge University Press.

Goodhart, Charles. 1988. "The International Transmission of Asset Price Volatility." In *Financial Market Volatility: A Symposium*. Jackson Hole, Wyo.: Federal Reserve Bank of Kansas City.

Goodman, John B. 1992. *Monetary Sovereignty: The Politics of Central Banking in Western Europe*. Ithaca, N.Y.: Cornell University Press.

Goodman, John B., and Louis W. Pauly. 1993. "The Obsolescence of Capital

Controls? Economic Management in an Age of Global Markets." *World Politics* 46 (October):50–82.

Gordon, Roger H., and Jeffrey K. Mackie-Mason. 1995. "Why Is There Taxation in a Small Open Economy: The Role of Transfer Pricing and Income Shifting." In *The Effects of Taxation on Multinational Corporations*, ed. Martin Feldstein, J. Hines, and Glenn Hubbard. Chicago: University of Chicago Press.

Gotschalk, Peter. 1993. "Changes in Inequality of Family Income in Seven Industrialized Countries." *American Economic Review* 2: 136–142.

Gottfries, Nils, and Henrik Horn. 1987. "Wage Formation and the Persistence of Unemployment." *Economic Journal* 97: 877–884.

Gourevitch, Peter A. 1986. *Politics in Hard Times*. Ithaca, N.Y.: Cornell University Press.

Gourevitch, Peter, et al. 1984. *Unions and Economic Crisis: Britain, West Germany and Sweden*. London: Allen and Unwin.

Graham, Andrew, and Anthony Seldon. 1990. *Government and Economies in the Postwar World*. London: Routledge.

Graham, Edward M., and Paul R. Krugman. 1989. *Foreign Direct Investment in the United States*. Washington, D.C.: Institute for International Economics.

Grant, Charles. 1994. *Inside the House that Jacques Built*. London: Nicholas Brealey.

Grant, Wyn. 1993. "Transnational Companies and Environmental Policy Making: The Trend of Globalization." In *European Integration and Environmental Policy*, ed. J. Duncan Liefferink, Philip D. Lowe, and A. P. J. Mol. London: Belhaven.

——— 1994. *Business and Politics in Britain*. 2nd ed. London: Macmillan.

Greenwood, Justin, Jürgen Grote, and Karsten Ronit, eds. 1992. *Organized Interests and the European Community*. London: Sage Publications.

Grilli, Vittorio, and Gian Maria Milesi-Ferretti. 1995. "Economic Effects and Structural Determinants of Capital Controls." *IMF Staff Papers* 42 (3): 517–551.

Grossman, Gene M., and Elhanan Helpman. 1990. "Comparative Advantage and Economic Growth." *American Economic Review* 80: 796–815.

Guger, Alois, and Wolfgang Polt. 1994. "Corporatism and Incomes Policy in Austria: Experiences and Perspectives." In *The Return to Incomes Policy*, ed. Ronald Dore et al. London: Pinter Publishers.

Haas, Ernst B. 1958. *The Uniting of Europe*. Stanford, Calif.: Stanford University Press.

Haavio-Mannila, Elina, ed. 1985. *Unfinished Democracy: Women in Nordic Politics*. Oxford: Pergamon.

Haberler, Gottfried. 1945. "The Choice of Exchange Rates after the War." *American Economic Review* 35: 308–318.

——— 1954. *Currency Convertibility*. Washington, D.C.: American Enterprise Institute.

Habermas, Jürgen 1961. "Über den Begriff der politischen Beteiligung." In *Student und Politik*, ed. Jürgen Habermas, Ludwig von Friedeburg, Christoph Oehler, and Friedrich Weltz. Neuwied am Rhein: Luchterhand.

——— 1973. *Legitimationsprobleme im Spätkapitalismus*. Frankfurt: Suhrkamp.

Habermas, Jürgen, Ludwig von Friedeburg, Christoph Oehler, and Friedrich Weltz. 1961. *Student und Politik*. Neuwied am Rhein: Luchterhand.

Hagen, Elisabeth, and Jane Jenson. 1988. "Paradoxes and Promises: Work and Politics in the Postwar Years." In *Feminization of the Labor Force: Paradoxes and Promises*, ed. Jane Jenson, Elisabeth Hagen, and Ceallaigh Reddy. New York: Oxford University Press.

Hagen, Kåre, 1992. "The Interaction of Welfare States and Labor Markets." In *The Study of Welfare State Regimes*, ed. Jon Eivind Kolberg. Armonk, N.Y.: M. E. Sharpe.

Hainsworth, Paul. 1992a. "The Extreme Right in Postwar France: The Emergence and Success of the National Front." In *The Extreme Right in Europe and the USA*, ed. Paul Hainsworth. London: Pinter Publishers.

1992b. "Introduction. The Cutting Edge: The Extreme Right in Post-War Western Europe and the USA." In *The Extreme Right in Europe and the USA*, ed. Paul Hainsworth. London: Pinter Publishers.

Hall, Peter A. 1986. *Governing the Economy*. New York: Oxford University Press.

1987. "The Evolution of Economic Policy under Mitterrand," In *The Mitterrand Experiment*, ed. George Ross and Stanley Hoffmann, 54–72. New York: Oxford University Press.

1989. "State and Market." In *Developments in French Politics*, ed. Peter A. Hall, Jack Hayward, and Howard Machin. London: Macmillan.

1993. "Policy Paradigms, Social Learning, and the State: The Case of Economic Policy-Making in Britain." *Comparative Politics* 25: 275–296.

1994. "Central Bank Independence and Coordinated Wage Bargaining: Their Interaction in Germany and Europe." *German Politics and Society* 31: 1–23.

Hallerberg, Mark. 1996. "Tax Competition in Wilhelmine Germany and Its Implications for European Union." *World Politics*. 48 (3): 324–357.

Halman, L., and Roek De Moor. 1993. "Comparative Research on Values." In *The Individualizing Society: Value Change in Europe and North America*, ed. Peter Ester, Loek Halman, and Ruud de Moor. Tilburg: Tilburg University Press.

Hamao, Yasushi, Ronald W. Masulis, and Victor Ng. 1990. "Correlations in Price Changes and Volatility across International Stock Markets." *Review of Financial Studies* 3 (3): 281–307.

Hancke, Bob. 1997. "Modernization without Flexible Specialization." Berlin: Wissenschaftszentrum für Sozialforschung.

Hancke, Bob, and Sylvie Cieply. 1996. "Bridging the Finance Gap for Small Firms." Berlin: Wissenschaftszentrum für Sozialforschung.

Hancke, Bob, and David Soskice. 1996a. "Coordination and Restructuring in Large French Firms." Discussion Paper of the Wissenschaftszentrum, Berlin.

1996b. "Von der Konstruktion von Industrienormen zur Organisation der Berufsausbildung. Eine vergleichende Analyse." Wissenschaftszentrum Berlin für Sozialforschung.

Hanson, Charles. 1991. *Taming the Trade Unions*. London: Macmillan.

Hanson, Charles, and Graham Mather. 1988. *Striking out Strikes*. London: Institute of Economic Affairs.

Hardin, Russell. 1982. *Collective Action*. Baltimore: Johns Hopkins University Press.

Harmel, Robert, Uk Heo, Alexander Tan, and Kenneth Janda. 1995. "Performance, Leadership, Factions and Party Change: An Empirical Analysis." *West European Politics* 18 (1): 1–33.

Harris, Richard A., and Sidney M. Milkis. 1989. *The Politics of Regulatory Change*. 2nd ed., 1996. New York: Oxford University Press.

Harrison, Bennett, and Barry Bluestone. 1988. *The Great U-Turn*. 2nd ed. New York: Basic Books.

Harrop, Martin, and William Miller. 1987. *Elections and Voters*. London: Macmillan.

Hayek, Friedrich A. 1980. *Unemployment and the Unions*. London: Institute of Economic Affairs.

Hayward, Jack. 1976. "Institutional Inertia and Political Impetus in France and Britain." *European Journal of Political Research* 4 (4): 341–351.

Heath, Anthony, and Bruno Paulson. 1992. "Issues and the Economy." *Political Quarterly* 63 (4): 432–447.

Heclo, Hugh, and Lester M. Salamon, eds. 1982. *The Illusion of Presidential Government*. Boulder, Colo.: Westview Press.

Helpman, Elhanan, and Paul R. Krugman. 1985. *Market Structure and Foreign Trade: Increasing Returns, Imperfect Competition, and the International Economy*. Cambridge, Mass.: MIT Press.

Hemerijck, Anton C., and Robert C. Kloosterman. 1994. "The Postindustrial Transition of Welfare Corporatism." Paper delivered at the Conference of Europeanists, Chicago, March 14–17.

Henning, C. Randall. 1994. *Currencies and Politics in the United States, Germany, and Japan*. Washington, D.C.: Institute for International Economics.

Hernes, Gudmund. 1991. "The Dilemmas of Social Democracies: The Case of Norway and Sweden." *Acta Sociologica* 34: 239–260.

Hernes, Helga Maria. 1987. *Welfare State and Women Power: Essays in State Feminism*. Oslo: Norwegian University Press.

Herrigel, G. 1993. "Large Firms, Small Firms and the Governance of Flexible Specialization: The Case of Baden-Württemberg and Socialized Risk." In *Country Competiveness: Technology and the Organizing of Work*, ed. B. Kogut, 15–35. New York: Oxford University Press.

1995. *Industrial Constructions*. Cambridge: Cambridge University Press.

Hibbs, Douglas A., Jr. 1977. "Political Parties and Macro-Economic Policy." *American Political Science Review* 71 (4): 1467–1486.

1982. "Economic Outcomes and Political Support for British Governments among Occupational Classes: A Dynamic Analysis." *American Political Science Review* 76: 259–279.

1987. *The American Political Economy: Macroeconomics and Electoral Politics*. Cambridge, Mass.: Harvard University Press.

1990. "Wage Dispersion and Trade Union Action in Sweden." In *Generating Equality in the Welfare State*, ed. Inga Persson. Oslo: Norwegian University Press.

Hibbs, Douglas A., Jr., and Håkan Locking. 1991. "Wage Compression, Wage Drift, and Wage Inflation in Sweden." FIEF Working Paper no. 87. Trade Union Institute for Economic Research (FIEF), Stockholm.

1995. "Wage Dispersion and Productive Efficiency: Evidence from Sweden." Unpublished manuscript, Trade Union Institute for Economic Research (FIEF), Stockholm.

1996. "Wage Compression, Wage Drift and Wage Inflation in Sweden." *Labour Economics* 3: 109–141.

Hinrichs, Karl. 1991. "Public Pensions and Demographic Change." *Society* 28 (6): 32–37.

Hirsch, Fred, 1980. *Die sozialen Grenzen des Wachstums: Eine ökonomische Analyse der Wachstumskrise*. Reinbek: Rowohlt.

Hirsch, Fred, and John. H. Goldthorpe, eds. 1978. *The Political Economy of Inflation*. London: Martin Robertson.

Hirschman, Albert O. 1979. "The Turn to Authoritarianism in Latin America and the Search for Its Economic Determinants." In *The New Authoritarianism in Latin America*, ed. David Collier. Princeton, N.J.: Princeton University Press.

Hix, Simon. Forthcoming. "Dimensions and Alignments in European Union Politics: Cognitive Constraints and Partisan Responses." *European Journal of Political Research*.

Hix, Simon, and Christopher Lord. 1996. *Political Parties in the European Union*. New York: St. Martin's Press.

Hobson, Barbara, and Marika Lindholm. 1997. "Women's Collectivities, Power Resources, and the Making of Welfare States." *Theory and Society* 26: 475–508.

Hobson, John Atkinson. 1965 [1938]. *Imperialism: A Study*. Ann Arbor: University of Michigan Press.

Hoerr, John. 1993. "Solidaritas at Harvard. Meet the Harvard of the Labor Movement. A Model of the New Unionism." *American Prospect* 14: 67–82.

Hoffmann, Stanley. 1982. "Reflections on the Nation-State in Western Europe Today." *Journal of Common Market Studies* 21: 21–37.

Höhne, Roland. 1990. "Die Renaissance des Rechtsextremismus in Frankreich." *Politische Vierteljahresschrift* 31: 79–96.

Hollingsworth, J. Rogers, and Robert Boyer. 1997. *Contemporary Capitalism: The Embeddedness of Institutions*. Cambridge: Cambridge University Press.

Hollingsworth, J. Rogers, Philippe Schmitter, and Wolfgang Streeck, eds. 1994. *Governing Capitalist Economies*. New York: Oxford University Press.

Hooghe, Liesbet, ed. 1996a. *Cohesion Policy and European Integration: Building Multi-Level Governance*. Oxford: Oxford University Press.

1996b. "Building A Europe with the Regions: The Changing Role of the European Commission." In *Cohesion Policy and European Integration: Building Multi-Level Governance*, ed. Liesbet Hooghe. Oxford: Oxford University Press.

1997. "Serving 'Europe.' Political Orientations of Senior Commission Officials." Paper prepared for the Workshop of European Consortium of Political Research, Bern, February 4.

Hoover, Kenneth, and Raymond Plant. 1988. *Conservative Capitalism*. London: Routledge.

Horsefield, John. 1969. *The International Monetary Fund, 1945–1965*. Washington, D.C.: International Monetary Fund.

Hout, Mike, Clem Brooks, and Jeff Manza. 1993. "The Persistence of Classes in Postindustrial Societies." *International Sociology* 3: 259–278.

Howell, Chris. 1992. "The Contradictions of French Industrial Relations Reform." *Comparative Politics* (January).

——— 1992. *Regulating Labor*. Princeton, N.J.: Princeton University Press.

Huber, Evelyne, Charles Ragin, and John D. Stephens. 1993. "Social Democracy, Christian Democracy, Constitutional Structure and the Welfare State." *American Journal of Sociology* 99 (3): 711–749.

Huber, Evelyne, and John D. Stephens. 1993a. "Political Parties and Public Pensions: A Quantitative Analysis." *Acta-Sociologica* 36: 309–325.

——— 1993b. "The Swedish Welfare State at the Crossroads." *Current Sweden* 394: 1–4.

——— 1996a. "Internationalization and the Social Democratic Welfare State: Crisis and Future Prospects." Paper prepared for the Tenth Conference of Europeanists, Chicago, March 14–17.

——— 1996b. "Political Power and Gender in the Making of the Social Democratic Service State." Paper presented at the annual meeting of the American Political Science Association, San Francisco, August 28–September 1.

——— 1998. "Internationalization and the Social Model." *Comparative Political Studies* (June).

Humphries, Jane, and Jill Rubery. 1988. "British Women in a Changing Work Place, 1979–1985." In *Feminiization of the Labor Force: Paradoxes and Promises*, ed. Jane Jenson, Elisabeth Hagen, and Ceallaigh Reddy. New York: Oxford University Press.

Husbands, Christopher. 1992a. "Belgium: Flemish Legions on the March." In *The Extreme Right in Europe and the USA*, ed. Peter Hainsworth. London: Pinter Publishers.

——— 1992b. "The Netherlands: Irritants on the Body Politic." In *The Extreme Right in Europe and the USA*, ed. Peter Hainsworth. London: Pinter Publishers.

Hyman, Richard. 1994. "Industrial Relations in Western Europe: An Era of Ambiguity?" *Industrial Relations* 33 (1): 1–24.

Ignazi, Piero. 1989. "Un nouvel acteur politique." In *Le Front national à découvert*, under the direction of Nonna Mayer and Pascal Perrineau.

——— 1992. "The Silent Counter-revolution." *European Journal of Political Research* 22: 1–30.

Immergut, Ellen. 1992. *Health Politics*. Cambridge: Cambridge University Press.

Income Data Services. 1996. *Industrial Relations and Collective Bargaining*. London: Institute of Personnel and Development.

Ingerslev, Olaf, and Lisbeth Pedersen. 1996. *Marginalisering, 1990–1994*. Copenhagen: Socialforsknings Instituttet.

Inglehart, Ronald. 1977. *The Silent Revolution: Changing Values and Political Styles among Western Publics*. Princeton, N.J.: Princeton University Press.

——— 1990a. "Values, Ideology, and Cognitive Mobilization in New Social Movements." In *Challenging the Political Order*, ed. Russel Dalton and Manfred Kuechler. Oxford: Polity Press.

——— 1990b. *Culture Shifts in Advanced Society*. Princeton, N.J.: Princeton University Press.

International Monetary Fund [IMF]. Various years. *Annual Report on Exchange Ar-*

rangements and Exchange Restrictions. Washington, D.C.: International Monetary Fund.

Various issues. *Balance of Payments Statistics Yearbook*. Washington D.C.: International Monetary Fund.

Various years. *International Financial Statistics Yearbook*. Washington D.C.: International Monetary Fund.

1995. *Private Market Financing for Developing Countries*. Washington, D.C.: International Monetary Fund.

Iversen, T. 1995. "Contested Economic Institutions: The Politics of Macro-Economics and Wage-Bargaining in Organized Capitalism." Political Science Department, Duke University. Mimeographed.

1998. "Power, Flexibility and the Breakdown of Centralized Wage Bargaining." *Comparative Politics* 28: 399–436.

Iversen, T., and Anne Wren. 1997. "Equality, Employment and Budgetary Restraint: The Trilemma of the Service Economy." Center for European Studies, Harvard University. Mimeographed.

Jachtenfuchs, Markus, and Beate Kohler-Koch. 1995. "Regieren im dynamischen Mehrebenensystem." In *Europäische Integration*, ed. Markus Jachtenfuchs and Beate Kohler-Koch. Opladen: Leske + Budrich.

Jacobs, Brian. 1993. *Fractured Cities*. London: Routledge.

Jeffrey, Charlie. 1996. "Conclusions: Sub-National Authorities and European Domestic Policy." *Regional and Federal Studies* 6 (2): 204–219.

Jencks, Christopher, and Paul E. Peterson, eds. 1992. *The Urban Underclass*. Washington, D.C.: Brookings Institution.

Jenson, Jane, Elisabeth Hagen, and Ceallaigh Reddy, eds. 1988. *Feminization of the Labor Force: Paradoxes and Promises*. New York: Oxford University Press.

Jenson, Jane, and Rianne Mahon. 1993. "Representing Solidarity: Class, Gender and the Crisis in Social Democratic Sweden." *New Left Review* 201: 76–100.

Jeon, Bang Nam, and George M. von Furstenberg. 1990. "Growing International Co-Movement in Stock Price Indexes." *Quarterly Review of Economics and Business* 30 (3): 15–30.

Johnson, Harry G. 1974. "The Case for Flexible Exchange Rates, 1969." In *International Trade and Finance*, ed. Robert E. Baldwin and J. David Richardson. Boston: Little, Brown.

Jordan, Grant, and Nigel Ashford, eds. 1993. *Public Policy and the Impact of the New Right*. London: Pinter Publishers.

Kalleberg, Arne L., and Tom Cølbjornsen. 1990. "Unions and the Structure of Earnings Inequality: Cross-National Patterns." *Social Science Research* 19: 348–371.

Kalyvas, Stathis N. 1996. *The Rise of Christian Democracy in Europe*. Ithaca, N.Y.: Cornell University Press.

Kane, Edward J. 1987. "Competitive Financial Regulation: An International Perspective." In *Threats to Financial Stability*, ed. R. Protes and A. Swoboda. Cambridge: Cambridge University Press.

Kangas, Olli. 1991. *The Politics of Social Rights*. Stockholm: Swedish Institute for Social Research.

Kareken, John, and Neil Wallace. 1977. "Portfolio Autarky: A Welfare Analysis." *Journal of International Economics* 7: 19–43.

Karlsson, Gunnel. 1996. *Från Broderskap till Systerskap. Det Socialdemokratiska kvinnoförbundets kamp för inflytande och makt i SAP*. Lund: Arkiv Förlag.

Kasman, Bruce, and Charles Pigott. 1988. "Interest Rate Divergences among the Major Industrial Nations." *Federal Reserve Bank of New York Quarterly Review* 13 (3): 28–44.

Katz, Harry. 1993. "The Decentralization of Collective Bargaining: A Literature Review and Comparative Analysis." *Industrial and Labor Relations Review* 47 (1): 3–22.

Katzenstein, Peter J., ed. 1978. *Between Power and Plenty*. Madison: University of Wisconsin Press.

———. 1984. *Corporatism and Change: Austria, Switzerland, and the Politics of Industry*. Ithaca, N.Y.: Cornell University Press.

———. 1985. *Small States in World Markets: Industrial Policy in Europe*. Ithaca, N.Y.: Cornell University Press.

———. 1987. *Policy and Politics in West Germany*. Philadelphia: Temple University Press.

———, ed. 1989. *Industry and Politics in West Germany*. Ithaca, N.Y.: Cornell University Press.

Kaufman, Franz-Xaver. 1989. *Religion und Modernität: Sozialwissenschaftliche Perspektiven*, Tübingen: J.C.B. Mohr Paul Siebeck.

Keech, William R. 1995. *Economic Politics: The Costs of Democracy*. Cambridge: Cambridge University Press.

Kenen, Peter B. 1985. "Macroeconomic Theory and Policy: How the Closed Economy was Opened." In *Handbook of International Economics*, ed. Ronald Jones and Peter Kenen. Amsterdam: North Holland.

Keohane, Robert, and Helen Milner. 1996. *Internationalization and Domestic Politics*. Cambridge: Cambridge University Press.

Kerbo, Harold R. 1982. "Movements of 'Crisis' and Movements of 'Affluence.'" *Journal of Conflict Resolution* 26: 645–663.

Kern, Horst, and Michael Schumann. 1984. *Das Ende der Arbeitsteilung?* Munich: C. H. Beck.

Kesselman, Mark, and Joel Krieger, eds. 1986. *European Politics in Transition*. New York: Heath.

Kim, Heung Sik. 1990. "Toward Building a Theoretical Model of Welfare Policy Development." Ph.D. dissertation, Northwestern University.

King, Desmond. 1987. *The New Right: Politics, Markets and Citizenship*. Chicago: Dorsey.

———. 1995. *Actively Seeking Work? The Politics of Unemployment and Welfare Policy in the United States and Britain*. Chicago: University of Chicago Press.

———. 1996. "Sectionalism and Policy Formation in the United States: President Carter's Welfare Initiatives." *British Journal of Political Science* 26: 337–367.

King, Mervyn A. 1994. "Debt Deflation: Theory and Evidence." *European Economic Review* 38: 419–445.

King, Mervyn A., and Sushil Wadhwani. 1990. "Transmission of Volatility between Stock Markets." *Review of Financial Studies* 3 (1): 5–33.

Kingdon, John. 1984. *Agendas, Alternatives and Public Policies*. Boston: Little, Brown.

Kircheimer, Otto. 1957. "The Waning of Opposition in Parliamentary Regimes." *Social Research* 24: 127–156.

Kitschelt, Herbert. 1989. "The Internal Politics of Parties. The Law of Curvilinear Disparity Revisited." *Political Studies* 37 (3): 400–421.

1990. "New Social Movements and the Decline of Party Organization." In *Challenging the Political Order*, ed. Russell Dalton and Manfred Kuechler. Oxford: Polity Press.

1991a. "Industrial Governance, Innovation Strategies, and the Case of Japan: Sectoral or Cross-national Analysis?" *International Organisation*.

1991b. "The 1990 German Federal Election and the National Unification." *West European Politics* 14 (4): 121–148.

1992. "The Formation of Party Systems in East Central Europe." *Politics and Society* 20: 7–50.

1993. "Class Structure and Social Democratic Party Strategy." *British Journal of Political Science* 23 (3): 299–337.

1994a. *The Transformation of European Social Democracy*. Cambridge: Cambridge University Press.

1994b. "Austrian and Swedish Social Democrats in Crisis: Party Strategy and Organization in Corporatist Regimes." *Comparative Political Studies* 27 (1): 3–39.

Kitschelt, Herbert, In collaboration with Anthony J. McGann. 1995. *The Radical Right in Western Europe: A Comparative Analysis*. Ann Arbor: University of Michigan Press.

1996 "Defense of the Status Quo as Equilibrium Strategy? New Dilemmas for European Social Democracy." Paper prepared for presentation at the annual meeting of the American Political Science Association, San Francisco, August 28–September 1.

Kjellberg, Anders. 1992. "Sweden: Can the Model Survive?" In *Industrial Relations in the New Europe*, ed. Anthony Ferner and Richard Hyman. Oxford: Basil Blackwell.

Knetter, Michael. 1989. "Price Discrimination by US and German Exporters." *American Economic Review* 79 (1): 198–210.

Knight, Jack. 1992. *Institutions and Social Conflict*. Cambridge: Cambridge University Press.

Knutsen, Oddbjorn. 1995. "Value Orientations, Political Conflicts and Left-Right Identification: A Comparative Study." *European Journal of Political Research* 28 (1): 63–93.

Kohl, Jürgen. 1981. "Trends and Problems in Postwar Public Expenditure Development in Western Europe and North America." In *The Development of Welfare States in Europe and America*, ed. Peter Flora and Arnold J. Heidenheimer. New Brunswick, N.J.: Transaction Books.

Kohler-Koch, Beate. 1994. "Changing Patterns of Interest Intermediation in the European Union." *Government and Opposition* 29 (2): 166–180.

Kolinsky, Eva. 1992. "A Future for Right Extremism in Germany?" In *The Extreme Right in Europe and the USA*, ed. Paul Hainsworth. London: Pinter Publishers.

1993. "Party Change and Women's Representation in Unified Germany." In *Gender and Party Politics*, ed. Joni Lovenduski and Pippa Norris. London: Sage Publications.

Koopmans, Ruud. 1996a. "Asyl: Die Karriere eines politischen Konflikts." In *Kommunikation und Entscheidung*, ed. Wolfgang van den Daele und Friedhelm Neidhardt. *WZB-Jahrbuch*. Berlin: edition sigma.

1996b. "Explaining the Rise of Racist and Extreme Right Violence in Western Europe: Grievances or Opportunities?" *European Journal of Political Research* 30: 185–216.

Koopmans, Ruud, and Dieter Rucht. 1996. "Rechtsradikalismus als soziale Bewegung?" In *Rechtsextremismus: Ergebnisse und Perspektiven der Forschung*, ed. Jürgen Falter et al. Opladen: Westdeutscher Verlag.

1995. "The Dynamics of Protest Waves." In *The Politics of New Social Movements in Western Europe: A Comparative Analysis*, ed. Hanspeter Kriesi et al. Minneapolis: University of Minnesota Press.

Korpi, Walter. 1983. *The Democratic Class Struggle*. London: Routledge & Kegan Paul.

1993. "Politik och Valjare bakom Valutgangen 1991." *Sociologisk Forskning* 1: 3–28.

Korpi, Walter, and Joakim Palme. 1994. "The Strategy of Equality and the Paradox of Redistribution." Paper presented at the International Sociological Association Meetings, Bielefeld, Germany, July 18–23.

Kriesi, Hanspeter. 1987. "Neue soziale Bewegungen: Auf der Suche nach ihrem gemeinsamen Nenner." *Politische Vierteljahresschrift* 28: 315–334.

1989. "New Social Movements and the New Class in the Netherlands." *American Journal of Sociology* 94: 1078–1116.

1993. *Political Mobilization and Social Change: Levels of Mobilization and Mobilization Potentials in the Dutch General Public*. Aldershot: Avebury.

1995. "Alliance Structures." In *The Politics of New Social Movements in Western Europe: A Comparative Analysis*, ed. Hanspeter Kriesi et al. Minneapolis: University of Minnesota Press.

Kriesi, Hanspeter, and Jan-Willem Duyvendak. 1995. "National Cleavage Structures." In *The Politics of New Social Movements in Western Europe: A Comparative Analysis*, ed. Hanspeter Kriesi et al. Minneapolis: University of Minnesota Press.

Kriesi, Hanspeter, Ruud Koopmans, Jan-Willem Duyvendak, and Marco G. Giugni. 1992. "New Social Movements and Political Opportunities in Western Europe." *European Journal of Political Research* 22: 219–244.

1995. *The Politics of New Social Movements in Western Europe: A Comparative Analysis*. Minneapolis: University of Minnesota Press.

Kriesi, Hanspeter, and Philip van Praag Jr. 1987. "Old and New Politics: The Dutch Peace Movement and the Traditional Political Organizations." *European Journal of Political Science* 15: 319–346.

Kurth, James R. 1979. "The Political Economy of the Product Cycle: Industrial History and Political Outcomes." *International Organization* 33 (1): 1–34.

Kurz, Karin, and Walter Müller. 1987. "Class Mobility in the Industrial World." *Annual Review of Sociology* 13: 417–442.

Kurzer, Paulette. 1993. *Business and Banking: Political Change and Economic Integration in Western Europe*. Ithaca, N.Y.: Cornell University Press.

Kuttner, Robert. 1983. "The Declining Middle." *Atlantic Monthly* (July): 60–72.

Ladrech, Robert. 1993. "Social Democratic Parties and E.C. Integration." *European Journal of Political Research* 24 (2): 195–210.

Lamfalussy, Alexandre. 1981. "Changing Attitudes towards Capital Movements." In *Changing Perceptions of Economic Policy*, ed. Frances Cairncross. London: Methuen.

Lane, Jan-Erik, and Svante O. Ersson. 1991. *Politics and Society in Western Europe*. London: Sage Publications.

Lange, Peter. 1984. "Unions, Workers and Wage Regulation: The Rational Bases of Consent." In *Order and Conflict in Contemporary Capitalism*, ed. John Goldthorpe. Oxford: Clarendon Press.

———. 1993. "Maastricht and the Social Protocol: Why Did They Do It?" *Politics and Society* 21: 5–36.

———. 1996. "The End of Corporatism? Wage Setting in the Nordic and Germanic Countries." In *Work and Society*, ed. Sanford Jacoby. New York: Oxford University Press.

Lange, Peter, and Geoffrey Garrett. 1985. "The Politics of Growth: Strategic Interaction and Economic Performance in the Advanced Industrial Democracies, 1974–1980." *Journal of Politics* 47 (3): 792–827.

Lange, Peter, George Ross, and Maurizio Vennicelli. 1982. *Unions, Change, and Crisis: French and Italian Union Strategy and the Political Economy, 1945–1980*. London: Allen and Unwin.

Lange, Peter, and Lyle Scruggs. 1996. "A Crisis of Unionism? Developments of Trade Union Power in the 1980's in Postwar Perspective." Paper presented at the annual meeting of the American Political Science Association, San Francisco, August 28–September 1.

Lange, Peter, Michael Wallerstein, and Miriam Golden. 1995. "The End of Corporatism? Wage Setting in the Nordic and Germanic Countries." In *Workers of Nations: Industrial Relations in a Global Economy*, ed. Sanford Jacoby. Oxford: Oxford University Press.

Langhammer, Rolf J., and Andre Sapir. 1987. *Economic Impact of Generalized Tariff Preferences*. London: Trade Policy Research Centre.

Lauber, Volkmar. 1992. "Changing Priorities in Austrian Economic Policy." *West European Politics* 1: 147–172.

Lawrence, Robert Z., and Matthew J. Slaughter. 1993. "International Trade and American Wages in the 1980s: Giant Sucking Sound or Small Hiccup?" *Brookings Papers on Economic Activity – Microeconomics* 2: 161–210.

Layard, Richard, Stephen Nickell, and Richard Jackman. 1991. *Unemployment, Macro-Economic Performance and the Labour Market*. Oxford: Oxford University Press.

Lazonick, William. 1991. *Business Organization and the Myth of the Market Economy*. Cambridge: Cambridge University Press.

League of Nations. 1938. *Report on Exchange Controls*. Geneva: League of Nations, Committee on Exchange Controls.

Leamer, Edward E. 1988. "Measures of Openness." In *Trade Policy Issues and Em-*

pirical Analysis, ed. Robert E. Baldwin. Chicago: University of Chicago Press; Cambridge, Mass.: National Bureau of Economic Research.

1992. "Wage Effects of a US-Mexican Free Trade Agreement." National Bureau of Economic Research working paper no. 3991. Cambridge, Mass.

Lehmbruch, Gerhard, and Philippe Schmitter, eds. 1982. *Patterns of Corporatist Policy-Making*. Beverly Hills, Calif.: Sage Publications.

Lehrer, M. 1996. "The German Model of Industrial Strategy in Turbulence: Corporate Governance and Managerial Hierarchies in Lufthansa." Berlin, Wissenschaftszentrum Berlin für Sozialforschung.

Leibfried, Stephan, and Paul Pierson. 1995. "Semi-Sovereign Welfare States: Social Policy in a Multi-Tiered Europe." In *Fragmented Social Policy: The European Union's Social Dimension in Comparative Perspective*, ed. Stephan Leibfried and Paul Pierson. Washington, D.C.: Brookings Institution.

1996. "Social Policy." In *Policy Making in the European Union*, ed. Helen Wallace and William Wallace, 185–208. Oxford: Oxford University Press.

Lemmen, Jan, and Sylvester Eijffinger. 1995. "The Fundamental Determinants of Financial Integration in the European Union." No. 95117. Center for Economic Research.

Leonardi, Robert, and Douglas A. Wertman. 1989. *Italian Christian Democracy: The Politics of Dominance*. Houndmills: Macmillan.

Lepsius, Rainer M. 1966. "Extremer Nationalismus. Strukturbedingungen vor der nationalsozialistischen Machtergreifung." In *Veröffentlichungen der Wirtschaftshochschule Mannheim*, vol. 15. Stuttgart: Kohlhammer.

Levich, Richard. 1987. "Macroeconomic Determinants of Capital Flight." In *Capital Flight and Third World Debt*, ed. Donald R. Kessard and John Williamson. Washington, D.C.: Institute for International Economics.

Levy, Frank. 1988. *Dollars and Dreams: The Changing American Income Distribution*. New York: W. W. Norton.

Levy, Frank, and Richard Murnane. 1992. "U.S. Earnings Levels and Earnings Inequality: A Review of Recent Trends and Proposed Explanations." *Journal of Economic Literature* 30: 1333–1381.

Levy, Jonah. 1994. "Tocqueville's Revenge: Dilemmas of Institution-Building in Post-Dirigiste France." Ph.D. dissertation, Massachusetts Institute of Technology.

Lewis, Jane, and Gertrude Aström. 1992. "Equality, Difference, and State Welfare: Labor Market and Family Policies in Sweden." *Feminist Studies* 1: 59–87.

Lewis-Beck, Michael. 1988. *Economics and Elections: The Major Western Democracies*. Ann Arbor: University of Michigan Press.

Lijphart, Arend. 1974. "The Netherlands: Continuity and Change in Voting Behavior." In *Electoral Behavior: A Comparative Handbook*, ed. Richard Rose. New York: Free Press.

1984. *Democracies: Patterns of Majoritarian and Consensus Government in Twenty-One Countries*. New Haven, Conn.: Yale University Press.

Lindbeck, Assar. 1974. *Swedish Economic Policy*. Berkeley: University of California Press.

ed., 1994. *Turning Sweden Round*. Cambridge, Mass.: MIT Press.

Lindbeck, Assar, and Dennis J. Snower. 1988. *The Insider-Outsider Theory of Employment and Unemployment*. Cambridge, Mass.: MIT Press.

Lindberg, Leon N., and Charles S. Maier, eds. 1985. *The Politics of Inflation and Economic Stagnation: Theoretical Approaches and International Case Studies*. Washington, D.C.: Brookings Institution.

Lindenius, Christina. 1990. "Exchange Deregulation – Short and Long Run Effects." *Sveriges Riksbank, Quarterly Review*.

Linz, Juan J. 1967. "Cleavage and Consensus in West German Politics: The Early Fifties." In *Party Systems and Voter Alignments: Cross-National Perspectives*, ed. Seymour Martin Lipset and Stein Rokkan. New York: Free Press.

Lipietz, Alain. 1987. *Mirages and Miracles: The Crisis of Global Fordism*. London: Verso.

Lipset, Seymour Martin, and Robert Bendix. 1959. *Social Mobility in Industrial Societies*. Berkeley: University of California Press.

Lipset, Seymour Martin. 1960. *Political Man*. New York: Doubleday Anchor.

——— 1964a. "The Changing Class Structure and Contemporary European Politics." In *A New Europe?*, ed. Stephen Graubard. Boston: Beacon Press.

——— 1964b. "The Changing Class Structure and Contemporary European Politics." *Daedalus* 93 (1).

——— 1981 [1961]. *Political Man*. Enl. ed. Baltimore: Johns Hopkins University Press.

——— 1991. "No Third Way: A Comparative Perspective on the Left." In *The Crisis of Leninism and the Decline of the Left*, ed. Daniel Chirot. Seattle: University of Washington Press.

Lipset, Seymour Martin, and E. Raab. 1978. *The Politics of Unreason: Right-Wing Extremism in America, 1790–1977*. 2nd ed. Chicago: University of Chicago Press.

Lipset, Seymour Martin, and Stein Rokkan. 1967a. *Party Systems and Voter Alignments: Cross-National Perspectives*. New York: Free Press.

——— 1967b. "Cleavage Structures, Party Systems and Voter Alignments: An Introduction." In *Party Systems and Voter Alignments: Cross-National Perspectives*, ed. Seymour Martin Lipset and Stein Rokkan. New York: Free Press.

Lister, Ruth. 1991. "Social Security in the 1980's." *Social Policy and Administration* 25 (2): 91–107.

Ljungqvist, Lars, and Thomas J. Sargent. 1995. "The European Unemployment Dilemma." Unpublished manuscript, Federal Reserve Bank of Chicago and the University of Chicago.

LO-Bladet. 1992. Landsorganisationen (LO). Copenhagen.

Locke, Richard M. 1995. *Remaking the Italian Economy*. Ithaca, N.Y.: Cornell University Press.

Locke, Richard M., and Kathleen Thelen. 1995. "Apples and Oranges Revisited: Contextualized Comparisons and the Study of Comparative Labor Politics." *Politics and Society* 23: 337–367.

Loesche, Peter, and Franz Walter. 1992. *Die SPD: Klassenpartei, Volkspartei, Quotenpartei*. Darmstedt: Wissenschaftliche Buchgesellschaft.

Longstreth, Fred H. 1988. "From Corporatism to Dualism? Thatcherism and the Climacteric of British Trade Unions in the 1980s." *Political Studies* 36: 413–432.

Lovenduski, Joni, and Pippa Norris. 1994. "Labour and the Unions. After the Brighton Conference." *Government and Opposition* 29: 201–217.

Lucardie, Paul, and Hans-Martien ten Napel. 1994. "Between Confessionalism and Liberal Conservatism: The Christian Democratic Parties of Belgium and the Netherlands." In *Christian Democracy in Europe: A Comparative Perspective*, ed. David Hanley. London: Pinter Publishers.

Lucas, Robert E. 1990. "Why Doesn't Capital Flow from Rich to Poor Countries." *American Economic Review* 80: 92–96.

Ludlow, Peter. 1992. *The Making of the European Monetary System*. London: Butterworth.

Lutz, S. 1993. *Die Steuerung industrieller Forschungskooperation*. Frankfurt am Main: Campus.

Machin, Howard, and Vincent Wright, eds. 1985. *Economic Policy and Policy-Making under the Mitterrand Presidency*. London: Pinter Publishers.

Machin, Stephen, and Alan Manning. 1994. "The Effect of Minimum Wages on Wage on Wage Dispersion and Employment: Evidence from the UK Wages Councils." *Industrial and Labor Relations Review* 47: 319–329.

Machlup, Fritz, Walster S. Salant, and Lorie Tarshis, eds. 1972. *International Mobility and Movement of Capital; A Conference of the Universities – National Bureau Committee for Economic Research*. New York: National Bureau of Economic Research.

MacInnes, John. 1987. *Thatcherism at Work*. Milton Keynes: Open University Press.

Mackie, Thomas T., and Mark N. Franklin. 1992. "Electoral Change and Social Change." In *Electoral Change: Responses to Evolving Social and Attitudinal Structures in Western Countries*, ed. Mark N. Franklin, Thomas T. Mackie, and Henry Valen. Cambridge: Cambridge University Press.

Mackie, Thomas T., and Richard Rose. 1991. *The International Almanac of Electoral History*. Houndmills: Macmillan.

MacKuen, Michael B., Robert S. Erikson, and James A. Stimson. 1992. "Peasants or Bankers? The American Electorate and the U.S. Economy." *American Political Science Review* 86 (3): 597–611.

Magee, Stephen P. 1980. "Three Simple Tests of the Stolper-Samuelson Theorem." In *Issues in International Economics*, ed. Peter Oppenheimer. London: Oriel Press.

Magee, Stephen P, William A. Brock, and Leslie Young. 1989. *Black Hole Tariffs and Endogenous Policy Theory: Political Economy in General Equilibrium*. Cambridge: Cambridge University Press.

Mahon, Rianne. 1995. "Swedish Unions in New Times: Women Workers as the Basis for Renewal?" Paper presented at the annual meeting of the American Political Science Association, Chicago.

Mair, Peter. 1993. "Myths of Electoral Change and the Survival of Traditional Parties." *European Journal of Political Research* 24 (2): 121–133.

Majone, Giandomenico. 1994. "The Rise of the Regulatory State in Europe." *West European Politics* 17 (3): 77–101.

_____. 1995. "The Development of Social Regulation in the European Community: Policy Externalities, Transaction Costs, Motivational Factors." Unpublished manuscript.

Malinvaud, Edmond. 1980. *Profitability and Unemployment*. Cambridge: Cambridge University Press.

Mannheimer, Renato. 1993. "L'elettorato della Lega Nord." *Polis* 7 (2): 253–274.

Mannheimer, Renato, and Giacomo Sani. 1987. *Il mercato elettorale.* Bologna: Il Mulino.

Mares, Isabela. Forthcoming. "Is Unemployment Insurable? Employers and the Institutionalization of the Risk of Unemployment." *Journal of Public Policy.*

Marglin, Stephen, and Juliet Schor, eds. 1990. *The Golden Age of Capitalism.* New York: Oxford University Press.

Marin, B. 1983. "Organising Interests by Interest Organisation." *International Political Science Review* 4: 197–216.

Marklund, Steffan. 1988. *Paradise Lost?* Lund: Arkiv.

Marks, Gary. 1986. "Neocorporatism and Incomes Policy in Western Europe and North America." *Comparative Politics* 17 (3): 253–277.

———. 1993. "Structural Policy and Multilevel Governance in the E.C." In *The State of the European Community,* vol. 2, *The Maastricht Debates and Beyond,* ed. Alan Cafruny and Glenda Rosenthal. Boulder, Colo.: Lynne Rienner.

———. 1996. "Exploring and Explaining Variation in E.U. Cohesion Policy." In *Cohesion Policy and European Integration: Building Multi-Level Governance,* ed. Liesbet Hooghe. Oxford: Oxford University Press.

Marks, Gary, Liesbet Hooghe, Kermit Blank. 1996. "European Integration since the 1980s: State-centric Versus Multi-Level Governance." *Journal of Common Market Studies* 34 (3): 343–378.

Marks, Gary, and Doug McAdam. 1996. "Social Movements and the Changing Structure of Opportunity in the European Union." *West European Politics* 19 (2): 249–278.

Marks, Gary, Jane Salk, Leonard Ray, François Nielsen. 1996. "Competencies, Cracks and Conflicts: Regional Mobilization in the European Union." *Comparative Political Studies* 29 (2): 164–192.

Marmor, Theodore R., Jerry L. Mashaw, and Philip L. Harvey. 1990. *America's Misunderstood Welfare State.* New York: Basic Books.

Marsh, David. 1992. *The New Politics of British Trade Unionism: Union Power and the Thatcher Legacy.* Ithaca, N.Y.: ILR Press.

Marsh, David, and R. A. W. Rhodes, eds. 1992. *Implementing Thatcherite Policies: Audit of an Era.* Milton Keynes: Open University Press.

Marsh, John, and Johan Olsen. 1989. *Rediscovering Institutions: The Institutional Basis of Politics.* New York: Free Press.

Martin, Andrew. 1979. "The Dynamics of Change in a Keynesian Political Economy: The Swedish Case and Its Implications." In *State and Economy in Contemporary Capitalism,* ed. Colin Crouch. London: Croom Helm.

———. 1996. "Macroeconomic Policy, Politics and the Demise of Central Wage Negotiations in Sweden." Working Paper no. 63. Harvard University, Center for European Studies. Cambridge, Mass.

Martin, Cathie Jo. 1994. "Business and the New Economic Activism: The Growth of Corporate Lobbies in the Sixties." *Polity* 27 (1): 49–76.

Martin, David. 1978. *A General Theory of Secularization.* Oxford: Basil Blackwell.

Mathieson, Donald J., and Liliana Rojas-Suarez. 1994. "Capital Controls and Capital Account Liberalization in Industrial Countries." In *Capital Mobility:*

The Impact on Consumption, Investment, and Growth, ed. Leonardo Leiderman and Assaf Razin. Cambridge: Cambridge University Press.

Matzner, Egon, and Wolfgang Streeck, eds. 1991. *Beyond Keynesianism*. London: Edward Elgar.

Maurau, Guy. 1993. "Regulation, Deregulation and Labor Market Dynamics." In *Employment Security and Labor Market Dynamics*, ed. Christoph F. Buechtemann. Ithaca, N.Y.: ILR Press.

Maurice, Marc, et al. 1986. *The Social Foundations of Industrial Power*. Cambridge, Mass.: MIT Press.

Maxfield, Sylvia. 1997. *Gatekeepers of Growth: The International Political Economy of Central Banking in Developing Countries*. Princeton, N.J.: Princeton University Press.

Maxfield, Sylvia, and James H. Nolt. 1990. "Protectionism and the Internationalization of Capital: US Sponsorship of Import Substitution Industrialization in the Philippines, Turkey and Argentina." *International Studies Quarterly* 34: 49–82.

Mayer, Karl Ulrich. 1993. "Changes in European Life Courses and Their Social, Political and Economic Determinants." Paper presented at the European Science Foundation Conference, Schloss Ringberg.

Mayer, Karl Ulrich, and Glenn R. Carroll. 1987. "Jobs and Classes: Structural Constraints on Career Mobility." *European Sociological Review* 3 (1): 14–38.

Mayer, Karl Ulrich, and Walter Müller. 1986. "The State and the Structure of the Life Course." In *Human Development and the Life Course: Multidisciplinary Perspectives*, ed. Aage B. Sorensen, Franz E. Weinert, and Lonnie Sherrod. Hillside, N.J.: L. Erlbaum Associates.

Mayer, Nonna, and Pascal Perrineau. 1989. "Conclusion. L'introuvable équation Le Pen." In *Le Front national à découvert*, under the direction of Nonna Mayer and Pascal Perrineau.

Mazey, Sonia, and Jeremy Richardson. eds. 1993a. *Lobbying in the European Community*. Oxford: Oxford University Press.

——— 1993b. "E.C. Policy Making: An Emerging European Policy Style?" In *European Integration and Environmental Policy*, ed. Duncan Liefferink and Philip Lowe. Scarborough, Ontario: Belhaven Press.

McAdam, Doug. 1982. *Political Process and the Development of Black Insurgency, 1930–1970*. Chicago: University of Chicago Press.

McGann, Anthony J., and Herbert Kitschelt. 1995. "Electoral Trade-Offs and Strategic Choices of Social Democratic Parties in the 1990s." Paper prepared for the annual meeting of the American Political Science Association, Chicago, August 31–September 3.

McGowan, Lee, and Stephen Wilks. 1995. "The First Supranational Policy in the European Union: Competition Policy." *European Journal of Political Research* 28: 141–169.

McKenzie, Richard B., and Dwight R. Lee. 1991. *Quicksilver Capital: How the Rapid Movement of Wealth Has Changed the World*. New York: Free Press.

McKeown, Timothy. 1991. "A Liberal Trade Order: The Long-Run Pattern of Imports to the Advanced Capitalist States." *International Studies Quarterly* 35 (2): 151–172.

McLaughlin, Andrew, and Justin Greenwood. 1995. "The Management of Interest

Representation in the European Union." *Journal of Common Market Studies* 33 (1): 143–156.

Mead, Laurence M. 1983. "Religion and the Welfare State." In *Comparative Social Research*, vol. 6, *The Welfare State, 1883–1983*, ed. Richard F. Tomasson. Greenwich, Conn.: JAI Press.

——— 1992. *The New Politics of Poverty*. New York: Basic Books.

Melucci, Alberto. 1989. *Nomads of the Present*. Philadelphia: Temple University Press.

Merkel, Wolfgang. 1993. *Ende der Sozialdemokratie?* Frankfurt: Campus Verlag.

Meunier-Aitshalia, Sophie. 1993. "Harmonization Policy in the European Community: A Reassessment in the Maastricht Era." Paper presented at the annual meeting of the American Political Science Association, Washington, D.C., August 28–September 1.

Middentorp, Cees P. 1993. "Authoritarianism: Personality and Ideology. Their Political Relevance and Relationship the Left-Right Ideology in the Netherlands (1970–1985)." *European Journal of Political Research* 24 (2): 211–228.

Milgrom, P., and J. Roberts. 1992. *Economics, Organization and Management*. Englewood Cliffs, N.J.: Prentice-Hall.

——— 1995. "Complementarities: Strategy, Structure and Industrial Change in Manufacturing." *Journal of Accounting and Economics* 19 (2–3): 179–208.

Miliband, David, ed. 1994. *What Is Left?* Oxford: Polity Press.

Milner, Simon. 1995. "The Coverage of Collective Pay-Setting Institutions in Britain, 1895–1990." *British Journal of Industrial Relations* 33: 69–91.

Milward, Alan. 1992. *The European Rescue of the Nation-State*. Berkeley: University of California Press.

Mingione, Enzo. 1991. *Fragmented Societies*. Trans. Paul Goodrick. Oxford: Basil Blackwell.

Ministerie van Sociale Zaken en Werkgelegenheid. 1996. *De Nederlandse verzorgingsstaat in internationaal en economisch perspectief*. Den Haag: SDU.

Mitchell, Deborah. 1991. *Income Transfers in Ten Welfare States*. Brookfield: Avebury.

Mitra, Subrata. 1988. "The National Front in France – A Single Issue Movement?" *West European Politics* 11: 47–63.

Mitscherlich, Alexander. 1963. *Auf dem Weg zur vaterlosen Gesellschaft*. Munich: Piper.

Mjøset, Lars, ed. 1986. *Norden Dagen Derpå*. Oslo: Universitetsforlaget.

——— 1987. "Nordic Economic Policies in the 1970s and 1980s." *International Organization* 41 (3): 403–456.

——— 1996. *Nordic Economic Policies in the 1980s and 1990s*. Paper presented to the Tenth International Conference of Europeanists, Chicago, March 14–17.

Moene, Karl Ove, Ragnar Nymoen, and Michael Wallerstein. 1995. "The Persistence of Slack and Tight Labor Markets." Center for Urban Affairs and Policy Research Working Paper 95–7. Northwestern University, Evanston, Ill.

——— 1997. "Labor Market Friction and Unemployment." In *Making Solidarity Work? The Norwegian Labour Market Model in Transition*, ed. Jon Erik Dolvik and Arild H. Steen. Oslo: Scandinavian University Press.

Moene, Karl Ove, and Michael Wallerstein. 1993a. "The Decline of Social Democracy." In *The Economic Development of Denmark and Norway since 1879*, ed. Karl Gunnar Persson. Gloucester: Edward Elgar.

1993b. "What's Wrong with Social Democracy?" In *Market Socialism: The Current Debate*, ed. Pranab Bardhan and John Roemer. Oxford: Oxford University Press.

1995a. "How Social Democracy Worked: Labor Market Institutions." *Politics and Society* 23 (2): 185–211.

1995b. "Full Employment as a Worker Discipline Device." In *Property Rights, Incentives and Welfare*, ed. John Roemer. London: Macmillan.

1996. "Egalitarian Wage Policies and Economic Performance." Paper presented at the annual meeting of the American Political Science Association, San Francisco, August 28–September 1.

1997. "Wage Inequality, and Job Creation." *Journal of Labor Economics*.

Moene, Karl Ove, Michael Wallerstein, and Michael Hoel. 1993. "Bargaining Structure and Economic Performance." In *Trade Union Behavior, Pay Bargaining and Economic Performance*, ed. Robert Flanagan, Karl Ove Moene, and Michael Wallerstein. Oxford: Oxford University Press.

Moran, Theodore. 1973. "Foreign Expansion as an 'Institutional Necessity' for Corporate Capitalism: The Search for a Radical Model." *World Politics* 25: 369–386.

Moravcsik, Andrew. 1991. "Negotiating the Single European Act: National Interests and Conventional Statecraft in the European Community." *International Organization* 45: 651–688.

1993. "Preferences and Power in the European Community: A Liberal Intergovernmental Approach." *Journal of Common Market Studies* 31: 473–524.

1994. "Why the European Community Strengthens the State: Domestic Politics and International Cooperation." Paper presented at the annual meeting of the American Political Science Association, New York, August 28–September 1.

Moses, Jonathon W. 1984. "Abdication from National Policy Autonomy: What's Left to Leave?" *Politics and Society* 22 (2): 125–148.

Müller, Wolfgang, and Barbara Steiniger. 1994. "Christian Democracy in Austria: The Austrian People's Party." In *Christian Democracy in Europe: A Comparative Perspective*, ed. David Hanley. London: Pinter Publishers.

Muller-Rommel, Ferdinand. 1984. "Zum Verhältnis von neuen sozialen Bewegungen und neuen Konfliktdimensionen in den politischen Systemen Westeuropas: Eine empirische Analyse." *Journal für Sozialforschung* 24: 441–454.

1985. "New Social Movements and Smaller Parties: A Comparative Perspective," *West European Politics* 8: 41–54.

1989. *New Politics in Western Europe*. Boulder, Colo.: Westview Press.

1990. "New Political Movements and 'New Politics' Parties in Western Europe." In *Challenging the Political Order*, ed. Russell J. Dalton and Manfred Kuechler. Cambridge: Polity Press.

Mundell, Robert. 1960. "The Monetary Dynamics of International Adjustment under Fixed and Flexible Exchange Rates." *Quarterly Journal of Economics* 74 (2): 227–257.

1962. "The Appropriate Use of Monetary and Fiscal Policy under Fixed Exchange Rates." *IMF Staff Papers* 9: 70–77.

1963. "Capital Mobility and Stabilization Policy under Fixed and Flexible Exchange Rates." *Canadian Journal of Economics and Political Science* 29: 475–485.

1964. "Capital Mobility and Size." *Canadian Journal of Economics and Political Science* 30: 421–431.

1968. *International Economics.* New York: Macmillan.

Murphy, Dale D., and Kenneth A. Oye. 1994. "Interjurisdictional Harmonization and Divergence across Open Economies." Unpublished manuscript, MIT Center for International Studies, Cambridge, Mass.

Murphy, Kevin M., and Finis Welch. 1991. "The Role of International Trade in Wage Differentials." In *Workers and Their Wages,* ed. Marvin Kosters. Washington, D.C.: American Enterprise Institute.

1992. "The Structure of Wages." *Quarterly Journal of Economics* 107: 285–326.

Murphy, Robert G. 1984. "Capital Mobility and the Relationship between Savings and Investment in OECD Countries." *Journal of International Money and Finance* 3 (3): 327–342.

Myles, John. 1984. *Old Age and the Welfare State.* Boston: Little Brown.

Myles, John, and Adnan Turegun. 1994. "Comparative Studies of Class Structures." *Annual Review of Sociology* 20: 103–124.

Myrdal, Hans-Goran. 1991. "The Hard Way for a Centralized to a Decentralized Industrial Relations System: The Case of Sweden and SAF." In *Employers' Associations in Europe: Policy and Organization,* ed. Otto Jakobi and Dieter Sadowski. Baden-Baden: Nomos Verlag.

Nathan, Richard, and Fred C. Doolittle, eds. 1987. *Reagan and the States.* Princeton, N.J.: Princeton University Press.

Nedelmann, Brigitta. 1987. "Individuals and Parties – Changes in Processes of Political Mobilization." *European Sociological Review* 3: 181–202.

Neidhardt, Friedhelm, and Dieter Rucht. 1993. "Auf dem Weg in die 'Bewegungsgesellschaft'? Über die Stabilisierbarkeit sozialer Bewegungen." *Soziale Welt* 44: 305–326.

Nelson, R. R., ed. 1993. *National Innovation Systems: A Comparative Analysis.* New York: Oxford University Press.

Newell, James, and Martin J. Bull. 1996. "The Italian General Election of 1996: The Left on Top or on Tap?" *Parliamentary Affairs* 49 (4): 616–647.

Niedermayer, Oskar, and Richard Sinnott, eds. 1995. *Public Opinion and Internationalized Governance.* Oxford: Oxford University Press.

Noel, Alain. 1987. "Accumulation, Regulation and Social Change: An Essay on French Regulation Theory." *International Organization* 41 (2): 303–333.

Nørby Johansen, Lars. 1986. "Denmark." In *Growth to Limits: The Western European Welfare States since World War II,* vol. 1, ed. Peter Flora. Berlin: Walter de Gruyter.

Nordhaus, William. 1975. "The Political Business Cycle." *Review of Economic Studies* 42: 169–190.

Norris, Pippa, and Joni Lovenduski. 1993. "Gender and Party Politics in Britain." In *Gender and Party Politics,* ed. Joni Lovenduski and Pippa Norris. London: Sage Publications.

North, Douglass C. 1990 *Institutions, Institutional Change, and Economic Performance.* Cambridge: Cambridge University Press.

Notermans, Ton. 1993. "The Abdication from National Policy Autonomy: Why the Macroeconomic Policy Regime Has Become So Unfavorable to Labor." *Politics and Society* 21 (2): 133–168.

Nugent, Neill. 1994. *The Government and Politics of the European Union.* London: Macmillan.

O'Brien, Richard. 1992. *Global Financial Integration: The End of Geography.* London: Pinter Publishers.

Offe, Claus. 1984. *Contradictions of the Welfare State.* Cambridge, Mass.: MIT Press.

——— 1985. "New Social Movements: Challenging the Boundaries of Institutional Politics." *Social Research* 52: 817–868.

ÖGB Nachtrichten Dienst. 1994.

Olson, Mancur. 1982. *The Rise and Decline of Nations: Economic Growth, Stagflation and Social Rigidities.* New Haven, Conn.: Yale University Press.

Organization for Economic Cooperation and Development [OECD]. Various issues. *Balances of Payments of OECD Countries.* Paris: OECD.

——— 1977. *Towards Full Employment and Price Stability.* Paris: OECD.

——— 1990. *Health Care Systems in Transition.* Paris: OECD.

——— 1991. *Employment Outlook.* Paris: OECD.

——— 1992a. *Employment Outlook: Historical Statistics, 1960–1990.* Paris: OECD.

——— 1992b. *Employment Outlook.* Paris: OECD.

——— 1992c. *International Direct Investment: Policies and Trends in the 1980s.* Paris: OECD.

——— 1993a. *Employment Outlook.* Paris: OECD.

——— 1993b. *Economic Surveys, 1992–1993: Germany.* Paris: OECD.

——— 1994a. *Economic Surveys: Sweden.* Paris: OECD.

——— 1994b. *New Orientations for Social Policy.* Paris: OECD.

——— 1994c. *Economic Surveys, 1993–1994: Netherlands.* Paris: OECD.

——— 1994d. *Economic Outlook.* Paris: OECD.

——— 1995a. *Economic Surveys, 1993–1994: Netherlands.* Paris: OECD.

——— 1995b. *The OECD Jobs Study.* Paris: OECD.

——— 1996a. *Employment Outlook.* July 1996. Paris: OECD.

——— 1996b. *Economic Surveys, 1995–1996: Germany.* Paris: OECD.

——— 1996c. *Economic Surveys, 1995–1996: Italy.* Paris: OECD.

——— 1996d. *Employment Outlook.* December. Paris: OECD.

——— 1997. "Economic Performance and the Structure of Collective Bargaining." *Employment Outlook.* Paris: OECD.

——— Forthcoming. "Economic Performance and the Structure of Collective Bargaining." *Employment Outlook.*

Osler, Carol L. 1991. "Explaining the Absence of International Factor-price Convergence." *Journal of Money and Finance* 10: 89–107.

Ostrom, Elinor. 1990. *Governing the Commons.* Cambridge: Cambridge University Press.

ÖTV-Magazin. 1994.

Paci, Massimo. 1973. *Mercato del lavoro e classi sociali in Italia.* Bologna: Il Mulino.

Padgett, Stephen, and Tony Burkett. 1986. *Political Parties and Elections in West Germany: The Search for a New Stability.* London: Hurst.

Padoa, Fiorella, and Schioppa Kostoris. 1996. "Excesses and Limits of the Public Sector in the Italian Economy." In *The New Italian Republic: From the Fall of the Berlin Wall to Berlusconi*, ed. Stephen Gundle and Simon Parker. London: Routledge.

Paldam, Martin. 1981. "A Preliminary Survey of the Theories and Findings on Vote and Popularity Functions." *European Journal of Political Research* 9 (2): 181–199.

Palme, Joakim. 1990. *Pension Rights in Welfare Capitalism*. Stockholm: Swedish Institute for Social Research.

Palmer, John L., ed. 1986. *Perspectives on the Reagan Years*. Washington, D.C.: Urban Institute.

——— ed. 1988. *The Vulnerable*. Washington, D.C.: Urban Institute.

Palmer, John. L., and Isabel V. Sawhill, eds. 1984. *The Reagan Record*. Cambridge, Mass.: Ballinger Publishing.

Panitch, Leo. 1980. "Recent Theorizations of Corporatism: Reflections on a Growth Industry." *British Journal of Sociology*.

Papadopoulos, Yannis. 1991. "Quel rôle pour les petits partis dans la démocratie directe?" *Annuaire suisse de science politique* 31: 131–150.

Pappi, Franz Urban. 1984. "The West German Party System." *West European Politics* 7: 7–27.

Pappi, Franz Urban, and Peter Mnich. 1992. "Federal Republic of Germany." In *Electoral Change: Responses to Evolving Social and Attitudinal Structures in Western Countries*, ed. Mark N. Franklin, Thomas T. Mackie, and Henry Valen. Cambridge: Cambridge University Press.

Park, Jong H. 1994. "Trading Blocs and US-Japan Relations in Pacific Trade and Cooperation." In *International Trade: Regional and Global Issues*, ed. Michael Landeck. New York: St. Martin's.

Parker, Simon. 1996. "Electoral Reform and Political Change in Italy, 1991–1994." In *The New Italian Republic: From the Fall of the Berlin Wall to Berlusconi*, ed. Stephen Gundle and Simon Parker. London: Routledge.

Parsons, Talcott. 1971. *The System of Modern Societies*. Englewood Cliffs, N.J.: Prentice-Hall.

Pasquino, Gianfranco, and Patrick McCarthy, eds. 1993. *The End of Post-War Politics in Italy: The Landmark 1992 Elections*. Boulder, Colo.: Westview Press.

Pauly, Louis. 1988. *Opening Financial Markets: Banking Politics on the Pacific Rim*. Ithaca, N.Y.: Cornell University Press.

Penati, Alessandro, and Michael Dooley. 1984. "Current Account Imbalances and Capital Formation in Industrial Countries, 1949–1981." *IMF Staff Papers* 31: 1–24.

Pennings, Pier. 1995. "De boodschap van de partijen." In *De Democratie op drift: Een evaluatie van de verkiezingen in 1994*, ed. Jan Kleinnijenhuis, D. Oegema, J. A. de Ridden, and H. S. Bos. Amsterdam: VU Press.

Perrow, Charles. 1989. "Eine Gesellschaft von Organisationen." *Journal für Sozialforschung* 29: 3–20.

Persson, Inga, ed. 1990. *Generating Equality in the Welfare State*. Oslo: Norwegian University Press.

Peters, B. Guy. 1992. "Bureaucratic Politics and the Institutions of the European

Community." In *Euro-Politics: Institutions and Policy-Making in the 'New' European Community*, ed. Alberta Sbragia. Washington, D.C.: Brookings Institution.

Peterson, John. 1995. "Decision Making in the European Union: Towards a Framework for Analysis." *Journal of Common Market Studies* 32 (3): 411–426.

Peterson, Paul, and Mark Rom. 1989. "Lower Taxes." In *The Reagan Legacy*, ed. Charles O. Jones. New Jersey: Chatham.

Pierson, Paul. 1994. *Dismantling the Welfare State?* Cambridge: Cambridge University Press.

1996a. "The New Politics of the Welfare State." *World Politics* 48 (2): 143–179.

1996b. "The Path to European Integration: An Historical Institutionalist Analysis." *Comparative Political Studies* 29: 123–162.

Piore, Michael J., and Charles F. Sabel. 1984. *The Second Industrial Divide: Possibilities for Prosperity*. New York: Basic Books.

Pizzorno, Alessandro. 1978. "Political Exchange and Collective Identity in Industrial Countries." In *The Resurgence of Class Conflict in Western Europe since 1968*, ed. Colin Crouch and Alessandro Pizzorno. London: Macmillan.

Plender, John. 1988. "London's Big Bang in International Context." *International Affairs* 63: 39–48.

Pollack, Mark. 1995. "Creeping Competence: The Expanding Agenda of the European Community." *Journal of Public Policy* 29: 123–163.

Pollins, Brian. 1993. "Global Capital: Two Financial Booms Compared." Unpublished manuscript, Department of Political Science, Ohio State University.

Pontusson, Jonas. 1992. "Introduction: Organizational and Political-Economic Perspective on Union Politics." In *Bargaining for Change, Union Politics in North America and Europe*, ed. Miriam Golden and Jonas Pontusson. Ithaca, N.Y.: Cornell University Press.

1995. "From Comparative Public Policy to Political Economy: Putting Political Institutions in their Place and Taking Interests Seriously." *Comparative Political Studies* 28: 117–147.

Pontusson, Jonas, and Peter Swenson. 1995. "Governing Labor Markets: Employers, Wage Bargaining and the Politics of Institutional Change in Sweden." *Comparative Political Studies* 1.

1996. "Labor Markets, Production Strategies and Wage-Bargaining Institutions: The Swedish Employer Offensive in Comparative Perspective." *Comparative Political Studies* 29 (2): 223–250.

Porter, Michael. 1990. *The Competitive Advantage of Nations*. New York: Free Press.

Powell, G. Bingham, and Guy D. Whitten. 1993. "A Cross-National Analysis of Economic Voting: Taking Account of the Political Context." *American Journal of Political Science* 37 (2): 391–414.

Przeworski, Adam. 1985. *Capitalism and Social Democracy*. Cambridge: Cambridge University Press.

1995. "Economic Reforms, Public Opinion, and Political Institutions: Poland in the Eastern European Perspective." In *Economic Reforms in New Democ-*

racies: A Social-Democratic Approach, ed. Luiz Carlos Bresser Pereira, José María Maravall, and Adam Przeworski. Cambridge: Cambridge University Press.

Przeworski, Adam, and John Sprague. 1986. *Paper Stones: A History of Electoral Socialism*. Chicago: University of Chicago Press.

Pugliese, Enrico. 1993. *La sociologia della disoccupazione*. Bologna: Il Mulino.

Pulzer, Peter. 1995. "Pointing the Way: The Electoral Transition from the Bonn Republic to the Berlin Republic." In *Superwahljahr: The German Elections in 1994*, ed. Geoffrey K. Roberts. Special issue of *German Politics* 4 (2).

Putnam, Robert. 1992. *Making Democracy Work*. Princeton, N.J.: Princeton University Press.

Quadagno, Jill. 1994. *The Color of Welfare*. New York: Oxford University Press.

Quinn, Dennis. 1997. "The Correlates of Change in International Financial Regulation." *American Political Science Review*. 91 (3): 531–551.

Quinn, Dennis P., and Carla Inclan. 1995. "Liberalizing Capital: A Twenty-One Country Study of International Financial Regulation, 1950–1988." Unpublished manuscript, Georgetown University School of Business, Washington, D.C.

Raaum, Oddbjorn, Hege Torp, and Harald Goldstein. 1995. "Employment Effects of Labor Market Training in Norway." Memorandum no. 8. Oslo: University of Oslo, Department of Economics.

Raaum, Oddbjorn, and Frederik Wulfsberg. 1995. "Unemployment, Labor Market Programs and Wages in Norway." Paper presented at the world meeting of the Econometric Society, Tokyo.

Rabinowitz, George, and Stuart Elaine MacDonald. 1989. "A Directional Theory of Issue Voting." *American Political Science Review* 83 (1): 93–121.

Rabinowitz, George, Stuart Elaine MacDonald, and Ola Listhaug. 1991. "New Players in an Old Game: Party Strategy in Multiparty Systems." *Comparative Political Studies* 24 (2): 147–185.

Radice, Hugo. 1984. "The National Economy: A Keynesian Myth?" *Capital and Class* 22: 11–140.

Raschke, Joachim. 1985. *Soziale Bewegungen: Ein historisch-systematischer Grundriss*. Frankfurt: Campus Verlag.

Reagan, Michael D. 1987. *Regulation: The Politics of Policy*. Boston: Little, Brown.

Reder, Melvin, and Lloyd Ulman. 1993. "Unionism and Unification." In *Labor and an Integrated Europe*, ed. Lloyd Ulman, Barry Eichengreen, and William T. Dickens. Washington, D.C.: Brookings Institution.

Regini, Marino. 1992. *Confini mobile*. Bologna: Il Mulino.

———. 1994a. "Firms and Institutions: The Production and Use of Human Resources in the 'Strong' Regions of Europe." Paper presented to the World Congress of the International Sociological Association, Bielefeld, Germany, July 18–23.

———. 1994b. "An Italian Variety of Capitalism." IRES, Milan.

———. 1995. *Uncertain Boundaries: The Social and Political Construction of European Economies*. Cambridge: Cambridge University Press.

Rehn, Gösta. 1952. "The Problem of Stability: An Analysis of Some Policy Proposals." In *Wages Policy under Full Employment*, ed. Ralph Turvey. London: W. Hodge.

Rhodes, Martin. 1993. "The Future of the Social Dimension: Labour Market Regulation in Post-1992 Europe." *Journal of Common Market Studies* 30 (1): 23–51.

Richardson, J. David. 1995. "Income Inequality and Trade: How to Think, What to Conclude." *Journal of Economic Perspectives* 9: 33–55.

Richardson, Jeremy, ed. 1982. *Policy Styles in Western Europe*. London: Allen and Unwin.

——— 1996. "Policy Making in the EU: Interests, Ideas and Garbage Cans of Primeval Soup." In *European Union: Power and Policy Making*, ed. Jeremy Richardson. London: Routledge.

Richardson, Jeremy, and W. Jordan, eds. 1978. *Policy Styles in Western Europe*, London: Macmillan.

Rigter, Daniele P., E. A. M. Van den Bosch, R. J. Van der Veen, and A. C. Hemerijck 1995. *Tussen sociale wil en werkelijkheid. Een geschiedenis van het ministerie van Sociale Zaken*. Den Haag: Vuga.

Risse-Kappen, Thomas. 1996. "Exploring the Nature of the Beast: International Relations Theory and Comparative Policy Analysis Meet the European Union." *Journal of Common Market Studies* 34 (1):53–80.

Ritter, Gerhard, and Meredith Niehuss. 1991. *Wählen in Deutschland, 1946–1991*. Munich: C. H. Beck.

Roberts, Geoffrey K., ed. 1995. *Superwahljahr: The German Elections in 1994*. Special issue of *German Politics* 4(2).

Rodgers, Gerry, and Janine Rodgers. 1989. *Precarious Jobs in Labor Market Regulation: The Growth of Atypical Employment in Western Europe*. Geneva: International Institute for Labor Studies.

Rodrik, Dani. 1996. "Globalization and Labor, or: If Globalization Is a Bowl of Cherries, Why Are There So Many Glum Faces around the Table?" Paper presented at the CEPR Conference on Regional Integration, La Coruña, Spain, April 26–27.

——— 1997. *Has Globalization Gone Too Far?* Washington, D.C.: Institute for International Economics.

Rødseth, Åsbjørn. 1994. "Vegen til Hog Arbeidsloyse." In *SNF AArbok 1994: Perspektiv paa Arbeidsledigheten*, ed. Agnar Sandmo. Bergen: Fagbokfórlaget.

——— 1997. "Why Has Unemployment Been So Low in Norway?" In *Making Solidarity Work? The Norwegian Labour Market Model in Transition*, ed. Jon Erik Dolvik and Arild H. Steen. Oslo: Scandinavian University Press.

Rødseth, Åsbjørn, and Steinar Holden. 1990. "Wage Formation in Norway." In *Wage Formation and Macroeconomic Policy in the Nordic Countries*, ed. Lars Calmfors. Oxford: Oxford University Press.

Roemer, John E. 1983. "Unequal Exchange, Labor Migration, and International Capital Flows: A Theoretical Synthesis." In *Marxism, Central Planning and the Soviet Economy: Essays in Honor of Padma Desai*, ed. Padma Desai. Cambridge, Mass.: MIT Press.

Rogowski, Ronald. 1987. "Trade and the Variety of Democratic Institutions." *International Organization* 41: 203–224.

——— 1990. *Commerce and Coalitions*. Ithaca, N.Y.: Cornell University Press.

Rose, Richard. 1974. *Electoral Behaviour: A Comparative Handbook.* New York: Free Press.

Rosenbluth, Frances McCall. 1989. *Financial Politics in Contemporary Japan.* Ithaca, N.Y.: Cornell University Press.

Rosenfeld, Rachel A., and Arne L. Kalleberg. 1990. "A Cross-National Comparison of the Gender Gap in Income." *American Journal of Sociology* 1: 69–106.

Ross, George. 1993. "The European Community and Social Policy: Regional Blocs and a Humane Social Order." *Studies in Political Economy* 40: 41–72.

 1995a. *Jacques Delors and European Integration.* Oxford: Oxford University Press.

 1995b. "Assessing the Delors Era in Social Policy." In *European Social Policy: Between Fragmentation and Integration,* ed. Stephan Leibfried and Paul Pierson. Washington, D.C.: Brookings Institution.

Roth, Dieter. 1990. "Die Republikaner." *Aus Politik und Zeitgeschichte* 37–38 (14): 27–39.

 1994. "Was bewegt die Wähler?" *Aus Politik und Zeitgeschichte* 11 (18):3–13.

Roth, Roland. 1991. "Herausforderung demokratischer Institutionen durch neue Formen politischer Mobilisierung. Zur Situation in der Bundesrepublik." *Schweiz: Jahrbuch für politische Wissenschaft* 31: 209–233.

Rothstein, Bo. 1992. "Labor-Market Institutions and Working-Class Strength." In *Structuring Politics: Historical Institutionalism in Comparative Analysis,* ed. Sven Steinmo, Kathleen Thelen, and Frank Longstreth. Cambridge: Cambridge University Press.

Rowthorn, Bob. 1992. "Corporatism and Labour Market Performance." In *Social Corporatism: A Superior Economic System?,* ed. Jukka Pekkarinen, Matti Pohjola, and Bob Rowthorn. Oxford: Clarendon Press.

Rubery, Jill, and Colette Fagan. 1994. "Equal Pay and Wage Regulation Systems in Europe." *Industrial Relations Journal* 25: 281–292.

Ruggie, Mary. 1984. *The State and Working Women: A Comparative Study of Britain and Sweden.* Princeton, N.J.: Princeton University Press.

Sabel, Charles F. 1981. "The Internal Politics of Trade Unions." In *Organizing Interests in Western Europe: Pluralism, Corporatism, and the Transformation of Politics,* ed. Suzanne Berger. Cambridge: Cambridge University Press.

 1991. "Moebius-Strip Organizations and Open Labor Markets: Some Consequences of the Reintegration of Conception and Execution in a Volatile Economy." In *Social Theory for a Changing Society,* ed. Pierre Bourdieu and James S. Coleman. Boulder, Colo.:Westview Press.

 1992. "Studied Trust: Building New Forms of Cooperation in a Volatile Economy." In *Industrial Districts and Local Economic Regeneration,* ed. Frank Pyke and Werner Sengenberger. Geneva: International Institute for Labor Studies.

 1993. "Studied trust. Building New Forms of Cooperation in a Volatile Economy." In *Technology and the Wealth of Nations: The Dynamics of Constructed Advantage,* ed. D. Foray and C. Freeman, 332–352. London: Pinter Publishers.

 1995a. "Bootstrapping Reform: Rebuilding Firms, the Welfare State, and Unions." *Politics and Society* 23 (1): 5–48.

1995b. "Design, Deliberation, and Democracy: On the New Pragmatism of Firms and Public Institutions." New York: Columbia Law School.

1995c. "Intelligible Differences: On Deliberate Strategy and the Exploration of Possibility in Economic Life." New York: Columbia Law School.

1996. "Learning by Monitoring: The Institutions of Economic Development." In *Handbook of Economic Sociology*, ed. Neil Smelser and Richard Swedberg. Princeton, N.J.: Princeton University Press.

Sabel, Charles F., and Jonathon Zeitlin, eds. 1997. *Worlds of Possibility*. Cambridge: Cambridge University Press.

Sainsbury, Diane. 1990. "Party Strategies and the Electoral Trade-Off of Class-Based Parties." *European Journal of Political Research* 18 (1): 29–50.

1992. "Welfare State Retrenchment and Restructuring." Paper presented at the meeting of the American Political Science Association, Chicago, September 3–6.

Salant, Walter S. 1997. *Worldwide Inflation*. Washington, D.C.: Brookings Institution.

Salminen, Kari. 1993. *Pension Schemes in the Making*. Helsinki: Central Pension Security Institute.

Sanders, David. 1993. "Why the Conservatives Won – Again." In *Britain at the Polls 1992*, ed. Anthony King. New Jersey: Chatham.

Sanders, David, D. Marsh, and H. Ward. 1987. "Government Popularity and the Falklands War: A Reassessment." *British Journal of Political Science* 17: 281–313.

Sandholtz, Wayne. 1996. "Membership Matters: Limits of the Functional Approach to European Institutions." *Journal of Common Market Studies* 34 (3): 403–429.

Sandholtz, Wayne, and John Zysman. 1989. "1992: Recasting the European Bargain." *World Politics* 42: 95–128.

Sbragia, Alberta, ed. 1992. *Euro-Politics: Institutions and Policy-Making in the 'New' European Community*. Washington, D.C.: Brookings Institution.

1993a. "The European Community: A Balancing Act." *Publius* 23: 23–38.

1993b. "EC Environmental Policy: Atypical Ambitions and Typical Problems?" In *The State of the European Community*, vol. 2, *The Maastricht Debates and Beyond*, ed. Alan W. Cafruny and Glenda G. Rosenthal. Boulder, Colo.: Lynne Rienner.

1996. "Environmental Policy: The 'Push-Pull' of Policy Making." In *Policy Making in the European Union*, ed. Helen Wallace and William Wallace. Oxford: Oxford University Press.

Schain, Martin A. 1987. "The National Front in France and the Construction of Political Legitimacy." *West European Politics* 10: 229–252.

Scharpf, Fritz W. 1987. *Crisis and Choice in European Social Democracy*. Ithaca, N.Y.: Cornell University Press.

1988. "Game-Theoretical Interpretations of Inflation and Unemployment in Western Europe." *Journal of Public Policy* 7 (1).

1991. *Crisis and Choice in European Social Democracy*. Ithaca, N.Y.: Cornell University Press.

1994. "Community and Autonomy: Multilevel Policy-Making in the European Union." *Journal of European Public Policy* 1: 219–242.

1996a. "Negative and Positive Integration in the Political Economy of European Welfare States." In *Governance in the European Union*, ed. Gary Marks, Fritz Scharpf, Philippe C. Schmitter, and Wolfgang Streeck. London: Sage Publications.

1996b. "Problem-Solving Capacity of Multi-Level Governance Structures." Paper presented at the European University Institute.

Schettkatt, Ronald. 1992. *The Labor Market Dynamics of Economic Restructuring*. New York: Praeger.

Schizzerotto, A. 1993. "La porta stretta: Classe superiori e processi di mobilita." *Polis* 1.

Schmidt, Manfred. 1982. "The Role of the Parties in Shaping Macroeconomic Policy." In *The Impact of Parties*, ed. Francis Castles. Beverly Hills, Calif.: Sage Publications.

1993. "Gendered Labour Force Participation." In *Families of Nations: Patterns of Public Policy in Western Democracies*, ed. Frances G. Castles. Aldershot: Dartmouth.

Schmidt, Vivien A. 1994a. "Community and Autonomy: Multi-level Policy-Making in the European Union." *Journal of European Public Policy* 1: 219–242.

1994b. "The New World Order, Incorporated: The Rise of Business and the Decline of the Nation-State." Paper prepared for the Daedalus Conference on the Twentieth Century State at the American Arts and Sciences, Cambridge.

Schmitt-Beck, Rüdiger. 1992. "A Myth Institutionalized: Theory and Research on New Social Movements in Germany." *European Journal of Political Research* 21: 357–383.

Schmitter, Philippe. 1969. "Three Neofunctional Hypotheses about International Integration." *International Organization* 23 (1): 161–166.

1974. "Still the Century of Corporatism." *Review of Politics* 36 (1):85–131.

1981. "Interest Intermediation and Regime Governability in Contemporary Western Europe and North America." In *Organizing Interests in Western Europe*, ed. Suzanne Berger. Cambridge: Cambridge University Press.

1990. "Sectors in Modern Capitalism: Modes of Governance and Variations in Performance." In *Labour Relations and Economic Performance*, ed. Renato Brunetta and Carlo Dell' Aringa. New York: New York University Press.

1996a. "Imagining the Future of the Euro-Polity with the Help of New Concepts." In *Governance in the European Union*, ed. Gary Marks, Fritz Scharpf, Philippe C. Schmitter, and Wolfgang Streeck. London: Sage Publications.

1996b. "How to Democratize the Emerging Euro-Polity: Citizenship, Representation, Decision-Making." Unpublished paper, Instituto Juan Madrid, March.

Schmitter, Philippe C., and Gerhard Lehmbruch, eds. 1979. *Trends toward Corporatist Intermediation*. Beverly Hills, Calif.: Sage Publications.

Schumpeter, Joseph. 1964. *Imperialism and Social Classes*. New York: Meridian Books.

1976 [1942]. *Capitalism, Socialism and Democracy*. New York: Harper and Row.

Shavit, Y., and Blossfeld, H. P. 1993. *Persistent Inequality: Changing Educational Attainment in Thirteen Countries.* Boulder, Colo.: Westview Press.

Shefter, Martin. 1994. *Political Parties and the State: The American Historical Experience.* Princeton, N.J.: Princeton University Press.

Shepsle, Kenneth A. 1991. *Models of Multiparty Electoral Competition.* Chur: Harwood Academic Publishers.

Shirley, Ian. 1993. "Experiments in the New Zealand Laboratory." Paper presented at the Conference on Comparative Research on Welfare States in Transition, Oxford University, September 9–12.

Shonfield, Andrew. 1969. *Modern Capitalism.* New York: Oxford University Press.

Sidoti, Francesco. 1993. "The Extreme Right in Italy: Ideological Orphans and Countermobilization." In *The Extreme Right in Europe and the USA*, ed. Paul Hainsworth, London: Pinter Publishers.

Silvia, Stephen J. 1996. "Globalization and the German Economy: Labor Unions." Paper prepared for the APSA annual meeting, San Francisco, August 28–September 1.

———. 1998. "Between Pattern and Participation: German Industrial Relations since 1980." In *The Changing Place of Labor in European Society*, ed. Andrew Martin and George Ross. Providence, R.I.: Berghahn.

Simmons, Beth A. 1997. "The International Politics of Harmonization: The Case of Capital Market Regulation." Unpublished manuscript, Department of Political Science, University of California at Berkeley.

Smeeding, Timothy, Michael O'Higgins, and Lee Rainwater. 1990. *Poverty, Inequality and Income Distribution in Comparative Perspective.* New York: Harvester/Wheatsheaf.

Smith, Gordon. 1992. *Democracy in Western Germany: Parties and Politics in the Federal Republic.* 2nd ed. London: Heinemann.

Sobel, Andrew. 1994. "Breaching the Levee, Waiting for the Flood: Testing Beliefs about the Internationalization of Securities Markets." *International Interactions* 19 (4): 311–338.

———. "Internationalization and Liberalization of Securities Markets." Unpublished manuscript, Department of Political Science, Washington University, St. Louis.

———. 1995. "The Capital Pool: Sink or Swim? Political Institutions and International Capital Markets." Paper presented for the annual meeting of the Midwest Political Science Association, Chicago.

Sorge, A., and M. Warner. 1987. *Comparative Factory Organisation: An Anglo-German Comparison of Manpower in Manufacturing.* Aldershot: Gower.

Soskice, David. 1978. "Strike Waves and Wage Explosion, 1968–1970: An Economic Interpretation." In *The Resurgence of Class Conflict in Western Europe since 1968: Comparative Analyses*, vol. 2, ed. Colin Crouch and Alessandro Pizzorno. New York: Holmes and Meier.

———. 1990a. "Wage Determination: The Changing Role of Institutions in Advanced Industrial Countries." *Oxford Review of Economic Policy* 6: 36–61.

———. 1990b. "Reinterpreting Corporatism and Explaining Unemployment: Coordinated and Uncoordinated Market Economies." In *Labour Relations and Economic Performance*, ed. Renato Brunetta and Carlo Dell'Aringa. London: Macmillan.

1991. "The Institutional Infrastructure for International Competitiveness: A Comparative Analysis of the UK and Germany." In *The Economics of the New Europe*, ed. Anthony B. Atkinson and Renato Brunetta. London: Macmillan.

1993. "Innovation Strategies of Companies: A Comparative Institutional Explanation of Cross-Country Differences." Paper presented at the Wissenschaft Zentrum, Berlin.

1994a. "Advanced Economies in Open World Markets and Comparative Institutional Advantages: Patterns of Business Coordination, National Institutional Frameworks and Company Product Market Innovation Strategies," Mimeographed, Wissenschafts zentrum, Berlin.

1994b. "Finer Varieties of Advanced Capitalism: Industry versus Group Based Coordination in Germany and Japan." Paper presented to the Conference on Varieties of Capitalism, Poitiers.

1997a. "Openness and Diversity: Thinking about Transatlantic Economic Relations." In *Transatlantic Economic Relations in the Post-Cold War Era*, ed. Barry Eichengreen. New York: New York Council on Foreign Relations.

1997b. "German Technology Policy, Innovation and National Institutional Frameworks." *Industry and Innovation* 4: 75–96.

Soskice, David, and Wendy Carlin. 1989. "Medium-run Keynesianism: Hysteresis and Capital Scrapping." In *Macroeconomic Problems and Policies of Income Distribution*, ed. Paul Davidson and Jan Kregel. Aldershot: Edward Elgar Press.

Spakes, Patricia. 1989. "A Feminist Case against National Family Policy: View to the Future." *Policy Studies Review* 8 (3): 610–621.

Stallings, Barbara. 1987. *Banker to the Third World: U.S. Portfolio Investment in Latin America, 1900–1986*. Berkeley: University of California Press.

Standing, Guy. 1993. "Labor Regulation in an Era of Fragmented Flexibility." In *Employment Security and Labor Market Behavior*, ed. Christoph F. Buechtemann. Ithaca, N.Y.:ILR Press.

Statistisk årsbok för Sverige 1992. Sveriges offentliga statistik. Statistiska Centralbyran.

Steinmo, Sven. 1993. *Taxation and Democracy*. New Haven, Conn.: Yale University Press.

Steinmo, Sven, Kathleen Thelen, and Frank Longsreth, eds. 1992. *Structuring Politics*. Cambridge: Cambridge University Press.

Stephens, John D. 1976. "The Consequences of Social Structural Change for the Development of Socialism in Sweden." Ph.D. dissertation, Yale University.

1979. *The Transition from Capitalism to Socialism*. London: Macmillan.

1994. "The Scandinavian Welfare States: Development and Crisis." Paper presented at the World Conference of Sociology, Bielefeld, Germany, July 18–23.

1996. "The Scandinavian Welfare States." In *Welfare States in Transition*, ed. Gøsta Esping-Andersen. London: Sage Publications.

Stokman, Frans N., Rolf Ziegler, and John Scott, eds. 1985. *Networks of Corporate Power: A Comparative Analysis of Ten Countries*. New York: Blackwell.

Stolper, Wolfgang, and Paul Samuelson. 1941. "Protection and Real Wages." *Review of Economic Studies* 9: 58–73.

Streeck, Wolfgang. 1994. "Neo-Corporatist Industrial Relations and the Economic Crisis in West Germany." In *Order and Conflict in Contemporary Capitalism*, ed. John Goldthorpe. New York: Oxford University Press.

———. 1987. "The Uncertainties of Management and the Management of Uncertainty: Employers, Labor Relations and Industrial Adjustment in the 1980s." *Work, Employment and Society* 1 (3):281–308.

———. 1991. "On the Institutional Conditions of Diversified Quality Production." In *The Socio-Economics of Production and Employment*, ed. Egon Matzner and Wolfgang Streeck. London: Edward Elgar.

———. 1992a. *Social Institutions and Economic Performance*. London: Sage Publications.

———. 1992b. "National Diversity, Regime Competition and Institutional Deadlock: Problems in Forming a European Industrial Relations System." *Journal of Public Policy* 12: 301–330.

———. 1993. "The Rise and Decline of Neocorporatism." In *Labor and an Integrated Europe*, ed. Lloyd Ulman, Barry Eichengreen, and William T. Dickens. Washington, D.C.: Brookings Institution.

———. 1995. "From Market-Making to State-Building? Reflections on the Political Economy of European Social Policy." In *European Social Policy: Between Fragmentation and Integration*, ed. Stephan Leibfried and Paul Pierson. Washington, D.C.: Brookings Institution.

———. 1996. "Neo-Voluntarism: A New European Social Policy Regime?" In *Governance in the European Union*, ed. Gary Marks, Fritz Scharpf, Philippe C. Schmitter, and Wolfgang Streeck. London: Sage Publications.

Streeck, Wolfgang, and Philippe Schmitter. 1985. *Private Interest Government*. Beverly Hills, Calif: Sage Publications.

———. 1991. "From National Corporatism to Transnational Pluralism: Organized Interests in the Single European Market." *Politics and Society* 19 (2): 133–164.

Strom, Kaare. 1990. "A Behavioral Theory of Competitive Political Parties." *American Journal of Political Science* 34 (2): 565–598.

Svalforss, Stefan. 1992. "Den Stabila Välfärdsopinionen: Attityder till Svensk Välfärdspolitik 1986–92." Sociologiska Institutionen, Umeå Universitet, unpublished paper.

Swank, Duane. 1993. "Social Democracy, Equity, and Efficiency in an Interdependent World." Paper presented at the meeting of the American Political Science Association, New York.

Sweden. Various years. *Statistisk Årsbok för Sverige*. Stockholm: Sveriges Offentliga Statistik. Statistiska Centralbyrån.

Swenson, Peter. 1989. *Fair Shares: Unions, Pay and Politics in Sweden and West Germany*. Ithaca, N.Y.: Cornell University Press.

———. 1991. "Bringing Capital Back In, or Social Democracy Reconsidered." *World Politics* 43 (4): 513–544.

———. 1992a. "Managing the Managers: The Swedish Employers' Confederation, Labor Scarcity, and the Suppression of Labor Market Segmentation." *Scandinavian Journal of History* 16: 335–356.

———. 1992b. "Union Politics, the Welfare State, and Intraclass Conflict in Sweden and Germany." In *Bargaining for Change: Union Politics in North America and Europe*, ed. Miriam Golden and Jonas Pontusson. Ithaca, N.Y.: Cornell University Press.

Taylor, Robert. 1993. *The Trade Union Question in British Politics, 1945–1992*. Oxford: Basil Blackwell.

Tesar, Linda L. 1991. "Saving, Investment, and International Capital Flows." *Journal of International Economics* 31: 55–78.

Thelen, Kathleen. 1991. *Union of Parts*. Ithaca, N.Y.: Cornell University Press.

1993. "West European Labor in Transition: Sweden and Germany Compared." *World Politics* 46 (1): 23–49.

1994. "Beyond Corporatism: Toward a New Framework for the Study of Labor in Advanced Capitalism." *Comparative Politics* 27 (1): 107–124.

Therborn, Göran. 1986. *Why Some Peoples Are More Unemployed Than Others: The Strange Paradox of Growth and Unemployment*. London: Verso.

1995. *European Modernity and Beyond: The Trajectory of European Societies, 1945–2000*. London: Sage Publications.

Tilly, Charles. 1978. *From Mobilization to Revolution*. Reading, Pa.: Addison-Wesley.

1994. "Globalization Threatens Labor's Rights." Working Paper No. 182. New School for Social Research, Center for Studies of Social Change, New York

Tingsten, Herbert. 1955. "Stability and Vitality in Swedish Democracy." *Political Quarterly* 22 (2): 140–151.

Titmuss, Richard A. 1974. *Social Policy*. London: Allen and Unwin.

Todd, Emanuel. 1988. *La nouvelle France*. Paris: Ed. du Seuil.

Togeby, Lise. 1994. "Political Implications of Increasing Numbers of Women in the Labor Force." *Comparative Political Studies* 2: 211–240.

Touraine, Alain. 1980. *La prophétie anti-nucléaire*. Paris: Ed. du Seuil.

Traxler, Franz. 1994. "Collective Bargaining: Levels and Coverage." In *OECD Employment Outlook*. Paris: OECD.

1995. "Farewell to Labour Market Associations? Organized versus Disorganized Decentralization as a Map for Industrial Relations." In *Organized Industrial Relations in Europe: What Future?*, eds. Colin Crouch and Franz Traxler. Aldershot: Avebury.

1996. "Collective Bargaining and Industrial Change: A Case of Disorganization? A Comparative Analysis of 18 OECD Countries." Paper presented at the annual meeting of the American Political Science Association, San Francisco, August 28–September 1.

Tsebelis, George. 1994. "The Power of the European Parliament as a Conditional Agenda Setter." *American Political Science Review* 88: 128–142.

1995. "Will Maastricht Reduce the Democratic Deficit?" *APSA-Comparative Politics Newsletter* 6 (1): 4–6.

Turner, Philip. 1991. "Capital Flows in the 1980s: A Survey of Major Trends." BIS Economic Papers no. 30. BIS, Monetary and Economic Department, Basle.

Ultee, Wout, Jos Dessens, and Wim Jansen. 1988. "Why Does Unemployment Come in Couples?" *European Sociological Review*. 4: 111–122.

United Nations Commission on Transnational Corporations. January 1991.

Van der Eijk, Cees, and Mark Franklin, eds. 1995. *Choosing Europe: The European Electorate and National Politics in the Face of the Union.* Ann Arbor: University of Michigan Press.

Van der Eijk, Cees, and Philip van Praag. 1991. "Partijen, kiezers en verkiezingen." In *Maatschappij, Macht, Nederlandse Politiek*, ed. Uwe Becker. 2nd ed. Amsterdam: Het Spinhuis.

Van Holsteyn, J. J. M., and Broer Niemöller, eds. 1995. *De Nederlandse kiezer 1994.* Leiden: DSWO.

Van Kersbergen, Kees. 1994. "The Distinctiveness of Christian Democracy." In *Christian Democracy in Europe: A Comparative Perspective*, ed. David Hanley. London: Pinter Publishers.

———. 1995. *Social Capitalism: A Study of Christian Democracy and the Welfare State.* London: Routledge.

———. 1997. "Between Collectivism and Individualism: The Politics of the Centre." In *The Politics of Problem-Solving in Postwar Democracies*, ed. Hans Keman. London: Macmillan.

Van Kersbergen, Kees, and Hans-Martien ten Napel. 1994. "The Philosophy, Policies and Perspectives of European Christian Democracy." *Allen Review* 10: 7–10.

Van Kersbergen, Kees, and Bertjan Verbeek. 1994. "The Politics of Subsidiarity in the European Union." *Journal of Common Market Studies* 32 (2): 215–236.

Vartiainen, Juhana. 1997a. "Can Nordic Social Corporatism Survive? Challenges to the Labour Market." In *The Challenge of Globalization and Institution Building: Lessons from Small European States*, ed. Randall W. Kindley and David F. Good. Boulder, Colo.: Westview Press.

———. 1997b. "Understanding State-Led Late Industrialization." In *Government and Growth*, ed. Villy Bergström. Oxford: Clarendon Press.

Vernon, Raymond. 1966. "International Investment and International Trade in the Product Cycle." *Quarterly Journal of Economics* 80: 190–207.

Vickers, John, and Vincent Wright, eds. 1989. *The Politics of Privatization in Western Europe.* London: Frank Cass.

Visser, Jelle. 1989. *European Trade Unions in Figures, 1913–1985.* Deventer: Kluwer Law and Taxation Publishers.

———. 1990. "In Search of Inclusive Unionism." *Bulletin of Comparative Labour Relations*, no. 18. Devener: Kluwer Law and Taxation Publishers.

———. 1991. "Trends in Trade Union Membership." In OECD, *Employment Outlook* (July): 97–134. Paris OECD.

———. 1992. "The Strength of Union Movements in Advanced Capitalist Democracies: Social and Organizational Variations." In *The Future of Labor Movements*, ed., Marino Regini. London: Sage Publications.

Vogel, Steven K. 1996. *Freer Markets, More Rules: Regulatory Reform in Advanced Industrial Countries.* Ithaca, N.Y. Cornell University Press.

Vogelheim, Elisabeth. 1988. "Women in a Changing Workplace: The Case of the Federal Republic of Germany." In *Feminization of the Labor Force: Paradoxes and Promises*, ed. Jane Jenson, Elisabeth Hagen, and Ceallaigh Reddy. New York: Oxford University Press.

Von Beyme, Klaus. 1988. "Right-Wing Extremism in Post-War Europe." *West European Politics* 11: 1–17.

von Furstenberg, George M., and Bang Nam Jeon. 1989. "International Stock Price Movements: Links and Messages." *Brookings Papers on Economic Activity* 1: 125–179.

Wallace, Helen. 1993. "European Governance in Turbulent Times." *Journal of Common Market Studies* 31: 293–303.

———. 1996. "The Institutions of the EU: Experience and Experiments." In *Policy-Making in European Union*, ed. Helen Wallace and William Wallace. Oxford: Oxford University Press.

Wallace, Helen, and Alasdair R. Young. 1996. "The Single Market: A New Approach to Policy." In *Policy-Making in the European Union*, ed. Helen Wallace and William Wallace. Oxford: Oxford University Press.

Wallace, William. 1983. "Walking Backwards Towards Unity." In *Policy-Making in the European Communities*, ed. William Wallace, Helen Wallace, and Carole Webb. London: John Wiley & Sons.

———. 1994. *Regional Integration: The West European Experience.* Washington, D.C.: Brookings Institution.

Wallerstein, Michael. 1987. "Collective Bargaining and the Demand for Protection." *American Journal of Political Science* 31: 729–752.

———. 1990. "Centralized Bargaining and Wage Restraint." *American Journal of Political Science* 34: 982–1004.

Wallerstein, Michael, and Miriam Golden. Forthcoming. "The Fragmentation of the Bargaining Society: Changes in the Centralization of Wage-Setting in the Nordic Countries, 1950–1992." *Comparative Political Studies*.

Wallerstein, Michael, Miriam Golden, and Peter Lange. 1997. "Unions, Employers' Associations and Wage-Setting Institutions in North and Central Europe, 1950–1992." *Industrial and Labor Relations Review* 50: 379–401.

Walsh, Janet. 1993. "Internalization vs. Decentralization: An Analysis of Recent Developments in Pay Bargaining." *British Journal of Industrial Relations* 3: 409–432.

Watts, Nicholas J. 1987. "Mobilisierungspotential und gesellschaftspolitische Bedeutung der neuen sozialen Bewegungen." In *Neue soziale Bewegungen in der Bundesrepublik Deutschland*, ed. Roland Roth and Dieter Rucht. Frankfurt: Campus Verlag.

Webb, Michael C. 1991. "International Economic Structures, Government Interests, and International Coordination of Macroeconomic Adjustment Policies." *International Organization* 45 (3): 309–342.

Weiler, Joe H. H. 1991. "The Transformation of Europe." *Yale Law Review* 100: 2403–2483.

Weir, Margaret. 1992. *Politics and Jobs.* Princeton, N.J: Princeton University Press.

Weir, Margaret, and Theda Skocpol. 1985. "State Structures and the Possibilities for Keynesian Responses to the Great Depression in Sweden, Britain and the United States" In *Bringing the State Back In*, ed. Peter Evans, Dietrich Rueschemeyer, and Theda Skocpol. Cambridge: Cambridge University Press.

Wertman, Douglas A. 1974. "The Electorate of Religiously-based Political Parties:

The Case of the Italian Christian Democratic Party." Ph.D. dissertation, Ohio State University.

1995. "The Last Year of the Christian Democratic Party." *Italian Politics: A Review* 9: 135–150.

Western, Bruce. 1993. "Postwar Unionization in Eighteen Advanced Capitalist Countries." *American Sociological Review* 58: 266–282.

1997. *Between Class and Market: Postwar Unionization in the Capitalist Democracies.* Princeton, N.J.: Princeton University Press.

Whiteley, Paul. 1985. "Perceptions of Economic Performance and Voting Behavior in the 1983 General Election in Britain." In *Economic Conditions and Electoral Outcomes: The United States and Western Europe*, ed. Heinz Eulau and Michael Lewis-Beck. New York: Agathon.

Whiteley, Paul, Patrick Seyd, Jeremy Richardson, and Paul Bissell. 1994. "Thatcherism and the Conservative Party." *Political Studies* 42 (2): 185–202.

Wickham-Jones, Mark. 1995. "Anticipating Social Democracy, Preempting Anticipation: Economic Policy-Making in the British Labor Party, 1987–1992." *Politics and Society* 23: 465–494.

Wiener, Antje. 1994. "The E.C. Citizenship Policy Packages – Constructive Citizenship in a Non-State." Paper prepared for the annual meeting of the American Political Science Association, Washington, D.C., August 28–September 1.

Wilensky, Harold. 1976. *The 'New Corporatism': Centralization and the Welfare State.* Beverly Hills, Calif.: Sage Publications.

Wilks, Stephen. 1992. "Models of European Administration: DG IV and the Administration of Competition Policy." Paper presented to the European Group of Public Administration Conference, Pisa. September 2–5.

1993. "Economic Policy." In *Developments in British Politics 4*, ed. Patrick Dunleavy et al. London: Macmillan.

Wilks, Stephen, and Maurice Wright, eds. 1987. *Comparative Government and Industry Relations.* Oxford: Oxford University Press.

Willems, Helmut. 1993a. *Fremdenfeindliche Gewalt: Einstellungen, Täter, Konflikteskalation.* Opladen: Leske + Budrich.

1993b. "Gewalt gegen Fremde. Täter, Strukturen und Eskalationsprozesse." In *Aggression und Gewalt*, ed. Landeszentrale für politische Bildung Baden-Württemberg. Stuttgart: Kohlhammer.

Williamson, Jeffrey G. 1992. "The Evolution of Global Labor Markets in the First and Second World since 1830: Background Evidence and Hypotheses." National Bureau of Economic Research Historical Paper no. 36. Cambridge, Mass.

Williamson, Oliver J. 1985. *The Economic Institutions of Capitalism.* New York: Free Press.

Windolf, P., and J. Beyer. 1996. "Cooperative Capitalism: Corporate Networks in Germany and Britain." *British Journal of Sociology* 47 (2).

Winkler, Jack. 1974. "Corporatism." *European Journal of Sociology* 17 (1): 100–136.

Wood, Adrian. 1994. *North-South Trade, Employment and Inequality: Changing Fortunes in a Skill-Driven World.* Oxford: Clarendon Press.

1995. "How Trade Hurt Unskilled Workers." *Journal of Economic Perspectives* 9: 57–80.

Wood, Stewart. 1996. "Labor Power and Employers' Preferences: The Ambiguous Reform of the West German Strike Payments Law (1984–87)." St. John's College, Oxford University. Mimeographed.

———. 1997. "Capitalist Constitutions: Supply-Side Reform in West Germany and the UK, 1960–1990." Ph.D. dissertation, Harvard University.

Wright, Erik O. 1985. *Classes.* London: Verso.

———. 1991. "The Conceptual Status of Class Structure in Class Analysis." In *Bringing Class Back In*, ed. Scott G. McNall et al. Boulder, Colo.: Westview Press.

Wright, Vincent, ed. 1994. *Privatization in Western Europe.* London: Frank Cass.

Wriston, Walter. 1988. "Technology and Sovereignty." *Foreign Affairs.* 67: 63–75.

WSI-Materialen. (previously: *WSI-Arbeitsmaterialen*). Various years. Wirtschafts-und sozialwissenchaftsliches Institut der DGB. Dusseldorf.

Zevin, Robert. 1992. "Are World Financial Markets More Open? If So, Why and with What Effects?" In *Financial Openness and National Autonomy: Opportunities and Constraints*, ed. Tariq Banuri and Juliet B. Schor. Oxford: Clarendon Press.

Ziegler, Nicholas. 1997. *Governing Ideas: Strategies for Innovation in France and Germany.* Ithaca, N.Y.: Cornell University Press.

Zweig, Ferdinand. 1971. *The Worker in Affluent Society.* New York: Free Press.

Zysman, John, 1984. *Governments, Markets, and Growth: Financial Systems and the Politics of Industrial Change.* Ithaca, N.Y.: Cornell University Press.

———. 1996. "How Institutions Create Historically-Rooted Trajectories of Growth." *Industrial and Corporate Change.*

Zysman, John, and Laura Tyson, eds. 1983. *American Industry in International Competition.* Ithaca, N.Y.: Cornell University Press.

INDEX